The LGBTQ Almanac

500 Years of Queer Culture in American History

DEBORAH G. FELDER

VISIBLE INK PRESS

DETROIT

About the Author

Deborah G. Felder is a graduate of Bard College, where she studied drama and literature. She worked as an editor at Scholastic, Inc., and has been a freelance writer and editor for over 30 years. The author of more than 20 publications, including fiction and nonfiction books and articles for middle grade, young adult, and adult readers, she has published such titles as *The 100 Most Influential Women of All Time: A Ranking Past and Present; A Century of Women: The Most Influential Events in Twentieth-Century Women's History*; and *A Bookshelf of Our Own: Works That Changed Women's Lives*. She has also written book reviews for the *New York Times Book Review, Kirkus Reviews*, and *Publishers Weekly*. For Visible Ink Press, she is the author of *The American Women's Almanac: 500 Years of Making History, Trailblazing Women!: Amazing Americans Who Made History*, and *The Handy Literature Answer Book: An Engaging Guide to Unraveling Symbols, Signs and Meanings in Great Works.*

She resides with her husband, Daniel Burt, in South Chatham, Massachusetts.

The LGBTQ Almanac

500 Years of Queer Culture in American History

DEBORAH G. FELDER

The LGBTQ Almanac: 500 Years of Queer Culture in American History

Visible Ink Press®
43311 Joy Rd., #414
Canton, MI 48187-2075

Visible Ink Press is a registered trademark of Visible Ink Press, LLC.

Most Visible Ink Press books are available at special quantity discounts when purchased in bulk by corporations, organizations, or groups. Customized printings, special imprints, messages, and excerpts can be produced to meet your needs. For more information, contact Special Markets Director, Visible Ink Press, www.visibleinkpress.com, or 734-667-3211.

Managing Editor: Kevin S. Hile
Cover Design: John Gouin, Graphikitchen, LLC
Page Design and Typesetting: Kevin S. Hile
Proofreaders: Larry Baker and Shoshana Hurwitz
Indexer: Shoshana Hurwitz

Cover and chapter title images: Shutterstock.

ISBNs:

Paperback: 978-1-57859-713-0
Library Hardbound: 978-1-57859-849-6
eBook: 978-1-57859-850-2

Cataloging-in-Publication data is on file at the Library of Congress.

Printed in the United States of America.

10 9 8 7 6 5 4 3 2 1

Also from Visible Ink Press

African American Almanac: 400 Years of Black Excellence, 2nd edition
By Lean'tin Bracks, Ph.D.
ISBN: 978-1-57859-780-2

The American Women's Almanac: 500 Years of Making History
By Deborah G. Felder
ISBN: 978-1-57859-636-2

Black Firsts: 500 Years of Trailblazing Achievements and Ground-Breaking Events, 4th edition
By Jessie Carney Smith, Ph.D.
ISBN: 978-1-57859-688-1

Freedom Facts and Firsts: 400 Years of the African American Civil Rights Experience
By Jessie Carney Smith, Ph.D., and Linda T. Wynn
ISBN: 978-1-57859-192-3

The Handy African American History Answer Book
By Jessie Carney Smith, Ph.D.
ISBN: 978-1-57859-452-8

Indigenous Firsts: A History of Native American Achievement and Events
By Yvonne Wakim Dennis, Arlene Hirschfelder, and Paulette F. Molin
ISBN: 978-1-57859-712-3

Latino Almanac: From Early Explorers to Corporate Leaders
By Nicolás Kanellos, Ph.D.
ISBN: 978-1-57859-611-9

Latino Firsts: Trailblazers and Milestones in United States History
By Nicolás Kanellos, Ph.D.
ISBN: 978-1-57859-848-9

Native American Almanac: More Than 50,000 Years of the Cultures and Histories of Indigenous Peoples
By Yvonne Wakim Dennis, Arlene Hirschfelder, and Shannon Rothenberger Flynn
ISBN: 978-1-57859-507-5

Native American Landmarks and Festivals: A Traveler's Guide to Indigenous United States and Canada
By Yvonne Wakim Dennis and Arlene Hirschfelder
ISBN: 978-1-57859-641-6

Originals! Black Women Breaking Barriers!
By Jessie Carney Smith, Ph.D.
ISBN: 978-1-57859-759-8

Trailblazing Women! Amazing Americans Who Made History
By Deborah G. Felder
ISBN: 978-1-57859-729-1

Please visit us at www.visibleinkpress.com.

Acknowledgments

We here at Visible Ink Press would like to thank the following people who have reviewed the content of this book and offered many helpful suggestions.

Bonnie Morris, Ph.D., is a lecturer at UC Berkeley's Department of History. She has a Ph.D. in women's history from Binghamton University and is the author of 19 books, including *The Feminist Revolution: The Struggle for Women's Liberation* and *Women's History for Beginners*. She is a consultant to the Smithsonian, an advisor to the National Women's History Museum, and an archivist/historian to Olivia Records, working on a documentary about women in music. She has also consulted to Disney Animation and introduced a course on Sports and Gender in U.S. History at UC.

Ronni Sanlo, Ed.D., is a retired UCLA professor and director emeritus of the UCLA LGBT Center. Prior to her work at UCLA and the University of Michigan LGBT Centers, Ronni was an HIV epidemiologist in Florida from 1987 to 1994. She is the founder of the award-winning Lavender Graduation and the founding chair of the Consortium of Higher Education LGBT Resource Professionals. Ronni is also the founder and director of the Lavender Graduation Legacy Project. Ronni spends her free time writing plays about the LGBTQ story, diligently searching for our family of sheroes, heroes, and they-roes. Ronni and her wife, Dr. Kelly Watson, and their dog, Popeye, spend much of their time on their boat, *Strait Knot*.

Robert David Sullivan is former editor of the LGBTQ weekly *The New York Blade*, former editor at the *Boston Phoenix, Boston Business Journal*, and *CommonWealth* magazine, and current production editor at *America Magazine*, the last of which is a Jesuit review to which he often contributes articles on American society and politics, including LGBTQ issues.

Acknowledgments

Table of Contents

Introduction

In her book *Redefining Realness: My Path to Womanhood, Identity, Love & So Much More*, producer and transgender activist Janet Mock writes, "I believe that telling our stories, first to ourselves and then to one another and the world, is a revolutionary act. It is an act that can be met with hostility, exclusion, and violence. It can also lead to love, understanding, transcendence, and community." Queer Americans, once forced to live publicly closeted for fear of suffering the social, professional, and legal consequences of their sexual orientation, could not safely tell their stories until the 20th century, when an ever-increasing activism, moving inexorably toward a revolutionary social and legal crescendo, made the telling possible. At the same time, scholars and academics worked to rectify what had been the erasure of the LGBTQ+ history that included these stories, and LGB, LGBT, and LGBTQ initialism began to signal a community and its expanding inclusiveness.

I grew up knowing about Christine Jorgenson, the first widely known American trans woman, and came of age when the Gay Liberation Movement began after the seminal event that was the Stonewall Uprising of 1969. I was familiar with gay enclaves in Greenwich Village, on Fire Island, and in Provincetown, where my Cape Cod grandmother, a retired New York City social worker, introduced me to a lesbian couple, one of whom she'd worked with.

I was living in Manhattan during the AIDS epidemic. When gay men, including a childhood friend, succumbed to the disease, there was little-to-no crisis response from the federal government, and "Silence = Death" could be seen written in chalk on city sidewalks. At the same time, popular leading man Rock Hudson, whose sexual orientation had been an open secret within the Hollywood community while he remained closeted to the public, disclosed that he had AIDS.

During the 1990s, a decade in which it seemed as if acceptance of LGBTQ people had finally begun to be achieved, it was a shock to learn that violence toward gay and trans men remained a reality with the murders of Brandon Teena and Matthew Shepard, both of whom were just 21 years old. Then, during the first two decades of the new century, I was glad when LGBTQ Americans could legally love—even marry—whomever they wished.

But there was so much about LGBTQ that I did not know. I wanted to enhance my knowledge and understanding of queer history from antiquity to the present and to discover more about the influential individuals who made invaluable contributions in the fight for LGBTQ+ civil rights and have achieved recognition in a variety of professions. I wanted to know the stories.

My research for this book led me to discoveries about LGBTQ+ history and the people who made the history that helped me toward a greater understanding of the marginalization and the persecution of LGBTQ Americans because of the laws and morality codes that made same-sex relationships and non-binary behavior a crime, allowed police harassment of LGBT individuals in social spaces, prohibited or diluted LGBT presence on stage and screen, and forced Hollywood in its so-called Golden Age to straightwash its movie stars. It was acceptable to deny employment to LGBTQ workers, label queer Americans as "deviant," and "mentally ill," and to use derogatory slang words to describe LGBT people. But research also led me to the people throughout American history who created a wealth of LGBTQ art, literature, and entertainment with LGBTQ themes and characters, the educators who created safe spaces for queer students to academically and socially thrive, religious leaders who welcomed LGBTQ parishioners when others would not, and the scientists who worked to end the suffering and death caused by HIV/AIDS. Equally inspiring was the quest for civil rights, which began with the assimilationist gay and lesbian homophile movement of the 1950s and its emphasis on education, community, legal and humanitarian equality, and peaceful protest.

The Homophile Movement gave way to the LGBT activists of the post-Stonewall Uprising era, who created new organizations and adopted more confrontational tactics to challenge societal norms and demand the rights and political representation they deserved and had been denied to them for too long. As the author of books on women's history, literature, and biography, I discovered more about the intersection of the women's movement of the late 1960s and 1970s and lesbian activism Finally, I learned which countries around the world have embraced equality for LGBTQ+ people and which nations have oppressed their queer citizens.

Queer identity, defined by the several ways in which the acronym LGBTQ can be written, signifies both a single community and a series of communities. With that in mind, I have tried to acknowledge each identity within LGBTQ+ initialism. Although there are pejorative slang words for LGBTQ+ people that have been reclaimed (most notably, "queer"), I have chosen to include only such words that are historically relevant or have been quoted by the subject of a biography. I have used the words "homosexual" and "homosexuality," still frequently seen (more often the latter word) but considered by many to be outdated clinical terms, in a historical or biographical context, and neutral pronouns when it was clear to me that they were indicated.

The list of influential LGBTQ+ Americans is long, and it was a challenge deciding which biographies to include. I chose to focus more completely on the stories of individuals who I felt best represented the historical trajectory of LGBTQ+ in America, and throughout the book are icons and trailblazers whose struggles and sacrifices, triumphs and achievements have defined the LGBTQ+ experience past and present.

The future is always difficult to predict, and as of this writing in 2025 it is full of uncertainty for the well-being of Americans. But after completing this book, one thing became very clear to me: LGBTQ+ Americans will never return to the shadows again nor allow their history and the civil rights they have earned to be erased. Queer Americans will not choose to be invisible and silent but instead will continue to proudly tell their stories. I feel honored to have had the opportunity to offer these stories in this book.

A Historical Overview

During the last three decades of the 20th century, when queer studies joined African American and women's studies in colleges and universities and the initialism that would become LGBTQ+ was evolving and beginning to expand, historians and scholars were beginning to fill in the gaps concerning queer history in America and throughout the world. One result was a greater understanding of queer orientation dating back to antiquity. Civilizations such as ancient Greece and Rome, pre-Meiji (before 1868) Japan, and China accepted and socially codified same-sex and bisexual relationships. The Hindu and Vedic texts, epic poetry, and stories of India describe same-sex relationships and gender nonconformity among the deities and Mughal emperors and nobles. The *hijira* of South Asia, also known as *kinnar* or *Khawaja sira*, are transgender communities that also date back to antiquity and are presently considered a third gender. Queer orientation is recorded in the histories of South Sea islanders, the Ottoman Empire, Persia, parts of Africa, Medieval and Renaissance Europe, and in the indigenous populations of the pre-Columbian Americas.

As Europeans explored and settled in what would become the United States and Canada and diplomats, traders, and Catholic missionaries began to arrive there, they recorded their encounters with transgender, gender-nonconforming, and gay indigenous peoples. In some tribes, transgender and gender-nonconforming individuals were recognized as an elite third gender who were allowed the privilege of polyamory. Explorers in California translated the indigenous word for queer Native Americans into the Spanish word *joyas* ("jewels"), while the French referred to queer First Nations peoples as *berdaches*, a word derived from Arabic that indicated a young, passive, male sexual partner. During the 20th century, anthropologists began to use *berdaches* to refer to transgender native peoples as well as gay indigenous peoples. In 1990, participants at a gay and lesbian conference in Winnipeg, Canada, introduced the pan-Indian descriptor "two spirit" to replace *berdaches*, which they considered outdated and offensive. While gaining mainstream approval in Canada and the United States, the term "two spirit" has also been criticized as too limited a term to encompass diverse tribal cultural and spiritual LGBTQ+ orientations, traditions, and observances, as well as being a form of queer identity erasure. In 2004, Cree writer, filmmaker, and performer T. J. Cuthand, who came out as a trans man in 2022, coined the term "Indiqueer," which has been used either alone or in tandem with "two spirit."

A modern perspective would find LGBTQ+ power dynamics in some ancient civilizations objectionable; for example, in the patriarchal, slave-owning society that was ancient Rome, same-sex and bisexual relationships were considered acceptable only for free-born, primarily male citizens of the patrician class, and although little is known about the private lives of women in the patriarchal ancient past, evidence suggests that Roman, Greek, Egyptian, and Indian women could be subject to fees or fines for the discovery of lesbian behavior. In general, however, a certain liberality of thought allowed for the presence of socially and culturally sanctioned LGBTQ+ orientation before the rising authority and influence of the Christian Church in Medieval and Renaissance Europe. These eras, together with the Protestant Reformation, mark the establishment and enforcement of the heteronormative and gender-normative doctrines the European explorers, missionaries, and colonists would bring with them to the New World. The result would be forced gender-conforming compliance of Native American converts; British, French, and Spanish colonial laws forbidding same-sex relationships and gender nonconformity; and, ultimately, the erasure of queer history and historical figures from the American history canon until modern historians began to rectify the ignorance and suppression concerning America's LGBTQ+ past.

The two-spirit flag (or Indiqueer flag) is a symbol of the LGBTQ community among many Native Americans.

The 17th and 18th Centuries

Since these centuries provide few accounts of the LGBTQ+ orientations and identities as we know them today, early LGBTQ+ history in America can be primarily defined by the laws and punishments that attempted to eradicate any behavior perceived to be sexually immoral and socially unacceptable. The colonists in British America centered their heteronormative and binary doctrines on what they extrapolated from the Bible and English common law forbidding what we refer to as "nonbinary" behavior and primarily male same-sex relationships, the latter of which, prior to the clinical introduction of the words "homosexual" and "homosexuality" in the late 19th century, were referred to as "buggery" and, more generally, "sodomy." The precedent in English common law and the colonial sodomy laws that followed date back to 1533, during the reign of Henry VIII, when Parliament, transferring ecclesiastical law to the secular domain, enacted the first statute against male same-sex relationships and made acts of sodomy a capital crime. The law, called the Buggery Act, was eventually repealed but reinstated during the Elizabethan Era and remained in force in the United Kingdom until 1861, when it was amended to being a crime punishable by imprisonment for 10 years to life.

The first gay man in North America known to have been convicted of sodomy and executed was likely an unnamed colonist from the French settlement of Fort Caroline, which had been conquered and absorbed into Spanish Florida in 1565. When British America crafted its laws, most of the colonies followed English common law and made male same-sex relationships a capital criminal offense. Little documentation exists regarding executions carried out in the colonies of British and Dutch America; the crime of sodomy, which included all forms of nonprocreative sex as well as nonmarital sex and sexual assault,

During the reign of England's Henry VIII, the Buggery Act of 1533 was passed. It was the first law restricting the act of sodomy in England.

was difficult to prove since two witnesses were required and such witnesses, who might then be accused as well, were often reluctant to come forward. The first known execution for the crime of sodomy in British America took place around 1625 in Virginia Colony, when Richard Cornish (sometimes known as William Cornish), a ship's master, was hanged for allegedly sexually assaulting his male indentured servant. Two witnesses, one of whom was Cornish's brother, testified that no assault had occurred, but they were not believed; instead, they were pilloried and whipped for lying in court.

In Puritan New England, the General Court of the Massachusetts Bay Colony codified its sodomy laws in 1631, ruling that engaging in male same-sex relationships was a sex crime comparable to rape, incest, adultery, and bigamy and punishable by whipping, banishment, or execution. In New Amsterdam, Dutch law also made male gay relationships a capital crime for both consensual relationships and sexual assault, the latter known as "forcible buggery." The colony's few existing court records document enslaved Africans as victims of the latter and were punished as well but usually by flogging. After Dutch New Amsterdam became British New York in 1664, the law was amended to read: "If any man lyeth with mankind as he lyeth with a woman, they shall be put to Death, unless one party were Forced or be under fourteen Years of age, in which Case he shall be punished at the Discretion of the Court of Assizes." Exceptions regarding execution for male same-sex relationships included the Quaker colonies of Delaware, East and West New Jersey, and Pennsylvania, the latter of which, under the leadership of its founder, William Penn, rejected the death penalty as another form of British–Anglican colonial tyranny as well as for religious reasons. It is recorded that in Pennsylvania, punishments for engaging in male same-sex relationships included whipping, forfeiture of one-third of a miscreant's estate, six months' imprisonment with hard labor, and life imprisonment for a second offense.

In 1702, East and West New Jersey were unified as a single royal colony and therefore subject to English common law regarding gay relationships. By 1719, Pennsylvania and Delaware were similarly forced to conform to English law and accept implementation of the death penalty for male same-sex relationships. In 1777, Thomas Jefferson, while working with the

Virginia legislature to reform the criminal code in Virginia, proposed a law abandoning execution for other penalties. In 1779, the legislature presented a version of Jefferson's bill that would replace execution for rape, polygamy, and sodomy "with man or with woman" with the punishment of bodily mutilation: "if a man, with castration, if a woman, by cutting thro' the cartilage of her nose, a hole of one-half inch diameter at the least." The proposed law, considered progressive by 18th-century standards, was not enacted.

The success of the American Revolution and the Enlightenment values that had formed the Declaration of Independence and was enshrined in the Constitution's Bill of Rights, together with the increasing sovereignty of the states, created an opportunity for the reform—but not the abolishment—of sodomy laws and punishments. In 1786, Pennsylvania, which had resented the imposition of English common law, replaced the death penalty for gay men with land forfeiture and imprisonment. Other states slowly followed Pennsylvania in abolishing execution for male same-sex relationships, but slaveholding states continued to uphold the death penalty for enslaved Africans in same-gender relationships. The last states to abolish execution for gay male relationships were North Carolina (1869) and South Carolina (1873). However, male same-sex relationships continued to be called "sodomy" and were classed as a felony in every state until the late 20th century, when states began to either repeal sodomy laws or use them as a justification for discrimination against gays. In 1973, the American Psychiatric Association removed the diagnosis of homosexuality from its second edition of the *Diagnostic and Statistical Manual of Mental Disorders (DSM-II)*, but it was not until the case of *Lawrence v. Texas* in 2003 that the U.S. Supreme Court constitutionally invalidated sodomy laws in all 50 states.

Like the word "homosexual," the word "lesbian" did not begin to describe same-sex relationships between women until the 19th century. The American colonies proposed laws forbidding female same-sex relationships, in some cases linking them with the crime of sodomy, but these laws were seldom enacted or enforced. In 1636, influential Puritan theologian John Cotton suggested amending the sodomy law in the Massachusetts Bay Colony to include execution for "unnatural filthiness" between women as well as men, but Cotton's proposed law was not enacted. When Massachusetts legislator Reverend Nathaniel Ward prepared the "Body of Laws and Liberties," a new legal code first published as a broadside in 1641–1642, laws forbidding male same-sex relationships were reiterated; women were liable

Thomas Jefferson was considered progressive for proposing that the crime of sodomy should not be punished with death but, instead, with castration (for men) or cutting the cartilage in the nose (for a woman).

to execution for witchcraft, murder, or bestiality. Court documents from the era show that the Puritan colonies did punish lesbian women, however. In 1642, Elizabeth Johnson, a servant in Massachusetts, was fined and "severely whipped" for "unseemly practices with another maid attempting to do that which man and woman do." Trial documents from 1648–1650 in Yarmouth on Cape Cod (then part of the Plymouth Colony of Massachusetts) record the case of Sarah White Norman, 25, and Mary Vincent Hammon, 15, both married women who were prosecuted for "lewd behavior each with the other upon a bed." Hammon was "cleared with admonition," possibly because of her youth. Norman was convicted, asked to publicly acknowledge her "vile behavior," and warned against committing future offenses, "lest… her punishment be the greater." By this time, Norman's husband had deserted her and their children and moved to England, where he eventually squandered all his money and died in poverty. Hammon reconciled with her husband and went on to have several children with him. It is not known whether the two women continued their relationship in secret.

Gender identity and expression in British America was strictly binary. Officially, two sexes—male and female—existed, and each was expected to conform to their birth-assigned physical and social gender roles in the community. An individual who was discovered straying from the binary clothing norm was subject to arrest and, sometimes, hefty fines. A few 17th- and 18th-century examples exist of cross-dressing men; however, a 1652 court case in Massachusetts mentions that Joseph Davis was convicted of "putting on women's apparel and going from house to house with a female." Davis was ordered to pay a fine and "to make public acknowledgement of his fault." Edward Hyde, Lord Cornbury (1661–1723), the colonial governor of New York and New Jersey, is alleged to have scandalously worn women's clothes in public "in face of the Sun and sight of the Town" and to have horrified legislators when he opened the New York Assembly in 1702 dressed as his cousin, Anne, then queen of Great Britain. Cornbury's political rivals may have invented or exaggerated the unpopular governor's cross-dressing appearances, but in any case, the strategy worked, and he was removed from office in 1708.

The 17th and 18th centuries offer examples of women who challenged binary norms, the most famous of whom was Deborah Sampson, who enlisted as a male soldier during the Revolutionary War. It is recorded that in 1692, Mary Henley, a Massachusetts resident assigned female at birth, was arrested for wearing men's clothes and charged with "seeming to confound the course of nature." In Virginia, Thomas/ine Hall (c. 1603–?), a nonbinary, probably intersex indentured servant assigned female at birth, labored at tasks as

This painting, currently maintained by the New York Historical Society, purportedly shows Lord Cornbury dressed as a woman.

Born Jemima Wilkinson, after a bout with typhus the Quaker preacher renamed themselves "the Public Universal Friend" and declared they were genderless.

both a male and a female for one employer and as a female with another employer. The men and women of the community, uncomfortable with Hall's nonbinary behavior and, unclear on whether they were a man or a woman after suspicions were raised concerning their suspected dalliance with a woman servant, decided to conduct inspections of Hall's genitals. They were found to have both male and female genitals, neither of which were fully formed, but the men who examined Hall decided that they were a man and should be prosecuted and punished for wearing women's clothes. In 1629, Hall appeared before the Quarter Court at Jamestown, told their story, and received the governor's remarkable verdict for its time: Hall was declared to be both a man and a woman and was instructed to wear both the breeches and shirt of a man and the cap and apron of a woman. Hall's life and status as an indentured servant after their court appearance is not recorded.

Jemima Wilkinson (1752–1819) was a Quaker and a preacher in Rhode Island and New York who abandoned traditional Quakerism when they became a believer in the tenets of the First Great Awakening, a religious revival movement that flourished in the 1730s and 1750s and encouraged individual spiritual enlightenment. In 1776, Wilkinson became ill with what was probably typhus and upon their recovery declared that they had been dead and resurrected as a genderless evangelist named the Public Universal Friend. The Friend renounced their birth name, wore androgynous clothing, and rejected gendered pronouns. They expected their followers, the Universal Friends, to do the same. Nineteenth-century historians claimed that the Friend's resurrection account and evangelicalism was a religious hoax, insisted on referring to them by their birth name, and regarded their rejection of gender identity as evidence of mental instability. Scholars in queer studies have cited the Public Universal Friend as an example of a public figure in LGBTQ+ history who lived outside the gender binary well before the term "transgender" was in use.

Romantic Friendships

The term "romantic friendship" dates from the late 18th century and has been used in historical scholarship to describe same-sex intimate and often lifelong relationships characterized by loving devotion and physical affection. In antiquity, such friendships among men were fostered in the heroic warrior tradition and are most evident in the literature of the time; for example, in Homer's *Iliad*, the Greek war-

The devoted relationship the biblical Ruth has for her mother-in-law, Naomi, has been considered an important source for the concept of romantic friendships in the 19th century. (Portrait of a woman as Ruth by Francesco Hayez, 1835).

rior Achilles describes his fellow warrior, tentmate, and best friend Patroclus as "the man I loved beyond all other comrades, loved as my own life." Homer does not explicitly refer to the two as lovers, but other classical literature featuring them, including works by Aeschylus and Plato, characterize their relationship as homoerotic. The Old Testament's Book of Samuel has David speak of his feelings for his close friend, Jonathan: "Your love was wonderful to me, passing the love of women," which has led some scholars to interpret their relationship in a sexual context. After becoming a widow, the biblical Ruth binds herself to her mother-in-law Naomi with a vow that suggests more than an oath of religious loyalty: "Entreat me not to leave you or to return from following you; for wither you go I will go, and where you lodge, I will lodge. Your people will be my people and your God my God. Where you die I will die, and there I will be buried. May the Lord deal with me ever so severely, if even death separates you and me" (Ruth 1:16–17). In *Surpassing the Love of Men: Romantic Friendship and Love Between Women from the Renaissance to the Present,* historian Lillian Faderman cites Ruth's speech, which has been used in same-sex wedding ceremonies as a foundation of 19th-century romantic friendships between women. In *Odd Girls and Twilight Lovers,* Faderman describes these friendships as fostering "heart values."

The same-sex romantic friendships of the 19th and early 20th centuries were rooted in the largely separate social and academic spheres traditionally occupied by men and women. Women often continued their intimate friendships after marriage; men were expected to give them up once they married. During the 19th century, with its ever-growing diverse population and increasingly educated middle class, gay, lesbian, and bisexual behavior gradually began to be considered socially unacceptable, unnatural, or deviant rather than immoral: "abnormal" at best, illegal at worst. Romantic friendships allowed men and women to express their feelings in open displays of affection, frequently in journal entries and loving letters written to each other and composed in the poetic, grandiose, and often sensual writing style of the time. Whether or not romantic friendships of the past can be described as simply close and loving relationships that evoke another time, evidence of 19th- and early 20th-century gay, lesbian, and bisexual cultures, or both, has been a subject of speculation and debate. In her influential article "The Female World of Love and Ritual," historian Carroll Smith-Rosenberg suggests that romantic friendships, with "their ambivalent and romantic rhetoric presents us with an ultimate puzzle: the relationship along the spectrum of human emotions between love, sensuality, and sexuality."

Romantic friendships allowed men to share lodgings without comment, and unmarried women could live together in same-sex partnerships that sometimes came to be known as "Boston marriages," a term derived from Henry James's 1886 novel *The Bostonians*, which featured two women characters living together in a long-term relationship. In most cases, lesbians were only accepted in society if they hid their orientation and presented themselves and their partners as intimate friends, but close associates and friends most likely knew and accepted (or preferred to ignore) the orientation of women who lived together. One example is diarist and poet Charity Bryant (1777–1851), the aunt of Transcendentalist poet William Cullen Bryant, and Sylvia Drake (1784–1868), who were partners in a tailoring business as well as in life and accepted as a married couple in their community of Weybridge, Vermont.

Other notable examples of couples in romantic friendships and Boston marriages include Secretary of State Daniel Webster (1782–1852) and New Hampshire state senator and representative James Hervey Bingham (1781–1859); abolitionist and U.S. senator Charles Sumner (1811–1874) and abolitionist and physician Samuel Howe (1801–1876); authors Annie Adams Fields (1834–1915) and Sarah Orne Jewett (1849–1909); suffragists Carrie Chapman Catt (1859–1947) and Mary Garrett Hay (1857–1928); and founder of Hull House settlement house and Nobel Peace Prize recipient Jane Addams (1860–1935) and philanthro-

First Lady Eleanor Roosevelt (second from the left in this 1933 photo) was most likely in a romantic, even sexual, relationship with journalist Lorena Hickock (far right).

pist Mary Rozet Smith (1868–1934). Letters from poet Emily Dickinson (1830–1886) to her sister-in-law, editor, and lifelong close friend Susan Huntington Gilbert Dickinson (1830–1913) are often lyrically romantic in nature and express, according to many scholars, homoerotic feelings. First Lady Eleanor Roosevelt (1884–1962), the most famous woman of her time, composed letters to journalist Lorena Hickok (1893–1968) that provide ample evidence of a romantic friendship as well as evidence of a sexual relationship.

Gender Identity

The 19th century saw an increase in nontraditional gender expression, some of which coincided with the expansion of the American frontier. Women who worried about their sexual safety while traveling west alone over long distances sometimes chose to identify as men. The California Gold Rush that began in 1848, together with the development of the railroad, brought large numbers of male laborers to the West and over the following decades created largely homogenous male societies in need of entertainment. The lack of women entertainers led to an opportunity for men to appear in drag as "female impersonators," but only onstage. Challenges to established expectations and social prohibitions concerning binary gender roles and identity were met with anti-cross-dressing laws in 34 cities between 1845 (New York) and 1900. These laws were designed to either arrest or harass people for "masquerading": publicly appearing "in a dress not belonging to his or her sex."

When women who dressed as men in order to obtain jobs were discovered and arrested for what was considered "immoral" and "disguised" behavior, they often cited financial need. One example of an immigrant who changed his gender identity after his arrival in the United States for that reason is Frank Woodhull (c. 1858–?), born Mary Johnson in Canada. In 1893, after struggling and failing to find work as a woman, he began living as a man and working at various jobs in California. In 1908, he returned from a vacation in England and was processed at Ellis Island in New York, where he were told that he would be screened for tuberculosis, a routine practice at the time for immigrants who had not yet become naturalized citizens. He admitted that he was a female living as a man and asked not to be examined. He was detained and confined in a private room at the Ellis Island Hospital until his case could be settled. *The New York Times*, which ran an article on Woodhull and interviewed him, reported, "If she is discharged, she must go from Ellis Island as a woman to meet the requirements of the law, but thereafter she will be free to choose her own manner of life." Two months later, the Ellis Island Board of Special Inquiry ruled that he "should be allowed to win her livelihood as she saw fit."

Since female enlistment in the military remained forbidden, several hundred people who were assigned female at birth enlisted as male soldiers in order to fight in Union or Confederate armies during the Civil War (1861–1865). Given the need for soldiers as the conflagration grew, the lack of physical examinations, and the assumption that enlistees would be male, female soldiers were able to conceal their gender unless they were outed by accident or had been wounded and were hospitalized. Most of the women who served returned to their cisgender lives after the war, but there were exceptions. Albert Cashier (1829–1915), an Irish immigrant born Jennie Hodgers, lived as a man before enlisting at the age of 18. He served in the Union Army for three years and fought in over 40 battles. After the war, he continued to live as a man until he was elderly, suffering from dementia and being confined to a state hospital for the insane in Illinois. While bathing him, attendants discovered

One of the most noted cases of a woman posing as a man during the U.S. Civil War was that of Jennie Hodgers, who served in the Union Army as Albert Cashier. When Cashier died in 1915, they were buried in uniform and with full military honors.

that he was a female and forced him to wear a dress for the first time since childhood. He died of injuries resulting from a fall caused when he tripped over his long skirt.

A notable example of a formerly enslaved transgender Black woman who reclaimed her gender identity after the Civil War and Emancipation is Frances Thompson (1840–1876). Thompson, a casualty of the Memphis Riots of 1866, was assigned male at birth, identified as a woman, and worked as a female launderer in Memphis. The rioting began after police attempted to break up a public gathering of Black soldiers, women, and children; they arrested two soldiers, and gunshots rang out. A white mob then went on a three-day rampage against the Black community, starting fires and killing and raping Black residents, including Thompson and her housemate, Lucy Smith. Thompson's testimony at the U.S. congressional hearing that followed the riots led to awareness of her gender identity. In 1876, she was fined $50 and jailed for "cross-dressing," and her testimony was discredited as Reconstructionist propaganda. She was sentenced to serve on the city's chain gang, forced to wear men's clothing, and died in Memphis of dysentery soon after her release.

An aspect of transgender and gender-nonconforming history that adds to the conversation concerning the complex expression of sexual orientation and gender identity are the accounts of "female husbands," people assigned female at birth who lived as men and were legally married to women. The term dates to 17th-century England and was popularized by British novelist Henry Fielding, whose 1746 novel *The Female Husband* is a fictionalized account of the trial of transgender spouse George (born Mary) Hamilton, who was prosecuted for vagrancy but also punished for sexual immorality after a public outcry. Both the British and American press further popularized the term and exploited it for sensational value. The most notable, and newsworthy, American example of a "female husband" is Joseph Lobdell (c. 1829–1912), born Lucy Ann Lobdell in New York. As Lucy Ann, he married George Slater and gave birth to a daughter. After his abusive husband abandoned his family, he sent his daughter to live with his parents and began presenting as a man and living as a backwoodsman. While working as an itinerant laborer in various towns, he was sometimes forced to leave on suspicion that he was female. He moved to Pennsylvania, where he reentered society, worked as a voice teacher, and became engaged to a young, female student. He was again forced to flee when the girl's rejected suitor began to suspect his birth gender and threatened to tar and feather him. While living in the poorhouse in Delhi, New York, he met Mary Louise Perry, whose husband had also deserted her. The two married around 1861 (Slater had been killed in the Civil War), and when the pair was arrested for vagrancy some time afterward, "discovery that the supposed man was a woman was made." After his release, Lobdell was arrested for wearing men's clothing, and in 1880, he was sent to an insane asylum in Willard, New York. In 1883, P. M. Wise, an "alienist" (the precursor descriptor for "psychiatrist") at the asylum, wrote an article on Lobdell titled "Case of Sexual Perversion," in which he referred to the Lobdells' marriage as "Lesbian love," reportedly the first use of the word "lesbian" in an American clinical publication. In 1900, Lobdell was transferred to another New York insane asylum, where he remained confined until his death.

Shown here around 1853, Joseph Lobdell led a diverse career as a singing teacher, fiddler, and laborer who successfully led a man's life for many years until they were arrested for vagrancy and discovered to be a woman.

An early example is documented of a transgender woman who was not a "female husband" but a woman who was assigned male at birth, lived as a woman, and legally married men. Lucy Hicks Anderson (1886–1954), a popular Prohibition Era African American socialite and chef, identified as female from an early age with her parents' support. After divorcing her first husband, Clarence Hicks, she worked as a domestic and chef in Oxnard, California, preparing lavish dinners for Oxnard's wealthy families. With the money she saved, she bought a boardinghouse that also served as a secret brothel and speakeasy and continued to host dinners attended by eminent citizens of the city. She remarried in 1944 to G.I. Reuben Anderson, and her gender identity remained unchallenged until 1945, when he was forced to undergo a medical examination after a sailor claimed that he had contracted a venereal disease at the brothel. Upon discovering Lucy's birth gender, the district attorney arrested her for lying on her marriage certificate and invalidated the marriage. The federal government then had both Andersons arrested and tried for fraud for receiving a spousal allotment under the G.I. Bill. The couple was sent to a men's prison, where Lucy was forbidden to wear women's clothing. After their release, the Andersons, barred from returning to Oxnard under penalty of further prosecution, relocated to Los Angeles, where they lived quietly and without harassment. In the words of Lucy at her first trial: "I have lived, dressed, acted just what I am, a woman."

The 20th century featured the first opportunities for transgender Americans to complete the process of gender reassignment through medical procedures initially known as "sex changes." In 1917, physician Alan Hart (1890–1962), born female, became the first documented trans man in the United States to undergo limited gender reassignment surgery. The first widely known person to hormonally and surgically transition was actress and singer Christine Jorgensen (1926–1989), born George, who began her gender transition in Denmark in 1952 and completed it in the United States as a patient of endocrinologist and sexologist Harry Benjamin. Although other individuals who had undergone gender reassignment surgery generated some press during the 1930s and 1940s, primarily in tabloid newspapers or niche magazines such as *Sexology*, Jorgensen's gender change became a worldwide media sensation. Jorgensen, who initially wanted to keep her transition a secret, was outed when a letter to her parents to inform them of her transition was leaked to the *Daily News*. In December 1952, the paper ran a story with the headline "Ex-GI Becomes Blonde Beauty: Operations Transform Bronx Youth," together with before and after photos. Other papers followed suit, and a slew of reporters interviewed Jorgensen at the airport after she returned to the United States in 1953. Subsequent articles and media coverage varied from noncommittal reportage to derision as well as questions concerning her mental health and the legitimacy of her womanhood. Throughout much of her post-transition life, Jorgensen embraced her celebrity as an opportunity to control her own narrative and to inform the public that her transition was both normal and worthy of acceptance at a time when transsexualism, like gay and lesbian behavior, was considered a perversion.

American singer and actress Christine Jorgensen had surgery done in Denmark and became famous for her 1967 book, Christine Jorgensen: A Personal Autobiography.

During the 1960s, in the wake of Jorgensen's transition, the first organizations, publications, and books such as Harry Benjamin's *The Transsexual Phenomenon* provided information and support for what was then a small transgender community. The result was a growing public awareness of transgenderism, which went on to gain wider exposure from pop artist and filmmaker Andy Warhol, whose Factory studio in New York City in the late 1960s and 1970s became a noted hangout for artists, musicians, and celebrities, including transgender actresses Holly Woodlawn and Candy Darling, who became known as Warhol Superstars. The 1970s, a decade that featured greater LGBTQ+ activism and the women's liberation movement, also saw an increase in the visibility of transgender activism as well as the start of advocacy and activist organizations for male cross-dressers, one of which was the Queens Liberation Front.

Despite the media attention paid to Christine Jorgensen and, later, ophthalmologist and tennis player Renée Richards, a trans woman who completed her transition in the 1970s, gender-affirming care during the 1980s and early 1990s was difficult to access because of the cost of transition, the lack of medical support, and the psychiatric community's labeling of transgenderism as a disorder. Individuals who could afford to transition and were able to find physicians who would complete it felt forced to hide their reassigned gender identities because of the stigma attached to transgender visibility and the threat of violence toward transgender individuals. For example, Brandon Teena, a 21-year-old trans man who sometimes claimed to be intersex and was hoping to medically transition when it was possible for him to do so, was raped and murdered in Nebraska in 1993. It was not unusual during the latter decades of the 20th century for young LGBTQ+ people to become unhoused after their families rejected their orientation. In 2022, the Trevor Project reported that overall, 28 percent of LGBTQ+ youth experienced homelessness or housing instability at some point during their lives. Over the years, many of these young people have reported episodes of harassment and abuse toward them at shelters, especially in shelters meant for adults.

Many young LGBTQ people get kicked out of their homes by parents who don't accept them. They often end up living on the streets, struggling to survive.

In 2008, a survey titled "The Lives of Transgender People," published by Columbia University Press, reported that the largest percentage of transgender individuals who were out to all their friends were aged 23–32; the largest percentage of those who remained in the closet were trans people aged 63 and over. When asked how they learned about their gender identity, respondents aged 18–52 cited reading/research, support groups, and TV; those 53 years old and above mentioned the above, together with mentioning Christine Jorgensen. In 2022, *The New York Times* published a report containing the estimate that as of 2020, teens and adults under the age of 25 made up 43 percent of the transgender population, while those aged 25–64 encompassed nearly 50 percent. A 2022 survey conducted by the National Center for Transgender Equality (NCTE), released in 2024, found that out of more than 90,000 survey participants, a considerable majority reported greater well-being after their transition.

Although the start of the 21st century saw social, political, employment, educational, and medical initiatives on behalf of transgender Americans, the second and third decades brought a backlash from some state and local governments against transgender individuals. Questions began to be raised as to whether gender-affirming care such as the administration of puberty blockers and hormone therapy were appropriate treatments for teens and children who identified as transgender, with some states beginning to ban their use for people under a certain age. Mandates insisted that transgender people use bathrooms according to their birth gender, and states began to restrict or ban drag performances, brunches, and library story hours for children. The challenging and banning of school and public library books with LGBTQ+ themes and content was an additional cause for concern that a sizable number of states were seeking to revert to the repressive values, discrimination, and legal prohibitions of the past, which could threaten not only the free expression of preferred gender identity but also the safety and well-being of the entire LGBTQ+ community.

A Sense of Community: LGBTQ-Friendly Spaces and Places

The criminalization and social rejection of LGBTQ+ Americans before the repeal of sodomy laws and a gradually increasing, if ambivalent, climate of acceptance that began toward the end of the 20th century led to the use and creation of social and residential spaces and places in cities and resort towns where LGBTQ+ people could openly and safely live, gather, and form romantic and sexual relationships, where they could be "out" without being "outed," the latter of which often led to lost jobs and loss of family ties as well as harassment and violence. The 21st century has seen welcoming and supportive LGBTQ+ retirement and assisted-living communities across the United States as the over-55 LGBTQ+ population has grown: In 2020, some four million LGBTQ+ people over the age of 65 lived in the United States, and it has been estimated that by 2030, over six million LGBTQ+ Americans will be of retirement age.

The number of older LGBTQ Americans is growing, and with it there has been increasing availability of LGBTQ retirement and assisted-living communities.

While most LGBTQ+-friendly enclaves have historically centered on cities and towns, the countercultural political, peace, and environmental "Back to the Land" movements of the late 1960s and 1970s saw young gay liberation and lesbian feminist groups begin experiments in collective living. The Lavender Hill Commune, a collective of writers, artists, and activists, grew out of an earlier Staten Island, New York, commune, the 25 to 6 Baking and Trucking Society, and was established in 1973 on 80 acres near Ithaca in upstate New York. The commune, which lasted for 11 years, focused on self-sufficiency and a connection with nature while also providing a safe space for its members to explore gender and sexual identity and to experiment with gender roles. On February 21, 2025, the Lavender Hill Commune was added to the National Register of Historic Places for its cultural significance in LGBTQ+ history.

LGBTQ+ in the City

In similar fashion to other persecuted and marginalized groups in American history, cities, with their larger and more culturally diverse populations, offered opportunities for LGBTQ+ life and culture to flourish. Beginning in the early 20th century with New York City's Greenwich Village, LGBTQ+ neighborhoods became established in many U.S. cities and have included Philadelphia's Gayborhood, Boston's South End and Jamaica Plain neighborhoods, Chicago's Andersonville area, and San Francisco's first gay neighborhood, Polk Gulch. By the mid-1960s, San Francisco had become known as the "Gay Capital of America," in part because of a 1964 *Life* magazine article titled "Homosexuality in America," the first article to focus on gay issues in the United States. During the early 1960s, San Francisco's Tenderloin district, an area that had long been home to marginalized groups such as the working class and people of color, saw an influx of LGBTQ+ residents after urban renewal projects priced them out of other neighborhoods.

Although subject to police raids and closings, drag balls, bathhouses, and gay and lesbian bars and nightclubs were the first spaces that allowed the queer community to openly socialize together and, like the straight community, to meet possible sexual and romantic partners.

Early on, city enclaves, sometimes known as "gayborhoods" or gay villages depending on their municipal status, included LGBTQ+-friendly businesses such as bookstores, restaurants, bars, and nightclubs. Although subject to police raids and closings, drag balls, bathhouses, and gay and lesbian bars and nightclubs were the first spaces that allowed the queer community to openly socialize together and, like the straight community, to meet possible sexual and romantic partners. Cities like New York, Chicago, and San Francisco also fostered LGBTQ+ subcultures, such as leather communities, which began to appear in the 1950s as offshoots from post–World War II motorcycle clubs. Once a subculture for primarily white gay men, sometimes known as leathermen, leather culture grew more inclusive over the decades with the addition of people of color, transgender people, and lesbians. In San Francisco during the late 1970s, lesbian activist Cynthia Slater fought for and achieved acceptance into the gay leather scene, and in 1976, the newly formed lesbian leatherwomen club Dykes on Bikes led the LGBTQ+ Pride Parade, the San Francisco Gay Freedom Day Parade, for the first time. The following year saw the formation of the lesbian biker club Leather and Lace in Los Angeles. During the AIDS crisis of the 1980s and early 1990s, lesbian leatherwomen often helped to care for gay male bikers who had been stricken with the disease. Various performers have been associated with leather culture, including the Village People, heavy metal band Judas Priest, Meat Loaf, Freddie Mercury of the rock band Queen, and Joan Jett.

Drag balls. An early form of city nightlife socializing, drag balls contributed to the establishment of LGBTQ+ culture and came to show ways in which race, gender, and sexual orientation could intersect and evolve. The balls were gala cross-dressing entertainments: part parties, part nightclubs. They originated from European cross-dressing "grand rag" masquerade costume parties and balls as well as the debutante balls for young women of the upper classes, intended to show that they were of an age to be "coming out" in society. Drag balls similarly allowed the LGBTQ+ community to abandon the secrecy of their orientation necessary in mainstream society and "come out" to one another. The first drag ball in the United States took place in 1869 at the Hamilton Lodge, a ballroom in the Harlem neighborhood of New York City. Known as the Masquerade and Civic Ball, the balls at the Hamilton Lodge became a popular annual event until 1916, when the Com-

Drag balls had grown into spectacles by the 1920s in places like Greenwich Village in New York. Webster Hall, recognized as the first modern night club, is shown here pulling out all the stops.

mittee of Fourteen, a moral reform organization founded in 1905 by members of the Anti-Saloon League and eventually disbanded in 1932 due to lack of funds, began to intermittently investigate the balls in person. The committee declared the balls to be scandalous events featuring "male perverts" and demanded their closure in a series of 130 detailed reports.

During Prohibition (1920–1933) and the Harlem Renaissance (1920–1935), the influential intellectual, cultural, and artistic movement that centered on Black life and activism, drag balls, including those at the Hamilton Lodge, the Savoy, and the Alhambra Ballroom, enjoyed such a huge resurgence in popularity as speakeasies, as well as nightclubs, that New York City police, despite harassment and raids, were disinclined to prevent them from continuing. Historian and LGBTQ+ activist George Chauncey has referred to the popularity of drag balls during this era as the "Pansy Craze." The balls attracted large numbers of gay, lesbian, and transgender people, which included such notable figures from the Harlem Renaissance as Alice Dunbar Nelson, Alain Locke, and Langston Hughes, and many partygoers outside of the LGBTQ+ and Black community, all of whom also came to see drag performers like blues singer and pianist Gladys Bentley and the beauty pageants featuring glamorous drag queens that were held there. Despite the balls' interracial presence, the Black contestants at the Hamilton Lodge had a prevailing sense that pageant judges associated glamour with whiteness, leading them to unduly favor white, Eurocentric features. In 1936, a Black contestant won the beauty pageant at the Hamilton Lodge for the first time, but questions concerning racial bias among pageant judges toward Black and Latinx contestants persisted as the drag balls expanded to include other major cities throughout the 20th century.

The late 20th century saw drag balls begin to transform from pageantry into a drag house ball subculture called Ballroom, where Black and Latinx drag queens would compete for trophies and cash prizes in competitions that featured a form of expressive dancing called "voguing," named after the fashion magazine *Vogue*. Houses, which have been founded in several U.S. cities, have also provided guidance, support, and shelter for transgender people who have been estranged from their families or are unable to take advantage of conventional support systems. Notable houses include the Royal House of LaBeija, founded by drag performer and Ballroom culture cofounder Crystal LaBeija, and the House of Aviance, founded by drag performer Mother Juan Aviance.

Many bath houses closed because of the AIDS epidemic, but this one in Portland, Oregon, survived and remained open until 2007.

Bathhouses. These gathering spaces for men, once known as Turkish baths, date back to ancient Greece and Rome and to the 15th century in Europe and the late 19th century in New York City. The first recorded police raid on a gay venue in New York took place at the Ariston Baths in 1903. Police arrested 34 patrons, of which 16 were charged with sodomy and 12 were held over for trial. The proprietor was charged with "keeping a disorderly house." Gay men also patronized Everard Baths, a former church converted to a bath by financier James Everard in 1888 until its closing in 1986 during the AIDS epidemic, when the operation of bathhouses became controversial. In 1919 and 1920, the police, at the behest of the New York Society for the Suppression of Vice, another of the several moral reform organizations of the day, raided Everard Baths and arrested the manager and several patrons. Everard Baths was a favorite of such notables in the arts as Alfred Lunt, Clifton Webb, Nöel Coward, Gore Vidal, Rudolf Nureyev, Lorenz Hart, and Truman Capote. Another popular early bathhouse was the Lafayette Baths, which was managed by lyricist and composer brothers Ira and George Gershwin and was a favorite of gay painter George Demuth. The 1950s saw the opening of exclusively gay bathhouses in the United States, which, like earlier baths, were subject to vice raids from time to time. During the 1960s and 1970s, baths were primarily under gay ownership and became fully licensed gay social establishments that hosted Pride parties and conducted voter registration drives on their premises. The most famous bathhouse during this era was the Continental Baths in New York's Ansonia Hotel, which opened in 1968. The Continental was operated by New York City Opera singer Steve Ostrow (1932–2024), who featured music and a DJ and, later, live public performances by many entertainers, including Bette Midler, Marvin Hamlisch, Patti LaBelle's group Labelle, Nell Carter, and Peter Allen. Ostrow canceled the live performances in 1974 when gay patrons began to leave because the presence of a non-LGBTQ+ performer made them feel uncomfortable. In 1976, he closed the Continental Baths, and the following year, he reopened the space as Plato's Retreat, a swingers' club for straight couples and bisexual women. San Francisco, which boasted 30 gay bathhouses by the late 1970s, began to close during the AIDS epidemic. The last to shutter was San Francisco's 21st Street Baths, which opened in the early 1960s and closed in 1987.

Bars. Opinion is divided on which American LGBTQ+ bar was the earliest. During the late 19th century, several bars in New York City's Bowery, the Lower East Side, and a lower Midtown area called the Tenderloin were patronized by gay men. The Slide, a basement saloon on Bleecker Street in Greenwich Village, hosted large groups of gay men in drag and was closed by police in 1892, with the manager arrested for "disorderly conduct," a catchphrase that would come to be used as an excuse for police raids on bars that served gays. The Atlantic House, a popular hotel, bar, and nightclub in Provincetown that dates to the late 19th century, discreetly served gay patrons during the Prohibition years of the 1920s and became openly gay friendly beginning in the 1950s. The Gangway in San Francisco was originally a dive bar that opened in 1910, became a speakeasy called the Larkin Street Grill during the Prohibition years, and, after 1933, operated as the Gangway until its closure in 2018. Other early 20th-century contenders for the oldest continuously operating gay bar that date to 1933 and the end of Prohibition include Café Lafitte in Exile in New Orleans; the Korner Lounge in Shreveport, Louisiana; the White Horse Inn in Oakland, California; and the Double Header in Seattle, Washington. Julius' in Greenwich Village, which opened in 1864 and received its current name in 1930, is often

New Orleans' Café Lafitte in Exile claims bragging rights to being the oldest gay bar in the United States. It was established in 1933.

cited as New York's oldest continuously operating gay bar. The first leather bar in the United States was the Gold Coast, which opened in San Francisco in 1958. Not far from Julius' is the most historically notable gay bar of them all, the Stonewall Inn at 53 Christopher Street, where resistance against a police raid in 1969 proved to be a flashpoint in the history of LGBTQ+ activism.

During much of the 20th century, it was illegal to serve alcohol to queer patrons and thus difficult for bars that openly served LGBTQ+ customers to obtain liquor licenses. If a gay bar was discovered breaking this law, the establishment could lose its license to operate and would close. After the repeal of Prohibition in 1933, the Mafia, which had provided alcohol for speakeasies (some of which also featured drag shows) during the 1920s, continued to maintain a stranglehold on nightlife and saw an opportunity for further profit in the ownership of bars catering to the vilified and shunned male gay community, particularly in Chicago and New York. By 1966, the Genovese crime family controlled nearly all the gay bars in New York's Greenwich Village, including the popular Stonewall Inn. One way to get around local liquor license laws was to label gay bars as private, members-only "bottle clubs," which could legally allow patrons to imbibe the Mafia's watered-down and expensive alcohol. However, despite owners' payoffs to police and bar payoffs to owners for "protection," LGBTQ+ bars continued to experience police raids and arrests for "disorderly conduct" and raids for breaking state liquor laws. Bar owners were also not above extorting money from wealthy, closeted customers in exchange for silence. During the Stonewall Uprising in June–July 1969, activists Fred Sargeant and Craig Rodwell printed and distributed 5,000 leaflets calling for an end to Mafia-run LGBTQ+ establishments and advocating on behalf of gay ownership of bars.

During the 1950s, when gay bars and clubs began to be scrutinized for the violation of anti-sodomy laws, owners often escaped raids and harassment of their patrons by bribing law enforcement officials.

Police harassment of LGBTQ+ bar patrons and raids on gay and lesbian bars were common in Los Angeles and San Francisco throughout the 20th century. The largest police raid in San Francisco history took place in September 1961 at the Tay-Bush Inn, during which 103 LGBTQ+ patrons, mostly gay men, were arrested. The same year, the "gayola" scandal in San Francisco, in which police were discovered to be extorting gay bars in exchange for the cessation of raids, led to the creation of the Tavern Guild, an association formed by gay bar owners and liquor wholesalers that lasted from 1962 to 1995.

In Seattle, the gay community patronized bars, cabarets, and nightclubs in the Pioneer Square section of the city beginning in the 1920s. The oldest continuously operating gay bar was the Double Header (1934–2015), located above the Casino, a dance club, café, pool room, and card room catering to gays and lesbians and popular with drag queens. During the 1950s, when gay bars and clubs began to be scrutinized for the violation of anti-sodomy laws, owners often escaped raids and harassment of their patrons by bribing law enforcement officials. In 2024, Seattle experienced its first bar raids since the 1990s. During one weekend in late January, the city's Joint Enforcement Team (JET), made up of Washington State Liquor and Cannabis Control Board (LCB) representatives and police, fire, and transportation officers, conducted unannounced investigations of four LGBTQ+ bars and clubs for liquor violations. At the Cuff, a gay bar, officers walked through with flashlights and took photos of patrons. The officers found no alcohol violations but identified "lewd conduct" at three venues because some of the patrons in the bars were shirtless or scantily clothed. According to the *Seattle Times*, no citations were issued, and members of the LGBTQ+ caucus in the state senate have proposed an amendment to the administrative code that would disallow citations for disobeying the long-standing "lewd conduct" regulation.

The AIDS epidemic that began in the early 1980s severely impacted gay bars, causing many to close their doors. Gay bars have long offered refuge for those impacted by HIV and have offered support through fundraising events, testing, and free condoms. During the AIDS epidemic, the Gangway hosted fundraising events on behalf of San Francisco General Hospital's Ward 5B, the first inpatient AIDS unit in the United States.

At a time in American history when women were barred from spaces serving alcohol, the earliest bar that may well have included lesbians among its patrons was the Café des Beaux Arts, a popular French restaurant and bar in New York City that opened the first known American "ladies' bar" in 1911. According to the website *Lost Womyn's Space*, the ladies' bar closed in 1921 when, like other drinking establishments, the Café des Beaux Arts was shuttered because of Prohibition. During the 1920s, women were allowed to drink in speakeasies, and in 1925, lesbians were welcomed, most notably at Eve's Hangout, a popular Greenwich Village nightclub also known, in speakeasy-speak, as Eve Adams's Tearoom, which included among its patrons famed photographer

The property at 129 MacDougal Street in Greenwich Village, where Eve's Hangout was once located, is now a pizza restaurant called La Lanterna di Vittorio.

Berenice Abbott. Its owner and manager, Polish immigrant Eva Kotchever, had previously hosted a gay and lesbian literary salon in Chicago and was the author of *Lesbian Love* under the pen name Evelyn Adams. In 1926, police officers of the New York City Vice Squad arrested Kotchever for obscenity and "disorderly conduct" and closed the nightclub. After a year in prison, Kotchever was deported back to Poland, where she was murdered in 1943 at the Auschwitz concentration camp. During the so-called post–World War II Lavender Scare of the 1950s, a time in American history that coincided with the Red Scare, gays and lesbians were targeted as leftists and Communists, and bars were routinely raided for political, as well as anti-LGBTQ+, reasons. Examples include Tommy's Place/12 Adler Place and Kelly's Alamo Club, both in San Francisco. The latter was raided by police in 1954, and 36 women were arrested for "frequenting a house of ill repute." During the 1960s, lesbian bars were subject to a peculiar form of police scrutiny during raids through the enforcement of old cross-dressing laws that remained in effect and required women to wear three items of "female apparel," sometimes known as the "three-article rule," which was also applied to men wearing drag. Police would inspect women's underwear and check their pants with flashlights to see if their flies were in the front, in the masculine fashion.

Twentieth-century lesbian bars notable for their longevity date from the late 1940s and include the Pied Piper in Provincetown, Massachusetts, which opened in the 1950s as the Ace of Spades and in the 1980s was known as the Pied Bar; the Palms in West Hollywood, California; and Phase 1 in Washington, D.C. (nearly 50 years). By the 1980s, some 200 lesbian bars existed across the nation, but the latter years of the decade began to see a steep decline in the number of both gay and lesbian bars, including establishments catering to gay and lesbian people of color. Reasons for a continuing decline include gentrification, the availability of online dating services and apps, the advent of bars reflecting the expanding LGBTQ+ community, and the COVID-19 pandemic of 2020–2022. In 2020, directors and writers Elina Street and Erica Rose founded the Lesbian Bar Project in Brooklyn, New York, to support the preservation of the remaining 15 lesbian bars across the country by sponsoring fundraising campaigns and to preserve this important aspect of lesbian history through documentaries on the subject. The decline in lesbian and gay bars has led to alternative venues allowing LGBTQ+ people to meet without relying on bars or dating apps. Boston, for example, has offered such organizations as Lesbian Nightlife, a series of nightclubs that produce events for lesbian, trans, and queer women; FLAG (Friends, Lesbians, and Gays) Flag Football; and the Boston Gay Professionals Meetup Group. In 2019, the Pied Bar became *Orange is the New Black* actress Lea DeLaria's jazz club The Club. In 2024, the space reopened as a seafood restaurant, Ocean 193.

LGBTQ+ Resort Communities

The early and mid-20th century saw the burgeoning of LGBTQ+-friendly residential and beachside resort areas as vacation sanctuaries. Among the earliest were Provincetown on Cape Cod, Key West in the Florida Keys, and Fire Island in New York. However, the Midwest had its own gay resort early in the century in the twin villages of Saugatuck and Douglas, Michigan, where an artists' colony founded in 1910 on Lake Michigan began to attract many gay artists by the 1920s. The 1960s through the 1990s saw Delaware's Rehoboth Beach and Florida's South Beach in Miami Beach become centers of LGBTQ+ life and nightlife. California's desert resort city Palm Springs, popular with Hollywood celeb-

The desert resort town of Palm Springs in southern California is a haven for the LGBTQ community. About half of the full-time residents are LGBTQ.

rities since the mid-20th century, began to attract the LGBTQ+ community by the 21st century and, as of 2023, had the largest proportion of LGBTQ+ residents in the nation. In 2020, Christy Holstege became the first female mayor of Palm Springs as well as reportedly the first openly bisexual mayor in the United States, and the following year saw Lisa Middleton elected as the first openly transgender mayor in California history.

Provincetown. One of the most queer-inclusive towns in the United States, this Cape Cod seaport village was primarily known early on for its Portuguese American whaling and fishing industries as well as affordable boardinghouses and a small number of summer visitors. After the turn of the 20th century, Provincetown began to attract artists, writers, actors, and "freethinkers" from Greenwich Village such as activists John Reed and Emma Goldman. Notable LGBTQ+ summer residents during these early years included painter Charles Demuth, writer Djuna Barnes, and 29-year-old playwright Tennessee Williams, who first arrived in Provincetown in the summer of 1940. During the 1950s, members of the town government (known as Selectmen) enacted regulations banning drag shows and forbidding, according to the local paper the *Provincetown Advocate*, bars and restaurants that encouraged "the habitual gathering of "home-sexuals (sic) of either sex." The ordinances were ignored, and in 1960, after Weathering Heights, a nightclub featuring cross-dressing wait staff and drag acts, was refused a liquor license and closed, town shopkeepers successfully pushed back against regulations targeting the LGBTQ+ community. By the 1970s, Provincetown had a significant LGBTQ+ population; by the 21st century, the queer community comprised the majority of Provincetown's some 3,000 residents and about 90,000 summer visitors. Considered by many to be the nation's unofficial LGBTQ+ summer capital, Provincetown continues to attract LGBTQ+ notables such as filmmaker John Waters; comedian, actress, and singer Lea DeLaria; painter Christopher Sousa; and photographer Ron Amato.

Key West. When the Great Depression of the 1930s economically devastated Key West, the federal organization Works Progress Administration (WPA) stepped in with strategies to revitalize the city by hiring writers and artists to create paintings for the city as well as postcards, brochures, and posters that were sent throughout the country to bolster tourism. By the late 1930s, the small city was beginning to attract such LGBTQ+ notables as Pulitzer Prize–winning poet and U.S. poet laureate Elizabeth Bishop. In 1941, Tennessee Williams and composer Leonard Bernstein visited Key West for the first time, with Williams settling there until his death in 1983 and Bernstein eventually purchasing a winter home in the city. Broadway luminaries such as playwrights James Kirkwood (*A Chorus Line*) and Terrence McNally (*Love! Valour! Compassion!*) and composer and lyricist Jerry Herman (*Mame*) were also Key West aficionados. In 1967, gay Key Wester businessman and native David Wolkowsky, who local media has referred to as "Mr. Key West," built the Pier House, the Keys' first high-end resort hotel. Other seminal events in Key West's LGBTQ+ history include the establishment of the Key West Business Guild to support LGBTQ+ businesses and encourage tourism (1978); the election of Richard Heyman, reportedly the first openly gay mayor in the United States (1983); and the election of Teri Johnston, the first openly lesbian to be elected mayor of a Florida city. One of Key West's most important testaments to LGBTQ+ history is its AIDS Memorial, created with private funding in 1997. The Friends of the AIDS Memorial, Inc., has been responsible for the Memorial's upkeep since 1998 and organizes an annual march and a reading of names for World AIDS Day on December 1.

Fire Island. The Fire Island hamlets of Cherry Grove, often called America's first gay and lesbian village, and Fire Island Pines, its historically more affluent and conservative close neighbor, have long been popular LGBTQ+-accepting recreational beach enclaves. Favored for its proximity to New York City, Fire Island first became known during the Prohibition years of the 1920s as a safe summer vacation haven for the city's queer community and, in much the same way as Provincetown and Key West, for its relative isolation and relaxed policing. In 1927, Frank Carrington (1893–1975), a prominent theater director and cofounder of the Cherry Lane Theatre in New York and the Paper Mill Playhouse in New Jersey, purchased a home near Fire Island Pines called Carrington House, where, throughout the 1930s and 1940s, he welcomed LGBTQ+ friends and colleagues. In 1948, Carrington helped to establish and incorporate the Arts Project of Cherry Grove, which held its first production, *The Cherry Grove Follies of 1948*, as a fundraising event. Today, the building in which the theater is housed is called the Community House.

After the Great Hurricane of 1938 destroyed the majority of the communities' cottages, straight homeowners began to rent to young city LGBTQ+ vacationers to defray the costs of rebuilding. During the 1940s and 1950s, the increasing population of Cherry Grove LGBTQ+ homeowners and visitors included such well-known writers as W. H. Auden, Patricia Highsmith, Frank O'Hara, and Truman Capote, who completed the first draft of *Breakfast at Tiffany's* at Carrington House. During the 1960s and 1970s, noted artists

A ferry full of drag queens arrives at the Fire Island town of Pines Harbor. The neighborhoods of Fire Island Pines and Cherry Grove are particularly gay-friendly on the island.

Andy Warhol and David Hockney were summer visitors, and the LGBTQ+ population began to expand to Fire Island Pines. An incident occurred in the latter community in 1976, when Cherry Grove drag queen Teri Warren was denied service at a restaurant there. Cherry Grove residents responded by dressing in drag and mounting an "invasion" of the Pines by water taxi, an event that is repeated annually on July 4.

The most iconic building in the Fire Island LGBTQ+ communities is Carrington House, considered the oldest surviving building in Cherry Grove. In 2014, it was listed on the National Register of Historic Places and is one of five sites recognized for its importance in LGBTQ+ history.

The Language of LGBTQ+

The language used to describe LGBTQ+ orientation was slow to evolve and even slower to shed its offensive connotations. In 1828, Connecticut lexicographer Noah Webster (1758–1843) published the first edition of his influential *Webster's American Dictionary of the English Language,* in which he included definitions of the same derogatory words for gay men that had been in use for centuries, some taken from stories in the King James Version (KJV) of the Bible such as "sodomite," the demonym for denizens of the immoral biblical city of Sodom. Webster also included "sodomite" as a definition for "abuser." He would not have known the words "homosexual" and "homosexuality," neologisms which first became widely known after German psychiatrist Richard von Krafft-Ebing used them, along with the word "heterosexual," in his 1886 book *Psychopathia Sexualis*. The first dictionary to include the word "homosexuality" was the 1909 *Merriam-Webster New International Dictionary*, where it was defined as a medical term meaning "morbid sexual passion for one of the same sex." "Homosexual" became the default descriptor of gay men and remains in use, although it has become increasingly less ubiquitous, given its history as a clinical term. Several new and revived post-World War II LGBTQ+ rights groups in Europe and the United States preferred the word "homophile" to emphasize same-sex love over sexuality, leading to a homophile movement that lasted until 1969 and the start of the gay liberation movement.

Webster broadly defined "disorderly" as "lawless, as in lawless assemblies" and "in a manner contrary to rules or established institutions." The word was commonly used as a euphemistic excuse for arrests during the 19th and 20th centuries in venues where LGBTQ+ people peacefully gathered, which were subject to frequent police raids; these included gay and lesbian bars and clubs, bathhouses, and drag balls, where patrons were arrested for "disorderly conduct" in a "disorderly house" or, simply, for being "disorderly."

Once often used as a word defining an event or a person as "merry," "lighthearted," or "carefree," "gay" had also been in use since the 17th century to describe people engaged in various forms of dissipation such as female and male prostitutes. Webster omitted that usage, but he did include a definition of the word to mean drunkenness and intoxication, adding that it was "a vulgar use of the word in America." "Gay" made its first appearance in the *Oxford English Dictionary* in 1951 as a slang term for "homosexual" and by 1955 was established in society as such; however, it had been used as a descriptor in underground gay social circles since the 1930s as well as a slur among heterosexuals to derisively define a man who was gay or thought to be gay. It was more widely reclaimed in the late 1960s and gained acceptance in gay and lesbian communities during the 1980s to describe anyone who preferred same-sex relationships. However, as late as the 1990s, "gay" was once again used as a derogatory term for people who were perceived to be acting "stupid" or "effeminate," as in "that's so gay," a phrase some in the gay community have also reclaimed. It is difficult to imagine a reclamation of the word "effeminate," another derogatory "feminine" descriptive used for gay men or men who were thought to be gay, which Webster and the lexicographers who came after him variously and pejoratively defined as "unmanly," "womanish," and "weak." "Pansy," which dated from the Elizabethan Era, similarly evoked effeminacy.

"Lavender," a descriptive word that evokes an image of violets (and pansies) but, more commonly, that of the lavender plant and lavender's delicate scent, was traditionally associated with the ancient Greek poet Sappho. She referenced girls wearing "violet tiaras" or garlands, and the lavender color became a coded symbol for gay men in Victorian queer culture. The gay British poet and playwright Oscar Wilde, who was known for his brightly colored style of dress, was reported to have worn lavender trousers during his American lecture tour in 1882.

Webster's definitions of the word "queer" stemmed from its original use in the 16th century to describe someone who was considered "odd" or "peculiar," "singular," or "whimsical."

Illinois conservative Republican senator Everett Dirksen used the phrase "lavender lads" during the U.S. government's post–World War II anti-homosexual campaign known as the Lavender Scare. *Confidential,* a gossip magazine of the era, picked up Dirksen's phrase to speculate on the sexual orientation of politicians and Hollywood stars. The term "lavender marriage," which dates from the early 20th century, primarily referred to a marriage of convenience between gay celebrities and straight women, which in Hollywood were sometimes arranged by the studios. Such marriages were part of a publicity strategy that would come to be known as "straightwashing," a word that describes Hollywood's concealment of actors' sexual orientation and enhancement of heteronormative masculinity in order to maintain their popularity with fans and to avoid the potential social, legal, and financial ramifications of outing that could cost the studios their bankable stars. A straight marriage or dating partner has also been referred to as a "beard" and the process of dating as "lavender" or "front" dating.

Webster's definitions of the word "queer" stemmed from its original use in the 16th century to describe someone who was considered "odd" or "peculiar," "singular," or "whimsical." The first person alleged to have publicly used it as an insulting slang word for a gay man was the Marquess of Queensberry, the father of Oscar Wilde's lover, Lord Alfred Douglas. When called to testify at Wilde's sensational 1895 trial for the crime of homosexuality, the Marquess described Wilde as a "snob queer," then a term for a gay man. The Marquess's use of the word "snob," which originally referred to someone "without nobility," also suggests an aristocrat's demeaning description of a lower- or middle-class person (Wilde was a doctor's son), no matter how well educated and brilliant, who imitates their betters; in Wilde's case, openly and publicly, with a persona that projected an exaggerated aura of aesthetic, witty-ironic, and sartorial affectation sometimes associated with the word "camp." The word "camp" and its usage is said to have variously originated from 16th-century theater, where it applied to male actors who dressed as women; from the Italian–Romani slang word *polari,* used particularly among a subculture of LGBTQ+ cross-dressing actors, circus and fairground workers, wrestlers, sailors, and sex workers; or from the French term *se camper,* meaning "posing [in front of someone] in an exaggerated manner." A camp sensibility has historically been perceived as merely "effeminate" artifice, a flamboyant aspect of LGBTQ+ and especially gay identity, but it is actually more allied with performance. Drag star RuPaul has suggested that the word "camp" refers to both celebration and subversion: the ability to "see the façade of life, the absurdity of life from outside yourself," a sensibility that Oscar Wilde understood very well.

By 1914, "queer" had been adopted as a slang word, which appeared as such in subsequent editions of Webster's dictionary as well as becoming widely established as a gay slur. The word "queer" began a process of reclamation as a positive self-label for the lesbian and gay community during the gay rights movement and the first gay Pride parades of the 1970s as well as during the AIDS epidemic that began in the 1980s, with the defiant activist chant, "We're here, we're queer, get used to it!" It was eventually added to the LGBT acronym and then became used as an umbrella term to describe LGBTQ+ diversity and inclusiveness. The letter "Q" can also signify the process of "questioning" one's gender and sexual orientation and is sometimes represented in variations of LGBTQ+ initialism as "Q2."

Once considered a slur, the word "queer" has now become a more positive label, one that is even used in scientific papers about LGBTQ subjects.

Not everyone in the LGBTQ+ community embraces the use of the word "queer" as an umbrella term; for many gay men especially, it remains an offensive word, one built on hate and homophobia. It especially recalls for older gay men a time when they commonly experienced harassment and were subjected to physical violence, sometimes called "gay bashing," and when the word "queer" was used as a slur, along with the slurs "fag" and "faggot," which were hurled at them during the commission of these hate crimes. Many LGBTQ+ people and allies question as to whether the word can be completely reclaimed because of its historical usage signifying the abnormality of the "other" and because homophobes continue to use it as a pejorative. The increasingly popular use of the word "queer" may be due in part to a generational shift: LGBTQ+ people who came of age in the 1980s and beyond and inherited a legacy of activism, a justifiable expectation of their civil rights, and an expansion of LGBTQ+ initialism may have a more comfortable and deliberately defiant relationship with the word "queer" as a reclaimed and positive descriptive of all aspects of LGBTQ+ orientation and uniqueness rather than as a verbal weapon of hate and ignorance. The meaning and usage of the word "queer" have also been subjects for discussion in college-level LGBTQ+ studies courses.

Cross-dressing, particularly men dressed as women, has been a feature of theatrical and traditional entertainments since ancient times, but Webster had no notion of "drag" as a form of cross-dressing and cross-dressing entertainment. The word's origin is unknown, but it first appeared in print in 1870 as theater slang for women's clothing worn by men and the feeling of long skirts "dragging" on the floor. The word "drag" is also thought to be an abbreviated form of the term "grand rag," frequently used to describe a masquerade ball. Webster's definition for the word "masquerade" was "disguise," and "rag" in this context would be slang for "clothing."

The closest Webster came to mentioning the word "lesbian" was the word "sapphic" to describe the verse of the ancient Greek lyric poet Sappho, who lived on the island of Lesbos in the Aegean Sea. Whether Sappho was lesbian, bisexual, or straight has long been the subject of scholarly debate, but it is generally accepted that her love poetry celebrates erotic and romantic feelings between women. "Sapphic," "sapphism," and "sapphistry" were the first words used to describe sexual relationships between women; by 1870, the words "lesbian" and "lesbianism," a reference to Lesbos, were in use, and in 1890, the term "lesbian" appeared in a medical dictionary to describe a sex position the lexicographer called "lesbian love." By 1925, the word "lesbian" had become a noun in medical literature to define the female equivalent of a "sodomite," a regressive definition that dates to the Colonial Era in America, which Webster defined as someone who committed sodomy, "a crime against nature." The word "dyke," also spelled "dike," was coined early on as a slang term to describe aggressive and masculine lesbian behavior and may have been a shortened version of "bull dyke," a term that came to have the same meaning. The word "dike," which Webster defined as "the same word as ditch," became a 19th-century slang word for vulva. Historian Lillian Faderman places the usage of the term "bull dyke" to describe lesbians within the Black Harlem lesbian subculture of the 1920s.

Nobody is certain what the origin of the word "drag" in reference to a man wearing women's clothing came from, though it might have something to do with long dresses dragging on the floor.

By the 1950s, straight people were using the terms "dyke" and "bull dyke," as well as their sister term "butch," as slang pejoratives. LGBTQ+ usage of the word "butch," which, during the early 20th century began to indicate either a tough kid or a type of men's haircut, is said to date back to the lesbian subcultures of the 1940s and 1950s. Conversely, using the terms "femme" and "lipstick lesbian" (also called "dolly dyke") to denote feminine-identifying lesbians came into use during the 1940s and 1980s, respectively. The term "Dykes on Bikes" (DOB) was a descriptive originally coined for a lesbian motorcycle club during its first appearance at the 1976 San Francisco Gay Freedom Day Parade. The DOB subsequently became a fixture at LGBTQ+ Pride events and the international athletic competition called the Gay Games and included 22 chapters as well as numerous affiliates. Like much of the derogatory language once used as a weapon against LGBTQ+ people, many lesbians have since reclaimed the disparaging words once intended to belittle and diminish them.

Webster ignored references to "bisexual" and "bisexuality," words that would not appear until the late 19th century. He included variations of "hermaphrodite," the precursor of the term "intersex," and he unconsciously hinted at sexual and gender fluidity with the word "bisexous," which he defined as "consisting of both sexes." The word "transvestite" to indicate a male cross-dresser was the invention of German sexologist Magnus Hirschfeld sometime during the 1910s, but the "trans" component of LGBTQ+ initialism began as "transsexual," a term coined by physician Harry Benjamin, the author of *The Transsexual Phenomenon* (1966), and adopted by famed sexologist Alfred Kinsey. In 1965, psychiatrist John Oliven offered the words "transgender" and "transgenderism," which he felt better described the spectrum of gender identities.

LGBTQ+ initialism began as LGB, which, during the 1980s, replaced "gay, lesbian, and bisexual" to form a shorter term defining a cohesive community and was expanded late in the decade to LGBT. During the same decade, the initialism sometimes began to appear as GLBT, for example by San Francisco's GLBT Historical Society. By the 1990s and into the 21st century, the acronym saw greater expansion as LGBT activism and advocacy began to include queer, questioning, nonbinary, gender fluid, genderqueer, asexual, aromantic (aro), pansexual, and intersex individuals as well as the advent of gender-neutral language, including a reintroduction of the honorific Mx. rather than Mr., Mrs., or Ms. More recently, LGBTQ+ initialism has sometimes been seen in such reconfigurations as LGBTQIA+, 2SLGBTQ+ to include "two spirit" First Nations/indigenous peoples, LGBTQ+/SGL (same-gender loving), and LGBTQQIP2SA. For those who simply embrace the umbrella term "queer," perhaps the slogan on a Pride rainbow T-shirt says it best: "Let Me Be Perfectly Queer."

In the late 1970s and early 1980s, some gays and lesbians expressed criticism that drag queens and kings were acting out male and female stereotypes and that bisexuals were primarily gays and lesbians who were afraid to come out and claim their sexual identity. Questions subsequently remained as to whether such broad inclusiveness signified by the ever-expanding acronym and its "+" has diluted the advocacy, activism, and uniqueness that defined the original acronyms of LGB and LGBT. However, it has also been argued that the expansion of the language of LGBTQ+ is a positive social evolutionary change that represents and celebrates a wide diversity and complexity of sexual and gender identity, fluidity, and expression. What all variations of LGBTQ+ initialism ultimately signify is what was so repressed in America's past: an open and intentional statement of orientation, identity, and inclusiveness that Noah Webster, that early 19th-century wordsmith, could never have imagined.

Activism

LGBTQ+ activism, from early resistance and the homophile movement that saw the founding of the first gay and lesbian organizations to the increasingly confrontational activist groups created after the Stonewall Uprising of 1969, was pivotal in changing the social and political landscape that had historically vilified, medicalized, and marginalized LGBTQ+ Americans and denied them acceptance, affirmation, and civil rights. The battle for social and political equality was due to the efforts of dedicated activists who were determined to end discrimination against LGBTQ+ Americans and to change long-held preconceived notions of what it means to be LGBTQ+.

TIMELINE

1888. One of the earliest documented cases of queer resistance and the first recorded instance of an LGBTQ+ American engaging in activism to defend the right of the queer community to gather takes place in Washington, D.C. William Dorsey Swann (1860–1925), a former enslaved African American and self-identified "queen of drag," angrily attempts to resist arrest during a police raid on one of a series of drag balls he hosted in what is known as the House of Swann. Twelve Black men are arrested along with Swann, and his parties and previous raids and arrests are reported in local newspapers, causing a risk to the reputations of future ball attendees. In 1896, while hosting a ball, Swann is arrested again for "keeping a disorderly house," a euphemism for "brothel," and is sentenced to 10 months in prison. His lawyer requests a pardon from President

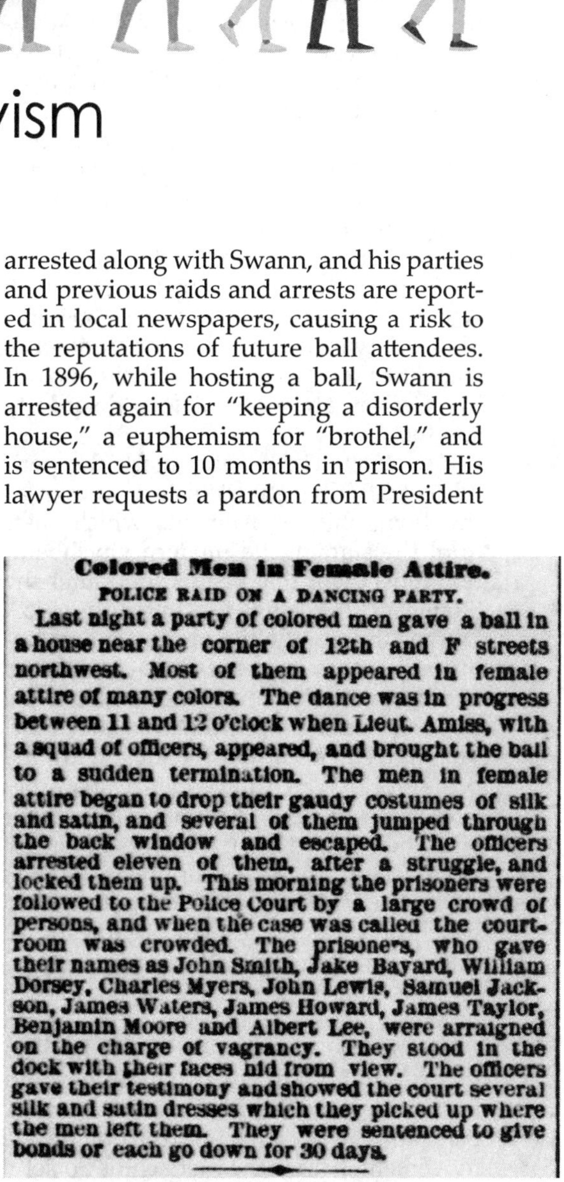

Colored Men in Female Attire.

POLICE RAID ON A DANCING PARTY.

Last night a party of colored men gave a ball in a house near the corner of 12th and F streets northwest. Most of them appeared in female attire of many colors. The dance was in progress between 11 and 12 o'clock when Lieut. Amiss, with a squad of officers, appeared, and brought the ball to a sudden termination. The men in female attire began to drop their gaudy costumes of silk and satin, and several of them jumped through the back window and escaped. The officers arrested eleven of them, after a struggle, and locked them up. This morning the prisoners were followed to the Police Court by a large crowd of persons, and when the case was called the courtroom was crowded. The prisoners, who gave their names as John Smith, Jake Bayard, William Dorsey, Charles Myers, John Lewis, Samuel Jackson, James Waters, James Howard, James Taylor, Benjamin Moore and Albert Lee, were arraigned on the charge of vagrancy. They stood in the dock with their faces hid from view. The officers gave their testimony and showed the court several silk and satin dresses which they picked up where the men left them. They were sentenced to give bonds or each go down for 30 days.

A newspaper clipping from the Evening Star *dated April 13, 1988, describes the Washington, D.C., raid in which William Dorsey Swann and other men were arrested by police at a drag ball.*

Grover Cleveland, but the application is denied. Police raids on drag balls in New York City and San Francisco become common during the 20th century, well into the 1960s.

1924. In Chicago, Henry Gerber founds the Society for Human Rights (SHR), the first recognized American LGBTQ+ advocacy organization. The SHR is chartered by the state of Illinois, and African American clergyman John T. Graves serves as its first and only president. The organization publishes the newsletter *Friendship and Freedom*, the first gay-interest publication in the United States, but few members are willing to receive it through the mail since postal inspectors, bound by the Comstock Act, will deem the newsletter obscene. The Society is disbanded in the summer of 1925 after several of its members, including Gerber, are arrested for "disorderly conduct."

1945–1969. These years mark the period in LGBTQ+ activist history known as the homophile movement, which lasts until the start of the modern gay liberation movement that begins soon after the Stonewall Uprising in June–July 1969. During the homophile era, gays and lesbians begin to coalesce as a community and formally organize and address the legal and social discrimination they face. The movement also coincides with the post–World War II Lavender Scare, a period when the U.S. government, together with the FBI and the CIA, investigate gay "infiltration" in the government and the military and, along with local police, keep watch on gay and lesbian organizations. The word "homophile," which replaces "homosexual," is chosen to emphasize same-sex love and community and to minimize the sexual aspect by which an unaccepting public solely defines gay and lesbian identity. Gay and lesbian rights organizations associated with the homophile movement include the Mattachine Society, the Daughters of Bilitis, the Janus Society, and the Homophile Action League.

1950. Harry Hay and other left-wing gay activists in Los Angeles found the Mattachine Society, one of the most influential LGBTQ+ organizations of its time. The founders draft a Statement of Purpose and initially structure the organization like a Communist cell: They remain anonymous in order to help safeguard the secrecy of the organization and call themselves the "Fifth Order." In 1952, after founder Dale Jennings is arrested for "lewd behavior," the society publicizes the case under the name "Citizens Committee to Outlaw Entrapment." The resulting publicity brings in financial support and increased membership that numbers over 2,000 in California by 1953. *The Mattachine Review* magazine begins publication in 1955, and two years later, the society's headquarters move to San Francisco. By the 1960s, chapters of the Mattachine Society have been organized in New York, Washington, D.C., and other cities with their own publications and newsletters. These chapters eventually become autonomous organizations. The San Francisco Mattachine Society lasts until 1967.

1952. Disaffected members of the Mattachine Society found ONE, Inc., a gay rights organization named for a quote by Victorian philosopher and essayist Thomas Carlyle: "A mystic bond of brotherhood makes all men one." "One" is also a reference to gay men as "one of us." ONE, Inc., accepts lesbians, who will prove essential to the group's early organizational success. The first LGBTQ+ organization to have its own office, ONE, Inc., is also notable for its publication of a monthly magazine, *ONE Magazine*, cofounded by Los Angeles gay activist Don Slater. *ONE Magazine* is openly sold on the streets of Los Angeles for 25 cents and becomes the focus of an obscenity lawsuit in 1954 that eventually reaches the U.S. Supreme Court. ONE, Inc., expands in 1956 with the establishment of the ONE Institute, which in 1981 becomes the first accredited institution of higher learning to offer master's and doctoral degrees in homophile studies. The archives of ONE, Inc., and a separate faction, the Homosexual Information Center (HIC), will become invaluable resources

The Ladder *was the first lesbian periodical to be published in the United States. It ran from 1956 to 1995.*

for scholars and students of LGBTQ+ history as a special collection of the University Library at California State University and the National Gay & Lesbian Archives at the University of Southern California. Included among the HIC online archives are copies of *Tangents*, a ONE, Inc., publication offered in Los Angeles from 1965 to 1970.

1955. On September 21, the Daughters of Bilitis, the United States' first major lesbian organization, is formed in San Francisco by Del Martin; her partner, Phyllis Lyon; and Rosalie "Rose" Bamberger. Founded as a private social club and alternative to lesbian bars, which are frequently raided, the DOB allows lesbians to openly meet one another and provides a place for them to dance together since same-sex dancing in public places is illegal. The organization is named for a character in the 1894 work *The Song of Bilitis* by French poet Pierre Louys, in which the female character Bilitis lives alongside Sappho on Lesbos. The word "daughters" is chosen to suggest a comparison with such venerable American social organizations as the Daughters of the American Revolution (DAR). At the start, the DOB eschews activism for the goal of assimilation within straight culture, which sparks an ongoing debate over "butch" versus "femme" proper dress at gatherings, with femme established as a rule that is often ignored. In 1956, the organization begins publishing *The Ladder*, the first nationally distributed lesbian publication in the United States and the primary method of communication for the DOB membership. The magazine is published monthly and, later, bimonthly until 1972. As its membership grows, with chapters in Los Angeles, New York, Rhode Island, and Chicago, the DOB begins to shift its focus to providing support for women who fear coming out and educating members on gay and lesbian history and their rights, with such *Ladder* articles as "What to Do in Case of Arrest," a guide for lesbians caught up in bar raids. By the mid-1960s, the DOB membership, through the medium of *The Ladder*, increasingly voices dissatisfaction with the organization's aim of assimilation and during the 1960s and 1970s begins to align itself with the growing feminist activism of the second women's movement, the women's liberation movement, which followed the women's suffrage movement of 1848–1920. The DOB's national organization ceases operation in 1970, although some local chapters continue until 1995.

1959. In May, police harassment and arrests of LGBTQ+ people, routine in Los Angeles during the late 1950s and 1960s, lead to a clash between members of the community and police at Cooper Do-Nuts, a popular queer hangout. When police arrest two drag queens, a male sex worker, and a gay man, onlookers begin throwing coffee, doughnuts, cups, and trash at them until they are forced to flee. Subsequent rioting in the street brings police backup, after which officers block off the street and beat and arrest several rioters. The incident becomes alternately known as the "Cooper Do-Nuts Riot" or the "Cooper Do-Nuts Uprising" and is often cited as the first physical confrontation between the LGBTQ+ community and the police.

1960. On May 27, the Daughters of Bilitis holds the first of five biannual national conventions during the national organization's 15-year history. Some 200 women attend the convention, where the San Francisco Police check to see if any of them are wearing men's clothing. Awards are given to the "Sons of Bilitis" (aka "SOB")—men such as the organization's lawyer and photographer, as well as members of the Mattachine Society, who have supported DOB initiatives and helped plan their convention.

1961. On August 5 at the Black Nite gay bar and nightclub in Milwaukee, Wisconsin, transgender drag performer and proprietor Josie Carter, wielding two beer bottles, fights off four young servicemen who attack her husband, the bouncer, after the men are asked to leave for refusing to provide identification. The men return with a cohort of 12 servicemen and begin to destroy the bar, prompting a brawl between them and 75 bar patrons. When the police arrive, they arrest the attackers and not the bar patrons, owing to good relations between them and Carter, who is later quoted as saying, "They took care of me and taught me how to stay out of trouble."

1962. The Janus Society, a homophile organization based in Philadelphia, is founded. It is notable as the publisher of *Drum* magazine, which focuses on gay culture and news and enjoys a wide circulation until the society ceases operations in 1969. The society also organizes several LGBTQ+ rights demonstrations and sponsors events such as a 1964 free lecture during which gay activist Frank Kameny discusses discrimination against the gay community in employment, education, and housing.

The monthly gay men's magazine Drum *was published by the Janus Society in Philadelphia from 1964 to 1969.*

1963. The East Coast Homophile Organizations (ECHO) is established in Philadelphia to initially foster cooperation between and coordinate activism among East Coast chapters of the Mattachine Society, the Daughters of Bilitis, and the Janus Society. ECHO sponsors monthly meetings and holds its first yearly conference from August 21 to September 1, 1963. At the 1964 conference held in Washington, D.C., in October, the participating groups set an activist agenda, which will take the form of picketing and other public protests. Since employment discrimination will be a focus of picketing, gay activists are required to wear jackets and ties and lesbians instructed to wear skirts. In 1966, ECHO is reestablished as the North American Conference of Homophile Organizations (NACHO) in order to coordinate more homophile organizations and chapters. Its subsidiary organization is the Eastern Regional Conference of Homophile Organizations (ERICHO), which by 1969 includes original ECHO members as well as New York's Council on Equality for Homosexuals, the Student Homophile League, and the West Side Discussion Group; Philadelphia's Homophile Action League; and Hartford's Institute for Social Ethics. NACHO disbands in 1970 during the activism that follows the Stonewall Uprising.

1964. The first organized protests in New York City take place. In what is considered the first planned U.S. gay rights demonstration, activist Randy Wicker organizes a group at the Whitehall Street Induction Center in September to protest the military's treatment of gays, specifically its violation of the confidentiality of gay men's draft records.

In December, Wicker organizes gays and lesbians in a protest at Cooper Union, where a psychiatrist is presenting a lecture titled "Homosexuality: A Disease." The protestors are given 10 minutes for a rebuttal of the psychiatrist's claims.

In July, the Council on Religion and the Homosexual (CRH), made up of religious leaders from various Protestant sects, is formed with the purpose of joining gay activists and religious leaders to confront oppression and violence. It is the first group to use the term "homosexual" in its name.

On New Year's Eve, the CRH, together with homophile organizations such as the Daughters of Bilitis and the Mattachine Society, hold a costume ball at California Hall in San Francisco as a mutual fundraising event. In attendance are over 600 people, including clergymen and their wives, as well as members of the LGBTQ+ community. The San Francisco Police Department is notified of the event and initially insists that attendees cannot dress in drag, but the CRH contends that the department cannot dictate what guests wear since the ball is a private event. Despite the department's agreement not to interfere, more than 20 police officers arrive, block the intersection, and photograph and harass guests entering the building from 9:00 P.M. to 1:00 A.M. Four lawyers representing the groups and a housewife protest and are arrested and charged with obstruction; a clergyman is threatened with arrest while escorting two guests to their car; and two other men are arrested for "disorderly conduct." The local American Civil Liberties Union (ACLU) announces its intention to defend the lawyers in court, thus taking on its first gay rights case. However, the judge instructs the jury to find the four not guilty before the defense begins its arguments. The legal victory in the case and the ensuing publicity generated by the CRH result in greater awareness of the group and an increase in its influence. The CRH goes on to help organize a forum for gay and lesbian voters, which in turn leads to the presence of LGBTQ+ candidates for office, the most well known of whom will be Harvey Milk, who is elected to the San Francisco Board of Supervisors in 1978 and assassinated the same year, along with Mayor George Moscone.

1965. On April 17, the day after *The New York Times* publishes a report on Cuba's plan to incarcerate gay men in forced labor camps, the Mattachine Society of Washington, D.C., led by activists Frank Kameny and Jack Nichols, along with lesbian activists, picket the White House in protest. The protest also offers a wider opportunity to address LGBTQ+ discrimination, with one picket sign reading: "Homosexuals Ask for Redress of Grievances." On April 18, members of the Mattachine Society of New York and other homophile activists picket the United Nations to protest the treatment of gays in both Cuba and the United States.

A historical marker in Philadelphia tells the story of the sit-in at Dewey's restaurant, where LGBTQ patrons followed the model of Black sit-ins to protest the restaurant's discriminatory policy.

On April 25, some 150 people are denied service at Dewey's, a popular lunch counter and hangout for LGBTQ+ Philadelphians, after the management implements a policy of refusing to serve "homosexuals," "masculine women," "feminine men," and "persons wearing nonconformist clothing." Three teenagers stage a sit-in in protest and are arrested for "disorderly conduct," along with Janus Society president Clark Polak, who had arrived to help the teens retain a lawyer. The following week, members of the Janus Society hold demonstrations outside Dewey's and distribute 1,500 leaflets advertising the five-day protest. At the same time, activist leaders meet with local authorities and Dewey's representatives. On May 2, when three people are again denied service and conduct a second sit-in, the police are called. However, this time, no one is arrested, and the protestors leave an hour later. As Polak later recalls, "I was quite politely told that we could stay in there as long as we wanted as the police had no authority to ask us to leave."

From May 26 to October 25, groups within the East Coast Homophile Organizations (ECHO) hold the first of a series of pickets in Washington, D.C. Targets are the White House, the Civil Service Commission, the Department of State, and the Pentagon. ECHO organizes pickets at Independence Hall in Philadelphia on July 4, which becomes known as the Annual Reminder and is held each year through 1969. The event is the brainchild of activist Craig Rodwell, and its name is chosen to remind Americans that a sizable number of their fellow citizens are denied the rights of "life, liberty, and the pursuit of happiness," enshrined in the Declaration of Independence.

On September 26, 30 people picket outside San Francisco's Grace Cathedral to protest the demotion of Episcopal priest Robert Cromey, a cofounder of the Council on Religion and the Homosexual (CRH) who had affirmed his support of gay rights and "love relationships with persons of the same sex" during an interview for the Religious News Service. The protest is not successful, but the cathedral gradually becomes more accepting of gay parishioners, and by 1969, several members of its congregation have openly identified as gay.

1966. On April 21, Julius', a Greenwich Village bar that had been the target of a police raid 10 days earlier, becomes the scene of a "sip-in" protest, derived from the sit-in protests of the civil rights movement. Four members of the Mattachine Society—Dick Leitsch, Craig Rodwell, John Timmons, and Randy Wicker—invite reporters to follow them as they visit bars in Greenwich Village, where they deliberately announce their sexual orientation to challenge the New York State Liquor Authority's regulation against the serving of alcoholic beverages to gay and lesbian customers in bars and restaurants because

Now on the National Register of Historic Places, Julius' Bar is located at 159 West 10th Street, just a block from the Stonewall Inn. The Sip-In that occurred there in April 1966 helped gay people gain the right to be served at public taverns in New York.

it considers their presence "disorderly." Two of the bars, one of which includes a sign reading "If you are gay, go away," close for the day. They are served at the Waikiki bar and refused service at Julius', where the bartender, after Dick Leitsch informs him that he is a homosexual, says, "I can't serve you," and he puts his hand over Leitsch's glass, which is photographed. The following day, *The New York Times* reports on the sip-in, with the headline "3 Deviants Invite Exclusion by Bars." Leitsch unsuccessfully files a complaint with the SLA; however, New York's human rights commission rules that discrimination against gay and lesbian customers cannot continue.

In May, 27-year-old Los Angeles leatherman and activist Steve Ginsburg (d. 2007) founds the group Personal Rights in Defense and Education (PRIDE). Ginsburg had previously founded Chutzpah (later known as Achvah, which means "declaration" in Hebrew), the first gay Jewish group on the West Coast. PRIDE is formed in response to the Los Angeles Police Department's (LAPD) harassment of gays at public meeting places and bars and, unlike earlier, more restrained forms of protest, favors large, loud, and aggressive demonstrations as well as political and social actions on behalf of gay sporting events, the right to political gatherings, to marry, and to access social services, especially among gay youth. The organization's meetings are held at The Hub, a gay bar, and are called "PRIDE nights." Although the organization only lasts until 1968, it sets the tone for future unapologetically assertive activist organizations such as the Gay Liberation Front and ACT UP, and its monthly newsletter evolves into the venerable and long-running LGBTQ+ publication *The Advocate*.

On May 21, Armed Forces Day, simultaneous demonstrations take place among a national coalition of gay and lesbian homophile organizations to protest the exclusion of gays in the military as well as the military's practice of discharging soldiers when their orientation is discovered. The protestors picket and hand out leaflets in Washington, D.C., Philadelphia, New York, Los Angeles, and San Francisco. It is the largest group of gay protestors in the United States up to that point. In Los Angeles, a motorcade consisting of more than a dozen cars with picket signs attached to them travels through the city and through Hollywood.

On July 19, young gay and transgender activists associated with Vanguard, the first known American queer youth organization (1965–1967), picket Compton's Cafeteria, a popular open-all-night meeting place for gay and transgender people, some of whom are sex workers, in the Tenderloin district of San Francisco. The protest is a response to a pattern of routine police harassment and arrests, particularly of trans women for "female impersonation" and drag queens for "cross-dressing," as well as management's recent hiring of Pinkerton security agents in an enhanced attempt to deny service to queer

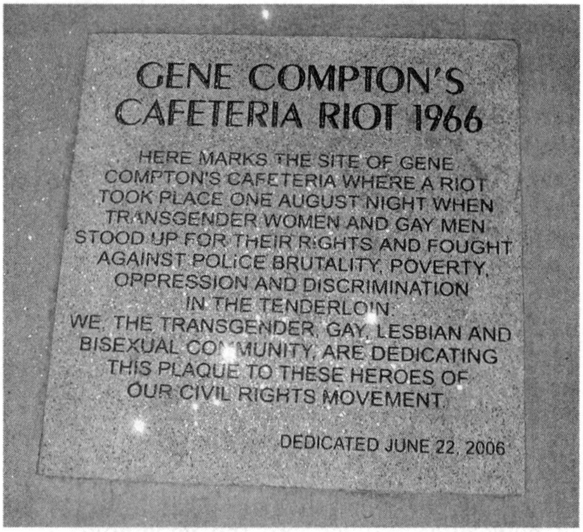

Forty years after the riot, a historical marker was placed at the site of the Compton's Cafeteria riot in San Francisco, once again advancing the rights of gay and transgender people.

customers and harass them into leaving the premises. Compton's management essentially considers them to be loiterers who cost the cafeteria other business and is additionally concerned that the illegality of cross-dressing, together with physical altercations between customers after midnight, could result in the cafeteria's closure. The July protest proves unsuccessful, and police harassment continues.

In August, the most violent confrontation between the LGBTQ+ community and police prior to the Stonewall Uprising of 1969 takes place when a Compton's Cafeteria worker calls the police to complain about raucous behavior from transgender customers. When police arrive, an officer grabs a trans woman and attempts to arrest them. They throw a cup of coffee in the officer's face, sparking an upheaval during which customers throw items from the restaurant, including furniture, at officers and the cafeteria's windows, breaking them. The protest becomes a pitched battle between customers and police and moves into the streets, where protestors damage a police car and burn down a newsstand as police attempt to arrest them and shove them into paddy wagons. The next evening, violence breaks out again as more protestors return to picket the cafeteria and smash its newly installed windows after Compton's management refuses to allow them to enter. These events lead to local initiatives to establish social, psychological, and medical support and advocacy services for transgender people and the creation of the National Transsexual Counseling Unit (NTCU) in 1968. Compton's Cafeteria closes in 1972 after six years of steadily declining business.

In the fall, bisexual Columbia University student and LGBTQ+ activist Stephen Donaldson (born Robert Martin) founds the Student Homophile League (later known as the Columbia Queer Alliance), the first collegiate queer student organization in the United States. The SHL begins with 10–12 members and is officially recognized by the university in April 1967 after nearly a year during which the organization grapples with the administration over such SHL stipulations as the right to keep members' names confidential. *The New York Times* covers the event with the headline "Columbia Charters Homosexual Group." The SHL inspires the establishment of similar organizations at Cornell, MIT, New York University, and Stanford University over the next two years. By 1970, more than 150 LGBTQ+ student groups in colleges and universities are founded throughout the United States.

1967. On New Year's Eve, undercover LAPD police officers infiltrate the Black Cat Tavern, a gay bar that opened two months earlier, to secure evidence of "homosexual" behavior such as hugging and kissing. The officers and uniformed police reinforcements beat up couples and two bartenders and arrest a total of 14 patrons for "assault and public lewdness." Two patrons, pursued by officers, flee to a nearby gay bar, New Faces, but are captured and arrested. Inside the bar, police demand to see the manager, a woman introduced to them as Lee Roy, who is wearing an evening gown. The officers hear the name as "Leroy," assume she is a cross-dressing male, and brutally beat her as well as a bartender who tries to intervene. Two of the 14 gay men who are arrested are later forced to register as sex offenders. The LAPD justifies its officers' use of excessive force as a response to "rioting."

On February 11, some 40 demonstrators, organized by the gay rights group PRIDE and Ukrainian American gay activist Alexei Romanoff, the owner of the New Faces gay bar, gather outside the Black Cat to protest the police raid on New Year's Eve. A sizable number of police officers show up, and although the protestors are angry, the demonstration remains orderly, somber, and peaceful so that police will not have cause to intervene and label the demonstration as a "riot." The event is intended to coincide with other demonstrations in the area to protest police raids and harassment at venues such as Pandora's Box, a straight nightclub on the Sunset Strip that the Los Angeles City Council has slated for closure and a planned demolition in the summer. When Pandora's Box owner, DJ and TV host Jimmy O'Neill, attempts to have the Black Cat call off its demonstration after learning that the word "homosexual" is going to be used, Black Cat protestors accede to pressure not to explicitly include the word on its picket signs. Instead, the signs feature such slogans as "End Illegal Entrapment" and "No More Abuse of Our Rights and Dignity." In 2008, the City of Los Angeles Cultural Heritage Commission installs a commemorative plaque on the building that housed the Black Cat Tavern. Pandora's Box is demolished in August 1967 and is now a traffic island.

1968. In a protest challenge to continuing police entrapment and harassment, over 200 people attend a St. Patrick's Day party at Griffith Park, a popular LGBTQ+ gathering and cruising spot in Los Angeles. The party is hosted by two drag queens known as "The Princess" and "The Duchess."

On April 28, amid a strike and student protests at Columbia University in New York City, members of the university's

The Black Cat Tavern is still in operation in the Silver Lake neighborhood of Los Angeles. Back in 1967, police entered the establishment on New Year's Eve and beat up several patrons. While this did not set off a riot, it did lead to a protest the following February attended by some 200 people.

Student Homophile League (SHL) picket and disrupt a panel of psychiatrists discussing homosexuality, which remains classified as a mental illness among members of the medical profession.

On May 9, 200 students protest after Charles E. Rollins, president of Bucks County Community College, cancels a talk to be given by Richard Leitsch, president of the Mattachine Society of New York. The counterculture of the late 1960s commonly describes gatherings as "happenings," "be-ins," or "love-ins."

On Memorial Day, what is advertised as a "Gay-In" takes place at the Crystal

Springs Picnic Ground at Griffith Park. The event is also billed as "this historic first, a gay day in the park" and is cosponsored by the Los Angeles *Advocate* and *Tangents* magazines; ONE, Inc.; the National League for Social Understanding; and the Southern California Council on Religion and the Homosexual. The featured speaker is Mike Hannon, a former LAPD police officer-turned lawyer and civil rights activist who is running for Los Angeles district attorney. His topic, "How to rebuild respect for the law," focuses on the challenges of being gay in a homophobic society.

On August 17, the late 1960s hippie mantra of "flower power" to symbolize and emphasize peace over war inspires a unique protest from customers of The Patch, a Los Angeles LGBTQ+ bar. Patch owner, comedian Lee Glaze, nicknamed "The Blond Darling," has repeatedly been warned by the LAPD that he can only stay in business if he prohibits drag queens, men dancing together, and more than one person in the bar bathrooms. Rather than observe these prohibitions, Glaze plays "God Save the Queen" on the jukebox whenever he spots police officers entering the bar in order to alert customers to the need to comply with the rules until he gives an all-clear signal. Glaze's compliance signal fails when undercover police officers of the LAPD Vice Squad enter The Patch. They eventually leave but return with uniformed officers to screen customers, demanding to see their IDs to check their assigned gender. After two men are arrested for cross-dressing, Glaze leads a group to a customer-owned flower shop, where they arm themselves with bouquets of flowers and proceed to the police station. There, they stage a peaceful all-night sit-in in the lobby of the station waiting to post bail for their arrested friends. The sit-in becomes known as the "Flower Power Protest."

1969. In April, San Francisco radio journalist Leo E. Laurence and steamship freight company employee Gayle Whittington found the Committee for Homosexual Freedom (CHF), a gay and lesbian rights organization. When the two are fired from their jobs after the underground newspaper the *Berkeley Barb* publishes a photo of them embracing, the CHF organizes protests at Whittington's employer, the State Steamship Company. The organization goes on to introduce a San Francisco municipal ballot measure that is a "declaration of policy concerning sexual freedom and homosexual employment rights." If the measure had passed, it would have banned discrimination in employment based on sexual orientation. In May, the CHF pickets Tower Records for several weeks until the store reinstates an employee who had been fired after he was suspected of being gay.

Stonewall

On June 24, 1969, the NYPD conducts an evening raid on the Stonewall Inn, a popular LGBTQ+ dive bar on Christopher Street in New York's Greenwich Village. The police confiscate an illegal supply of alcohol, arrest some bar employees, and afterward plan another, more intensive raid to take place on the following Friday in the hope of shuttering the bar for good. The second police raid does not go as planned; instead, it sparks a series of spontaneous protests and violent confrontations between police and the local LGBTQ+ community. These acts of resistance, also referred to as the Stonewall Rebellion, the Stonewall Riots, or simply Stonewall, prove to be a turning point in the history of LGBTQ+ activism and the fight for queer rights in the United States.

Events at the Stonewall Inn unfold around midnight on June 28. Some 200 drag queens and gay and lesbian customers are drinking and dancing at the bar when undercover male and female police officers arrive and identify cross-dressing

In 2003, at a time when it was unoccupied, the Stonewall Inn's exterior remained as unremarkable as it had been back in 1969, when the gay community certainly did not wish to draw unwarranted attention to itself. It would reopen four years later after being renovated.

customers to be arrested for "masquerading." Police also plan to arrest bar employees and any Mafia members who happen to be present and to confiscate the rest of the bar's beer and liquor supplies. After one of the officers uses the bar's pay phone to summon backup, four plainclothes and two uniformed police officers enter the bar through its double doors, turn off the music, turn on the lights, and block the outside doors and the doors to the bathrooms to prevent escape. Customers who are arrested refuse to leave with police officers, other customers decline to provide identification, and the already tense atmosphere grows when, according to witnesses, police grope cross-dressing lesbian customers while frisking them. Police allow customers who have not been arrested to exit the bar by the front door, but rather than leave the area, they join a crowd outside that soon swells to an estimated 100 to 150 onlookers, many of them young, homeless gay men for whom the Stonewall Inn has always been a safe space. As the police, sometimes roughly, lead the arrested in handcuffs to a patrol wagon and squad cars to transport them to the 6th Precinct, the growing crowd becomes restless, yelling at police, taunting them, and throwing objects such as garbage cans, bottles, rocks, and bricks at them. Police respond with tear gas and beatings. Garbage is set on fire and thrown into the bar. As street violence escalates, several police officers barricade themselves inside the building, prompting a group of protestors to break down the door and battle with the officers inside the bar.

By around 4:00 A.M., New York's Tactical Police Force has managed to break the siege inside the Stonewall and clear the streets. Thirteen people have been arrested, among them straight folk musician, left-wing activist, and Greenwich Village resident Dave Von Ronk, who has joined the uprising in support and, like an unnamed number of LGBTQ+ protestors, has been beaten by police. Despite the destruction of its interior because of protestors' altercations with police, the burned and blackened bar defiantly reopens, leading to sporadic and infrequently violent confrontations between protestors and police that continue over the next several evenings.

During the Stonewall siege, activists Fred Sargeant and Craig Rodwell prepare and hand out some 5,000 leaflets, the first of which is headlined "Get the Mafia and the Cops Out of Gay Bars," lists details about police corruption, and is signed by the "Homophile Youth Movement." It begins:

> The nights of Friday, June 27, 1969 and Saturday, June 28, 1969 will go down in history as the first time that thousands of Homosexual men and women went out into the streets to protest the intolerable situation which has existed in New York City for many years—namely, the Mafia (or syndicate) control

> of this city's Gay bars in collusion with certain elements in the Police Dept. of the City of New York. The demonstrations were triggered by a Police raid on the Stonewall Inn late Friday night, June 27th. The purported reason for the raid was the Stonewall's lack of a liquor license. Who's kidding whom? Can anybody really believe that an operation as big as the Stonewall could continue for almost 3 years just a few blocks from the 6th Precinct house without having a liquor license? No! The Police have known about the Stonewall operation all along. What has happened is the presence of new "brass" in the 6th Precinct which has vowed to "drive the fags out of the Village."

The Stonewall Inn in New York City's Greenwich Village is now a historic landmark.

Sargeant and Rodwell also notify the New York press about the events taking place at the bar. The *New York Post*, the *Daily News*, and *The New York Times* cover the uprising but exclusively quote police sources in their stories. The *Times*, for example, features the headline "4 Policemen Hurt in 'Village' Raid" and goes on to describe "hundreds of young men" on a "rampage" after "a force of plainclothes men" raid "a bar well known for its homosexual clientele." The *Daily News* headline is predictably sensational and offensive: "Homo Nest Raided, Queen Bees are Stinging Mad." Howard Smith and Lucian Truscott IV, reporters from *The Village Voice*, then Greenwich Village's popular hometown newspaper and the Stonewall Inn's neighbor, are among the first journalists on the scene, with Smith trapped inside the bar with police during the siege. The *Voice* is the only paper to feature the uprising on its front page, with firsthand accounts and quotes from both protestors and police. But while the paper is often politically and socially left of center, it is also known for its homophobic slant during its early years, and its writers are liberal with their use of the terms "faggot" and "dyke" throughout their articles on the uprising, referring to the protestors as "limp wrists" and the "forces of faggotry" and the event as the "Great Faggot Rebellion." Smith wrote of his experience inside the Stonewall Inn: "The sounds filtering in doesn't suggest dancing faggots any more. It sounds like a powerful rage bent on vendetta." The *Voice*'s unflattering coverage and use of slurs leads to a large and angry protest outside the paper's offices on July 2, which brings a final confrontation between protestors and police that lasts until late in the evening.

The Stonewall Inn closes in October 1969 after a failed attempt to convert the business to a juice bar, and various establishments occupy the building during the 1970s and 1980s. In 1990, Jimmy Pisano purchases the inn's original location, reopens it as a bar called Stonewall, and, with his partner, runs it until his death due to AIDS in 1994. In 2007, the whole building is renovated and reopened as the Stonewall Inn.

Although it was not the first significant activist event in LGBTQ+ history, Stonewall has been popularly considered the most transformative. It marks a shift from the relatively staid activism of the homophile movement, with its emphasis on assimilation rather than aggressive confrontation, into a more radical movement emphasizing LGBTQ+ liberation, power, and pride as well as equality. In the words of Stonewall patron and activist Michael Fader, "Everyone in the crowd felt that we were never going to go back. The bottom line was, we weren't going to go away. And we didn't."

Activism After Stonewall

The aftermath of the Stonewall Uprising sees an abandonment of the Old Left activism upon which the Mattachine Society was founded in favor of a gay liberation (sometimes shortened to "gay lib") movement that parallels and intersects with liberal New Left social movements of the 1960s and 1970s such as the anti-Vietnam War, feminist, and Black Power movements.

1969. The Gay Liberation Front (GLF), formed in New York City on July 24, 1969, chooses its name to align with militant and left-leaning counterculture political groups of the era like the Indochinese National Liberation Front (NLF) and the Black Panther Party, whose cofounder, Huey Newton, views gays and lesbians as oppressed groups and supports gay liberation. In addition to its platform supporting gay rights and nontraditional gender roles, the GLF denounces racism and embraces anti-capitalist initiatives such as support for Third World nations. In November 1969, the GLF launches its newspaper, *Come Out!*, which ceases publication in 1972. Gay Liberation Front chapters are founded in several countries around the world and, like the American GLF chapters, members go on to found other LGBTQ+ activist groups. The GLF holds the first of 24-hour weekly protests at the New York Women's House of Detention (1932–1974) on August 2. Located near the Stonewall Inn, the jail's inmates, many of whom are women of color, support the uprising by leaning out the windows chanting "Gay Power! Gay Power!" and setting fire to the few possessions allowed in their cells.

On September 12, the GLF stages a large demonstration at *The Village Voice* to protest the paper's disparaging coverage of LGBTQ+ issues.

Come Out! *newspaper was published by the Gay Liberation Front, but it only had a short run of three years, shutting down in 1972.*

In San Francisco on October 31, some 50–100 members of the city's GLF chapter, the Committee for Homosexual Freedom (CHF), and the Gay Guerilla Theater gather at the *San Francisco Examiner* building to protest a disparaging article on LGBTQ+ bars and clubs on Folsom Street. The "expose" refers to these establishments as "deviate" sites for "sick" LGBTQ+ patrons and labels them as "semi-males," "members of the pseudo-fair sex," and "women who aren't exactly women." In response, *Examiner* employees throw a plastic bag of printer ink out a second-story window onto protestors (some sources say the roof), who use the ink to scrawl "Gay Power" and other slogans on the building's walls and windows and stamp surfaces throughout downtown San Francisco with purple handprints. The city's tactical police squad arrives to harass and arrest demonstrators, treating them roughly in the process, which later results in a GLF demonstration at City Hall to protest police brutality.

The October 31 protest becomes known alternately as the "Friday of the Purple Hand" or the "Bloody Friday of the Purple Hand" and inspires some gay and lesbian activists to adopt the purple handprint in much the same way as the organized crime symbol of the "Black Hand": as a method of extortion, in this case as a warning to the authorities against anti-LGBTQ+ attacks. On October 3, New York Mattachine Society member and drag queen Lee Brewster founds the Queens Liberation Front (QLF) to advocate for the rights of cross-dressers. Primarily active during the 1970s, the QLF works to overturn a New York City ordinance against cross-dressing and from 1971 to 1983 publishes *Drag Queens: A Magazine About the Transvestite*.

1970s. The decade sees a gay liberation movement that results in new LGBTQ+ groups being formed and a continuation of the confrontational activism that began to evolve during the 1960s and increased after Stonewall. With a new sense of confidence and power, LGBTQ+ activists take to the streets, demanding their rights and shouting, "Say It Loud. Gay and Proud." Drag queens and kings, who helped spark the uprising, take a more activist role as part of the wider LGBTQ+ community, and bisexuals and gays and lesbians of color begin to make their voices heard. Lesbian activism becomes more visible and includes lesbian feminist "separatist" groups, in part empowered by second-wave feminism.

A 1971 poster by the Gay Activists Alliances advertises their Firehouse Dance at their headquarters at 99 Wooster Street in New York City.

1970. The Gay Activists Alliance (aka the GAA or, simply, the Alliance), formed on December 21, 1969, in New York, with chapters across the country appearing soon afterward, becomes the most influential LGBTQ+ activist group during the first years of the decade. Founded by eight disaffected members of the Gay Liberation Front, the GAA is as confrontational in its approach as the GLF, but its goal is to take a neutral political stance and focus explicitly on gay and lesbian rights. The organization adopts the lowercase spelling of the Greek letter lambda, which represents "wavelength" in physics, as its symbol to signify an exchange of energy. On March 8 in New York, the GAA and the GLF organize an angry demonstration to protest a police raid at the Snake Pit, an after-hours basement bar on West 10th Street, which had resulted in 167 arrests and seriously injured bar patron Diego Viñales, age 23, when he jumped out a window of the precinct while attempting to escape detention and was impaled on a fence. Some 500 people attend the protest, which sees widespread mainstream media coverage.

Its visibility established, GAA cofounder Marty Robinson conceives a form of group protest called "zaps": surprise, generally nonviolent and often humorous confrontations with homophobic politicians and corporate and government entities that are designed to embarrass them, force them to address gay and lesbian discrimination and rights, and gain media attention on LGBTQ+ issues. Notable targets of GAA zaps include the New York City Marriage License Bureau to demand marriage rights for gays; Fidelifacts, a homophobic background-check agency that assists employers in identifying and discriminating against LGBTQ+ job seekers; and the New York Taxi Commission, which requires gay cabbies to obtain approval before employment.

During a zap at *Harper's Magazine* to protest a homophobic article, GAA members bring coffee, doughnuts, and cookies with them and proceed to conduct an all-day sit-in at the magazine's offices. The GAA forms several subcommittees to address specific employment, political, and social issues, such as fostering a sense of community, including among lesbians, who are less well represented in the organization. The *Gay Activist*, the GAA newspaper, is published until 1980. The following year, members of the Alliance vote to officially disband the organization because it is felt that the group had become too much like the GLF, which also ceases operations around that time. However, both groups' legacies of confrontation live on in the LGBTQ+ activist groups that follow.

On May 1, a feminist lesbian group comprised of disaffected members of the Gay Liberation Front and the National Organization for Women (NOW), calling themselves the Lavender Menace, "zaps" the opening session of NOW's Second Congress to Unite Women in New York to challenge the anti-lesbian sentiment within the organization. The group is protesting NOW president Betty Friedan's omission of the New York chapter of the Daughters of Bilitis from the organization's list of sponsors the year before in the fear that lesbian participation was a threat to NOW's ability to effect serious mainstream political change. The group's name stems from Friedan's reported description

A flyer for the 1970 San Francisco Gay-In

of lesbian visibility in NOW as a "lavender menace." After the group stations itself in the auditorium with placards and passes around copies of its manifesto, "The Woman-Identified Woman," 40 Lavender Menace members take the stage amid cheers of support; women in the audience begin a positive dialogue with them, which leads to lesbian-related workshops and resolutions over the next two days. The Lavender Menace later changes its name to the Radicalesbians.

May 27 and 28 mark the first simultaneous Pride parades in the United States in Chicago, San Francisco, New York City, and Los Angeles in observance of the first anniversary of the Stonewall Uprising. The Chicago and San Francisco parades take place on June 27 to correspond with the last Saturday in June, with the San Francisco parade being a whole Pride weekend featuring a march on the 27th and a "Gay-In" on the 28th. Los Angeles's Pride Parade is organized by Reverend Troy Perry, founder of the gay-friendly Metropolitan Community Church in 1968, and Morris Kight of the Los Angeles chapter of the Gay Liberation Front, with Kight receiving death threats throughout the process. The parade receives coverage from *The Advocate*, which reports that "over 1,000 homosexuals and their friends staged, not just a protest march, but a parade down world-famous Hollywood Boulevard."

New York City's Pride Parade is the result of a resolution at the Philadelphia Eastern Regional Conference of Homophile Organizations (ERICHO) on November 2, 1969, that called for the abandonment of the Annual Reminder in favor of a Christopher Street Liberation Day March to commemorate the events of Stonewall. The organizers call themselves the Christopher Street Liberation Day Umbrella Committee (CSLDUC) and include Craig Rodwell (the creator of the Annual Reminder), Fred Sargeant, Ellen Broidy, Linda Rhodes, Brenda Howard, and many others. The committee solicits donations for the parade from national homophile organizations and sponsors as well as from the GLF and the customer mailing list of Rodwell's Oscar Wilde Memorial Bookshop.

On June 28, a few thousand participants take part in the Christopher Street Liberation Day Parade, which covers 50 blocks. New York's parade eventually becomes the largest such event in the world. Despite the relatively small numbers, the first Pride parades, initially known as "Gay Liberation Marches," "Gay Liberation Day," or "Gay Freedom Marches," lead to hundreds of parades in cities and towns throughout the United States and around the world.

Despite the relatively small numbers, the first Pride parades, initially known as "Gay Liberation Marches," "Gay Liberation Day," or "Gay Freedom Marches," lead to hundreds of parades in cities and towns throughout the United States and around the world.

By the 1980s, many parade organizers begin to replace the words "liberation" and "freedom" with the phrase "Gay Pride Parade." As the LGBTQ+ Pride movement spreads across the nation, June begins to be designated as Pride Month. President Bill Clinton officially declares June "Gay and Lesbian Pride Month" in 1999; in 2009, President Barack Obama declares "LGBT Pride Month"; and President Joe Biden declares "LGBTQ Pride Month" on June 1, 2021. Pride Month is also observed by several LGBTQ+-affiliated churches. In July, Black and Latinx gay and lesbian members of the Gay Liberation Front split from the GLF to form the Third World Gay Revolution (TWGR). The TWGR's ambitious platform confronts the politics and, in 21st-century language, the intersectionality of homophobia, heterosexism, racism, and classism and allies itself with the Black Panther Party (BPP) and the Latinx Young Lords Party (YLP). Although the TWGR

A pin made for the Christopher Street Liberation Day event designed to mark the first anniversary after the Stonewall riots.

lasts for only a few months, it is successful in raising consciousness concerning the struggles and challenges of gays and lesbians of color.

On September 20, activist groups, including New York University Gay Student Liberation, the Gay Liberation Front, and the Radicalesbians, hold a five-day sit-in at the university to protest the administration's cancellation of four "Dance-a-Fairs." Coordinated by the Christopher Street Liberation Day Committee (CSLDC), the dances are intended as fundraisers to help with legal, medical, and housing issues for the LGBTQ+ community. The networking that takes place during the sit-in inspires drag queens Sylvia Rivera and Marsha P. Johnson, who are members of the Gay Liberation Front and the Gay Activists Alliance, to form the Street Transvestite Action Revolutionaries (STAR). The organization operates as a collective to provide shelter, food, and other support to LGBTQ+ prisoners and homeless youth, especially young people of color. STAR lasts until 1973.

1971. The Furies Collective, a short-lived commune consisting of 12 lesbian feminist separatists, is founded in Washington, D.C. The commune's members view lesbianism as a political rather than sexual choice and consider straight women, together with the patriarchy, white supremacy, and imperialism, as obstacles to revolution. The collective published its own newspaper, *The Furies*, from 1972 to 1973. In 2016, the Furies's communal house became the first lesbian site on the National Register of Historic Places.

1972. Members of the Radicalesbians and the Lesbian Liberation Committee, a subcommittee of the Gay Activists Alliance, split from both groups to form the

The Furies Collective based themselves at this Washington, D.C., home at 219 11th St., SE.

Lesbian Feminist Liberation. The new group works to increase lesbian visibility at LGBTQ+ Pride marches, lobbies the New York City Council to add sexual orientation to its antidiscrimination ordinance, and stages demonstrations to protest anti-lesbianism and sexism in films and TV shows.

1973. The first formal meeting of Parents and Friends of Lesbians and Gays (PFLAG), the first and largest advocacy group to bring together families and allies of LGBTQ+ people, takes place on March 11 in New York City. PFLAG is the brainchild of elementary school teacher Jeanne Manford, who conceived the idea in 1972, after her son, Morty, was severely beaten during a Gay Activists Alliance protest. Mother and son subsequently appear together at New York's Pride Parade, with Jeanne receiving an enthusiastic response from the crowd for her sign reading "Parents of Gays Unite in Support of Our Children." Despite a slow start, PFLAG gains traction, with over 400 chapters in cities and rural communities across the country by the 21st century.

During the 1990s, PFLAG expands to include bisexual and transgender people and adds the word "Families" to its name. In 2014, the organization votes to rename itself as simply PFLAG to acknowledge LGBTQ+ diversity. In October, several prominent gay and lesbian activists found the National Gay Task Force in New York City. Its mission is to create a unified and organized national presence in the gay rights movement and to gain greater public acceptance of gays and lesbians.

Jeanne Manford, the founder of PFLAG, is seen here marching at the 1972 New York City Pride Parade.

On March 26, 1977, the Task Force, together with other gay and lesbian activists, meet with presidential aide Midge Costanza at the White House, the first such meeting in LGBTQ+ history. Topics under discussion include support of a presidential bill to end discrimination in the federal work force, the military, and housing as well as the ban on the granting of U.S. citizenship to gay immigrants.

In 1985, the group renames itself the National Gay and Lesbian Task Force and in 2014 becomes the National LGBTQ Task Force. Lambda Legal, aka the Lambda Legal Defense and Education Fund, holds its first meeting in New York City on November 10. Founded in 1971 by gay attorney William J. Thom but denied incorporation until 1973, when the New York Court of Appeals overturns the lower court decision that "there was no demonstrable need for its existence," Lambda Legal becomes known for its success in helping to secure full federal and state civil rights for LGBTQ+ people as well as those living with HIV. The scarcity of openly gay lawyers leads Lambda Legal to form an advisory board of prominent gay-supportive New Yorkers, including U.S. congressional representative Bella Abzug, state senator Carol Bellamy, and City University of New York professor and gay rights activist Martin Duberman. Lambda Legal's commitment to diversity for its board of directors presents a similar challenge during the early 1970s because of the unwillingness of lesbian lawyers, who fear risking their careers by openly allying themselves with an activist organization and instead prefer to work within the legal system to end discrimination. However, by the

1980s, Lambda's board includes an equal number of men and women.

1974. In New York, the Black Lesbian Caucus, which split off from the Gay Activists Alliance in 1971, reforms as the Third World Gay Women's Association and is popularly known as the Salsa Soul Sisters. The oldest Black lesbian organization in the United States, the group provides safe spaces for lesbian women of color as alternatives to lesbian and gay bars and is active in protests and community organizing. The group's publications include the magazine *Azalea* (1977–1983) and the newsletter *Salsa Soul Gazette* (1982). In 1979, the group leads the first National March on Washington for Lesbian and Gay Rights, carrying the official march banner. In 1993, the Soul Sisters separate into two groups: the African Ancestral Lesbians United for Societal Change, representing African-diaspora lesbians, and Las Buenas Amigas for Latinas.

1977. Berkeley School of Law graduate Donna Hitchens founds the Lesbian Rights Project, later renamed the National Center for Lesbian Rights (NCLR), to advance the civil rights of lesbians through legal, policy, and legislative initiatives. In Des Moines, Iowa, gay activist Thom Higgins (1950–1994), credited for coining the term "gay pride" in the wake of the Stonewall Uprising, throws a banana pie in the face of Florida singer and anti-gay campaigner Anita Bryant. Bryant is appearing at a televised pre-concert press conference to discuss her plan for opening Anita Bryant Centers, where "homosexuals" could be rehabilitated. Higgins does not face criminal charges, and Bryant responds, "At least it's a fruit pie."

In Des Moines, Iowa, gay activist Thom Higgins (1950–1994), credited for coining the term "gay pride" in the wake of the Stonewall Uprising, throws a banana pie in the face of Florida singer and anti-gay campaigner Anita Bryant.

1978. The National Coalition of Black Gays, renamed the National Coalition of Black Lesbians and Gays (NCBLG) in 1984, is founded in Columbia, Maryland. It is the only group to provide a national forum specifically for Black LGBTQ+ Americans to communicate their experiences and perspectives and eventually includes chapters in many cities across the country. The Coalition's magazine *Black/Out*, first published in 1986, features articles by such prominent Black activists as Bayard Rustin and Audre Lorde. The NCBLG ceases operations in 1990.

The Gay & Lesbian Advocates & Defenders (GLAD), later renamed the GLBTQ Legal Advocates & Defenders (GLAD Law), is founded in Boston, Massachusetts. The organization is formed in response to a sting operation during which the Boston police arrest over 100 men suspected of using a men's room at the Boston Public Library for sex. The arrests lead to GLAD's first case, *Doe v. McNiff*, with the result that all the defendants either have the charges against them dismissed or are found not guilty. In 1980, GLAD successfully defends the rights of a high school student to bring a same-sex date to a school prom. The organization subsequently becomes known for its work in legalizing same-sex marriage.

The first Pride Flag, aka the Rainbow Flag, makes its debut at the San Francisco Gay Freedom Day Parade on June 25. The flag is the creation of artist Gilbert Baker and is designed at the request of San Francisco city supervisor Harvey Milk. The colors of the rainbow featured on the flag signify life, healing, sunlight, nature, harmony, and spirit. During the 21st century, the flag undergoes two redesigns to signify the trajectory of LGBTQ+ history, and individual Pride flags appear to represent all people within the LGBTQ+ community.

1979. On October 14, during the year that marks the 10th anniversary of the

The original Pride Flag was designed by artist Gilbert Baker and adopted for use in 1978.

Stonewall Uprising, some 75,000 to 100,000 people attend the first National March on Washington for Lesbian and Gay Rights. Comedian Robin Tyler emcees the march, which features a lineup of speakers that includes straight allies as well as prominent members of the LGBTQ+ community. The march takes place during a five-day Third World Conference from October 11 to 15. On the last day, deemed "Constituency Lobby Day," some 500 marchers meet with 50 senators and 150 congressional representatives to discuss LGBTQ+ rights legislation.

1980. LGBTQ+ activist and Gay Rights National Lobby member Steve Endean establishes the Human Rights Campaign Fund, a political action committee (PAC) focused on advancing the cause of LGBTQ+ equality and lobbying on behalf of and in opposition to local, state, and federal regulation and candidates for office and, later, the expansion and protection of queer civil rights. In 1995, the organization drops the word "fund" from its name and forms new advocacy programs relating to families, the workplace, and the clergy, particularly regarding support for same-sex marriage. In June 2023, the HRC declares a "national state of emergency" in response to several states' enactment of anti-LGBTQ+ legislation.

1983. The Lesbian and Gay Community Center (now called the Lesbian, Gay, Bisexual & Transgender Community Center) purchases the former Food and Maritime Trades School in New York City's West Village. During the 1980s and early 1990s, the space becomes a major meeting place for many LGBTQ+ activist groups as well as the home of the New York chapter of the Gay and Lesbian Switchboard (1972–1997), considered the oldest operating LGBTQ+ hotline in the world, which was subsequently renamed the LGBT Switchboard of New York.

1985. GLAAD, originally known as the Gay & Lesbian Alliance Against Defamation, is founded in New York in response to the *New York Post*'s defamatory and sensationalized coverage of the AIDS epidemic. GLAAD's successes in changing media coverage of LGBTQ+ topics in New York leads to chapters in other cities, most notably in Los Angeles, where GLAAD also focuses on changing portrayals of lesbians and gays in Hollywood and greater queer representation in the entertainment industry.

1987. AIDS activist Larry Kramer, a cofounder of the Gay Men's Health Crisis (GMHC) in 1982 during the burgeoning AIDS epidemic, founds the AIDS Coalition to Unleash Power (ACT UP) in New York City on March 12. It was founded as a political direct-action group to force so far largely unresponsive federal and state governments and their elected officials, public health agencies, pharmaceutical and insurance companies, and religious organizations to protect people with AIDS and those at risk of HIV. Artist Avram Finkelstein founds the Silence=Death Project, a six-person collective best known for its

Located in New York's Greenwich Village at 208 West 13th Street, the Lesbian, Gay, Bisexual & Transgender Community Center is in a former elementary school that was built in 1925.

iconic "Silence=Death" political poster, used by ACT UP as a central image to protest the lack of public awareness and acknowledgment of the devastating AIDS epidemic. "Silence=Death" also appears in chalk on various New York City sidewalks. On October 11, over 750,000 people attend the Second National March on Washington for Lesbian and Gay Rights, also known as the "Great March." Its focus is on the AIDS crisis and the political inaction regarding the devastating epidemic and also marks the unveiling of the NAMES Project AIDS Memorial Quilt, a massive patchwork quilt honoring those lost to the virus. Several marches follow: the March on Washington for Lesbian, Gay, and Bi Equal Rights and Liberation (1993), the Millennium March on Washington (2000), the National Equality March (2009), and the National Pride March (aka the Equality March for Unity and Pride and the LGBT Resist March), held on June 11, 2017. The latter march commemorates the 49 victims murdered in the June 12, 2016, mass shooting at the Orlando, Florida, gay nightclub Pulse.

1988. At the height of the AIDS epidemic, the first National Coming Out Day (NCOD) takes place on October 11, the first anniversary of the Second National March on Washington for Lesbian and Gay Rights. New Mexico psychologist Robert Eichberg and Jean O'Leary, founder of the Lesbian Feminist Liberation and head of the National Gay Rights Advocates in Los Angeles, inaugurate the observance to celebrate LGBTQ+ orientation and identity and focus attention on the power of queer visibility as a transformative political force. At a time when much of the public justifies its homophobia because of the AIDS epidemic, Eichberg maintains that "it is imperative that we come out and let people know who we are and disabuse them of their fears and stereotypes." Sadly, Eichberg succumbs to AIDS in 1995.

1990. Outraged at the escalation of crimes against gays and lesbians in New York City and continuing anti-gay discrimination, four HIV/AIDS activists from ACT UP gather at the Lesbian and Gay Community Center in Greenwich Village on March 20 to form Queer Nation (the name is formally adopted on May 17).

During the early 1990s, chapters are developed in such cities as Atlanta, Denver, Houston, and San Francisco. Queer Nation's actions in New York during its first year include "Queer Nights Out" invasions of straight bars and demonstrations and marches to protest acts of violence such as a march and candlelight vigil on August 18 in Jackson Heights, Queens, to protest the refusal of police to classify the anti-gay-motivated murder of resident Julio Rivera as a bias crime.

On July 22, Queer Nation and ACT UP march through the exclusive enclave of Muttontown on Long Island, where they protest outside the home of state senator Ralph Marino, who has been instrumental in ensuring that a New York hate crime bill is not passed. Queer Nation's rallying cry during marches and demonstrations is "We're here! We're queer! Get used to it!"

1992. In New York City, six lesbian activists, feeling that their priorities are often sidelined by gay and women's rights groups, form the Lesbian Avengers. Its goal is to make lesbians more visible, as theater director and cofounder Ana Simo describes it, "on the street." Avengers tactics include zaps and agitprop humor to counter the stereotype of lesbians as somber and cheerless, such as posters and flyers with the motto "We Recruit," one of which features an image of 1970s blaxploitation action star Pam Grier sporting

U.S. congresswoman Nancy Pelosi is seen at the 1987 Second Nation March in Washington, D.C.

a rifle, and hosting parties and fundraisers. On the eve of the March on Washington for Lesbian, Gay, and Bi Equal Rights and Liberation in 1993, the Avengers hold the first Dyke March, which draws some 20,000 lesbians. By the time the group disbands in 1997, it has expanded to include 50 chapters across the country, hosted a TV network called Dyke TV, and has been featured on the covers of the mainstream magazines *Time* and *Vanity Fair*.

1994. The first LGBTQ+ History Month is observed in October. Originally called Gay and Lesbian History Month, the celebration is founded by Rodney Wilson, a Missouri high school history teacher and the first openly gay public school teacher in the state. In 2012, two school districts, in Florida and California, become the first to celebrate LGBTQ+ History Month in classrooms. Several countries around the world have celebrated LGBTQ+ History Month since the first decades of the 21st century, although not all countries do so in October.

1999. A group of transgender women

Examples of promotional materials used by the Houston branch of Queer Nation.

in Massachusetts found the Transgender Day of Remembrance (TDoR) to memorialize Rita Hester and Chanelle Pickett, two Black transgender women who had been murdered three years earlier. The event, also known as the International Transgender Day of Remembrance, serves to raise awareness of victims of transphobia and is observed annually on November 20.

2003. On December 8, eight Black civil rights leaders announce the formation of the National Black Justice Coalition (NBJC) during a press conference held at the National Press Club in Washington, D.C. The coalition's mission is to empower Black LGBTQ+ people and end discrimination by promoting social, economic, and political visibility and inclusivity. Over the years, the coalition has sponsored such initiatives as the Black Church Summit; the Black, Trans, and Proud campaign; and the Emerging Leaders Initiative.

On December 12, transgender woman Mara Keisling, with the support of the National Gay and Lesbian Task Force, establishes the National Center for Transgender Equality (NCTE) in Washington, D.C. The organization's mission is to end discrimination and violence toward transgender people. In 2023, the NCTE merges with the Transgender Legal Defense and Education Fund to become Advocates for Trans Equality (A4TE).

2004. Attorney, filmmaker, transgender activist, and trans man Alexander L. Lee founds the Transgender Gender-Variant & Intersex Justice Project (aka TGI or TGIJP) in San Francisco. A nonprofit organization working to end human rights abuses against transgender, gender-variant, and

(Left to right) Lexi Adsit, Mia "Tu Mutch" Satya, Shawn Demmons, and Nya are shown on stage during the 2016 Transgender Day of Visibility in San Francisco.

intersex people, TGI particularly focuses on trans women of color in California prisons and detention centers.

2009. The first International Transgender Day of Visibility (TDOV or Trans Day of Visibility) is held on March 31. It is the creation of Michigan transgender activist Rachel Crandall as a celebration of transgender people and a counterpoint to the Transgender Day of Remembrance. By 2014 and 2015, activists around the world celebrate the event, and it is widely publicized on social media platforms. In 2021, President Joe Biden officially proclaims the March 31 event, calling on Americans to "join in the fight for full equality for all transgender people."

2015. In commemoration of the Stonewall Uprising of 1969, the Stonewall Inn becomes a New York City landmark and the first LGBTQ+ landmark so designated. The following year, President Barack Obama officially declares the site as the Stonewall National Monument, making it the first national monument to be dedicated as an LGBTQ+ historic site. When an LGBTQ+ Rainbow Flag is raised at the memorial in 2017, it becomes the first officially maintained LGBTQ+ flag at a federal monument. Inside the Stonewall Inn is the National LGBTQ Wall of Honor, unveiled on June 27, 2019, during Stonewall 50—WorldPride NYC events.

BIOGRAPHIES

Sidney Abbott (1937–2015)

Lesbian Activist, Women's Rights Activist, Writer

One of the most vocal and active members of the National Organization for Women on behalf of lesbian inclusion in the feminist movement, Sidney Abbott was a member of the Lavender Menace and the Radicalesbians as well as the coauthor with Barbara Love of *Sappho Was a Right-On Woman: A Liberated View of Lesbianism.*

Born in Washington, D.C., Abbott grew up in a military family. Her father, a West Point graduate, served as an aide to General Douglas MacArthur during World War II. After attending Smith College, she completed her undergraduate studies at the University of New Mexico with a degree in art history. She went on to study urban planning at Columbia University before working as a project developer in New York City, serving as the first openly lesbian or gay appointee to a community planning board.

In 1969, Abbott joined the National Organization for Women (NOW), becoming a leading spokeswoman for lesbian rights on the organization's panels. At the time, Betty Friedan, the president of NOW, did not support her efforts, fearing that if NOW openly supported lesbian rights, it could compromise the larger agenda of women's equality, and she dubbed the lesbian presence in NOW as "the lavender menace." This became the term that she and other lesbian feminists chose in 1970 for their group, which protested the exclusion of lesbian issues from the mainstream feminist agenda. As a member of the Radicalesbians, she helped distribute a manifesto, "The Woman-Identified Woman," at the Second Congress to Unite Women in New York City in protest of the exclusion of lesbian speakers.

Abbott was instrumental in helping to normalize lesbianism. In 1972, she coauthored, with Barbara Love, the groundbreaking book *Sappho Was a Right-On Woman: A Liberated View of Lesbianism*. Published at a time when the American Psychiatric Association continued to classify lesbian and gay orientation as a mental illness, the book was, as Love described it, "the first book that came out with a positive view of lesbianism." In the introduction, they asserted that their main ambition in writing the book was not to be tolerated as freaks but, instead, "to be the most ordinary people." Abbott was also one of the founding board members of the National Gay Task Force as well as the founder of the nonprofit organization Women's Rights Are Human Rights.

Abbott died in a house fire in her home in Southold, Long Island, at the age of 77. In her eulogy, writer and activist Rita Mae Brown said, "Sidney put her shoulder to the wheel on feminist issues and she understood the pressure against lesbians."

Gloria Allen (1945–2022)

Transgender Activist

Gloria Allen, known as "Mama Gloria," was a transgender activist whose experiences running a charm school for at-risk transgender youth inspired both the acclaimed documentary *Mama Gloria* and the play *Charm*.

Born in Bowling Green, Kentucky, Allen was raised in Chicago, the eldest of eight children. She transitioned in the 1950s and credited her coming out to the love and support of her mother, Alma, a showgirl and former *Jet* magazine centerfold, and her grandmother, Mildred, a seamstress for cross-dressers and strippers. She worked as an X-ray technician, a licensed practical nurse, a motel clerk, and a nurse's aide caring for the elderly. Her personal life included several abusive relationships, including a decade-long relationship with an abusive boyfriend who she shot and injured, but he did not report the shooting to the authorities.

Before the Stonewall Uprising, which ignited the gay rights movement, Allen was a celebrated figure in the transgender rights movement in Chicago. In 2012, she opened her charm school out of a community center for LGBTQ+ people on Halsted Street in Chicago's Lakeview neighborhood. Most students were transgender people in their teens or early 20s from economically deprived backgrounds. Her school was informal and free, and lessons covered table manners, dating etiquette, hygiene, dressing, makeup, and job-interviewing skills in order to help students find both jobs and confidence and develop a sense of pride. As Philip Dawkins, who wrote the 2015 play *Charm*, based on Allen's work with the school, observed, "History was very important to Mama. It was very important to her to teach her babies that they were not the first people to walk this struggle. She wanted them to know they were not alone."

Called by the *Chicago Tribune* the "Emily Post of Halsted Street," Allen continued running the school for nearly a decade. In 2014, she received the Living Legend Award at the Trans 100 awards, a ceremony celebrating 100 transgender leaders. President Biden paid tribute to her at a Pride Month reception at the White House, saying, "We're in a battle for the soul of the nation. But when I look around this room here—and all of you here today, it's a battle I know we will win. We will do so on the shoulders of so many people who are no longer with us, but who paved the way for us. People like Gloria Allen, known as 'Mama Gloria,' who transitioned in the 1950s."

After Allen's death in an LGBTQ+ senior living facility, Luchina Fisher, director of the documentary *Mama Gloria*, eulogized her friend by saying that "Gloria stood for liberation; she lived it. She liked to joke about how she was 'out' when she came out of her mother's womb."

Wanda Alston (1959–2005)

Activist, Government Official

One of the inaugural 50 American "pioneers, trailblazers, and heroes" to be featured on the National LGBTQ Wall of Honor within the Stonewall National Monument, Wanda Alston was known for her activism and advocacy on behalf of LGBTQ+ Americans. She worked for the Human Rights Campaign and the National Organization for Women (NOW) and served as the special assistant to the mayor of Washington, D.C., for Lesbian, Gay, Bisexual, and Transgender Affairs.

Born in Newport News, Virginia, Alston earned a B.S. in mass communication from Norfolk State University and an M.B.A. in international management from Southeastern University in Washington, D.C. From 1992 to 1996, she served as the executive assistant to Patricia Ireland, president of NOW, and as a special project director, organizing four national marches on Washington and one in San Francisco.

She co-led the NOW delegation to the World Conference of Women in Beijing in 1995 and served as the staff liaison to the National Rainbow Coalition. Ireland recalled her colleague: "When she plugged into feminist activism, I think she found a whole new world overall—whether it was LGBT, civil rights, D.C. statehood, or electoral politics, she was an organizer like the rest of us and did it to keep her balance in an unjust world."

Beginning in 2001, as director of the D.C. Mayor's Office of LGBT Affairs, Alston was also the liaison between the district government and the LGBTQ+ community. Her efforts led to greater representation for the LGBTQ+ community on district government boards and commissions. She also worked with the Office of Human Rights and the Department of Employment Services to establish sensitivity training for all government agencies and was a fierce advocate for housing programs for homeless and at-risk LGBTQ+ youth.

Alston's life was tragically cut short in 2005, when she was stabbed to death in her home by 38-year-old William Parrott, who lived nearby. She was found by her partner, Stacey Long. Parrott was apprehended after taking Alston's car and credit cards and subsequently sentenced to a 24-year prison sentence.

News of her senseless and brutal murder shocked the D.C. community and her colleagues, who mourned the loss of a woman who had worked tirelessly to increase the visibility of LGBTQ+ Americans, particularly queer Americans of color. As Keith Boykin, president of the LGBTQ+ rights group National Black Justice Coalition, said, "Wanda was one of the toughest, most determined people I have ever met in my life."

Virginia Apuzzo (1941–)

Activist, Government Official

An executive director of the National LGBTQ Task Force (formerly known as the National Gay and Lesbian Task Force), Virginia "Ginny" Apuzzo is a former nun and gay rights and AIDS activist who served as associate deputy secretary of labor and assistant to the president for management and administration in the Clinton administration.

Apuzzo was born in the Bronx in New York City, where her father owned a gas station, and her mother worked as a waitress, factory worker, and salesperson. After attending a Catholic high school, she graduated from the State University of New York, New Paltz, in 1963 with a BS in history and education and became a teacher and chair of the Social Studies Department at the Marlboro Central District in Marlboro, New York.

At 26, she became a nun at the Sisters of Charity convent in the Bronx. She knew at the time that she was a lesbian, later recalling, "I tried to play by the rules. I thought I'd have to live my life with this deep dark secret." After the Stonewall Uprising, she decided to come out publicly and left the convent to begin teaching education at Brooklyn College, where she was later awarded tenure and continued to teach until 1986. She joined the National Gay and Lesbian Task Force, serving for many years as its executive director, and in 1978, she cofounded the Lambda Independent Democrats.

In 1979, Apuzzo served as the assistant commissioner for operations in the New York City Department of Health, becoming one of the earliest and most vocal female AIDS activists in the country. In 1980, she became one of the first openly lesbian delegates at the Democratic National Convention and authored the first gay and lesbian civil rights plank for the Democratic Party.

In 1997, President Bill Clinton appointed her to the White House senior staff as assistant to the president for administration and management, making her the highest-ranking openly lesbian federal employee. When she joined the Women's Caucus with her partner, Achebe Betty Powell, who was the first Black lesbian on the group's board, both worked to make lesbian rights more prominent in the women's movement. In 1999, she rejoined the NGLTF as the first holder of the Virginia Apuzzo Chair for Leadership in Public Policy.

Apuzzo cofounded the Hudson Valley LGBTQ+ Community Center in Kingston, New York, in 2005 and in 2007 was appointed to New York's Commission on Integrity, a position she held util her retirement.

Gilbert Baker (1951–2017)

LGBTQ+ Activist, Artist

Calling himself the "gay Betsy Ross," Gilbert Baker is the creator of the iconic Rainbow Flag. He would go on to achieve two world records for the largest flags ever created: a mile-long Rainbow Flag honoring the 25th anniversary of Stonewall in 1994 and a mile-and-a-quarter-long flag commemorating the 25th anniversary of the Rainbow Flag in 2003.

Born in Chanute, Kansas, Baker's mother was an educator, and his father served as a lawyer and a judge. As a child and teen, he had an outgoing and friendly personality but felt ostracized because of his gay identity. After graduating from high school, he attended college for a year before the Army drafted him. He was stationed in San Francisco just as the gay liberation movement was beginning to take shape and remained in San Francisco after leaving the Army in 1972.

During the 1970s, Baker participated in drag shows and joined the Sisters of Perpetual Indulgence, an LGBTQ+ advocacy group whose members dressed as nuns in order to bring attention to gender and sexual intolerance. Friends often asked him to make banners for protests and marches, and his early efforts often included the pink triangle, which protesters reclaimed as a positive symbol from its initial connotation in Germany during the Nazi era. When city supervisor Harvey Milk asked him to create an emblem for the 1978 Pride Parade, Baker, with the help of volunteers, filled trash cans with dye in the attic of the San Francisco LGBT Community Center and pieced together the first flags. He recalled, "We stood there and watched and saw the flags, and their faces lit up. It needed no explanation. People knew immediately that it was our flag." The first flags had eight colors, each stripe symbolic: pink for sex, red for life, orange for healing, yellow for sun, green for nature, turquoise for magic, blue for peace, and purple for spirit. He refused to apply for a trademark for his creation, regarding it as his gift to the world.

Since its introduction, the Rainbow Flag has become a universal symbol of LGBTQ+ pride, inclusion, peace, and love. After the U.S. Supreme Court legalized gay marriage in 2015, more than 26 million people on Facebook changed their profile photo to include the flag. Over the years, the flag has changed, going to six colors from eight. Baker explained that pink fabric was too expensive, so it was removed, and turquoise and blue were combined into one color, royal blue.

Baker's 1994 mile-long and 30-foot-wide Rainbow Flag, commissioned for the 25th anniversary of Stonewall, was carried by 10,000 people in the New York City Pride Parade. Both this flag and his mile-and-a-quarter-long flag, created in 2003 for the 25th anniversary of the first Rainbow Flag, were cut up and disseminated to more than 100 cities worldwide.

Baker's life is celebrated in the documentary *Rainbow Pride* (2003), and the sewing machine he used to create the first flag is on display at the GLBT Historical Society in San Francisco.

Wayne Besen (1970–)

LGBTQ+ Rights Advocate

A former spokesperson for the Human Rights Campaign, Wayne Besen founded the organization Truth Wins Out in 2006 to fight anti-gay religious extremism and counter the notion that a person's sexual orientation can be changed.

Born in Jacksonville, Florida, Besen attended high school in Honolulu and graduated in 1993 with a degree in broadcast journalism from the University of Florida. While still in college, he helped cofound his first nonprofit organization, Sons & Daughters of America, to increase public awareness of gay and lesbian injustices. The impetus to start the Truth Wins Out organization followed his experience coming out to his parents, who urged him to accept conversion therapy and the so-called ex-gay movement.

Besen's research has led him to interview hundreds of former and current "ex-gays" in order to document the truth of their experiences. He is an outspoken critic of Homosexuals Anonymous, who try to "cure" individuals of their sexual orientation. In September 2000, he photographed ex-gay activist John Paulk, chairman of Exodus International, a major organization in the ex-gay movement, at a Washington, D.C., gay bar, which led to Paulk's removal from Exodus International and ultimately to the organization's demise in 2013.

Besen is the author of *Anything but Straight: Unmasking the Scandals and Lies Behind the Ex-Gay Myth* (2003) and *Bashing Back: Wayne Besen on GLBT People, Politics and Culture* (2006). He was recognized in *The Advocate* magazine's "People of the Year" issue in 2006.

Elizabeth Birch (1956–)

Attorney, LGBTQ+ Rights Activist

From 1995 to 2002, Elizabeth Birch served as executive director of the Human Rights Campaign, the largest LGBTQ+ organization in the United States. Under her leadership, the HRC increased membership from 100,000 to 1.1 million.

Birch is the daughter of a Canadian Air Force officer, born at Wright-Patterson Air Force Base in Dayton, Ohio. She graduated from the University of Hawaii and earned her law degree at the Santa Clara University School of Law. She would later earn a Ph.D. from the University of Hawaii in 2004. In 1989, she joined Apple Inc. as the worldwide director of litigation and general counsel for its Claris subsidiary; she lef in 1995.

Birch's LGBTQ+ political activity began as a member of the Bay Area Municipal Elections Committee, an LGBTQ+ political action committee. She cochaired the National Gay and Lesbian Task Force from 1992 to 1994. In 1995, she joined the Human Rights Campaign as executive director, serving until 2004, when she left to spend more time with her partner, Hilary Rosen, and their children. The couple separated in 2006. She became the first leader of an LGBTQ+ organization to address a national political convention when she gave a prime time speech at the Democratic National Convention in 2000.

In 2004, Birch launched a consulting firm, Birch & Company. She also ran Rosie O'Donnell's production company, KidRo Productions, and oversaw O'Donnell's foundation, Rosie's For All Kids Foundation, until 2007. The Black-Tie Dinner, the largest LGBTQ+ fundraising dinner in existence, presents an annual Elizabeth Birch Equality Award to the individual, organization, or company that has made a significant contribution to the LGBTQ+ community. She was the first recipient of the award in 2004.

Lorena Borjas (1960–2020)

Transgender Activist, Immigrant Rights Activist

Described by her friend, activist Cecilia Gentili, as the "mother of the trans Latinx community" in Queens, New York, Lorena Borjas has been recognized for her work on behalf of immigrants and transgender women contending with human trafficking, health issues, and possible deportation.

Born in Veracruz, Mexico, Borjas, who identified as gay, ran away from home at 17 and came to the United States in 1981 after living on the streets of Mexico City for three years. When she first arrived, she shared an apartment in Queens, New York, with 20 transgender women who survived as sex workers and then underwent a successful gender transition under medical supervision. She remained undocumented until 1986, when she was granted amnesty under the Immigration Reform and Control Act (IRCA), enacted during the Reagan administration, and became a legal permanent resident in 1990. The same year, she was arrested on charges of prostitution and trafficking even though she had been a human trafficking victim herself. Her subsequent convictions meant that she was living under the constant threat of deportation because she could not renew her status as a permanent resident or become a U.S. citizen.

In 1995, despite the risk, Borjas began her work as an activist, organizing a transgender march to protest police policies and working to help transgender women with HIV/AIDS and protect transgender victims of human trafficking, slavery, and violence, offering shelter in her own apartment to trans women who had been rejected by their families. She provided trans women sex workers with food and condoms, connected them with social services, and facilitated access to HIV testing and hormone therapy. As Chase Strangio of the LGBT and HIV Project at the ACLU stated, she "was so connected to the community that when someone would get arrested, the first phone call was to Lorena." In 2011, they founded the Lorena Borjas Community Fund to put up bail for transgender people and help them break the cycle of arrest–jail–deportation.

In 2017, New York governor Andrew Cuomo granted Borjas a pardon, finally ending her long-held fears of deportation. Her attorney, Lynly Egyes of the Transgender Law Center, said that "Lorena has done more than anyone else I know to shine a light on the epidemic of trafficking in transgender communities and to help other trans women escape exploitation."

Ivy Bottini (1926–2021)

Activist, Artist

A pioneering activist for women's and LGBTQ+ rights, Ivy Bottini helped found the New York chapter of the National Organization for Women (NOW) and was elected its president in 1968. The same year, she designed the famous NOW logo and held a public forum titled "Is Lesbianism a Feminist Issue?," which marked the first time lesbian concerns were introduced into NOW's agenda.

Born Ivy Gaffney in Lynbrook, Long Island, New York, Bottini was the only child of a cab driver father and housewife mother. An avid athlete and talented artist, she received a full scholarship from the Pratt Institute of Art and Design to study advertising, graphic design, and illustration, and after graduating, she worked for several art and advertising agencies in New York City. She had realized that she was attracted to girls at an early age, but because of the cultural norms of the time, she did not pursue lesbian relationships. During her engagement to Eddie Bottini, she began to feel the physical symptoms of anxiety and was referred to a psychiatrist, who insisted that she was not a lesbian and advised her to solely rely on her soon-to-be husband for her well-being. In 1952, she married Eddie, with whom she had two daughters. The marriage lasted for 16 years.

Bottini regarded 1966 as the beginning of the turning point in her life. While working at *Newsday*, the major Long Island newspaper, she learned about Betty Friedan and her 1963 book *The Feminine Mystique* from a coworker who insisted that she go with her to a meeting of a group that would form the first chapter of the National Organization for Women (NOW). In 1968, she accepted her identity as a lesbian and was elected president of the New York chapter of NOW, creating a rise in feminist and lesbian consciousness within the chapter. In 1970, she joined the Lavender Menace, a group of disaffected radical feminist members of NOW, in occupying the Statue of Liberty and hanging a 40-foot banner, which read "Women of the World Unite" on its top balcony. Later in the year, Friedan forced her out of NOW in fear that having lesbians in leadership positions in the organization would threaten gains for the women's movement.

In 1971, Bottini relocated to California, where she continued her activism as a founder of the Los Angeles Lesbian/Gay Police Advisory Board as well as serving as cochair of the Lesbian and Gay Advisory Board for the city of West Hollywood. Appointed by Governor Jerry Brown as commissioner for the California Commission on Aging in 1981, she was the first out lesbian or gay person to be appointed to a California board or commission. In 1983, she cofounded AIDS Project Los Angeles and in 1993 cofounded the nonprofit organization Gay & Lesbian Elder Housing. Her initiatives during the 2000s included designing the T-shirts for the 2011 Los Angeles Dyke March. In 2019, she published her memoir, *The Liberation of Ivy Bottini: A Memoir of Love and Activism.*

Lee G. Brewster (1943–2000)

Transgender Activist, Performer

A drag queen and transgender and cross-dresser activist, Lee G. Brewster was a cofounder of the pre-Stonewall activist group the Queens Liberation Front and the publisher of *Drag* magazine. He also operated the Mardi Gras Boutique and hosted the annual Mardi Gras Ball for transgender people and the drag community.

Brewster was born in Honaker, Virginia, and raised in West Virginia, where his father was a coal miner. After working for the Federal Bureau of Investigation (FBI) for two years during the early 1960s, he was fired for being gay. He relocated to New York City, where he became involved with the Mattachine Society of New York and the Street Transvestite Action Revolutionaries (STAR). In 1969, he cofounded the Queens Liberation Front, an activist group, whose purpose was "to legalize the right to dress in the attire of the opposite sex in public without fear of police harassment." Founded in part to protest the relegation of drag queens to the back of the precursor to the Pride Parade, the Christopher Street Liberation Day March, in 1970, the QLF successfully used litigation to overturn a New York City ordinance against cross-dressing.

In 1969, Brewster opened the Mardi Gras Boutique, the first retail store to cater to drag performers as well as costume designers for such productions as *La Cage aux Folles* and *Tootsie.* The store, which began as a mail-order business in his apartment before moving to a retail space, sold clothing, shoes, accessories, wigs, and makeup as well as a variety of books and publications on transgender topics; it also served as a transgender community center. From 1971 to 1983, he published the magazine *Drag,* which included a mix of articles, editorials, and photo spreads of drag queens. His last Mardi Gras Ball in 1973 featured as guests author Jacqueline Susann, musical comedy actress Carol Channing, and actress Shirley MacLaine. After the Mardi Gras Boutique permanently closed in 2000 following his death, employee and friend Antoinette Scapinato commented, "For want of a better phrase, he was really the mother to us all."

Michael Callen (1955–1993)

AIDS Activist, Musician

Playwright Tony Kushner called Michael Callen "one of the omnipresent,

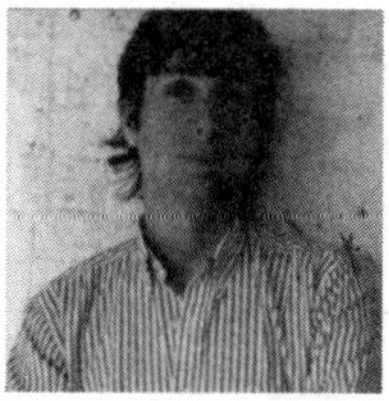

one of the titans" because of his pioneering and extensive advocacy during the AIDS epidemic on behalf of those suffering from the disease. Diagnosed with AIDS in 1982 at a time when the disease was called "Gay Related Immune Deficiency," he coined the term "people with AIDS" to replace the early characterization of AIDS victims as only gay men and supported numerous initiatives to empower the gay community, which included publishing the first guide to safe sex, *How to Have Sex in an Epidemic,* in 1983.

Born in Rising Sun, Indiana, and raised in Hamilton, Ohio, Callen attended Boston University on a music scholarship and graduated in 1977. After college, he moved to New York City, singing in cabarets and with the New York City Gay Men's Chorus. After his AIDS diagnosis, he spread the message of survival in books, magazines, newspapers, films, concerts, and television appearances. He was one of the earliest proponents of what came to be called safe-sex practices. In 1983, he was a plaintiff in the nation's first AIDS discrimination lawsuit, successfully fighting eviction from a Greenwich Village co-op for treating people with AIDS. The same year, he was a member of the founding board of the Lesbian and Gay Community Center in Greenwich Village. In 1985, he was one of the founders of the People With AIDS Coalition, whose programs included maintaining a toll-free phone line staffed entirely by people with AIDS and the largest AIDS treatment information library in New York City.

Even with his diagnosis and activism, Callen contributed significantly with his music. In 1998, his solo album, *Purple Heart,* was released, and the same year, he was a founding member of the Flirtations, an openly gay and politically active a cappella quintet that toured nationally and released two albums. He also wrote the song "Living in Wartime," which was performed in Larry Kramer's play *The Normal Heart*, and, with Peter Allen and Marsha Malamet, wrote "Love Don't Need a Reason," which became a gay anthem. His 1990 book *Surviving AIDS* tells the story of 14 long-term survivors, and he attributed his own longevity surviving with AIDS to "luck, Classic Coke, and the love of a good man!" The latter was Richard Dworkin, who met him in 1982 after answering a classified ad that Callen had placed looking for gay and lesbian musicians. As Dworkin later said, "He got a drummer, I got a vocalist and keyboard player, and we got the love of our lives." Shortly before his death, he completed work on new music released as a double CD and titled *Legacy*, a final testimony to his commitment to his gay identity and tireless advocacy.

Mandy Carter (1948–)

LGBTQ+ Activist, Civil Rights Activist

A self-described "out, southern, black, lesbian, social justice activist," Mandy Carter cofounded two groundbreaking rights organizations, Southerners On New Ground (SONG) and the National Black Justice Coalition (NBJC), to help forge connections between civil rights and LGBTQ+ organizations.

Born in Albany, New York, Carter was raised in orphanages and the foster care system. In high school, she excelled as a student but received a failing grade in Spanish that necessitated her attending a two-year college. As she recalled, "That F in Spanish is partly responsible for my being an activist. It turned out to be a good thing." She attended Hudson Valley Community College in Troy, New York, before dropping out and moving to New York City in 1967. There, she happened upon the headquarters of the League of Spiritual Discovery, an organization founded by psychedelic drug champion Timothy Leary, answering phones for the organization in exchange for food and a place to sleep. She next headed for San Francisco, where she joined the War Resisters League (WRL) and came out to her colleagues as a lesbian. In 1982, she secured a position as a full-time organizer of the WRL in Durham, North Carolina, and in 1993 cofounded the social justice organization Southerners On New Ground (SONG) to integrate work against homophobia into the ongoing equal rights struggle in the South.

Carter would go on to serve on countless committees for regional and national lesbian and Gay Pride marches, including the historic 1987 Second National March on Washington for Lesbian and Gay Rights. In 2003, she and Matt Foreman, executive director of the National LGBTQ Task Force, were the two official LGBTQ+ speakers at the Lincoln Memorial Rally marking the 40th anniversary of the March on Washington for Jobs and Freedom. The same year, she cofounded the National Black Justice Coalition, a national civil rights organization dedicated to the empowerment of Black LGBTQ+ people in combatting both homophobia and racism. In 2012, along with Chicana historian Elizabeth "Betita" Martinez and peace activist Matt Meyer, she coedited *We Have Not Been Moved: Resisting Racism and Militarism in 21st Century America.*

Carter has been the recipient of awards and honors, including the 2006 Spirit of Justice Award from Boston's Gay & Lesbian Advocates & Defenders (GLAD), induction into the International Federation of Black Pride's Black LGBT Hall of Fame during the Martin Luther King Jr. holiday in 2012, and inclusion on the 2012 Campus Pride student-created "hot list" of the nation's top 25 LGBTQ+ speakers, lecturers, and performers.

Gloria Casarez (1971–2014)

LGBTQ+ Activist, Community Organizer

Philadelphia's first director of LGBTQ+ affairs, Gloria Casarez served as the executive director of the Gay and Lesbian Latino AIDS Education Initiative (GALAEI) from 1999 to 2008.

Born in Philadelphia and raised Catholic, Casarez came out as a lesbian at the age of 17. She began her activism while attending West Chester University, where she was president of the Latino Student Union and a student representative to the Commission on the Status of Women. She earned a degree in criminal justice and political science in 1993. From 1991 to 1996, she served as a community organizer for Empty the Shelters, which focused on housing rights. As she later explained, "I was moved over and over again by women who were poor but always put their families first and tried to make things better."

As executive director of GALAEI, Casarez increased resources and developed programs serving men of color and the transgender community, including the first health program in Philadelphia that provided services to transgender people. During her tenure as director, she pushed for legislation protecting LGBTQ+ rights, including trans-inclusive access to health care, gender-neutral bathrooms in city-controlled buildings, and the right for a trans person to request name and gender changes. Legislation also included the nation's first Equality Tax Credit, a tax credit for employers who offer health benefits to same-sex couples, life partners, and transgender employees. In 1999, *Out* magazine named her one of the 100 Most Influential Leaders of the New Millennium.

Casarez married her longtime partner, Tricia Dressell, in 2011. In 2015, the Philadelphia City Council passed a resolution naming a block in Center City, a neighborhood in Philadelphia, Gloria Casarez Way, a street that also includes a mural titled *A Tribute to Gloria Casarez.*

June Chan (1956–)

Lesbian Activist, Neurobiologist

As the cofounder of the Asian Lesbians of the East Coast (ALOEC), June Chan has been instrumental in raising awareness of LGBTQ+ issues concerning the Asian American community.

Born in New York City to Chinese American parents who worked in Chinatown, Chan said that her activism stemmed from childhood memories of tourists displaying racist attitudes toward the people who lived and worked in the neighborhood. She graduated from the Bronx High School of Science in 1973 and went on to earn her bachelor's degree in biology at City College in 1977 and her master's degree from the State University of New York, Buffalo. After graduate school, she came out as a lesbian to her family, who was supportive.

In 1983, Chan met activist Katherine Hall, with whom she began working on projects documenting Asian lesbians in history and literature. The project included a pioneering slideshow that expanded the context for understanding Asian and Pacific Islander peoples, American people of color, and the lesbian community. They formed ALOEC the same year as a response to the mainly white and male LGBTQ+ community at the time and to provide support for Asian American lesbians. Conducting workshops and publishing a newsletter, ALOEC eventually formed the Asian Pacific Lesbian Network (later called the Asian Pacific Bi-Sexual Lesbian Network), the only philanthropic organization working exclusively to advance LGBTQ+ human rights around the world.

James Dale (1970–)

Gay Rights Activist

Gay rights activist James Dale is best known for his role in *Boy Scouts of America v. Dale,* the landmark Supreme Court case that challenged the Boy Scouts of America's (BSA) policy of excluding gays from leadership positions. He has been honored for his activism by numerous civil rights groups, including the American Civil Liberties Union (ACLU).

A New Jersey native, Dale was involved in scouting from the age of 8, becoming an Eagle Scout in 1988. While a student at Rutgers University, he served as copresident of the Bisexual, Lesbian, and Gay Alliance and in 1990 was a featured speaker at the Rutgers School of Social Work conference on the health needs of LGBTQ+ teens. During the same year, he gave an interview to the *Newark Star Ledge,* in which he was quoted as stating that he was gay. The BSA subsequently expelled him from his position as an assistant scoutmaster, basing their action on "the standards for leadership established by the Boy Scouts of America, which specifically forbid membership to homosexuals."

Dale then filed suit in the New Jersey Superior Court under the grounds that the BSA had violated the state statute prohibiting discrimination on the basis of sexual orientation in places of public accommodation. The Superior Court ruled against him in 1995, with Judge Patrick L. McCann labeling him as an "active sodomite"; however, in 1998, the Court's decision was overturned on appeal. After the BSA counter-appealed to the New Jersey Supreme Court and lost, the organization took its case to the U.S. Supreme Court and in 2000, in a 5–4 decision, the Court sided with the BSA and overturned the New Jersey Supreme Court's decision. The majority opinion held that the First Amendment right to freedom of "expressive association" allows a private organization like the BSA to exclude members who they feel would express a viewpoint that is contrary to the organization's mission. The dissenting minority opinion held that BSA principles say nothing about matters pertaining to sexuality or sexual orientation.

Dale has continued to advocate against the BSA ban, appearing in a 2001 documentary, *Scout's Honor,* about his experiences. In 2012, the BSA's National Council approved a resolution to remove the restriction denying membership to youth on the basis of sexual orientation but leaving in place the ban on gay adult scout leaders. However, in 2015, BSA national president Robert Gates stated that the continuing ban on gay adult leaders "cannot be sustained" and that he would no longer seek to revoke the charters of chapters that accepted gay adult leaders.

Stormé DeLarverie (1920–2014)

LGBTQ+ Activist, Entertainer

Stormé DeLarverie long asserted (with the confirmation of several eyewitnesses) that she threw the first punch at the Stonewall Inn, which served as the spark that spurred the crowd to action and ignited the June 1969 Stonewall Uprising. For this, she has come to be known as "the Rosa Parks of the gay community." A cofounder of the Stonewall Veterans' Association, she served as a leader of the organization and was a regular participant in New York Pride parades.

DeLarverie was born Viva May Thomas in New Orleans to a white father and a Black mother. She was never issued a birth certificate (she celebrated her birthday on December 24). While growing up, she was so often bullied, attacked, and beaten by peers for being of mixed race that her father ultimately sent her away to a private school for her own safety. When she was about 18, she realized that she was a lesbian and decided to move to Chicago, fearing that she would be murdered if she stayed in the South. Around this time, she began performing as a singer, first as a woman and later in male drag. From 1955 to 1969, she was the MC of the touring Jewel Box Revue, billed as "an unusual variety show," in which she dressed as a man and the rest of the cast, all men, dressed as women. It was the first integrated drag revue drawing both Black and white audiences in venues that included Harlem's Apollo Theater.

It remains a subject for debate whether or not DeLarverie was indeed the "cross-dressing lesbian" referenced in accounts of the Stonewall Uprising who attacked a policeman after he allegedly told her to "move along, faggot," thinking she was a man. Whether true or not, she has been seen as an icon of the gay liberation movement: the catalyst for the June 1969 rebellion that would initiate the increased LGBTQ+ activism of the 1970s. After Stonewall, she was on hand during the official formation of the Stonewall Veterans' Association and served in leadership positions in the organization for the rest of her life.

DeLarverie stopped performing after the death of her longtime partner, Diana, shortly after the Stonewall Uprising. She became a bodyguard for wealthy families during the day and a bouncer at several lesbian bars in Greenwich Village at night until she was 85. In 2001, she was the subject of the documentary *A Stormé Life*, and in 2019, she was one of the inaugural 50 pioneers, trailblazers, and heroes inducted on the National LGBTQ Wall of Honor within the Stonewall National Monument.

Stephen Donaldson (1946–1996)

LGBTQ+ Rights Activist, Author

Also known by his pseudonym, Donny the Punk, Stephen Donaldson was a bisexual rights activist best known for his pioneering activism in LGBTQ+ rights and prison reform as well as for his writings on the punk rock subculture. He was a founder of the first gay student group at Columbia University in 1965, the first to contest and prevail against a dishonorable military discharge for homosexual conduct, and a leader of the organization Stop Prisoner Rape and, later, Just Detention International.

The son of a career naval officer, Donaldson spent his early childhood in different seaport cities in the eastern United States and Germany. In a 1995 anthology titled *Bisexual Politics*, he wrote about his expulsion from the Boy Scouts for engaging in sexual behavior with other boys. His family responded by sending him first to his stepmother's relatives in Germany so that they could watch over him and then to a military boarding school, where he continued his sexual activity. He recalled the development of his sexual identity: "I ... learned that if I loved another boy I had to be a 'homosexual.' ... I could only find two books on the subject, which confirmed this label, and mentioned the Mattachine Society in New York as an organization of 'homosexuals.' So on a school expedition to the 'wicked city,' I slipped away, visited their office, and became a member...thus giving my new identity official status."

In 1965, Donaldson was admitted to Columbia University as a "known homosexual" under condition that he "undergo psychotherapy and not attempt to seduce other students." The following year, he began a relationship with gay activist Frank Kameny, who became an important mentor. Through Donaldson's efforts, the Student Homophile League, the first student gay rights group at Columbia and the first known LGBTQ+ student movement, was established in 1967. Chapters of the SHL were created around the country at Cornell, New York University, Stanford, and MIT, among others.

After graduating from Columbia in 1970, Donaldson enlisted in the U.S. Navy and served as a radioman on a NATO base in Italy. When the Navy announced its intention to release him on grounds of suspected homosexual involvement, he took the unprecedented step of mounting a public campaign against his discharge, eventually winning the support of U.S. Congress members Bella Abzug and Edward I. Koch. He lost his fight and was released in 1972, though he was later granted an honorable discharge.

Donaldson settled in the Washington, D.C., area and worked as a Pentagon correspondent for a privately owned newspaper distributed to American servicemen stationed in Europe. In 1973, he was arrested at a Quaker peace protest at the White House and was subsequently raped by inmates in the district's jail. This experience led to him becoming an outspoken activist on the issue of sexual victimization of male prisoners. During the 1980s and 1990s, he volunteered as a counselor to male victims of sexual assault and wrote articles on such topics as punk rock, prison conditions, Buddhism, and sexuality, often under the byline "Donny the Punk." He was also the assistant editor of the *Encyclopedia of Homosexuality* (1990) and coeditor of the 13-volume *Studies in Homosexuality* (1994).

After Donaldson's death due to an AIDS-related illness in New York City, the SHL, now known as the Columbia Queer Alliance, renamed its student lounge in his honor. Stop Prisoner Rape and Just Detention International continued the campaign for prisoners' rights that he had begun, gaining passage of the first U.S. law against rape in prison, the Prison Rape Elimination Act of 2003.

Julie Dorf (1965–)

Human Rights Activist

Founder and director of the International Gay and Lesbian Human Rights Commission (IGLHRC) to protect the rights of all people and communities subjected to discrimination and a leader in the global LGBTQ+ rights movement, Julie Dorf also cofounded the Council for Global Equality.

Dorf was raised in Milwaukee, Wisconsin, to parents who were involved in several social justice issues, including the plight of Soviet Jewry. In 1984, while she was a Wesleyan University student majoring in Soviet studies, she was an exchange student in Russia. There, she was one of the few "out" lesbians in Russia, where gay men were routinely imprisoned and lesbianism was classified as a form of schizophrenia. She began organizing within the nascent dissident underground, working with lesbian filmmakers and smuggling documentation of queer life back and forth across national borders, giving momentum to a significant grassroots organization in the seemingly impenetrable Eastern Bloc.

Dorf founded the IGLHRC (now OutRight Action International) in 1990 and served as its executive director until 2000. The organization reflects her intention to combat global human rights abuses on the basis of sexual orientation, gender identity, and HIV status. In 2008, she founded the Council for Global Equality, a coalition of 30 organizations working on U.S. foreign policy and global rights issues. She has also served as director of philanthropic services for Horizons Foundation, a San Francisco foundation for the LGBTQ+ community, and written extensively on social justice issues ranging from marriage equality to reparations for gay victims of the Nazi regime and Israeli–Palestinian relations.

Felicia Elizondo (1946–2021)

Transgender Activist, AIDS Activist

Latina trans woman Felicia Elizondo was a prominent San Francisco LGBTQ+ rights activist who was present at the historic 1966 community uprising at Compton's Cafeteria in San Francisco.

Born in San Angelo, Texas, and assigned male at birth, Elizondo grew up struggling with gender identity issues and suffered from bullying by her peers and sexual molestation by an older man. At the age of 14, she moved with her family to San Jose, California, and by the age of 16, she was spending time in San Francisco's Tenderloin district and at Gene Compton's Cafeteria, one of the few places in the city where drag queens and transgender people could congregate publicly and the site of one of the first LGBTQ+–police confrontations in U.S. history. She would be featured in a 2005 documentary on the uprising, *Screaming Queens: The Riot at Compton's Cafeteria*. At the age of 18, she joined the Navy and volunteered to serve in Vietnam. She recalled thinking, "If the military couldn't make me a man, nothing would." However, when she told her commanding officer that she was gay, she was interrogated by the FBI and the CIA before being discharged by the Navy as "undesirable" (she later successfully petitioned to have the discharge reclassified as honorable).

In 1973, after seeing *The Christine Jorgensen Story*, a film about the first nationally known transgender woman, Elizondo embraced her transgender identity and completed gender reassignment surgery. She subsequently worked as a drag performer at gay clubs with the stage name Felicia Flames. In 1987, she tested positive for HIV and began working with community organizations such as the San Francisco AIDS Foundation to improve the quality of life for people living with HIV/AIDS as well as performing her drag act at charity events, which raised funds for numerous HIV/AIDS nonprofits. She contributed panels to the NAMES Project AIDS Memorial Quilt, helped raise funds for such nonprofit organizations as the San Francisco LGBT Community Center, and worked with other transgender women of color to battle racism toward the community. In 2015, she served as lifetime grand marshal in the San Francisco Pride Parade and the following year spearheaded an initiative to rename the 100 block of Taylor Street Gene Compton's Cafeteria Way to commemorate the events of the Compton's Cafeteria riot there.

Ruth Ellis (1899–2000)

Lesbian Trailblazer, Entrepreneur

Ruth Charlotte Ellis, who lived to be 101, was openly lesbian at a time when few publicly expressed a nonheterosexual identity. She proudly asserted, "I was always out of the closet. I didn't have to come out." During her long life, she would become a trailblazer for the LGBTQ+ community in Detroit, particularly for African Americans.

Ellis was born in Springfield, Illinois, the youngest of four children. Her mother, Carrie, died when she was a teen; her father, Charles, was the first Black mail carrier in Illinois. When she was a teenager, her father became aware of his daughter's sexual orientation and was supportive. As she recalled, "He wouldn't let me go with the boys. He would say, 'Books and boys don't go together.' So, I think he was kind of glad I was with women because that way I wouldn't have a baby." She graduated from Springfield High School in 1919 during a time when fewer than 7 percent of African Americans graduated from secondary school. During the 1920s, she met her partner of 34 years, Ceciline "Babe" Franklin, and in 1937, the couple moved to Detroit, Michigan, where, having worked for a printing company in Springfield, she opened her own press out of the home she shared with Franklin. Ellis & Franklin Printing Co. was the first woman-owned printing shop in Michigan.

Ellis and Franklin's home was not just a location for their business; it also became a central location for gay and lesbian parties and a place of refuge for young, Black gays and lesbians, whom she supported with books, food, and assistance with college tuition. During the 1950s and into the 1960s, their home was known to generations of Midwestern African American gays and lesbians as the "Gay Spot." She proposed a variation on the Big Brothers/Big Sisters program, in which young gays and lesbians would be matched as social companions with gay and lesbian seniors according to similar interests. In her later years, she traveled with a group called the Golden Threads, an organization of elder lesbians.

As Ellis approached the century mark as possibly the oldest living African American lesbian in the nation, she earned national attention and acclaim through newspaper profiles and interviews. All the attention struck her as odd: She insisted that she was "just an ordinary person." In 1999, the Ruth Ellis Center was created to provide shelter and aid for LGBTQ+ youth in Detroit, and the same year, her extraordinary life was chronicled in the acclaimed documentary *Living with Pride: Ruth Ellis @ 100.* The City of Detroit recognizes her contributions every February during Black History Month by celebrating Ruth Ellis Day.

Reed Erickson (1917–1992)

Transgender Activist, Philanthropist

Reed Erickson was the founder of the first

transgender rights organization, the Erickson Education Foundation (EEF), which contributed millions of dollars to the early development of LGBTQ+ studies and advocacy between 1964 and 1984. As sociologist Aaron H. Devor has asserted, Erickson's philanthropy informed "almost every aspect of work being done in the 1960s and 1970s in the field of transsexualism in the US and, to a lesser degree, in other countries."

Born Rita Mae Erickson in El Paso, Texas, Erickson was raised in Philadelphia and attended the Philadelphia High School for Girls and Temple University, where he began using the nickname Eric when among friends. After he and his family moved to Baton Rouge, Louisiana, in 1940, he worked in the family's lead smelting business, graduating from Louisiana State University's school of mechanical engineering. After his father's death in 1962, he inherited a major interest in the family enterprises, running them successfully until he sold them in 1969. He amassed a personal fortune, estimated at over $40 million, due to investments in oil-rich real estate.

From 1963 to 1965, Erickson underwent gender reassignment surgery as a patient of endocrinologist and sexologist Dr. Harry Benjamin, who had overseen Christine Jorgensen's transition, and changed his name to Reed Erickson. In 1964, he launched the Erickson Education Foundation (EEF), with the stated goal "to provide assistance and support in areas where human potential was limited by adverse physical, mental or social conditions, and where the scope of research was too new, controversial or imaginative to receive traditionally oriented support." EEF grants supported the early homophile organization ONE, Inc., as well as such areas as acupuncture, dream research, homeopathy, and dolphin communication studies. However, the main focus of his attention through the EEF was transsexualism. The EEF funded almost every aspect of work being done in the 1960s and 1970s in the field of transsexualism in the United States, including the founding of the Johns Hopkins University Gender Identity Clinic. The EEF also functioned as an information and counseling resource for transgender people, creating a referral network of physicians and psychologists and publishing educational materials for transgender people and their families. In 1977, the EEF transferred its work to the Janus Information Facility.

Erickson was married four times between 1963 and 1987 and was the father of two children. During the 1970s, he began to experiment with drugs, which led to substance abuse, a series of arrests for illegal drug possession, and, eventually, a deterioration of his mental and physical health. In 1987, he fled to Mexico, where he married his fourth wife and remained for the rest of his life.

Arden Eversmeyer (1932–2022)

Elder Lesbian Rights Activist

Jean Arden Eversmeyer is notable as the founder of the Lesbians Over Age Fifty (LOAF) social organization and codirector of Old Lesbians Organizing for Change (OLOC). She also created the Old Lesbian Oral Herstory Project (OLOHP) to ensure that the stories of elder lesbians across the nation would be preserved in their own voices and in their own words.

Eversmeyer was born in Stevens Point, Wisconsin. The family moved to Dallas, Texas, in 1943. She earned a BS in health and physical education from Texas State College for Women in 1951 and a master's degree in education from Sam Houston State University in 1964. She worked in Texas public schools for 30 years teaching health, physical education, and driver's education and serving as a secondary school counselor, spending most of her career in the Pasadena and Houston Independent School districts before her retirement in 1981.

After her longtime partner, Tommie Russum, died of cancer in 1985, Eversmeyer, at the age of 54, felt alone and adrift, with few opportunities to meet single women her age. Finding no organizations to help, she decided to create one herself. She started Lesbians Over Age Fifty in 1987 to create safe meeting places and a social network for midlife and older lesbians in Houston. LOAF, the only lesbian organization of its kind in the United States, has grown from six to more than 150 members, who meet monthly.

In 1998, Eversmeyer founded the Old Lesbian Oral Herstory Project, which includes interviews with lesbians aged 70 and older to record their personal stories and document the lives of lesbians in the 20th century. The Project has collected over 800 stories of women from around the world and published two oral histories: *A Gift of Age: Old Lesbian Life Stories* (2009) and *Without Apology: Old Lesbian Life Stories* (2012). She often said, "You don't have to climb Mount Everest to be interesting. Everyone has an amazing story." In 2018, she married Charlotte Avery, her partner since 1987.

For her story as well as her service on behalf of older lesbians, Eversmeyer has been honored nationally and was the recipient of the Woman of Character, Courage, and Commitment Award from the National Women's History Project. The Arden Eversmeyer Endowed Scholarship in Multicultural Women's and Gender Studies was established at her alma mater, Texas Woman's University.

Leslie Feinberg (1949–2014)

Genderqueer Activist, Writer

Describing herself as an "anti-racist

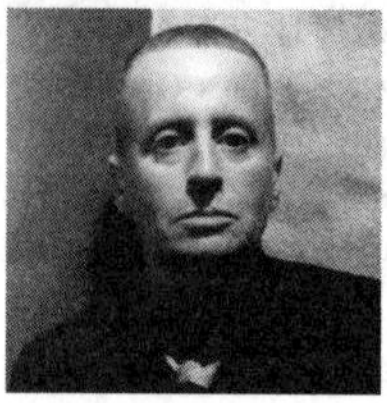

white, working-class, secular Jewish, transgender, lesbian, female revolutionary communist," Leslie Feinberg was an unapologetic advocate for those she saw as oppressed because of their LGBTQ+, ethnic, or racial identities. Her 1993 novel *Stone Butch Blues*, commonly described as a genderqueer narrative, has been called "a landmark in the contemporary literature of gender complexity."

Feinberg was born in Kansas City, Missouri, and grew up in Buffalo, New York. She was assigned female at birth but presented outwardly as male while growing up. "I am female-bodied," she stated. "I am a butch lesbian, a transgender lesbian." Her working-class Jewish family was hostile to her sexuality and gender expression, and she left home as a teenager. She subsisted on a variety of temporary, low-wage jobs, including washing dishes, working in a book bindery, cleaning out ship cargo holds, and as a sign language interpreter.

In her 20s, Feinberg met members of the Workers World Party, a Marxist–Leninist Communist group that had split with the Socialist Workers Party and joined the Buffalo branch of the party. After moving to New York City, she was active in anti-war, anti-racist, and pro-labor demonstration on behalf of the WWP. She began writing in the 1970s and was the editor of the political prisoners' page of the Workers World Party's newspaper for 15 years, becoming its managing editor in 1995.

Feinberg's first book, *Stone Butch Blues* (1993), is a coming-of-age novel, drawn at least in part from her own life. The protagonist is a young person, born female, who grows into adulthood at odds with her family, who eventually comes to grips with her complicated, unconventional sexual and gender identity. The novel received the Lambda Literary Award and the 1994 American Library Association Gay & Lesbian Book Award and is considered a pioneering work for raising issues of gender intersectionality that would later enter the mainstream. Writer Shauna Miller said that the novel "changed queer history. It changed trans history. It changed dyke history. And how it did that was by honestly telling a brutally real, beautifully vulnerable and messy personal story of a butch lesbian." Her other books include *Transgender Liberation: A Movement Whose Time Has Come* (1992) and *Transgender Warriors: Making History from Joan of Arc to Dennis Rodman* (1996). In *Transgender Warriors*, she defined "transgender" as "all people who cross cultural boundaries of gender."

In addition to writing, Feinberg pursued many causes as an activist. In 1974, she organized a march against racism in Boston, and she helped rally support for AIDS patients in the early days of the disease. A longtime advocate for women's reproductive rights, she returned to Buffalo in 1998 to work for that cause after an abortion provider was murdered in his home there.

In 2011, Feinberg married Minnie Bruce Pratt, a professor at Syracuse University. Her final words were reported to be, "Hasten the revolution! Remember me as a revolutionary communist."

James M. Foster (1934–1990)

Gay Rights Activist, Political Strategist

Regarded as a founding father of the early gay rights movement, historically known as the homophile movement, James M. Foster was a member of the San Francisco Health Commission for more than 25 years. A leader in efforts by gay organizations to achieve political influence, he became the first openly gay person to speak at a national party gathering when he addressed the Democratic National Convention in 1972.

Foster was born in Manhasset, Long Island, New York, and began his activism after he was dishonorably discharged from the U.S. Army in 1959 for being gay. He moved to San Francisco and in 1963 founded the Society for Individual Rights (SIR), the first political action group to successfully press local politicians for their support of gay rights. In 1971, he, along with Daughters of Bilitis cofounders Del Martin and Phyllis Lyon, transformed the SIR into the Alice B. Toklas Memorial Democratic Club, the first gay Democratic Party club in the United States, which is now known as the Alice B. Toklas LGBTQ Democratic Club.

After helping presidential candidate George McGovern win the 1972 California Democratic primary, Foster and fellow delegate Madeline Davis became the first openly LGBTQ+ people to address a national party convention. He was originally given a prime time speaking slot, but his slot was moved to 3:00 A.M. based on campaign manager Gary Hart's decision that the McGovern campaign needed to tone down its "radical" image. He stated, "We do not come to you begging your understanding or pleading your tolerance. We come to you affirming our pride in our lifestyle, affirming the validity of our right to seek and to maintain meaningful emotional relationships and affirming our right to participate in the life of this country on an equal basis with every citizen."

In 1973, fledgling gay politician Harvey Milk sought Foster's endorsement for his first campaign for city supervisor. However, he believed that it would be best for the gay community to work with liberal establishment politicians rather than to try to elect gay candidates and refused to support Milk's candidacy, a position that led to enmity between the two men that lasted until Milk's assassination in 1978. In 1980, he worked for Senator Ted Kennedy's presidential campaign and was a founding member of the San Francisco Health Commission. Five years after his partner, Larry Ludwig, died, he succumbed to an AIDS-related illness at his San Francisco home.

Cecilia Gentili (1972–2024)

Transgender Rights Activist

An advocate for the transgender community, sex workers, and people living with HIV, Cecilia Gentili was the driving force behind two New York State bills to aid trafficking victims and to end the "walking while trans" law, an anti-loitering law that police used to harass transgender people. When she died in February 2024, she was believed to have been the first transgender woman to have a funeral service at New York City's St. Patrick's Cathedral.

Born in Argentina, Gentili was raised as a boy and came out as gay at the age of 12. Although her mother was supportive, she found her maternal grandmother, an indigenous woman from the countryside, to be more open to conversations concerning gender identity. As a child, she had been sexually abused by a neighbor; bullied as a gay, cross-dressing teen; and harassed by local authorities since cross-dressing was illegal in Argentina. While attending college, she met a transgender person for the first time and began to fully identify as a woman. She lived in Brazil for a time, and in 1998, she moved to the United States, first to Miami, where she had difficulty finding a job because of her undocumented status. Within two weeks of arriving, she was arrested for prostitution and placed in a men's jail. Over the next five years, she struggled with drug addiction, engaged in sex work, and spent more time in prison.

In 2003, Gentili moved to New York City, where she was arrested for drug possession, jailed, and detained by U.S. Immigration and Customs Enforcement but released with an ankle bracelet since she could not be safely incarcerated with either men or women after being assaulted in prison by both groups. In 2011, she was granted asylum in the United States, entered an addiction-recovery program, and devoted herself to activism. She began an internship at New York City's LGBT

Center (now the Lesbian, Gay, Bisexual & Transgender Community Center), working with the NYC Anti-Violence Project. From 2012 to 2016, she was the transgender health program coordinator at the Apicha Community Health Center in New York City and from 2016 to 2019 served as the director of policy at the GMHC (formerly the Gay Men's Health Crisis), an AIDS service organization and the world's first organization dedicated to HIV/AIDS prevention.

She helped the Gender Expression Non-Discrimination Act become New York state law in 2019 and the same year cocreated the DecrimNY campaign to decriminalize sex workers in New York. She was also the driving force behind the Lorena Borjas Transgender and Non-Binary Wellness and Equity Fund, named after the New York Latina transgender and immigrant rights activist, which provided $1.8 million to organizations serving transgender people.

A performer and actor as well as an activist, Gentili performed in *The Knife Cuts Both Ways*, a 2017 comedic one-woman show based on her life. In 2022, she released *Faltas: Letters to Everyone in My Hometown Who Isn't My Rapist*, which won a Stonewall Book Award. She performed Off-Broadway in *Red Ink* in 2023, which was based on the book.

Over 1,000 mourners attended Gentili's funeral at St. Patrick's Cathedral. Afterward, the archdiocese of New York condemned the funeral, calling it an insult to the Catholic faith and saying it was unaware of the identity of the deceased—or her vocal atheism—when it agreed to host the service. Her family and friends denounced the Church's comments, accused the archdiocese of "hypocrisy and anti-trans hatred," and stated that the LGBTQ+ community would continue to celebrate her for the way she "ministered, mothered, and loved all people."

Henry Gerber (1892–1972)

Early Gay Activist

In 1924, Henry Gerber founded the Society for Human Rights (SHR), the oldest documented gay rights organization in the United States. The SHR's newsletter was *Friendship and Freedom*, the nation's first known American gay publication.

Born Heinrich Joseph Dittmar in the German province of Bavaria, Gerber arrived at Ellis Island in 1913 with family members, all of whom settled in Chicago because of its large German immigrant population. In 1917, during World War I, he was committed to a mental institution because he was gay and given the choice of internment as an enemy alien or service in the army. He chose the latter, and from 1920 to 1923, he served with the Allied Army of Occupation in Coblenz, Germany. During visits to Berlin, he discovered a thriving German gay subculture and gay emancipation movement, subscribed to a German homophile magazine, and learned about physician and sexologist Magnus Hirschfeld's Scientific-Humanitarian Committee in Berlin, which sought to reform anti-homosexual German law.

Returning to Chicago in 1924, Gerber went to work at the post office. Inspired by Hirschfeld, he set out to establish an organization to protect the rights of gay men. The Society for Human Rights secured a state charter in December 1924. The SHR newsletter *Friendship and Freedom* only lasted for two issues because the majority of members feared that postal inspectors would deem it obscene under the provisions of the Comstock Act, which was not repealed until 1958. He and SHR president John Graves decided to limit membership to gay men and to exclude bisexual men and did not know that the organization's vice president, Al Weningar, was married with children. In 1925, Weningar's wife reported the SHR to a social worker, calling the organization a group of "degenerates." The police raided Gerber's house, interrogated him, and then arrested him,

Graves, Weningar, and another man. The *Chicago Examiner* newspaper reported the story under the headline "Strange Sex Cult Exposed." He was prosecuted for deviancy, but after three trials, the charges were dropped. However, he had lost his life savings defending himself as well as his job at the post office for "conduct unbecoming a postal worker."

Gerber moved to New York City and reenlisted in the U.S. Army, serving for 17 years. During the 1930s, he managed a personal correspondence club and wrote articles for gay publications under a pseudonym. The correspondence club eventually became a national communications network for gay men. In 2015, his Chicago home was designated the second LGBTQ+ National Historic Landmark. An early stalwart in the pursuit of gay rights, he famously declared, "Nobody believes we can do it—reporters, opponents—except ourselves."

Barbara Gittings (1932–2007)

LGBTQ+ Rights Activist

Barbara Gittings organized the New York chapter for the early lesbian group the Daughters of Bilitis and edited the DOB magazine *The Ladder*. She was involved in the first picket lines that brought attention to the ban on employment of gay people in the U.S. government, lobbied the American Psychiatric Association to change its stance on homosexuality as a mental disorder, and worked to make information about gay men and lesbians more widely available in libraries as the head of the American Library Association's Gay Task Force.

Gittings was born in Vienna, Austria, where her father was a member of the U.S. diplomatic corps. After returning to the United States at the outbreak of World War II, the family settled in Wilmington, Delaware. She knew she was gay from a young age but did not know the word "homosexual" until she was rejected from her high school's National Honor Society for what one teacher believed were "homosexual inclinations." She enrolled at Northwestern University to study drama but spent much of her time in Chicago's libraries researching homosexuality. "I had to find bits and pieces under headings like 'sexual perversion' and 'sexual aberration' in books on abnormal psychology," she recalled. "I kept thinking, 'It's me they're writing about, but it doesn't feel like me at all.'" She left Northwestern after her freshman year and returned home, where she continued her research. This included reading such lesbian novels as *The Well of Loneliness* and taking a night course in abnormal psychology, where she had her first affair with another woman student. At 18, she left home for Philadelphia, where she worked in clerical jobs and hitchhiked to New York City on weekends. In New York, she visited gay bars dressed as a man as a way to connect with the gay community during her early exploration of her orientation.

Gittings traveled to California in 1956 to visit the early homophile organization ONE, Inc., and in 1958, she met Phyllis Lyon and Del Martin, the founders of the Daughters of Bilitis, who asked her to start a DOB chapter in New York City. She founded the New York DOB chapter in September 1958, served as its first president, and edited *The Ladder* until 1963. In 1961, she met photographer Kay Lahusen, who would become her partner for the next 46 years.

While working closely with Frank Kameny, founder of the Washington, D.C., chapter of the Mattachine Society, Gittings participated in many of the earliest LGBTQ+ actions in the United States, including the first gay picket lines at the White House, the Department of State, and at Independence Hall in Philadelphia protesting the federal government's policy on discrimination of homosexuals.

David Carter, author of *Stonewall: The Riots That Sparked the Gay Revolution* (2004), stated that she "was one of the rare people in the homophile movement—before Stonewall—who took a militant stance. And she not only took a militant stance, but she was in the forefront." In the early 1970s, she helped lobby the American Psychiatric Association to change its stance on homosexuality; it rescinded its definition of homosexuality as a mental disorder.

Gittings combined her activism with scholarship, serving for 16 years as head of the American Library Association's Gay Task Force, the first gay caucus in a professional organization, overseeing and editing the association's comprehensive bibliography of literature by and about gay men and lesbians. In retirement, with her partner in an assisted-living facility, one of her last acts was to come out in the newsletter published by the facility. She summed up her career as an activist in 1999 by saying, "As a teenager, I had to struggle alone to learn about myself and what it meant to be gay. Now for 48 years I've had the satisfaction of working with other gay people all across the country to get the bigots off our backs, to oil the closet door hinges, to change prejudiced hearts and minds, and to show that gay love is good for us and for the rest of the world too."

Harry Hay (1912–2002)

Gay Rights Activist

Actor, Communist labor organizer, musicologist, gay theoretician, and political activist, Henry "Harry" Hay has been called the "founder of the modern gay movement" and the "father of gay liberation." He was the cofounder of the Mattachine Society, the first sustained gay rights group in the United States, and a catalyst for the American gay rights movement.

Born in England, Hay suffered periodic beatings from his father, who disapproved of what he considered his son's "sissified" behavior. His family moved to Los Angeles in 1919, where, in 1934, he met actor Will Geer (best known as Grandpa Walton on *The Waltons* television series), who became his lover for many years. Geer introduced him to the Communist Party, and Hay served as an active trade unionist, skills he would later employ as an advocate for gay rights. In 1938, he married Anita Platky; the couple adopted two daughters and divorced in 1951. From 1963 until his death, his longtime partner was gay rights activist and inventor John Burnside.

In 1950, Hay, his then lover Rudi Gernreich, Bob Hull, Chuck Rowland, and Dale Jennings founded a gay rights group they named the Society of Fools. In 1951, he and new member James Gruber were discussing the "mattachines," a medieval French masque group of performers that protested oppression, when Gruber suggested that the group change its name to the Mattachine Society. Hay and other members agreed. Most historians regard the founding of the Mattachine Society as the beginning of the organized gay movement in the United States and Hay, as the writer of the society's first political manifesto, the identifier of gay men as an oppressed group. His wife divorced him when his involvement with the organization became known; he was expelled from the Communist Party for being gay and ultimately ejected by the Mattachine Society for being a Communist, but he persisted on behalf of gay rights. After the 1969 Stonewall Uprising, he was elected the first chair of the Southern California Gay Liberation Front and in 1979 cofounded the Radical Faeries, which was, in the words of his biographer, Stuart Timmons, "a mixture of a political alternative, a counterculture, and a spirituality movement." Noted for his anti-assimilation views, he believed that society must change and accept gays on their own terms as part of a distinct "sexual minority," a viewpoint that was decades ahead of its time.

In 2002, Hay was the subject of the documentary *Hope Along the Wind*. In 2019, he was honored as one of the inaugural 50 American "pioneers, trailblazers, and heroes" to be named to the National LGBTQ Wall of Honor within the Stonewall National Monument, the first U.S. national monument dedicated to LGBTQ+ activist history.

Brenda Howard (1945–2005)

LGBTQ+ Rights Activist

Called the "mother of Pride," Brenda Howard was a bisexual rights activist and sex-positive polyamorous feminist who played an instrumental role in the Pride March known as the Christopher Street Liberation Day Parade, which took place one year after the Stonewall Uprising. The event would evolve into the annual New York City Pride March and Pride celebrations around the world. An activist for LGBTQ+ rights for over three decades, she was an active member of the Gay Liberation Front and chaired the Gay Activists Alliance's Speaker's Bureau.

Howard was born in the Bronx, New York City, and grew up on Long Island. She graduated from Syosset High School and Manhattan Community College with an AAS in nursing. During the 1960s and 1970s, she was active in the anti–Vietnam War and second-wave feminist movements as well as participating in LGBTQ+ rights activism as a member of groups that included the Gay Liberation Front, the Coalition for Lesbian and Gay Rights, ACT UP, and Queer Nation. In 1987, she participated in the Second National March on Washington for Lesbian and Gay Rights. She helped found the New York Area Bisexual Network to help coordinate services for the bisexual community and was also an active member of the early bisexual political activist group BiPac. As one of the organizers of the 1993 March on Washington for Lesbian, Gay, and Bi Equal Rights and Liberation, she successfully lobbied to have the term "Bisexuals" included in the title of the march.

In 2005, after Howard's death, PFLAG created the annual Brenda Howard Memorial Award, the first award given by a major LGBTQ+ organization presented to a group or individual advocating on behalf of the bisexual community. In 2019, she was one of the inaugural 50 American "pioneers, trailblazers, and heroes" to be inducted on the National LGBTQ Wall of Honor within the Stonewall National Monument.

Dale Jennings (1917–2000)

Gay Rights Activist, Playwright, Novelist

One of the founders of the first enduring gay rights organizations in the United States, the Mattachine Society, William Dale Jennings was also the founder of ONE, Inc., later the ONE Institute, the oldest active organization dedicated to archiving materials on LGBTQ+ history through education, the arts, and social justice programs. He was also the editor in chief of *ONE Magazine*, which became the early voice of the American gay and lesbian activist movement. In 1954, under the provisions of the Comstock Act, the U.S. postmaster in Los Angeles confiscated the magazine as "obscene, lewd, lascivious and filth." In 1958, the Supreme Court unanimously reversed lower court rulings in the case of *One, Inc. v. Olesen* that upheld the post office, a decision that established an important legal journalistic precedent.

Jennings was born in Amarillo, Texas, and grew up in Denver, Colorado. He and his sister, Charlotte Elaine, excelled at music and performed on local radio, with his sister playing the violin and him on the piano. He also developed an early love of dance and as a teenager joined the Lester Horton dance troupe, which gave performances in venues throughout the United States. In his late teens, he moved to Los

Angeles with the intention of becoming a writer and theater director, eventually launching a theater company called the Theatre Caravan, for which he wrote and produced some 60 plays. During this time, he pursued relationships with women in order to avoid suspicions about his sexual orientation and married an aspiring actress at the Theatre Caravan, whom he divorced after serving in World War II. During the war, he was stationed at Guadalcanal and received several medals, including a bronze star. In 1946, after his honorable discharge from the military, he returned to California, where he studied film for two years at the University of Southern California.

In 1950, Jennings, along with his then boyfriend Bob Hull, met with labor union organizers Harry Hay and Chuck Rowland to form a group to work for gay civil rights. The group considered the names the International Bachelors Fraternal Order for Peace and Social Dignity, the Society of Fools, and the Mattachine Foundation before settling on the Mattachine Society. Its mission was to gain acceptance through positive communication between gays and heterosexuals and to establish gay men as one of America's largest minority communities.

In 1952, Jennings would become the Mattachine Society's first hero when he was arrested in a Los Angeles park for sexual solicitation, entrapped by vice detectives posing as gays. He decided to contest his arrest in court, something that was almost never done, with most gay men pleading guilty rather than face an accusation of homosexual conduct in an open court. During a 10-day trial, he acknowledged being gay but denied the solicitation. When the jury deadlocked 11–1 for acquittal, the judge dismissed the charge. The publicity resulted in a surge of membership in the Mattachine Society. In 1953, he, along with activists Don Slater and Dorr Legg, left the Mattachine Society to found ONE, Inc., which began publishing *ONE Magazine*, the first national magazine for gays, for which he wrote articles and book and movie reviews. Along with Slater, he founded the Homosexual Information Center (HIC) in 1965 and remained involved with the organization until 1997.

Jennings published his first novel, *The Ronin*, in 1968. His 1971 novel *The Cowboys* was turned into a 1972 film starring John Wayne and sparked some controversy for its homoerotic content. He continued to write until shortly before his death. He said about his own legacy, "I was one of the founders of the first homosexual organizations in U.S. history.... Our basic argument was that changes in sex laws would not benefit us alone but everyone."

Marsha P. Johnson (1945–1992)

LGBTQ+ Activist

Known as the "mayor of Christopher Street" and a most prominent figure of the post-Stonewall gay rights movement in New York City, Marsha P. Johnson was a tireless advocate for LGBTQ+ youth, those affected by HIV/AIDS, and gay and transgender rights. As cofounder of the Street Transvestite Action Revolutionaries (STAR), she worked to provide housing for LGBTQ+ youths living on the street.

Born Malcolm Michaels Jr. in Elizabeth, New Jersey, into a working-class family, Johnson, who was gender nonconforming and would self-identify as gay, was around 5 years old when she began to wear dresses, eventually stopping because of bullying and a sexual assault by an older teenager. After graduating from high school in 1963, she moved to New York City with $15 and a bag of clothes. As "Black Marsha," she worked as a prostitute and was often arrested (she claimed to have stopped counting after 100 times). She eventually chose the name Marsha P. Johnson, stating that the middle initial stood for "pay it no mind," a phrase she often used when questioned about her gender and lifestyle. She became well known in the LGBTQ+ community for her colorful wigs (often crowned with flowers and artificial fruit), red heels, sparkly robes, and multiple strands of costume jewelry. She modeled for artist Andy Warhol and performed for a time with the drag performance group Hot Peaches.

Johnson began frequenting the Stonewall Inn in Greenwich Village in the late 1960s and was one of the demonstrators during the Stonewall riots in 1969. According to David Carter in his book *Stonewall: The Riots That Sparked the Gay Revolution,* she was one of "three individuals known to have been in the vanguard" against the police. She denied starting the riot, and the claim that she threw the first brick in the riot has been disproved.

Following the 1969 Stonewall Uprising, Johnson joined the Gay Liberation Front and was active in the GLF Drag Queen Caucus. She marched in the first Gay Pride March, the Christopher Street Liberation Day March, on the first anniversary of Stonewall and in the same year founded, with transgender activist Sylvia Rivera, the Street Transvestite Action Revolutionaries (STAR), which insisted on being represented in gay Pride parades. She also established a shelter for homeless gay and trans youth.

During the 1980s, Johnson, who was HIV positive herself, became an AIDS activist and joined ACT UP in order to bring attention to the AIDS epidemic and sang with the New York City Gay Men's Chorus at a 1980s AIDS memorial. Suffering from mental illness throughout her life, she was in and out of psychiatric hospitals and would say about her condition, "I may be crazy, but that don't make me wrong." In 1992, her body was found floating in New York's Hudson River. The police ruled her death a suicide, but family and friends contested that ruling, insisting that it ignored a prominent head wound. In 2012, the police, under public pressure, reopened the case and reclassified her death as a drowning from undetermined causes, and the case remains unsolved. She has been the subject of several film projects, including the 2017 documentary *The Death and Life of Marsha P. Johnson,* which focused in part on the efforts of transgender activist Victoria Cruz to investigate her death. In 2020, New York State named a waterfront park in Brooklyn for her.

Cleve Jones (1954–)

LGBTQ+ Rights Activist, AIDS Activist

Cleve Jones is known for conceiving the NAMES Project AIDS Memorial Quilt, one of the world's largest pieces of community folk art, to commemorate the lives of those who have died of AIDS.

Born in West Lafayette, Indiana, Jones and his parents moved to Scottsdale, Arizona, when he was 14. He did not reveal his sexual orientation to his parents until he was 18. After attending high school and then Arizona State University for a time, he moved to San Francisco, where he was befriended by gay rights leader Harvey Milk, for whom he worked as a student intern while studying politics at San Francisco State University. In 1981, he went to work in the district office of State Assemblyman Art Agnos. In 1982, when AIDS was a new and largely underestimated threat, he cofounded the San Francisco AIDS Foundation (then called the Koposi's Sarcoma Research and Education Foundation).

In 1985, while planning an annual candlelight march to honor Harvey Milk, who had been assassinated in 1978, Jones learned that more than 1,000 San Franciscans had died of AIDS-related illnesses. He asked each of his fellow marchers to write the names of friends and loved ones who had died on placards, and at the end of the march, he and others taped the placards to the walls of the San Francisco Federal Building. The wall resembled a patchwork quilt, and that inspired the creation of the NAMES Project AIDS Memorial Quilt, first displayed in Washington, D.C., in 1987. He said at that dedication, "Today we have borne in our arms and on our shoulders a new monument to our nation's capital. It is not made of granite or steel and was not built by stonecutters and engineers. Our monument is sewn of fabric and thread and was created in homes across America and wherever friends and families gathered to remember their loved ones lost to AIDS." The quilt has grown to over 54 tons and memorializes the lives of over 85,000 Americans killed by AIDS.

In an interview in 2016, Jones described his status as HIV positive and said that he first learned of this in the 1980s. He fought the virus in the earliest drug trials, attributing his activism to saving his life because of his efforts to push the FDA to stop doing double-blind trials and to release the life-saving drugs as soon as possible. He is the author of a memoir, *When We Rise: My Life in the Movement* (2016), which was adapted as a 2017 television miniseries directed by Gus Van Sant. He is prominently featured in *And the Band Played On*, Randy Shilts's 1987 book on the AIDS epidemic in the United States, as well as in the 1985 documentary film *The Castro.*

ABilly S. Jones-Hennin (1942–2024)

LGBTQ+ Rights Activist

Active in African American organizations within the LGBTQ+ rights movement, ABilly Jones-Hennin was a cofounder of the first national Black LGBTQ+ organization in the United States, the National Coalition of Black Gays (NCBG), the first national advocacy group of its kind for Black gays and lesbians. He is also notable for his activism on behalf of AIDS victims during the 1980s. He identified as bisexual+ and queer and advocated for greater acceptance of bisexuality within the gay and lesbian rights movement.

Born Lannie Bess in St. John's, Antigua, Jones-Hennin was adopted when he was 3 years old and raised in Richmond, Virginia, by parents who renamed him Allen Billy Scott Jones. He later went by his middle name, adding the "A" initial in acknowledgment of a godparent. As a teenager in the 1950s, he attended civil rights protests with his family, participating in lunch counter sit-ins, and, as a young adult, was present at the 1963 March on Washington for Jobs and Freedom. After graduating from high school, he briefly served in the U.S. Marine Corps and graduated from Virginia State University in 1967 with a degree in business and accounting. He later earned a master's degree in social work at Howard University and worked as a qualitative researcher.

Jones-Hennin realized at an early age that he was attracted to men and initially identified as gay but, acting on the advice of his father, chose to marry a woman. He and his wife separated after seven years, with him maintaining joint custody of the couple's three children. After the separation, he moved to Washington, D.C., in 1977 and began to identify as bisexual. His children, as well as his parents, had always been supportive of his orientation, and after his father's death, he learned that his father had also been bisexual. In the late 1970s, he met his partner and later husband, Chris Hennin. The two were married in 2014.

Jones-Hennin once stated, "I have never separated my blackness from my gayness" and, to that end, cofounded the National Coalition of Black Gays (NCBG) in 1978. In 1979, he served as logistics coordinator of the first National March on Washington for Lesbian and Gay Rights and, during the same weekend, helped organize the National Third World LGBT Conference at Howard University, which would inspire the creation of the Lambda Student Alliance, the first LGBTQ+ student organization at a historically Black college or university. The same year, the NCBG organized the first delegation of gay people to meet with presidential representatives. Around that time, he also founded the Gay Married Men's Association (GAMMA), cofounded the Washington, D.C., chapter of Black and White Men Together, and founded the D.C. Coalition of Black Gays.

As the HIV/AIDS epidemic grew in the 1980s, Jones-Hennin worked with Chris Hennin to develop healthcare programs at Washington's Whitman-Walker Clinic and advocated for public education and support for those diagnosed with HIV/AIDS. In 1989, he was appointed minority affairs director of the National AIDS Network. During the 1990s, after he was diagnosed with spinal stenosis, he devoted much of his advocacy to disability justice. In 2007, he received the Community Pioneer Award from the Rainbow History Project for his activism and was named chair of the Washington, D.C., Mayor's LGBT Advisory Committee. During his later years, he suffered from Parkinson's disease and spoke out against homophobia in health care. After his death due to complications of Parkinson's, Hennin said this of his spouse of 45 years: "He was a person totally dedicated to turning adversity into hope."

Frank Kameny (1925–2011)

Gay Rights Activist

Notable as one of the most significant figures in the American gay rights movement, Frank Kameny was the first openly gay person to testify before Congress. A cofounder and first president of the Washington, D.C., chapter of the Mattachine Society in 1961, he helped lead some of the earliest public protests by gays and lesbians, including a picket line at the White House in 1965. In 1971, he became the first openly gay candidate for U.S. Congress when he ran in the District of Columbia's first election for a nonvoting congressional delegate. Although defeated, he and his campaign organization created the Gay and Lesbian Activists Alliance in Washington, D.C., to lobby the government on behalf of LGBTQ+ civil rights. He was the one who coined the phrase "Gay is Good."

Kameny's background and professional aspirations could not have predicted that he would spend most of his life as a gay rights activist. Born in New York City and raised in the borough of Queens, he entered high school at the age of 12. After his graduation in 1941, he attended Queens College to study physics. Drafted into the U.S. Army, he served in the European theater throughout World War II, and after the war, he returned to Queens College, earning a B.A. in physics in 1948. He then went on to attend Harvard, earning a master's degree in 1948 and a doctorate in astronomy in 1956. He was described by author Douglass Shand Tucci as "the most conventional of men, focused utterly on his work." The same year, while attending an American Astronomical Society meeting in San Francisco, plainclothes police officers arrested him and another man on a charge of "lewd conduct." He cooperated with the police, pleaded guilty, and paid a fine. He was told that his criminal record would be expunged after serving three years' probation.

Kameny taught for a year in the Astronomy Department of Georgetown University and was hired in 1957 by the U.S. Army Map Service. However, when it learned of his San Francisco arrest, he was fired and, in 1958, barred from future federal government employment. This experience radicalized him, and he appealed his firing through the courts, the first gay man to do so. He lost his case twice before seeking a review from the Supreme Court, which declined to consider the case. He would never hold a paid job again and instead devoted himself exclusively to activism. Despite his many outspoken public stances, he kept his personal life private and never had any long-term relationships with other men, saying merely that he had no time for them. In 1963, he and the Mattachine Society campaigned to overturn Washington, D.C.'s sodomy laws, and he personally drafted the bill that was finally passed in 1993. He and Daughters of Bilitis member Barbara Gittings successfully worked to remove the classification of homosexuality as a mental disorder from the second edition of the American Psychiatric Association's *Diagnostic and Statistical Manual of Mental Disorders (DSM-II)*. He consistently opposed the notion that homosexuality was inferior to heterosexuality, arguing that "not only is homosexuality, whether by inclination or overt act, not immoral, but that homosexual acts engaged in by consenting adults are moral, in a positive and real sense, and are right, good, and desirable, both for the individual participants and for the society in which they live." During the 1970s, he was appointed the first openly gay member of the District of Columbia's Human Rights Commission. Under the leadership of the National Gay Task Force, he, together with 12 other members of the gay and lesbian community, met with White House Office of Public Liaison officer Midge Costanza in 1977 to discuss needed changes in federal laws and policies, the first official gay rights discussion at the White House. In 1980, after officials at the National Security Agency discovered the sexual orientation of gay NSA linguist Jamie Shoemaker and attempted to convince him to resign, Kameny stepped in to try to prevent his de facto dismissal, with the result that Shoemaker became the first openly gay government employee.

In 2007, the Smithsonian included the picket signs that Kameny carried in front of the White House in 1965 in an exhibit titled *Treasures of American History*. In 2009, his home in Washington was designated a historic landmark by the District of Columbia's Historic Preservation Review Board. In 2012, the American Astronomical Society issued a posthumous certificate of appreciation to him, recognizing "his exemplary lifelong commitment to promoting equal rights for homosexual men and women." In the same year, the International Astronomical Union named an asteroid Frankkameny in his honor.

Arnie Kantrowitz (1940–2022)

LGBTQ+ Activist, Educator, Writer

A post-Stonewall champion of gay rights, Arnold "Arnie" Kantrowitz served as secretary and vice president of the Gay Activists Alliance in 1970 and in 1985 was a founding member of the Gay & Lesbian Alliance Against Defamation (GLAAD), a media monitoring group initially formed to counter inaccurate and slanderous media coverage of gays and lesbians generated during the early years of the AIDS crisis. His memoir, *Under the Rainbow: Growing Up Gay* (1977), is an important account of the difficulties that he and his gay contemporaries faced in the 1950s and 1960s and chronicles formative events in the gay rights movement.

Kantrowitz was born in Newark, New Jersey. After graduating from high school, he was accepted by Columbia and Princeton, but because he was gay and Jewish, he did not enroll in either because, as he later recalled, "I felt 'other,' I felt different from what my parents wanted me to be." Instead, he attended Rutgers University–Newark, graduating in 1961. After earning a master's degree in English literature from New York University, he taught at the State University of New York, Cortland, from 1963 to 1965 before moving to the City University of New York's College of Staten Island, where he introduced one of the earliest gay studies courses, was named chair of the English Department in 1999, and continued teaching until his retirement in 2006.

Kantrowitz came out as gay in 1970 and, early in the decade, was one of the first openly gay individuals to appear on popular radio and television talk shows. On September 1, 1973, the same year the American Psychiatric Association changed its classification of homosexuality as a mental illness, *The New York Times* published an article of his titled "We Are Already Your Children." In it, he calls for gay and lesbian equality and argues a comparison between the gay and lesbian community and other marginalized and persecuted Americans. "Homosexuals, the longest and most deeply suppressed of all groups," he writes, "are similarly spread throughout society. More than unnoticed, we are invisible, afraid even to declare our existence…." He ends his article by asserting, "The right to self-determination is a foundation of a truly free society. We are your children, your brothers and sisters, even your parents, your teachers and lumberjacks, your athletes and artists, your scientists and philosophers." He concludes, "Accepting the beauty of homosexual love is not a threat to the American way of life: It is a challenge to American ideals."

In addition to his memoir *Under the Rainbow*, Kantrowitz authored *Walt Whitman* (2005), a biography of the poet, which is part of the Stonewall Inn Classic series on the lives of gay and lesbian writers. He lived in New York City with his life partner, Lawrence D. Mass, a physician and writer, before dying of complications of COVID-19. After his death, he was eulogized as "a true sage and champion." Sarah Kate Ellis, president of GLAAD, said of him: "Arnie Kantrowitz's activism paved the way for the growing visibility, protections, and acceptance of the LGBTQ+ community that we see today."

Mara Keisling (1959–)

Transgender Rights Activist

Mara Keisling is the founding director of the National Center for Transgen-

der Equality, the first professionally staffed, transgender-specific national organization in the United States. She also served as the cochair of the Pennsylvania Gender Rights Coalition.

One of seven siblings, Keisling grew up as Mark in Harrisburg, Pennsylvania, where her father was the chief of staff to the governor. She graduated from Penn State and pursued graduate work in American government at Harvard before beginning a 25-year career in social marketing and public opinion research while also teaching government at George Mason University and Marymount University.

Keisling came out as a transgender woman and began transitioning during the 1990s after telling friends and family that she had felt like a woman since childhood. When she directly saw the discrimination faced by transgender people, she returned to Pennsylvania to cochair the Pennsylvania Gender Rights Coalition and serve on the steering committee of the Statewide Pennsylvania Rights Coalition. In 2003, sensing the need for a cohesive national voice in Washington on behalf of transgender people, she moved back to the capital and founded the National Center for Transgender Equality (NCTE), a social justice organization dedicated to advancing equality through advocacy, collaboration, and empowerment. As its executive director, she co-led United ENDA in 2007, a coalition of over 400 LGBTQ+ rights organizations lobbying for an Employment Non-Discrimination Act with explicit protection for transgender individuals. Even though the bill ultimately failed to pass, it was the first-ever transgender-inclusive legislation proposed to the U.S. Congress and produced the first-ever congressional hearing on transgender rights issues. In 2008, the NCTE, with the National LGBTQ Task Force, launched the "National Transgender Discrimination Survey," then the largest study of transgender individuals in the United States. This was followed by an even larger survey of nearly 28,000 trans people. During the administration of President Barack Obama, the NCTE secured a modification of Department of State regulations, which allowed transgender people to change the gender marker on their passports without having physically completed transition. In 2016, she, along with other demonstrators, was arrested for holding a sit-in at the North Carolina State Legislative Building to protest the enactment of the Public Facilities Privacy & Security Act, a law mandating that individuals may only use restrooms and changing facilities that correspond to the gender listed on their birth certificates.

Between 2019 and 2021, when Keisling stepped down from NCTE leadership, she and the organization drew criticism for alleged internal racism, which led to the withdrawal of employees of color. Nevertheless, through her leadership as a professional, strategic, and political advocate, the transgender community has become an unavoidable constituency that politicians can no longer ignore. She said, "Folks know we vote. Folks know we're serious about voting. We've built not just visibility, but political power."

Morris Kight (1919–2003)

Gay Rights Activist

A self-described "gay liberationist," Morris Kight is regarded as a pioneer of the LGBTQ+ rights movement in the United States. Active since the 1940s on behalf of peace and civil rights movements as well as labor rights groups, he also founded or cofounded several gay rights organizations during the 1950s, including the Committee for Homosexual Freedom (CHF), a homophile organization that would become the Gay Liberation Front in 1969.

Born in Comanche County, Texas, Kight grew up on the family farm. He recognized his sexual orientation early on and began exploring his sexuality while in high school, recalling that he "didn't have a trace of guilt feeling about that." He graduated from Texas Christian University in 1941 and moved to New Mexico, where he discovered underground gay communities in Alburquerque and Santa Fe. He was married from 1950 to 1955 and fathered two daughters. He later kept his marriage secret from all but his closest friends in the belief that it would affect his credibility as an activist for gay rights. His partner from 1978 until his death was Roy Zucheran.

From 1950 to 1955, Kight acted in the Summerhouse Theater and the Old Town Players in Albuquerque. Both companies brought in actors from California, who brought with them some of the new homophile organizations' pamphlets, which contained information on the Mattachine Society. In 1952, he worked with other members of the gay community to elect Democratic presidential candidate Adlai Stevenson.

Kight moved to Los Angeles in 1958, supporting himself for a number of years as a novelty vendor at Dodger Stadium during baseball games. His activism began with protests against the Vietnam War, founding in 1967 the Dow Action Committee, an anti-war group protesting the chemical company's production of Agent Orange. He tried to connect his social activism with gay rights concerns but found resistance in the more visible homophile groups such as the Mattachine Society, which he regarded as elitist. In 1969, after the Stonewall Uprising, he founded the third branch of the Gay Liberation Front (GLF) in Los Angeles. One of the GLF's first actions was a protest against Barney's Beanery, a West Hollywood chili parlor popular with actors and singers that displayed a sign that read, "Fagots [sic] Stay Out." When the owner, who never denied anyone service, responded to the group's demand to remove the sign by putting up more anti-gay signs, the protestors responded by ordering a single item and remaining in the restaurant for hours. After three months of losing money, the owner removed the signs and handed them over to Kight and others. The owner actually replaced the original sign after the protesters and media attention ceased, and it only came down for good in 1984, when Valerie Terrigno, the first lesbian mayor of West Hollywood, removed it herself as soon as the city council passed an antidiscrimination ordinance. Kight also helped to organize the first Christopher Street West Gay Pride Parade in Los Angeles in 1970. In 1971, he cofounded the Gay Community Services Center (later the Los Angeles Gay & Lesbian Community Services Center), the first nonprofit organization in America to have the word "gay" in its name. A provider of programs and services for lesbian, gay, bisexual, and transgender people, it became the largest facility in the world providing services to LGBTQ+ people.

Kight's radical politics and more confrontational, disruptive tactics put him at odds over the years with others in the LGBTQ+ movement who urged a policy of gaining acceptance in the wider society for LGBTQ+ people. Recalling his impatience with the early homophile movement in Los Angeles in the 1950s and 1960s, he maintained that it was "preoccupied with respectability rather than with achieving respect." He remained a committed activist until the end of his long life and challenged the ways in which respect could—and should—be achieved.

Kiyoshi Kuromiya (1943–2000)

LGBTQ+ Activist, AIDS Activist

Cofounder of the Gay Liberation Front's Philadelphia chapter, Kiyoshi Kuromiya revolutionized the way in which HIV/AIDS patients received reliable information about the virus. He referred to himself as the "Forrest Gump of activism" because of his activist career, which also included the civil rights and anti–Vietnam War movements.

Kuromiya was born at the Heart Mountain Relocation Camp, a Japanese American internment camp in Wyoming, to parents who had been born in California and were American citizens. The family eventually relocated to Monrovia, California, where he grew up. Kuromiya, who went by the name "Steve" at the time, knew that he was gay from an early age and, in a 1997 interview for the Philadelphia LGBT History Project, recounted that while still a child, he was arrested in a public park for lewd behavior with an older boy and sent to juvenile hall for three days. The judge told his parents that the boy was "in danger of living a lewd and immoral life." His activism began in 1962 while he was a student at the University of Pennsylvania with organizing events for civil rights and participating in the Congress of Racial Equality (CORE) diner sit-ins. He attended the 1963 March on Washington for Jobs and Freedom and met Martin Luther King Jr., with whom he worked closely until King's death. He joined the "Armies of the Night" anti-war demonstration in Washington, D.C., in 1967 and the following year organized an anti-war demonstration at the University of Pennsylvania that attracted thousands of protestors.

Kuromiya, who had officially come out as gay during the first Annual Reminder protest at Independence Hall in 1965, cofounded the Philadelphia Gay Liberation Front in 1969 following the Stonewall Uprising. In 1970, in the interest of gaining support for the Gay Liberation Front, he represented the GLF as the first openly gay delegate to the Black Panther Party Convention at Philadelphia's Temple University. During the early years of the AIDS epidemic in the early 1980s, he founded the Philadelphia chapter of ACT UP (AIDS Coalition to Unleash Power). After his AIDS diagnosis in 1989, he further educated himself on the disease, creating the ACT UP Standards of Care; disseminating AIDS information in the newsletter

The Critical Path, which he mailed to incarcerated people; eventually built a website, together with a network of computers in his apartment, to provide free internet access to people with HIV/AIDS; and ran a 24-hour hotline dispensing AIDS information. In 1997, he testified before the Supreme Court in the case of *Reno v. ACLU* regarding freedom of speech rights that would protect sexually explicit information about AIDS on the internet, with the result that the Court struck down part of the Clinton administration's Communications Decency Act, which had been signed into law in 1996. In 1999, he initiated a class-action suit, *Kuromiya v. The United States of America*, to make the case for the legalization of marijuana for medical use for people with AIDS.

In June 2019, Kuromiya was one of the inaugural 50 American "pioneers, trailblazers, and heroes" to be inducted on the National LGBTQ Wall of Honor within the Stonewall National Monument in New York City's Stonewall Inn. In 2022, he was honored with a Google Doodle.

Louise Lawrence (1912–1976)

Transgender Activist

Called by historian Susan Stryker "an unheralded founder of the transgender community in the United States," Louise Lawrence was dedicated to educating the public on gender nonconformity. She organized a network of gender-nonconforming people across the country beginning in the 1940s, advocated for transgender issues, and was a cofounder of the magazine *Transvestia.*

Assigned male at birth and named Lew, Lawrence enjoyed dressing as a female from an early age at home but presented as male in public for the first 30 years of her life. She worked as a bank clerk after graduating from high school, married at the age of 18 in 1930, and remarried after the death of her first wife five years later. Her second wife accepted her husband's cross-dressing, but the strain of keeping the secret led to her nervous breakdown, and the couple divorced in 1944. After the divorce, she moved to San Francisco, where she began to live full time as Louise Lawrence, writing in one of her journals: "I consider Louise to be my true identity even though the birth records say differently. And on this I will stand. For to me, as to most people who know me, I AM Louise."

During the 1950s, Lawrence befriended drag performers at San Francisco's legendary North Beach club Finocchio's, joined the city's chapter of the Mattachine Society, and facilitated an interface between her transgender network and medical researchers to correct the prevailing understanding that transgenderism and transvestitism were mental disorders. After meeting German American endocrinologist and sexologist Harry Benjamin, who coined the term "transsexual," she introduced him to her transgender contacts in order to help further his research. Under Benjamin's guidance, she experimented with hormone treatment and considered but ultimately rejected gender reassignment surgery. During this decade, she worked with sexologist Alfred Kinsey to provide data for his research. She set up interviews for him with cross-dressers, professional female impersonators, transvestites, and transsexuals; prepared a typed record of their life histories; and copied manuscripts of transvestite fiction, an underground literary genre known as petticoat discipline. She also provided Kinsey with her diary during the year she began her transition. Her contribution to Kinsey's research helped to bring early attention to gender nonconformity, including transsexualism.

In 1960, Lawrence, along with transgender activist Virginia Prince, published the first edition of *Transvestia*, which would last until 1986. They used Lawrence's address book from her research for its initial subscription list and her extensive network of LGBTQ+ people to raise enough money to launch the publication. Canadian transgender scholar Aaron Devor has described *Transvestia* as "a lifeline for people to communicate with each other, to learn that there were others like them." During the 1960s and 1970s, she continued as an advocate for the transgender community, as a documentarian and activist, and working with such organizations as WPATH (the World Professional Association for Transgender Health) and Tri-Ess, an organization for heterosexual cross-dressers and their loved ones, founded respectively in 1972 and 1976.

The work that Lawrence began in documenting the lives and struggles of transgender people continues in an archive in Vallejo, California, and is called the Louise Lawrence Transgender Archive. It is dedicated "to increasing the understanding of transgender people and encourage new scholarship by making transgender historical materials available to students, scholars, and the public."

Dick Leitsch (1935–2018)

Gay Rights Activist

President of the Mattachine Society in the 1960s, Richard Joseph "Dick" Leitsch spearheaded the 1966 "sip-in" at Julius' bar in New York City, one of the earliest acts of gay civil disobedience in the United States. The lawsuit that followed ended the liquor authority practice of using gay patronage as an excuse for revoking licenses and opened the way for licensed gay bars. He was also a pivotal figure in ending the policy of police entrapment of gay men.

Leitsch was born in Louisville, Kentucky; grew up in a Roman Catholic household; and attended parochial schools. When he came out while in high school, his parents were supportive, and he was living openly as a gay man by the 1950s. He attended Bellermine University to study theater but dropped out before graduating and, in 1959, moved to New York City, where he supported himself in subsequent years as a journalist, waiter, bartender, and painter. Soon after arriving in New York, he met then bartender Craig Rodwell, who persuaded him to attend a meeting of the Mattachine Society. Leitsch became the society's president in 1964.

Inspired by Frank Kameny, one of America's earliest gay rights activists, the Mattachine Society began to follow the model of the civil rights movement's protests. Leitsch, Rodwell, and others in 1966 staged a "sip-in" at Julius' bar in Greenwich Village, which had been discreetly serving a gay clientele since the 1950s even though the State Liquor Authority (SLA) prohibited bars from doing so under the pretext that gay customers were disorderly. They sat at the bar wearing suits and ties, and when the bartender came to take their order, Leitsch announced, "We are homosexual. We are orderly, we intend to remain orderly, and we are asking for service." The bartender refused to serve them, saying, "I think it's the law." The moment was captured by a photographer from *The Village Voice*, and the next day, *The New York Times* ran a story with the headline: "3 Deviants Invite Exclusion by Bars." He and the Mattachine Society brought a lawsuit against the SLA in an attempt to overturn the policy that prohibited bars from knowingly serving alcohol to gays. In 1967, New York State courts struck down the premise that homosexuals were inherently disorderly and therefore could be refused bar service as well as the statute that mandated gay patronage as a legitimate excuse for revoking licenses. As historian George Chauncey, the author of *Gay New York* (1964), observed, "Dick Leitsch was one of the country's most militant and important gay activists in the decade before Stonewall. The sip-in he organized at Julius' is a brilliant example of lessons he took from the black civil rights movement about how to stage events that reframed public understanding."

Leitsch was the first gay journalist to

report on the Stonewall Uprising with an account that first appeared as a special Mattachine Society newsletter before being reprinted in *The Advocate.* On the morning after the initial raid, he received a call from Mayor Lindsay, who pleaded with him "to stop this." Leitsch reportedly replied, "Even if I could, I wouldn't. I've been trying for years to get something like this to happen." However, he would work with the Lindsay administration to end a police policy of entrapment of homosexuals. David Carter, author of *Stonewall: The Riots That Sparked the Gay Revolution* (2005), has asserted that Leitsch's work ending entrapment and helping to legalize gay bars "constituted a liberalization that was the most essential precondition of the Stonewall uprising."

Leitsch continued his journalism, writing frequently for *Gay*, New York City's first gay newspaper, and is credited with writing the first published interview with then unknown singer Bette Midler. His longtime partner, Timothy Scofield, died in 1989 of AIDS, and he died of liver cancer at the age of 83. When news of his illness became public, he received a letter from President Barack Obama, stating, "Thank you for your decades of work to help drive our nation forward on the path toward LGBT equality. Our journey as a nation depends, as it always has, on the collective and persistent efforts of people like you."

Scott Long (1963–)

International LGBTQ+ Rights Activist

An advocate for LGBTQ+ rights around the world, Scott Long is the founder of the Lesbian, Gay, Bisexual, and Transgender Rights Program at Human Rights Watch, the first international program on LGBTQ+ rights at a major human rights organization. His research on the violence of human rights violations based on sexual orientation, gender identity, and HIV status has involved extensive work in the United States and in such countries as Egypt, Iraq, Romania, South Africa, Zambia, and Zimbabwe.

Born in Radford, Virginia, Long graduated from Radford University at the age of 18 and went on to receive a Ph.D. in literature from Harvard in 1989. The following year, he moved to Hungary to teach literature at Eotvos Lorand University in Budapest, became involved with the lesbian and gay movement in Hungary during the country's transition from a Soviet republic to a democracy, and organized the university's first course on sexuality and gender. In 1992, he began a Fulbright professorship teaching American studies at the University of Cluj-Napoca in Romania. He joined underground Romania activists campaigning for LGBTQ+ rights, which included campaigning for the removal of the Romanian penal code that criminalized consensual homosexual acts with five years' imprisonment. In 1993, he conducted the first-ever mission to Albania to investigate LGBTQ+ rights and meet gay activists there, documenting arrests and abuses that led to the repeal of Albania's sodomy law.

After returning to the United States in 1996, Long accepted a position with the International Gay and Lesbian Human Rights Commission (IGLHRC), first as its advocacy director and then as its executive director. He led the IGLHRC's lobbying efforts for the groundbreaking 2001 UN General Assembly Special Session on HIV/AIDS in order to secure a global commitment to combating the virus. Blocked from speaking by conservative Islamic states and the Vatican, the IGLHRC forced a vote by the General Assembly. "This was the first time," he commented, "a gay and lesbian issue has ever been debated on the floor of the General Assembly." In 2010, Long, who had been serving as the executive director of the IGLHRC since 2004, suffered a heart attack and resigned from Human Rights Watch on doctor's orders in order to recuperate. His resignation letter, in part, said that "Human Rights Watch—and other international organizations like it—needs a far deeper understanding of what social movements are, why they are important, how they turn human rights into living values rather than legal abstractions."

In 2018, Long, whose activism has endeavored to save countless lives around the world, was himself the victim of a near-fatal attack. While returning to his Oakland, California, home, he was struck from behind with an iron bar. He remembers hearing only the word "you—" before sustaining massive injuries that required reconstructive surgery and a long recovery. He would say of his experience, "We are an angry society, new reasons for anger keep appearing, festering, exploding, and this in some ways is a reminder."

Barbara Love (1937–2022)

Lesbian Activist, Writer

A member of the National Organization for Women (NOW), Barbara Joan Love helped found the Lavender Menace, a coalition of NOW lesbians disenchanted with the lack of lesbian acceptance within the organization. One of the first lesbian feminists to join the gay liberation movement, she also served on the board of the National Gay Task Force for nearly a decade.

Love grew up in Ridgewood, New Jersey, to politically conservative parents, with whom she often clashed because of her progressive, proto-feminist views on the status of women. She graduated from Syracuse University in 1959 with a degree in journalism and then taught at an American school in Italy during the early 1960s. She moved to Greenwich Village in New York City where, during the pre-Stonewall era, she frequented lesbian bars in Greenwich Village, which were often raided by the police. After cutting her hair short and dressing in less feminine clothing at the request of a girlfriend, she was approached by a group of men who stopped to help when her car had broken down and then beat her up after seeing her masculine appearance. In 1968 at the age of 31, she came out to her parents. Her mother, Lois Love, proved supportive and would go on to join her daughter on gay rights marches and in Pride parades as well as taking a role in the founding of Parents and Friends of Lesbians and Gays (PFLAG).

After joining the New York chapter of NOW, which had been founded in 1967, Love helped to organize and participated in several demonstrations, such as the Colgate Dump-In, in which activists poured Colgate-Palmolive products into a toilet set up at the company's Park Avenue headquarters to protest the treatment of women on the company's assembly line, and at *The New York Times* classified advertising office to protest the paper's policy of gender segregation in the "Help Wanted" listings (a policy the *Times* soon changed). In 1970, she, along with author Rita Mae Brown, activist Sidney Abbott, and others formed a consciousness-raising group of lesbian feminists in response to NOW founder and president Betty Friedan, who viewed the concerns of lesbians as a threat to the political aims of the women's movement. Out of their discussions came the formation of the Lavender Menace, named for the term Friedan first used in 1969 to negatively describe NOW's dissident lesbian feminists. During NOW's Second Congress to Unite Women in 1970, the women of the Lavender Menace wore T-shirts with the phrase and carried placards declaring, "We are your worst nightmare, your best fantasy."

A writer and editor as well as an activist, Love had a long career as an editor for trade publications, and for a few years in the late 1960s, she worked as a censor at CBS to enforce the network's standards. With her then partner Sidney Abbott, she coauthored the groundbreaking book *Sappho Was a Right-On Woman: A Liberated*

View of Lesbianism (1977), a compassionate exploration of lesbianism depicting how lesbians gained acceptance in the women's movement and, in the words of one reviewer, "how [lesbians] have emerged—almost existentially—as women like others." They declared that their ambition was to be ordinary: "Our goal is to go about our lives—as human beings, as women, as Lesbians—un-self-consciously, and to be able to spend all our energy and time on work or fun, and none on the arts of concealment or on self-hatred." She spent nearly a decade as the coeditor of *Feminists Who Changed America, 1963–1975* (2006), which featured biographies of 2,200 second-wave feminists and a record of the important events of that period. In 2021, she published a memoir titled *There at the Dawning: Memories of a Lesbian Feminist*.

Love married her partner, Donna Smith, in 2018 in a ceremony officiated by the former mayor of New York, David N. Dinkins. After her death, the Veteran Feminists of America said of her, "If Second Wave activists were graded according to their contributions, Barbara Love would be in the top ten."

Phillis Lyon

See Del Martin and Phyllis Lyon

Jeanne Manford (1920–2013)

Gay Rights Advocate

In 1973, Jeanne Sobelson Manford cofounded Parents of Gays (later PFLAG), a support program in New York City that would become the largest LGBTQ+ organization uniting parents, families, and friends, with over 400 chapters across the United States and more than 200,000 members and supporters.

Born in Flushing, Queens, New York, Manford was married and the mother of three when she graduated from Queens College in 1964. For the next 26 years, she worked as an elementary school math teacher in a public school in Queens. After the Manfords' son, Charles, died of a drug overdose in 1966, his younger brother, Morty, sought support from a therapist who informed his parents that their son was homosexual. Ethan Geto, a gay rights activist and friend of the Manfords, reported that when Morty was outed to his parents, "their reaction was, 'I am not going to lose another son because this society is so prejudiced against gay people. I want my son to thrive." In 1968, while he was a student at Columbia University, Morty joined the Student Homophile League and helped form a group called the Gay People. In 1969, he participated in the Stonewall Rebellion and then was a cofounder of the Gay Activists Alliance.

In 1972, the Gay Activists Alliance "zapped" the prestigious Inner Circle dinner at the Hilton Hotel to protest the lack of attention on the part of news media and the government regarding gay issues. They were ejected from the ballroom and a fight ensued, during which Michael Maye, then president of New York's Uniformed Firefighters Association, assaulted Morty and beat him up. Dismayed by the negative press coverage her son received, Jeanne wrote a letter to the *New York Post* defending her son and attacking the police for standing by and not doing anything about his attack. The same year, she marched in the annual Pride Parade commemorating the anniversary of Stonewall, carrying a sign that read, "Parents of Gays Unite in Support of Our Children." Later that year, the Manfords and others met at the Metropolitan Community Church in Greenwich Village to form Parents of Gays, a self-help support group that would become Parents of Gays and Lesbians and then, simply, PFLAG. As journalist Dan Savage asserts, Manford "put it in people's heads that gay and lesbian people had parents, that we were somebody's children, and that was the first real big step in the movement

Phyllis Lyon, 79, left, and Del Martin, 83, right, are seen here shortly after they became the first same-sex married couple in San Francisco. Behind them are (left to right) Kate Kendell, executive director of the National Center for Lesbian Rights; Raberta Achtenberg, senior vice president of the San Francisco Chamber of Commerce; Joe Caruso, head of Neighborhood Services; Steve Kawa, chief of staff; and Joyce Newstat.

toward full acceptance of lesbian, gay, bi and trans people."

Morty, who became assistant New York State attorney general, died in 1992 at the age of 42 of complications from AIDS. Jeanne, who retired from teaching in 1990, continued her involvement with the organization she helped create and in support of the LGBTQ+ community. In 1996, she moved to Minnesota to help care for her great-grandchild while her granddaughter attended medical school. Afterward, she moved to California to spend her remaining years with her daughter, Suzanne. In 2013, President Barack Obama honored Manford posthumously with the 2012 Presidential Citizens Medal, the second highest civilian award given by the United States, for her work in cofounding PFLAG and her lifetime of LGBTQ+ advocacy.

Del Martin (1921–2008) and Phyllis Lyon (1924–2020)

Lesbian Activists

Partners in life and activism, Del Martin and Phyllis Lyon, together with six other lesbian women, formed the Daughters of Bilitis (DOB), the first national lesbian organization in the United States. In 2008, they became the first couple to be married in San Francisco after the California Supreme Court ruled that same-sex marriage was legal.

Martin was born Dorothy L. Taliferro in San Francisco. She studied journalism at the University of California, Berkeley, and at San Francisco State College (later

University). At the age of 19, she married James Martin, but the marriage ended in divorce four years later. While working for a construction trade journal in Seattle, Martin met Lyon, an employee at the same firm, and the two entered into a permanent relationship in 1953. Lyon was born in Tulsa, Oklahoma, and her family moved to Sacramento in the early 1940s. She graduated from the University of California, Berkeley, in 1946 with a degree in journalism. She worked as a newspaper reporter in Chico, California, before moving to Seattle in 1953.

The couple returned to San Francisco and joined three other lesbian couples to found the Daughters of Bilitis in 1955. Initially founded as a group where lesbians could meet and socialize, the Daughters of Bilitis became an activist, as well as social, organization with established branches around the country. As Lyon recalled, "There were a lot of laws that were anti-gay, and there were more things to do than just party." In 1956, the DOB began publishing *The Ladder*, a newsletter, then a magazine, that became the first in the United States to address the lack of information about lesbians that they faced growing up and went on to feature articles on issues concerning gay rights. Lyon was the first editor of its newsletter, *The Ladder*, in 1956, and Martin took over editorship from 1960 to 1962. The couple also cowrote two books: *Lesbian/Woman* (1972) and *Lesbian Love and Liberation* (1973).

Martin and Lyon were among the first lesbians to join the National Organization for Women, and Martin is believed to have been the first openly gay woman to be elected to NOW's board of directors. On a local level, they were both members of the Alice B. Toklas LGBTQ Democratic Club in San Francisco, founded in 1971, which was the first gay political organization to advocate for passage of a bill to ban employment discrimination based on sexual orientation.

Martin and Lyon had been partners for 55 years when they were finally legally allowed to marry. Martin passed away a few months later, and Lyon continued her activism until her death at the age of 95. Summarizing their lives together as activists, she insisted, "If you got stuff you want to change, you have to get out and work on it. You can't just sit around and say, 'I wish this or that was different.' You have to fight for it."

Jeffrey Montgomery (1953–2016)

LGBTQ+ Rights Activist

Jeffrey Montgomery was a founding director of the Triangle Foundation (1991), an anti-violence, victim-advocacy organization serving Michigan's LGBTQ+ community, which later became known as Equality Michigan. His and other members' efforts helped to form the Equality Federation, a social justice and advocacy organization supporting a collation of state-based equality groups.

Montgomery was born in Detroit and grew up in Grosse Pointe, Michigan. His father, John, worked in public relations for Chrysler. After graduating from Michigan State University in 1976 with a degree in social science, he became the public relations director for Detroit's annual Thanksgiving Day Parade and worked for nearly 13 years (until 1989) on the restoration project of Detroit's Orchestra Hall. His activism began after his partner, Michael, was shot to death outside a Detroit gay bar in 1984 and the murder was not treated as a possible hate crime but as "just another gay killing" case that was not investigated and never solved. In response, he cofounded the Triangle Foundation to assist victims of anti-gay crimes and to work with police and prosecutors to change how anti-LGBTQ+ crimes were handled. Triangle, with Montgomery as its first executive director, widened its focus to lobby at the state and national levels for an end to discrimination in housing and employment. In addition, he was cochair of the National Coalition of Anti-Violence Programs and served as its national spokesman. He was also a founding board member of the Woodhull Freedom Foundation, a nonprofit organization advocating for sexual freedom as a fundamental human right.

Before his death, Montgomery had been working on a feature-length documentary on his work in Detroit's LGBTQ+ community, and the film, *America You Kill Me*, was released in 2002. His various contributions were summed up by Tim Retzloff, a professor of LGBTQ Studies at Michigan State University: "No other local activist for LGBTQ+ rights and sexual freedom from the past twenty-five years has had the potent impact on our history as Jeffrey Montgomery. His unflagging devotion to queer justice and social justice will be a model for generations to come."

Jack Nichols (1938–2005)

Gay Rights Activist

The founder, along with Frank Kameny, of the Mattachine Society's chapter in Washington, D.C., after the national Mattachine Society disbanded, John Richard "Jack" Nichols helped to organize some of the country's earliest gay and lesbian civil rights demonstrations and was the founder of *Gay*, the first gay weekly newspaper in the United States.

Nichols was born in Washington, D.C., the son of an FBI agent, and raised in Chevy Chase, Maryland. He dropped out of school at the age of 12 and came out as gay to his parents as a teenager and, as early as 1955, was sharing Donald Webster Cory's influential 1951 book on the status of gay men, *The Homosexual in America* (1951), with his gay friends.

In 1961, Nichols cofounded the Mattachine Society of Washington, D.C., the first gay civil rights organization in the capital. Two years later, he chaired the Mattachine Society Committee on Religious Concerns, later the Washington Area Council on Religion and the Homosexual, to strengthen links between the nascent gay rights movement and the National Council of Churches. In 1965, he led the first gay rights march on the White House, one of the first organized gay rights demonstrations. From 1965 to 1969, he also participated in the Annual Reminder, pickets held in front of Independence Hall in Philadelphia each Fourth of July, and joined other activists to lobby the American Psychiatric Association for removal of homosexuality as a mental illness from its journals. In 1967, he became one of the first Americans to talk openly about his homosexuality on national television, appearing on the CBS documentary *The Homosexuals*. He allowed himself to be interviewed on camera but used the pseudonym Warren Adkins at the request of his FBI agent father. As a result of his appearance, he was fired from his job at the International Inn hotel the day after the show aired.

Nichols relocated to New York City and in 1968, with his partner, Lige Clarke, began writing "The Homosexual Citizen" column for *Screw* magazine, the first LGBTQ+-interest column in a non-LGBTQ+ publication. A year later, they founded *Gay*, the first weekly newspaper for gay people in the United States, which was published until 1974. In 1975, 32-year-old Clarke was murdered on a road trip through Mexico, leaving Nichols bereft. From 1977 to 1978, he was the editor of *Sexology* magazine before being hired in 1981 as the news editor of the *San Francisco Sentinel*. His books include *Men's Liberation: A New Definition of Masculinity* (1975), *The Gay Agenda: Talking Back to the Fundamentalists* (1996), and *The Tomcat Chronicles: Erotic Adventures of a Gay Liberation Pioneer* (2004).

After his death, Nichols was eulogized by Malcolm Lazin, executive director of Equality Forum, who stated, "Jack helped launch the movement from the mid '60s, when the federal government would not hire gays and lesbians, the American Psychiatric Association considered gays per se mentally ill, and many states had criminal sanctions precluding gays from congregating in bars. Jack was among the gay pioneers who stepped out of a debilitating closet and helped crack the cocoon of invisibility."

Jean O'Leary (1948–2005)

LGBTQ+ Rights Activist

A former nun, Jean O'Leary organized the first White House meeting of gay leaders. A founder of Lesbian Feminist Liberation, one of the first lesbian activist groups in the women's movement, she was also an early member and codirector of the National Gay and Lesbian Task Force and cofounded National Coming Out Day.

Born in Kingston, New York, O'Leary grew up in Cleveland and, just out of high school, joined the Sisters of Holy Humility to "have an impact on the world." In 1971, after graduating from Cleveland State University with a degree in psychology, she left the convent after five years to pursue a doctorate in organizational development at Yeshiva University in New York. She subsequently became involved in the emerging gay rights movement, joining the National Gay and Lesbian Task Force and the Gay Activists Alliance. She created the Lesbian Feminist Liberation to draw attention to gay issues related to women and, in 1977, organized the first meeting of gay activist leaders at the White House. During the event, she said, "This is the first time…a president [Jimmy Carter] has seen fit to acknowledge the rights and needs of some 20 million Americans." During the 1980s, she was active in National Gay Rights Advocates, the largest national LGBTQ+ group in the United States at the time and one of the first groups to respond publicly to the HIV/AIDS crisis. In 1988, she, along with psychologist and activist Rob Eichberg, established the first National Coming Out Day, intended for gay men and lesbians to publicly declare their sexual orientation. She would go on to serve on the Democratic National Committee for 12 years as the chair of the committee's Gay and Lesbian Caucus from 1992 to 2002. From 1993 until her death, her partner was Lisa Phelps, with whom she shared a daughter and a son. After her death, AIDS activist Bob Hattoy said of O'Leary: "Jean taught gay men about feminism, she taught lesbians about AIDS, she taught feminists about gay and lesbian issues, and she taught Democrats about everything."

Clark Polak (1937–1980)

Gay Activist, Publisher

Clark Polak was the president of the Philadelphia-based Janus Society (1963–1969); the creator, publisher, and editor of *Drum* magazine (1964–1969); and the leader of the Homosexual Law Reform Society (1965–1969).

Polak was born into a middle-class, Jewish family in Philadelphia, Pennsylvania. He would later assert that he knew he was gay as early as the age of 5 and had a reputation as a "queer" in high school. After withdrawing from Penn State, he became a businessman in Philadelphia and owner of Frankford Personnel and Northeast Advertising Service.

In 1962, influenced by Donald Webster Cory's book on the status of gay men, *The Homosexual in America* (1951), Polak joined the Janus Society, an early homophile organization based in Philadelphia. He organized public lectures on LGBTQ+ topics, raised money for LGBTQ+ causes, advocated for LGBTQ+ civil rights, and presented pro-LGBTQ+ positions in the media. One example of his activism was his involvement in the 1965 Dewey's sit-in, carried out by three teens protesting the diner's refusal to serve queer people. The three were arrested, along with Polak, who had arrived at the scene to offer legal support. Another of his achievements was the publication of *Drum*, a gay-interest magazine whose circulation of approximately 15,000 exceeded that of the other early homophile periodicals—*The Mattachine Review, ONE Magazine*, and *The Ladder*—combined.

Polak also argued for the importance of gay sexual liberation, which had been avoided by earlier homophile organizations. He put his views into practice by opening several sex businesses, publishing and distributing gay pornographic material, and running three pornographic bookstores in Philadelphia. Taking the profits from *Drum* and his sex businesses, he founded the Homosexual Law Reform Society to push forward several important LGBTQ+ rights cases, including *Val's Bar, Inc. v. Division of Alcoholic Beverage Control*, which established the right of LGBTQ+ people to assemble in bars.

Polak was targeted by federal, state, and local officials who routinely harassed him for alleged violations of obscenity laws. He was ultimately convicted on federal charges and, in 1972, accepted a plea bargain, under which he agreed to abandon his pornography businesses. He closed down Janus and the HLRS and moved to California. There, he established the Stonewall Democratic Club and the Gay Rights Chapter of the ACLU, supported the Los Angeles gay community center, and funded the International Gay and Lesbian Archives while running an art gallery, writing art criticism, and amassing a second fortune in real estate. However, by the late 1970s, he was losing money and using drugs. He committed suicide at the age of 42.

Despite the many controversies that surround Polak's life and activist career, his efforts to move the homophile movement into a more militant, more radical, more pro-gay, and more sex-positive movement predicted many of the new directions the LGBTQ+ movement was headed after Stonewall.

Achebe Betty Powell (1940–2023)

LGBTQ+ Activist

One of the first Black women with a leadership role in the lesbian and gay liberation movement in the 1970s, Achebe Betty Powell was a founder of the Astraea Lesbian Foundation for Justice and was the first Black lesbian to serve on the board of directors of the National Gay Task Force.

Powell was raised in Florida and graduated with a B.A. from the College of St. Catherine and an MA in French language and literature from Fordham University. She became a French language teacher in the New York City schools and a professor of linguistics at Brooklyn College. She was an activist since high school, when she joined the National Conference of Christians and Jews. She would go on to work with the Gay Academic Union, the National Black Feminist Organization, and the National Gay Task Force.

Powell has been described by Trudy Ring in *The Advocate* as "among the small group of multiracial, multiclass, feminist activists who came together in 1977 to create a new way of bringing resources to movements led by lesbians and women of color, to, in [Powell's] words, 'generate the justice that our communities need, right here, right now.'" The Astraea Lesbian Foundation for Justice, which she cofounded, "works to connect the LGBTQ+ community to philanthropists and activists around the world." Also in 1977, she attended the historic meeting between the government and lesbian and gay leaders at the Carter White House.

After Powell's death due to complications from COVID-19, Kierra Johnson, executive director of the National LGBTQ Task Force, eulogized her as "a pioneer, a visionary, an inspiration, and trailblazer in a movement that was in its early organizing days." In a 2019 interview for *Time* magazine on the 50th anniversary of the Stonewall Uprising, Powell addressed intersectionality as a component of LGBTQ+ activism: "Could you imagine the power if we linked with the NAACP or La Raza [the prior name of UnidosUS, a national Latino advocacy organization] in a way that was fundamental? There are people yelling at this moment, 'We're almost there,' but we're not there until we have addressed race and gender and class in context of sexual orientation."

Sylvia Rivera (1951–2002)

Trans Activist, Community Organizer

A trans Latina, Sylvia Rivera was one of most prominent figures of the Stonewall Riots and a founding member of both the Gay Liberation Front and, later, the Gay Activists Alliance. Along with Marsha P. Johnson, she created STAR, a group dedicated to helping homeless trans youth. STAR was also one of the first political organizations for transgender rights in the world.

Born in the Bronx, New York, Rivera, assigned male at birth, had a difficult childhood. Her Puerto Rican father left when she was a baby, and her Venezuelan mother died of suicide when she was three years old. She was then raised by her grandmother, and she was beaten for wearing women's clothes and makeup. She ran away from her home when she was 11 and became a child prostitute, working in the Times Square area. Meeting a group of drag queens who welcomed her into their group, she became "Sylvia" and identified as a drag queen.

Rivera's biggest support came from Marsha P. Johnson, an African American drag queen and activist. She said of Johnson that "she was like a mother to me." Johnson would become her best friend, protector, and mentor. In 1969, at the age of 17, they participated in the Stonewall Uprising, which became a catalyst not only of the gay liberation movement but also for Rivera's activism. She cofounded the Gay Liberation Front and, with Johnson, cofounded the Street Transvestite Action Revolutionaries (STAR) to push for the recognition of transvestites in the emerging gay rights movement and the establishment of the first shelter for homeless gay and transgender youths. Defiant of labels, Rivera—poor, trans, a drag queen, a person of color, a former sex worker, a sometime drug addict, incarcerated, and homeless—crossed over so many categories that she refused to confine her activism to one type, advocating not only for gay and trans rights but also for racial, economic, and criminal justice issues.

Rivera, impatient with the gay movement being led by gay, middle-class, white men and lesbian feminists who did not share her passion for marginalized groups within the gay community, delivered a fiery speech at the Christopher Street Liberation Day Parade in 1973 amid boos from the crowd. Her "Y'all Better Quiet Down" speech declared, "You all tell me, go and hide my tail between my legs. I will no longer put up with this…I have been beaten. I have had my nose broken. I have been thrown in jail. I have lost my job. I have lost my apartment. For gay liberation, and you all treat me this way?" Feeling betrayed by the movement she had helped to create and fought so long and hard for, she disappeared from activism for the next 20 years. On the 25th anniversary of Stonewall, she participated in New York City's Pride Parade and reflected, "The movement had put me on the shelf, but they took me down and dusted me off. Still, it's beautiful. I walked down 58th Street and the young ones were calling from the sidewalk, 'Sylvia, Sylvia, thank you, we know what you did.' After that, I went back on the shelf. It would be wonderful if the movement took care of its own."

After Rivera's death, activist Riki Wilchins said of her, "In many ways, Sylvia was the Rosa Parks of the modern transgender movement." The Sylvia Rivera Law Project continues her legacy, working to guarantee that "all people are free to self-determine their gender identity and expression, regardless of income or race, and without facing harassment, discrimination, or violence." In 2005, the intersection of Christopher and Hudson streets, two blocks from the Stonewall Inn, was renamed Sylvia Rivera Way.

Marty Robinson (1942–1992)

Gay Activist

A participant in the Stonewall Uprising, activist Martin "Marty" Robinson led the first Christopher Street Liberation Day March in 1970 and cofounded the Gay Liberation Front, writing its newspaper, *Come Out!* He cofounded the Gay Activists Alliance and was a founding member of ACT UP, the National Gay Task Force, and GLAAD. He is credited with developing the concept of "zaps" protesting—the GAA's inventive and confrontational protests to attract press attention—and was known as "Mr. Zaps."

Robinson was born in Brooklyn, New York. He attended New York University for a time before working as a union carpenter, specializing in residential remodeling. A member of the Mattachine Society, he was a participant in the Stonewall Uprising, making speeches from the front door of the Stonewall Inn on the second night of rioting, urging the crowd to fight back. For him, what happened at Stonewall was a catalyst for his activism on gay rights. A month after the riot, he led the first Christopher Street Liberation Day March. He joined the Mattachine Society and cofounded the Gay Liberation Front before also founding the Gay Activists Alliance (GAA). According to historian David Carter, "It was [the Gay Activists Alliance] more than any other organization that made the gay liberation movement spread—and Marty Robinson was the primary genius behind that organization."

The effectiveness of the GAA under Robinson and others' leadership was avoiding the inaction of other civil rights organizations due to excessive regard for rigid hierarchical and endless wrangles over parliamentary procedure. The GAA focused exclusively on a single issue, gay and lesbian rights, such as the end of discriminatory practices in housing and employment, the repeal of the consensual sodomy statute, and the end of police harassment. The group specialized in direct confrontational actions, or "zaps," to challenge homophobic practices and politicians' reluctance to take stands on issues concerning the rights of gays and lesbians. He and the leadership of the GAA attempted to plan their "zaps" to leverage the power of the gay and straight media, a strategy that involved infiltrating an event, seizing the microphone, and upstaging the proceedings. In one example, "zappers" interrupted Mayor John V. Lindsay's speech at a ceremony marking the Metropolitan Museum of Art's 100th anniversary in order to prod him into stronger support for gay rights legislation.

Robinson was one of the founding members of the National Gay Task Force in 1973, which became the National Gay and Lesbian Task Force in 1985. In 1985, he helped form the Gay & Lesbian Alliance Against Defamation (GLAAD) and was the founding member of ACT UP in 1987, which brought attention to the AIDS crisis. He left GLAAD in 1986 to create the Lavender Hill Mob in order to carry out "zaps" on the issue of AIDS unresponsiveness, disrupting the Alfred E. Smith charity event of wealthy New York Catholics and Cardinal John O'Connor and a Mass at St. Patrick's Cathedral, with two members dressed as priests and nine others unfurling a banner as O'Connor delivered his sermon.

After nearly three decades of activism, Robinson died of AIDS in 1992 at the age of 49. His activism epitomized a shift in a gay rights movement following Stonewall that did not ask to be accepted; instead, he and the activists who joined him shouted their demands on the streets with an implacable urgency: "What do we want? Gay rights! When do we want them? Now!"

Craig L. Rodwell (1940–1993)

Gay Rights Activist

A gay rights pioneer whose activism spanned both the pre- and post-Stonewall eras, Craig L. Rodwell founded the Oscar Wilde Memorial Bookshop in New York City in 1967, the first bookstore devoted to gay and lesbian writers. He participated in the 1969 Stonewall Rebellion and was central in the creation of NYC Pride and its annual Gay Pride Parade, co-organizing the first one in 1970.

Rodwell was born in Chicago to parents who separated before his first birthday. When he was 6, his mother sent him to a Christian Scientist-affiliated school for "problem boys," where he first experienced same-sex relationships. When he was 14, he was charged and convicted by the Chicago police for juvenile delinquency when he was caught walking home after having sex with a man in his 30s. The experience set him on the road to becoming a self-described "angry queer."

After graduating from a public high school, Rodwell, who studied ballet in Boston, gained a scholarship in 1958 to the School of American Ballet in New York City. He also joined the gay rights organization the Mattachine Society of New York. In 1962, he had his first serious relationship with Harvey Milk, who would later become the first openly gay politician to be elected to public office in California.

Their relationship ended in part due to Milk's conflicted reaction to his early activism and to Rodwell's arrest and incarceration when he was picked up while cruising in New York's Washington Square Park. In 1967, he opened the Oscar Wilde Memorial Bookshop in Greenwich Village, first on Mercer and then relocating to Christopher Street in 1973, not far from the Stonewall Inn. In the same year, he began the Homophile Youth Movement group in the neighborhood and began to publish its periodical, *HYMNAL.* He conceived of the first yearly gay rights protest, the Annual Reminder, picketing Independence Hall in Philadelphia each July 4 from 1965 to 1969.

In the early morning hours of June 28, 1969, Rodwell was on his way home with his partner, Fred Sargeant. As they passed the Stonewall Inn, they discovered a plainclothes police raid underway. As the police began to bring those arrested from the bar to a paddy wagon, he led the chant of "Gay Power," and the police retreated back into the bar as the riot began. They called the press, with the result that the event was covered in *The Village Voice*, *The New York Times*, and the *Daily News*. They prepared leaflets denouncing the police and the Stonewall Inn's criminal management, and throughout the nights of rioting that followed, they distributed some 5,000 copies of their flyers throughout the city. He subsequently suggested suspending the Annual Reminders in favor of an event commemorating the anniversary of Stonewall, and in November, he, Sargeant, and activists Ellen Broidy and Linda Rhodes proposed an annual march, which was approved at a meeting of the Eastern Regional Conference of Homophile Organizations (ERICHO) in Philadelphia with one abstention from the Mattachine Society. The event was known as the Christopher Street Liberation Day March, held on June 28, 1970, and remembered as the first New York City Gay Pride Parade.

Rodwell would remain a consequential figure in the gay liberation movement of the 1970s and 1980s. He sold his bookstore in 1993, although it continued to operate until 2009. In 2019, he was one of the inaugural 50 American "pioneers, trailblazers, and heroes" to be inducted on the National LGBTQ Wall of Honor within the Stonewall National Monument in New York's Stonewall Inn, the first U.S. national monument dedicated to LGBTQ+ rights and history.

Vito Russo (1946–1990)

Gay Rights Activist, Film Historian

Vito Russo was the author of *The Celluloid Closet*, an analysis of the depiction of homosexuality in the movies that is widely regarded as an essential reference work on homosexuality in the U.S. film industry. In 1985, he cofounded the Gay & Lesbian Alliance Against Defamation (GLAAD), a media watchdog organization that seeks to end anti-LGBTQ+ bias and advocates for LGBTQ+ inclusion in popular media.

Russo was born in the Italian American enclave of East Harlem in New York City. Early on, he developed a fascination with the movies and a growing awareness of his own sexuality and that he was "different." Thinking back on his youth, he stated, "I don't know what was different about the way I was raised or the way I reacted, but I never once, not for a second, believed that it was wrong to be gay, that it was a sin, that homosexuality was evil."

Russo obtained his undergraduate degree from Fairleigh Dickinson University and his master's degree in film from New York University in 1971. While completing his graduate degree, he worked in the film departments at the Lesbian and Gay Community Center and New York's Museum of Modern Art. His gay activism began after witnessing the Stonewall Riots and other instances of anti-gay behavior. He joined the Gay Activists Alliance in 1970 and later became a founding member of the Gay & Lesbian Alliance Against Defamation. In the early 1980s, he became involved in AIDS-related issues, raising money for several organizations and speaking frequently at political rallies.

Russo's research on the depiction of homosexuality in the movies that led to the publication of *The Celluloid Closet* in 1981 was preceded by his traveling throughout the country from 1972 to 1982 lecturing and screening film clips. In 1983, he wrote, produced, and hosted a series that was focused on the gay community called *Our Time* for WNYC-TV public television. Concerned over how LGBTQ+ people were presented in the media, he cofounded GLAAD in 1985 in order to pressure media organizations to end homophobic reporting. As a result of GLAAD pressure, *The New York Times* changed its editorial policy to use the word "gay."

In 1985, Russo was diagnosed with HIV and would write powerfully about his illness: "So, if I'm dying from anything, I'm dying from homophobia. If I'm dying from anything, I'm dying from racism. If I'm dying from anything, it's from indifference and red tape, because these are the things that are preventing an end to this crisis. If I'm dying from anything, I'm dying from Jesse Helms. If I'm dying from anything, I'm dying from the President of the United States. And, especially, if I'm dying from anything, I'm dying from the sensationalism of newspapers and magazines and television shows, which are interested in me, as a human-interest story—only as long as I'm willing to be a helpless victim, but not if I'm fighting for my life." He died of AIDS-related complications in 1990 at the age of 44. His biography, *Celluloid Activist*, was published in 2011, and a film documentary of his life, *Vito*, was released in 2012.

Bayard Rustin (1912–1987)

Political Activist

Bayard Rustin was a prominent leader

in social movements for civil rights and gay rights. He was a key organizer of the 1963 March on Washington for Jobs and Freedom and was one of Martin Luther King Jr.'s closest advisers. Once called the "Socrates of the civil rights movement" and "an intellectual engineer behind the scenes," he was involved in nearly every major civil rights effort from the 1940s on. An openly gay man at the center of the civil rights movement, he faced discrimination both within and outside the civil rights movement, which threatened to overshadow his considerable achievements.

Rustin was born in West Chester, Pennsylvania, the ninth of his parents' 12 children, and raised by his maternal grandparents, who were relatively wealthy local caterers. NAACP leaders such as W. E. B. Du Bois and James Weldon Johnson were frequent guests in the Rustin home, and under their influence, young Bayard campaigned against the racially discriminatory Jim Crow laws. His grandmother was a Quaker who passed on her faith to her grandson. At an early age, he confessed to his grandmother that he preferred to spend time with males rather than females. She responded, "I suppose that's what you need to do."

In 1932, Rustin attended Wilberforce College, a historically Black college in Ohio, but was expelled in 1936 after organizing a strike. He moved to Harlem in 1937 and began studying at City College, where he became involved in efforts to defend and free the Scottsboro Boys, nine young, Black men in Alabama who were accused of raping two white women. Active in the Communist Party and later the Socialist Party, he, along with George Houser, James Farmer, and activist Bernice Fisher, participated in the creation of the Congress of Racial Equality (CORE) in 1942. A conscientious objector who refused induction into the military during World War II, he was imprisoned from 1944 to 1946. In 1947, he and Houser organized the Journey of Reconciliation, the first Freedom Ride to test the 1946 Supreme Court ruling that banned racial discrimination in interstate travel.

In 1953, Rustin was arrested in California for sexual activity in a parked car with two men. He pleaded guilty to a charge of "sex perversion" (as "sodomy" was legally designated in California at the time) and served 60 days in jail. His arrest was the first time that his homosexuality had come to public attention. Since homosexual activity was still criminalized throughout the United States, he resigned from leadership positions and shifted to behind-the-scenes roles in several civil rights organizations.

In 1956, at the time of the Montgomery, Alabama, Bus Boycott, Rustin, who had traveled to India to study Gandhi's nonviolent resistance practices, became an adviser to 27-year-old Martin Luther King Jr. on nonviolent tactics. The following year, they began organizing the Southern Christian Leadership Conference (SCLC) over the objection of many African American leaders who were concerned about Rustin's sexual orientation and past Communist membership. In 1960, U.S. representative Adam Clayton Powell threatened to leak to the press the false rumor of a gay affair between Rustin and King, which caused King to distance himself from Rustin, who resigned his position in SCLC. However, King would reach out to him again in 1962 to help organize the 1963 March on Washington for Jobs and Freedom. A few weeks before the march, South Carolina senator Strom Thurmond attacked Rustin as a "communist, draft-dodger, and homosexual" and had his entire Pasadena arrest file entered in the public record. Thurmond also produced a photograph of Rustin talking to King while King was bathing, implying that they were lovers, which both men denied. Despite efforts to discredit him, Rustin was instrumental in organizing the march, training marshals, and scheduling the podium speakers. NAACP chairman

Roy Wilkins did not want him to receive any credit, however, saying, "This march is of such importance that we must not put a person of his liabilities at the head." Despite Wilkins's objection, Rustin appeared with fellow organizer A. Philip Randolph on the cover of *Life* magazine as "the leaders" of the March.

From 1965 to 1979, Rustin served as head of the A. Philip Randolph Institute, the AFL-CIO's African American constituency group, working to integrate unions and union membership. In the 1980s, Rustin, at the urging of his partner, Walter Naegle, became part of the LGBTQ+ movement as an advocate for AIDS education. Before same-sex marriage was legalized, Rustin, in order to protect their union legally, adopted Naegle in 1982. Giving testimony in 1986 on behalf of New York State's Gay Rights Bill, he declared that "the new 'niggers' are gays.... It is in this sense that gay people are the new barometer for social change.... The question of social change should be framed with the most vulnerable group in mind: gay people."

In a 2011 *Washington Post* article, journalist Steve Henrix wrote that Rustin "faded from the shortlist of well-known civil rights lions" due, in part, to public discomfort with his sexual orientation and former Communist affiliation. However, in 2013, President Barack Obama posthumously awarded him the Presidential Medal of Freedom, which he presented to Walter Naegle. A 2023 biopic, *Rustin,* was released to great acclaim, with actor Colman Domingo earning an Academy Award nomination for his performance as the title character.

Fred Sargeant (1948–)

Gay Rights Activist

A same-sex rights activist and Stonewall veteran who campaigned against Mafia-owned gay bars in New York City, Frédéric André "Fred" Sargeant was a central participant in the June 1969 Stone-

wall Uprising whose interview on New York's WBAI radio just days afterward may be the only existing contemporary audio eyewitness account of the event. He is also notable as one of the proposers and organizers of the 1970 Christopher Street Liberation Day March, an event that commemorated the first anniversary of Stonewall.

Sargeant was born in Fontainebleau, a suburb of Paris, to a French mother and a father who was an American G.I. and grew up in Connecticut. He graduated from Joel Barlow High School in Reading, Connecticut, in 1966. At 19, he moved to New York City, where he met and began a relationship with Craig Rodwell, who had recently opened the Oscar Wilde Memorial Bookshop in Greenwich Village. It was the first gay and lesbian bookstore in the nation and a gathering place for young, gay activists, who comprised Rodwell's Homophile Youth Movement (HYMN), which operated out of the store. Sargeant became the bookstore's manager and vice chairman of HYMN.

At around 1:00 A.M. on June 28, 1969, as Sargeant and Rodwell were on their way home, they discovered a plainclothes police raid underway at the Stonewall Inn, a gay bar owned by the Genovese organized crime family. As the police began to bring those arrested from the bar to a paddy wagon, Rodwell led the chant of "Gay Power," and the police retreated back into the bar as a riot began.

After they called the press, the event was covered in *The Village Voice, The New York Times,* and the *Daily News*. Throughout the nights of rioting, they prepared and handed out some 5,000 leaflets denouncing the collusion between police and the Stonewall Inn's Mafia management and demanding change such as the legalization of gay bars and a boycott of Mafia-owned bars "like the Stonewall."

In November 1969, Sargeant, Rodwell, and activists Ellen Broidy and Linda

Rhodes proposed a march to commemorate the Stonewall Uprising, which was approved at a meeting of the Eastern Regional Conference of Homophile Organizations (ERICHO) in Philadelphia with one abstention from the Mattachine Society. The Christopher Street Liberation Day March was held on June 28, 1970, and became the annual event known as the New York City Pride Parade.

Sargeant returned to Connecticut in 1971 and, in 1973, became a police officer, eventually rising to the rank of lieutenant in the Stamford Police Department. He explained his reasons for pursuing police work in the 2010 PBS documentary *American Experience*: "Who was at Stonewall? I wanted to see if I could make a difference and having seen the situation at Stonewall and how the NYPD handled that, I thought I could do it differently. Stonewall wasn't the only riot I saw. I'd been caught up in riots in the Village before and watched what the police did." After his retirement, he moved to Provincetown, Massachusetts, where he chaired a variety of boards and committees, including harbor development and regulations, community relations, community-oriented policing, and the development of goals for the hiring of a new police chief.

An invaluable resource on the history of the Stonewall Uprising, Sargeant appeared in the 2010 Peabody Award-winning documentary film *Stonewall Uprising*. The same year, he married his partner, with whom he lives in Vermont. In 2014, he led and was honored as a founder of Gay Pride at the 44th annual New York City Pride Parade. In 2022, he appeared as a historical character in Archie Bongiovanni's graphic novel *The Stonewall Riots: Making a Stand for LGBTQ Rights*.

José Sarria (1922–2013)

Gay Activist

The first openly gay person to run for public office, José Julio Sarria was a well-

known performer in the San Francisco drag scene as well as an activist. He dedicated his life to the fight for queer rights, organizing the first gay nonprofit corporation in California, the League for Civil Education, which became SIR, the Society for Individual Rights.

Sarria was born in San Francisco, the only child of a Colombian mother and a father who had no role in his life. He was raised by other families while his mother worked as a nanny. He attended several schools, including the Rafael Military Academy, and graduated from Commerce High School in San Francisco. From an early age, he favored dressing in girls' clothing, and he was allowed to go on family outings dressed as he wished.

When the United States entered World War II after the attack on Pearl Harbor, Sarria enlisted in the army despite his height, which, at 5 feet tall, made him too short to meet the Army's height requirement. Sarria, who had mastered four languages, was assigned to Army Intelligence. However, following a routine background check, he was rejected. He recalled, "I wasn't the most masculine guy in town.... So I think they figured that I was a little bit gay." He served with the Signal Corps, then trained as a cook and a scout before being assigned to the motor pool. He was discharged from the Army in 1947 with a rank of staff sergeant.

Following his military service, Sarria returned to San Francisco and enrolled in college with plans to become a teacher. However, he was arrested and convicted for solicitation in a sting operation at the St. Francis Hotel. He knew that his conviction meant that he could never become certified as a teacher and dropped out of college. Unsure of what to do next, he took the advice of a local drag performer to enter a drag contest, in which he took second place. He said, "I decided then to be the most notorious impersonator or homosexual or fairy or whatever you wanted to call me—and you would pay me for it."

In the meantime, he supported himself as a cocktail waiter at the famous Black Cat Bar (aka the Black Cat Cafe) in North Beach, one of San Francisco's most famous hangouts for Beatniks and bohemians, eventually attracting a large gay clientele. He began singing while delivering drinks, which led to regular performances. Billed as "The Nightingale of Montgomery Street," he parodied popular torch songs and eventually reworked the opera *Carmen* to be set in modern-day San Francisco. At closing time, he would lead patrons in the singing of "God Save Us Nelly Queens" (to the tune of "God Save the Queen"). His popularity with clients made the Black Cat one of the most famous gay bars in the United States and a place of community for gay men.

During a time of significant police harassment of the LGBTQ+ community, Sarria's performance developed into a pioneering gay political theater, with him encouraging patrons to stand up for themselves and reject second-class status, with the slogan, "United we stand, divided they arrest us one by one." He helped found a number of homophile organizations, including the League for Civil Education (1960) and the Tavern Guild of San Francisco (1962).

Although he was defeated in his bid to win a seat on the board of supervisors in 1961, his first campaign as an openly gay candidate would pave the way for later successful candidates, such as Harvey Milk, who was elected to the board of supervisors 16 years after Sarria's bid. Terence Kissack of the GLBT Historical Society stated that Sarria "put the gay vote on the map." Sarria observed, "From that day on, nobody ran for anything in San Francisco without knocking on the door of the gay community."

In the mid-1960s at San Francisco's first public drag ball, Sarria was named the Queen of the Ball but, declaring himself "already a queen," gave himself the grander title of "Empress." Drag ball culture led Sarria, known as Mama José, to found the Imperial Court of San Francisco (now the International Court System) in 1965, an association of charitable organizations that raises money for gay causes. With nearly 70 chapters in North America, it has become one of the largest LGBTQ+ organizations in the world.

Sarria was one of the inaugural 50 American "pioneers, trailblazers, and heroes" to be inducted on the National LGBTQ Wall of Honor within the Stonewall National Monument in New York's Stonewall Inn.

Mark Segal (1951–)

Gay Rights Activist, Journalist

A veteran of the 1969 Stonewall Uprising, activist Mark Allan Segal has been called "the Energizer Bunny of the gay rights movement" for his seemingly boundless energy as an activist for the cause of gay rights.

Segal was born in Philadelphia and raised in the only Jewish household in his public housing project. At the age of 8, he refused to sing "Onward, Christian Soldiers" at school. "Activism has always been a part of my life," he later recalled. "Poverty, anti-Semitism—you always have to fight." By the age of 13, he was marching in his first civil rights demonstration alongside his grandmother, who had been a suffragist. He knew from an early age that he was gay and has humorously credited the male models in the Sears catalogs with helping him recognize his sexuality.

Segal attended public schools in Philadelphia and, after graduating from high school, moved to New York City where, a month later, he took part in the June 1969 Stonewall Uprising, which was the catalyst for his activism. Following Stonewall, he was one of the young activists who formed the Gay Liberation Front, which, as he recalled, "focused on self-identity rather than letting society identify us—community. I honestly believe that the Gay Liberation Front created the LGBTQ+ community." He was also a member of the Christopher Street Liberation Day Committee, which organized the first Gay Pride Parade in 1970.

During the early 1970s, Segal became well known for his public acts of civil disobedience to protest the defamation of homosexuals on television and in public life and to seek fair representation in broadcast media. He formed the radical group the Gay Raiders, which, like the Gay Activists Alliance, began staging "zaps," disruptive events that drew public attention to the gay and lesbian rights movement. The Raiders performed stunts like handcuffing themselves to the Liberty Bell, interrupting a Nixon fundraiser, and, perhaps most famously, zapping the *CBS Evening News,* hosted by Walter Cronkite. Pretending to be a college newspaper reporter, he received permission to watch the broadcast inside the studio. Fourteen minutes into the program, he stationed himself in front of the camera, sending his "Gays Protest CBS Prejudice" sign into the homes of 20 million Americans. As he was being wrestled off the set, Cronkite asked for "that young man's contact information," and six months later, the *CBS Evening News* ran a feature on gay rights. "Part of the new morality of the '60s and '70s," Cronkite told his viewers, "is a new attitude toward homosexuality." Those appearances, coupled with scheduled appearances on various national and local television and radio talk shows, fulfilled one of the goals for his activism, "to show the nation who gay people are: our sons, daughters, fathers, and mothers." As comedy writer and actor Bruce Vilanch has asserted, "Before *Will and Grace* and *Ellen*, there was Mark Segal."

In 1976, Segal founded the *Philadelphia Gay News,* one of the longest-running LGBTQ+ publications in the United States. His activism during the 21st century has included partnering with the Obama administration on the creation and construction of LGBTQ+-friendly senior affordable apartments in Philadelphia, known as the John C. Anderson Apartments, which opened in 2013. In July 2014, he married his partner, Jason Villemez, in a ceremony officiated by Judge Dan Anders, Philadelphia's first openly gay judge. The following year, he published his memoir, *And Then I Danced: Traveling the Road to LGBT Equality,* which was named Best Book by the National Lesbian and Gay Journalists Association. In 2018, he donated 50 years' worth of personal documents and artifacts to the Smithsonian.

Ruth Simpson (1926–2008)

Lesbian and Gay Activist, Author

A president of the New York chapter of the Daughters of Bilitis, Ruth Simpson was the founder of the first lesbian community center in the United States and author of the influential book *From the Closet to the Courts*. She also produced the weekly cable TV talk show *Minority Report*.

Simpson was born and raised in Cleveland, Ohio, the daughter of Ethel and Edward Simpson, both pioneers in the labor movement. By the age of 12, she was accompanying her parents on picket lines. She graduated from Case Western Reserve University in 1947 with degrees in drama and English and worked through the 1950s and 1960s as a public relations executive with various New York City firms, including J. Walter Thompson.

Simpson joined New York's Daughters of Bilitis chapter in the late 1960s, becoming its president from 1969 to 1971. In response to the Stonewall Uprising and after an event in October 1970 during which two police officers arrived at the DOB headquarters and threatened to arrest her for the lack of an occupancy permit on the wall, she steered the DOB to organize gay rights demonstrations and opened what is regarded as the first-ever lesbian community center. In a groundbreaking 1971 article in *The New York Times*, "The Disciples of Sappho, Updated," journalist Judy Klemesrud reported on the arrest threat and the well-attended opening of the center chaired by Simpson, whom she described as a "woman with a big voice and a pixyish quality reminiscent of Claudette Colbert." Klemesrud quotes her as rousing her audience with the question "Is gay proud?" and reporting the audience's response: "Right on!" Simpson continued, "If we get enough gay people to say that, then we have no fears for the future." She went on to read several letters from young lesbians asking for help in coming out. The same year, she participated in the Gay Activists Alliance "zap" against Fidelifacts, a private investigating agency accused of gathering information on the sex lives of LGBTQ+ people and selling it to prospective employers. In an interesting coincidence, the protest appeared in the opening sequence of the movie *Shaft*, in which the title character, played by actor Richard Roundtree, is shown winding his way through the activists, providing a rare live color documentation of a GAA action.

In 1976, Simpson and her partner of 37 years purchased a home in Woodstock, New York, where she helped to organize Woodstock's first gay group. She also published *From the Closet to the Courts: The Lesbian Transition*, a detailed and well-received memoir of her time in the gay rights movement as well as being a critique of social and political attitudes toward lesbians in such spheres as religion, psychiatry, the legal system, and within the women's and gay rights movements. In 1982, she began a weekly cable talk show on politics, *Minority Report*, taping the last show the week before her death.

Aimee Stephens (1960–2020)

LGBTQ+ Rights Activist

Aimee Stephens is notable for bringing the first transgender rights legal case to the Supreme Court, which received a full hearing in 2020 and led to a historic 6–3 decision prohibiting employment discrimination against LGBTQ+ workers.

Born in Fayetteville, North Carolina, Stephens graduated from Mars Hill University in 1984 with a degree in religious education. She obtained a degree in mortuary science from Fayetteville Technical Community College in 1988. Stephens, who was assigned male at birth and lived as a man well into her late 40s, had thought of herself as a girl from childhood and struggled between her sense of identity and the life she led, living as a woman at home with her wife, Donna, and their child and working as a male funeral director in Livonia, Michigan, a suburb of Detroit.

Stephens's gender dysphoria was so severe that she contemplated suicide, but she resisted and instead wrote a coming-out letter to her employer and coworkers, saying, "I intend to have sex reassignment surgery. The first step I must take is to live and work full-time as a woman for one year. At the end of my vacation on August 26, 2013, I will return to work as my true self, Aimee Australia Stephens, in appropriate business attire." Her employer responded with her dismissal and an offer of a severance package contingent on her agreeing to stay quiet. She refused and reached out to the ACLU and the Equal Employment Opportunity Commission (EEOC), which took her case to federal court. She lost her case but then won after appealing in the circuit court. Her former employer appealed, and the case headed to the Supreme Court. In the meantime, she could not find work. Even with her years of experience, no funeral home in the Detroit area would hire her. She retrained as a medical assistant and found a job, but her health, undermined by a period without health insurance, deteriorated so that she could no longer work.

By the time her case reached the Supreme Court, the EEOC had reversed its initial position that Stephens's firing constituted discrimination "because of sex," which is prohibited by the Civil Rights Act of 1964. The Justice Department now claimed that it was legal to discriminate against people because they are transgender. However, the Supreme Court agreed with her that she was protected under Title VII of the federal Civil Rights Act of 1964, with Justice Neil Gorsuch declaring that the statute was clear and acknowledging that "Congress likely did not have the LGBTQ+ community in mind when it banned discrimination on the basis of sex." She did not live to hear the Supreme Court's judgment in her favor. She died of kidney failure before the ruling was announced. She said about her thought process ahead of the Supreme Court hearing, "I knew there were hundreds of people like me. There had to be.... But it was not until I came out of the building on October 8 that I realized that this number was in the thousands, not hundreds.... If I can put my name to this and lead the march forward for fairness and truthfulness, then I'm proud to do that."

At a considerable cost to her livelihood and ultimately to her life, Stephens helped to change U.S. history, establishing equal protection under the law for gay, lesbian, and transgender employees from discrimination based on LGBTQ+ orientation. In June 2020, she was added to the list of American "pioneers, trailblazers, and heroes" on the National LGBTQ Wall of Honor on the Stonewall National Monument inside the Stonewall Inn.

Carmen Vázquez (1949–2021)

LGBTQ+ Activist

Self-described as "a Puerto Rican, a butch lesbian, and a socialist," Carmen Vázquez was a longtime force for LGBTQ+ rights and issues, first in San Francisco and then in New York. A board member of the National Gay Task Force (later the National LGBTQ Task Force) during the 1990s, she cofounded and worked with an impressive number of organizations that focused on a variety of LGBTQ+ causes.

The oldest of seven children, Vázquez was born in Puerto Rico and raised in Harlem. She began to explore her sexual orientation at an early age and was reputedly expelled from high school for kissing a girl. She earned a bachelor's degree in American literature and a master's degree in education at the City University of New York.

In 1975, she moved to San Francisco, where she cofounded and was director of the Women's Building, a women-led, nonprofit arts and education community center that focused on gender equality and social justice; helped found and became executive director of the Lavender Youth Recreation and Information Center and the National Network for Immigrant and Refugee Rights; and cofounded and cochaired the Central American Women's Solidarity Network.

In 1993, as coordinator of lesbian and gay health services for the city's Department of Public Health, she initiated a survey of lesbian health needs and sexual practices. Regarding the changes in San Francisco's lesbian community, particularly among lesbians of color, over her two decades in the city, she observed, "We went from underground to most definitely front and center in the political spectrum of San Francisco."

In 1994, Vázquez returned to New York, where she became the first director of public policy for the Lesbian and Gay Community Center and, in 2003, became deputy director of Empire State Pride Agenda, a lobbying group. Her other work on behalf of LGBTQ+ activism included serving as the coordinator of the Health and Human Service Unit of the New York State Department of Health AIDS Institute, a cochair of the Equality Federation from 2004 to 2006, and a founder of Causes in Common, a national coalition of LGBTQ+ liberation and reproductive activists.

After her death due to COVID-19-related causes in 2021, Vázquez was eulogized by Rea Carey, executive director of the National LGBTQ Task Force: "The loss of Carmen tears open a hole in the heart of the LGBTQ+, social justice, immigration, reproductive justice, and sexual freedom movements. I'm deeply sad that one of our movement's most brilliant activists is no longer with us. Rest in power, Carmen. We will continue your work for liberation."

Lilli Vincenz (1937–2023)

Lesbian Activist

The first lesbian member of the Mattachine Society of Washington, D.C., Lilli Vincenz is believed to be the first self-identified lesbian to picket the White House on behalf of gay rights in 1965. The following year, she became the first lesbian with her face showing to appear on the cover of a national gay magazine, the Daughters of Bilitis publication *The Ladder*. In 1969, she created the *The Gay Blade*, the country's oldest LGBTQ+ newspaper.

Vincenz was born in Hamburg, Germany, and grew up during World War II. Her father died when she was 2 years old, and in 1949, when her mother married an American, the family moved to Fort Lee, New Jersey. She recognized her sexuality at an early age and recalled that "it became painful after a while to realize that I was gay and I didn't know anyone else who was gay. I was extremely lonely."

She graduated from Douglass College, part of Rutgers University, in 1959 with bachelor's degrees in French and German and in 1960 earned a master's degree in English from Columbia. She planned to continue her studies to earn a doctorate but instead went to work as an editor in publishing before deciding to join the U.S. Women's Army Corps because she had heard that it was "a hotbed of gay people." Once her sexual orientation was discovered, she was discharged from the service after nine months while training as a neuropsychiatric technician at the Walter Reed Military Hospital in Washington, D.C.

Vincenz remained in the area and, in 1963, joined the Mattachine Society of Washington, D.C., making her one of the first lesbians to join a homophile group predominantly composed of gay men. She was the first and only openly lesbian participant in the group's 1965 picketing outside of the White House in what is thought to be the first demonstration of its kind for gay rights. She later explained her involvement with the organization: "to be with gay people, help the movement, help unmask the lies being told about us, correct the notion of homosexuality as a sickness and present it as it is, a beautiful way to love." She filmed two important gay rights demonstrations, the earliest films to document the gay rights movement: the July 4, 1968, Annual Reminder in Philadelphia and *Gay and Proud*, documenting the 1970 Christopher Street Liberation Day March, marking the first anniversary of the Stonewall Uprising.

In 1971, Vincenz, together with activists Barbara Gittings, Barbara Love, and three other lesbians, appeared on the PBS talk show *The David Susskind Show* to debate long-held stereotypes about gays with Susskind. From 1971 to 1979, she held a weekly session at her home for lesbians in the Washington area to safely discuss lesbian-related issues and gay activism. The sessions came to be known as the Gay Women's Open House (GWOH).

It was around this time that she began dating Nancy Ruth Davis, a writer and activist, who would become her partner until Davis passed away in 2019. To enhance her skills in addressing the needs of lesbians, she earned a master's degree in psychology from George Mason

University and started a psychotherapy practice, eventually earning a doctorate from the University of Maryland in 1990. In 2013, her papers, films, and other memorabilia were donated to the Library of Congress.

In a 1999 interview with activist Jack Nichols, Vincenz reflected on her involvement in the LGBTQ+ movement: "I saw myself as being able to make a difference, as a pioneer working with other pioneers. Philosophically I was totally prepared for this role. It was an exhilarating time!"

Janet Weinberg (1955–2018)

LGBTQ+ Activist

An executive member and fundraiser in social service organizations such as the Gay Men's Health Crisis, the Educational Alliance, and the Lesbian, Gay, Bisexual & Transgender Community Center, Janet Inez Weinberg devoted herself to advocating on behalf of people with disabilities and those with HIV/AIDS.

Weinberg was born in Manhattan, New York, and grew up in Highland Park, New Jersey. After attending Hofstra University in Hempstead, New York, she graduated with a degree in occupational therapy from York College in Queens. She began her career as an occupational therapist at VTA Management Services, a company providing rehabilitation therapy services, working with children with learning disabilities, traumatic injuries, and neuromuscular diseases, eventually rising to a supervisory position, overseeing the work of more than 1,000 therapists. Known for her activism on behalf of people with HIV, she witnessed homophobia in 1985 during an incident in Rockway Beach, Queens, when the community angrily attempted to block a proposal to house dying homeless AIDS patients in a local nursing home rather than in a hospital. She experienced homophobia firsthand during the 1980s when she was hospitalized for a non-AIDS-related illness and the hospital staff refused to come into her room because she was a lesbian. She would become disabled and require the use of a wheelchair.

During the mid-1990s, Weinberg served on the board of the Lesbian, Gay, Bisexual & Transgender Community Center, where she worked for many years as its development director. In 2005, she joined the Gay Men's Health Crisis, becoming the senior managing director of development there until 2009. She organized AIDS Walk New York, a charity benefit that became the largest single-day AIDS fundraiser in the world. In 2008, it had 45,000 participants, raising $7.4 million. In 2011, two months after same-sex marriage was legalized in New York State, she wed her longtime partner, Rosalyn H. Richter, who was an associate justice of the Appellate Division of the New York Supreme Court. The following year, she was diagnosed with breast cancer. Instead of retiring as she had planned, she took on consulting work for the Educational Alliance, whose community centers serve residents of the Lower East Side and the East Village. She worked as EA's executive vice president from 2014 to 2018.

Weinberg also served on the board of the New York City AIDS Memorial, which was erected at 12th Street and Greenwich Avenue in Greenwich Village in 2016 to honor the 100,000 New Yorkers who had died of AIDS. In 2019, she was one of the inaugural 50 people to be inducted on the National LGBTQ Wall of Honor within the Stonewall National Monument, which she helped to create.

Randy Wicker (1938–)

Gay Rights Activist

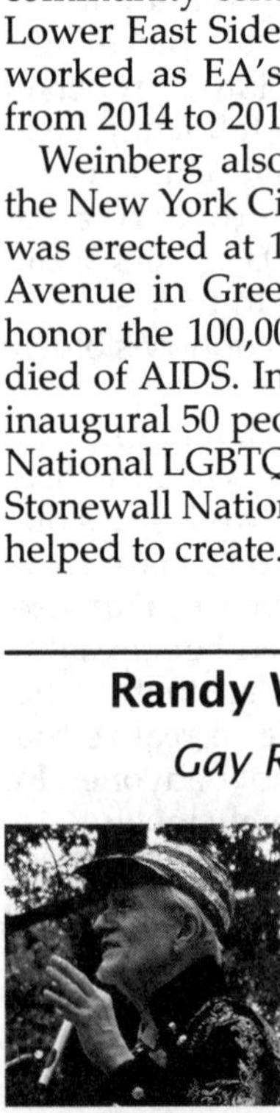

One of the most visible gay rights activists in New York City during the 1960s and early 1970s, Randy Wicker is credited with leading the first organized protest for gay rights when he and nine other members of the Sexual Freedom League demonstrated in front of the U.S. Army Induction Center on September 19, 1964, to protest confidentiality violations of gay men's draft records. He is also believed to have been the first openly gay person to appear on East Coast television without a fake name or disguise in the same year.

Born Charles Gervin Hayden Jr. in Plainfield, New Jersey, and raised in Florida by his grandparents, he later used the pseudonym Randolfe Hayden Wicker at the request of his family when he told them of his involvement in gay rights activism and legally changed his name in 1967. While attending the University of Texas during the mid to late 1950s, he ran for student body president, but his campaign proved unsuccessful after he was outed, along with his roommate, to the dean as gay. He first became aware of a gay rights movement after discovering a copy of *ONE Magazine* and in 1958 affiliated himself with the New York City chapter of the Mattachine Society, spending the summer in New York to work with the organization. After graduating from college, he relocated permanently to New York City and tried to shift the conservative focus of the Mattachine Society to a more radical, activist policy. When that failed, he created the Homosexual League of New York in 1962. After the New York radio station WBAI broadcast a program featuring a panel of psychiatrists espousing the theory of homosexuality as a mental illness, he convinced the station to put him and other openly gay men on the air to talk about their lives. This is believed to be the first time that gay men discussed homosexuality on the radio. In 1966, he took part in the Mattachine Society's "sip-in" protest at the Greenwich Village bar Julius' in order to challenge the New York State Liquor Authority's regulation against serving gays.

After the Stonewall Uprising, Wicker temporarily channeled his activism into writing for the tabloid newspaper *Gay* in 1970 and in 1972 appeared as coauthor, with *The Ladder* art director and writer Kay Lahusen, of the book *The Gay Crusaders*, profiles of early gay rights leaders. Lahusen, who had written the book under the pen name Kay Tobin, did not enjoy public speaking, and Wicker agreed to promote it for her. He returned to direct activism, joining the Gay Activists Alliance (GAA) in order to concentrate on gay rights issues and participating in a series of "zaps," or occupational-style actions. He would continue pursuing a more confrontational style as a member of the Radical Faeries, whose activities he began documenting in 2009. He also reported on GAA zaps for such media outlets as *Gay* and *The Advocate*. He roomed with Stonewall veteran, Gay Liberation Front Drag Queen Caucus member, and Street Transvestite Action Revolutionaries (STAR) cofounder Marsha P. Johnson from 1982 until her death in 1992. In 2023, he served as grand marshal of the New York City Pride March. The same year, he started a petition to have the statue of Civil War general Philip Sheridan, which stands in Christopher Park within a portion of the Stonewall National Monument, removed because of Sheridan's 1868–1869 war against and dispossession of the Southern Plains Indians.

Shirley Willer (1922–1999)

Lesbian and Gay Activist

President of both the New York City and national chapters of the Daughters of Bilitis, Shirley Willer helped to enhance the homophile movement and its commitment to gay and lesbian rights during the 1960s, helping to pave the way for the post-Stonewall gay rights movement that followed.

Willer was born in Chicago, where she and her younger sister were raised by a single working mother who had left her abusive husband. At 19, while working toward a bachelor's degree in nursing at the University of Chicago in 1941, she realized that she was a lesbian during a nursing class lecture on women's attraction to other women. She recalled, "I thought, 'Oh gee, I'm one of those things!'" She learned that what she considered normal and natural was considered deviant after she confessed to identifying as a lesbian to her professor and was sent to a psychiatrist for six months; later, when she came out to her mother, her reaction was, "Where did I go wrong?" After receiving her degree, she worked for most of her professional career as a registered nurse in a Chicago hospital. The death of a fellow gay nurse in 1947 motivated her activism. Seriously injured in an apartment fire, he "didn't receive good care because he was queer. They didn't even change his dressings," she recalled. She began her activism by providing sanctuary and support for LGBTQ+ people in Chicago, taking in young men and women who had no place to go and most of whom were teenagers. "We encouraged these kids to be themselves," she explained, "to stop trying to hide it. We knew at the time that we couldn't do much to change the laws in Chicago, but we could give these kids a sense of self-esteem."

In 1962, Willer moved to New York City and joined the Daughters of Bilitis, becoming president of the New York chapter in 1963 and national president in 1966. Under her leadership, she helped to get the term "lesbian" removed from the lexicon of mental illness and to convince *The New York Times* to substitute "homosexual" for "pervert" in its coverage. She also encouraged the DOB to work closely with the Mattachine Society to form alliances based on common causes between lesbians and gays.

During the 1960s, Willer formed a long-term relationship with a DOB founding member, Marion Glass, and they remained partners for life. Stepping down from the DOB in the 1970s, they moved to Key West, Florida, where they spent their last years together, both active in the growing lesbian and gay community in Key West. The second episode of season 2 of the podcast *Making Gay History* is devoted to the life and work of Willer.

Phill Wilson (1956–)

HIV/AIDS Activist

A community organizer, activist, and educator, Phill Wilson founded the Black AIDS Institute, served on the Presidential Advisory Council on HIV/AIDS, and sits on the Strategic Working Group for the National Institute of Allergy and Infectious Diseases. He also cofounded and cochaired the National Black Lesbian and Gay Leadership Forum.

Born in Chicago, Wilson was involved in the gay community of Chicago through sports and social activities. He earned BAs in theater and Spanish at Illinois Wesleyan University and, upon graduating in 1982, moved to Los Angeles. His activism began after he and his partner, Chris Brownlie, were both diagnosed with HIV in the early 1980s. At the time, AIDS was believed to be an exclusively gay disease, with outreach primarily focused in white, gay communities. He believed that AIDS affected Black communities much more. "Black people represented 25% of the new cases in the U.S.," he said. "Even as early as then, Black women represented over 50% of women diagnosed with HIV and AIDS. So Black people were always disproportionately impacted, over-represented in disease, underrepresented in advocacy, underrepresented in resources dedicated to fighting the disease." After Brownlie died of an AIDS-related illness in 1989, Wilson channeled his grief into activism, addressing the lack of attention paid to AIDS in the Black community.

Wilson began working as the director of

policy and planning for AIDS Project Los Angeles and served as the AIDS coordinator for Los Angeles. From 1990 to 1995, he served as cochair of the Los Angeles HIV Health Commission and in 1995 became a member of the Health Resources and Service Administration (HRSA) AIDS Advisory Committee. He took a break from work in 1997, when his disease became too immobilizing. However, he went back to work in 1999, when he founded the Black AIDS Institute. In 2010, he was appointed to President Obama's Presidential Advisory Council on HIV/AIDS, becoming the cochair of the disparities subcommittee.

Originally told that he had only a few months to live, four decades later, Wilson continues to battle. As he recalls, "The dying would take care of itself, that wasn't my job. My job was to focus on the living." He concludes that "it's been a journey and a gift of a journey that I'm very, very happy about."

William E. Woods (1949–2008)

Gay Rights Activist

Called "the father of Hawaii's gay rights movement," in 1990, William E. Woods helped to initiate the court cases that would eventually lead to the legalization of same-sex marriage in the United States. He also founded the Gay and Lesbian Education and Advocacy Foundation (GLEAF) and worked for legislation to prohibit workplace discrimination against gay people.

Born in Decatur, Illinois, Woods attended Millikin University before transferring to the University of Hawaii, where he graduated in 1971. He began working in the Hawaii Department of Health before founding the Sexual Identity Center, a social services organization for gay people. In 1974, he was defeated in his campaign for a seat in the Hawaiian Senate, the first of many failed attempts to win election to a state-level position as an openly gay candidate.

Woods is probably best known for orchestrating a challenge to the ban on same-sex marriage. In December 1990, he brought three same-sex couples to the Hawaii Department of Health's main office in Honolulu to fill out marriage licenses. He expected them to be turned down and intended to next go to the ACLU office for support. Previously, ACLU lawyers had belittled his plan, but the media attention from this attempt forced the ACLU to take it seriously. This initiated a series of court cases that ended in the Supreme Court of Hawaii's 1993 decision that denying same-sex marriage violated the right to equal protection granted by the state constitution. However, a 1998 amendment that defined marriage as the union of a man and a woman made the ruling irrelevant. Despite ultimately failing to secure same-sex marriage in Hawaii, his efforts would eventually succeed.

As journalist Sasha Issenberg commented, "Not a single gay-rights group formally embraced marriage rights for its core constituency until the Hawaii Supreme Court in May 1993 gave unexpected blessing to the cause, the unexpected outcome of the legal process that Bill Woods began." Issenberg would go on to describe the initial events of 1990 as the beginning of "a chain of events" that led to legal same-sex marriage in the United States in all 50 states in 2015.

In 1990, Woods founded the Gay and Lesbian Education and Advocacy Foundation (GLEAF), one of Hawaii's most important gay rights organizations, which spearheaded the fight for antidiscrimination protection in employment, housing, and other areas. In 2003, he married his partner, Lance W. Bateman, in Vancouver, less than a year before the first legal same-sex marriage took place in the United States in Massachusetts in 2004. He reflected, "My own pursuit of legal gay marriage did not begin as a personal goal. Why would anyone need a piece of paper to demonstrate they had a loving relationship? I thought. But it was a choice I believed should be available for all."

Education

LGBTQ+ Advocacy in Schools

The activism that culminated in the Stonewall Uprising of 1969 and helped fuel the gay liberation movement of the 1970s, together with activism during the AIDS crisis in the 1980s and the increasing initiatives to gain civil rights for all those who identified as queer, led to greater visibility for the LGBTQ+ community. However, coming out as queer remained problematic for many young people as well as for adults. Families that rejected their children's orientation left young people at risk of homelessness, poverty, and suicide as well as subject to harassment, bullying, and violence, especially in high schools, with chronic truancy and high dropout rates prevalent among LGBTQ+ students. The last decades of the 20th century began to see both educators and students dedicated to ensuring safe educational and social environments for queer young people in American schools.

In 1979, after learning about an unhoused, 15-year-old boy who had been beaten and forced to leave an emergency shelter because he was gay, New York City educators and partners Emery Hetrick and A. Damien Martin founded a social services and advocacy organization called the Institute for the Protection of Lesbian and Gay Youth (IPLGY), renamed the Hetrick-Martin Institute (HMI) in 1988. Drs. Hetrick and Martin went on to establish Harvey Milk High School in 1985 as a safe and productive educational space for LGBTQ+ teens. Named after San Francisco city supervisor Harvey Milk, the first openly gay man to be elected to public office in the United States and assassinated in 1978, the school conducted classes at the Washington Square United Methodist Church and subsequently in a designated classroom at the HMI offices before moving to its current space, a 12-story former loft building in Greenwich Village.

The school became a fully accredited public high school in 2003, administered by the New York City Department of Education, which had allocated funds to expand the school with the approval of Mayor Mike Bloomberg. At the same time, State Senator Ruben Diaz (D-Bronx) filed a lawsuit against the Department of Education, claiming that Harvey Milk High School violated the department's antidiscrimination policies and the rights of heterosexual students, many of whom were students of color attending overcrowded and underperforming public schools. Attorney Norman Siegel, former executive director of the New York Civil Liberties Union, agreed and called for a general initiative to support citywide public school programs to tackle the problem of institutional homophobia.

Both parties reached a settlement in 2006, when the Department of Education

Originally located at the Washington Square United Methodist Church at 135 West 4th St. in New York City, Harvey Milk High School (shown here) is now at 2-10 Astor Place in the East Village.

agreed to allow non-LGBTQ+ students to attend the school. Harvey Milk High School has so far been unique to New York City, which has long offered public schooling catering to a variety of educational needs and interests.

Initiatives to provide social and educational support for bullied and disenfranchised LGBTQ+ students aged 13 through high school began in 1984 with Project 10, founded in Los Angeles by Fairfax High School educator and counselor Virginia Uribe after noting the experience of an openly gay high school student who had been rejected by his parents after coming out to them and had dropped out of four high schools because of continued sexual harassment. Uribe, who would become Project 10's full-time coordinator, named the pioneering program after an Alfred Kinsey sex research statistic that theorized that 10 percent of the male population was gay. By 1986, Project 10 included all Los Angeles Unified School District (LAUSD) schools, and the Friends of Project 10, Inc., a nonprofit organization, was formed in order to expand the program to other district schools. The program faced attempts to abolish it during the late 1980s and 1990s, the first of which was spearheaded in 1988 by Marian LaFollette, a Republican member of the California Assembly who, together with the Traditional Values Coalition, unsuccessfully tried to pass a resolution to deny funds to the LAUSD unless it abandoned the program. Project 10 is also known for introducing the first LGBTQ+ prom and for helping to implement the 2011 FAIR (Fair, Inclusive, and Respectful) Education Act in California, which required the inclusion of LGBTQ+ people of note in public K–8 school textbooks and social studies curricula.

The 1990s saw the further emergence of state and nationwide programs dedicated to ending discrimination, harassment, and bullying of LGBTQ+ students and ensuring inclusive, safe, and affirming educational environments for queer students and their allies. GLSEN (pronounced "glisten"), founded in 1990 by Massachusetts high school history teacher Kevin Jennings as the Gay, Lesbian & Straight Education Network, has worked to provide developmentally relevant and helpful resources for educators and has encouraged student-led programs in K–12 schools throughout the United States. One example of a state-led initiative is Massachusetts's Safe Schools Program, initiated in 1993. The Trevor Project, which provides crisis and suicide intervention materials for educators, was founded in 1998 by the filmmakers who produced and directed the 1994 film *Trevor*, the story of a young, gay teen who attempts suicide after he is rejected by his friends because of his sexual orientation. In 2008, PFLAG created the program Cultivating Respect: Safe

Schools for All, which formed a coalition in 2021 with GLBTQ Legal Advocates & Defenders (GLAD Law), GLSEN, and the National Center for Lesbian Rights (NCLR) to create a social, educational, and legal resource website for students, educators, family members, and trusted allies. In June 2021, the U.S. Department of Education's Office of Civil Rights confirmed that Title IX of the Education Amendments of 1972, the law that prohibits discrimination based on sex in federally funded schools, protects students from discrimination based on sexual orientation and gender identity.

Despite the welcome anti-bullying initiatives of the late 20th century and the first decades of the 21st century, anti-LGBTQ+ legislation and rhetoric in some states represented a backlash toward queer young people, leading to an increase in bullying incidents in schools as well as cyberbullying. A widely reported incident occurred in Oklahoma in February 2024, when 16-year-old transgender student Nex Benedict (2008–2024) was severely beaten by a group of girls during an altercation in a school bathroom and died the next day. News coverage of Benedict's beating and death led to a 200 percent increase in crisis contact calls to the Rainbow Youth Project, a national LGBTQ+ suicide prevention group. An autopsy conducted in March determined that the cause of Benedict's death was suicide and not from physical injuries they had sustained from the beating. The same year also saw a continuation of support from allies for LGBTQ+ young people in grades 9–12, with Pride proms planned in communities across the United States.

After being beaten by students at their high school for going into the girls' bathroom, binary youth Nex Benedict died of an overdose of Prozac and Benadryl.

LGBTQ advocacy on college campuses began in the 1970s, when members of activist groups such as the Gay Liberation Front and the Radical Lesbians began to form centers to support gay and lesbian students. The first LGBTQ center was established at the Ann Arbor campus of the University of Michigan in 1971. During the 1990s, the center expanded its initiatives to include support for bisexual and transgender students, and in the 2000s it was renamed the Spectrum Center to reflect all aspects of LGBTQ initialism. In 1995 educator Ronni Sanlo, director of the University of Michigan's LGBTQ center, created the first Lavender Graduation ceremony during commencement week to honor LGBTQ students and ally students and to acknowledge their achievements and contributions to the university. Dr. Sanlo chose lavender to signify the color's importance in LGBTQ history. By 2001, over 45 Lavender Graduations were celebrated at colleges and universities nationwide; by 2022, that figure had risen to 200.

Queer-Straight Alliances

The gay liberation movement and the formation of new activist groups, such as the Gay Activists Alliance, inspired high school students to organize their own

Concord Academy in Massachusetts is where the first Gay-Straight Alliance was formed in 1988 by Kevin Jennings.

school-based gay liberation clubs. One notable example was the Gay International Youth Society, founded in 1972 at George Washington High School, an ethnically diverse, overcrowded, and, at the time, underperforming public high school in New York City. The club was first proposed by Elie Lamadrid, a GWHS student who described herself as a "Third World woman," which indicated in the phraseology of the era that she was a student of color. She found support for the club among teachers, and its diverse roster of members included lesbians, gays, and straight allies. The Gay International Youth Society's manifesto set out its ambitious anti-homophobia agenda, which included, among its demands, "the right to be treated as equal human beings, which includes the removal of all textbooks and other educational media that treat homosexuality as an aberration, rather than, as an integral and important part of human sexuality."

The most widely known faculty-sponsored, student-led club that was committed to encouraging positive relationships between queer and straight students and providing them with safe and supportive environments has been the Gay–Straight Alliance (GSA). Kevin Jennings (later the founder of GLSEN) formed the first GSA in 1988 at Concord Academy, a private school in Massachusetts. Jennings had recently come out and conceived the idea for the club after a straight student approached him with concerns about the treatment of gay students at the school. A similar scenario took place in 1992 at Newton South High School, a public school in Newton, Massachusetts, after Robert Parlin, a 9th-grade history teacher, came out as gay during a school meeting and was then approached by a student who wanted to start a GSA club. GSA clubs were established at other Massachusetts schools and began to be formed at schools in other states. In 1998, strategy consultant Carolyn Laub founded the Gay–Straight Alliance Network (also abbreviated as the GSA Network) in order to assist students in forming GSA clubs, first in the San Francisco Bay Area and then statewide by 2001. The National Association of GSA Networks was formed in 2005 in order to broaden the initiative to include GSAs in schools across the United States and would grow to include 40 organizations in California, representing more than 4,000 GSA clubs nationwide.

In 2016, at the behest of GSA youth leaders, the organization changed its formal name to the Genders & Sexualities Alliance Network in order to reflect the diverse orientation and identity contained within LGBTQ+ initialism. In 2018, a GLSEN/GSA report that was published by the National Institutes of Health (NIH) detailed positive outcomes for both LGBTQ+ and non-LGBTQ+ students in GSA clubs, citing "fewer anti-LGBTQ remarks, feeling safer at school regarding their sexual orientation and gender identity, experiencing lower levels of victimization, and having peers more accepting of LGBTQ people."

Not all schools and school districts have welcomed GSA clubs. One example is the Board of Education in Kentucky's Boyd County, which shut down all extracurricular clubs at K–12 district schools in 2002 in order to silence controversy over the formation of a GSA club at one high school. The ACLU took the case to federal court, successfully arguing that the shutdowns were unconstitutional and a violation of the Equal Access Act, which, as Title VIII of the Education for Economic Security Act of 1984, compels federally funded public high schools to provide equal access to extracurricular student clubs. The research group Child Trends reported that between 2016 and 2018, more than half of the high schools in 10 states supported GSA clubs, with Rhode Island supporting the most (72 percent) and Mississippi the fewest (15 percent). In Florida, the policies of Governor Ron DeSantis and his administration, which have eroded LGBTQ+ rights through the enactment of anti-LGBTQ+ legislation pertaining to schools, has affected the membership of GSA clubs and, with it, their status as safe spaces for queer students. In August 2023, the Florida Board of Education, using the state's Parental Rights in Education statute, aka the "Don't Say LGBTQ" or, more colloquially, the "Don't Say Gay" law, bypassed the Equal Access Act and enacted a new regulation requiring students to obtain parental permission slips before joining any extracurricular school activity. The result has been a significant drop in GSA memberships, as well as in other LGBTQ+-supportive school clubs, for fear among students that they would be outed to their parents when they were not ready or willing to do so.

LGBTQ+ in the Classroom

Discrimination against teachers who were suspected or known to be gay or lesbian emerged in force after World War II, when the anti-Communist Red Scare and Lavender Scare of the 1950s resulted in the federal and state persecution of Americans, considered to be a threat to postwar concepts of patriotism, national security, and heteronormative conformity.

During the 1940s until the early 1970s, short, educational "social guidance" films for children, teens, and adults on topics ranging from good citizenship to personal hygiene to dating to staying safe in certain situations were popular with school administrators, although students often considered them laughably melodramatic. In 1961, former child actor Sid Davis, producer and director of such films, offered *Boys Beware*, a 10-minute film made with the cooperation of the Inglewood, California, police department that featured a police

The 1961 short film Boys Beware *produced with the help of the Inglewood, California, Police Department and school district portrays homosexuals as being middle-aged murderers and pedophiles who are out to lure young boys into their depraved traps.*

detective as the film's narrator. The film warned young teens about gay men, who are depicted as sexual predators, child molesters, and hebephiles, and characterized "homosexuality" as a mental illness. Color versions of the film, retitled *Boys Aware*, with different actors, were released in 1973 and 1979. In 2015, a teacher at the Raymore-Peculiar High School in Kansas City, Missouri, was fired after showing the film to his class.

The postwar era saw a nationwide purge of gay and lesbian educators, who lost their jobs and, often, their teaching credentials, and was the harshest in Florida. Between 1957 and 1963, the Florida Legislative Investigation Committee, aka the Johns Committee, named for right-wing segregationist Governor Charley Johns, actively pursued and investigated known or "suspected" gay and lesbian teachers and professors without due process, threatened them with imprisonment for perjury if they refused to out themselves or their colleagues, and dismissed any defense concerning character and privacy.

The activism of the 1970s led to more teachers challenging their dismissals in court, and local and state legislative initiatives began to prohibit employment discrimination on the basis of sexual orientation. However, in 1977, a political coalition calling itself Save Our Children, Inc., based in Miami, Florida, mounted a campaign together with Christian fundamentalists to overturn a recently adopted anti-discrimination ordinance in Dade County.

The coalition's head was singer/celebrity Anita Bryant, a well-known brand ambassador for the Florida Citrus Commission who was featured in national TV commercials touting Florida orange juice. Bryant claimed that the ordinance discriminated against her right to teach her children biblical morality since it included parochial as well as public schools and labeled gay and lesbian educators as "recruiting" children for the "survival and growth of homosexuality." Other coalition members cited "militant homosexuals" as threats to children.

The tactic was successful, and the ordinance was repealed by a vote of 69–31 percent. The trajectory of the campaign received heavy mainstream and gay press attention, and the result led to protests from gay activists and orange juice boycotts, which helped to derail Bryant's career but did not succeed in convincing Dade County legislators to reestablish the antidiscrimination ordinance. In 1978, California conservative state legislator John Briggs spearheaded the Briggs Initiative, formally known as Proposition 6, a similar legislative initiative to prohibit gays, lesbians, and supporters of gay rights from teaching in California public schools. The proposition was defeated.

During the late 1980s, the AIDS/HIV crisis led some states to begin to enact censorship laws restricting any discussion of "homosexuality" and/or AIDS in sex and health education classes.

Oklahoma enacted a similar law, which was overturned in the state's Court of Appeals on the basis of First Amendment rights and challenged in *National Gay Task Force v. Board of Education of Oklahoma City* by the U.S. Supreme Court in 1985. The outcome was an even split between the justices, who supported the First Amendment "free speech" portion of the argument but not the "equal protection" clause of the 14th Amendment, also cited by attorneys for the National Gay Task Force. The SCOTUS deadlock allowed the favorable Court of Appeals decision to stand.

LGBTQ+-inclusive curricula have long been a contentious issue in American K–12 school districts. During the late 1980s, the AIDS/HIV crisis led some states to begin to enact censorship laws restricting any discussion of "homosexuality" and/or AIDS in sex and health education classes. The first states to do so were Louisiana and Oklahoma in 1987, followed by South Carolina (1988), Arizona and Texas (1991), Alabama (1992), North Carolina (1995), Mississippi (1998), and Utah (2001). Some states eventually repealed these laws, but as of 2023, censorship laws restricting LGBTQ+ inclusion in sex and health education classes remained on the books in Louisiana, Oklahoma, Mississippi, and Texas.

During the 1980s in New York City, gay and lesbian activist groups advocated for the inclusion of the discussion of same-sex relationships in New York public school curricula. After the highly publicized 1989 slaying of Black teen Yusef Hawkins and the 1990 murders of two gay men, the New York City Board of Education created the Children of the Rainbow Curriculum: First Grade in 1991 in order to promote multicultural understanding and help decrease racism and bigotry. The curriculum's 443-page resource guide for teachers suggested lessons and reading material and included a section called "Families" that focused on gay and lesbian couples, recommending the books *Heather Has Two Mommies* (1989), *Daddy's Roommate* (1990), and *Gloria Goes to Gay Pride* (1991). New York City Board of Education chancellor Joseph Fernandez, whose new curriculum, which included AIDS education and support for condom distribution in the city's high schools, was causing controversy, approved the Children of the Rainbow Curriculum.

In September 1992, a week before the new school year was scheduled to begin, Mary Cummins, head of Community School District 24 in the New York borough of Queens, refused to adopt it, writ-

There is a definite split among teachers, students, and their parents as to the appropriateness of teaching about sexual orientation and gender identity. Most opposed were elementary school teachers (62%) and parents (54%), and less than a third of students (29%) were comfortable with the topic being taught.

ing to parents that it would "have teachers telling their first-graders that gay/lesbian couples are 'family' just like any other family unit" and going on to state, "we will not accept two people of the same sex engaged in deviant sex practices as a 'family.'" Cummins's letter influenced school districts in other boroughs to reject the curriculum, and the Christian Coalition of America mobilized to oppose it, with the result being that the Children of the Rainbow Curriculum was defeated.

Although the Children of the Rainbow Curriculum suffered a defeat, mainstream interest in teaching LGBTQ+ history increased during the 1990s and into the following decades with the creation of LGBTQ+ History Month in 1994 and the National Park Service's report on LGBTQ+ historic sites in 2016.

Some state laws explicitly required public school curricula to include LGBTQ+ people and history in history, civics, or social studies classes or called for a state's board of education to create an LGBTQ+-inclusive curriculum but did not require schools to use it. According to the Movement Advancement Project (MAP), a nonprofit organization that tracks equality and inclusivity in the United States, as of 2023–2024, California, Colorado, Illinois, Nevada, New Jersey, and Oregon required the former, while Connecticut adopted the latter option. Five states required parental notification of LGBTQ+ curricula that allowed parents to opt out or required parents to opt in, and seven states censor the discussion of LGBTQ+ people or topics throughout school curricula through "Don't Say LGBTQ" laws. Twenty-nine states, the District of Columbia, and the five U.S. territories had no LGBTQ+-specific curricular laws. Florida's controversial "Don't Say LGBTQ" law, which forbade any discussion of sexual orientation and gender identity in school curricula, suffered a partial defeat in March 2024, when state legislators and the Board of Education agreed to allow "conversations" on sexual orientation and gender identity in schools but not instruction of these topics. The core "Don't Say Gay" law remained the same.

A Pew Research Center study on the national debate over what K–12 schools are or should be teaching about sexual orientation and gender identity and how teens and adults in general feel about the teaching of these subjects was released in February 2024. According to those surveyed, 41 percent of teachers felt that the debate had a negative effect on their jobs. The majority of K–12 teachers accepted that students can be recognized as different from their birth-assigned gender, but 50 percent felt that gender identity should not be taught in school, with the largest percentage among elementary and middle school teachers (62 percent and 45 percent, respectively). Twenty-nine percent of teens felt comfortable when topics related to sexual orientation or gender identity are brought up in class and that the majority of adults (54 percent) should be able to opt their children out of learning about LGBTQ+ issues in school.

Queer Studies and Queer Theory

The academic disciplines of queer studies and queer theory, often taught within the same course, are sometimes mistaken for each other, but while both areas of study use empirical observations on historical, cultural, and geographic variations in gender and sexual orientation as a starting point, queer studies classes focus on topics that begin with the study of LGBTQ+ literary theory and history and expand to include the study of a wide variety of academic disciplines within an LGBTQ+ context as well as the ways in which intersectionality can broaden and influence that context. A term coined by Black feminist scholar and activist Kimberlé Crenshaw in 1989, intersectionality explores the points at which economic, social, and institutional power, according to Crenshaw, "comes and collides, where it interlocks and intersects. It's not simply that there's a race problem here, a gender problem here, and a class or LGBTQ problem there." Such a framework, Crenshaw maintains, "erases what happens to people who are subject to all of these things."

The college-level program known variously throughout its history as Gay, Lesbian, and Queer Studies, Sexual Diversity Studies, Gender (or Queer) and Sexuality Studies, Queer Studies, or LGBTQ+ Studies originated as Gay and Lesbian Studies in the 1970s and emerged from several factors: the formation of some 1,000 LGBTQ+ college student groups, beginning with Columbia's Student Homophile League in 1967; the introduction of ethnic and women's studies courses; the post-Stonewall activism that generated the gay liberation movement; and studies on LGBTQ+ life and culture that led to the first publication of works on previously suppressed gay history.

The first undergraduate course in LGBTQ+ studies was offered at the University of California, Berkeley, in the spring of 1970, with the City University of New York establishing the first university program in gay and lesbian studies (1986) and the College of San Francisco offering one of the first gay literature courses and claiming the establishment of the first Department of Gay and Lesbian Studies in the United States in 1989. Yale University became a notable center of gay and lesbian studies in the late 1980s and early 1990s. In upstate New York during the late 1990s, Hobart and William Smith Colleges was among the first school to offer a major in LGBTQ+ studies and remained one of the few schools to maintain a specific tenure track in queer studies when many schools began to absorb their programs into the overlapping disciplines of gender and women's studies.

The use of the term "queer theory" among scholars began in the 1990s with renewed interest in *The History of Sexuali-*

ty, a 1976 work by French philosopher Michel Foucault. It emerged as an interdisciplinary field from lesbian, gay, and gender studies as a challenge to traditional notions of heterosexual and same-sex desire as the norm and expanded its perspective to critically analyze the nature and fluidity of gender identity, sexual practices, and orientations that exist outside of the accepted constructs of cisgender/binary and racial classifications. Queer theorists and thinkers are critical of the essentialist, absolutist view that individuals and members of racial, ethnic, and sexual communities possess intrinsically separate and characteristic natures that define them and view this concept as a phenomenon that has been socially and culturally constructed. Despite the controversial nature of the word "queer," queer theorists and many academics in other disciplines have so far embraced the reclamation of the word to consider the possibilities that can define all aspects of gender and sexual identity.

BIOGRAPHIES

Gloria E. Anzaldúa (1942–2004)

Scholar, Author

Gloria E. Anzaldúa, who called herself a "*tejana patlache* [queer] *nepantlera* [spiritual activist]," was a pioneer in establishing the contemporary Chicano/Chicana movement and scholar of lesbian and queer theory and development. She is perhaps best known for coediting *This Bridge Called My Back: Writings by Radical Women of Color* (1981) with Cherrie Moraga, which argued that feminism should fully embrace lesbian voices and concerns. Her classic book of poems and essays, *Borderlands/La Frontera*, in the words of one critic, "established the Mexican American border as a metaphor for different types of transgressions—racial, sexual, social, and cultural"—that is "still painfully relevant."

Anzaldúa was born in Raymondville, Texas, near the U.S.–Mexican border. She was a descendant of Spanish settlers who came to the Americas in the 16th and 17th centuries. She has described her father's family as "very poor aristocracy, aristocracy anyway" and his mother as "very indian [indigenous], working class." At the age of 6, she was diagnosed with a rare hormonal condition that caused her to go through puberty much younger than other children, which in turn ended bone growth early. She first experienced discrimination growing up in the Rio Grande Valley, which would inform her later research and writing about the area. After graduating from high school in 1962, she attended Texas Woman's University before transferring to Pan American University, graduating with a bachelor's degree in English in 1968. She went on to earn a master's degree in English from the University of Texas in 1972 and began work on a Ph.D. in comparative literature. While at UT, she first participated in Chicano and feminist activism and, in 1977, moved to California in order to devote herself to writing. Of her own sexuality, she would explain that she identified herself as a lesbian and had always been attracted to women but that the word "lesbian" was "not an adequate term" to describe herself; she "became a lesbian in my head first, the ideology, the politics, the aesthetics" and that the "touching, kissing, hugging, and all came later." She would write extensively about her queer identity and the marginalization of queer people, particularly in communities of color.

In California, Anzaldúa supported herself through her writing, lectures, and occasional teaching about feminism, Chicano studies, and creative writing at San Francisco State University; the University of California, Santa Cruz; Florida Atlantic

University; and other universities. Her many published works include *This Bridge Called My Back: Writings by Radical Women of Color* (1981) (with Cherrie Moraga), *Borderlands/La Frontera: The New Mestiza* (1987), *This Bridge We Call Home: Radical Visions for Transformation* (2002) (with AnaLouise Keating), *The Gloria Anzaldúa Reader* (2009), and *Light in the Dark/Lux en lo Oscuro: Rewriting Identity, Spirituality, Reality* (2015). Her poems and essays explore the anger and isolation of occupying the margins of culture and collective identity. She was awarded the Lambda Literary Awards' Lesbian Small Press Award, a Sappho Award of Distinction, and many other prizes. Her work represents foundational texts in the Chicano and Chicana movement as well as lesbian/queer theory.

Anzaldúa died at the age of 61 of complications of diabetes while working on her doctorate in literature, which was awarded to her posthumously by the University of California, Santa Cruz. In the essay "Speaking in Tongues: A Letter to Third World Women Writers" (1981), she offers a justification for her career: "Why am I compelled to write? Because the writing saves me from this complacency I fear. Because I have no choice. Because I must keep the spirit of my revolt and myself alive. Because the world I create in the writing compensates for what the real world does not give me. By writing I put order in the world, give it a handle so I can grasp it. I write because life does not appease my appetites and hunger. I write to record what others erase when I speak, to rewrite the stories others have written about me, about you."

Lauren Berlant (1957–2021)

Scholar, Social Theorist

Widely regarded as one of the most esteemed and influential literary and cultural critics in the United States, Lauren Gail Berlant was a key theorist of affect theory and queer theory. Her scholarly project in several groundbreaking books charted the emergence of the U.S. political sphere as an affective space of attachment and identification. Pairing literary criticism and historical analysis, she explored the territory of this intimate public sphere through close readings of U.S. women's literary works and their stage and film adaptations.

Berlant was born in Philadelphia and grew up in Penn Valley, Pennsylvania, an affluent suburb. When her attorney father and interior decorator mother divorced and declared bankruptcy, Berlant, who was attending Oberlin College, used scholarships, jobs, and loans to gain a degree in English in 1979 and a Ph.D. in English at Cornell University in 1985. Just before completing a dissertation, she began teaching at the University of Chicago in 1984, remaining on the faculty until 2021. She offered courses in lesbian and feminist theory, and in 1996, she helped found the Center for the Study of Gender and Sexuality at the University of Chicago. Courses included "Problems in the Study of Sexuality" and "Theories of Gender and Sexuality." Her colleagues, professors Debbie Nelson and Kristen Schitt, stated that she "was inarguably the most important scholar and theorist of gender and sexuality of their generation.... [Berlant's] work raised significant questions about people's desires for normativity, conventionality, and social belonging—and about the cultural forms and representational strategies that minoritarian groups have developed to express them."

Berlant produced a trilogy on "national sentimentality" that fundamentally revised the understanding of the relationship between gender and citizenship—*The Anatomy of National Fantasy: Hawthorne, Utopia, and Everyday Life* (1991), *The Queen of America Goes to Washington City: Essays on Sex and Citizenship* (1993), and *The Female Complaint: On the Unfinished Business of Sentimentality in American Culture* (2008). Other important books she authored include *Cruel Optimism* (2011), *Desire/Love* (2012), and *On the Inconvenience of Other People* (2022).

So powerful and influential have Berlant's writings been in capturing the contemporary world, they have been described as "the era of Berlant." Judith Butler, the eminent theorist of gender, wrote that she "redefines 'brilliant' for our times, and hers is a brilliance that attends closely to our times, its sufferings and potentials for affirmation."

Berlant died of cancer at the age of 63, survived by partner Ian Horswill. In *The Queen of America Goes to Washington City*, she summarizes many of the key concepts that dominated her teaching and writing for nearly four decades: "I found, when circulating chapters from this book, that some readers feel I am too hard on heterosexuality. I do not mean to be coming out against it. I simply do not see why the nation has to have an official sexuality, especially one that authorizes the norm of a violent gentility; that narrows the field of legitimate political action; that supports the amputation of personal complexity into categories of simple identity; that uses cruel and mundane strategies both to promote shame for non-normative populations and to deny them state, federal, and juridical supports because they are deemed morally incompetent to their own citizenship. This is the heterosexuality I repudiate."

John Boswell (1947–1994)

Scholar, Historian

One of the most significant scholars in gay and lesbian studies, John Boswell was a historian at Yale University whose best-known book is *Christianity, Social Tolerance, and Homosexuality: Gay People in Western Europe from the Beginning of the Christian Era to the Fourteenth Century* (1980), which won the 1981 American Book Award for history. He challenged the social constructionist view that gay identities originated in modern Western societies by documenting a highly developed gay subculture in Western Europe from the mid-11th century, proving that not only was homosexuality tolerated in the Middle Ages but that same-sex unions were celebrated liturgically.

Boswell was born in Boston and earned his B.A. at the College of William and Mary and his Ph.D. from Harvard University in 1975 before joining the faculty at Yale University, becoming a full professor in 1982. He was a medieval philologist who spoke several Scandinavian languages as well as German, French, Spanish, Italian, Latin, Greek, and early and modern Russian. In 1987, he helped organize the Lesbian and Gay Studies Center at Yale.

A convert to Roman Catholicism as a teenager, Boswell, in *Christianity, Social Tolerance, and Homosexuality*, set out, in his words, "to rebut the common idea that religious belief—Christian or other—has been the cause of intolerance in regard to gay people." In *The Marriage of Likeness: Same-Sex Unions in Pre-Modern Europe* (1994), he documented that early Christians did on occasion accept same-sex relationships, uncovering the liturgical ceremonies used to sanctify same-sex unions. Historian Paul Robinson called his work "revolutionary…for it tells of things heretofore unimagined and sets a standard of excellence that one would have thought impossible in the treatment of an issue so large, uncharted and vexed." His contentions were controversial, with one professor of history stating that "the mainstream reaction was that he raised some interesting questions, but had proven his case."

Boswell died of an AIDS-related illness at the age of 47. He partnered with Jerone Hart for some 20 years until Boswell's death. Since his death, other scholars, such as Terry Castle, Ruth Vanita, and Rictor Norton, have extended his scholarship, proposing that categorizations of humans by sexual predilection predate the modern period in the West and other cultures. Fellow historian Martin Duberman eulogized him, saying, "I regard him as one of the major innovative figures in gay and lesbian scholarship. John was very brave and pioneering. And very brilliant."

Judith Butler (1956–)

Scholar, Educator, Author

Judith Butler's groundbreaking theories of the performative nature of gender and sexuality have been influential in the fields of cultural theory, queer theory, and philosophical feminism. In their best-known work, *Gender Trouble: Feminism and the Subversion of Identity*, and its sequel, *Bodies That Matter: On the Discursive Limits of "Sex,"* they explore the assumption that gender is socially constructed rather than innate and that conventional notions of gender and sexuality serve to perpetuate the traditional domination of women by men and justify the oppression of homosexuals and transgender people.

Butler was born in Cleveland, Ohio. Their family was of Hungarian–Jewish and Russian–Jewish descent, with most of their maternal grandmother's family murdered in the Holocaust. They have said that their first training in philosophy came from the classes on Jewish ethics they took in the Hebrew school they attended. They transferred from Bennington College in order to study philosophy at Yale University, earning a B.A. (1978), an M.A. (1982), and a Ph.D. (1984). They have taught at Wesleyan University, George Washington University, Johns Hopkins University, and the University of California, Berkeley.

In the 1985 essay "Performative Acts and Gender Constitution: An Essay in Phenomenology and Feminist Theory," Butler articulated the core concept that gender is performative—that is, not a static identity or role but a set of ever evolving acts—and that gender identity is established through behavior and it is possible to construct different genders via different behaviors. They would explore these and other gender-related concepts in the best-selling *Gender Trouble* (1990) and in such works as *Imitation and Gender Insubordination* (1991), *Bodies That Matter* (1993), *Excitable Speech* (1997), *Precarious Life* (2004), and *Undoing Gender* (2004). Their work has shaped and influenced feminist and queer theory, cultural studies, and philosophy. Their theory of gender performativity has helped to define understandings of gender and queer identity both in academia and queer activism internationally. Scholar Darin Barney stated, "Butler's work on gender, sex, sexuality, queerness, feminism, bodies, politic speech and ethics has changed the way scholars all over the world think, talk and write about identity, subjectivity, power and politics. It has also changed the lives of countless people whose bodies, genders, sexualities and desires have made them subject to violence, exclusion, and oppression."

Beyond their scholarship, Butler has been an activist on queer and feminist issues, serving for a time as the chair of the board of the International Gay and Lesbian Human Rights Commission. They have spoken out on issues ranging from affirmative action and gay marriage to anti-war protests. Some of their positions and comments have angered many. After they were awarded the Adorno Prize from the City of Frankfurt (2012) in honor of their contributions to feminist and moral philosophy, protests occurred in Israel over their call for a boycott of Israel over its treatment of the Palestinian people. Their effigy was burned before a 2017 democracy conference in Brazil and depicted as an "antichrist" because of their gender theories and Jewish identity.

Butler is a lesbian, legally nonbinary, and uses neutral pronouns. They have indicated being "never at home" with the assignment of female at birth. Asked in an interview to reflect on the key concept of *Gender Trouble* more than 30 years after publication, they explained, "Gender...becomes a negotiation, a struggle, a way of dealing with historical constraints and making new realities. When we are 'girled,' we are entered into a realm of girldom that has been built up over a long time—a series of conventions, sometimes conflicting, that establish girlness within society. We don't just choose it. And it is not just imposed on us. But that social reality can, and does, change." Ultimately, all of their writings have been informed by one central drive: "We need to rethink the category of woman."

Martin Duberman (1930–)

Scholar, Author, Gay Rights Activist

Considered one of the preeminent scholars of the LGBTQ+ movement, Martin Baumi Duberman founded the Center for Lesbian and Gay Studies at CUNY. A prolific and eclectic author of biography, history, plays, and fiction, his works include *Stonewall* (1993), regarded as the definitive account of the Stonewall Uprising.

Born in New York City, Duberman was the son of a Jewish father born in Ukraine who emigrated initially to work as a manual laborer but later founded a successful clothing business that allowed him to attend the Horace Mann School, an elite prep school, before attending Yale University in 1948 and receiving his M.A. and Ph.D. from Harvard University. From 1957 to 1961, he was a history instructor at Yale before joining the faculty at Princeton University, becoming a full-time professor in 1967.

Duberman's initial historical field was American history during the Civil War and Reconstruction, publishing *Charles Francis Adams, 1807–86* (1961) and *Antislavery Vanguard: New Essays on the Abolitionist* (1965). He also wrote several plays, notably *In White America* (1964). After documenting instances of homophobia in his history book *Black Mountain: An Exploration of Community* (1971) and experiencing homophobic attacks from his academic peers, he became involved in gay activism and, with fellow gay scholars, founded the Gay Academic Union (1973) and joined the National Gay and Lesbian Task Force. In 1971, he left Princeton to become the distinguished professor of history in the field of gay and lesbian studies at Lehman College, part of the City University of New York. A year later, he came out publicly in an essay in *The New York Times.* He was the founder and first director of the Center for Lesbian and Gay Studies at CUNY. His many books include *The Uncompleted Past* (1969), *The Memory Bank* (1970), *About Time: Exploring the Gay Past* (1986), *Hidden from History: Reclaiming the Gay and Lesbian Past* (1989), *Cures: A Gay Man's Odyssey* (1991), *Stonewall* (1993), *Midlife Queer: Autobiography of a Decade, 1971–1981* (1996), *A Queer World: The Center for Lesbian and Gay Studies Reader* (1997), and *Left Out: The Politics of Exclusion* (2002).

Duberman met his partner, Eli Zal, in 1987 at an ACLU gay rights event. They married in 2016. His latest book, *Reaching Ninety* (2023), is a memoir recalling the people, events, and works of a long and extraordinarily productive life. His many honors include the Vernon Rice/Drama Desk Award, three Lambda Literary awards, a special award from the National Academy of Arts and Letters for his contributions to literature, and the 2007 Lifetime Achievement Award from the American Historical Association. He's been a Pulitzer Prize and National Book Award finalist.

Lillian Faderman (1940–)

Scholar, Historian, Author

Called the "mother of lesbian history" for her pioneering research and writings on lesbian culture, literature, and history, Lillian Faderman is a retired professor from California State University, Fresno, where she helped to establish its Department of Women's, Gender, and Sexuality Studies, one of the first of its kind in California.

Faderman was born in New York during World War II and raised by her mother and aunt, who had emigrated from a *shtetl* in Latvia to work in the garment industry. The remainder of her family died in

Europe during the Holocaust. She moved with her mother and aunt to Los Angeles as a teenager. To help pay for her education, she did nude modeling and made softcore films. Her experiences in the porn industry are described in her memoir, *Naked in the Promised Land* (2003). She stated that her sexual attraction to women first occurred in her early teens, but "I did not think of myself as homosexual until later." She discovered the underground gay bar scene in Los Angeles and eventually came out as a lesbian in 1956 at the height of the so-called Lavender Scare.

Faderman enrolled at the University of California, Berkeley, and later at the University of California, Los Angeles, paying for her education by working as a stripper. She became an English professor at California State University, Fresno, and her first published work was a college anthology of multiethnic literature, one of first anthologies of its kind. She would become one of the first academics to publish books about female same-sex relationships.

Her many books include *Surpassing the Love of Men* (1981), *Odd Girls and Twilight Lovers* (1991), *The Gay Revolution* (2015), *Harvey Milk: His Lives and Death* (2018), and *Woman: The American History of an Idea* (2022). Her works have won six Lambda Literary awards, two American Library Association awards, and listings as notable books of the year and among the best books about radical history and LGBTQ+ life.

Following her retirement in 2007, Faderman served as historian in residence for the Lambda Archives of San Diego and embarked on a project to document the queer bars and clubs that defined the Los Angeles gay scene that she experienced. "For queer people," she said, "having a history is crucial. When I came out…it was like we had invented this stuff. I had no idea that there were generations before me." Asked why it is so important for the younger generation to study gay history, she explains, "I think we need to know that we've had enemies before and that we figured out how to organize and fight. And if you fight, you can be victorious. It's vital to know that."

Few scholars and writers have done more than Faderman to ensure that the past history of gay life in America is remembered and understood, saying, "My writing has been my activism."

Anne Fausto-Sterling (1944–)

Academic, Author

A developmental biologist who is considered a leading expert on biology and gender, Anne Fausto-Sterling was a professor of biology and gender studies at Brown University, where she was a faculty member for more than four decades. Her 1985 book *Myths of Gender: Biological Theories About Women and Men* is regarded as a core text in the investigation of what makes us male or female, shifting old assumptions about how humans develop particular traits. In 1993, she challenged that accepted gender binary in the essay "The Five Sexes: Why Male and Female Are Not Enough."

Both of Fausto-Sterling's parents were writers. She received her B.A. in zoology from the University of Wisconsin in 1965 and her Ph.D. in developmental genetics from Brown University in 1970, after which she joined the Brown faculty and was appointed the Nancy Duke Lewis Professor of Biology and Gender Studies.

Fausto-Sterling has written extensively on the social construction of gender, sexual identity, gender roles, and intersexuality. Historian of science Evelynn M. Hammonds has described her as one of the most influential feminist scientists of her generation. Her first book for a general audience, *Myths of Gender* (1985), was praised by one reviewer as offering "profound challenges to scientific research, the creation of social policy, and the future of feminist and gender theory." She laid out a challenge to the conception of two sexes in the 1993 essay "The Five Sexes" that offers an alternative model of gender as five sexes: male, female, merm, ferm, and herm. She has described the essay as "intended to be provocative" but "with my tongue firmly in cheek." A second book for the general reader, *Sexing the Body: Gender Politics and the Construction of Sexuality,* appeared in 2000, urging a much wider understanding of gender and the social basis for gender identity. In a 2001 interview, she said, "When people say 'it's nurture' or 'it's nature' in making us male or female, I take the middle ground and say that it's a combination of both. That's not a popular position to take in today's environment, but it is the one that makes the most sense."

One of the key subjects of Fausto-Sterling's research and the basis of much of her gender theories is infants born with ambiguous genitalia, who were once called hermaphrodites, but she prefers the term "intersexuals." She explains, "From them, we can literally see how society's ideas about male and female are constructed. When infants with ambiguous genitalia are born, everyone—parents, doctors—are very upset, and the physicians often suggest drastic surgeries to assign a specific gender to the child.... In the end, the doctors take a body that was clearly neither male or female and turn it into one they can represent to the world as 'male' or 'female.'" She has advocated that sexual-assignment surgeries on infants should be halted: "People deserve to have a choice about something as important as that. Infants can't make choices. And the doctors often guess wrong."

Fausto-Sterling published a third book for the general reader, *Sex/Gender: Biology in a Social World* (2012), that attempts to show the interaction between biology and socialization in gender determination and identity. She married Paula Vogel, Yale professor and Pulitzer-winning playwright, in 2004 and retired from Brown University in 2014 after 44 years on the faculty.

Aaron Fricke (1962–)

Gay Activist, Author

Aaron Fricke is best known for the legal case *Fricke v. Lynch,* in which gay teens won the First Amendment right to attend their proms with the dates of their choice. In 1980, while attending Cumberland High School in Cumberland, Rhode Island, he came out as gay and began dating a fellow male student.

When the school refused to allow the two to attend prom together for fear that student reaction would disrupt the dance and might result in physical harm to those attending, Fricke, represented by John Ward of Gay & Lesbian Advocates & Defenders (GLAD), filed suit in the District Court of Rhode Island. He stated, "I feel I have the right to attend. I feel I want to go to the prom for the same reason any other student would want to go."

Aaron Fricke v. Richard B. Lynch would become a milestone in protecting the rights of LGBTQ+ students. GLAD founder and co-counsel John Ward argued that in not allowing Fricke to bring a male date to his prom, Cumberland High School violated his First Amendment rights of association and free speech and his 14th Amendment right to equal protection under the law. The court issued an injunction in his favor just in time for him to attend the dance with his date. The case gained significant national recognition and ended up encouraging schools around the country to change their policy and make it possible for LGBTQ+ students to attend their proms with the date of their choice, same-sex or otherwise.

Fricke continued his activism on behalf of LGBTQ+ rights and published two books, *Reflections of a Rock Lobster: A Story about Growing Up Gay* and *Sudden Strangers: The Story of a Gay Son and His Father.*

Marilyn Frye (1941–)

Philosopher, Educator

A radical feminist theorist, Marilyn Frye has written widely on gay and lesbian marginalization, oppression, and justice issues surrounding women and gay people. She taught at Michigan State University for many years. Her book *The Politics of Reality: Essays in Feminist Theory* (1983) is regarded as a classic of feminist philosophy.

Born in Tulsa, Oklahoma, Frye earned her bachelor's degree in philosophy from Stanford University and her doctorate in philosophy from Cornell University in 1969. She taught at the University of Pittsburgh, the University of Michigan, and the University of Washington before joining the faculty at Michigan State University. In 2001, she was awarded the Distinguished Woman Philosopher Award by the Society for Women in Philosophy.

Frye is the author of two influential books of essays on feminist theory: *The Politics of Reality* (1983) and *Willful Virgin: Essays in Feminism* (1992). The first book includes her most reprinted essay, "Oppression," which explores how women can be said to be oppressed. She described two characteristics of women's oppression: by holding positions that make them responsible yet powerless to effect decisions and by internalizing and self-policing their limitations and restrictions. In this and other writings, she further illuminates the oppression of sexual minorities by heterosexuals and the oppression of minority races, connecting these to the project of feminism. In *Willful Virgin*, she explored heterosexism as manifested in feminism and society at large and the myriad ways in which heterosexuality is taken to be normative. In the essay "Willful Virgin, or Do You Have to Be a Lesbian to Be a Feminist," she argues, "The central constitutive dynamic and key mechanism of the global phenomenon of male domination, oppression, and exploitation of females is near-universal female heterosexuality." She concludes that sexism exists because most women willingly tolerate being subordinate to and serving men.

Frye, who is openly lesbian, has achieved distinction in the field of philosophy, which she was discouraged to enter. As a woman colleague expressed it, "If you were a woman and a philosopher, you were just a living, breathing contradiction." She took this as a challenge while devoting her philosophical work to the questions of gender roles, identity, and justice. Asked to advise other women who might want to follow her into philosophy, she urges, "Do it feminist. Bring your life into it. Turn out philosophy that comes out of women's lives. Philosophy comes out of lives.... Some people are going to head off into 'What is it?' and 'How does it work?' Other people are going to head off into 'What does it mean?' That's me."

David M. Halperin (1952–)

Educator, Author

A prominent theorist in the fields of gender studies, queer theory, and critical theory, David M. Halperin is known for his combination of classics and the history of homosexuality in his studies of contemporary sexuality, social theory, and material and visual culture. The author of many important works, including *One Hundred Years of Homosexuality* (1990) and *How to Be Gay* (2012), he was the cofounding editor of *GLQ: A Journal of Lesbian and Gay Studies* from 1991 to 2006.

Born in Chicago, Halperin graduated from Oberlin College in 1973 and earned a Ph.D. in classics and humanities from Stanford University in 1980. He was a professor of literature at the Massachusetts Institute of Technology from 1979 to 1996 and a lecturer in sociology at the University of New South Wales from 1996 to 1999, where he remained an honorary professor until 2006.

He is currently the W. H. Auden Collegiate Professor of the History and Theory of Sexuality at the University of Michigan, where he is also a professor of English, women's studies, comparative literature, and classical studies.

In 1990, Halperin published *Before Sexuality: The Construction of Erotic Experience in the Ancient Greek World* and *One Hundred Years of Homosexuality: and Other Essays,* the title of which refers to the centenary of Charles Gilbert Chaddock's 1892 translation of Krafft-Ebing's *Psychopathia Sexualis.* Chaddock is credited with the first use of the term "homosexual" in English in this translation, which Halperin contends marks an important change in the understanding of homosexuality. His other books include *Saint Foucault: Towards a Gay Hagiography* (1995), *How to Do the History of Homosexuality* (2002), *What Do Gay Men Want? (2007), How to Be Gay* (2012), and *The War on Sex* (2017).

Halperin, who is openly gay, opposed the presence of the ROTC on the MIT campus on the grounds that it discriminated against gay and lesbian students. His protest prompted death threats. In 2003, the American Family Association of Michigan tried unsuccessfully to ban his course "How to Be Gay: Male Homosexuality and Initiation."

Emery Hetrick (1931–1987) and A. Damien Martin (1933–1991)

Educators

In 1979, Emery Sylvester Hetrick and his companion, A. Damien Martin, founded the Institute for the Protection of Lesbian and Gay Youth, an advocacy agency devoted to serving the needs of lesbian, gay, bisexual, and transgender youth between the ages of 13 and 24 and their families. It was renamed the Hetrick-Martin Institute (HMI) in honor of the founders. In 1985, HMI established the Harvey Milk High School, the first high school in the United States specifically catered toward LGBTQ+ students.

Hetrick was born in Columbus, Ohio. He was a 1953 graduate of Ohio State University and graduated in 1957 from Cornell University Medical School. He was an attending psychiatrist and supervisor at the Harlem Hospital Center and associate medical director of the Roerig division of Pfizer, Inc., a New York drug company, from 1979 until his resignation for health reasons in 1986. Martin, a Philadelphia native, was a psychiatrist who taught speech pathology at New York University's School of Education. Hetrick and Martin became life partners after meeting in 1975. Their life together was featured in a 1984 *New York Times* feature in the Style section on gay couples in committed relationships.

In 1979, after hearing about a 15-year-old boy who had been beaten and thrown out of an emergency shelter because he was gay, Hetrick and Martin founded the nonprofit organization that would become the Hetrick-Martin Institute. As Martin later stated, "Blacks, Jews, and Hispanics are not thrown out of their families or religion at adolescence…. Gay and lesbian kids are." After four years of lobbying and fundraising, the institute opened in 1983 as a drop-in center and developed counseling programs for at-risk LGBTQ+ youth in New York City.

In 1985, the Institute established the Harvey Milk High School in cooperation with the New York City Department of Education. Named for the slain gay San Francisco city councilman, the school provides an alternative public education for LGBTQ+ youth. It is the largest school of its kind in the world. Programs include job training, HIV education, and internships. Martin said that the school was founded "for gay youths, partly because violence inflicted on young homosexuals made it impossible for some to stay in other schools."

Both men died of AIDS-related complications. Before his death, Martin reflected on the significance of the Institute and its importance: "I think that the institute is probably one of the most, if not the most, radical thing that the movement has done. Because we took what was the most effective political charge against us, the biggest hate campaign, that we're a danger to children and to families, and we've, as you said, turned it around. I mean, what we said was, 'No, that's not true. What you people are doing is a danger to children and to our children in particular.'"

Loraine Hutchins (1948–)

Educator, Bisexual Activist

A founder and leader of the bisexual rights and liberation movement, Loraine Hutchins was the editor of *Bi Any Other Name: Bisexual People Speak Out*, an important early anthology that proved to be a catalyst of the bi movement.

Hutchins was born in Washington, D.C. She graduated with a degree in English and American literature in 1970 from Shimer College in Mount Carroll, Illinois. Growing up during the activism of the 1960s and 1970s, she realized that she was bisexual and found herself unwelcome in both the gay rights and women's movements, which she passionately embraced. She set out to create the first-ever safe space in both movements for bisexual folks. She cofounded BiNet USA in order to spread bisexual awareness, share resources, and build a community; served on BiNet's board of directors; and spearheaded the foundation of a direct-action group called the Alliance of Multi-Cultural Bisexuals (AMBi). In 1991, she coedited (with Lani Ka'ahumanu) *Bi Any Other Name: Bisexual People Speak Out*. In 2011, she coedited (with H. Sharif Williams) her second anthology: *Sexuality, Religion and the Sacred: Bisexual, Pansexual and Polysexual Perspectives*.

In 1993, Hutchins led BiNet's media campaign for the March on Washington for Lesbian, Gay, and Bi Equal Rights and Liberation, and in 1998, she became the first bisexual grand marshal for the Capital Pride Parade, literally leading the charge for equality and bi-visibility.

Some 30 years after receiving her B.A., Hutchins earned her Ph.D. in cultural studies from Union Institute and University in Cincinnati with a dissertation, "Erotic Rites," which explored the relationship between sexuality and spirituality.

As a teacher, speaker, and writer, Hutchins has devoted her career to bisexual activism and, perhaps more than anyone else, deserves the credit for the "B" in LGBTQ+. She still has much to do: "Bottom line, the bi movement has a long way to go in that we are still fighting erasure and exclusion. You wouldn't know we are the most populous of the LGB cohort, would you, but that is what current research shows. It's even a higher percentage of B's in the younger and more of color sub-sets. Yet most of the media attention and fundraising support still goes to the G's, and the L's. Doesn't make any sense, does it? Well, but it does, because of how invisible we still are. And trivialized, when we are recognized."

Karla Jay (1947–)

Educator, Author

An early member of New York's Gay Liberation Front and its first woman member, Karla Jay taught English, women's studies, and LGBTQ+ studies courses at Pace University for 39 years. As an activist, she participated in many of the important early protests of the gay and lesbian movements. Her many publications include *Out of the Closets: Voices of Gay Liberation* (1972), *Lavender Culture* (1979), *Lesbian Texts and Contexts* (1990), *Dyke Life: From Growing Up to Growing Old, A Celebration of the Lesbian Experience* (1995), and *Tales of the Lavender Menace: A Memoir of Liberation* (1999).

A Brooklyn, New York, native, Jay was

the caregiver from a young age of her mother, who suffered from mental illness. She earned a B.A. in French from Barnard in 1968 and a doctorate in comparative literature from New York University. In 1969, she became a member of the Redstockings, a radical feminist group dedicated to advancing the women's liberation agenda. She had been aware of her lesbianism since high school and came out to her Redstockings colleagues. In the aftermath of Stonewall, she became a member of the Gay Liberation Front and participated in several actions, including the Gay-In in Los Angeles in 1970, the sit-in at *Ladies Home Journal*, and the Wall Street "Ogle-In," in which a large group of feminists sexually harassed male Wall Streeters on their way to work with catcalls and crude remarks. She became a member of the Lavender Menace, a group formed to protest the exclusion of lesbians from women's liberation groups, and participated in the "Lavender Menace Zap" at the Second Congress to Unite Women in New York City, which is widely regarded as being a turning point in the history of second-wave feminism.

Having coedited (with Allen Young) *Out of the Closets: Voices of Gay Liberation* in 1972, a pioneering anthology, Jay realized that she needed to be open about her sexuality as she began her teaching career at Pace University. She faced opposition and a lack of support from other gay academics, who devoted their mentoring to other men, not to lesbians. She persisted with a steady stream of work detailing the challenges faced by gays and lesbians, including *After You're Out: Personal Experiences of Gay Men and Lesbian Women* (1975) (also with Allen Young) and *The Gay Report: Lesbians and Gay Men Speak Out about Sexual Experiences and Lifestyles* (1979).

Jay taught for nearly 40 years until her retirement as professor emerita of English and women's and gender studies. She lives with her spouse, Karen F. Kerner, a retired physician, on the Upper West Side of Manhattan. Asked in 2017 to provide advice for young LGBTQ+ activists, she said, "College students don't realize that when they get out of college, they're going to be discriminated against. Not everybody is going to think [being gay] is really cool. And I think that they have to keep fighting for women's rights, for the rights of minorities, for the rights of LGBTQ people, for all of these groups. Then they have to turn around and help other people. They have got to continue fighting for basic human rights for everybody."

Kevin Jennings (1963–)

Educator, Administrator, Author

In 1988, while a history teacher at Concord Academy in Massachusetts, Kevin Brett Jennings, who had just come out as gay, established the first Gay–Straight Alliance (GSA) in order to address the conditions for gay students at the school. Other GSA groups were subsequently founded in middle schools, high schools, colleges, and universities across the United States. He would go on to cofound the Gay, Lesbian & Straight Education Network (GLSEN) in Boston in 1990. He served as an assistant deputy secretary of education in the Obama administration, followed by directing the Arcus Foundation, the world's largest foundation of LGBTQ+ rights organizations, and was the CEO of Lambda Legal.

Jennings was born in Fort Lauderdale, Florida, the son of an itinerant Southern Baptist preacher. He grew up in the rural South and was bullied and beaten up by classmates for what they considered to be effeminate behavior. He attempted suicide after realizing he was gay. Moving to Hawaii, he completed high school in Honolulu and entered Harvard University, earning a B.A. in history in 1985. He became a high school history teacher first at Moses Brown School in Providence, Rhode Island

(1985–1987) and then at Concord Academy, Concord, Massachusetts (1987–1995).

While at Concord Academy, Jennings started the nation's first GSA with a female student and helped to spread the Alliance's mission through the Gay and Lesbian Independent School Teacher Network. In 1992, he was appointed cochair of the Education Committee of the Governor's Commission on Gay and Lesbian Youth in Massachusetts. He was the principal author of "Making Schools Safe for Gay & Lesbian Youth," a commission report that led to Massachusetts becoming the first state in the United States to outlaw the discrimination of public school students on the basis of sexual orientation in 1993.

Besides Jennings's career in government service and being active in multiple foundations, he is the author or editor of several books, including *Becoming Visible: A Reader in Gay & Lesbian History for High School & College Students* (1994), *Telling Tales Out of School: Gays, Lesbians, and Bisexuals Revisit Their School Days* (1998), and *Mama's Boy, Preacher's Son* (2006), a memoir of growing up as a closeted gay student.

Jonathan Ned Katz (1938–)

Scholar, Author

A historian of human sexuality, Jonathan Ned Katz is the author of many works that helped create the field of LGBTQ+ history. He is the founder of *OutHistory.org*, a major website on LGBTQ+ history. He is one of the great exceptions in scholarship as a pioneering historian who lacks any kind of college degree.

Katz grew up in Greenwich Village in New York City and graduated from New York's High School of Music & Art, concentrating in art. He went on to study at several colleges, including Antioch, City College, and Hunter College, but never completed a degree. The Stonewall Uprising became a catalyst for his activism and research, joining the Gay Activists Alliance (GAA), a community offering, in his words, "a hope that we could change things and make things better—more just—for gay people and lesbians." The GAA in 1972 produced his documentary play, *Coming Out!*, and it caused him to come out to his mother when she saw an advertisement for the play in *The Village Voice* with his name as the author. "So that was a big coming out," he later recalled, "and after a few years, my mother got used to the idea, and by 1975, she was helping me edit this first book on LGBTQ U.S. history that I wrote, called *Gay American History: Lesbians and Gay Men in the USA.*"

He would produce the first comprehensive history of the gay community in the United States, which is now considered a foundational text in LGBTQ+ historical studies. Preferring to call himself a detective rather than a historian, his work explores the social organization of human sexual activity, relationships, and identities historically and culturally. His other books include *Gay/Lesbian Almanac* (1983), *The Invention of Heterosexuality* (1995), *Love Stories: Sex Between Men Before Homosexuality* (2001), and *The Daring Life and Dangerous Times of Eve Adams* (2021).

Katz regards his research as activism: "It gives us back to ourselves. The more I know about queer history, the more fascinating and complex it becomes." In 2012, he was honored by SAGE (Services & Advocacy for LGBT Elders) for being a veteran activist and a champion of change. Asked how he has managed to remain so prolific in his 80s, he says, "I've been lucky. Some people are only recognized after their death. In my 60s, I came out as 'old' and started talking publicly about being old and gay. I want to reclaim the word old as positive, the way we reclaimed the word queer."

Suzanne Kessler (1946–)

Academic, Social Psychologist

Suzanne Kessler, who taught psychology at the State University of New York, Purchase, pioneered the application of ethnomethodology to the study of gender and sex in *Gender: An Ethnomethodological Approach* (1978) (coauthored with her faculty colleague, Wendy McKenna). Kessler and McKenna were two of the first people to argue that the distinction between gender and sex is a socially constructed one. Their work would become part of the foundational principles for gender theorists such as Judith Butler, Anne Fausto-Sterling, and Kate Bornstein. Her other important book is *Lessons from the Intersexed* (1998).

Born in Pittsburgh, Pennsylvania, Kessler received her Ph.D. in social psychology from the City University of New York Graduate Center in 1972 after receiving a B.A. from Carnegie Mellon University in 1968. She taught psychology at the State University of New York, Purchase, for three decades and became the dean of the School of Natural and Social Sciences and then the dean of the School of Liberal Arts and Sciences and vice provost for academic affairs.

Kessler, with her colleague, Wendy McKenna, in *Gender: An Ethnomethodological Approach* (1978), applied the concept of ethnomethodology, the study of how social order is produced in and through processes of social interaction, to an understanding of gender. They would pioneer the theory that became known as the social construction of gender that determination by biological markers alone is too restrictive. Their pioneering work would open up the field of gender study, which would be further developed by scholars such as Judith Butler, Kate Bornstein, Candace West, and Anne Fausto-Sterling.

Lessons from the Intersexed (1998) details the medical treatment of intersex children, those born with ambiguous genitalia, and the dubious system of determining gender based on "acceptable infant penis and clitoris sizes." Again, Kessler demonstrates how biological determinations of gender conflict with social attitudes.

In 2000, most of the journal *Feminism & Psychology* was devoted to the importance of Kessler and McKenna's work. Gender theorist Mary Crawford wrote that "they not only made the claim that sex is a belief system rather than a fact, but went on to analyze the interpretive practices that enable each of us to create the 'fact' of two and only two sexes.

The continuing importance of Kessler and McKenna's work is twofold: First, it provides compelling, lived examples of the social construction of gender in interaction. The second reason is: the current multiplicity of theoretical positions on gender mutability, coupled with the increased visibility of transgendered and intersex people."

Alain LeRoy Locke (1885–1954)

Educator, Philosopher, Cultural Critic

As the first African American Rhodes Scholar in 1907, Alain LeRoy Locke has been described as the "dean and father of the Harlem Renaissance" and as the leader and chief interpreter of the most influential movement in African American literary and cultural history. He contributed five seminal essays to the landmark *The New Negro* (1925), which has been called the "first national book" of African American history.

Born in Philadelphia, Locke graduated with a B.A. in philosophy from Harvard in 1907. As the first Black Rhodes Scholar, he studied at Oxford (1907–1910) and the University of Berlin (1910–1911), receiving his Ph.D. in philosophy from Harvard in

1918. For almost 40 years until his retirement in 1953, he, as head of the Department of Philosophy, taught at Howard University in Washington, D.C.

Throughout his teaching and writing career, Locke was a tireless promoter of African American culture and the arts. He urged Black painters, sculptors, and musicians to look to African sources for identity and discover materials and techniques for their work. He encouraged Black authors to reflect the African American experience. He helped to introduce to the wider American audience the achievements of the Harlem Renaissance in *The New Negro*, an anthology of fiction, poetry, drama, and essays. His many books included *Four Negro Poets* (1927), *Frederick Douglass, a Biography of Anti-Slavery* (1935), *Negro Art—Past and Present* (1936), and *The Negro and His Music* (1936).

Locke would define his aesthetic philosophy as "cultural pluralism," emphasizing the necessity of the individual to determine values of conduct and interrelationships. He was a closeted homosexual based on the discriminatory laws against homosexuality at the time.

It is believed that he encouraged and supported other gay African Americans who were part of the Harlem Renaissance, most notably Countee Cullen and Zora Neale Hurston. Although describing his life as a gay man as "paralyzingly discreet," he did not question the legitimacy or rightness of his gayness nor did he disguise his identity by attempting to pass himself off as heterosexual, as many at the time did. His sexual identity was well known to his close associates, and he described his situation as "vulnerable/invulnerability," signifying both risk and endurance.

He retired to New York City in 1953, where he was looked after during his final illness by his friend and protégée, English professor and civil rights activist Margaret Butcher.

A. Damien Martin

See Emery Hetrick and A. Damien Martin

José Esteban Muñoz (1967–2013)

Educator, Author

A Cuban American academic in the fields of performance studies, queer theory, and cultural studies, José Esteban Muñoz's first book, *Disidentifications: Queers of Color and the Performance of Politics* (1999), examines queer people of color from the perspective of performance studies. He was a professor in and former chair of the Department of Performance Studies at New York University's Tisch School of the Arts.

Born in Havana, Cuba, Muñoz relocated with his parents to Hialeah, Florida, when he was an infant. He earned his B.A. in comparative literature from Sarah Lawrence College in 1989. In 1994, he earned his doctorate from Duke University, working with queer theorist Eve Kosofsky Sedgwick, and was influenced by the works of Chicana feminists such as Gloria Anzaldúa and Cherrie Moraga.

Muñoz's scholarship attempted to redress the absence in queer theory that overlooked the role of race and ethnicity and ignored the unique perspective of queers of color. He focused on queers of color, who were often ignored by academia, drawing on his own adolescent experiences as a punk queer in a community of Cuban American exiles. His most influential writing on the subject was *Disidentifications: Queers of Color and the Performance of Politics* (1999), a work that revolutionized the discussion of how queer artists of color employ and manipulate their hybrid identities. Published a decade later, *Cruis-*

ing Utopia: The Then and There of Queer Futurity (2009) details essential survival strategies for the queer community and the utopian potential of queer aesthetics and performance.

Muñoz died while working on his third book, *The Sense of Brown: Ethnicity, Affect and Performance* (published in 2020), at the age of 46. As social theorist John Andrews observes, "José's serious engagement with artists' lives, practice, and work has changed how many academics conceive the practice of theorizing. His work as a theorist countered the more rarefied modes of how academics and art critics use and produce theory."

Janice G. Raymond (1943–)

Academic, Author

A former nun and radical feminist who became open about her lesbianism, Janice G. Raymond was a professor of women's studies at the University of Massachusetts, Amherst. She wrote extensively against violence, sexual exploitation, and "medical abuse" of women. Her most controversial work was *The Transsexual Empire* (1979), the first feminist critique of transsexualism. In it, she argues that the notion of transgender identity is based on the "patriarchal myths" of "male mothering" and the "making of woman according to man's image." For her views, she has been criticized by many in the LGBTQ+ and feminist communities as being transphobic, accused of trafficking in hate speech against transsexual men and women, and labeled the "original TERF" (trans-exclusionary radical feminist).

After graduating from Salve Regina College in Rhode Island with a B.A. in English literature in 1965, Raymond received a master's degree in religious studies from Andover Newton Theological School in 1971 and was a member of the Sisters of Mercy congregation. She left the convent as an outspoken lesbian and feminist and gained a Ph.D. in ethics and society from Boston College in 1977. She became a faculty member at the University of Massachusetts, Amherst, from 1978 until her retirement in 2002.

Derived from Raymond's dissertation, *The Transsexual Empire: The Making of the She-Male* (1979) investigates the role of transgender people in society. In it, she argues that transgender identities are based on traditional gender stereotypes in order "to colonize feminist identification, culture, politics, and sexuality" and that "all transsexuals rape women's bodies by reducing the real female to an artifact, appropriating this body for themselves.... Transsexuals merely cut off the most obvious means of invading women, so that they seem non-invasive." The book was well received in the mainstream media, with psychiatrist Thomas Szasz commenting that it "has rightly seized on transsexualism as an emblem of modern society's unremitting—though increasingly concealed—antifeminism." In 1980, lesbian trans feminist Carol Riddell wrote the first feminist critique of the book, stating that the book is "dangerous to transsexuals because it does not treat us as human beings at all, merely as the tools of a theory" and that *The Transsexual Empire*, if it did not invent anti-transsexual prejudice, "did more to justify and perpetuate it than perhaps any other book ever written."

Raymond was unrepentant in her position. She would follow it up with other important feminist works such as *Women as Wombs: Reproductive Technologies and the Battle Over Women's Freedom* (1993), *A Passion for Friends: Toward a Philosophy of Female Affection* (1996), and *Doublethink: A Feminist Challenge to Transgenderism* (2021). In *Doublethink*, she takes on the "doublethink" of the transgender movement that "defines men as women, women as men, he as she, dissent as heresy, science as sham, and critics as fascists." In a positive review by critic Claire Heuchan in *Lesbian and Gay News*, she is praised for "a directness that is characteristic of her work" in which she "cuts through the culture of fear and intellectual dishonesty that defines many discussions around gender identity." Heuchan's words can serve to summarize Raymond's decades of research and advocacy, which challenge and provoke accepted assumptions about gender identity and its conflicts.

Gayle S. Rubin (1949–)

Educator, Activist

Cultural anthropologist and theorist Gayle S. Rubin is the author of a pioneering work in feminist theory and queer studies. Her 1984 essay "Thinking Sex" is widely regarded as a founding text of gay and lesbian studies and queer theory. She has been branded by conservative cultural critic David Horowitz as one of the "101 most dangerous academics in America."

Rubin was raised in a middle-class, Jewish home in South Carolina, attending segregated public schools. Her experience gave her "an abiding hatred of racism in all its forms." Attending the University of Michigan in 1968, she wrote on feminist topics for the campus newspaper. In 1970, she helped found the Radicalesbians, an early lesbian feminist group. In 1975, she gained prominence in the essay "The Traffic in Women: Notes on the 'Political Economy' of Sex," which defined a "sex/gender system" by which "a society transforms biological sexuality into products of human activity and in which these transformed sexual needs are satisfied."

In 1978, Rubin moved to San Francisco for doctoral research in anthropology on the gay male leather subculture. She would eventually complete her Ph.D. in anthropology at the University of Michigan with the dissertation "The Valley of Kings: Leathermen in San Francisco, 1960–1990." In 1984 in "Thinking Sex," she examined the value system that social groups attribute to sexuality, defining some behaviors as good and natural and others (such as homosexuality or BDSM) as bad and unnatural. The social coding of sexuality that she articulates would become a core concept in gay and lesbian studies, sexuality studies, and queer theory.

At the trial of David DePape, who was accused of attacking and severely injuring Paul Pelosi, the husband of then Speaker of the House Nancy Pelosi, it was revealed that the 2022 attack was intended to be a kidnapping in an effort to get to Rubin, who was "Target 1" on a list that included such high-profile individuals as Tom Hanks, Adam Schiff, and Bernie Sanders. DePape accused her of being a "pedo activist" who was working to turn schools into "pedo factories."

A professor of anthropology and women's studies at the University of Michigan, Rubin is the author of *Deviations: A Gayle Rubin Reader* (2012), which is regarded to be the definitive collection of her writings. Judith Butler said of her work, "It is rare to find an intellectual who founded an entire field of sexuality studies, whose theoretical contributions have been so far-reaching, and who continues to make rich, surprising, and singular inventions."

Edward Sagarin (1913–1986)

Academic, Author

Writing under the pen name Donald Webster Cory, Edward Sagarin published the pioneering book *The Homosexual in America: A Subjective Approach,* which has been called one of the most influential works in the history of the gay rights movement and earned him the honorific of "father of the homophile movement" for asserting that gay men and lesbians deserved civil rights as members of an unrecognized or condemned minority. However, a decade and a half after his pathbreaking 1951 book, Sagarin, as a tenured sociologist at New York's John Jay College of Criminal Justice, began to insist on pathologizing homosexuality, earning himself, as a conspicuous critic of the gay liberation movement of the 1970s that he, as Donald Webster Cory, helped to inspire, yet another honorific as the "Dr. Jekyll–Mr. Hyde of the American homophile movement."

Sagarin was born in Schenectady, New York, to Russian-immigrant, Jewish parents. His mother died when he was 5 years old, and when his father remarried, the family relocated to New York City. From birth, he suffered from scoliosis, a curvature of the spine, which produced a noticeable hump on his back. A sensitivity to his own physical difference and its trauma may explain why he developed an academic interest in social deviants of all kinds from homosexuals to dwarfs and schizophrenics. After graduating from high school, he traveled to France, where he met André Gide, and despite his sexual attraction to men, in 1936, he married Gertrude Liphshitz, with whom he had a son. He established himself in the perfume and cosmetics business, publishing *The Science and Art of Perfumery* in 1945.

In 1951, under the name Donald Webster Cory, Sagarin wrote *The Homosexual in America: A Subjective Approach*, the first widely read nonfiction book in the United States to present a knowledgeable and sympathetic account of the plight of homosexuals. His book contrasted with Alfred Kinsey's report in *Sexual Behavior in the Human Male* (1948) in its personal and anecdotal approach documenting what it was like to be a homosexual in 1950s America and argued forcefully for the civil rights of homosexuals. "We are a minority," he declared, "not only numerically, but also as a result of a caste-like system in society … our minority status is similar, in a variety of respects, to that of national, religious, and other ethnic groups; in the denial of civil liberties; in the legal, extra-legal and quasi-legal discrimination; in the assignment of an inferior social position; in the exclusion from the mainstreams of life and culture.… On the other hand, one great gap separates the homosexual minority from all others, and that is its lack of recognition, its lack of respectability in the eyes of the public, and even in the most advanced circles."

The Homosexual in America was reprinted several times in the 1950s, and it was particularly popular among members of the budding homophile movement of the day, immediately making Cory a hero in homophile circles.

Sagarin lost his job when his employer somehow found out that he was Donald Webster Cory, but he persisted, publishing other books using his pseudonym, including *Twenty-One Variations on a Theme* (1953), a pioneering anthology of short stories dealing with homosexuality by various authors. He joined the editorial board of *ONE Magazine*, published by the Mattachine Society, and regularly contributed articles.

In 1958, Sagarin returned to college, entering an accelerated program at Brooklyn College, and completed his B.A. in the same class as his son. He went on to earn a Ph.D. in sociology from New York University in 1966, completing a dissertation called "Structure and Ideology in an Association of Deviants," which was a study of the Mattachine Society. He began his academic career at Baruch College of the City University of New York, rising in the ranks and prominence as a specialist in deviancy.

During the 1960s, he opposed the radicalism of the new generation of gay activists, such as Frank Kameny, and their rejection of the "sickness theory" of homosexuality. In *The Homosexual and His Society* (1963) (coauthored with John LeRoy), he claimed that there was no such thing as a "well-adjusted homosexual." In the 1970s, he would become a conspicuous critic of the gay liberation movement (despite his own pursuit of an active homosexual sex life). He argued that although homosexuality should be decriminalized and injustices to homosexuals redressed, homosexuality was a pathology, and he urged homosexuals to seek therapy and attempt to become heterosexual. In 1974 at a sociological society convention, he was "outed" by a colleague as Donald Webster Cory. He subsequently withdrew from the public debate over homosexuality.

At the time of his death, he was serving as dean of the graduate school of John Jay College of Criminal Justice in New York City.

Eve Kosofsky Sedgwick (1950–2009)

Scholar, Literary and Social Theorist

Eve Kosofsky Sedgwick was an influential literary and social critic who focused on sexual identity and was one of the originators of queer theory in foundational works such as *Between Men: English Literature and Male Homosocial Desire* and *The Epistemology of the Closet.* A professor at Hamilton College, Boston University, Amherst College, Duke University, and the Graduate Center of the City University of New York, she was renowned for using literary criticism to question dominant discourses of sexuality, race, gender, and the boundaries of literary criticism.

Born in Dayton, Ohio, Sedgwick grew up in Bethesda, Maryland. It was at Cornell University, where she earned a bachelor's degree in English in 1971, that she met and married her life partner, Hal Sedgwick, who became a professor of visual perception at New York's State College of Optometry. She went on to earn a master's degree and a doctorate in English at Yale University, beginning her teaching career first at Hamilton College, then Boston University, then Amherst, during which she began to explore the hidden sociosexual subplots in writers like Charles Dickens and Henry James.

In 1989 at the annual meeting of the Modern Language Association, she delivered a paper, "Jane Austen and the Masturbating Girl," that argued that the restless Marianne Dashwood in Austen's *Sense and Sensibility* should be understood in relation to contemporary thoughts on the evils of "self-abuse." Teasing out disguised subtexts, especially the repressed themes of same-sex love, making readers more alert to the "potential queer nuances of literature," she became a provocative and notorious force among theorists who would develop the key concepts of queer theory. Despite the boldness of her views, *Rolling Stone* dubbed her "the soft-spoken queen of the constructionists." She would describe the function of queer theory by saying, "It's about trying to understand different kinds of sexual desire and how the culture defines them. It's about how you can't understand relations between men and women unless you understand the relationship between people of the same gender, including the possibility of a sexual relationship between them."

Sedgwick would publish several foundational books in the field of queer theory, including *Between Men: English Literature and Male Homosocial Desire* (1985), *The Epistemology of the Closet* (1990), and *Tendencies* (1993). In 1991, after being diagnosed with breast cancer, she wrote *A Dialogue on Love,* chronicling her treatment, her feelings on death, and her gender uncertainty before her mastectomy and chemotherapy. Her last published work of literary and social criticism, *Touching Feeling: Affect, Pedagogy, Performativity* (2003), attempted to link queer theory to the emotions.

Sedgwick's life and work were sources of confusion for many because she was a leading queer theorist who was heterosexual and never publicly identified as anything but straight. It was the very narrow conception of both gender and sexuality that she contended with throughout her distinguished academic career.

Her colleague, Cathy Davidson, recalled that she "was praised, but she was also criticized from every side—feminists who didn't know why she was talking about men, gay men who didn't like her feminism, lesbians who scorned her for being married. It's easy to lionize and forget what courage goes into that kind of lionization. That what made her brave and prolific and wonderful and a Buddhist and inspiring and a teacher."

Lucy Diggs Slowe (1865–1937)

Educator, Athlete

The first African American woman to serve as dean of women at an American university, Lucy Diggs Slowe was also the one of the original founders of Alpha Kappa Alpha, the first sorority founded by African American women. She was also a tennis champion, becoming the first African American woman to win a national championship in any sport.

Slowe was born in Berryville, Virginia, and, after her parents' early death, was raised by her aunt in Lexington, Virginia, before moving to Baltimore when she was 13. She attended the Baltimore Colored School and became the first person from her school to attend Howard University, the top historically Black college in the United States. After graduation in 1908, she returned to Baltimore to teach high school and earned her M.A. from Columbia in 1915. She next went to Washington, D.C., to teach and, in 1919, created the first junior high school in the District of Columbia, becoming its principal, a position she held until 1922. While teaching at one of three D.C. high schools and serving as the dean of girls, in 1917, she won the first women's title at the American Tennis Association's national tournament.

In 1912, Slowe met Mary Burrill (1881–1946), an educator, playwright, and poet. They hid their romantic relationship from all but their closest friends and lived together for more than two decades in a house in northeast Washington that, in a 2019 application for National Historic Landmark status, described the residents as "the best-known example of a same-sex couple in Washington."

In 1922, Howard University appointed Slowe as their first dean of women, and she would serve as a college administrator at Howard for the next 15 years until her death in 1937. She also helped organize and served as the first president of the National Association of College Women, an organization dedicated to advancing women in higher education. She argued, "If a college accepts women students and employs women faculty, it should give them the same status as it gives male students and teachers, respectively." So respected was her work on behalf of raising the status and standards for women in higher education that in 1931, she was invited to address the predominantly white National Association of Women Deans, becoming the first African American to do so.

Slowe has rightly been described a woman of many firsts and a pioneering educator committed to women's and civil rights. The Slowe-Burrill House, which she shared with her partner and where she hosted innumerable salons and intellectual gatherings, was designated a National Historic Landmark in 2020.

Barbara Smith (1946–)

Scholar, Author, Activist

The first scholar to coin the term "identity politics" to describe the intersecting modes of identity that create unique forms of oppression for women of color, especially Black lesbian women, Barbara Smith is an authority on Black feminism in the United States. She was among the first to define an African American women's literary tradition and to build Black women's studies and Black feminism in the United States.

Smith was born in Cleveland, Ohio, and, along with her twin sister, Beverly, was raised by her grandmother while their mother worked as a nurse's aide and store clerk before her death when the girls were 9. Attending public schools, she gained entrance to Mount Holyoke College in 1965 and, after a year at the New School for Social Research in New York City, graduated from Mount Holyoke in 1969. She went on to earn an M.A. in literature at the University of Pittsburgh in 1971 and completed all but her dissertation for her doctoral studies at the University of Connecticut by 1981. During her graduate school days, she was active in the women's movement and the gay liberation movement, becoming a well-known activist for Black, feminist, and LGBTQ+ issues.

Smith was a cofounder of the Combahee River Collective in 1975. Named after a successful military operation that Harriet Tubman led during the Civil War at a river in South Carolina, the CRC was a Black, feminist, lesbian, socialist organization that argued that neither the white feminist movement nor the civil rights movement was addressing the needs of Black women and, more specifically, Black lesbians. The organization is best known for its Combahee River Collective Statement (1977), coauthored by Smith, her sister, and Demita Frazier, as one of the earliest explorations of the intersection of multiple oppressions, including racism and heterosexism, critiquing both sexual oppression in the Black community and racism within the wider feminist movement.

The first known written appearance of the term "identity politics" appeared in the Statement, and the coinage has been credited to Smith. The Collective disbanded in 1980, and Smith, realizing that very few publishing opportunities existed for female scholars of color, established Kitchen Table: Women of Color Press, the first U.S. publisher for women of color to reach a wide national audience, and broke new literary ground by integrating Black, lesbian voices with those of other Black women.

Smith has been a visiting professor, writer in residence, and lecturer at numerous universities and research institutions, including the Schomburg Center for Research in Black Culture (1995–1996). She entered politics and was elected to the Albany (New York) Common Council in 2005. The same year, she was nominated for a Nobel Peace Prize.

Carroll Smith-Rosenberg (1936–)

Scholar

A groundbreaking and influential scholar of U.S. women's and gender history, Carroll Smith-Rosenberg published the article "The Female World of Love and Ritual: Relations between Women in Nineteenth-Century America," which has been described as one of the first and most influential explorations of the history of lesbianism in the United States.

Smith-Rosenberg was born in Yonkers, New York. She received a B.A. from Connecticut College and a Ph.D. from Columbia University in 1968. Her earliest scholarship focused on 19th-century urban America, and she began to consider gender as a category of historical analysis at a time when this was a novel, if not revolutionary, approach. She married medical historian Charles Rosenberg and began her teaching career at the University of Pennsylvania, where she helped organize Penn's women's studies program. "We were making it up as we went along," she said.

A lesbian relationship led Smith-Rosenberg to end her marriage as she began to explore the history of lesbianism more widely in societal and cultural terms. In 1975, she published "The Female World of Love and Ritual" in the feminist journal *Signs*. Combining archival, historiographical, and psychoanalytic approaches to interpreting 19th-century women's correspondence with one another, she pioneered the understanding of human sexuality and gender identity as fluid, relativistic, and susceptible to wide-ranging cultural and social forces. Her approach in "The Female World of Love and Ritual" would become a template for studying sexuality and gender in the decades that followed.

Leaving UPenn in 1995, Smith-Rosenberg taught at the University of Michigan until her retirement in 2008. Her major works include *Disorderly Conduct: Visions of Gender in Victorian America* (1985) and *This Violent Empire: The Birth of an American National Identity* (2010). Her books and many articles have become essential course material in women's studies and queer studies courses nationally. She has described her principal goal as a scholar to "redefine the canons of traditional history that the events and processes central to women's experience assume historic centrality and women are recognized as active agents of social change." She is considered by the generation of scholars who have followed her a game changer.

Asked in an interview if she regards herself as a crusader, Smith-Rosenberg replied, "Heavens no! I'm just a historian with two small cats. As historians, we tell stories and hope that you believe them!"

Sandy Stone (1936–)

Academic, Artist

Regarded as one of the founders of transgender studies, Allucquére Rosanne "Sandy" Stone was a professor at the University of Texas, Austin, and the founding director of the Advanced Communication Technology Lab and the New Media Initiative in the Department of Radio-TV-Film. Before her academic career, she worked as a recording engineer, overseeing the recordings of Jimi Hendrix, the Byrds, Van Morrison, and many others.

She went on to become a member of the Olivia Collective, which founded the women's music label Olivia Records, and wrote the 1987 essay "The Empire Strikes Back: A Posttranssexual Manifesto," widely considered the founding text in transgender studies.

Born in Jersey City, New Jersey, Stone was designated male at birth but reported always feeling uncomfortable with that designation. Disliking formal education and preferring to follow her interests on her own, she eventually graduated from St. John's College (Annapolis, Maryland) in 1965. Her first career was as a recording engineer, first at Record Plant Studios in New York City and later on the West Coast. In 1974, she settled in Santa Cruz, California, and underwent gender reassignment surgery through the Stanford Gender Dysphoria Program.

From around 1976 until 1978, Stone was the sound engineer at the Olivia Collective, a group that in 1973 founded Olivia Records, a women's music label started by lesbians from the Washington, D.C., area to promote the lesbian expression. In 1979, lesbian feminist scholar Janice Raymond attacked her in *The Transsexual Empire: The Making of the She-Male*, accusing her of subverting the work of Olivia Records with "male energy." Raymond threatened to out her as transgender without realizing that she had already informed the Collective of her transgender status. The Collective publicly defended Stone, who continued with the Collective until dissension over her transgender status, exacerbated by Raymond's book, culminated in 1979 in a threatened boycott of Olivia products, and Stone left the group.

In 1987, while studying for her doctorate at the University of California, Santa Cruz, Stone wrote "The Empire Strikes Back: A Posttranssexual Manifesto" in answer to Raymond's *The Transsexual Empire*. In it, she refuted the narrow conception of womanhood in Raymond's attack on transgender status. She called for transgender people to come out as a means of empowerment. By doing so, she applied for the first time a core concept of the radical gay and lesbian movement to the transgender community. Instead of being either ignored or deprecated by the gay or lesbian community, transgender identity, articulated by her essay, would, in the words of *The Transgender Studies Reader*, become the catalyst for "a gradual but steady body of new academic and creative work by transgender people" as well as "new critical perspectives on gender."

Stone, while completing her doctorate, began teaching in the Sociology Department of the University of California, San Diego, in 1987 and, in 1992, at the University of Texas, Austin. Receiving her doctorate in 1993, she published her dissertation as *The War of Desire and Technology at the Close of the Mechanical Age* (1996). At the University of Texas, where she earned tenure despite conservative faculty members' objections, she directed the Advanced Communication Technology Lab and the New Media Initiative. She has taught courses in and written about film, music, neurology, engineering, and computer programming.

In 1995, Stone married Jeffrey Prothero (Cynbe ru Taben), a researcher and programmer. They divided their time between Santa Cruz and Austin. In 2010, she retired from the University of Texas but continues speaking and performing widely. Over an incredibly productive, influential, and eclectic career, she fully embodies the empowerment concepts she proclaimed in 1987 in urging transgender people not to hide from but embrace their identity and its possibilities.

Susan Stryker (1961-)

Scholar, Historian, Author, Filmmaker

Professor of gender and women's studies at the University of Arizona, Susan O'Neal Stryker was the former director of the Institute of LGBT Studies and founder of the Transgender Studies Initiative at the

University of Arizona. A transgender woman, she is the author of several books on LGBTQ+ history and culture and is a leading scholar of transgender history.

Stryker grew up in Oklahoma while also spending time in Arkansas, Texas, Germany, and Hawaii as part of her father's military service. She received a B.A. from the University of Oklahoma in 1983 and a Ph.D. in history at the University of California, Berkeley, in 1992. It was shortly after earning her doctorate that she came out as transgender and began to transition. From her earliest memory, she "always felt [she] was a girl though [she] had a male body at birth." In 1992, she cofounded, with Anne Ogborn, Transgender Nation, a direct-action activist group. "When I came out as transsexual in 1992," she recalled, "I was acutely conscious, both experientially and intellectually, that transsexuals were considered abject creatures in most feminist and gay or lesbian contexts, yet I considered myself both feminist and lesbian."

In 1994, Stryker published her first academic article, "My Words to Victor Frankenstein About the Village of Chamounix," in Duke University Press's *Journal of Lesbian and Gay Studies*, one of the first articles ever to be published in a scholarly academic journal by an openly transgender author. She used the analogy of Frankenstein's monster to reflect transgender identity and reclaim the comparison of transgender people as monsters. "Words like 'creature,' 'monster,' and 'unnatural,'" she stated, "need to be reclaimed by the transgendered. By embracing and accepting them, even piling one on top of another, we may dispel their ability to harm us." From 1999 to 2003, she was the executive director of the GLBT Historical Society in San Francisco. Teaching stints followed at Macquarie University in Sydney, Australia; Fraser University in Vancouver, Canada; Harvard University; and other schools until she was finally appointed associate professor of gender and women's studies and director of the Institute of LGBT Studies at the University of Arizona in 2011, retiring in 2020.

Stryker's first book was *Gay by the Bay: A History of Queer Culture in the San Francisco Bay Area* (coauthored with Jim Van Buskirk) (1996). Her other books include *Queer Pulp: Perverted Passions from the Golden Age of the Paperback* (2001), *The Transgender Studies Reader* (coedited with Stephen Whittle) (2006), *Transgender History* (2008), and *The Transgender Studies Reader 2* (coedited with Aren Aizura) (2013).

Stryker directed the Emmy-winning documentary *Screaming Queens: The Riot at Compton's Cafeteria* (2005), which brings together eyewitness accounts of trans women and drag queens who fought police harassment in San Francisco in August 1966.

In her essays, books, and films, Stryker has documented both the history of transgender people and the challenges they face. Asked how she would like to be remembered, she explained, "I was just doing my thing, in whatever world opened up in front of me, to unfold the mystery of my transness to myself, and to help make more room for trans experience for others."

Virginia Uribe (1933–2019)

Educator

A high school counselor and science teacher, concerned over the trouble faced by gay students, Marilyn Virginia Uribe in 1984 founded Project 10, a dropout-prevention program for LGBTQ+ youth. High schools throughout the United States incorporated aspects of Project 10.

Born in Los Angeles, Uribe grew up in an Italian family. She went to a Catholic elementary school, high school, and college. Early on, she was attracted to women, but she eventually married and had two children before the marriage ended in divorce. In 1988, she met Gail Rolf, and they were later married in 2008, remaining together until her death. Uribe went to work as a science teacher and counselor at Fairfax High School in the Los Angeles Unified School District.

The plight of one student who had been kicked out of his house and dropped out of four different high schools due to sexual harassment was the catalyst for Uribe to take action by founding Project 10, which focused on building school-based support for LGBTQ+ teens by training school personnel in conflict resolution and suicide prevention as well as providing education and counseling programs for students. Project 10 was the first program in the United States to address anti-LGBTQ+ harassment in public schools and became a model for school districts throughout the country and around the world. According to its mission statement, "[Project 10] works to assure that public schools are in compliance with state and federal laws regarding sexual orientation and gender identity, and that academic achievement should not be limited by being part of a marginalized social group."

The program met resistance from conservative groups who lobbied for funding cuts for the program, but she prevailed at court hearings. In 1998, when she retired from teaching after 42 years, she became the executive director of Friends of Project 10, Inc., funding programs not covered by the school district, including a gay and lesbian prom.

In 1992, Uribe received the National Education Association's Annual Human and Civil Rights Award for Creative Leadership in Human Rights, now renamed the Virginia Uribe Award for Creative Leadership in Human Rights. She has been honored by the Lambda Legal Defense and Education Fund, the Hollywood Chamber of Commerce, the California Senate and California Assembly, the Los Angeles City Council, and the American Civil Liberties Union.

In 2019, Uribe was one of the inaugural 50 American "pioneers, trailblazers, and heroes" to be inducted on the National

LGBTQ Wall of Honor within the Stonewall National Monument.

Michael Warner (1958–)

Scholar, Author

American literary critic and political theorist Michael Warner is considered one of the founders of queer theory. He is the Seymour H. Knox Professor of English at Yale University and has written widely on early American literature and print culture as well as more theoretical works on social and cultural movements. His book *The Trouble with Normal* (1999) contended that queer theory and the ethics of a queer life serve as a critique not just of heterosexuality but also of existing social and economic structures. It and his other works, such as *Fear of a Queer Planet Public: Queer Politics and Social Theory* (1993) and *Publics and Counterpublics* (2002), have helped focus debate among LGBTQ+ activists and academics.

Warner received his Ph.D. in English from Johns Hopkins University in 1986 after completing two MAs from the University of Wisconsin and Johns Hopkins in 1981 and 1983, respectively. He first taught at Northwestern University (1985–1990) and Rutgers University (1990–2007) before becoming the Seymour H. Knox Professor of English at Yale University in 2007.

Warner's first book, *The Letters of the Republic: Publication and the Public Sphere in Eighteenth-Century America* (1990), established his reputation as a leading scholar of early American literature, print culture, and public sphere theory. *The Trouble with Normal* (1999) is one of the foundational texts of queer theory in which he challenges the efforts of gay and lesbian rights advocates to accommodate and assimilate to heteronormative standards in an effort to join the public, constituted by the dominant heterosexual society. As he notes, these efforts effectively undermine the transformative qualities that queerness can bring to a society in refiguring the way sex and relationships are regarded. He argues that the gay rights' struggle for marriage equality is a struggle for normalcy and privacy, which comes at the cost of those who do not marry and choose to conduct themselves in the public sphere.

Warner's collection of essays, *Publics and Counterpublics* (2002), explores the question "What is public?" and traces the history of debates over public and private spheres, particularly around the women's liberation and gay rights movements. One chapter, "Something Queer About the Nation State," discusses queer politics and activism. Queer theorist Ken Plummer stated that *Publics and Counterpublics* extended the public/private debate and contributed to the development of queer theory.

Warner's scholarship has extended the groundbreaking work by Eve Kosofsky Sedgwick, *The Epistemology of the Closet,* and Judith Butler's *Gender Trouble,* both published in 1990, examining the meanings cultures attach to gender, sex, and sexuality and how these meanings change over time and create power dynamics and social inequalities. His works have been recognized by numerous awards, including the 1993 Crompton-Noll Award for Best Essay in Lesbian and Gay Studies and the 2001 Foerster Prize for Best Essay in American Literature.

Randi Weingarten (1957–)

Educator, Labor Leader

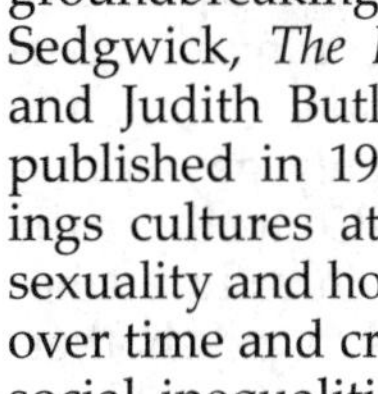

The president of the American Federation of Teachers (AFT) and the former president of the United Federation of Teachers (UFT), Randi Weingarten became the first openly LGBTQ individual to be elected president of a national American labor union.

Born in New York City, Weingarten grew up in Rockland County, New York, and developed an early interest in labor unions and politics when her mother—a teacher—went on strike. Weingarten attended Cornell University and received her juris doctor (J.D.) degree at the Cardoza School of Law at Yeshiva University. In 1986, she became counsel to the president of the United Federation of Teachers, representing the union in several important cases, and by the early 1990s she was the union's chief contract negotiator.

From 1991 to 1997, Weingarten also taught history at Clara Barton High School in Crown Heights, Brooklyn. She was elected the union's assistant secretary in 1995, treasurer in 1997, and finally president in 1998, a position she held for 12 years, before becoming president of the American Federation of Teachers in 2008.

In 2007 Weingarten publicly came out as a lesbian when she accepted the Empire State Pride Agenda Community Service Award from Christine Quinn, the first woman and first openly gay speaker of the New York City Council. At the presentation, Weingarten introduced her then-partner, Liz Margolies, a psychotherapist and health care activist. In 2012 she was in a relationship with New York Rabbi Sharon Kleinbaum. The couple married in March 2018.

As president of the UFT, Weingarten fought for higher salaries and better training for teachers, as well as merit pay. As president of the AFT, she has worked to put educational reform on the national agenda, to change how teachers are evaluated, and to improve access for all students.

Weingarten has long advocated a "bottom up" approach to education reform that addresses the needs of teachers and their students. Worried about the consequence of certain market-based proposals that she fears will result in the "eventual elimination of public education altogether," Weingarten sees the role of private charter schools as complementing, rather than competing with, public schools. "Charter schools should be laboratories for innovation and creative ideas," she has asserted, "that can be scaled up so they can enrich communities."

A tireless advocate for teacher's rights and responsibilities as well as one of the nation's most effective labor leaders, Weingarten has often been a lightning rod for the contentious issues surrounding education in America. This has been especially evident during the second presidency of Donald Trump and his administration's efforts to end government funding for public education, to use public funds to support private and charter schools, and to affect curriculum and cultural identity teaching in the classroom. When the administration announced its intention to dismantle the Department of Education in March 2025, Weingarten responded with a statement on behalf of the AFT that called for Congress "to make clear to the president that the federal government will not, in the face of this order, abdicate its responsibility to all children, students, and working families, who deserve a future full of promise and possibility, not diminished dreams."

Mary Emma Woolley (1867–1947)

Educator

The first woman student to be accepted at Brown University, Mary Emma Woolley would serve as the 11th president of Mount Holyoke College from 1901–1937, presiding over a series of reforms that raised the standard for women's higher education, which would become a model for other institutions.

The daughter of a Congregational minister, Woolley grew up in Connecticut and Rhode Island. She attended several smaller schools run by women before completing her secondary education at the Wheaton Seminary (now Wheaton College) in Massachusetts. She returned to teach there from 1885 to 1891. She agreed to become one of the first female students at Brown University, earning her B.A. and M.A. there.

In 1895, Woolley began teaching biblical history and literature at Wellesley College, where she was eventually promoted to full professor, and served as a department chair. In 1900, at the age of 38, she was named president of Mount Holyoke College, becoming one of the youngest college presidents in the United States. The same year, she became the first woman to receive an honorary degree from Amherst College. Over her 36-year tenure as president, she was instrumental in raising academic and admission standards, salaries, and benefits while overseeing 16 major building constructions and increasing the endowment tenfold to nearly $5 million. She abolished the college's domestic work system, which required students to cook and clean for economic reasons. She was a respected supporter of female higher education, arguing that women's education needed to be justified on intellectual grounds alone and that an educated woman could achieve anything.

In 1899, while teaching at Wellesley, Woolley formed a relationship with Jeannette Augustus Marks (1875–1964) that lasted 46 years. Marks followed Woolley to Mount Holyoke, where she was a professor of English literature. They never publicly acknowledged a lesbian relationship, but they lived together until Woolley's death in 1947.

When Woolley retired in 1937 at the age of 74, the board of trustees, fearing that Mount Holyoke was becoming too "feminized" with male faculty in the minority, appointed a male president to succeed her. She opposed the decision and refused to return to campus for the rest of her life. She was an outspoken activist for women's suffrage and pacifism. She served as vice president of the American Civil Liberties Union and was an early member of the Association of Collegiate Alumnae, which in 1881 became the American Association of University Women, serving as its president from 1927 to 1933. She is the subject of the play *Bull in a China Shop*, written by Mount Holyoke alumna Bryna Turner, which premiered at Lincoln Center in 2017. At Mount Holyoke, the Lesbian, Bisexual and Transgendered Community Center was renamed the Jeannette Marks House.

Religion

When the English first came to settle in what would become British America during the 17th century, they brought their religious observances and their laws with them, both of which would influence secular, as well as spiritual, life long after the American colonies became the United States. In Puritan New England, church and state were not separate spheres, and for spiritual and secular guidance, the Puritans relied upon both the Old and New Testaments in the popular Geneva Bible (1560). A translation from the Greek New Testament and scholarly editions of the Hebrew scriptures, the Geneva Bible was unique in that it featured extensive marginal notes to assist readers in interpreting biblical passages, which could then be used in everyday life.

The Puritans inherited from John Calvin, a central figure in the Protestant Reformation, the Calvinist belief in predestination, the concept that one is chosen by God before birth to be either the "elect," who is granted salvation in the hereafter, or to be condemned to eternal damnation. Since the Puritans had no way of knowing their eternal destiny, they lived in a perpetual state of anxiety, which could only be assuaged by Puritan theologians, the most influential members of the community, interpreting the scriptures in such a way as to avoid any behavior that might be construed as a sin that prevented them from living a righteous life and attaining God's divine grace. The Puritans had a predilection for binary and gender-conforming behavior to begin with, but what they found in the books of Deuteronomy, Romans, and Corinthians were passages that reinforced their notion that cross-dressing was an "abomination," shameful, and deceptive as well as being a demonstration of disbelief in God and a rebellion against divine order. Among the sins to be avoided were all forms of sexual lust, which the Puritans characterized as "our cursed natures," and included same-sex relationships, whose "abominations" were largely interpolated from the prohibitions mentioned in the books of Genesis (the story of Sodom's downfall), Leviticus, Romans, Corinthians, and Timothy.

The non-separation of church and state allowed the Puritans to apply these prohibitions to the legal statutes that, derived from the scriptures, governed their lives. Puritanism began to wane in the early 18th century and was superseded by the Congregational Church by 1740, but differences between the two sects were largely in name only.

The Jamestown colony, which preceded the Plymouth colony of the Puritan pilgrims by 13 years, was comprised of English Anglicans who also believed in the Calvinist doctrine of predestination but differed from the Puritans in their belief that following the teachings and pronouncements of Jesus would make them worthy of salvation. They also conflated church and state but in a different—and

The Revised Standard Version of the Bible was published in 1952 by the National Council of the Churches of Christ in the USA. It was the first version of the Bible to contain the word "homosexual."

crucial—way. Anglicans belonged to the Church of England, whose supreme head was the monarch, and, thanks to Henry VIII, the first Church of England monarch, the Jamestown Anglicans were the inheritors of 16th-century English common law, condemning same-sex relationships. They did not need the scriptures to help justify their prosecution of gay men. However, the Jamestown colonists, who also used the Geneva Bible, would have known the same biblical passages and marginal notes that influenced the Puritans regarding same-sex relationships as well as nonbinary/cross-dressing behaviors.

The first Bible to include the word "homosexual" was the Revised Standard Version (RSV), which was retranslated and replaced the 1901 American Standard Version (ASV) with a view toward offering a more readable and accurate modern Bible. Its publisher, the Division of Christian Education of the Federal Council of Churches (formed in 1908 and renamed the National Council of the Churches of Christ in 1950, usually shortened as the National Council of Churches), came out with the New Testament in 1946 and added the Old Testament in 1952. When Bible scholars retranslated the apostle Paul's first epistle to the Corinthians from the Greek New Testament into English, they replaced the descriptive terms "effeminate" and "abusers of themselves with mankind" in the King James Version (KJV) with the single noun "homosexual."

While researching the roots of anti-LGBTQ+ theology, gay biblical historian and researcher Ed Oxford and Christian author and LGBTQ+ ally Kathy Baldock subsequently discovered evidence that the use of the word "homosexual" represents misinterpretations of the ancient Greek words *malakoi* and *arsenokoitoi* in Corinthians. The first word refers to someone who is "effeminate," which in the ancient Greek means anyone who is given to laziness and indolence and who pursues pleasurable and decadent pursuits. The second word translates to "male bed," which translators construed in a gay context but was more likely to refer to abusive, predatory sexual behavior and pederasty. It has been suggested that those who translated the widely read Revised Standard Version for publication and chose to interpret the Greek words as indicating "homosexuality" helped to fuel the persistent and damaging homophobia of the Christian right.

The New Revised Standard Version (NRSV), published in 1971, replaced the word "homosexual" with "sexual perverts," an even more inflammatory descriptor for conservative Christian Bible readers who were likely familiar with the 1946 RSV translation as well.

An ecumenical partnership of mainline Protestant, Eastern Orthodox, African American, evangelical, and peace churches, the latter of which have included the Amish and the Mennonites, the National Council of Churches (NCC) has, since its founding as the Federal Council of Churches, championed a variety of progressive civil causes. However, given the number and variety of its member churches, the Council has faced opposition from some members regarding LGBTQ+ inclusion and the acceptance of LGBTQ+-friendly churches into the organization. The Council took a unified stance in 2010 when, along with other national faith leaders, it called on the "Church Universal to join us in working to end the violence and hatred against our lesbian, gay, bisexual and transgender brothers and sisters" and signed a pledge to "LGBT and straight people of faith standing together for the shared values of decency and civility, compassion and care in all interactions."

The affirmation of LGBTQ+ inclusion in church communities is a fairly recent occurrence. Throughout U.S. history, openly queer Americans, particularly lesbian, gay, and bisexual people, have often faced condemnation rather than spiritual solace when endeavoring to practice their religion together with straight congregations and, as a result, many have been forced to leave their organized religious communities.

During the 20th century, some religious parishioners and faith leaders stepped into the breach with LGBTQ+-affirming churches. The first of these was formed in 1946 in Atlanta, Georgia, after a priest at the Sacred Heart Roman Catholic Church refused to administer the sacraments to parishioners who admitted they were gay. In response, a group of some 20 gay and straight Sacred Heart parishioners founded the Eucharistic Catholic Church with funding from the management of a local gay bar. The new church, which welcomed both Catholic and Protestant parishioners, conducted its first service on Christmas Eve 1946, with Father (later Bishop) George Hyde presiding. Hyde, a former seminarian expelled on charges of sexual misconduct with another man, had been ordained as a priest by Greek Orthodox bishop John Kazantks, who had been suspended from his parish in Greece after defending priests charged with "homosexual" behavior and immigrated to the United States, where he worked as a Greek language teacher in the Atlanta public school system. Among the Eucharistic Catholic Church's affirmations is the "full inclusion of LGBTQ people as gifts from God in the life of the Church, including ordained ministry and the Sacrament of Marriage."

Two historically notable LGBTQ+-affirming churches are the Glide Memorial Church and the Metropolitan Community Church. In 1929, San Francisco Methodist philanthropist Lizzie Glide founded the Glide Foundation, which was built in 1931 as the Glide Memorial Church in the Tenderloin district to serve as a nondenominational place of worship. In 1964, the church redefined its pastoral mission to include the district's marginalized populations, among them a large number of LGBTQ+ residents.

In 1965, the church served as the headquarters of the Council on Religion and the Homosexual (CRH), which sought to bring clergy and gay rights activists together and, in 1966, sponsored the LGBTQ+ gay rights youth organization Vanguard. In 1972, the Glide Publications

Glide Memorial Church in San Francisco is a nondenominational church that has worked diligently to ease poverty and social injustice in its community.

division of the church published the influential book *Lesbian/Woman* by Daughters of Bilitis founders Del Martin and Phyllis Lyon, considered the first positive book on lesbianism as well as a foundational text of lesbian feminism. The Glide Memorial Church, popularly known as GLIDE, has identified itself as a "radically inclusive, just, and loving community" and has sponsored a number of social justice programs the church defines as a mission to "alleviate suffering and break the cycles of poverty and marginalization."

In October 1968, gay former Pentecostal minister Troy Perry founded the Metropolitan Community Church (MCC), a nondenominational Protestant church in Huntington Park, California, as a welcoming and affirming place of refuge and worship for gay, lesbian, and straight allies. Twelve people attended the MCC's first service, which was held at Perry's home, but by 1969, the congregation had grown to around 200 people and was subsequently housed in such venues as a nearby women's club, a Methodist church, an auditorium, and a theater before purchasing and consecrating a building in Los Angeles in 1971. In 1973, a blaze that the fire department deemed of "suspicious origin" destroyed the building. The MCC went on to establish churches elsewhere in Los Angeles and in several other U.S. cities, including Washington, D.C., as well as in Canada. In the same year as the destruction of the MCC's building in Los Angeles, the church's venue in New Orleans, a gay bar called the UpStairs Lounge, was the target of an arson attack that killed MCC reverend Bill Larson and a number of parishioners. Sometimes known as the "Gay Church" during the 1970s, the "AIDS Church" in the 1980s, and, more recently, the "Queer Church," the MCC has become

A ceremony dedicated to the Transgender Day of Rememberance is shown here at the Metropolitan Community Church's Washington, D.C. church.

a global pastoral presence, with over 200 churches around the world.

LGBTQ+ Catholics, rejected by the Church, discovered an advocate in Augustinian Catholic priest Father Pat Nidorf, who founded Dignity in 1969. Now known worldwide as DignityUSA, the organization became a lay-led group in 1971 after a bishop ordered Father Nidorf to stop his ministry. Since 1986, when the Vatican published a document banning Dignity groups from meeting in Catholic spaces, congregants have conducted their religious services, social events, and community service programs in other churches and community centers.

The first openly LGBTQ+-inclusive synagogue in the world was founded in Los Angeles in 1972. Called Beth Chayim Chadashim (BCC), Hebrew for "House of New Life," the Reform synagogue was founded by four gay and lesbian Jews who had been attending the Metropolitan Community Church. During the 1980s, BCC helped found the World Congress of Gay and Lesbian Jewish Organizations, conducted its first bat mitzvah, and hired its first ordained rabbi and first long-term cantor. In addition, BCC began to host PWA (People With AIDS) dinners. The 1990s saw BCC's membership grow to 250 people, 90 percent of whom were LGBTQ+, and an outreach to women members with the BCC Sisterhood, later called *Nashim L'Nashim* ("Women for Women"), which included women-led services and feminist discussion groups.

In 2010, BCC hired Juval Porat, a gay, Israeli-born cantor who was notable as the first cantor to be ordained in post-Holocaust Germany. BCC continues to be known for its inclusivity and progressive stance, which includes programs focusing on issues concerning gender and sexuality.

In 2020, the Williams Institute School of Law at the University of Southern California analyzed the data from a national Gallup daily tracking survey on religiosity and LGBTQ+ Americans and found that nearly half of LGBTQ+ adults identified as either highly or moderately religious. An increasing number of Christian, Jewish, and Islamic denominations, organizations, and scholars have officially spoken out in support of LGBTQ+ inclusion, civil rights, same-sex marriage, and the ordination of openly queer clergy, while others have held firm to their anti-LGBTQ+ religious traditions.

A 2024 survey conducted by the Public Religion Research Institute (PRRI) found that 47 percent of respondents . . . left their church because of increasingly negative attitudes toward LGBTQ+ people and issues.

A 2024 survey conducted by the Public Religion Research Institute (PRRI) found that 47 percent of respondents, a large percentage of which were Americans under 30, left their church because of increasingly negative attitudes toward LGBTQ+ people and issues. Some switched faith traditions, a practice known as "religious churning."

According to the Southern Poverty Law Center, some 70 LGBTQ+ hate groups existed in the United States in 2021. Among them were so-called Christian groups that have been openly hostile to LGBTQ+ religious inclusion and LGBTQ+ people in general. These include the Traditional Values Coalition, based in Washington, D.C., which follows a Puritan-style, Bible-based condemnation of the queer community; the Stedfast Baptist Church, based in Fort Worth, Texas, and Oklahoma City, which celebrated the 2016 mass shooting at the Pulse nightclub in Orlando and whose pastor, Dillon Awes, has advocated for the execution of gay people; and the Faithful Word Baptist Church, a fundamentalist Baptist church based in Tempe, Arizona, whose founder, Steve Anderson, has been well known for his anti-gay and anti-transgender rhetoric.

The headquarters of the Westboro Baptist Church in Topeka, Kansas, makes no bones about its hatred of an America that embraces diversity and human rights. The grafitti on the sign in front says, "God Hates the Phelps," a reference to the family that has led the church since its 1955 founding.

Perhaps the most notorious LGBTQ+ religious hate group is the Westboro Baptist Church (WBC), based in Topeka, Kansas, which is anti-Semitic, Islamophobic, transphobic, and what the Anti-Defamation League has described as "virulently homophobic." Its congregants, who are primarily members of founder Fred Phelps's family, first came to the public's attention in 1988, when CNN reported its picketing of the funeral of slain gay man Matthew Shepard.

The group, with its multicolored picket signs featuring homophobic slurs, has habitually protested nationwide at the funerals of LGBTQ+ people and Pride events as well as churches that support same-sex marriage, the funerals of military personnel and victims of school shootings, and any other entity or funeral of a high-profile person they deem to be either directly or tangentially supporting "homosexuality." Counter-protests are often held at funerals where members of the WBC appear; for example, when the group protested at the 2011 funeral of Elizabeth Edwards, the wife of former senator John Edwards and a supporter of gay marriage, a large group of counter-protestors calling itself the "Line of Love" also arrived to promote "proper respect for funerals."

In 2016, after the Pulse nightclub shooting, some 200 people formed a human chain that blocked the main street in Orlando, Florida, to counteract the presence of the WBC there. A more quiet but equally effective counter-protest occurred in 2012, when Aaron Jackson, cofounder of the humanitarian organization Planting Peace, purchased a house directly across the street from the Westboro Baptist Church. The following year, Jackson, who had named the house "Equality House," painted it in the colors of the Rainbow Flag.

BIOGRAPHIES

Robert Carter (1927–2010)

Roman Catholic Priest

Robert Earl Carter was a Jesuit and early leader of Dignity New York, a support group for gay Catholics who helped found the National Gay Task Force. He was one of the first Roman Catholic priests in the United States to declare publicly that he was gay.

Carter was born in Chicago and grew up in Lakewood, Ohio, and, later, Park Ridge, Illinois. His parents were Protestants, and Carter, who won a scholarship to attend the University of Chicago, converted to Catholicism when he graduated in 1946, having been introduced from reading James Joyce's *A Portrait of the Artist as a Young Man* to "the centrality of Catholicism in the history of Western civilization." By 1949, he completed a master's degree in Greek studies and a Ph.D. in 1953. He entered the Society of Jesus in 1954, becoming a Jesuit priest in 1963 and a teacher of classics and historical theology. He would earn a master's degree in social work from Columbia in 1981.

With fellow Jesuit John McNeill, Carter hosted the first meeting of Dignity New York at their New York Jesuit residence in 1972. He became one of the group's board members and advisers. As he recalled, "No longer was I just the professor of Early Church Studies and a research scholar. Now I was giving hope and new life to many gay Catholics." After marching with Dignity in the 1973 Gay Pride March in New York City, he was invited by New York City health commissioner Howard Brown (who had just come out publicly) to serve on the board of the National Gay Task Force. When a *New York Times* article about the group named Carter, who became one of the first openly gay Catholic priests in the 1970s, he was subject to irate demands for his expulsion from the priesthood by parents and alumni, but he was not disciplined by the Jesuits. The Catholic Church at the time held that while homosexual attraction was deemed "disordered," gay people who were celibate were not considered inherently sinful (in 2005, however, the Vatican declared that the Church would not admit to a seminary or ordain "those who practice homosexuality, present deep-seated homosexual tendencies or support the so-called 'gay culture'"). Catholic authorities did rule that Dignity could not meet on church property, and he celebrated Mass at meetings in apartments all around Manhattan, leading blessing ceremonies for gay couples, and testifying in 1986 in support of the gay rights law that was proposed by Mayor Edward I. Koch. He counseled AIDS patients at Lincoln Hospital in the Bronx and later became a supervisor of the outpatient AIDS program at Bellevue Hospital in Manhattan.

Carter would write in his memoir, "I consider myself to have been most fully a Jesuit, 'a companion of Jesus,' when I came out publicly as a gay man, one of the social rejects of my time. It was only by coming out that society's negative stereotypes would be overcome and we would gain social acceptance." According to gay rights activist Brendan Fay, "Bob Carter helped me move from self-hate to self-acceptance and then to a place of gay activism. He was like a Catholic Harvey Milk."

Robert Warren Cromey (1931–2025)

Episcopal Priest, Therapist

Although gay, married, and with children, Reverend Robert Warren Cromey devoted his ordained life to fighting for the rights of LGBTQ+ people. In 1964, he co-organized the Council on Religion and the Homosexual, the first organization to have the word "Homosexual" in its name. He was an early celebrator of gay marriage

(1964) and had a private practice as a therapist serving the LGBTQ+ community. In the 1980s, his church had funerals for over 70 men who died of AIDS.

Cromey was a native New Yorker who studied at New York University and the General Theological Seminary, becoming an Episcopal priest in 1956. He moved to San Francisco in 1962, where he served as a clergyman at several area churches, becoming a rector at Trinity Episcopal Church. In 1963, he preached a sermon about homosexuality and the Christian concern for the outcast. He was widely castigated as a "queer lover." He recalled, "I was called a homosexual sympathizer in the early 1960s, but 'fag priest' was the only nickname I really loved. Because I became a fag priest and outspoken advocate for gay rights. It made me relatively famous. In the Bay Area and San Francisco, I was on every radio and TV show and interviewed innumerable times by the newspapers. These nicknames helped because I had a reputation, and I got a great deal of attention because of them—they were a good thing."

In 1964, Cromey participated in a weekend conference for clergy and homosexuals, and after that event, a group of clergy members, including Cromey, and gay men and lesbians founded the Council on Religion and the Homosexual in order to develop dialogue between straights and gays in local churches. In 1964, several gay groups sponsored a New Year's Eve costume ball, with proceeds to go to the Council. As guests arrived, police photographers took pictures, and several were arrested. Cromey and others denounced the police and their discrimination against gays. Later, a judge admonished the police for their actions, and all charges were dropped.

In 1968, Cromey performed a wedding ceremony for a lesbian couple in St. Aidan's Episcopal Church, where he was vicar. In 1982, as rector of Trinity Episcopal Church, he allowed a gay couple to be married in the church. In 1996, a wedding of a gay couple, in which he gave the final blessing, was filmed by ABC television and aired nationally on ABC's *Turning Point.* In 1992, he published *In God's Image: Christian Witness to the Need for Gay/Lesbian Equality in the Eyes of the Church.* In 2013, he wrote an essay, "My Part in the GLBT Rights Movement." In 2017, he published *Joy Years: My Retirement Memoir.*

Darlene Onita Garner (1948–)

Minister

Cofounder of the National Coalition of Black Lesbians and Gays (NCBLG), Darlene Onita Garner was the first African American elder in the Metropolitan Community Church, an LGBTQ+-affirming Protestant Christian denomination.

Of African, Cherokee, and Irish descent, Garner was born in Columbus, Ohio. After her parents divorced when she was 2 years old, she was raised in the National Baptist Convention before being raised by her great-uncle and aunt. She attended Ohio State University, got married, and had three children. She said that she got married "to prove to myself that the feelings that I had for women were something other than being, as my family would say, being—that way." The marriage ended in divorce after several years.

In 1973, Garner came out as a lesbian and relocated with her three children to Washington, D.C., and in 1976, she joined the Metropolitan Community Church (MCC), the "world's first church group with a primary positive ministry to gays, lesbians, bisexual, and transgender persons." Although welcomed at the inclusive MCC, she remained conflicted: "It felt as though I had to choose between being Black and being lesbian." In 1978, she cofounded the National Coalition of Black Gays (later called the National Coalition of Black Lesbians and Gays), believed to be the first national LGBTQ+ organization devoted to the Black community. She would reflect on the experience: "We knew that we were making history. What we were doing had the capacity to change the face of history. Our youth and naiveté helped us do it with a boldness. If we had been seasoned activists, we might not have taken it on. We know that if it was not us, there might be no one. So we took it on."

In 1986, Garner entered Lancaster Theological Seminary and was ordained at MCC in 1988. Her first full-time ministry was as executive director of the Philadelphia Mayor's Commission on Sexual Minorities. She also served as a pastor at MCC in Philadelphia, Baltimore, and Fairfax, Virginia. In 1993, she was elected to the MCC Board of Elders and traveled internationally on behalf of MCC, living for a time in South Africa and Mexico. In 2010, she and her partner, Reverend Candy Holmes, were one of the first same-gender couples to apply for a marriage license in the District of Columbia.

Robert Allan "Laud" Humphreys (1930–1988)

Episcopal Priest, Sociologist

Robert Allan Humphreys, known as Laud Humphreys, is noted for his pioneering research into sexual encounters between men in public bathrooms, published as *Tearoom Trade* (1970). It elicited charges of unethical research methods but would also influence subsequent scholars' research on sexuality and sexual identity.

Born in Chickasha, Oklahoma, Humphreys graduated from Colorado College in 1952. Although his family was Methodist, he was drawn to the Episcopal Church and attended Seabury-Western Theological Seminary in Evanston, Illinois, graduating in 1955 when he took the name "Laud" from William Laud, Archbishop of Canterbury in the 17th century. Ordained an Episcopal priest, he served several parishes over the next 10 years in Oklahoma, Colorado, and Kansas. His strong public advocacy for the civil rights movement produced tension in his parishes, and when he was dismissed from his parish in Wichita, Kansas, he left the church and enrolled in graduate school in sociology at Washington University.

In 1960, Humphreys married Nancy Margaret Wallace, and they adopted two children. He received his Ph.D. in 1968 with a dissertation on men who sought sexual encounters with other men in public restrooms in the St. Louis area. It was published as *Tearoom Trade* and won the C. Wright Mills Award of the Society for the Study of Social Problems. Its methodology of covert research of an illegal behavior without gaining his subjects' consent was also attacked, and an unsuccessful attempt was made to rescind his Ph.D..

Humphreys became an academic, teaching sociology at Southern Illinois University, SUNY Albany, and Pitzer College in Claremont, California, from 1972 until his death due to lung cancer in 1988. In 1972, he published *Out of the Closets: The Sociology of Homosexual Liberation.* In 1974, he came out as a gay man and cofounded the Sociologists' Gay Caucus. In 1980, he separated from his wife, began living with Brian Miller, and opened a private practice as a psychotherapist.

Through these years, Humphreys was conflicted over the Episcopal Church: Although he was drawn to its rituals and heritage, he abhorred its political conservativism and treatment of gay people. His article "Jesus Christ, a Sexual Person?" offered a queer interpretation of Jesus and Paul that influenced subsequent LGBTQ+ theologians. During his final years, he resumed some priestly functions at St. Thomas Church in Hollywood.

George Hyde (1923–2010)

Clergyman, Minister to the Gay Community

George Augustine Hyde led the first known church to minister to openly gay parishioners. He later served as archbishop of the Orthodox Catholic Church of America from 1970 to 1983. With an active pastoral outreach to gay people as members and priests, the Orthodox Catholic Church of America developed a reputation as an exclusively "gay church" rather than as a church with a mission of inclusiveness and empowerment for all parishioners regardless of sexual orientation.

Born in Chattanooga, Tennessee, Hyde grew up in Atlanta. Even though he was raised as a Southern Baptist, he became interested in Roman Catholicism and enrolled in St. Mary's Seminary in Perryville, Missouri, to become a priest. He found adjustment to seminary life difficult and, after being accused of same-sex conduct by fellow students, was expelled.

Returning to Atlanta, he became a public high school teacher and met John Kazantks, a bishop in the Greek Orthodox Church who had been cast out of his church position and left Greece after being accused of being gay. Together, they established a new church designed for those who were in quest of an ecclesiastical life outside the Roman Catholic and other "institutional churches."

Throughout the late 1940s, they expanded their outreach to the gay community around Georgia, and the network they established would become what is considered the first group of explicitly gay-affirmative religious congregations in the United States. Hyde recalled that the church ministered to "a population of traumatized people. They had gone to church since kids, little kids, and been told from the pulpit, 'You people are no good'.... They were so afraid of being discovered that they had no confidence in themselves. I was disturbed because I think the [established] church was guilty of this. The church was hypocritical."

Hyde, who had been ordained by Bishop Kazantks in 1946, moved to Washington, D.C., in 1950, where he joined some colleagues in a worker–priest community called the Society of Domestic Missionaries, with the intention of taking "the church to where the people were." In 1957, he was consecrated as a bishop of what would become the Orthodox Catholic Church of America and became its leader. The church's pastoral mission was inclusion of gays and Blacks as members and priests. He led the church until 1983, when he retired for health reasons and moved to Florida, where he lived until his death.

Mychal Judge (1933–2001)

Roman Catholic Priest

Mychal Judge, who served as chaplain for the New York City Fire Department, was the first identified casualty of the attacks on September 11, 2001. Having rushed into the North Tower of the World Trade Center after learning that people were trapped in the wreckage, he was killed during the collapse of the South Tower and subsequently classified as "Victim 0001."

Born Robert Emmett Judge, he was the son of Irish immigrants. His father worked in a grocery store in Brooklyn and died when he was 6 years old. He attended St. Francis Preparatory School in Brooklyn for a year before entering St. Joseph's Seraphic Seminary in Callicoon, New York, at the age of 15. In 1955, he completed his novitiate as a cloistered Franciscan friar, professing the vows of poverty, chastity, and obedience in 1958, and was ordained a priest in 1961, taking the name "Father Michael Fallon Judge" but later choosing the name Mychal to reflect his Irish heritage.

Judge served for several years in parishes in New Jersey and New York City. In 1985, he moved into the friary at the Church of St. Francis of Assisi in New York City, where he lived for the rest of his life, active in serving the homeless in the neighborhood and occasionally assisting the city's fire department chaplain.

During this time, in private writings, he confessed to having sexual attractions to men, although he remained committed to his vow of chastity. At the height of the AIDS crisis, he established the St. Francis AIDS Ministry at the friary. Attending funerals of those who died of AIDS and befriending gay activists, he often met with disapproval from the archdiocese of New York.

In 1992, Judge was appointed chaplain for the New York City Fire Department. In 2000, he marched with gay rights activists in New York City's first gay-inclusive St. Patrick's Day parade, held in Queens. He accompanied firefighters to the World Trade Center on September 11, 2001, and was inside the North Tower reportedly administering last rites to a fallen firefighter when he was killed by falling debris from the South Tower. The photograph of rescue workers carrying his body away from the World Trade Center became one of the enduring images of the September 11 attacks. More than 3,000 mourners attended his funeral Mass, which was televised.

In 2002, Congress passed the Mychal Judge Police and Fire Chaplains Public Safety Officers' Benefit Act, which made fire and police chaplains who were killed in the line of duty eligible for federal death benefits and provided extended eligibility of qualifying beneficiaries to anyone named, not just spouses, children, or parents. The act was the first of its kind to extend equal benefits to domestic and same-sex partners listed as beneficiaries.

Support for the canonization process for Judge began soon after his death. However, neither the New York archdiocese nor his Franciscan order have acted to begin the process. It is widely considered that his homosexuality is the major obstacle to his canonization, which should be, according to Kathleen Cummings, director of the Cushwa Center for the Study of American Catholicism at the University of Notre Dame, "a slam dunk," considering the heroic way he died and his well-documented spirituality and ministries.

Elliot Kukla (1974–)

Transgender Rabbi

The first openly transgender person to become an ordained rabbi, Elliot Kukla (he/they) came out six months before his ordination. At the request of a transgender friend, he wrote the first blessing sanctifying the gender-transition process to be included in the Union for Reform Judaism's resource manual for gay, lesbian, bisexual, and transgender congregants.

In a 2023 interview with the *Them.us* website, Kukla described himself as a child of "hippie parents." He was raised in Toronto and on the Big Island of Hawaii in a culturally Jewish household, but his spiritual journey led him to Hinduism and Buddhism and "about every religion except for Judaism." As a teenager, he enrolled in an ultra-Orthodox yeshiva, but after realizing how incompatible ultra-Orthodox Judaism was with queerness, he moved to Modern Orthodox, then to Conservative, and, finally, to ordination in Reform Judaism "to try to find a queer and trans Judaism." He characterized his entire journey through Judaism as "a series of slamming doors and then opening them."

In 2006, Kukla was ordained by a Reform seminary, the Hebrew Union College of Los Angeles, becoming the first openly transgender rabbi to be recognized by a mainstream Jewish denomination. His Jewish blessing for transition, right before coming out as trans, was published in 2007 and went viral around the world. The same year, he cofounded *TransTorah*, the first website to address transgender issues in Judaism. From 2008 to 2021, he served as a rabbi at the Bay Area Jewish Healing Center, where he codirected Kol Haneshama, an award-winning spiritual care hospice program.

Kukla, who suffers from lupus, is also a disability activist and, with a degree in religion and visual studies from the University of Toronto, he is a visual artist with

Sins Invalid, a political arts and education group that helped to create the disability justice movement in the early 2000s. He currently lives in Oakland, California, with his partner and their child.

John J. McNeill (1925–2015)

Catholic Priest, Theologian

Called the "patron saint of LGBTQ+ Catholics," Father John J. McNeill, an openly gay Jesuit priest, pushed the Church to be more welcoming to gay men and lesbians and was expelled from his order as a result. He was the author in 1976 of *The Church and the Homosexual*, which has been called "the primary text that is still considered the key in transforming the conversation on religion and homosexuality."

McNeill was born in Buffalo, New York. His mother died when he was 4 years old, and in order to rear him and his four older siblings, his mother's sister married his father, agreeing to live celibately as brother and sister. He recalled that "we children grew up with the burden of our responsibility for our parents' frustrations and unhappiness." At the age of 17, during World War II, he served in the U.S. Army and was taken prisoner by the Nazis, who kept him in a sealed boxcar for days without food or water. After the war, he graduated from Canisius College in Buffalo and earned graduate degrees from Bellarmine College in New York and Woodstock College in Maryland. In 1959, he was ordained by New York's Cardinal Spellman through the Society of Jesus (the Jesuit order).

While studying for his doctorate at the Catholic University of Leuven, Belgium, McNeill was lonely and considering suicide when he fell in love with another man. "The experience of the joy and peace that comes with that…" he stated, "it was a clear indication to me that homosexual love was in itself a good love and could be a holy love."

After receiving his doctorate in philosophy in 1964, McNeill joined the faculty of Le Moyne College in Syracuse, New York. He began ministering to gay Catholics in 1970, later training as a psychotherapist. He helped found the New York chapter of DignityUSA, a support group for LGBTQ+ Catholics, in 1972 and began speaking publicly on gay Catholic issues. In 1976, he published *The Church and the Homosexual*, a scholarly analysis showing that the Bible does not condemn same-sex relationships as well as being a call for the Catholic Church to end its homophobic practices. The Vatican first approved the book but withdrew its support as he became more widely known as a gay rights champion. In 1977, the Vatican ordered him not to speak or write publicly on the subject, an order he obeyed for nearly a decade, although he continued quiet pastoral work with gay men and lesbians. The AIDS epidemic and the 1986 Vatican pastoral letter "On the Pastoral Care of Homosexual Persons," declaring homosexuality as an intrinsic moral evil, prompted him to break his silence, condemning the Vatican in *The New York Times* and the *National Catholic Reporter*. In 1987, he was expelled from the Society of Jesus.

Although his expulsion was painful to him, McNeill said that it was also liberating. He continued his psychotherapy practice and even served as the grand marshal of the 1987 New York City Gay Pride Parade. He taught at Fordham University and published *Taking a Chance on God: Liberating Theology for Gays, Lesbians, and Their Lovers, Families and Friends* (1988) and *Freedom, Glorious Freedom: The Spiritual Journey of Life for Gays, Lesbians and Everybody Else* (1995).

Brendan Fay, director of *Taking a Chance on God*, a 2011 documentary about McNeill, stated, "John McNeill is one of the most important voices in the history of the LGBT civil rights movement." Catholic feminist theologian Mary E. Hunt said of her friend, "He was a gay man who was a Jesuit priest—and being a gay man who is a Jesuit priest, by the way, is not an unusual thing. The difference is that John McNeill was honest, and he was honest early. And being honest early meant that he paid a large price."

Patrick "Pax" Nidorf (1932–2023)

Catholic Priest

Father Pinchus Patrick "Pax" Nidorf, an Augustine priest from San Diego, was the founder in 1969 of the support group Dignity for gay and lesbian Catholics, the first group of its kind in the institutional Catholic Church. It has the distinction of being one of the only pre-Stonewall LGBTQ+ organizations still in existence. Dignity was declared "untenable" by Los Angeles archbishop Timothy Manning, and Nidorf became one of the first American priests to be censured for his work with gay and lesbian Catholics.

Born in Phoenix, Arizona, Nidorf entered the Augustinian monastic order after his early training studying art and was ordained a Catholic priest in 1960 in San Diego. He also pursued a degree as a psychologist and was a teacher at St. Augustine High School in San Diego, where he met students who struggled with their sexuality. According to Dignity leader Pat McArron, "Early in 1969, [Nidorf]…began a ministry for gay and lesbian Roman Catholics as an extension of his professional work. He chose the name 'Dignity' to stress his basic goal; to bring dignity into the spiritual and social lives of gay and lesbian Catholics." Dignity was established at a time when the American Psychiatric Association's first edition of the *Diagnostic and Statistical Manual of Mental Disorders (DSM-I)* categorized homosexuality as a mental disorder and the *Catechism of the Catholic Church* regarded homosexual acts to be among the grave sins against chastity. Word of his ministry spread by word of mouth as well as through advertisements that he placed in the *Los Angeles Free Press* and *The Advocate*. As he recalled on the occasion of the 25th anniversary of Dignity in 1994, "When I started Dignity in 1969, in the eyes of the world it was probably a very small thing. However, in the microcosm of my own life, it was a monumental gamble." Eventually, the San Diego chapter of Dignity became the seed for DignityUSA, with chapters nationwide.

In 1971, after Nidorf opened the Los Angeles chapter of Dignity, he was censured by Los Angeles archbishop Timothy Manning, and the support group was banned from the use of church property. He resigned as Dignity's leader, and the organization became a lay-led group. He would later change his name to Pax and leave the priesthood, and in 1973, he married Dacia St. John, also a psychologist. The couple were happily married for 26 years until her death in 1999. He continued to serve gays and lesbians as a therapist in private practice.

Nidorf has been described as "the spark that lit the flame" for DignityUSA, an organization that has supported thousands of queer Catholics since it began more than half a century ago. As DignityUSA president Meli Barber stated on his passing at the age of 91, "Because Pax had the compassion, the vision, and the courage to understand that LGBTQIA+ Catholics needed a safe space to pray and find a spiritual home, people my age have never had to live in a world without Dignity…. What an amazing gift to so many, and to the whole church."

Troy Perry (1940–)

Religious Leader

A gay rights and human rights activist and founder of the Metropolitan Community Church (MCC), serving LGBTQ+ Christians,

Troy Perry, a minister in the Pentecostal Church, performed the first public same-sex wedding ceremony in the United States in 1969. He has been credited with originating the concept of a West Coast gay Pride parade as a commemoration of the 1969 Stonewall Uprising, cofounding the Christopher Street West organization in Los Angeles that held the Gay Pride Parade on June 28, 1970.

Born in Tallahassee, Florida, Perry ran away from home after being sexually abused by his stepfather. He was ordained as a Baptist minister at the age of 15. Although at an early age he accepted his homosexuality, he married a minister's daughter, and the couple moved to the Midwest, where Perry, having joined the Pentecostal Church of God, studied at Midwest Bible College in Summit, Illinois, while serving as a pastor of a church in Joliet, Illinois. He would subsequently be expelled from the Moody Bible Institute in Chicago for being involved in a homosexual relationship. He moved to southern California, keeping his gayness a secret, and joined another Pentecostal church, but he was defrocked as the pastor and got divorced when his sexuality became known.

After serving in the U.S. Army from 1965 to 1967, Perry moved to Los Angeles, where he held a worship service in his home for a small group of 12 in 1968, most of whom were homosexuals. From this beginning, he founded the Metropolitan Community Church (MCC), which was open to all individuals regardless of sexual orientation, and focused its outreach to homosexual, bisexual, transgender, and queer Christians. The MCC has grown, now with over 400,000 members in 222 congregations in 37 countries.

In 1969, Perry performed the first same-sex wedding ceremony in the United States. In 1972, he published an autobiography, *The Lord Is My Shepherd and He Knows I'm Gay*. In 1979, Perry, with Robin Tyler, planned the National March on Washington for Lesbian and Gay Rights. In 2003, he and his spouse, Phillip Ray De Blieck, were married under Canadian law. In 2004, they filed suit against the State of California, seeking the state's recognition of their Canadian marriage. In 2008, the California Supreme Court ruled in their favor.

Brandan Robertson (1992–)

Religious Leader

Brandan Robertson, theologian, author, and LGBTQ+ activist, serves as the pastor of Sunnyside Reformed Church in New York City and is also known as the "TikTok Pastor," with over 215,000 followers and 5.5 million views of his theological digital content, which explores the connections between spirituality and sexuality.

Raised in a Maryland trailer park, Robertson was taken to church by a Baptist neighbor at the age of 12 and embraced his new faith. He received his bachelor's degree in pastoral ministry and theology from Moody Bible Institute in Chicago, Illinois, in 2014. There, he began to question his own sexuality and, as a condition for his graduation, had to spend his senior year in weekly gay-conversion therapy sessions. "By the time I came to the end of senior year," he recalled, "I knew more certainly than ever that I was attracted to men." He went on to earn a master's degree in theological studies, focusing on sexual and gender justice, from Iliff School of Theology in 2017 and a master's degree in political science from Eastern Illinois University in 2021. As of 2024, he was pursuing a doctorate in religion at Drew University.

In 2014, Robertson was named the national spokesman of Evangelicals for Marriage Equality, an organization created in order to encourage evangelicals to support civil marriage equality. In the same year, he led the effort to convene a historic meeting between Southern Baptist leaders and LGBTQ+ movement leaders. Frustrated about the Evangelical Church's lack of movement on LGBTQ+ issues, in a 2016 op-ed for *Time* magazine, he declared that he could not "in good conscience, remain aligned with the modern manifestation of the [evangelical] movement," and he ceased espousing traditional doctrines of a particular religious denomination in order to focus on mindfulness, contemplation, and progressive Christianity that emphasizes inclusion and empowerment regardless of sexual orientation.

A prolific author, Robertson has written *Our Witness: The Unheard Stories of LGBT Christians* (2017), *True Inclusion: Creating Communities of Radical Embrace* (2018), *The Gospel of Inclusion: The Christian Case for LGBT+ Inclusion* (2019), and *Dry Bones and Holy Wars: A Call for Social and Spiritual Renewal* (2022). During the pandemic, he found a new way to spread a more inclusive, modern gospel through TikTok, becoming one of the digital leaders of the so-called Christian Left, a social justice–minded counterpoint to conservative evangelicalism. In his posts, he debunks verses of the Bible that have been interpreted as a condemnation of homosexuality. "The first time the word 'homosexuality' ever appeared in the Bible was in 1946," he points out. "I use religion to create justice in the world by empowering communities to do what's right," he said. "I went from organized religion to religion for organizing."

V. Gene Robinson (1947–)

Episcopal Bishop

V. Gene Robinson has the distinction of being the first openly gay priest to be consecrated a bishop in a major Christian denomination. His election caused controversy in the Church, resulting in many theologically traditional Episcopalians in the United States breaking from the Episcopal Church to form the Anglican Church in North America.

Born in Kentucky to tobacco sharecropper parents who had been expecting a girl, Robinson suffered temporary paralysis due to childbirth complications and almost died as a baby. He was raised in the Disciples of Christ denomination but joined the Episcopal Church while attending the University of the South in Sewanee, Tennessee, where he graduated in 1969. He received an MDiv from General Theological Seminary in New York and was ordained in 1973. While serving as a chaplain at the University of Vermont, he began dating his future wife, Isabella "Boo" Martin, to whom he confessed his homosexuality. They decided to go ahead with the marriage in 1972. Eventually, the couple moved to New Hampshire and opened a horse camp for children. They would have two children of their own.

In 1986, Robinson came out to a friend, and he and his wife amicably divorced. In 1987, he met his partner, Mark Andrew. They were married in a private civil union in 2008 and got divorced in 2014. In 1988, he served as canon or executive assistant to the bishop of New Hampshire for the next 17 years until he was elected bishop in 2003.

Robinson's election was contentious. He faced death threats and an accusation from a parishioner of inappropriate "touching," which was investigated and dismissed. A group of 19 bishops warned of a possible schism in the Episcopal Church and the Anglican community worldwide. Some disaffected Episcopalians did disaffiliate from the Episcopal Church in order to form the Convocation of Anglicans in North America. He would point out that gay bishops have always existed in the Episcopal Church: "I'm just the first openly gay one." He would later reflect on the controversy: "I can tell you from my own experience, and it's one of the things that led to my coming out: It's an awful thing to stand in a pulpit and encourage people to live authentic lives when you know you're not being authentic. It's why God called me out of the closet." He published a memoir in 2008 of his reflections on the controversy, *In the Eye of the Storm: Swept to the Center by God.* In 2009, he led the invocation at the ceremonies preceding the inauguration of Barack Obama and was influential in the 2009 decision by the Episcopal Church in the United States affirming the rights of gays and lesbians to be ordained. He retired in 2013, citing the strain over his election on both him and the diocese. He would later become a senior fellow at the Center for American Progress and vice president of religion and senior pastor at the Chautauqua Institution until his final retirement in 2021. Between 2010 and 2022, the Episcopal Church elected five gay and lesbian active bishops.

Mary Alfreda "Freda" Smith (1935–2019)

Minister

In 1972, Mary Alfreda "Freda" Smith became the first woman minister and the first lesbian to be ordained by the Metropolitan Community Church, the first LGBTQ+-affirming Christian denomination in the United States. In 1975, in Denver, Colorado, she performed, with Catholic priest Robert Sirico of the Metropolitan Community Church in Seattle, Colorado's first gay wedding with a government-issued civil marriage license.

Smith was born in Pocatello, Idaho, to parents who had left Great Depression–era Oklahoma to settle in Idaho shortly before she was born. Growing up, Smith, whose grandmother was a Nazarene minister, was deeply involved in the Nazarene Church and felt a calling to become either a preacher or a poet. She also began recognizing her lesbianism and prayed for a "cure" before accepting that God did not want to change her but wanted her to use her passion as she was and help others who were struggling with their sexual identity. She attended Idaho State College, majoring in speech and journalism, before transferring to California State University, Sacramento, and ultimately earning a master's degree and becoming a licensed marriage and family therapist.

Smith was active in Robert Kennedy's 1968 presidential campaign in California and, after his assassination, decided to come out as a lesbian and feminist in order to work to change discriminatory laws in California. At the time, homosexuality was still against the law in California, condemned by the Church, and considered a mental disease. She became cochair of the California Committee for Sexual Law Reform and learned of the Metropolitan Community Church, founded by Reverend Troy Perry in 1968. Satisfying her long-desired wish to become a preacher, she joined the church and, in 1972, became its first woman minister and the first lesbian to be ordained by the MCC. She served as senior pastor of MCC Sacramento from 1972 to 2005.

During her ministry, Smith successfully convinced the MCC to change its bylaws to use the pronouns "he" and "she" and, in 1973, became the first woman to be elected to its Board of Elders. A champion of same-sex marriage, she also pushed the MCC to become a leader in Christian social action and the ordination of women clergy. She is also known for her narrative poem "Dear Dora, Dangerous Derek Diesel Dyke: An American Tragedy," which she read before the California legislature in the 1970s while serving as cochair of the California Committee for Sexual Law Reform and working on behalf of the Consenting Adult Sex Law bill. Her signature sermon was "Purple Grass," which was about a lamb that was rejected by society because it liked eating purple grass instead of green grass. In the poem, the Good Shepherd assures the lamb of God's unfailing love regardless of its choice. Her sermon became the name of an MCC award that honors exceptional individuals in evangelicalism and preaching. She was survived by her life partner of nearly 50 years, Kathleen Meadows.

Abby Stein (1991–)

Rabbi, Transgender Activist, Author

Rabbi Abby Chava Stein is the first woman and the first openly transgender woman to be ordained by an Orthodox Jewish denomination, having received her rabbinical degree in 2011 before coming out as transgender. Her first book, *Becoming Eve: My Journey from Ultra-Orthodox Rabbi to Transgender Woman* (2019), became a bestseller.

A 10th-generation descendant of the Baal Shem Tov, the professed founder of Hasidic Judaism, Stein grew up in Williamsburg, Brooklyn, as a male named Yisroel and was expected to continue the family's vocation as a rabbi. She grew up speaking Yiddish and Hebrew and was educated at a traditional, all-boys Jewish day school, living in a community highly segregated by gender. However, from the age of 5, she identified as a girl. She always felt different but felt pressured to keep her identity a secret and follow the more traditional path of living as a man, getting married, and becoming a rabbi.

After high school and completing her rabbinical education in 2011, Stein, who had married, came out to her family as transgender shortly after her son was born. This led to a split with her father, who told her, "You should know that this means I might not be able to talk to you ever again." She left the Hasidic community and, in 2015, made headlines by publicly coming out and starting her physical transition, founding a support group for trans people from Orthodox backgrounds. In 2016, she celebrated her transition and name change to Abby Chava Stein. In 2018, she cofounded Sacred Space, a multifaith project celebrating women and nonbinary people of all faiths. After publishing her memoir in 2019, she re-embraced her title and various roles as a rabbi while advocating on behalf of the LGBTQ+ community, with an emphasis on transgender people. In 2019, she served on the Women's March steering committee and, during the rally that followed, was a featured speaker along with other clerics. In her speech, she called for unity, asserting that "a lot of people in the media are trying to divide us. What brings us together is not the fact that we are all the same. What brings us together are our differences." In 2023, she began working as a rabbi and scholar in residence at the New Shul, a progressive, nondenominational synagogue in New York's Greenwich Village.

Cecil Williams (1929–2024)

Pastor, Community Activist

Active in the civil rights movement, Cecil Williams became one of the first African Americans to become involved in the gay rights movement. As the pastor of Glide Memorial Church (also known as GLIDE) in San Francisco for more than 60 years, he has been called a founding father of modern-day San Francisco as a tireless advocate for racial equality and LGBTQ+ rights. He was one of the first clergymen to preside over same-sex weddings, four decades before the legalization of gay marriage.

Born in San Angelo, Texas, and raised in the segregated South, Williams earned his B.A. in sociology from Huston-Tillotson University in Austin in 1952 and became one of the first five African Americans to graduate from Perkins School of Theology at Southern Methodist University in 1956. He served as a pastor in New Mexico and Kansas City, Missouri, before becoming the pastor of Glide Memorial Church, an affiliate of the Methodist Church, in 1963 in San Francisco's Tenderloin district. At the time, GLIDE had a small, white, affluent congregation, and in 1964, at a time when homosexuality was a crime in California and considered a mental disorder by the medical profession, Williams, drawing on his experience in the civil rights movement, urged gays to use their votes to gain power, much to the consternation of his congregation. He opened the church to jazz music, gays, hippies, addicts, the poor, the homeless, and anyone else who wanted to come. He hosted political rallies and services and speeches by Angela Davis and the Black Panthers. "The true church stays on the edge of life," he declared, "where the real moans and groans are. Most church folks settle in, get comfortable and build doctrinal walls to protect themselves from anyone who thinks or looks differently than they do."

Assisted by his wife, Janice Mirikitani (1941–2021), a Japanese American poet and activist, Williams grew his racially, ethnically, and sexually diverse congregation to over 10,000 members, with worshippers that included Maya Angelou and Warren Buffett. He would make GLIDE a safe haven for the LGBTQ+ community, with GLIDE becoming one of the fastest-growing United Methodist churches in North America and the Glide Foundation becoming San Francisco's largest social service provider, feeding 3,500 people a day and offering job training and programs for HIV-related services, alcohol abuse, and domestic violence, with more than 1,700 volunteers. He retired as GLIDE's pastor in 2000 but found a position with a nonprofit organization that allowed him to continue his service on behalf of the church and the community until he stepped down in 2023. The intersection of the streets in San Francisco that marked the location of the Glide Memorial Church was renamed Reverend Cecil Williams Way in 2013.

Arts and Entertainment

Art

The visual art created by LGBTQ+ artists has often been called "Queer Art," a descriptor that speaks to the reclamation of a word once used as a slur and can broadly and fluidly refer to various modern and contemporary art styles that draw on queer imagery and issues relevant to sexual and cultural aspects of communities within LGBTQ+ initialism. It has also been used to define the work of past LGBTQ+ artists before the use of present-day terms describing queer sexual and gender identity.

Queer Art has its roots in the art and culture of antiquity and in artwork that either openly depicted or used "queer code" in the form of symbols or language to express forbidden and hidden LGBTQ+ identities and orientation. A vase painting from around 500 B.C.E. depicts the Greek warriors Achilles and Patroclus in which Achilles is attentively bandaging Patroclus's arm and both of whom, in Homer's *Iliad,* are portrayed as devoted friends. In Plato's *Symposium* and other Greek works of literature as well as in Shakespeare's *Troilus and Cressida,* the two are characterized as lovers. The life-sized, reclining Greek statue *Sleeping Hermaphrodite* in the Louvre Museum is an Early Imperial Roman copy of the original by Greek sculptor Polycles in around 150 B.C.E. that is based on the Greek myth of the intersexed child of Aphrodite and Hermes. In gay French painter Jacques-Emile Blanche's 1895 portrait of British illustrator Aubrey Beardsley, whose sexual orientation remains a question, the subject wears a pink flower in his buttonhole as a symbol of gay support (violets had long been a symbol of lesbian love).

In the early 1900s, Norwegian photographer Marie Høeg, who challenged gender roles in her work, was often photographed with her partner, Bolette Berg, both wearing men's clothing, sporting moustaches, and smoking cigarettes, which was garb and behavior then considered, along with being lesbian, as scandalous for women. The subject of *The Sorcerer of Hiva Oa,* a 1902 Paul Gauguin painting, is a transgender Micronesian indigenous Mahu healer. *Medallion,* a 1936 painting by lesbian British painter Gluck, who was born Hannah Gluckstein and created a gender-neutral identity through her name choice, shows the profiles of Gluck and her lover, Nesta Oberma, and was created as a defiantly public declaration of their relationship.

As art historian Alex Pilcher has observed, LGBTQ+ artists were historically dismissed, downplayed as such, or "diagnosed" as "celibate," "asexual," or "sexually confused," with their queer subjects considered "friends" or "comrades." In 20th-century America between World War I and World War II, the presence of LGBTQ+ artists at speakeasies, nightclubs,

A circa 1900 photograph of the Norwegian Marie Høeg (left) and her partner, Bolette Berg, both of whom would commonly dress in men's clothing for photo shoots like this one.

and bars in Harlem and Greenwich Village helped to foster a certain general social acceptance of people in the arts who were rumored or known to be queer. However, given the legal and cultural ramifications of openness, LGBTQ+ artists continued to create coded artwork throughout most of the era.

Queer coding is present in the paintings of vaudeville performers, sailors, and Turkish baths by gay artist Charles Demuth (1883–1935), whose most famous work is *I Saw the Figure 5 in Gold* (1928). Art historians Jonathan David Katz and Andrew Graham-Dixon have pointed to the works of abstract painters Agnes Martin, Robert Rauschenberg (in his 1954 Combine painting *Bantam*, with its gay iconography), and Jasper Johns (*White Flag*, 1955) as examples of modern artists who used coding to allude to their orientation.

In the 1960s, artist and filmmaker Andy Warhol made use of gay iconography with his series of silkscreen paintings featuring the actress Marilyn Monroe, titled *Shot Marilyns* (1964). Toward the end of the decade, photographer Robert Mapplethorpe began to openly—and controversially—document the gay male BDSM scene in New York City. The last three decades of the 20th century saw more LGBTQ+ artists openly use queer imagery in their artwork, in part due to the confrontational LGBTQ+ activism sparked by the Stonewall Uprising and the AIDS epidemic, which contributed to the formulation of an increasingly visible queer identity and a refusal to remain closeted.

Early on, this influenced the formation of agitprop groups such as the Guerrilla Girls, queer and straight feminist artists who, since 1985, have utilized "culture

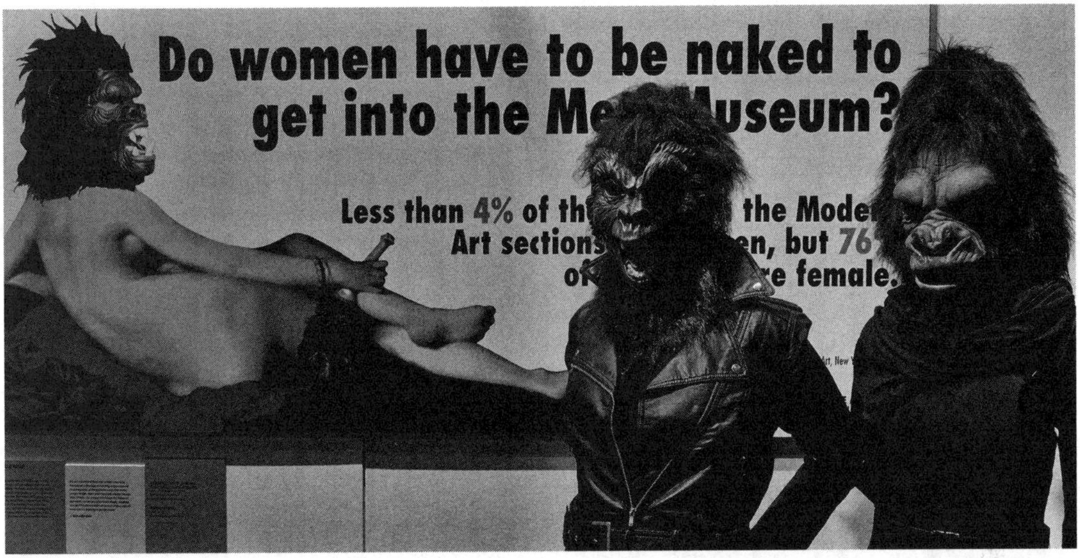

The Guerilla Girls—shown here at an exhibit at London's Victoria and Albert Museum—is a feminist artist group that was founded in 1985 to inform the public about racism and sexism in the business world of art.

jamming"—criticizing consumerism and forms of media, including advertising—in their artwork to protest gender and racial inequality within the arts community as well as in society at large. When the Silence=Death Project collective created the eponymous and iconic Silence=Death AIDS poster in 1987, the work included a pink triangle as a reference to Nazi persecution.

Artist Keith Haring's 1989 painting *Silence=Death* includes the words "Ignorance=Fear" and "Fight AIDS/Act Up." In 1991, the lesbian feminist art collective fierce pussy was founded in New York City to work with the AIDS Coalition to Unleash Power (ACT UP) and address issues of lesbian identity and visibility through their art. In 2017, the Silence=Death image was installed on the façade of New York's Leslie-Lohman Museum of Art with the words "Be Vigilant. Refuse. Resist."

Literature

American LGBTQ+ fiction began with novels featuring romantic friendships between men, some with hints of homoeroticism. An early example is Herman Melville's *Moby-Dick* (1851), in which Ishmael, a schoolmaster, sailor, and first-person narrator of much of the novel, and Queequeg, a harpooner, Pacific Islander, and cannibal, share a bed the night before the doomed voyage on the *Pequod*. Queequeg embraces Ishmael in the morning, declares them to be married, and the two go on to develop an affectionate, even romantic, friendship. When the titular whale destroys the ship, it is Queequeg's coffin, which he built aboard the ship, that saves

Ishmael, the only survivor of the crew, from drowning. *Cecil Dreame* was an 1861 semi-autobiographical novel by Connecticut-born Civil War officer Major Theodore Winthrop that was published posthumously after Winthrop was killed the same year in the Battle of Big Bethel. The novel tells the story of Robert Byng, who forms a romantic friendship described as "closer than brothers" with the eponymous character, a fellow lodger and artist at a fictional American college (based on New York University) who possesses a "singular, refined beauty." Byng, who loves Cecil with "a love passing the love of women," is simultaneously both attracted to and repelled by the wealthy, charismatic, and sinister debauchee Densdeth, who offers him a life of unspecified sinful acts and later dies in his arms, prompting Byng to remark, "There was a man whom I should have loved if I had not hated." In a gender-bending twist, the character "Cecil Dreame" is revealed to be a woman hiding from the nefarious Densdeth in disguise. In 2016, NYU Press reissued the novel, calling it "one of the queerest American novels of the 19th century." Whether or not Winthrop was a closeted gay man has been the subject of speculation. An early fictional work that features the stereotype of a gay relationship ending unhappily or in death (or both) is the 1889 novel *A Marriage Below Zero*, written by British-born, New York–based author and drama critic Alan Dale (1861–1928). In it, Elsie Revener, a young, married woman, discovers that her husband, Arthur, has been in a long-standing love affair with another man. After attending a church service during which the minister rails against sodomy, Arthur leaves his wife, who later finds him dead in a Paris hotel room, a victim of suicide.

In contrast, *Imre: A Memorandum* (1906) by Xavier Mayne, the pen name of New York journalist and novelist Edward Prime-Stevenson (1858–1942), is a romance set in Budapest in which a British aristocrat and the title character, a Hungarian military officer, become friends, then lovers, and remain happily coupled at the end of the novel. Five hundred copies of the original were published in Naples, Italy, and the Canadian academic publisher Broadview Press reissued the novel in 2003. Nothing is known for certain regarding Prime-Stevenson's sexual orientation, though he is generally assumed to have been gay and has been described as the first modern gay American author. Prime-Stevenson went on to publish *The Intersexes* (1908), a sexology study that used science, law, history, and the author's personal viewpoint to defend homosexuality.

A contender for the first mainstream American gay novel is *Bertram Cope's Year* (1919) by Chicago novelist and essayist Henry Blake Fuller (1857–1929). A subtly suggestive dark comedy of manners, the

Henry Blake Fuller was perhaps the first established author to seriously address the theme of homosexuality in his fiction with his novel Bertram Cope's Year.

novel's title character is a young, handsome, and socially ambitious graduate student and English instructor who becomes the object of social and sexual desire to an older society woman; two older men; and three eligible, young women, none of whom know that Cope's primary emotional attachment is to his roommate and best friend, Arthur Lemoyne, who may not be quite as closeted as Cope may think he is. Bisexual author Carl Van Vechten (1880–1984), known for his many photo portraits of notable Harlem Renaissance figures and other celebrated people in the arts, admired *Bertram Cope's Year* as a "skillful," "delicate," and "studiously restrained" "ironic comedy" on a subject that is "generally taboo in English literature."

Van Vechten's 1925 Jazz Age novel *The Firecrackers* features a similar central character, a handsome, mysterious, young man who becomes the object of sexual fascination and desire to the men and women who occupy the same sophisticated, pleasure-seeking social circle as he. The same year, Clarkson Crane (1894–1971), an adjunct professor at the University of California, published *The Western Shore*, which draws on Crane's experiences as a student at USC Berkeley and is notable for its inclusion of a gay English professor and the frankness of students questioning their sexual orientation. In 1926, writer and artist Richard Bruce Nugent (1906–1987), one of the few openly gay Harlem Renaissance figures, published "Smoke, Lilies, and Jade," a short story in which the protagonist struggles to understand his bisexuality.

Strange Brother (1931) by novelist and travel writer Mary Blair Niles (1880–1959), who wrote under the name Blair Niles, explores the themes of a closeted gay man forming a close platonic friendship with a straight woman, the fear of coming out, and the tragic consequence of doing so. In *Serenade* (1937), a complicated and violent work by early noir novelist James M. Cain, the author of *Double Indemnity* (1936) and *Mildred Pierce* (1941), the main character is

Author and noted photographer Carl Van Vechten was a patron of the Harlem Renaissance and noted for his 1926 bestseller, Nigger Heaven.

a self-hating, closeted opera singer whose passionate relationship with an Indio Mexican prostitute, an attraction to a gay conductor, and an inability to reconcile his sexual identity ends in tragedy. Homophobia and gay bashing in the military is the main subject of prolific filmmaker and sometime novelist Richard Brooks's (1912–1992) World War II stateside murder mystery *The Brick Foxhole* (1945), which would form the basis of the 1947 film *Crossfire*. The film version of Brooks's novel changed the motive for murder from homophobia to anti-Semitism because Hays Code censorship guidelines prohibited any mention of "homosexuality," then seen as a sexual perversion.

Notable post–World War II gay and bisexual novels include *The City and the Pillar* (1948) by Gore Vidal; *Quatrefoil* (1950) by James Baldwin; *Giovanni's Room* (1956) by James M. Fugate (1922–1995), who used the pen name James Barr; and *Advise and Consent* (1959) by Allen Drury (1918–1998). Vidal's novel, in which the author describes bisexuality as a "natural human state" and which he revised in 1965, is a coming-of-age wartime story in which the protagonist discovers and accepts the fact that he is gay, unlike the childhood friend he loves, who marries and remains closeted. Despite its unhappy ending, *The City and the Pillar* has been praised as the first postwar novel to feature a gay protagonist in a sympathetic manner.

Unhappy outcomes are also a feature of *Quatrefoil*, *Giovanni's Room*, and *Advise and Consent*, which explore the necessity of keeping gay or bisexual orientation hidden. In the case of Baldwin's bisexual protagonist, David, this necessity takes the form of internalized homophobia that results in his abandonment of his male lover, Giovanni, who is later executed for murder, and guilt over his abandonment. Finally, David's fiancée, who cannot accept David's bisexuality, leaves him. Despite its unhappy ending, *Quatrefoil*, a love story, is considered a groundbreaking novel for its positive depiction of a gay relationship. The novel received a boost in popularity with the distribution of free copies to 75 gay bars in the United States and Canada. Drury's political bestseller, released a few years after the Red Scare, included a Lavender Scare, which targeted gays as well as alleged Communists in the government and the military; a main character is a young, married anti-corruption senator who commits suicide after his wartime same-sex liaison is exposed and used to blackmail him in favor of the opposition.

In 1966, screenwriter and novelist George Baxt (1923–2003) achieved a first in mystery/crime fiction with *A Queer Kind of Death*, the first in a five-book series featuring the character Pharoah Love, a Black gay New York City detective who was the first American gay detective in the genre. Baxt would go on to win the Lambda Literary Award for Gay Mystery four times, including two awards for Pharoah Love novels. Another Lambda Literary Award winner was novelist and poet Joseph Hansen (1923–2004) for his similarly groundbreaking detective series featuring gay insurance investigator David Brandstetter, introduced in Hansen's 1970 novel, *Fadeout*. The spy thriller, which became popular after the success of former British intelligence officer Ian Fleming's *James Bond* series of novels and films, led to spoofs of the genre, most notably on TV. Novelist Victor J. Banis (1937–2019), whom the Wildside Press has called the "godfather of modern popular gay fiction," contributed to the craze in 1966 with *The Man from C.A.M.P.*, the first in a series of gay pulp spy novels written under the pen name Don Holliday that featured fictional superspy Jackie Holmes. Banis's inspiration for his series and its protagonist came from the popular 1960s TV spy spoof series *The Man from U.N.C.L.E.* and *Batman*, a spoof of comic book superheroes Batman and Robin.

During the 1970s, the gay novel genre included such notable American fiction as Allen Drury's *The Throne of Saturn* (1971), which explores the unrequited love of one male astronaut for another; *Dancer from the Dance* (1978) by Andrew Holleran (under the pen name Eric Garber), which concerns a young lawyer who leaves his straight life in the Midwest for New York City's gay scene during the 1970s and his relationship with a man variously described as a socialite, speed addict, and drag queen; and Armistead Maupin's *Tales of the City* (1978), the first volume in a long-running series.

The last decades of the 20th century saw such notable novels with gay and bisexual themes as Edmund White, who published *A Boy's Own Story*, the first book in an autobiographical trilogy, in 1982; Bret Easton Ellis's *The Rules of Attraction* (1987); and Annie Proulx's short story "Brokeback Mountain" (1997), upon which the acclaimed 2005 film was based.

American pulp fiction featured prominently in LGBTQ+ fiction. Paperback books that were so-called for the rough,

Although she is often thought of for writing the short story "Brokeback Mountain" that was adapted as an award-winning movie of the same title, Annie Proulx has also won the National Book Award for Fiction, the Pulitzer Prize for Fiction, and (the first woman to do so) the PEN/Faulkner Award for Fiction.

cheap wood pulp paper on which they were printed; their small "pocket" size; and their inexpensive pricing, pulp novels had been popular as "dime novels" since the 19th century. By the 1950s, pulp novels, which covered a variety of genres, including Western, detective, and science fiction, often featured lurid, colorful, and sexually provocative cover art as well as a focus on sensational and traditionally proscribed subjects such as gangs, drug use, interracial relationships, and "erotica." The latter suggested sexual couplings, but gay pulp novels, which appeared in the mid-1960s, became more sexually explicit after the relaxation of censorship laws during the decade. Less explicit were pulp novels featuring lesbian characters, many of which were written to exploit the topic of lesbianism; these were written by men or by women with male pen names and marketed to straight men in order to feed their sexual fantasies.

In 1950, Gold Medal Books, a newly minted paperback book subsidiary of magazine publisher Fawcett Publications, published *Women's Barracks*, a fictionalized account of French author Tereska Torrès's World War II experiences serving with Free French Forces. The first American-published pulp novel to include a lesbian relationship in its story, *Women's Barracks* is considered a pioneering example of lesbian fiction and is credited as the first American best-selling original paperback. The novel, with its lesbian content, suggestive cover art, and popularity with readers, was banned in Canada as "nothing but a description of lewdness from beginning to end" and was also banned in several U.S. states.

In 1952, the newly formed U.S. congressional House Select Committee on Current Pornographic Materials referred to the novel as an example of books promoting "moral degeneracy." Fawcett avoided the specter of a nationwide ban when it agreed to publish a second edition of the novel with a narrator who voiced a disapproval of the lesbian characters' behavior in order to instruct readers on morality and the "problem" of lesbianism.

Eager to replicate the popularity and financial success of *Women's Barracks: The Frank Autobiography of a French Girl Soldier*, Gold Medal Books next published *Spring Fire*, the first pulp novel to focus on a lesbian relationship. The novel concerns a love affair between two sorority sisters who continue to date men in order to remain closeted and seem "normal" and whose relationship results in the characters' repudiation of lesbianism and the mental breakdown and institutionalization of one of them because of it. The novel's author,

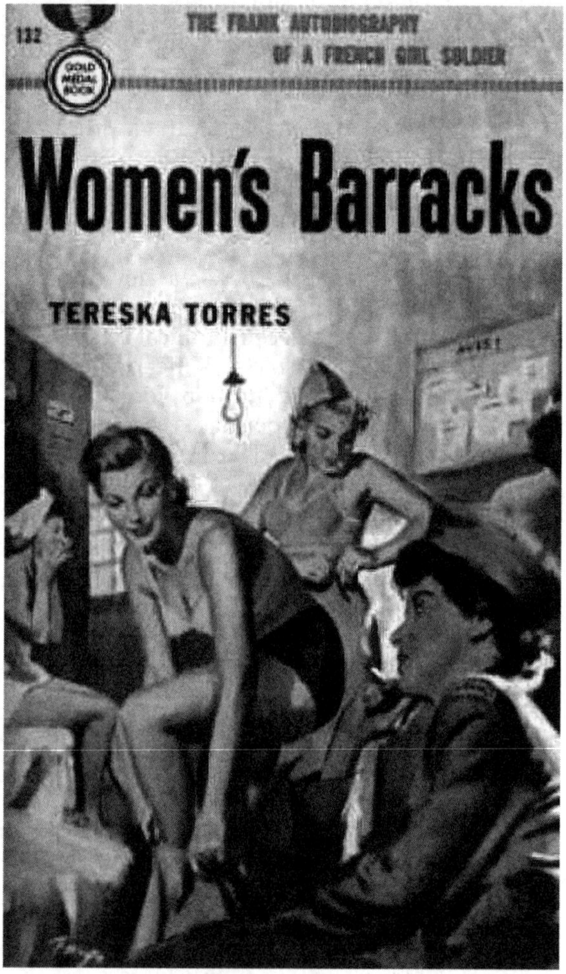

Tereska Torrès' 1950 book, Women's Barracks: The Frank Autobiography of a French Girl Soldier, *is considered the first lesbian pulp fiction book published in the United States. It was loosely based on the author's personal experiences during World War II.*

Marijane Meaker (1927–2022), who was commissioned to write *Spring Fire* under the pen name Vin Packard, was instructed by her editor to have the characters reject "homosexuality" as immoral so that the postal service, acting under provisions of the Comstock Act (which was established in 1873), would not consider the novel "obscene" and refuse to ship it. *Spring Fire* sold nearly 1.5 million copies during its first three printings, attracted a great deal of positive attention from women readers, and inspired other authors to write lesbian pulp fiction that would become classics of the genre.

One example is author and professor Ann Weldy (1932–) who, under the pen name Ann Bannon, wrote six influential lesbian pulp novels titled *The Beebo Brinker Chronicles*, which were published from 1957 to 1963. The series, which centered on a young lesbian who discovers and becomes more confident with her sexual identity, earned Weldy the title "Queen of Lesbian Pulp Fiction."

During the 1960s, *The Beebo Brinker Chronicles* received poor reviews in *The Ladder*, the Daughters of Bilitis publication, and from future Naiad Books publisher Barbara Grier (under the pseudonym Gene Damon). However, later critics have pointed to the novels as unique for their relative accuracy in portraying lesbian relationships. Author Katherine V. Forrest, creator of Kate Delafield, the first American fictional lesbian detective, has cited Beebo Brinker's influence on her own sexual identity and has referred to the character as "arguably the most iconic figure in lesbian fiction." A New York stage adaptation based on three books in the series, produced in the 2000s by Lily Tomlin and Jane Wagner, received the GLAAD Media Award.

Also considered a classic of lesbian pulp fiction and praised for its influence is Valerie Taylor's (1913–1997) *The Girls in 3-B* (1959), in which three young women from the same small town move to Chicago to find jobs and face the challenges of navigating big-city life. The novel explores such themes as sexual harassment, drug use, workplace discrimination, the pressure to marry, and the necessity of remaining closeted. Both the *Beebo Brinker* series and *The Girls in 3-B* have been cited as sympathetic and positive examples of lesbian pulp fiction authored by women and marketed as such, unlike earlier novels in the genre, which, as historian Lillian Faderman has observed, "warned females that lesbianism was sick or evil and that if a woman dared to love another woman she would end up lonely and suicidal."

The commercial and affordable genre-driven paperback pulp novel made the topic of lesbianism accessible to a wide number of readers, but lesbian and bisexual women characters had been present in literary fiction since the advent of the novel in the 18th century.

In Kate Chopin's 1899 landmark feminist novel *The Awakening*, married protagonist Edna Pontellier is romantically and sexually attracted to men, but gender studies theorist Mary Biggs has suggested that Edna's quest for social and sexual independence includes a capability for "responding physically to a woman and of loving a woman."

The early to mid-20th century continued to offer stylistically and thematically complex lesbian-focused fiction, the most influential of which was the groundbreaking 1928 novel *The Well of Loneliness* by British author Radclyffe Hall (1888–1943), born Marguerite Antonia Radclyffe Hall and, in adulthood, known as John. Hall's novel, considered by many to be a classic of LGBTQ+ literature, focuses on the love affair between an upper-class British woman named Stephen and Mary, a fellow ambulance driver, during World War I and explores the couple's social isolation and rejection because of their same-sex relationship as well as the sexual and gender implications suggested by Stephen's male name.

A defense of lesbianism, the novel was judged "obscene" by a British court and not published again until 1949; however, legal challenges in New York State and in the U.S. Customs Court failed to prevent bookstores from offering it. The publicity that accompanied the novel's legal battles led to a rise in lesbian visibility in British and American culture and, as the best-known English-language lesbian novel of the era, was often the first source on the subject for young women readers.

The first American-published, lesbian-centered novel was *Ladies Almanack* (1928) by artist, poet, and novelist Djuna Barnes (1892–1982), an illustrated, thinly disguised *roman à clef* concerning amorous pursuits among the lesbian writers (recast as pseudonymous characters) that she frequently encountered at American expatriate writer and hostess Natalie Clifford Barney's Parisian literary salon, including Radclyffe Hall and her partner, Una Vincenzo. Barnes would go on to author *Nightwood* (1936), notable for its explicit portrayal of lesbianism, intense prose style, modernist technique and for its ed-

The Awakening

By

KATE CHOPIN

Author of "A NIGHT IN ACADIE," "BAYOU FOLKS," Etc.

HERBERT S. STONE & COMPANY
CHICAGO & NEW YORK
MDCCCXCIX

A novel ahead of it's time, The Awakening *by Kate Chopin, features a female protagonist, Mrs. Pontellier, who challenges social norms, explores infidelity, questions the values of motherhood, and expresses sexual desires—all in ways considered outrages at the time of its 1899 publication.*

itor, poet, playwright, and future Nobel laureate T. S. Eliot.

Educator and writer Frances Rummel (1907–1969) drew upon her own life for her novel *Diana: A Strange Autobiography* (1939), which concerns the eponymous heroine's discovery of her lesbian identity and was unique for its sympathetic and positive portrayal of lesbianism and its happy outcome. *Diana* was published under the pen name Diana Fredericks; the author's real name was not known until after her death. The cover art of the original edition simply shows the statuelike figure of a woman, but the 1955 mass-market paperback version published by Berkley Books, retitled *Diana: A Strange Love,* featured a cover that was the erotically suggestive, stereotypical hallmark of pulp fiction.

Patricia Highsmith's romance novel *The Price of Salt* (1952), set in Manhattan and drawing from the author's experiences, concerns the love affair between two lonely women: Therese, a young, aspiring set designer unhappily dating a man, and Carol, a wealthy, soon-to-be divorced woman in her early 30s. The novel explores issues such as the recognition of sexual identity and the need to remain closeted, especially for a divorced woman with children, who would undoubtedly lose custody if her sexual orientation were known. English professor Susan Fraiman has called *The Price of Salt* an example of queer "shelter writing," in which lesbian protagonists need to find and arrange safe spaces to meet. Highsmith's publisher rejected her manuscript, and her agent warned that its publication would end her career. However, another hardcover publisher accepted it, using Highsmith's pen name, Claire Morgan. A pulp edition was published in 1953 as well as a mass-market paperback edition in 1969, after which the book remained out of print until 1983, when Naiad Press offered to publish the book under Highsmith's pen name. The acclaimed 2015 Todd Haynes film *Carol,* starring Cate Blanchett and Rooney Mara, is based on Highsmith's novel.

English professor Susan Fraiman has called* The Price of Salt *an example of queer "shelter writing," in which lesbian protagonists need to find and arrange safe spaces to meet.

A Place for Us (1969) by Alma Routsong (1924–1996) is a historical novel set in 1816 based on the 19th-century Boston marriage of painter Mary Ann Wilson and farmer Florence Brundage. The novel, which tells the story of two Connecticut women who fall in love and leave their homes to start a new life together on a farm in upstate New York, explores gender and sexual identity and orientation as well as the roles of women and religion in early 19th-century America.

After mainstream publishers rejected the manuscript, Routsong self-published 1,000 copies of the novel through Bleecker Street Press, which she created and named for the apartment she shared with her partner, Elizabeth Deran. Published under her pen name, Isabel Miller, an anagram of "lesbia" and her mother's maiden name, Routsong sold copies of her novel on the streets of New York City and at meetings of the Daughters of Bilitis, which promoted the book in its house publication *The Ladder*.

In 1971, the novel received the first-ever Gay Book Award under the auspices of the newly created Stonewall Book Awards for fiction and nonfiction, sponsored by the American Library Association. The novel's popularity inspired Routsong to resubmit the manuscript, which was accepted by mainstream publisher McGraw-Hill and republished in 1971 under the title *Patience and Sarah*. The opera *Patience and Sarah,* adapted from the novel, received positive reviews after its 1998 premiere at the Lincoln Center, and the novel became an award-winning screenplay in 2009. Arsenal Pulp Press, which published a 2005 paperback edition of the novel in its Little Sister's Classics series, has described *Patience and Sarah* as a "touchstone for the burgeoning gay and women's activism of the late 1960s and early 1970s."

In 1976, Catherine Nicholson and Harriet Ellenberger started the venerable *Sinister Wisdom* in Charlotte, North Carolina, a lesbian literary and art journal that has featured the works of such celebrated authors as Audre Lorde and Adrienne Rich. The 1980s and 1990s saw lesbian literature begin to diversify into genre fiction such as fantasy and science fiction, and a milestone was reached in lesbian feminist nonfiction in 1983 with the publication of Anita Cornwell's *Black Lesbian in White America,* the first collection of essays by an African American lesbian author.

It is also worth noting the positive fictional lesbian characters in comic books such as Maggie Sawyer of the Metropolis Special Crimes Unit, who has appeared in *Superman, Batman, Action Comics,* and *Detective Comics* as well as in the live-action series based on the comics, *Smallville* and *Supergirl*. Sawyer, who made her debut in 1987, had been married to a fellow police officer but later came out as a lesbian. An earlier example is the *Flash* newspaper city desk editor Hank O'Hair, the stereotypical butch-masculine-presenting sidekick and confidant of straight intrepid reporter Brenda Starr, the beautiful, red-haired title character of Dale Messick's long-running comic strip (1940–2011). When Hank was introduced in the early 1940s, many readers considered her character to be a lesbian, with the result being that Messick felt compelled to marry her off to a male artist in 1948.

Supergirl, a cousin of the Kryptonian Superman, first appeared in issue #123 of the Superman comic book, published in 1958. While Supergirl is not a lesbian, she is one of a growing number of women fictional characters in the genre, a sign that comic books are becoming less masculine-oriented.

Novels with transgender and gender identity themes emerged in the early 21st century, but a few 19th- and 20th-century examples are noteworthy. The 1891 fantasy novel *A Florida Enchantment* by writer and sometime publisher Archibald Clavering Gunter explores the boundaries of gender, sexuality, and social norms in the story of Lillian, a young woman on vacation in Florida who discovers a magical seed that grants her the power to change people's gender. She proceeds to transform a variety of colorful characters into the opposite gender, including herself, with scandalous and humorous results. The novel, now recognized as a queer classic, was well received in its day, but an 1896 stage adaptation was lambasted by *Variety* and *The New York Times,* which described it as "vile stuff" with a "most disagreeable theme."

The earliest 20th-century transgender novel prior to Stonewall and the first to feature a main character transitioning to a woman was Gore Vidal's satirical, epistolary, and often sexually graphic *Myra Breckinridge* (1968). The novel became a worldwide bestseller despite conservative book critics of the era who disregarded *Myra Breckinridge* as pornography and has since been recognized as a queer classic among some critics for its skewering of conventional gender and sexual identity and behavior. The 1970 film adaptation was universally panned; Vidal's 1974 sequel, *Myron*, was published soon after the Supreme Court's anti-pornography ruling in *Miller v. California*, which left the decision of what is considered pornography up to individual communities, is most notable for the author's replacement of profanity in the novel with the names of the five justices who voted for the decision as well as the names of well-known anti-pornography crusaders.

Stories with LGBTQ+ themes for preschool and beginning readers began to appear in the 1970s and, along with books for middle school and young adult (YA) readers, would become more numerous by the 21st century. LGBTQ+ picture books through the decades have focused on human families, though some have been "metaphor" books that featured animals as characters. Notable early picture books include *When Megan Went Away* and *Lots of Mommies* (Jane Severance, 1979, 1983); *Heather Has Two Mommies* (Lesléa Newman, 1989); and *Daddy's Roommate* (Michael Willhoite, 1990). Early picture books with themes of gender identity include *William's Doll* (Charlotte Zolotow, 1972); *Oliver Button Is a Sissy* (Tomie dePaola, 1979); and *Jesse's Dream Skirt* (Bruce Mack, 1979).

According to the American Library Association, parental and political activism regarding book bans has escalated, with more than 4,000 books being targeted for censorship and wholesale removal by 2022.

A few 20th-century novels featured gay teens as protagonists or supplementary characters, but it was not until the late 1960s that the term "young adult" (YA) began to be commonly used to describe and market realistic fiction written specifically for readers generally aged 12 to 18. The earliest LGBTQ+ YA novel was *I'll Get There. It Better Be Worth the Trip* by John Donovan, published in 1969, in which a lonely, young, gay teen struggles with his mother's homophobia and feelings of guilt over his sexual orientation when she discovers his relationship with a male classmate. LGBTQ+ literature has represented a relatively small fraction of the entire book market, with 136 titles for children and YA readers published in 2017, according to a study conducted by the Cooperative Children's Book Center (CCBC) at the University of Wisconsin's School of Education.

Larger publishing houses have often rejected titles with LGBTQ+ themes and characters because of perceived smaller profits and the additional possibility of controversy; however, some smaller presses have specialized in LGBTQ+ fiction for adult, child, and YA readers, most notably Alyson Books, based in New York City but founded in Boston in 1980 by writer and businessman Sasha Alyson.

Attempts have been made for decades to ban some books representing a variety of LGBTQ+ themes and content in public libraries, especially in classrooms and school libraries, throughout the United States. In recent years, many more books have been labeled "sexually explicit," "pornographic," "indecent," or academically and politically "undesirable."

According to the American Library Association, parental and political activism regarding book bans has escalated, with more than 4,000 books being targeted for censorship and wholesale removal by 2022. During the same year, according to *The New York Times*, more than 150 bills in 35 states were aimed at restricting or removing access to school and public library materials and called for the punishment of staff who refused to comply. Targeted books have included those with profanity and sexual content; books with LGBTQ+ themes and individuals; books about peo-

The 2019 graphic memoir Gender Queer *by Maia Kobabe is about an honest portrayal of an adolescent exploring their gender identity and sexuality as they enter adulthood. It has been widely banned in American schools.*

ple of color, including queer people of color; and Black history, the latter of which has been incorrectly conflated with the academic discipline known as critical race theory.

In 2023, the majority of the top 10 most challenged books contained LGBTQ+ themes. First on the list was *Gender Queer: A Memoir* (2019), a graphic novel by cartoonist and author Maia Kobabe, which has been the most consistently banned LGBTQ+ book in American school districts since its publication. Second and third on the list of challenged books were George M. Johnson's *All Boys Aren't Blue* (2021), a YA memoir about Johnson's experience as a queer, Black man growing up in New Jersey.

By 2025, some school libraries removed or covered shelves containing books with LGBTQ+ content as well as books on Black history. In June 2025 in a 6–3 decision, the U.S. Supreme Court, in the case of *Mahmoud v. Taylor*, ruled that parents of elementary school-aged children had the right to opt out of classroom instruction featuring books that addressed gender identity and sexual orientation.

In 1989, the annual Lambda Literary Awards, also known as the "Lammys," was instituted in order to acknowledge queer excellence in adult, YA, and children's fiction, nonfiction, and poetry; to increase visibility for LGBTQ+ writers and their works; and to bring attention to LGBTQ+ publishers and bookstores. The first awards focused on gay and lesbian works and AIDS literature, but the program dropped the category as the HIV crisis began to recede and added categories for bisexual and transgender literature. The first Lambda Literary Awards honored books written in 1988, and the winners included Paul Monette (*Borrowed Time: An AIDS Memoir*); Edmund White (*The Beautiful Room Is Empty*); George Baxt (*Who's Next*); Dorothy Allison (*Trash: Short Stories*); and Carl Morse and Joan Larkin (*Gay & Lesbian Poetry in Our Time*).

Music

The 20th century saw the emergence of American classical, popular, and rock music by LGBTQ+ composers, songwriters, and performers who would become among the most celebrated musical artists in the world. Many of them were closeted to all but their close friends and colleagues until later in the century for fear of public rejection, but there were exceptions. Sam-

Musician, composer, and lyricist Billy Strayhorn collaborated with Duke Ellington and penned such hits as "Take the A Train" and "Chelsea Bridge."

uel Barber (1910–1981), a classical composer celebrated for his operas and his exquisite, highly popular 1938 composition *Adagio for Strings*, lived openly with his longtime partner, Italian American opera composer Gian Carlo Menotti (1911–2007). Their careers did not suffer because of their orientation; Menotti was best known for the classic Christmas opera *Amahl and the Night Visitors* (1951) and was a two-time recipient of the Pulitzer Prize for his operas *The Consul* (1950) and *The Saint of Bleecker Street* (1955), both of which enjoyed successful runs on Broadway. Composers Virgil Thompson (1896–1989) and Ned Rorem (1923–2022) were also open, if discreet, about their lovers and partners.

The 1966 publication of Rorem's Paris and New York diaries, in which he wrote openly and frankly about his sexuality and relationships, garnered praise for Rorem as a gay icon and pioneer of gay liberation. Giants of 20th-century classical and popular music such as Aaron Copland, Leonard Bernstein, and the incomparable songwriter Cole Porter remained publicly closeted. Composer, lyricist, arranger, and pianist Billy Strayhorn (1915–1967), who collaborated with bandleader Duke Ellington for nearly 30 years and composed, among other works, the band's signature tune "Take the A Train," was openly gay to band members and his friends.

Queer representation in popular music during the early to mid-20th century included such popular African American singers, songwriters, and recording artists as "Mother of the Blues" Gertrude "Ma" Rainey (1886–1939) and "Empress of the Blues" Bessie Smith (1894–1937), both of whom began their careers on the Black vaudeville circuit, and Lucille Brogan (1897–1948), who recorded some of the most explicitly sexual songs in the genre. Rainey's 1928 song "Prove It on Me Blues" alludes to a 1925 incident in which Rainey was arrested for participating in an orgy with the women in her chorus. An ad for a recording of the song featured Rainey in a three-piece suit, a skirt, and a man's fedora talking to two stylish African American "flappers," with a white police officer lurking behind them in the shadows. Scholar Angela Davis has credited "Prove It on Me Blues" as an influential song during the 1970s lesbian cultural movement.

Memphis-born jazz and blues singer–songwriter Alberta Hunter (1895–1984) was a closeted lesbian who began her jazz and blues career in a Chicago brothel, became a headliner at well-known city nightclubs, and, during the 1920s, undertook a successful European tour, where she replaced bisexual star Josephine Baker at the Casino de Paris music hall. In 1954, Hunter abandoned her singing and recording career to become a nurse; made a sensational comeback with a series of well-attended appearances at the Cookery, a Greenwich

Village restaurant and nightclub, beginning in 1977; and continued performing and recording until her death. Hunter's primary romantic and sexual relationship was with Lottie Tyler, the niece of Black vaudevillian Bert Williams, but she had a brief, unhappy, and unconsummated marriage to African American labor leader Willard Saxby Townsend from 1919 to 1923. Maxene Andrews (1916–1975), the middle sister of the highly popular and influential close harmony trio the Andrews Sisters, married music publisher Lou Levy in 1941 despite having had a relationship with her manager, Lynda Wells, since 1937. Andrews separated from Levy in 1949, and she and Wells eventually became longtime partners.

During the 1950s and 1960s, LGBTQ+ singers and songwriters remained closeted or did not publicly come out until later in their lives and careers. San Francisco-raised crooner Johnny Mathis (1938–), a Grammy Lifetime Achievement Award winner and the third best-selling pop and jazz musical artist of the 20th century, managed to keep his sexual orientation private and, unlike other celebrities of the era, was not either personally or professionally compelled to date women in order to appear straight. In a 1982 article in *Us Weekly* magazine, Mathis was quoted as saying, "Homosexuality is a way of life that I've grown accustomed to," a remark he claimed was intended to be off the record and would not discuss for many years because of subsequent death threats. In 2017, Mathis revisited the article during an interview on *CBS News on Sunday Morning* and confirmed that he was gay.

The 90-year-old Johnny Mathis still performs concerts as of 2025. A successful performer since the 1950s, he didn't come out until much later in his life.

The media frequently speculated on the sexual orientation of British singer Dusty Springfield (1939–1999), considered to be one of pop music's most iconic solo performers in the United States as well as in Britain. Springfield feared the loss of her career if it became known that she was a lesbian, but after the subject was raised in a newspaper interview in 1970, she admitted to her five-year relationship with American singer–songwriter Norma Tanega and came out publicly as bisexual. Mid-1960s pop star Lesley Gore (1946–2015), popular for her songs about teen girl–boy angst with the hit "You Don't Own Me," knew she was a lesbian by the age of 20. Gore lived with LGBTQ+ rights activist Lois Sasson from 1963 until her death but kept her orientation and her relationship with Sasson private until 2005.

Critically acclaimed singer–songwriter Laura Nyro (1947–1997), whose songs, such as "Wedding Bell Blues," "Eli's Coming," and "Stoney End," became commercial hits with artists like the Fifth Dimension and Barbra Streisand, was bisexual, a fact known only to her closest friends. Nyro had several relationships with men and one marriage and, in 1980, began living with painter Maria Desiderio (1954–1999) in a relationship that lasted until Nyro's death.

The last decades of the 20th century began to see more openly LGBTQ+ American musical artists, though some solo performers and band members, like those who came before them, did not officially come out as queer until later in their careers. Soft rock performer Barry Manilow (1943–) kept his orientation secret because he did not want to disappoint his mostly female fan base. Manilow did not officially come out as gay until 2017, three years after marrying his manager and longtime partner, TV executive Gary Kief. At the time, Manilow also mentioned his early, two-year marriage to Susan Deixler, with whom he had been in love, stating that their marriage did not fail because of his sexual orientation.

The first openly gay rock musician to be signed to a major record label was glam rocker Jobriath, born Bruce Wayne Campbell (1946–1983), whose first album *Jobriath*, with Elektra Records, debuted in 1973. The following year, he appeared on the popular TV music show *The Midnight Special*. The disco era of the late 1970s saw the formation of the Village People, a popular group named in recognition of Greenwich Village as a gay village and costumed to symbolize aspects of American machismo gay fantasy culture, with such personas as cowboy, sailor, leather biker, police officer, and construction worker. Only two of the original members were openly gay. The Village People was the brainchild of French disco producers Jacques Morali and Henri Belolio, who moved to New York in 1977 and teamed up with straight singer–songwriter Victor Willis (1951–), who would become the group's lead singer. Intended to appeal to a gay audience, the Village People quickly crossed over into the mainstream with such hits as "Macho Man" and "YMCA" (both 1978).

A group that is known for covering a wide range of musical genres is the gay men's chorus, the world's first openly gay chorus, which was founded as the San Francisco Gay Men's Chorus (SFGMC) in 1978 by gay music pioneer Jon Reed Sims. The group's 1981 national tour and companion recording sparked an LGBTQ+ choral movement that saw the formation of gay men's chorus groups in several cities in the United States as well as in Canada and Australia. Jay Davidson, a founding member of the SFGMC, went on to create the Gay and Lesbian Association of Choruses, an international association of LGBTQ+ choruses also known as the GALA Choruses, which made its debut at the 1982 Gay Games in San Francisco.

Pop crooner Barry Manilow made a career making women swoon since the 1970s, but he didn't come out until 2017.

A lesbian music movement began to emerge during the early 1970s at the same time as a lesbian-feminist-separatist movement, the latter formed as a reaction against the heteronormativity of the women's liberation movement that began in the mid to late 1960s and a lack of lesbian representation in the wake of the post-Stonewall gay rights movement.

In 1973, members of the lesbian separatist group the Olivia Collective, named after the title character in a 1949 coming-of-age novel by bisexual English author Dorothy Bussy, founded Olivia Records in Washington, D.C., the first women-owned record label. Olivia Records would relocate to California in 1976, first to Los Angeles and then to Oakland in 1977. The label's founders included political activist and Furies Collective member Ginny Berson, singer–songwriter Meg Christian, entrepreneur Judy Dlugacz, and seven other Olivia Collective members. Olivia Records' first best-selling artists were Meg Christian and singer–songwriter and activist Cris Williamson, who were featured with separate songs, "Lady" (Christian) and "If It Weren't for the Music" (Williamson), on each side of the label's first 45 record.

By the late 1970s, Olivia Records had begun to promote Black artists such as singer–songwriter Linda Tillery and composer and pianist Mary Watkins. In 1977, Olivia Records responded to singer and orange juice promoter Anita Bryant's anti-gay campaign Save Our Children with the well-received album *Lesbian Concentrate: A Lesbianthology of Songs and Poems*, a compilation of lesbian music and the spoken word. The album's cover featured a can of orange juice labeled "Lesbian Concentrate," a nod to Bryant's role as spokesperson for the Florida Citrus Commission. In 1983, Meg Christian left the label, and by 1988, despite three large-grossing anniversary concerts at Carnegie Hall during the decade, Olivia Records faced financial difficulties as well as the dispersal of five of its founding members. The Olivia brand restructured its business model and be-

Singer-songwriter Meg Christian has been active in the women's music movement since the 1970s. Favoring folk music as a genre, she tries to make audiences more aware of political issues regarding women.

came a lesbian travel agency.

Olivia Records' historical influence can also be seen in the advent of women's music festivals, which also addressed the underrepresentation of women in the music industry and at the same time contributed to the need for safe spaces for women, especially lesbian women, to connect, network, and perform music. The festivals helped launch and advance the careers of lesbian musical artists, including Olivia Records musicians Meg Christan and Cris Williamson as well as singer–songwriters Holly Near and Alix Dobkin (1940–2021), the latter of whom would go on in 1979 to become the first lesbian feminist musician to do a European concert tour.

The first large and most enduring women's music festival was the National Women's Music Festival (NWMF), which was founded in 1974 at the University of Illinois, expanded in 1976, and incorporated as Women in the Arts/ National Women's Music Festival, Inc. (WIA/NWMF) in 1982. As of 2025, the WIA/ NWMF was based in the Madison, Wisconsin, area. The Michigan Womyn's Music Festival (MWMF), also known as Michfest, was held annually from 1976 to 2015 on privately owned woodland in Oceana County. During the 1990s, the MWMF drew criticism for its policy of excluding trans women from such LGBTQ+ activist groups as the Human Rights Campaign, GLAAD, the National LGBTQ Task Force, and the National Center for Lesbian Rights. The group Camp Trans held annual demonstrations at the festival.

The first large and most enduring women's music festival was the National Women's Music Festival (NWMF), which was founded in 1974 at the University of Illinois. . . .

Some women musical artists whose careers began to flourish during the 1980s and 1990s have refused to bow to speculation regarding their sexual orientation, while others have declared themselves as openly lesbian. Emily Sailers (1963–) and Amy Ray (1964–), who comprise the folk-rock duo the Indigo Girls and are considered LGBTQ+ icons for their activism on behalf of queer rights, came out as lesbians in 1989, although in recent years, they have identified as queer in acknowledgment of the complex nature of sexual and gender identity.

The music and success of the Indigo Girls, together with the songs of such late century chart-toppers as singer–songwriter Melissa Etheridge (1961–), whose demo tape was rejected by Olivia Records in 1975, and Canadian pop and country singer–songwriter k. d. lang (1961–) resonated with their young lesbian fans and helped pave the way for lesbian musicians of the 21st century, one of whom, singer–songwriter Brandi Carlile (1981–), has been nominated for 27 Grammy awards, has received 10 Grammys, and is a two-time Emmy Award winner.

The music industry has included a number of LGBTQ+ and straight American and British artists who have been celebrated over the years as queer icons and allies, some of whom are also known for their work onstage and on the screen: Ethel Merman, Doris Day, Liza Minnelli, Barbra Streisand, Cher, Diana Ross, Bette Midler, Dolly Parton, Dusty Springfield, Madonna, Lady Gaga, Taylor Swift, Elton John, Freddie Mercury, George Michael, and Culture Club's Boy George.

The legendary singer–actress Judy Garland (1922–1969), born Frances Gumm, stands out as the first and perhaps the most special gay icon. Garland first attained iconic status with her role as Dorothy in the 1939 film *The Wizard of Oz*; additionally, the term "friend of Dorothy" came to be used to describe a gay man. One of the most shining and admired performers of her generation and beyond, Garland, who solidified her status with her powerful, richly voiced, and emotionally rendered performances in films such as *A Star Is Born* (1954), in concert, and on television, had nevertheless been exploited early on by MGM Studios for her talent and endured a lifetime of personal

Judy Garland (shown here in her iconic role as Dorothy Gale in the 1939 movie The Wizard of Oz*) became an icon of the gay community, and "friend of Dorothy" became a term to describe gay men.*

and professional struggle, which ended with her death due to a barbiturate overdose just days before the Stonewall Uprising. Garland's uniqueness as a performer, together with her difficult life and tragic death, touched all of her fans but perhaps resonated most with the gay community, who saw her as a reflection of their own struggles in a homophobic society. Garland's rendering of "Over the Rainbow" would become the first American gay anthem.

Subsequent LGBTQ+ anthems have included Doris Day's rendition of "Secret Love," which she performed in the 1953 film *Calamity Jane*; Barbra Streisand's "Don't Rain on My Parade" (1968); songs by the Village People (1970s); Gloria Gaynor's 1978 disco hit "I Will Survive"; Diana Ross's "I'm Coming Out" (1980); Madonna's "Vogue" (1990); Lady Gaga's 2011 cover of Carl Bean's 1977 song "I Was Born This Way"; and Hayley Kiyoko's "Girls Like Girls" (2015).

A notable queer ally in the music world has been pop star Cyndi Lauper, whose original rendition of the 1986 Billy Steinberg and Tom Kelly hit song "True Colors" has also become a gay anthem; she cofounded the True Colors Fund, a nonprofit organization dedicated to ending LGBTQ+ youth homelessness. Lauper would go on to supply the music for *Kinky Boots*, a stage musical based on the 2005 British film of the same name in which a shoe factory owner forms an unlikely partnership with Lola, a cabaret star and drag queen. In 2022, Lauper performed "True Colors" at the ceremony during which President Joe Biden signed the Respect for Marriage Act into law.

Theater

During the 19th and early 20th centuries, popular American theater catered to rural and urban audiences with variety entertainments such as traveling medicine shows, the Wild West shows of Buffalo Bill Cody, circuses, burlesque shows, and the Ziegfeld Follies. A form of variety theater called vaudeville, an American version of the British music hall, began in the 1860s and remained popular until the 1930s and was notable for featuring vaudevillians performing comedic skits, circus acts, and musical numbers, many of whom would go on to lucrative radio, film, and television careers and worldwide stardom.

Moms Mabley (born Loretta Mary Aiken, 1897–1975), one of the first openly queer comedians, parlayed a successful career on the Black vaudeville circuit, then called the Chitlin' Circuit, into recording, movie, and TV fame. She came out as a lesbian in 1921, recorded lesbian-themed stand-up routines, and, in 1939, became

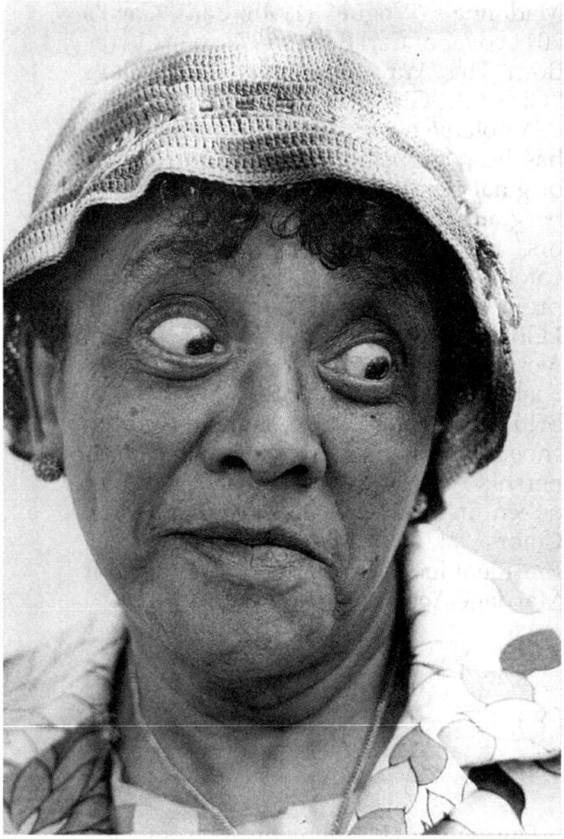

Jackie "Moms" Mabley appearing in character on a 1968 episode of The Smothers Brothers Comedy Hour. *Mabley was not secretive about being queer and had relationships with both men and women.*

the first woman comedian to perform at Harlem's Apollo Theater.

Vaudeville also merits a place in LGBTQ+ history for its drag stars, then billed as "female impersonators," some of whom were closeted gay men and, in rare cases, openly gay. Two examples are Karyl Norman (1897–1947), born George Peduzzi, and Barbette (1899–1973), born or self-named either Vander Clyde or Vander Clyde Broadway. Norman was a popular and likely closeted headliner who billed himself as the "Creole Fashion Plate," appeared in stage plays and musical comedies as well as in vaudeville, toured internationally, and headlined at the famed vaudeville venue the Palace Theatre in 1923 in an act titled *Glorifying the American Boy–Girl*, an allusion to impresario Florenz Ziegfeld's Follies, which was advertised as "Glorifying the American Girl."

Barbette, a high-wire performer and trapeze artist who performed his acts in full drag, made his debut at the Harlem Opera House in 1919 and went on to tour the vaudeville circuit and appear in such Parisian venues as the Moulin Rouge and the Folies Bergère. Barbette's engagement at the London Palladium was cut short and his permit to work in England permanently rescinded when he was discovered having sex with another man. He found a champion and admirer in gay French avant-garde artist, playwright, and filmmaker Jean Cocteau, with whom he had a brief affair and who cast him in a scene in his first film, *The Blood of the Poet* (1930), where the performer appeared dressed in a gown designed by Coco Chanel. After his performing career ended, Barbette became a consultant on several films, including the quasi-drag comedy *Some Like It Hot* (1959), where he coached actors Jack Lemmon (playing Daphne) and Tony Curtis (playing Josephine) on the art of gender illusion.

Gay and lesbian characters were present in early to mid-20th-century plays and musical theater prior to the 1960s either in coded references, through innuendo, or stereotyped as the public often saw them, with gay characters in vaudeville and burlesque presented as "effeminate" and "flamboyant" and termed "pansy characters" or "Nances" (a slang pejorative derived from "Nancy" or "Nancy Boy") and lesbians characterized as "manly." The perception that to be seen as gay or lesbian was shameful was further enhanced by the obscenity laws that allowed police to close down theaters showing plays that were deemed objectionable.

Change began during the 1960s as an LGBTQ+ theater movement began to take shape as a specific genre, thanks to the advent of downtown Off-Off-Broadway avant-garde theaters and performance spaces such as the Limbo Lounge, Joe Ci-

Fashion designer Ellen Stewart started La MaMa Experimental Theatre Club in 1961 in New York's East Village above her basement boutique, where she sold her original designs.

no's Caffe Cino, Ellen Stewart's La MaMa Experimental Theatre Club, and Al Carmines's Judson Poets' Theatre, venues that, together with Off-Broadway theaters, would come to feature the work of openly gay playwrights who wrote about visibly gay characters as well as plays and sketches within the popular subgenre of drag theater. However, Broadway remained an elusive goal for the genre until the 1970s and 1980s, stereotyping of LGBTQ+ people in stagecraft often endured, and lesbian representation was sparse.

The LGBTQ+ theater movement would lead to the proliferation of queer New York theater companies such as Charles Ludlam's Ridiculous Theatrical Company in 1967 and playwright Doric Wilson's The Other Side of Silence Theatre Company (TOSOS) in 1973 as well as San Francisco's Theatre Rhinoceros (aka Theatre Rhino aka The Rhino) in 1977 and Boston's Triangle Theater Company in 1980. San Francisco's avant-garde drag theater group the Cockettes (1969–1972), founded by actor and performance artist Hibiscus (George Edgerly Harris III, 1949–1982), first offered parodies of musical comedies and went on to perform their own works. One of the Cockettes's most notable members was openly gay African American singer Sylvester (born Sylvester James Jr., 1947–1988), who achieved success in a variety of popular musical genres, including disco. In 1978, the Gay Theatre Alliance was founded in order to help promote gay and lesbian theater across the country, and New York's National Queer Theater (NQT), founded in 2018, would go on to cofound the Queer Theatre Alliance in 2020, a national network of theaters for LGBTQ+ artists and audiences.

Plays

The first known 20th-century play to feature a lesbian scene was *God of Vengeance*, a 1906 Yiddish drama written by Sholem Asch and set in a Jewish brothel. After a six-month run in Berlin, Germany, in 1907, the play was brought to Broadway, where it was alternately reviled and praised by reviewers in the Jewish community for its provocative content. A 1922 production at the Provincetown Playhouse in Greenwich Village moved to the Apollo Theater on Broadway the following year and was shut down less than a month later for violating the New York Penal Code, with everyone involved with the production, including the theater owner, arrested and indicted on obscenity charges. The convictions were overturned after a lengthy court battle.

A 2015 play by prolific Pulitzer Prize–

winning lesbian dramatist Paula Vogel titled *Indecent* concerns the controversy over *God of Vengeance* and was produced on Broadway in 2017. *The Captive*, a 1926 three-act French melodrama by Edouard Bourdet in which a young Parisian woman in a passionate lesbian love affair must choose between her lover and the man who loves her and to whom she is engaged was a scandalous hit on Broadway and ran for 160 performances before police shut it down. The ensuing court cases over *The Captive*, along with *The Drag* (marketed as "a male *Captive*") and *Pleasure Man*, which were gay/drag plays written and produced by the irrepressible future movie star Mae West under the pen name Jane Mast, as well as West's prostitution drama, *Sex*, in which she appeared, led to the Wales Act, aka the Wales Padlock Law, in 1927.

A precursor of Hollywood's 1930 Motion Picture Production Code, also known as the Hays Code, which was implemented to set moral standards for movies, the Wales Act, sponsored by New York state senator B. Roger Wales, amended the penal obscenity code to ban plays "depicting or dealing with, the subject of sex degeneracy, or sex perversion" and allowed the closure of productions and padlocking of theaters. The last Broadway show impacted by the Wales Padlock Law was *Trio*, a lesbian drama by Dorothy and Howard Baker that was based on Dorothy Baker's 1943 novel, which concerns the rivalry between a woman professor and a young man for the affections of a female graduate student. The play ran from late November 1945 to February 1946 before it was shut down.

Lillian Hellman's acclaimed first play, *The Children's Hour*, which ran on Broadway from 1934 to 1936 and was a critical and financial success as well as being a

The original cast of the 1934 Broadway production of The Children's Hour *included (left to right) Robert Keith, Anne Revere, Florence McGee, Katherine Emery, and Katherine Emmet.*

contender for the Pulitzer Prize for Drama, tells the story of close friends Martha and Karen, who own and operate a girls' boarding school in New England and whose lives and livelihoods are destroyed after a spiteful student falsely accuses them of having a lesbian relationship. Martha ultimately confesses her love for Karen, with further tragic results that reflect the literary trope of queerness perceived as somehow shameful. *The Children's Hour* escaped the Wales Padlock Law in New York only to be banned in Boston at the behest of the city's censorship organization, the Watch and Ward Society, as well as in Chicago. In London, Lord Chamberlain, the royally appointed censor, banned a public performance of the play, which was then presented in private at the independent Gate Theatre Studio. *The Children's Hour* was revived on Broadway in 1952, nine years before Hollywood's straight-washed film version was released.

The first known American play with a suggestive gay theme was Henry Blake Fuller's melodrama At Saint Judas' . . .

In 1959, Broadway debuted one of the most celebrated plays in the history of American theater: Lorraine Hansberry's *A Raisin in the Sun*, the story of a Black family's experiences in South Chicago. A closeted lesbian, Hansberry was a member of the Daughters of Bilitis while she was writing the play and was later married to producer and songwriter Robert Nemiroff for nine years.

Lesbian themes and characters onstage were not perceived as commercially viable until the 1980s and 1990s. A notable early example is Jane Chambers's two-act play *Last Summer at Bluefish Cove*, which premiered Off-Broadway at the Actors' Playhouse in 1982. The play focuses on the friendships of lesbian friends and a straight outsider who share a summer cottage and is considered to be the first mainstream lesbian drama.

In 1990, the Five Lesbian Brothers, a lesbian theater troupe formed in the 1980s that first performed as satirists at New York's WOW Café, produced their first play, *Voyage to Lesbos*, set in the town of Lesbos, Illinois, during the 1960s, and performed it at WOW. The troupe went on to write and produce the satirical comedies *Brave Smiles* (1992) and *The Secretaries* (1994), the latter as the more successful and well reviewed of the two, both of which were shown at the New York Theatre Workshop (NYTW).

The first known American play with a suggestive gay theme was Henry Blake Fuller's melodrama *At Saint Judas'*, which was included in his 1896 anthology of 12 one-act plays titled *The Puppet Booth* and intended to be read and not performed. The play takes place in a church sacristy and is a dialogue between two characters who are military officers: the unnamed Best Man and the Bridegroom, who is about to be wed. The two are close friends in the tradition of physically affectionate, though apparently not sexually intimate, 19th-century romantic friendships, but when the jealous Best Man confesses his passionate love for the Bridegroom and attempts to sabotage the wedding ("I have loved you all my life.... The thought of *her* made me desperate... made me mad..."), the Bridegroom becomes enraged, draws his rapier, and exhorts the Best Man to use it to commit suicide in order to expiate his shameful confession, which he does.

British imports to Broadway, such as Nöel Coward's *The Vortex* (1925) and Mordaunt Shairp's *The Green Bay Tree* (1933), raised speculation concerning the sexual orientation of their characters. In Coward's play, the adult son of an aging, promiscuous beauty is addicted to cocaine, considered at the time as code for gayness. When reviewing a revival of *The Green Bay Tree* in 1951, *New York Times* theater critic Brooks Atkinson referred to the play's exploration of a "half-suggested homosexual relationship." In American playwright Eugene O'Neill's *Strange Interlude* (1928), the trajectory of main character Richard

Marsden throughout the play suggests an ambiguous sexual orientation in contrast to the straight sexual desires of the characters with whom he interacts.

Two popular mid-century plays by straight playwrights, Robert Anderson's *Tea and Sympathy* (1953) and Arthur Miller's *A View from the Bridge* (1955), featured plot elements that reflected the long-held view that it was unmasculine, shameful, and altogether socially abnormal to be gay or to be perceived as gay. Tennessee Williams and Edward Albee, two of three prominent gay playwrights of the 1940s, 1950s, and 1960s, did not hide the fact that they were gay, while the third, William Inge, remained closeted. All three were Pulitzer Prize recipients best known for classic American plays that focus on straight characters who were often in difficult or dysfunctional friendships and familial, marital, sexual, and romantic relationships. However, Inge also wrote three short plays that include gay characters, one of which, *The Boy in the Basement* from the early 1950s, concerns a middle-aged, closeted gay man who lives with his parents.

Queer references exist in the plays of both Williams and Albee. In Williams's *Cat on a Hot Tin Roof* (1955), it is suggested that alcoholic main character Brick, who has rejected sexual and emotional intimacy with his beautiful wife, Maggie, the "cat" of the title, may be denying his romantic and sexual attraction to his close college friend, Skipper, whose advances he had rejected and who committed suicide for reasons not revealed in the play. *The Zoo Story* (1959), Albee's two-character, one-act play on the theme of social alienation, has been seen as a coded gay allegory.

After Albee's *Tiny Alice* premiered on Broadway in 1964, the play received a scathing indictment from author Philip Roth in *The New York Review of Books* titled "The Play That Dare Not Speak Its Name." In it, Roth castigates the play's codified "pansy rhetoric and repartee—all of this can be traced to [Albee's] own unwillingness or inability to put its real subject at the center of the action."

The same year, the earliest play in the nascent LGBTQ+ theater movement to gain mainstream critical attention, Lanford Wilson's *The Madness of Lady Bright*, opened at Caffe Cino. The one-act play, primarily a monologue delivered by Leslie Bright, an aging, lonely drag queen reflecting on his life and work, is one of the first to explicitly feature realistic, non-stereotyped, openly gay characters. The actor who originated the lead role of Leslie Bright won an Obie Award for his performance, and the play went on to tour internationally and has frequently been revived. Roth's review of

The film version of Tennessee Williams' Cat on a Hot Tin Roof *(1958) starred Elizabeth Taylor (as Maggie the Cat) and Paul Newman (as Brick). The story is about a family that keeps secrets to themselves, including Brick's concealed homosexuality.*

(Left to right) Frederick Combs, Cliff Gorman, Reuben Greene, Kenneth Nelson, and Keith Prentice in a scene from the 1970 adaptation of The Boys in the Band, *a tale of complex relationships and homosexual angst that was considered a milestone in gay cinema.*

Tiny Alice and Wilson's play, as well as the less socially constricted world of Off- and Off-Off-Broadway, would likely not have escaped the notice of conventional Broadway-oriented theater critics, one of whom was writer and editor Stanley Kauffmann (1916–2013).

In January 1966, during an eight-month stint as theater critic for *The New York Times*, Kauffmann wrote an article titled "Homosexual Drama and Its Disguises," in which he, in effect, called for the end of queer-coded theater. Kauffmann, who cited but did not name "three of the most successful American playwrights of the last twenty years...(reputed) homosexuals," was presumably referring to Tennessee Williams, William Inge, and Edward Albee when he argued that the work of the "homosexual dramatist" offers "a badly distorted picture of American women, marriage, and society in general." Instead, he went on to assert, a gay playwright "must be free to write truthfully of what he knows, rather than try to transform it to a life he does not know, to the detriment of his truth and ours."

Given the enduring power and popularity of the works written by the three playwrights in question as well as the freedom and ability of a writer to successfully provide dramatic conflict out of their own particular experiential and creative predilections, Kauffmann's thesis seems ignorant and offensive (his writings have sometimes been criticized as homophobic), but at the same time, it was a liberating call for gay playwrights to write their own uncloseted truth.

A playwright who was about to do just that was Mart Crowley, whose groundbreaking and well-received ensemble drama *The Boys in the Band* offered a candid, pre–gay liberation movement portrayal of gay lives and perspectives. After having difficulty in finding an agent willing to pitch a "gay" play and a lack of interest from producers and theater owners, Crowley gained support from Edward Albee and producer–director Richard Barr, who headed the Playwrights Unit and was president of the League of American Theatres and Producers. *The Boys in the Band* debuted Off-Broadway in 1968, a year after the repeal of the Wales Padlock Law, and enjoyed a successful run until 1970, when the original cast appeared in a feature film based on the play, which was notable as a milestone in the history of gay cinema. A revival of the play debuted on Broadway in 2018, and a second movie adaptation was released on Netflix in 2020. Crowley's limited-run sequel, *The Men from the Boys*, premiered at San Francisco's Conservatory Theater Center in 2002.

Noteworthy post-Stonewall plays by gay playwrights that achieved Broadway status were Terrence McNally's comedy *The Ritz* (1975), set in a gay bathhouse and featuring Rita Moreno in a Tony Award–winning performance; Martin Sherman's *Bent* (1979), concerning the persecution of gay men in Nazi Germany; and Harvey Fierstein's *Torch Song Trilogy*, starring Fierstein as a gay drag queen and torch singer, which debuted Off-Broadway at La MaMa Experimental Theatre Club in 1978 and moved to Broadway in 1982.

Despite the increasing visibility of the post-Stonewall queer community overall and its unwillingness to remain in the shadow of the closet, public condemnation and blacklisting continued to represent a threat, even in the theater world where, unlike most workplaces, there was a greater tolerance of gay colleagues. Theatrical agents persisted in urging their gay clients to escort women to awards shows rather than their partners and to eschew any mention of partners or lovers in public. Then, at the 1983 Tony Awards ceremony, producer John Glines became the first person to directly acknowledge a same-sex relationship on a nationally televised awards show when

Harvey Fierstein (right) and Matthew Broderick play Arnold Beckoff and his young boyfriend Alan, who is beaten to death by a homophobic gang in 1988's Torch Song Trilogy.

he accepted the Tony for *Torch Song Trilogy* as Best Play and thanked "my partner and my lover, Lawrence Lane" during his speech. The public response was swift: Glines received death threats, but many more people across the country wrote heartfelt letters to thank him for his statement. Glines's choice to mention his partner came at a historical moment when the queer community was facing a new disease that would threaten LGBTQ+ social gains and at the same time necessitate a positive change in public attitudes concerning gay visibility and acceptance in American society.

Early awareness came on May 18, 1981, when the influential biweekly gay newspaper the *New York Native* published the first report of a type of pneumonia affecting some gay men that would come to be known as AIDS and would take the lives of many gay theater professionals, including five of the actors appearing in the original production of *The Boys in the Band* as well as *Boys* director Robert Moore and producer Richard Barr. At the same time, the HIV/AIDS crisis produced not only an activism driven by the epidemic's toll on a still marginalized population but also some of the most powerful plays in LGBTQ+ history and the history of American theater.

Plays during the first decades of the AIDS epidemic include *The AIDS Show (Artists Involved with Death and Survival)*, a collaboratively written theater piece that explored the impact of AIDS on the queer community, which was produced by San Francisco's Theatre Rhinoceros in 1984; William Hoffman's *As Is* and AIDS activist Larry Kramer's *The Normal Heart*, both produced in 1985 and set in New York City during the rise of the epidemic; Tony Kushner's complex, operatic, multi-award-winning two-part play *Angels in America*, subtitled *A Gay Fantasia on National Themes*, which made its Broadway debut in its entirety in 1993 after *Part One: Millennium Approaches* and *Part Two: Perestroika* premiered separately in San Francisco, Los Angeles, and London; and Terrence McNally's award-winning *Love! Valour! Compassion!*, in which eight gay friends of differing personalities, professions, and stages in life and love, two of whom are suffering from AIDS, come together on each of the three summer holiday weekends at one character's lakeside vacation home north of New York City.

Musical Theater

The early 20th century saw the evolution of the operetta into a distinctly American Broadway musical comedy form beginning with the immensely popular productions of George M. Cohan, which were stories heavy with musical interludes and songs that would become American classics. Musical theater would become more complex and sophisticated with such musical comedies and dramas as Jerome Kern and Oscar Hammerstein's *Showboat* (1927); Cole Porter's *Anything Goes* (1934); and Rodgers and Hammerstein's *Oklahoma!* (1943), the latter of which would define the form for decades to come, not least because it was the first musical to feature choreography integral to the plot.

One notable musical comedy lyricist was Lorenz Hart (1895–1943), whose collaboration with composer Richard Rodgers (the same Rodgers of Rodgers and Hammerstein) on such hit Broadway musicals as *Babes in Arms* (1937) and *Pal Joey* (1940) supplied lyrics for show tunes that have since become classic standards, including "My Funny Valentine," "Bewitched, Bothered, and Bewildered," and "Manhattan." Hart was considered among his colleagues and social circle to be gay and closeted, and his lyrics, like those of his contemporary, Cole Porter, have often been interpreted as queer coded.

Broadway musicals featured the first openly LGBTQ+ character in 1969, when actor René Auberjonois appeared as stereo-

The wildly successful Broadway musical A Chorus Line *tells the stories of various members of the backup dancers, including one who describes his difficult coming out to friends and family.*

typically flamboyant gay costume designer Sebastian Baye, the nasty nemesis of Katharine Hepburn's Coco Chanel in the Alan Jay Lerner and André Previn musical *Coco*. The following year, the Betty Comden and Adolph Green musical *Applause*, based on the Oscar-winning 1950 film *All About Eve*, featured the genre's first likeable gay character, hairstylist Duane Fox, as well as including a scene in a gay bar. *Seesaw* (1973), a musical adaptation of William Gibson's 1958 play *Two for the Seesaw*, netted the first of several Tony Awards for the multitalented Tommy Tune as openly gay choreographer David as well as Tonys for director and choreographer Michael Bennett, who also authored the musical's book.

Bennett would go on to win a Tony for his direction and choreography of the long-running hit musical *A Chorus Line*, which debuted on Broadway in 1975. One of the highlights of *A Chorus Line* is a heartfelt monologue delivered by Paul, one of two gay actor–dancers auditioning for a spot on the line, who relates his experience of discovering his sexuality and coming out to his family and friends. Matron "Mama" Morton, who presides over the women's block of the Cook County Jail in the 1975 musical comedy *Chicago*, is a butch lesbian who reveals how she can influence the career ambitions of the central women characters, Roxie Hart and Velma Kelly, with the song "When You're Good to Mama."

One of the first popular musicals to feature gender and sexual fluidity, most notably through central drag character Dr. Frank-N-Furter, was *The Rocky Horror Show*, which began its Broadway run in 1975. A humorous tribute to science fiction and horror B movies of the early 1960s, *The Rocky Horror Show* became the cult classic film *The Rocky Horror Picture Show* in 1975 and has toured nationally and internationally as a stage show since its first production in London's West End theater district in 1973.

A milestone in musical theater was reached in 1983 when *La Cage aux Folles*, with lyrics by Jerry Herman and book by Harvey Fierstein, opened on Broadway. The first hit Broadway musical to center on a gay relationship, the musical's central characters are Georges, the manager of the eponymous St. Tropez nightclub featuring drag shows, and his partner, Albin, the club's star attraction. The musical's first-act finale features Albin singing "I Am What I Am," a song that became a gay anthem and was first covered by disco star and gay icon Gloria Gaynor the same year.

In the 1989 musical *Grand Hotel*, based on the 1929 Vicki Baum novel and the 1932 film, the character of Rafaela reveals to the audience through the songs "22 Years/Villa on a Hill" and "How Can I Tell Her?" that she is deeply, and hopelessly, in love with her straight employer, prima ballerina Elizaveta, one of the show's central characters.

The first show to feature a lesbian couple is the 1992 sung-through Broadway musical *Falsettos*. A musical with two acts comprising of and named for the one-act Off-Broadway musicals *March of the Falsettos* (1981) and *Falsettoland* (1990), the second and third in a trio of musicals that begins with *In Trousers* (1979), *Falsettos* centers on gay characters, with lesbian couple Cordelia and Charlotte being introduced in *Falsettoland*. The two-act musical is set in New York City in 1979 and 1981 and includes the second-act song "Something Bad is Happening," sung by physician Charlotte, who is alluding to the onset of the AIDS epidemic.

RENT, a 1996 musical based on Giacomo Puccini's 1896 opera *La Bohème*, concerns struggling, young, straight and queer artists living in the Alphabet City area of Manhattan, some of whom are HIV positive and one of whom has AIDS. One of the longest-running shows on Broadway at 12 years, *RENT* was critically acclaimed and received a Tony Award for Best Musical as well as a Pulitzer Prize.

A scene from the 2005 movie adaptation of RENT.

Broadway has traditionally represented the gold standard for American theatrical productions, and the arrival of musical theater featuring LGBTQ+ characters and themes was a historical moment in queer history, one that reflects the increased visibility of the LGBTQ+ community during the last decades of the 20th century and into the 21st century.

But the 1989 Off-Off-Broadway musical *Elegies for Angels, Punks and Raging Queens* is notable for its enhancement of queer visibility in a very personal way. The creation of composer Janet Hood and Tony-nominated librettist and lyricist Bill Russell (1949–) that was inspired by the NAMES Project AIDS Memorial Quilt and Edgar Lee Masters's classic *Spoon River Anthology* (1915), the musical, set to a blues, jazz, and rock score, comprises more than 30 free-verse poems offering the perspective of the people named on the quilt who lived with AIDS and lost their lives to the disease as well as the feelings of family and friends who were left behind to cope with their loss. *Elegies* was first staged in New York City's Soho at the TWEED New Works Festival and, since the 1990s, has seen productions at various venues in New York, in London, and in various countries around the world.

Film

LGBTQ+ representation, whether queer coded or open, has been present in film ever since silent movies inaugurated the medium in the first decades of the

20th century. During the silent film era, cross-dressing and gender reversal was a staple of comedy films starring such popular actors as Charlie Chaplin, Mabel Normand, Wallace Beery, Oliver Hardy, and Fatty Arbuckle, often in the plot as a prelude to the slapstick antics common in the genre.

A 1914 silent film that LGBTQ+ film historians consider to be one of the earliest on-screen depictions of cross-dressing that includes gender *and* sexual role reversal with lesbian, transgender, and bisexual characters is *A Florida Enchantment*, a comedy–fantasy based on Archibald Clavering Gunter's 1891 novel.

LGBTQ+ characters began to effectively disappear with the advent of the "talkies" and the moral guidelines and studio self-censorship guided by the National Legion of Decency (aka the Catholic Legion of Decency), founded by John T. MacNicholas, the archbishop of Cincinnati, and the Hays Code, which were both created in 1934. Named for Will H. Hays, president of the Motion Picture Producers and Distributors (MPPDA), the Hays Code's Hollywood enforcer from 1934 to 1954 was Catholic journalist Joseph Breen and would be supplanted in 1968 by the Motion Picture Association of America's ratings code, which remains in effect today. The Legion's influence ceased in 1980 soon after its reorganization into the National Catholic Office for Motion Pictures (NCOMP).

Censorship codes included a variety of prohibitions relating to "moral standards" and included proscriptions against depictions of miscegenation (interracial relationships) and explicit sexuality and/or "any inference of sex perversion," which *de facto* meant homosexuality even though sexual orientation was not specifically mentioned. Films with cross-dressing characters escaped censorship if they were comedies or if the characters were clearly heterosexual.

Some 1930s and mid-century films featuring plots that revolved around gender reversal include *Sylvia Scarlett* (1935), a box-office failure starring Katharine Hepburn as a woman con artist presenting as a young man to evade police; *Charley's Aunt* (1941), based on the stage farce and starring comedian and radio star Jack Benny as the titular character; and *I Was a Male War Bride* (1949), a post–World War II comedy with Cary Grant in drag as an Army nurse so that he can join his wife, played by Ann Sheridan, on a transport ship.

Some Like It Hot (1959) adds an interesting element to its comical drag premise of two male musicians who disguise themselves as women and join a women's band in order to evade the murderous gangsters hot on their trail. The two succeed so successfully in presenting as women that they both become objects of desire to a horny bellboy; a wealthy, old yachtsman, who proposes marriage; and the gangsters. *Some Like It Hot*, which became an enormous hit and is rated as one of the greatest films of all time, might have raised eyebrows at the Hays office had it not been a screwball comedy helmed independently by Billy Wilder as producer and director and distributed at a time when Hays's influence was beginning to wane.

The 1919 German film *Anders als die Andern* (*Different from the Others*) is con-

In a scene from the 1919 German movie Different from the Others, *Paul Körner (left) is a violinist struggling with his sexuality when he meets "the Doctor," an intellectual who believes that alternative sexualities are just as legitimate as socially accepted ones.*

sidered to be the first film to openly and positively depict a gay couple. Set during the post–World War I years of the Weimar Republic, the film concerns Paul Körner, a famous violinist who, after first rejecting and then accepting his orientation, is the target of a would-be extortionist who has seen him holding hands with his lover. When the scandal becomes public, Körner's career is destroyed, and he commits suicide. The film was cowritten by gay German sexologist Magnus Hirschfeld (1868–1935) and starred Conrad Veidt (1893–1943), both of whom would escape Nazi Germany: Hirschfeld to France and Veidt eventually to America, where he would gain everlasting fame as the villainous Major Strasser in *Casablanca.* The film led to new censorship laws in Germany, and the film's opponents labeled Hirschfeld and his cowriter, director and producer Richard Oswald, both of whom were Jewish, as promoting the "Jewish vice of homosexuality." When the Nazis came to power in 1933, *Different from the Others* joined the regime's many banned "decadent" works, and prints of the film were burned.

OutFest, a national LGBTQ+-centered nonprofit organization that sponsors film festivals, a streaming platform, and educational services for filmmakers, screened the film at events in Los Angeles and New York in 2012 and 2016. *Different from the Others* inspired the 1961 British film *Victim,* starring Dirk Bogarde as a closeted lawyer who, like Veidt's Körner, stands up to his would-be blackmailer in court. A 2022 article in *The Advocate* points to the film's patronizing take on gay men as "poor souls who just can't help themselves" but praises the film's call for tolerance and its "stand against the criminalization of homosexuality," which "enables blackmail."

Pandora's Box (1929), a German silent film starring American actress Louise Brooks (1908–1985) as a beautiful, seductive, and destructive 1920s courtesan, features an openly lesbian subplot that was groundbreaking for its time, which was either eliminated from the film or re-edited, depending on the censorship laws in the countries in which it was shown. Brooks never declared a straight, lesbian, or bisexual orientation but claimed to be sexually fluid and to have had lesbian dalliances, including one with likely bisexual film legend Greta Garbo.

The 1920s and pre-Code 1930s saw a variety of social, romantic, and sexual themes expressed in film, but opinion is divided on which early film was the first to feature a same-sex kiss.

The 1920s and pre-Code 1930s saw a variety of social, romantic, and sexual themes expressed in film, but opinion is divided on which early film was the first to feature a same-sex kiss. During the previous decade, director D. W. Griffith's multi-timeline, three-hour-long epic *Intolerance* (1916) included a close embrace and a kiss between Babylonian prince Belshazzar and his beloved warrior, the Mighty Man of Valor (played by Elmo Lincoln of early *Tarzan* fame). Director Cecil B. DeMille, best known for the 1956 remake of his silent version of *The Ten Commandments*, used the dramatic trope of a selfish, thrill-seeking young woman who must pay the price for her willfulness in his 1922 drama *Manslaughter*, notable as one of the first films to include an orgy as well as an erotic lesbian kiss.

William Wellman's Academy Award–winning 1927 silent and synchronized sound film *Wings*, the story of two World War I fighter pilots who are best friends in love with the same woman, features a well-executed tracking scene of couples at tables at the Café de Paris, one of which is an affectionate lesbian couple. Toward the end of the film, when one of the friends is mortally wounded in combat, the other holds him close and kisses him tenderly.

The 1930 pre-Code drama *Morocco*, starring the openly bisexual Marlene Dietrich and directed by Josef von Sternberg, has Dietrich, after performing at a cabaret in a top hat, white tie, and tailcoat, bestow a kiss on a woman in the audience.

The first gay bar in film appears in a brief scene during the 1932 pre-Code wild-girl-gone-wrong melodrama *Call Her Savage,* in which two waiters in drag perform a song about sailors. Gays and lesbians were portrayed in several other pre-Code films, with both often appearing according to derogatory stereotypes: gay characters as high-voiced and flighty; lesbians as burly and butch.

The 1933 Fox Film Corporation musical *My Weakness* is said to be the first mainstream film to use the word "gay" to indicate a same-sex male relationship; in this case, it was as a solution proposed by one man to another when neither of the two can elicit a romantic interest from the woman they love. The pre-Code censors at Fox's Studio Relations Committee (SRC) insisted that the word had to be muffled, and by 1933, the Hays office warned that all gay characters would be removed from films.

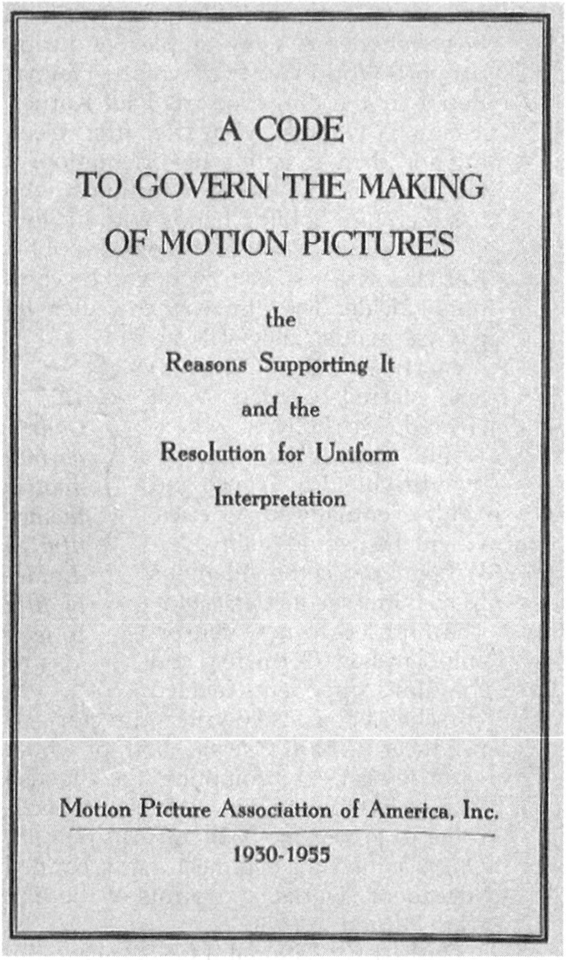
A CODE
TO GOVERN THE MAKING
OF MOTION PICTURES
the
Reasons Supporting It
and the
Resolution for Uniform
Interpretation
Motion Picture Association of America, Inc.
1930-1955

The Motion Picture Production Code (or Hays Code, as it was called, after Will H. Hays, the president of the Motion Pictures Producers and Distributors of America) set rules as to what was acceptable to show in movies. It was enforced from 1934 to 1968, when it was replaced by the Motion Picture Association of America's rating system.

Morals clauses permitting studios to discontinue actors' salaries "if they forfeit the respect of the public" were fixtures in stars' contracts even before the beginning of Hollywood's "Golden Age" (1927–1960) and the introduction of the Hays Code. Such clauses would remain in force after the gay liberation movement following the 1969 Stonewall Uprising, keeping many LGBTQ+ actors and actresses closeted for fear of losing their fans and their careers, although there were some who preferred to keep their orientation private even when it became potentially less career damaging to come out.

Morals clauses, along with the Hays Code influencing film production and distribution, prompted Hollywood studios and their publicists and "fixers" to mount campaigns to ensure that the public believed that their favorite LGBTQ+ movie and, later, television stars were straight and to counteract rumors in gossip columns and fan magazines such as *Confidential* that they were not, a practice known as "straightwashing."

One way to hide their stars' orientation was through pairing them with straight men and women (aka "beards") in arranged dates ("front dating") and "lavender marriages," the most famous of which was the 1955–1958 lavender marriage between closeted gay Universal Studios heartthrob Rock Hudson and Phyllis Gates, who was the secretary of a Hollywood talent agent. An earlier example is the 1919 arranged marriage between actress Jean Acker (1892–1978) and silent film sex symbol Rudolph Valentino (1895–1926), both of whom were rumored to be queer. Acker, a member of a group of closeted lesbian and bisexual Hollywood actresses nicknamed the "sewing circle" whose film career lasted from 1913 to 1955, reportedly locked her new husband out of their hotel room on their wedding night and divorced him in 1923.

One gay Hollywood star who refused to publicly deny his orientation was popular leading man William Haines (1900–1973). Forced to choose between his rising film career and his life partner, Jimmie Shields, Haines chose his partner and in 1935 left the film business to set up with Shields what would become a successful interior design firm that included many of Haines's Hollywood friends among his clients.

Movie heartthrob Rudolph Valentino, who died young from sepsis after an appendicitis, made women swoon in the 1920s but was rumoured to be gay.

With morals clauses and Hays Code censorship firmly in place and, together with the Catholic Legion of Decency, also founded in 1934, attempting to govern morality on and off the screen and legislating to studios and moviegoers the approval or disapproval of a film's production and distribution, directors managed to elude censorship regarding sexuality and sexual orientation through the creative use of queer coding to suggest gay and lesbian identity. At the same time, many queer-coded characters continued to be subject to prevailing negative public stereotypes of lesbians and gays as abnormal, disturbed members of society: comically mannish or effeminate; dramatically criminal, psychopathic, tragic, or mentally ill; misfits deserving of a shameful end; or, at the very least, only worthy of ridicule.

The musical film *Wonder Bar* (1934), which barely escaped Hays Code censorship, is another relic of the ways in which gay men were often stereotyped. The film, starring popular singer Al Jolson (1886–1950), includes a scene in which a handsome man asks to cut in on a dancing couple. The woman partner readies herself to dance with the man, who ignores her and begins dancing with her male partner. This elicits a response from Jolson's character, who flaps his wrist in effeminate fashion and exclaims, "Boys will be boys! Woo!"

Another contender for the first use of the word "gay" in a same-sex context is director Howard Hawks's 1938 screwball comedy *Bringing Up Baby*. When Cary Grant's mild-mannered, priggish paleontologist, David, throws on a woman's feather-trimmed robe because airheaded love interest Susan (Katharine Hepburn) has sent his own clothes to the cleaners, David's appearance prompts Susan's aunt to indignantly ask him why he is wearing "these" clothes. Grant's frenetic ad-libbed response is "Because I just went GAY all of a sudden!" Grant's ad-lib most likely avoided censorship because of its ubiquitous presence as a word indicating "merry" or "cheerful" as well as the comedic silliness of Grant's delivery, which hearkens back to the comic cross-dressers of silent movies.

Each character in the nonhuman trio accompanying Dorothy and Toto to the Emerald City in the classic 1939 film *The Wizard of Oz* is played for laughs, but Bert Lahr, who, like Jolson, started his show business career in vaudeville, played the Cowardly Lion as a comic stereotypical stage "sissy," a self-proclaimed, wrist-flapping "dandy-lion," code words for queer.

In *The Women* (1939), based on Clare Booth Luce's Broadway play and helmed by gay director George Cukor, successful, financially independent writer Nancy Blake is stereotypically queer coded as the only unmarried and working woman and also the only one who prefers mannish suits in contrast to her coterie of wealthy women friends, who dress in the height of late 1930s feminine fashion. Nancy, who describes herself as "what nature abhors. I am an old maid. A frozen asset," responds to her friends and their romantic machinations with gentle comic ironic disdain.

A slightly more overtly coded character is Mrs. Danvers, the housekeeper in Alfred Hitchcock's *Rebecca* (1940), based on Daphne du Maurier's best-selling 1938 gothic novel. Judith Anderson, who plays Mrs. Danvers, makes it abundantly clear to the audience that her character was—and remains—unrequitedly and obsessively in love with the deceased title character.

Gay and lesbian subtexts are present in films of the 1940s and 1950s. Peter Lorre's queer-coded, stereotypically prissy villain Joel Cairo in the film noir classic *The Maltese Falcon* (1941) is written as gay in Dashiell Hammett's 1930 novel, but when director John Huston was writing the

The villain Joel Cairo (played by Peter Lorre, at right, shown with Sydney Greenstreet) in the classic film noir The Maltese Falcon is a prissy character with obvious queer undertones.

screenplay, the Hays office warned him not to try to give Joel a "Nancy" quality.

A gay subtext is present in the relationship between characters Brandon (John Dall) and Phillip (Farley Granger), young, sophisticated, well-to-do intellectuals who share a Manhattan penthouse apartment in Alfred Hitchcock's 1948 psychological crime thriller *Rope*. Enthralled by the notion of German philosopher Friedrich Nietzsche's intellectually superior *übermench* (superman), Brandon and Phillip kill their visiting prep school classmate, David, as an exercise in committing the perfect murder. They hide the body in a chest in their apartment, where it lies while they host a party, and deflect questions from David's parents and aunt concerning David's whereabouts until all unravels, thanks to their suspicious headmaster (James Stewart), who is appalled that his rhetoric on the "superman" inspired his former students to commit the crime. The film's screenwriter, Arthur Laurents, when interviewed for Vito Russo's 1981 book *The Celluloid Closet*, suggested that Hays censors "didn't have a clue what was and what wasn't [in the film], that's how it got by."

Films set in prisons, particularly in women's prisons, often lent themselves to a lesbian-coded subtext with pulp fiction flair, as in James Cromwell's grim, socially conscious 1950 film *Caged*, adapted from screenwriters Virginia Kellogg and Bernard C. Schoenfeld's short story "Women Without Men."

In Hitchcock's *Strangers on a Train* (1951), adapted from Patricia Highsmith's 1950 novel, tennis star Guy befriends wealthy, sexually ambiguous psychopath Bruno (Robert Walker) while traveling by train to Washington, D.C., by way of his hometown. Bruno proposes an exchange of murders: He will kill the promiscuous wife that Guy plans to visit and has been unsuccessfully trying to divorce so that he can marry a senator's daughter, and Guy will kill Bruno's hated father. When Bruno, unbidden, kills Guy's wife, Guy refuses to reciprocate and desperately tries to distance himself, whereupon Bruno attempts to frame him for his wife's murder. Film professor and historian Robert L. Carringer offered a political subtext to the film that is embodied in the similarly sexually ambiguous and therefore vulnerable character of Guy who, Carringer suggests, represents the harassed victims of the homophobic Lavender Scare during the Cold War climate of hysteria that pervaded Congress in the early to mid-1950s.

During the late 1950s, studios often edited or eliminated gay or gay-coded characters and themes from films adapted from plays. *Tea and Sympathy* (1956) presented the central character, a young, questioning prep school student as sexually naïve but straight, while the film version of *Cat on a Hot Tin Roof* (1958) eliminated nearly all suggestions of main character Brick's romantic and sexual feelings for his dead fraternity brother, much to the reported dismay of playwright Tennessee Williams.

By the 1960s, films with LGBTQ+ themes and characters started to become more visible, if subject to the same defining LGBTQ+ stereotypes, because of a gradual relaxation of Hays censorship. Hays liberalization was due to a variety of factors: the 1952 Supreme Court case *Joseph Burstyn, Inc., v. Wilson*, which determined that film as an artistic medium was entitled to First Amendment protection regarding free speech; studios' willingness to ignore the Code in some cases in order to compete with television; a shift toward independent filmmaking and producing; access to more socially liberal international films; and moviegoers' increasing disinclination to rely on the Catholic Church or conservative Protestant groups to inform them about what and what not to see.

The 1936 film version of Lillian Hellman's play *The Children's Hour*, directed by William Wyler, had been adapted to conform to the Hays Code, with the plot changed to reflect a heterosexual love triangle and the title changed to *These Three*. When the play's second film adaptation, starring Shirley MacLaine and Audrey Hepburn, was released in 1961, it retained

Hellman's title and kept its lesbian subplot largely intact.

A more widely seen breakthrough film was David Lean's Oscar-winning epic biographical film *Lawrence of Arabia* (1962), which concerns the exploits of British army officer and Middle East diplomat T. E. Lawrence. Lean's film suggests that the complicated Lawrence, whose sexuality has been much debated, was gay as well as sexually masochistic, the latter opinion shared by Lawrence's biographers. As Lean later stated: "We thought we were being very daring at the time: Lawrence and Omar [Omar Sharif, who played Lawrence's Arab friend Sherif Ali], Lawrence and the Arab boys."

During the 1960s and 1970s, pop artist Andy Warhol offered an avant-garde and queer approach to filmmaking, with a long catalog of underground films starring the straight and LGBTQ+ artists, musicians, and literary figures who frequented his New York studio, the Factory. These included such "Warhol Superstars" as gay sex symbol Joe Dallesandro (*Flesh*, 1968 and *Trash*, 1970) and transgender actress Holly Woodlawn (*Trash* and *Women in Revolt*, 1971). Woodlawn is also notable as the "Holly" in musician Lou Reed's 1972 hit song "Walk on the Wild Side." Reed was a regular at the Factory, along with members of his and John Cale's band, the Velvet Underground.

During the 1960s and 1970s, pop artist Andy Warhol offered an avant-garde and queer approach to filmmaking, with a long catalog of underground films starring the straight and LGBTQ+ artists, musicians, and literary figures who frequented his New York studio, the Factory.

Notable documentaries on queer subculture during the 1960s included *Portrait of Jason* (1967), a cinéma verité film by Shirley Clarke on the life of Black gay nightclub owner, performer, and hustler Jason Holiday, considered controversial for its white filmmaker's perceived mockery of a Black gay man, and *The Queen* (1968), directed by Frank Simon, which explores the world of drag culture through competitors in the Miss All-America Camp Beauty Contest.

The film trope of homosexuality as shameful and potentially career or even life-ending persisted during the 1960s in such political dramas as *Advise and Consent* (1962), which was based on Allen Drury's novel in which a young senator commits suicide when a previous same-sex liaison threatens to become public and includes a scene in a gay bar, and *The Best Man* (1964), based on Gore Vidal's play, which features a presidential candidate who was accused of having had a gay relationship. Films began to treat gay characters more sensitively as the 1970s progressed in the wake of Stonewall and gay liberation.

Early in the decade, films such as *The Boys in the Band* (1970) and the prison film *Fortune and Men's Eyes* (1971), which was based, like *The Boys in the Band*, on a stage play, portrayed gay men in a sympathetic manner. In 1978, feminist filmmaker Barbara Hammer (1939–2019), whose *Dyketactics* (1974) is considered the first lesbian film made by a lesbian, released *Double Strength*, the last in a series of avant-garde films exploring lesbian identity, desire, and sexuality through her then relationship with a trapeze artist. Hammer's first feature, *Nitrate Kisses*, an award-winning documentary concerning the marginalization of LGBTQ+ people in the 20th century, was released in 1992.

The 1980s in LGBTQ+ film began with the psychological thriller *Windows*, the only movie directed by famed cinematographer Gordon Willis. In it, a recently divorced New York woman is the subject of her psychopathic lesbian next-door neighbor's obsession. The film elicited many protests from queer activists for its homophobia and hateful lesbian stereotypes as well as a negative review from *New Yorker* critic David Denby, who described the film as only existing "in the perverted fantasies of men who hate lesbians so much they will concoct any idiocy in order to slander them."

On the heels of *Windows* came the poorly received film *Cruising* (1980), directed by William Friedkin of *Exorcist* fame and starring Al Pacino as an undercover police officer investigating the serial killings of gay men picked up in New York City's West Village gay bars. The film was the target of many protests by the gay and lesbian community during production and after its release over Hollywood's long campaign to present gay men, as one activist pamphlet put it, "one-dimensional sex-crazed lunatics, vulnerable victims of violence and death." For the protestors, *Cruising* invited violence against the gay community: "This is not a film of how we live: it is a film about why we should be killed...." In the main, however, there was a slowly growing tolerance of the queer community during the decade. That tolerance would be tested with the rise of religious fundamentalist groups and the emergence of the HIV/AIDS epidemic, which, before AIDS was fully understood, attempted to validate the negative stereotypes of gays as the "sex-crazed lunatics" referenced in the abovementioned pamphlet protesting *Cruising* or by labeling gay men as disease-spreading drug addicts.

However, like the playwrights of the 1980s and 1990s, filmmakers rose to the challenge, offering films that featured characters with AIDS such as *Longtime Companion* (1989), the first to be released in theaters; *Parting Glances* (1986), considered influential in the history of LGBTQ+ cinema for its evocative and detailed representation of New York gay and gay-friendly urbanites; the documentary *Paris Is Burning* (1991), a chronicle of 1980s drag ball culture comprised of gay, Black, Latino, and transgender communities; and *Philadelphia* (1993), Jonathan Demme's legal drama, in which an attorney (Tom Hanks) hires a homophobic lawyer (Denzel Washington) to sue the employer that fired him after learning he was gay and had AIDS. The widely released and positively re-

Tom Hanks (right) plays a gay lawyer who hires an attorney played by Denzel Washington to sue his employer after he was fired for being gay and having AIDS in the critically acclaimed 1993 film Philadelphia.

viewed film netted an Oscar for Best Actor for Tom Hanks, and Bruce Springsteen received an Academy Award for Best Original Song for "Streets of Philadelphia."

The Hollywood star most often mentioned as an LGBTQ+ ally and well known for her advocacy on behalf of the queer community, especially during the AIDS crisis, was Elizabeth Taylor (1932–2011), whose close friends and colleagues included the celebrated, closeted actors Montgomery Clift (1920–1966) and Rock Hudson (1925–1985). In 2000, she was presented with the Vanguard Award at the annual GLAAD (Gay & Lesbian Alliance Against Defamation) Media Awards for her work in increasing the visibility and understanding of the LGBTQ+ community. During her acceptance speech, Taylor referenced the ignorance concerning the disease that led to the rampant discrimination against gay men in the early to mid-1980s as well as the Reagan administration's lack of support for the gay community during the crisis. Her speech also advocated for gay marriage and the legal right for LGBTQ+ couples to adopt.

Notable documentaries during the 1980s include Rob Epstein's Oscar-winning *The Times of Harvey Milk* (1984), the story of the assassinated California political figure, with playwright and actor Harvey Fierstein as narrator, and Greta Schiller and Robert Rosenberg's *Before Stonewall* (1984), a chronicle of the LGBTQ+ community prior to the modern gay rights movement that featured interviews with many influential LGBTQ+ artists and activists.

The 1980s also saw more sympathetic and creatively conceived films with lesbian themes and characters, such as Lizzie Borden's dystopian drama *Born in Flames* (1983) and John Sayles's *Lianna* (1983), which, along with Donna Deitch's *Desert Hearts* (1985), are notable as films about lesbians in love with happy endings.

The genre of LGBTQ+ cinema (also known as queer cinema) centered on queer themes and characters and was recast as New Queer Cinema, a term coined by film scholar and editor of *Film Quarterly* B. Ruby Rich in 1992 to describe a growing movement of LGBTQ+ independent films covering all aspects of the queer experience, often challenging traditional assumptions of LGBTQ+ identity, gender, class, family, and society. The use of the word "queer" reflected aspects of queer theory in 1980s and 1990s academic writing and differed from ways in which the word began to be used as an inclusive description of LGBTQ+ identity and experience.

Todd Haynes's *Poison* (1991), Tom Kalin's *Swoon* (1992), Gregg Araki's *The Living End* (1992), and the Wachowskis' crime thriller *Bound* (1998) are pioneering examples of New Queer Cinema's focus on explicitly lesbian and gay protagonists and themes and the genre's sometimes hostile approach toward straight culture.

Queer cinema of the 1990s, as Wilson Chapman of the film industry and film criticism website *IndieWire* observed, "set the bar high for the many LGBTQ films to follow." These would include critically praised and award-winning 21st-century American gay-, lesbian-, transgender-, and genderqueer-focused films such as *Hedwig and the Angry Inch* (2002), based on the 1998 Broadway rock musical comedy; Ang Lee's modern cowboy romance *Brokeback Mountain* (2006), the first LGBTQ+ film to be nominated for a Best Picture Oscar; the comedy–drama *Tangerine* (2015), which sparked the first Academy Awards campaign to include openly transgender actresses among the nominees; Todd Haynes's widely acclaimed lesbian romance *Carol* (2015), based on Patricia Highsmith's novel and starring Cate Blanchett as the titular character; *Moonlight* (2016), a coming-of-age drama praised for its representation of the Black and LGBTQ+ community and the first film in the genre to win an Academy Award for Best Picture; the heartfelt American, Italian, and French coming-of-age romantic drama *Call Me By Your Name* (2017), based on Italian American writer André Aciman's 2007 novel and the recipient of several awards as well as four

Heath Ledger (left) and Jake Gyllenhaal play straight-looking cowboys who fall in love in the 2005 film Brokeback Mountain *based on the story by Annie Proulx.*

Academy Award nominations, earning an Oscar for Best Adapted Screenplay; and prolific and influential film and television producer and director Greg Berlanti's teen romantic comedy *Love, Simon* (2018), which concerns issues relating to closeting, coming out, acceptance, and concepts of normativity.

Milestones in TV

1948. One of the most popular entertainments offered on the fledgling medium of television are comedy–variety programs featuring such former vaudevillians as comedians Milton Berle, Bob Hope, and Jack Benny. In 1948, Berle becomes the permanent host of the *Texaco Star Theater,* which is renamed the *Milton Berle Show* in 1955. Popularly known as "Uncle Miltie" and "Mr. Television," Berle routinely dresses in female drag during the variety show's comedy skits, including in a skit with Bob Hope, who is also in drag. Characters and performers in drag would appear in several shows throughout television history, one of the most influential of which was the reality show *RuPaul's Drag Race,* which debuted in 2009.

1961. *The Rejected,* the first made-for-television documentary film about gay men, is produced independently by John W. Reavis for the San Francisco TV station KQED, which broadcasts the program on September 11. Reavis's goal is to present "as objective analysis of the subject [of homosexuality] as possible without being overly clinical." To that end, the film features interviews with gay men and the opinions of professionals and community leaders such as anthropologist Margaret Mead, Episcopal bishop James Pike, psychiatrist Karl Bowman, and openly gay Mattachine Society president Hal Call together with other society members. The documentary is later syndicated to National Education Television (NET) stations across the United States.

1967. The TV career of iconic costume and fashion designer Bob Mackie (1939–) takes off when he begins an 11-year engagement as designer for *The Carol Burnett Show.* Among his many memorable costume designs is the famous curtain dress worn by Burnett in "Went with the Wind," the show's well-loved spoof of the classic film *Gone with the Wind.* Mackie's designs for singer–actor Cher become equally famous. Mackie had been discovered by legendary costumer Edith Head at Paramount Pictures in 1961 and received his first big break in 1963 designing for *The Judy Garland Show,* where he met his life partner, designer Ray Aghayan (1928–2011).

1972. The *ABC Movie of the Week* broadcasts the made-for-television drama *That Certain Summer,* which concerns a father in a same-sex relationship who must come out to his 14-year-old son. The realistic and sympathetically rendered film is considered to be the first television drama to

Cher poses in a Bob Mackie creation (Farrah Fawcett stands behind; inset of Bob Mackie).

positively depict a stable, same-sex couple and the first to feature a gay parent. TV's first recurring openly gay character appears on summer replacement sitcom *The Corner Bar*, featuring the denizens of a New York City tavern called Grant's Toomb. The gay character, Peter Panama, is stereotyped as a flamboyant, ascot-wearing set designer.

1973. A new TV genre, the reality show, debuts on PBS with *An American Family*, which chronicles the lives of Santa Barbara, California, couple Pat and Bill Loud and their five children over 12 one-hour, weekly episodes. A significant moment in television and LGBTQ+ history happens in the second episode, when eldest son, Lance (1951–2001), comes out to his parents as gay. The charismatic Lance becomes the popular show's leading personality and is seen as a gay icon.

1977. *Soap*, a sitcom parody of daytime soap operas, debuts on ABC. The series features comedian–actor Billy Crystal as Jodie Dallas and is the first recurring openly gay leading character in a prime-time series. A complex character seen navigating relationships with other men and considering gender reassignment surgery, Jodie marked an important step toward greater visibility for LGBTQ+ characters on mainstream television. The show faces criticism before its debut from the International Union of Gay Athletes and the National Gay Task Force over concerns about the way Jodie and his closeted pro football player lover, Dennis, will be portrayed and, after its airing, from religious groups for its "raunchiness."

As the show continues, Jodie and Dennis break up and Jodie becomes engaged to a woman, sparking some backlash from LGBTQ+ groups over the character's inconsistency concerning his sexual identity. On October 1, the first serious depiction of a transgender character on network television comprises the storyline of a season 4 episode of the popular sitcom *The Jeffersons*, in which George Jefferson's Navy buddy Eddie reveals that he has undergone gender transition and is now living as Edie. On October 9 in a critically acclaimed, Emmy Award–winning episode of *All in the Family*, Edith Bunker discovers that her cousin, Liz, who has recently passed away, had been in a long-term lesbian relationship. The plot revolves around a valuable tea set that was treasured by the couple, which has been left to Edith as part of her cousin's estate. Edith must convince Archie that Liz's partner, Victoria, deserves to keep the family heirloom.

1981. The prime-time soap opera *Dynasty* is the first soap to include an openly gay character, Steven Carrington. The character's arc addresses his struggles with his sexual orientation and his relationships.

1982. *All My Children* becomes the first daytime soap opera to feature an openly LGBTQ+ character and the first openly lesbian character, psychologist Dr. Lynn Carson.

The cast of the soap opera spoof Soap *is pictured here in 1977. Billy Crystal (seated at far left) played Jodie Dallas, the first recurring gay character on American TV.*

1985. The NBC TV film *An Early Frost,* which tells the story of a young, gay man who returns home to tell his family that he has AIDS, is the first major American television program to address the HIV/AIDS crisis. The film is groundbreaking for its depiction of the struggles faced by those with HIV/AIDS as well as the challenges of being openly gay.

1989. The NBC legal drama *L.A. Law* features the first same-sex kiss on American television, shared by characters Abby Perkins (Michele Greene) and C. J. Lamb (Amanda Donohoe).

1994. Enrique "Rickie" Vasquez (Wilson Cruz) on the teen drama *My So-Called Life* is the first openly gay teenager portrayed on American television. The show offers an honest and empathetic look at the struggles of a gay teen, including bullying and the search for acceptance.

1997. The character Ellen Morgan in the sitcom *Ellen* comes out as gay shortly after the show's star, Ellen DeGeneres, came out. The episode, known as "The Puppy Episode," makes television history and is a positive watershed moment for lesbian and gay visibility, but it also ignites some controversy over its subsequent queer content, prompting ABC to add a parental advisory at the beginning of each episode.

1998. The influential sitcom *Will & Grace* debuts and becomes one of the most successful sitcoms ever to feature gay characters, with Will Truman (Eric McCormack) and Jack McFarland (Sean Hayes) portrayed as openly gay men. The show helps to normalize LGBTQ+ characters and relationships on mainstream television and is praised for its positive representation of the gay community.

2000. The American version of the British series *Queer as Folk* premieres on the

Eric McCormack (left) plays openly gay attorney Will, who is friends with his flamboyant friend Jack (Sean Hayes) in the popular TV sitcom Will & Grace.

premium TV station Showtime. Set in Pittsburgh, Pennsylvania, it is the first American television drama to focus entirely on the lives of gay men and depicts a network's first explicit sex scene between two men. The series includes a lesbian couple and addresses such topics as relationships, diversity within the community, HIV/AIDS, coming out, and family acceptance. Showtime debuts *The L Word,* a groundbreaking series focusing on the lives of a group of lesbian and bisexual women in Los Angeles. A drama that explores the complexities of the characters' relationships and identity, *The L Word* has remained an iconic series within the queer community. A sequel, *The L Word: Generation Q,* brought back fan-favorite characters and introduced new ones and ran from 2019 to 2023.

2003. The first reality show with LGBTQ+ hosts, *Queer Eye,* initially broadcast as *Queer Eye for the Straight Guy,* premieres on Bravo and becomes a cultural phenomenon. The series features five openly gay men, professionals in a variety of fields, performing lifestyle makeovers for straight men. A positive and celebratory portrayal of gay men, the show challenges stereotypes and helps to expand the public's view of gay men in American society. A short-lived spin-off, *Queer Eye for the Straight Girl,* debuts in 2005 and features four host–experts made up of three gay men and a woman, Honey Labrador, who is a lesbian.

2009. On July 16, Andy Cohen, an executive producer of *The Real Housewives* franchise, makes TV history as the first openly gay late night talk show host when his show *Watch What Happens Live!* debuts on Bravo. The same year sees the debut of the critically acclaimed, multi-award-winning ABC sitcom *Modern Family* (2009–2020), which centers on three interrelated suburban Los Angeles families, one of which is headed by openly gay couple Mitchell Pritchett and Cameron Tucker. The characters quickly become fan favorites, and the series, which includes the first same-sex wedding on prime-time network TV, is praised for its portrayal of a family that reflects a diverse America.

2013. Netflix's women's prison comedy–drama *Orange Is the New Black* debuts and earns accolades for its diverse cast of LGBTQ+ characters, which includes inmate Sophia Burset, a transgender woman of color played by transgender actress and activist Laverne Cox. Cox becomes the first openly transgender person to be nominated for an Emmy Award and the first trans woman to win one in 2015 when she receives a Daytime Emmy as executive producer of *Laverne Cox Presents: The T Word.*

2015. The cast of *Empire,* a Fox music drama centered on a fictional hip-hop music and entertainment company, includes Jussie Smollett as an openly gay musician struggling to gain acceptance from his father. The groundbreaking show is the first to feature a Black gay man as a central character in a major network drama and addresses issues of homophobia in the African American community and the music industry. *Transparent,* the first comedy–drama series to center around a transgender character, premieres on Amazon and stars Jeffrey Tambor as trans parent Maura Pfefferman. The series goes on to win multiple awards for its groundbreaking portrayal of transgender issues, including

Billy Porter, shown here in a scene from Pose, *became the first openly gay Black actor to win an Emmy for best leading actor.*

a Golden Globe and two Emmys for Tambor as Outstanding Lead Actor in a Comedy Series.

2017. *Pose,* an FX series exploring the lives of LGBTQ+ African American and Latinx communities involved in New York's drag ball culture in the 1980s and 1990s, makes history with the largest cast ever of transgender actors of color in regular roles for a scripted series. *Pose* is also groundbreaking for its representation of the transgender community and for bringing the stories of queer people of color to mainstream audiences. Cast member Billy Porter becomes the first openly Black gay actor to win an Emmy Award in the Outstanding Lead Actor in a Drama Series category.

2018. Notable for its portrayal of queer Latina women and its exploration of cultural identity, family dynamics, and gentrification, the Starz series *Vida* concerns two sisters who move back to their childhood home in Los Angeles after their mother's death. There, they discover that their mother had a secret lesbian relationship.

2019. The superhero series *Batwoman,* based on the DC Comics character, debuts on the CW network, with Ruby Rose as the openly lesbian title character Batwoman/Kate Kane, a cousin of caped crusader Batman/Bruce Wayne. Although *Batman: The Animated Series* (1992–1995) is the first TV series to include a lesbian superhero in the character of Renee Montoya, a police officer who becomes a crime-fighter known as The Question, *Batwoman* is the first live-action series in the action genre to be centered around a lesbian character.

2020. *Love, Victor,* a series focusing on a gay teen that was inspired by the 2018 comedy film *Love, Simon,* debuts on the streaming platform Hulu. The series receives critical acclaim as well as several awards during its three seasons.

2021. Despite the greater inclusion of LGBTQ+ themes and characters on TV in the 21st century, bisexuality has remained underrepresented. Bisexuality is a feature of the HBO Max comedy series *Hacks,* which stars Hannah Einbinder as a young, openly bisexual comedy writer hired to write a new act for veteran Las Vegas standup comedian Deborah Vance (Jean Smart).

BIOGRAPHIES

Berenice Abbott (1898–1991)

Photographer

Called the dean of American photographers, Berenice Abbott left an indelible mark on the medium through her groundbreaking work capturing the essence of modern urban life. With a keen eye for composition and a commitment to documenting the evolving landscape of cities, her photographs serve as invaluable historical records, offering viewers a glimpse into the past while also challenging perceptions of space and time. Her mastery of light and shadow, coupled with her innovative use of perspective, transformed photography into a powerful tool for artistic expression and social commentary.

Abbott was born in Springfield, Ohio, and raised by her divorced mother. She attended Ohio State University for two semesters but left in 1918 when her English professor was dismissed because he was a German. She moved to New York City, where she studied sculpture and painting, and in 1921 went to Paris to study sculpture with Emile Bourdelle. While in Paris, she became an assistant to American surrealist artist Man Ray, who wanted someone with no previous knowledge of photography. In 1925, she set up her own photography studio and established a successful career as a portrait photographer, creating several well-known portraits of artists and writers, including James Joyce, Coco Chanel, Marcel Duchamp, and Max Ernst. She also created vivid portraits of lesbians and bisexuals, including Margaret Anderson, Jane Heap, Sylvia Beach, Bryher, Djuna Barnes, and others. She made images as well of such gay or bisexual men as André Gide and Jean Cocteau.

Returning to New York City in 1929, Abbott set out to document the changing face of the city. Eventually published in 1939, her photo book *Changing New York* focused on architectural details and important historical buildings as well as bridges and skyscrapers. These photographs captured the dynamic energy and stark contrasts of the cityscape from its bustling streets and towering skyscrapers to its quieter neighborhoods and historic landmarks. One of her most famous images from this series is *Nightview, New York*, a mesmerizing nighttime shot of the city illuminated by the glow of streetlights and neon signs. Her use of light and shadow as well as her keen eye for composition helped to define her distinctive style and cement her reputation as one of the foremost photographers of her time.

Abbott was known to have had relationships with women throughout her life, although she was private about her personal life and never publicly identified as gay. In 1935, she moved into a Greenwich Village loft with art critic Elizabeth McCausland, with whom she lived until McCausland's death in 1965.

Abbott's major project beyond New York was to photograph U.S. Highway 1 from Maine to Florida. Shortly after finishing that project, she underwent a lung operation and was advised to move away from New York City due to air pollution. She moved to Blanchard, Maine, to a house along the banks of the Piscataquis River. She would reside in Maine until her death at the age of 93.

Throughout her career, Abbott was a determined advocate for photography and her documentary approach. She argued that photography was uniquely a descriptive medium. "Photography can never grow up," she argued, "if it imitates some other medium. It has to walk alone; it has to be itself."

Adrian (1903–1959)

Costume Designer, Fashion Designer

One of Hollywood's most influential costume designers who was most well known to audiences and fashion aficionados through his on-screen credit "Gowns by Adrian," Adrian is best known for his work at MGM, where he designed costumes for over 250 films, including iconic outfits for stars like Greta Garbo, Joan Crawford, and Judy Garland. Some of his most famous designs include Dorothy's ruby slippers in *The Wizard of Oz* and the glamorous gowns in *Grand Hotel*. His contributions to costume design not only helped define the look of Hollywood's Golden Age but also influenced fashion trends for decades.

Born Adrian Adolph Greenburg in Naugatuck, Connecticut, Adrian developed an early passion for fashion design that led him to the New York School of Fine and Applied Arts, where he honed his skills before furthering his education in Paris. His career began in earnest in 1924 when he started designing costumes for *George White's Scandals*, a popular series of Broadway variety revues, then for silent films, which set the stage for his remarkable career in Hollywood.

In 1928, Adrian joined Metro-Goldwyn-Mayer (MGM) as head costume designer, a role that would solidify his place in fashion history. Throughout the 1930s and 1940s, he designed some of the most iconic costumes in film, dressing Hollywood stars like Greta Garbo, Joan Crawford, and Katharine Hepburn. His designs, such as the *Letty Lynton* dress—a white, cotton, organdy gown with large, ruffled sleeves, puffed at the shoulders and worn by Joan Crawford, who starred in the 1932 film of the same name—became cultural phenomena, influencing mainstream fashion and becoming some of the most copied styles of the era. His other memorable designs included wardrobes for Joan Crawford in *Grand Hotel* (1932), Jean Harlow in *Dinner at Eight* (1933), the fashionably turned-out women in *The Women* (1939), and Katharine Hepburn in *Philadelphia Story* (1940). His ability to blend theatricality with elegance made his costumes beloved by stars and audiences alike.

In 1939, Adrian married actress Janet Gaynor in what has been called a lavender marriage since he was openly gay within the film community and Gaynor was rumored to be either gay or bisexual. The couple went on record to say that they were happily married, and they remained together until his death in 1959. They had one son, Robin, born in 1940. In 1941, seeking to expand his influence beyond costume design, he left MGM and opened his own fashion house, Adrian, Ltd. His high-end, ready-to-wear collections continued to reflect his impeccable taste and innovative design sense, attracting a loyal clientele who appreciated his flair for sophistication and drama. Slowed by a heart attack in 1952, Adrian, who never assigned work to assistants, retired and closed Adrian, Ltd., although he came out of retirement in 1958 to design costumes for *At the Grand*, a musical version of *Grand Hotel*. In 1959, he was hired to design costumes for the Broadway musical *Camelot* and, while working on the project in his studio, suffered a fatal heart attack. He was posthumously awarded the Tony Award for Best Costume Design in a Musical.

Alvin Ailey (1931–1989)

Choreographer, Dancer

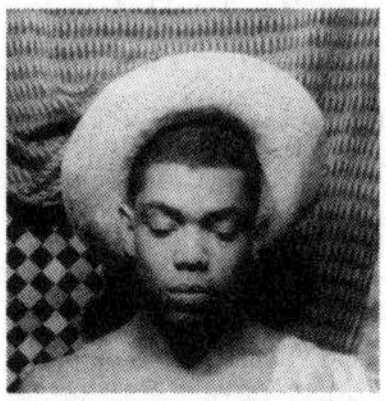

Alvin Ailey transformed the landscape of American modern dance. As the founder of the Alvin Ailey American Dance Theater, he created a platform that celebrated African American cultural expression and broke down racial barriers in the performing arts. His innovative choreography and dedication to social justice have left an indelible mark on the dance world, making him a pivotal figure in modern dance history.

Ailey was born in Rogers, Texas. Raised by a single mother during the Great Depression, he experienced the harsh realities of racial segregation and economic hardship from an early age. His family moved to Los Angeles when he was 12, where he was introduced to the world of dance by attending performances of the Ballet Russe de Monte Carlo and the Katherine Dunham Dance Company. He began his formal dance training with mentors such as Lester Horton, whose techniques and inclusive approach to dance profoundly influenced his artistic development. Horton's mentorship provided him with a solid foundation in various dance styles and the importance of storytelling through movement.

In 1958, Ailey founded the Alvin Ailey American Dance Theater in New York City, aiming to provide a platform for African American dancers and promote modern dance. His most famous work, *Revelations* (1960), is considered a masterpiece that draws from African American spirituals, gospel songs, and blues, encapsulating the African American experience with profound emotional and cultural resonance. His choreography often addressed social issues and celebrated African American culture, making his work both artistically significant and socially relevant. Other notable works include *Cry* (1971), a solo piece dedicated to his mother that was performed by Judith Jamison and highlights the struggles and resilience of Black women, and *Blues Suite* (1958), which reflects the African American experience in the rural South. His innovative approach to dance and commitment to diversity in the arts earned him numerous accolades, including a Kennedy Center Honors award in 1988 and a posthumous Presidential Medal of Freedom in 2014.

Ailey kept his personal life private, but he was openly gay within his close circles. His experiences as a Black gay man in mid-20th-century America influenced his work and his advocacy for marginalized communities. He struggled with mental health issues and battled the stigma associated with being gay, especially within the conservative cultural context of his time. Despite these challenges, he remained dedicated to his artistic vision and social advocacy until his death due to AIDS-related complications. His legacy continues to inspire discussions about the intersections of race, sexuality, and art.

Edward Albee (1928–2016)

Playwright

Edward Albee is regarded as the foremost American playwright of his generation and a successor to Eugene O'Neill, Arthur Miller, and Tennessee Williams as a dominating voice in American drama. His best-known work was also his first full-length play and Broadway debut, *Who's Afraid of Virginia Woolf?*, which won a Tony Award in 1963 for Best Play and electrified and shocked theatergoers in its portrait of a toxic marriage in academia. Decades later, he would write that the play had "hung about my neck like a shining medal of some sort—really nice but a trifle onerous."

Born near Washington, D.C., Albee was given up for adoption within days of his birth and adopted by Reed Albee, a millionaire theater owner, and his wife, Frances. His childhood was unhappy because he felt like an outsider in his parents' home. With a passion for art and writing, he reported disappointing his parents: "I think they wanted somebody who would be a corporate thug of some sort, or perhaps a doctor or lawyer or something respectable. They didn't want a writer on their hands." He confessed in interviews that he knew he was gay by the time he was 8, began writing poetry at 9, and had his first homosexual encounter at 12.

In 1949, after attending several private schools, boarding schools, and Trinity College in Hartford for a time, Albee moved to Greenwich Village, working at unskilled jobs while attempting to establish his writing career amid a circle of painters, writers, and musicians, including playwright William Inge and composers David Diamond, Aaron Copland, and William Flanagan, who became his lover. Struggling to find his voice as a poet and a short story writer, he recalled, "I knew

I was a writer and failed basically at all other branches of writing, but I was still a writer. So I did the only thing I had not done. I wrote a play. It was called *The Zoo Story*."

The Zoo Story, influenced by European drama and the Theatre of the Absurd, made Albee something of a spokesperson for new, experimental American drama which, he contended, should challenge audiences' complacency. His next three plays, also one act each—*The Sandbox, The American Dream*, and *The Death of Bessie Smith*—were successes Off-Broadway. *Who's Afraid of Virginia Woolf?* dramatizes a late-night boozy encounter between married couple George, a history professor, and Martha, the daughter of the college president, and two campus newcomers, Nick and his wife, Honey, which embodies Albee's assaultive dramatic method. Few other characters on the American stage had ever gone at one another so mercilessly or exposed their psychological core in language that drama historian Ruby Cohn called "the most adroit dialogue ever heard on the American stage." The play propelled Albee into the front rank of American dramatist, and he would go on to dominate American drama in the 1960s and 1970s. As President Bill Clinton said to the playwright at the Kennedy Center Honors ceremony in 1996, "In your rebellion, the American theater was reborn." Albee's subsequent plays include *Tiny Alice* (1964), *A Delicate Balance* (1966), *All Over* (1971), *Seascape* (1975), *The Lady from Dubuque* (1978), and *Three Tall Women* (1991).

Although open about his gayness, Albee was reluctant to be defined or limited by it, saying that a writer who "happens to be gay or lesbian must be able to transcend self. I am not a gay writer. I am a writer who happens to be gay." By transcending his self, he suggested that the goal of the writer is to transition from the personal to the universal. As critic Ben Brantley wrote, "Mr. Albee has unsparingly considered subjects outside the average theatergoer's comfort zone: the capacity for sadism and violence within American society; the fluidness of human identity; the dangerous irrationality of sexual attraction and, always, the irrefutable presence of death."

Dorothy Arzner (1897–1979)

Film Director

Dorothy Arzner was a pioneering figure in Hollywood known for being one of the first female directors in the American film industry. From 1927 until her retirement in 1943, she was the only female director working in Hollywood. Her trailblazing career broke barriers in a male-dominated field, and her innovative techniques and compelling narratives left an indelible mark on cinema. Her work not only highlighted her technical prowess but also often explored complex themes of gender and identity, making her an influential and progressive voice in early Hollywood.

Arzner was born in San Francisco, California, and raised in Los Angeles. Her father owned a restaurant that was frequented by many silent film stars, including Mary Pickford, Mack Sennett, and Douglas Fairbanks, and would be her first contact with the movie business. She initially studied medicine at the University of Southern California but left to pursue a career in the film industry. Starting as a typist at Paramount Pictures, she became a script supervisor, an editor, and, eventually, a director. She soon realized, "If one was going to be in this movie business, one should be a director because he was the one who told everyone else what to do."

Arzner edited 52 films, including Rudolph Valentino's *Blood and Sand* (1922), in which she intercut the bullfighting scenes with stock footage, saving the studio thousands of dollars. After serving as director

James Cruze's "right arm" on several films, she was given her first directing job on the film *Fashions for Women* (1927). Its success led to her directing three more silent films; then, she was given the assignment to direct Clara Bow in her first talkie, *The Wild Party* (1929). She was one of the first Hollywood directors who had to contend with the challenges of sound, and she had a technician rig a microphone to the end of a fishing rod to maneuver the mic, inventing the "boom microphone."

One of Arzner's most notable achievements is her direction of the 1933 film *Christopher Strong*, starring Katharine Hepburn. This film, along with others, like *Dance, Girl, Dance* (1940), showcased her ability to create strong, complex female characters and address themes of gender and independence. In 1932, she left Paramount to freelance for other studios. When MGM released *The Bride Wore White* (1937), it advertised it as "A Woman's Love Directed by Hollywood's Only Woman Director." Over her career, she directed over 20 films, many of which received critical acclaim and commercial success. During World War II, she made training films for the Women's Army Corps. She retired after her 1943 film *First Comes Courage*, weary of the studio system. Her work was rediscovered by feminist critics in the 1970s who were reviewing older films to screen at film festivals, and in 1975, she was honored by the Director's Guild. Katharine Hepburn sent her a congratulatory telegram, reading, "Isn't it wonderful that you had such a great career when you had no right to have a career at all?"

Arzner's personal life and sexuality were also notable aspects of her identity. As an openly lesbian woman in Hollywood, she navigated an industry and a society that were often hostile to LGBTQ+ individuals. She had affairs with actresses Alla Nazimova and Billie Burke before eventually settling down with choreographer Marion Morgan, living together for 40 years until Morgan's death in 1971. Despite the challenges of being a lesbian woman in Hollywood (it has been speculated that her early retirement from directing was due to the film industry becoming increasingly difficult for marginalized individuals), she achieved a distinguished career and a fearlessness in expressing in her sexual identity, serving as an inspiration to many in the LGBTQ+ community. Her openness about her sexuality and her ability to thrive professionally provided a powerful example of resilience and authenticity.

John Ashbery (1927–2017)

Poet, Art Critic, Educator

Recognized as one of the greatest 20th-century American poets, John Ashbery's poems pushed the limits of language while probing the landscape of consciousness. He published more than 30 volumes of poetry and won nearly every major American award for poetry, including the Pulitzer Prize in 1976. As critic Langdon Hammer remarked in 2008, "No figure looms so large in American poetry over the past 50 years as John Ashbery."

Born in Rochester, New York, the son of a farmer and a biology teacher, Ashbery was educated at Deerfield Academy, where he began to read the poetry of W. H. Auden and Dylan Thomas and began writing poetry, although his first ambition was to be a painter. He graduated from Harvard University in 1949 and received an MA from Columbia University in 1951. He worked as a copywriter in New York from 1951 to 1955 and lived in France through 1965. He wrote art criticism for various periodicals, including *ARTnews*, where he became an editor upon his return to New York. From 1974 to 1990, he was a professor of English at Brooklyn College and went on to teach at Bard College until his retirement in 2008.

Ashbery's early collections of verse include *Turandot and Other Poems* (1953), *Some Trees* (1956), *The Tennis Court Oath* (1962), and *The Double Dream of Spring* (1970). *Self-Portrait in a Convex Mirror* (1975) won the Pulitzer Prize, the National Book Award, and the National Book Critics Circle Award. The collection's title poem is considered to be one of the masterpieces of late 20th-century American poetry. His poetry was initially greeted with puzzlement and hostility because of its extreme difficulty, characterized by arresting imagery, intricate form, and sudden shifts in tone and subject. Subsequent collections, including *Houseboat Days* (1977) and *As We Know* (1979), reinforced his reputation as a poet of free-flowing verse with extensive linguistic play and considerable humor, reflecting the play of the human mind. His later works, such as *Girls on the Run* (1999), *Chinese Whispers* (2002), *Where Shall I Wander?* (2005), *Quick Question* (2012), *Breezeway* (2015), and *Commotion of the Birds* (2016), are notably elegiac as the poet contemplates death and dying.

While Ashbery's verse resists autobiographical interpretations, his gayness is nevertheless increasingly being recognized critically as a cornerstone of his poetics. He identified as gay as an adolescent and endured bullying for being a "sissy." In college, he hid his sexuality from his hetero peers. In the 1950s, he worried that he would not be able to work because of the homophobia of the McCarthy era. However, he actually came out to the draft board and was exempted from military service during the Korean War. He met art dealer David Kermani in 1970, who became his partner (and later spouse) for close to 50 years. As his biographer, Karin Roffman, observes, "I don't think Ashbery planned to be evasive in his poetry. He was drawn aesthetically to restraint," yet Roffman detects an "emotional boldness" in his work. This can be seen quite clearly in his poem "How to Continue," an elegy for queer life before AIDS with its final stanza:

> And when it became time to go
> they none of them would leave without the other
> for they said we are all one here
> and if one of us goes the other will not go
> and the wind whispered it to the stars
> the people all got up to go
> and looked back on love

James Baldwin (1924–1987)

Writer, Activist

Novelist, essayist, and playwright James Baldwin wrote with eloquence and passion on the subject of race in America, exploring the psychological implications of racism for both the oppressed and the oppressor. He was also one of the first Black writers to include queer themes in fiction, most notably in *Giovanni's Room* (1956), with an unprecedented and controversial frankness. In the early 1960s, he began to criticize discrimination against gay men. As critic Benjamin DeMott has asserted, he is one of "the few genuinely indispensable American writers."

Baldwin was born James Arthur Jones in Harlem, New York, and was raised by a single mother. He never knew the identity of his biological father. His mother, Emma Jones, had fled racial segregation in the South during the Great Migration, arriving in Harlem at the age of 19. In 1927, she married David Baldwin, a laborer and Baptist preacher, and James took his stepfather's name and eventually became the eldest of nine brothers and sisters. Recognized as gifted in his Harlem public school, he attended DeWitt Clinton High School in the Bronx, which had a predominantly white and Jewish student body, graduating in 1941. Having begun writing poems, short stories, and plays at a young age, he declared in his high school yearbook his ambition to become a "novelist–playwright." Feeling guilty about being attracted to men rather than women, he sought refuge in religion and served as a youth minister in a Harlem Pentecostal church from the ages of 14 to 16.

After graduating, Baldwin worked menial jobs to support his family before moving to Greenwich Village in 1943 and, disillusioned by American racial discrimination, to Paris in 1948, where he completed his first novel, *Go Tell It on the Mountain* (1953), an autobiographical account of a young man growing up in Harlem. He recalled that *Mountain* was "the book I had to write if I was ever going to write anything else. I had to deal with what hurt me most." His next novel, *Giovanni's Room* (1955), is the story of an American living in Paris contending with his sexuality. It has been called by one critic as "probably the first novel to deal so openly with tragic homosexual love." Love between men was also explored in a later novel, *Just Above My Head* (1978). He also treated interracial relationships in his novel *Another Country* (1962).

Although Baldwin saw himself primarily as a novelist, his most enduring contribution to literature may well be his collections of essays. The three most important are *Notes of a Native Son* (1955), *Nobody Knows My Name* (1961), and *The Fire Next Time* (1963), essential reflections during the years of the civil rights movement that have earned him a reputation as one of America's greatest essayists of the 20th century.

Despite Baldwin's writing on race and homosexuality, he remained uncomfortable with others labeling him as a Black writer or a gay writer, seeing this as limiting. This reluctance drew criticism from various groups that wanted to claim him as a spokesperson. "I was a maverick," he recalled, "…in the sense that I depended on neither the white world nor the black world. That was the only way I could've played it. I would've been broken otherwise. I had to say, 'A curse on both your houses.' The fact that I went to Europe so early is probably what saved me. It gave me another touchstone—myself." Scholar Chris Freeman has described him as "intersectional before there was a classification of intersectional. He is the reason we even have the word." According to scholar Michelle Gordon, it was his intersectional identity that made him an outsider: "Being a Black American in Europe. Being Black and gay in the world. It all gives him outsider status, which allows him the ability to see the world so clearly, because he did not quite fit."

If being either Black or gay alone insufficiently captures Baldwin's complex sense of self-identity, the combination has mattered. As Charles Stephens, executive director of the Counter Narrative Project, observed, "Black gay men in particular have found in Baldwin a kind of father figure. There isn't a single Black gay writer of literary fiction or nonfiction that has not been influenced by James Baldwin on some level. As we seek to navigate our current political moment, we believe that James Baldwin offers a necessary blueprint for how we continue to fight for social justice."

Djuna Barnes (1892–1982)

Writer, Artist

Avant-garde writer and artist Djuna Barnes was one of the first creators of lesbian literature, including her most acclaimed novel, *Nightwood* (1936), which has become both a cult classic of lesbian fiction and an important work of modernist literature. Dylan Thomas described *Nightwood* as "one of the three great prose books ever written by a woman," while William S. Burroughs called it "one of the great books of the twentieth century." She never duplicated the achievement of *Nightwood* and never gained the acclaim of fellow modernist writers like T. S. Eliot and William Faulkner. She called herself "the most famous unknown of the [20th] century."

Barnes was born in Cornwall-on-Hudson, New York, and educated at the Pratt Institute and the Art Students League of New York. She worked as a journalist and also published some stories in *The Dial* and *Vanity Fair*. Her first collection of poems and stories appeared in *The Book of Repulsive Women* (1915), which satirized the stereotypes of female sexuality. Several plays followed in 1919, including *Three from the Earth*, *Kurzy of the Sea*, and *An Irish Triangle*.

In 1920, Barnes left for Paris, where she lived for 12 years. She arrived with letters of introduction to Ezra Pound and James Joyce and entered the Parisian world of expatriate bohemians, a circle that included Gertrude Stein, Mina Loy, Kay Boyle, and Peggy Guggenheim. In 1922, she moved in with the "great love" of her life, artist Thelma Ellen Wood. They separated in 1928, the same year that two of Barnes's major works appeared: *Ryder*, drawing heavily on her childhood experiences in a succession of styles parodying writers like Chaucer and Rossetti, and *Ladies Almanack*, a *roman à clef* about a lesbian social circle centering on her friend Natalie Clifford Barney's salon in Paris.

Barnes achieved fame with the publication of *Nightwood* in England in 1936, edited and introduced by T. S. Eliot. Set in 1920s Paris, the novel reflects the circumstances surrounding the ending of her relationship with Wood. Due to concerns about censorship, Eliot softened any language relating to sexuality and religion (which was restored in later editions) and called it "so good a novel that only sensibilities trained on poetry can wholly appreciate it." Despite such praise from Eliot and others, the book did not sell, and she began a long period of decline, eventually returning to New York, living in a small apartment in Greenwich Village, where she lived reclusively for the last 41 years of her life. During this period, she only managed to produce two additional works, *The Antiphon* (1958), a verse play drawing on her family history, and *Creatures in an Alphabet* (1982), a collection of short, rhyming poems. Because of the reputation of *Nightwood*, she became a lesbian icon, with admirers hanging around outside of her street in order to catch a glimpse of her. Under such scrutiny, she drew back from any role as a lesbian leader, saying at one point, "I am not a Lesbian, I just loved Thelma." When women affectionately named their nearby feminist bookstore Djuna Barnes after her, she demanded a name change. She died in her apartment at the age of 90.

A pioneer of what can be termed lesbian modernism, Barnes consistently rejected any attempt to consign her or her work to simple categories. Joanne Winning, in a critical assessment, writes that her resistance was "a repudiation of belonging or identification with any fixed identity, a refusal to succumb to a narrative of identity formation."

James Beard (1903–1985)

Chef

James Andrew Beard was a seminal figure in American culinary history, often referred to as the "dean of American cookery." His influence extends far beyond his cookbooks and television appearances, as he played a pivotal role in shaping American cuisine and elevating the nation's culinary standards. His legacy continues to inspire chefs, home cooks, and food enthusiasts, solidifying his status as a key figure in the gastronomic world.

Beard was born in Portland, Oregon. He developed an early appreciation for food through his mother, who managed a boardinghouse and prepared elaborate meals, and his father, who was a part-time fisherman. According to his memoir, "By the time I was seven, I knew I was gay." He attended Reed College in Portland but was expelled in 1922 after just one year for homosexuality, having had relationships with "one or more male students and a professor," he reported. He then pursued a career in acting and singing, which took him to Europe, where he further developed his palate and appreciation for diverse cuisines. In Paris, he first experienced French cuisine and became a self-confessed "Francophile." He returned to the United States in 1927, living in Portland, Hollywood, and New York and attempting careers in acting, costume and set design, and radio.

In 1937, Beard moved to New York City and opened a catering company. This led to lecturing, teaching, and writing about food. He published his first cookbook in 1940, *Hors d'Oeuvre and Canapés*, a compilation of his catering recipes. According to fellow cooking enthusiast Julia Child, the book put him on the culinary map.

Beard's contributions to American cuisine are vast. He authored over 20 cookbooks, including classics such as *The James Beard Cookbook* (1959) and *Beard on Bread* (1973). These works demystified cooking techniques and emphasized the importance of using fresh, quality ingredients. He was also a pioneer in television, hosting one of the first cooking shows, *I Love to Eat*, on NBC in 1946. His efforts extended to education as well with the establishment of the James Beard Cooking School in New York City and Oregon. Perhaps his most enduring legacy is the James Beard Foundation, established in 1986, which honors culinary excellence and continues to support and celebrate chefs and food professionals through awards, scholarships, and advocacy.

Beard came out in 1981 in a revised version of his memoir, *Delights and Prejudices.* Gino Colacci was his "lifetime companion" of 30 years. Beard died of heart failure at the age of 81. He was celebrated by fellow food writer Craig Claiborne, who said, "Mr. Beard, more than any other person, helped shape the change in American dining habits. He was an innovator, an experimenter, a missionary in bringing the gospel of good cooking to the home table."

Michael Bennett (1943–1987)

Writer, Director, Choreographer

Widely regarded as the most influential theater director and choreographer of his generation, Michael Bennett was the cocreator of *A Chorus Line* as well as responsible for such shows as *Company*, *Follies*, and *Dreamgirls*, works that defined the contemporary Broadway musical. He received Tony Award nominations for every musical with which he was associated, winning eight.

Bennett, whose original name was Michael Bennett DiFiglia, was born in Buffalo, New York, the son of a machinist and a secretary. He started dance lessons at the age of 3 and, by the age of 12, was adept in tap, ballet, modern, and folk dancing. Just before he was supposed to graduate from high school, he joined a company performing *West Side Story* and spent a year in Europe with the show. When the tour ended, he came to New York City and worked as a chorus dancer onstage and on television.

Bennett's first work as a choreographer came with the short-lived flops *A Joyful Noise* (1966) and *Henry, Sweet Henry* (1967). His first hit came in 1968 with *Promises, Promises*, and in the next few years, he choreographed *Coco* (1969) with Katharine Hepburn and two Stephen Sondheim musicals, *Company* (1970) and *Follies* (1971), along with *Seesaw* (1973), on which he was also the director and librettist. *Seesaw* is the second Broadway musical after *Applause* (1970) to feature a homosexual character. *A Chorus Line* would be the third.

A Chorus Line originated when two Broadway dancers, Michon Peacock and Tony Stevens, set out to create a theater troupe consisting of Broadway dancers who wanted to create workshops and their own productions, approaching Bennett with their idea. They brought a group of dancers together in 1974 to share their stories and experiences, and Bennett knew he had the material for a radically new kind of musical: a completely ensemble show with no star, a backstage drama that was a kind of anti-musical musical. He pitched the idea to Joseph Papp, founder of the New York Shakespeare Festival, to develop it into a workshop, and he brought in Nicholas Dante and, later, James Kirkwood to develop the dancers' stories into monologues and got Marvin Hamlisch to write the score and Edward Kleban to write the lyrics. The show was a massive hit when it premiered at The Public Theater, and it was quickly transferred to Broadway, running from 1975 to 1990 and becoming the longest-running Broadway production ever until *Cats* beat the record in 1995. His next musical was the short-lived *Ballroom* (1978), but he had one more major hit with *Dreamgirls* in 1981, which earned him his seventh and final Tony Award.

Bennett identified as bisexual. He had two primary heterosexual relationships, the first of which being with fellow dancer and actor Donna McKechnie, whom he married in 1976 but divorced four months later. He promised to wed Sabine Cassel but did not. He had long relationships with dancers Larry Fuller, Scott Pearson, Richard Christopher, and Gene Pruitt. He died at the age of 44 of AIDS-related lymphoma, leaving a sizable portion of his estate to fund research to fight the AIDS epidemic.

Gladys Bentley (1907–1960)

Singer, Musician

Gladys Bentley was a trailblazing blues singer and pianist during the Harlem Renaissance, renowned for her powerful voice, charismatic stage presence, and unapologetic defiance of gender norms. Performing in men's clothing and openly embracing her sexuality, she challenged societal conventions and became a symbol of resistance and liberation for the LGBTQ+ community. Her bold performances and significant contributions to music and culture underscore her importance as a pioneering figure in both African American and LGBTQ+ histories, paving the way for future generations of artists and activists.

Bentley was raised in Philadelphia, Pennsylvania. Her mother was from Trinidad, and she reported that she was originally from Port-au-Spain, Trinidad. She was the eldest of four siblings and remembered her childhood as an unhappy one, as her mother had wanted a son. She came to believe that her mother's rejection helped shape the gender nonconformity she exhibited at an early age. In school, she faced ridicule for wearing boys' clothing and for her crushes on female teachers. Doctors eventually diagnosed her with "extreme social maladjustment." In 1923, at the age of 16, no longer able to endure the abuse she received from her family and peers, she moved to Harlem in New York City.

Bentley arrived during the explosion of African American arts and culture of the Harlem Renaissance, and she quickly became a prominent figure in the vibrant nightlife scene of the 1920s and 1930s. Her performances at the Clam House and later the Ubangi Club were legendary, drawing large crowds who were captivated by her talent and audacious persona. She became known for her deep, growling voice and her ability to play the piano with impressive skill. She was also known for her flamboyant style, often performing in men's clothing, complete with a top hat and tails, which was highly unconventional at the time. Her repertoire included bawdy and humorous songs, many of which she wrote herself, and her performances were characterized by their unabashed celebration of sexuality and gender fluidity.

Despite the challenges she faced due to her race and gender, Bentley enjoyed considerable popular success and was one of the best-known entertainers of the Harlem Renaissance. Her recordings, such as "Worried Blues" and "Moanin'," showcased her unique style and contributed to the popularity of the blues genre. Her willingness to live openly as a lesbian and defiance of traditional gender roles made her a pioneering figure in both the LGBTQ+ community and the broader cultural landscape of her time. Although interracial and same-sex marriage was illegal, she married a white woman in 1931 in a public civil ceremony. In 1937, she moved to Los Angeles, but some club owners forced her to wear dresses. In the more repressive 1950s, in order to continue her career, she tried to transform her image, announcing in 1953 in *Jet* magazine that she had transitioned from the "third sex" to a "true female," dressing as a woman and claiming to have married a man.

Bentley died of pneumonia at the age of 52. At one time, she had been known as the most famous lesbian in Harlem. Writer Langston Hughes praised her as "an amazing exhibition of musical energy—a large, dark, masculine lady, whose feet pounded the floor while her fingers pounded the keyboard—a perfect piece of African sculpture, animated by her own rhythm." According to Jim Wilson, author of *Bulldaggers, Pansies, and Chocolate Babies: Performance, Race, and Sexuality in the Harlem Renaissance,* "Gladys Bentley should be remembered for being a gender outlaw. She was just defiant in who she was, and for the gender and sexuality studies today, she shows the performance of gender."

Leonard Bernstein (1918–1990)

Conductor, Composer

Acclaimed as the "monarch of music," Leonard Bernstein was one of the most influential figures in 20th-century music. One of the first American-born conductors to lead world-class orchestras and achieve global fame, he was a composer, conductor, pianist, and educator with boundless creativity and passion for music and left an indelible mark on both classical and popular music.

Born Louis Bernstein in Lawrence, Massachusetts, to Jewish parents who both immigrated to the United States from Ukraine, he was called Lenny or Leonard by his family, which he officially renamed himself at the age of 16. He began playing piano at the age of 10. He attended Boston Latin School and Harvard University, graduating in 1939. He went on to study music at the Curtis Institute of Music in Philadelphia (1939–1940) and conduct at the Berkshire Music Center, now known as the Tanglewood Music Center. In 1943, he was appointed assistant conductor of the New York Philharmonic, making his conducting debut on short notice after guest conductor Bruno Walter got the flu. The notoriety he received propelled him to instant fame, and over the next two years, he made conducting debuts with 10 different orchestras in the United States and Canada.

Bernstein conducted the New York City Center orchestra from 1945 to 1947. He became the first American to conduct at La Scala in Milan. From 1958 to 1969, he was the conductor and musical director of the New York Philharmonic, becoming the first American-born person to hold those posts. His popularity increased due to his appearances on television on such programs as *Omnibus* and *Young People's Concerts,* in which he explained classical music to young listeners.

As a composer, Bernstein was noted for his skillful use of different themes and musical forms, exploring biblical themes in *Symphony No. 1* (1942) and *Chichester Psalms* (1965), jazz rhythms in *Symphony No. 2* (1949), and Jewish liturgical themes in *Symphony No. 3* (1963). His best-known works, however, were on Broadway and in films, including the musicals *On the Town* (1944, filmed 1949); *Wonderful Town* (1953, filmed 1958); *Candide* (1956); and *West Side Story* (1957, filmed 1961), in collaboration with Stephen Sondheim and Jerome Robbins. He also wrote the scores for the ballets *Fancy Free* (1944), *Facsimile* (1946), and *Dybbuk* (1974) as well as the music for the film *On the Waterfront* (1954).

In addition to his musical accomplishments, Bernstein was also a passionate advocate for social justice and political activism. He used his platform to address issues such as civil rights, nuclear disarmament, and advocacy for AIDS research and patient care, participating in one of the earliest HIV/AIDS fundraisers in 1983.

Regarding his sexuality, Bernstein's personal life has been the subject of speculation and scrutiny. While he was married to Chilean actress Felicia Montealegre for over 25 years and had three children with her, his relationships and encounters with men have been documented by biographers and acquaintances. He sought the advice of composer Aaron Copland and musician David Oppenheim in 1943 about living as a gay man in the public eye. The year he married Montealegre, she wrote a letter to him, saying, "You are a homosexual and may never change—you don't admit to the possibility of a double life, but if your peace of mind, your health, your whole nervous system depend on a certain sexual pattern, what can you do?" He managed a loving relationship with his wife in a marriage that lasted 25 years while still having various affairs with men. In 1976, after a "trial separation" from his wife, he lived for a time with musical scholar Tom Cothran but returned to care for his wife, who had been diagnosed with lung cancer, until she died in 1978. A friend, Shirley Rhoads Perle, observed that he "required men sexually and women emotionally."

Bernstein continued to set a seemingly inexhaustible pace during his last two decades: conducting, composing, teaching, and producing television specials up until his announced retirement from conducting in 1990. He died five days later at the age of 72 of a heart attack. Asked to justify his diverse interests and activities, he once stated, "I don't want to spend my life, as Toscanini, studying and restudying the same 50 pieces of music. It would bore me to death. I want to conduct. I want to play the piano. I want to write for Hollywood. I want to write symphonic music. I want to keep on trying to be, in full sense of that wonderful word, a musician."

Marc Blitzstein (1905–1964)

Composer, Lyricist, Librettist

Composer Marc Blitzstein was renowned for his contributions to musical theater and opera. His work is celebrated for its social and political themes and his innovative approach to musical storytelling that has had a lasting influence on American theater. His best-known work, *The Cradle Will Rock* (1937), is a groundbreaking musical that was both controversial and critically acclaimed for its unabashedly pro-labor message. His compositions often addressed issues of labor, social justice, and the human condition, reflecting his deep commitment to progressive causes. He has the distinction of introducing a diversity of social class voices and issues that earlier Broadway musicals had never attempted.

Blitzstein was born in Philadelphia, Pennsylvania, the son of a banker. A musical prodigy, at the age of 3, he was playing by ear works by Offenbach and Mendelssohn. He made the first of many public appearances at the age of 6 and performed piano concertos with the Philadelphia Orchestra by the age of 15. He studied at the University of Pennsylvania from 1921 to 1923 on a scholarship and at the Curtis Institute of Music. In 1927, he continued his education in Berlin, where he was influenced by prominent composers such as Arnold Schoenberg and Nadia Boulanger.

His early exposure to diverse musical styles and techniques laid the groundwork for his eclectic and pioneering approach to composition.

In 1933, Blitzstein married Eval Goldbeck, a New York writer. At the time, he was conflicted over his sexuality. He had had his first gay sexual relationship at the age of 19, although he was also in a relationship with Goldbeck, whom he eventually married. He identified as bisexual, although Goldbeck began to view their union as a "social gesture" in order to serve his musical ambitions. Struggling with breast cancer and anorexia, she died in 1936.

One of Blitzstein's most notable achievements was his musical *The Cradle Will Rock* (1937), a controversial and politically charged work that critiqued corporate greed and corruption. Directed by Orson Welles, the production faced significant opposition from the government, leading to its famous premiere in which the cast performed from the audience due to a theater lockout and union restrictions, with only Blitzstein onstage at the piano performing the score. This bold and unorthodox approach highlighted his commitment to artistic integrity and social justice. Another significant work, *Regina* (1949), an adaptation of Lillian Hellman's play *The Little Foxes*, showcased his ability to blend classical and popular music styles, earning critical acclaim. His other operas and musicals included *Triple-Sec*; *The Harpies*; *The Condemned*; *Parabola and Circula*; *Reuben, Reuben*; and *Juno*, which was based on Sean O'Casey's *Juno and the Paycock*. His most popular contribution to the musical stage was his translation from the German of Kurt Weill and Bertolt Brecht's *The Threepenny Opera*. An opera based on the executions of Sacco and Vanzetti was left unfinished at the time of his death.

In 1964 on the French island of Martinique, Blitzstein was brutally attacked and robbed by three sailors after attempting to proposition one of them at a bar. Before dying of a ruptured liver caused by the severe beating, he identified his assailants but asked that his family be told that he was injured in a car accident since, although openly gay, he had kept his homosexuality private from his family. His assailants were later convicted of involuntary homicide and theft.

When he learned of Blitzstein's death, Leonard Bernstein said, "I cannot even begin to measure our loss of him as a composer. I can think only that I have lost a part of me; but I know also that music has lost an invaluable servant. His special position in musical theater is irreplaceable." Despite the circumstances of his passing, his career is a testament to his innovative spirit, his commitment to social justice, and his influence on American musical theater.

Kate Bornstein (1948–)

Writer, Actor, Gender Theorist

A trailblazer in their writing, acting, and activism, Kate Bornstein has been exploring their identification as nonbinary—not a man and not a woman—for nearly three decades. They are the author of *Gender Outlaw: On Men, Women, and the Rest of Us* (1995) and the subject of the documentary *Kate Bornstein Is a Queer & Pleasant Danger* (2014).

Assigned male at birth in Ashbury Park, New Jersey, Bornstein grew up in a Conservative Jewish family. After graduating from Brown University in 1969, they joined the Church of Scientology but were later disillusioned and formally left the movement in 1981. From an early age, they concluded that they weren't a boy and didn't want to grow up to be a man. In 1984, they began transitioning to female, which was completed in 1986. They settled into the lesbian community in San Francisco, writing art reviews for the gay and lesbian paper the *Bay Area Reporter*.

However, they realized that being a woman was no less play acting and pretending than being male and gave up the idea of being a woman in favor of adopting a nonbinary identity.

Bornstein began performing, creating several performance pieces and one-person shows to dramatize their experiences as well as teaching workshops and publishing gender theory books and novels. These include *Gender Outlaw* (1995), *My Gender Workbook* (1998), *Hello, Cruel World* (2006), *Gender Outlaws: The Next Generation* (2010), and the memoir *A Queer and Pleasant Danger* (2012).

Bornstein appeared in the 2017 film *Saturday Church* and, in 2018, performed on Broadway in the play *Straight White Men.* They lecture and perform at colleges and high schools and have earned praise and awards for their work on suicide prevention. In a summation of a career that is on the front line of gender debates, they wrote in 2019: "My own gender is a continuum that stretches from a 4-year-old who stood in the wrong gender line to the 71-year-old who just doesn't capitulate to binaries anymore. It's a Pride time of year, and I'm proud to be a loving auntie and granny to thousands of nonbinary people around the world. That's a whole lot of nothing going on, and it makes me positively giddy to think what that might mean for the future."

Rita Mae Brown (1944–)

Author, Activist

Rita Mae Brown, a writer known for her commitment to the feminist and gay liberation movements, is famous for her coming-of-age autobiographical novel *Rubyfruit Jungle* (1973), a hilarious and insightful account of one woman's intellectual and sexual odyssey which, because of its erotic lesbian content, was rejected by several publishers before becoming a bestseller. Gloria Steinem praised it as "the rare work of fiction that has changed real life." Brown has subsequently published over 50 works of fiction, nonfiction, and poetry, including the *Mrs. Murphy* mystery series and the *Sister Jane* fox-hunting novels.

Born in Hanover, Pennsylvania, to an unmarried, teenage mother and her mother's married boyfriend, Brown, as a newborn, was left at an orphanage before being adopted by her mother's cousin to be raised in York, Pennsylvania, and, later, Fort Lauderdale, Florida. She attended the University of Florida in 1962 but was expelled from the racially segregated university for her participation in the civil rights movement. She hitchhiked to New York City, where she lived from 1964 to 1969, sometimes homeless, while attending New York University. She earned BAs in classics and English and a certificate in cinematography in 1968. Eventually, she would receive a Ph.D. in literature from Union Institute & University (1976) and a second doctorate in political science from the Institute for Policy Studies in Washington, D.C.

From the late 1960s, Brown was an activist, joining the Gay Liberation Front and the fledgling National Organization for Women, but she resigned in 1970 over anti-lesbian comments by Betty Friedan. She would play a leading role in the Lavender Menace "zap" of the Second Congress to Unite Women protesting Friedan's remarks and the exclusion of lesbians from the women's movement. Brown and other lesbian activists formed the Radicalesbians and the Furies Collective, a separatist lesbian feminist collective in Washington, D.C., that held that heterosexuality was the root of all oppression. She was exiled from the Furies after a few months.

After the publication of *Rubyfruit Jungle*, Brown became one of the most public lesbians in the United States. Regarding her sexuality, she said, "I don't believe in straight or gay. I really don't. I think we're all degrees of bisexual. There may be a few people on the extreme if it's a bell curve who really truly are gay or really truly are straight. Because nobody had ever said these things and used their real names. I suddenly became the only lesbian in America. It was hysterical. It was a misnomer, but it's okay. It was a fight worth fighting."

In 1978, Brown moved to Charlottesville, Virginia, where she lived briefly with American actress and writer Fannie Flagg. In 1979, she met and fell in love with tennis great Martina Navratilova, with whom she bought a horse farm in Charlottesville. Navratilova eventually ended their relationship over concerns that coming out would hurt her application for U.S. citizenship. Brown still resides on the estate in Charlottesville, where in addition to her writing, she enjoys humane fox hunting and has a large collection of horses, dogs, and cats.

Brown, who rejects the term "lesbian writer," has focused her work on dramatizing the lot of women on the edge of society, including women of color, lesbians, and working-class women, in such politically charged books as *The Hand That Cradles the Rock* (1971), *Songs to a Handsome Woman* (1973), *A Plain Brown Rapper* (1976), *Six of One* (1978), *Southern Discomfort* (1982), *Sudden Death* (1983), *High Hearts* (1987), *Venus Envy* (1994), *Dolley: A Novel of Dolley Madison in Love and War* (1995), *Riding Shotgun* (1996), and *Alma Mater* (2002).

Over a long and incredibly prolific career, Brown has remade herself many times over from best-selling author to feminist and lesbian icon to fox-hunting mystery writer, always viewing the world from a fresh, if odd, angle. "The reward for conformity," she said, "is that everyone likes you but yourself."

Mary Burrill (1881–1946)

Playwright, Educator

Mary Powell Burrill was an African American playwright of the Harlem Renaissance known for her powerful works, which addressed social issues and depicted the realities of African American life. Her contributions to American theater in the early 20th century were significant, as she used her platform to highlight issues such as racial discrimination, gender inequality, and social justice. Her plays, including *Aftermath* and *They That Sit in Darkness*, were celebrated for their poignant storytelling and incisive commentary on the African American experience.

Burrill was born in Washington, D.C. She graduated from the M Street High School (now Dunbar High School), one of the first high schools for Black students in the United States. While there, she shared a romance with fellow student Angelina Weld Grimké, a great-niece of abolitionists and women's rights activists Sarah Moore and Angelina Emily Grimké, who helped ignite her passion for writing. After high school, she moved to Boston, where she received her degree from Emerson College in 1904, being the first woman of color to graduate from Emerson. She then worked as a teacher at Armstrong Manual High School (1905–1907), the Washington Conservatory of Music and School of Expression (1907–1911), and Dunbar High School (1911–1944), teaching English, speech, and drama.

In 1912, Burrill met her long-term romantic partner, educator Lucy Diggs Slowe, and they eventually moved in together in Washington. To combat discrimination due to their sexual orientation, they never publicly revealed that they were a couple, though they were recognized as such by their closest friends. Slowe would become, in 1922, the first dean of women at Howard University.

Burrill's first play, *The Other Wise Man*, was completed in 1905. The two plays for which she is best known are *They That Sit in Darkness*, set in the rural South and depicting the realities of being a young mother with multiple children and the effects of poverty that trapped African Americans and, in particular, Black women, and *Aftermath*, which depicts a young,

African American soldier returning to rural South Carolina to find that his father has been lynched and must face the reality that his service did not free him or his community.

Burrill's importance extends beyond her contributions to literature and theater. As an educator, she influenced many young, African American students, instilling in them a sense of pride and a commitment to social justice. Her dedication to education and her impact on her students further solidified her legacy as a pioneer in both the arts and the fight for equality. The house where Burrill and Slowe lived, known as the S Street Salon, was considered a refuge for Howard University's female students, and they regularly hosted get-togethers to mentor students. She would teach many writers who would become prominent in the New Negro Movement or the Harlem Renaissance such as Willis Richardson, who became the first Black playwright to have one of his plays performed on Broadway, and May Miller, whose play *Pandora's Box* was written while she was a student of Burrill's at Dunbar. In 2020, the Slowe-Burrill House, where the couple lived for 15 years, was added to the National Register of Historic Places by the National Park Service.

Burrill's achievements in playwriting and education, along with her courage in her personal life, have left an indelible mark on American culture and history. Her work continues to be celebrated for its depth, social relevance, and the powerful way it captures the African American experience.

Charles Busch (1954–)

Actor, Playwright

Preferring the term "male actress" to drag queen, Charles Busch is a stage and film actor and a prolific playwright of such shows as *Vampire Lesbians of Sodom*, which ran for five years Off-Broadway, and the Broadway hit *The Tale of the Allergist's Wife*. He starred in the film versions of his plays *Psycho Beach Party* and *Die Mommie Die*. A drag icon, he has performed his cabaret act around the world.

Busch grew up in Hartsdale, New York. His mother died when he was 7 years old, and his aunt brought him to live with her in Manhattan, where he developed an intense interest in films, particularly those from the 1930s and 1940s. He attended the High School of Music and Art in Manhattan and graduated from Northwestern University in 1976 with a major in drama. While at the university, he had difficulty being cast in plays and began to write his own material. Male roles did not interest him, and he discovered that his talent and passion was in playing leading ladies. As he recalled, "Playing a female role gave me a freedom of movement and vocal variety I had never known. Drag for me was not an expression of outrage or even satire, but rather a passageway to channel the feminine in my nature, which turned out to be a place of authority."

Busch has credited seeing a performance of Charles Ludlam's play *Eunuchs of the Forbidden City* by New York's Ridiculous Theatrical Company with giving him the idea of combining his beloved classic Hollywood references with his desire to play leading ladies. After graduation, he toured his own one-man (non-drag) show *Alone with a Cast of Thousands* around the United States from 1978 to 1984. As venues for his style of cabaret performance shrank, he wrote a play called *Vampire Lesbians of Sodom* about a lesbian vampire-turned-actress who was locked in a 2,000-year-long rivalry with another lesbian vampire actress, with himself and a friend in the roles. It would run at the Provincetown Playhouse in Greenwich Village for five years, one of the longest-running plays in Off-Broadway history. Additional plays, revues, and television and movie work followed. In 2000, *The Tale of the Allergist's Wife*, a comedy about an Upper West Side woman facing an existential crisis, earned him a Tony nomination for Best Play. In 2023, he published his memoir, *Leading Lady: A Memoir of a Most Unusual Boy*, which tells his story of managing a creative life as a male actress, creating the roles he wanted to play regardless of gender restrictions.

Paul Cadmus (1904–1999)

Artist

Paul Cadmus, one of the first openly gay American artists who also unabashedly made artworks with queer themes, was renowned for his provocative and meticulously detailed works, which often explored themes of sexuality, social critique, and the human condition. His unique style and willingness to address controversial subjects made him a significant figure in 20th-century American art.

Cadmus was born in New York City, the son of artists. His father worked as a commercial artist; his mother illustrated children's books. He demonstrated an artistic talent from a young age and, at the age of 15, he left school to attend the National Academy of Design for six years. He enrolled in the Art Students League of New York in 1928, taking life-drawing lessons while working as a commercial illustrator at a New York advertising company. He furthered his education while traveling through Europe from 1931 to 1933 with fellow artist Jared French, who became his lover for a time. Running out of money, he returned to the United States and became one of the first artists to be employed by the New Deal art programs, painting murals at post offices.

At the age of 29, in 1934, Cadmus created his most famous work while working for the Public Works of Art Project, *The Fleet's In!* It depicted sailors on shore leave engaging in various rowdy activities, including flirtation and drunkenness. The homoerotic undertones and portrayal of sailors in compromising situations led to its controversial removal from an exhibition by the U.S. Navy and catapulted him to national prominence, launching his career.

Cadmus's art is notable for its explicit and implicit homoerotic themes, making him a significant figure in the history of LGBTQ+ art. His frequent depiction of male bodies, often in intimate and sensual contexts, challenged conventional norms and emphasized their beauty and physicality. Works like *YMCA Locker Room* (1934) portray men in close, sometimes flirtatious, interactions, suggesting deeper, homoerotic connections. *Aspects of Suburban Life: Main Street* (1935) provided a critical look at suburban existence and was part of his broader commentary on American society. *The Herrin Massacre* (1940) depicted the 1922 violent labor dispute in Herrin, Illinois, using stark realism to convey the brutality of the event, demonstrating his engagement with historical and political themes in his works. Additionally, he used allegory and symbolism to explore desire and sexuality, as seen in *The Seven Deadly Sins* (1936), and his portraits, particularly those of his partner, Jon Anderson, convey affection and intimacy, capturing the nuances of their relationship.

Cadmus's work was groundbreaking for its open exploration of homosexual themes during a time of significant social stigma. By providing representation and visibility for the LGBTQ+ community, he challenged societal norms and celebrated gay identity. His influence extended to later generations of LGBTQ+ artists, inspiring them to explore similar themes. Through his art, he critiqued moral hypocrisy and societal attitudes toward sexuality, contributing to cultural discourse on these issues. His enduring legacy lies in his technical excellence and his role in advancing LGBTQ+ visibility and acceptance in the art world, securing his place as a pioneering figure in LGBTQ+ art history.

John Cage (1912–1992)

Composer

John Milton Cage Jr. was an avant-garde composer and influential figure in 20th-century music known for his innovative approaches to composition and performance. He challenged conventional ideas about music, sound, and silence with one of his most famous works, *4′33″*, consisting of four minutes and 33 seconds of silence. This piece encouraged audiences to focus on ambient sounds, redefining the concept of music. His experimentation with prepared pianos, chance operations, and electronic music pushed the boundaries of what was considered music, making him a pivotal figure in the development of experimental and contemporary classical music.

Cage was born in Los Angeles but spent part of his childhood in Detroit and Ann Arbor, Michigan, before returning to California. He had his own weekly radio show in Los Angeles when he was 12 years old and began studying the piano, and his program featured his own performances. In 1930, after two years at Pomona College, he went to Paris, working with an architect, and devoted himself to the study of contemporary piano works. Returning to California in 1931, he worked as a cook and gardener while giving lectures on modern art. In the 1930s, he studied music with notable figures such as Henry Cowell and Adolph Weiss and was strongly influenced by the music of Arnold Schoenberg, which laid the foundation for his avant-garde approach to composition.

In 1937, Cage gravitated to the world of dance, moving to Seattle, where he worked as a composer and accompanist for dance classes. There, he met and began his lifelong collaboration with dancer and choreographer Merce Cunningham. It was Cage who persuaded Cunningham to start his own dance company, with which he toured as composer, accompanist, and music director.

Called by his mentor Schoenberg "not a composer but an inventor of genius," which greatly pleased Cage, he experimented with prepared pianos, placing different objects between the strings for different sounds, spoken text compositions, and electronic music pushing the boundaries of what was considered music, making him a pivotal figure in the development of experimental and contemporary classical music. His *Europera 5*, for example, juxtaposes 19th-century operatic arias, his own instrumental music, radio broadcasts, and silent television pictures. He said, "There is no noise, only sound. I haven't heard any sounds that I consider something I don't want to hear again, with the exception of sounds that frighten us or make us aware of pain, I don't like meaningful sound. If sound is meaningless, I'm all for it."

Cage's importance extends beyond his compositions; he was a philosopher and writer whose ideas influenced a wide range of artistic disciplines. His book *Silence: Lectures and Writings* is a seminal text that explores his thoughts on sound, silence, and the role of the artist in society. He collaborated with many notable artists and was an influence on many, including Cunningham, Jasper Johns, and Robert Rauschenberg. His interdisciplinary approach fostered collaborations across music, dance, visual arts, and literature, making him a central figure in the postwar American avant-garde movement.

Cage's legacy is marked by his radical rethinking of music and sound, his philosophical writings, and his contributions to various art forms through his interdisciplinary collaborations. His openness about his sexuality and his partnership with Cunningham also left a lasting impact, helping to pave the way for a greater acceptance of LGBTQ+ individuals in the arts.

Truman Capote (1924–1984)

Author

An acclaimed writer of fiction and nonfiction and celebrity, Truman Capote was both a colorful and controversial presence on the literary and social scene. Openly gay, he battled homophobia throughout his career but managed to become one of the best-known writers of the postwar period and a fixture among the rich and fashionable.

Born in New Orleans, Capote was largely neglected by his parents, often left in the care of others, and spent much of his childhood in the care of his mother's relatives in Monroeville, Alabama, where he became friends with future author Harper Lee (Dill Harris, in Lee's *To Kill a Mockingbird,* is believed to have been based on a young Capote). In 1932, he went to New York to live with his mother and her second husband. He wrote short stories from the age of 11 and attended a string of prep schools and a military school. His early work defied the social conventions of his conservative, Southern background by sympathetically portraying characters normally deemed immoral or amoral. His stories were published widely in *The Atlantic Monthly, Harper's, Mademoiselle, The New Yorker,* and other publications. He won the O. Henry Award in 1948 for the story "Shut a Final Door." His first novel, *Other Voices, Other Rooms* (1948), a best-selling, semi-autobiographical account of his childhood in Alabama, brought him critical acclaim and some notoriety for dealing with homosexuality. *A Tree of Night and Other Stories* (1949) followed.

Breakfast at Tiffany's: A Short Novel and Three Stories appeared in 1958. The title novella centered on the free-spirited Holly Golightly and became the first of two of Capote's major works. It prompted Norman Mailer to call him "the most perfect writer of my generation." His second great achievement, a considerable departure for the writer, was *In Cold Blood: A True Account of a Multiple Murder and Its Consequences* (1965), detailing the unexplained murder of the Clutter family in rural Holcomb, Kansas. He traveled there, interviewing everyone involved in the investigation and most of the town's residents. He labeled it a "nonfiction novel." It became an international bestseller (and blockbuster film) and one of the leading achievements of the evolving New Journalism movement. He would never complete another novel after it.

Capote continued to publish journalism and short prose pieces, collected in *Then It All Came Down* (1976) and *Music for Chameleons* (1980), while trading on his celebrity to enter the world of the jet set. He was a seemingly ubiquitous presence on talk shows and at exclusive social gatherings. In 1966, he hosted the legendary Black and White Ball for ultra-A-list celebrities. His long-delayed and much anticipated tell-all of his experience among the rich and famous, *Answered Prayers,* was left unfinished, though the incomplete book was published in 1987 after his death.

His early work defied the social conventions of his conservative, Southern background....

In his later years, Capote struggled with alcohol and drug addiction. Outspoken and honest about his gayness, he claimed multiple affairs but spent the majority of his life partnered with fellow writer Jack Dunphy. He never embraced the gay rights movement, but his own frankness about his sexuality and encouragement of honesty in others made him a notable gay icon. He said that he "never had any problem about being homosexual.... I didn't look like anybody else, and I wasn't like anybody else. People start out by being put off by something that's different, but I very easily disarmed them. Seduction—that's what I do.... I was totally self-created."

Willa Cather (1873–1947)

Novelist, Short Story Writer, Essayist

Willa Cather can be described as the last great 19th-century American writer. Adrift and dispossessed by the modern world, she celebrated in her writing the departed world of the past. However, she contributed far more than nostalgia for the bygone by exploring the emotional contours of the past while offering a definition of the American identity based on its frontier and immigrant experience. She would explain America's present by investigating its past.

Born in Virginia, Cather moved to the Nebraska prairie village of Red Cloud as a child, leaving for schooling at the state university in Lincoln. After graduating in 1895, she went to work editing a home magazine in Pittsburgh and later was a drama and music reviewer for a Pittsburgh newspaper. After a stint as a high school English teacher, in 1906, she began work as an editor for *McClure's* magazine, a job she held until 1911, when she resigned to pursue a writing career. Encouraged by Maine regionalist writer Sarah Orne Jewett to focus on the region she knew best, she produced her Prairie Trilogy—*O Pioneers* (1913), *The Song of the Lark* (1915), and her masterpiece, *My Antonia* (1918)—all drawing on her Nebraskan experience.

My Antonia, though Cather's fourth novel, was the first to most completely reflect her realization that "life began for me when I ceased to admire and began to remember." The novel would celebrate both the elemental landscape of the Nebraska prairie and the intensity and idiosyncrasies of its inhabitants, who first carved lives from the unforgiving wilderness. Its vivid depiction of people and places is focused on the life of a Czech farm girl, Antonia Shimerda, and the impact she had on the narrator, Jim Burden, over her lifetime, telling the story of the settling and transformation of the Nebraskan frontier. The novel is one of the greatest pastoral elegies in American literature, celebrating all that is primal and archetypal through its heroine, Antonia, one of a core group of essential characters in American literature.

Cather's subsequent work continued to explore her past, the most distant past, and an increasingly disappointing present in comparison. *One of Our Own* (1921) is set during World War I. *A Lost Lady* (1923) is based on a woman she knew in Red Cloud. *Death Comes for the Archbishop* (1926) is based on the life of 19th-century French missionaries in New Mexico. *Shadows on the Rock* (1931) is set in 17th-century Quebec. *The Professor's House* (1935) is about a man's midlife crisis and many of her own anxieties during the period. *Sapphira and the Slave Girl* (1940) takes place in the village of her birth in the years before the Civil War.

Over her long and productive career, Cather remained dedicated to her art, foregoing matrimony and children to pursue her writing. Since most of her close relationships were with women, she has been claimed as an early example of a lesbian author. In 1911 at *McClure's,* she met editor Edith Lewis, forming a domestic partnership with her that lasted 40 years. Lewis was described as her personal secretary, and the author destroyed letters and diaries that treat her sexuality. It has been argued that Cather was a closeted lesbian, but little evidence contradicts the facts of her celibacy and her primary relationship with her art.

Ilene Chaiken (1957–)

Writer, Director, Producer

Ilene Chaiken is a writer, producer, and director best known for her groundbreaking work in television. As the creator of the iconic series *The L Word,* she has been instrumental in bringing nuanced and authentic LGBTQ+ stories to mainstream media. Her work has significantly contributed to the visibility and representation of LGBTQ+ characters and narratives, making her a prominent figure in the entertainment industry and a powerful advocate for the LGBTQ+ community.

Chaiken was born in Elkins Park, Pennsylvania, outside of Philadelphia. She grew up in a Jewish family and showed an early interest in storytelling and the arts. She attended Rhode Island School of Design to study graphic design but eventually shifted her focus to film and television. After graduating, she moved to Los Angeles to pursue a career in the entertainment industry.

Chaiken began her career working in the mailroom at Creative Artists Agency (CAA) and later became an executive for Aaron Spelling Productions. She then transitioned into screenwriting and producing, contributing to projects like the action film *Barb Wire* (1996) and the television film *Dirty Pictures* (2000), which won a Golden Globe Award. Additionally, she worked as a staff writer for the popular sitcom *The Fresh Prince of Bel-Air* and as a writer and producer for the medical mystery–comedy drama series *Diagnosis: Murder*.

Chaiken came out as a lesbian during the time of her first romantic relationship with a woman and its breakup. She has discussed how this relationship led her to pitch a series to Showtime for a show about lesbians in Los Angeles, mirroring the lives of her and her friends. The network resisted, considering it too far outside the mainstream. However, after the success of a similar show about gays, *Queer as Folk,* she tried again, and *The L Word* finally aired from 2004 to 2009. The series was revolutionary as one of the first mainstream television shows to focus on the lives of lesbian and bisexual women. *The L Word* not only provided representation but also tackled complex issues such as identity, relationships, and societal acceptance. She served as the showrunner and executive producer, ensuring that the series remained true to its authentic portrayal of LGBTQ+ experiences.

Chaiken would go on to help create the TV adaptation of *The Handmaid's Tale* but left during its development in 2015 to become the executive producer and showrunner for the series *Empire,* which aired from 2015 to 2020. *Empire* centered on an African American family involved in the hip-hop and entertainment industry and featured an openly gay main character, showcasing the intersectionality of race and sexuality. In its final season, *Empire* featured a transgender character, portrayed by transgender actress and singer Alexandra Grey. In 2020, Chaiken cocreated *Law & Order: Organized Crime* and produced a sequel to *The L Word, The L Word: Generation Q,* which ended in 2023. She is thought to be currently working on a New York–set reboot of the original series.

Chaiken has been married to LouAnne Brickhouse, a former executive at Disney, since 2013. She is a coparent to twin daughters with her former partner, English architect Miggi Hood. In many ways, her career is remarkable as a woman and a lesbian in an era when Hollywood still struggles with diversity, especially behind the cameras. "Clearly, it's still a boys' club," she observed. "As a gay person, there still is just an uphill road for us to hoe. We are underrepresented vastly, and we haven't been represented in all of the ways in which we live in the world. I think it's incremental, the progress that we see in that regard."

Jane Chambers (1937–1983)

Playwright

Jane Chambers was a pioneering playwright whose work brought lesbian themes and characters to the forefront of American theater. Her plays challenged the prevailing social norms and provided a much-needed voice for the lesbian community, contributing to greater visibility and acceptance. Her commitment to authentic representation and courage in addressing taboo subjects made her a significant figure in LGBTQ+ history.

Chambers was born in Columbia, South Carolina. She attended Rollins College in Florida, intending to become a playwright, but dropped out after she encountered discrimination as a woman there. After studying acting at the Pasadena Playhouse in 1956, she moved to New York City and then to Poland Spring, Maine, where she worked at its television station. She enrolled in Goddard College in Vermont, completing her degree in 1971. There, she met Beth Allen, who would become her partner and manager.

Chambers's most notable achievements came from her contributions to lesbian theater. *A Late Snow* (1974) was one of the first plays to feature openly lesbian characters. *Last Summer at Bluefish Cove* (1980) is considered one of the first plays to present lesbian characters in a positive and realistic light. The play, which centers on a group of lesbian friends vacationing together, was groundbreaking for its honest portrayal of lesbian relationships and its challenge to the stereotypical depictions of lesbians in the media. *My Blue Heaven* (1981) is one of the first American plays featuring a same-sex marriage and follows two women who leave Manhattan for country life when one loses her job for writing an openly gay book. In *Kudzu* (1981), four elderly people, two gay and two straight, face the realities of aging in a domestic comedy set in the rural South. *Kudzu* was in rehearsals for a Broadway run when she was diagnosed with a brain tumor; she was unable to make the necessary revisions, and the Broadway production was subsequently cancelled. It would have made her the first lesbian to stage a play about happy, well-adjusted lesbians on Broadway. Over her brief life—she died a month short of her 46th birthday—she wrote at least 35 plays, 17 novels, 32 screenplays and television scripts, numerous short stories, a poetry collection, and dozens of articles.

Chambers was openly lesbian and used her work to advocate for lesbian rights and visibility. Her personal experiences and relationships deeply influenced her writing, allowing her to create authentic and relatable characters. Her courage in living openly and addressing lesbian themes in her work made her a role model for many in the LGBTQ+ community. Her plays continue to be celebrated for their pioneering role in lesbian theater and impact on LGBTQ+ representation.

Montgomery Clift (1920–1966)

Actor

Edward Montgomery Clift was a groundbreaking actor whose intense and sensitive portrayals redefined Hollywood's approach to the creation of character in film. A key figure in the post–World War II wave of method actors, he brought a raw emotional depth to his roles that challenged the era's conventional leading man archetypes. His work in film not only garnered critical acclaim but also left a lasting impact on future generations of actors, solidifying his place as a cinematic legend.

Clift was born in Omaha, Nebraska. Raised in a privileged but emotionally tumultuous household, his early life was marked by extensive travel and private tutoring. He developed a passion for acting at a young age and moved to New York City in his teens, where he quickly made a name for himself on Broadway. By the age of 20, he had become a respected stage actor, performing in plays like *There Shall Be No Night* and *The Skin of Our Teeth*, earning acclaim for his intense and naturalistic performances.

Clift's transition to film was marked by his debut in *Red River* (1948) followed by a starring role in *The Search* (1948), for which he received his first Academy Award nomination. His subsequent films, including *A Place in the Sun* (1951), *From Here to Eternity* (1953), and *Suddenly, Last Summer* (1959), showcased his exceptional range and ability to convey complex emotional states. His collaborations with directors like Alfred Hitchcock in *I Confess* (1953) and John Huston in *The Misfits* (1961) further demonstrated his versatility. Despite a severe car accident in 1956 that affected his looks and career, he continued to deliver powerful performances, earning additional Oscar nominations for *From Here to Eternity*, *The Young Lions* (1958), and *Judgment at Nuremberg* (1961).

Clift's car accident, driving home from a party at Elizabeth Taylor's, is one of the most infamous incidents in Hollywood history, significantly impacting both his career and personal life. The physical and emotional toll of the accident exacerbated his struggles with substance abuse; he became increasingly dependent on alcohol and painkillers, leading to erratic behavior and further affecting his health and career. Friends and colleagues noted that the once vibrant and handsome actor had become a shadow of his former self, struggling with his demons while still delivering powerful performances.

Clift's personal life was as complex and intense as his on-screen roles. Early biographers attributed his decline into alcohol and drugs to self-loathing due to his homosexuality. Later critics and researchers who have looked more closely at the evidence show an actor far less closeted than fellow actor Rock Hudson, one who readily embraced his sexual preferences and willingly accepted his reputation as a contrarian and outsider. His untimely death at the age of 45 in 1966 from a heart attack left a poignant mark on his legacy, highlighting the often painful intersection of personal struggle and public persona. His legacy as an actor remains profound. His bravery in continuing to work and deliver compelling performances, even as he battled immense personal difficulties, has garnered admiration, and his story is often cited as an example of the intense pressures and vulnerabilities faced by actors in the spotlight.

Walter W. Cole (Darcelle XV) (1930–2023)

Entertainer

Walter Willard Cole, known onstage as Darcelle XV, was a legendary drag performer and LGBTQ+ icon. Founder of the Darcelle XV Showplace in Portland, Oregon, he created a vibrant and inclusive space for drag. Recognized as the world's oldest performing drag queen by Guinness World Records, he was celebrated for his dazzling performances and advocacy for LGBTQ+ rights.

Cole was born in Portland, Oregon, an only child who was bullied by classmates, who called him "sissy boy" and, when he got glasses, "four-eyed sissy boy." His mother died when he was 10, and he was sexually abused by his alcoholic father. In 1951, he married his high school sweetheart, Jeanette Rossini, before being drafted into the U.S. Army, where he served for two years in the Signal Corps in Italy. After being discharged, he returned to Portland and used money saved from his military service to buy a coffeehouse and a jazz club.

In 1967, Cole purchased a derelict tavern in northwest Portland, then considered the city's Skid Row, which became the Darcelle XV Showplace, a drag cabaret. He confessed to his wife that he was gay soon after buying the tavern. He subsequently moved in with Roc LeRoy Neuhardt, a dancer and choreographer. Cole never divorced his wife. He first wore women's dresses in 1967; by 1969, he developed the alter ego Darcelle, after French actress Denise Darcel; came out publicly as gay; and regularly performed at the Showplace. His specialty was performing Barbra Streisand songs. The club quickly became a cornerstone of the drag scene and a sanctuary for the LGBTQ+ community. Under his leadership, the Showplace became renowned for its extravagant performances and inclusive atmosphere. His performances, characterized by dazzling costumes, sharp wit, and a warm stage presence, established him as a trailblazer in the drag world. In the early 1970s, he was crowned the 15th "Empress" of the Imperial Sovereign Rose Court of Oregon, an LGBTQ+ organization; he then added XV to his stage name and renamed the club the Darcelle XV Showplace.

Over the years, Cole became an important advocate for Portland's LGBTQ+ community and an indefatigable fundraiser for many causes. During the AIDS crisis in the 1980s and early 1990s, he helped to raise money for medical research, facilities for people with AIDS, and children whose lives were affected by the disease. A granite sculpture to honor Oregonians who had died of AIDS was named the Darcelle XV AIDS Memorial in 2017. In 2020, the Darcelle XV Showplace was added to the National Register of Historic Places for its contribution to LGBTQ+ history.

"She touched the lives of so many, not only through her performances but also through her fearless community advocacy and charitable works," said Todd Addams, director of Basic Rights Oregon. "She was nothing short of an icon." After his death, Oregon senator Ron Wyden declared that "Darcelle carved out an unforgettable chapter in Portland's history" with "pioneering courage."

Aaron Copland (1900–1990)

Composer

Regarded as the "dean of American composers," Aaron Copland was an impassioned champion of American music in every style. His works, like the ballets *Appalachian Spring*, *Billy the Kid*, and *Rodeo* and the orchestral pieces *Fanfare for the Common Man* and *Third Symphony*, defined a distinctive American classical music style. His style is often described as "American Romanticism," featuring melodies inspired by folk and jazz music. Perhaps more than any other American composer, he democratized classical music, widening the appeal and popularity of serious music to a wide, general audience.

Born in Brooklyn, New York, Copland was the son of Russian–Jewish immigrants and attended public schools. An older sister taught him to play the piano, and by the age of 15, after attending a concert by Polish composer–pianist Ignacy Jan Paderewski, he decided that he wanted to become a composer, initially through a correspondence course to learn harmony and then with noted music teacher Rubin Goldmark.

In 1921, Copland attended a newly founded school for Americans in France where he studied with French composer Nadia Boulanger, becoming her first American student in composition. Returning to New York in 1925, he was given a commission by Boulanger to write a new symphony for her upcoming American tour. When *Symphony for Organ and Orchestra* premiered in 1925, conductor Walter Damrosch declared, "If a young man can write a piece like that at the age of 24, in five years he will be ready to commit murder!"

In the decade that followed, Copland became world famous while attempting to capture the American experience in music, incorporating a range of styles in his works that included jazz and folk elements. His best-known pieces include *Piano Variations* (1930), *Dance Symphony* (1930), *Lincoln Portrait* (1942), and *Fanfare for the Common Man* (1942). He later composed the music for Martha Graham's 1944 dance, *Appalachian Spring*, which won him the Pulitzer Prize. He was a renowned composer of film scores as well, including *Of Mice and Men* (1939), *Our Town* (1940), and *The*

North Star (1943), which were all nominated for Academy Awards. He eventually won an Oscar for *The Heiress* (1949).

In the 1950s, Copland became a target during the Red Scare for his allegedly leftist politics. When his work as a composer declined, he concentrated on conducting, touring the world with his own works and those of other great American musicians. He was also an active teacher at Tanglewood, Harvard, and New York's New School. He was also the author of five books and traveled globally in an attempt to elevate the status of American music abroad.

While Copland's sexuality has been a subject of speculation and debate, he never publicly identified as gay during his lifetime. However, biographers and historians have noted that he maintained close relationships with several men throughout his life, including artist Emil Antonucci and photographer Victor Kraft. Although he was never outspoken on the subject, he felt little to no angst about his sexuality. He never went to great lengths to hide his relationships, most of which were with talented, young men who ran in his cultural sphere. Nor did his homosexuality interfere with his success as a composer, though it may have contributed to his blacklisting during the Red Scare. At one point, Leonard Bernstein pressured his mentor and friend to publicly come out. Copland wryly responded, "I think I'll leave that to you, boy."

Copland died after a long illness at the age of 90, easily one of the most acclaimed and important figures in 20th-century American music.

Laverne Cox (1972–)

Actor, Producer

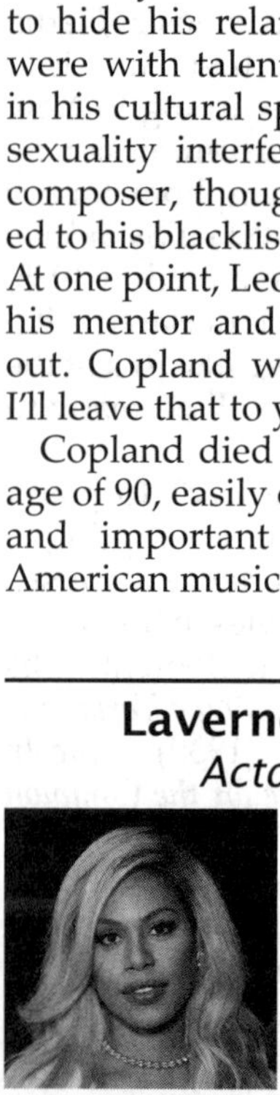

Laverne Cox is a trailblazing actress and advocate known for her role as Sophia Burset on *Orange Is the New Black,* earning her a historic Emmy nomination as the first openly transgender nominee. She is a vocal advocate for transgender rights and LGBTQ+ visibility. In 2014, she became the first transgender person to be featured on the cover of *Time* magazine. She is the first trans woman to produce and star in her own TV show, the makeover series *TRANSform Me.* Producing documentaries like *Laverne Cox Presents: The T Word,* she has significantly advanced transgender representation and acceptance in mainstream media.

Born Roderick Laverne Cox in Mobile, Alabama, Laverne was designated male at birth but from a young age identified as female, recalling about her youth, "I was very feminine and I was really bullied, majorly bullied." She also said, "I internalized a lot of shame about who I was as a child," surviving a suicide attempt when she was in the 6th grade. After attending high school at the Alabama School of Fine Arts in Birmingham, Alabama, she attended Indiana University and graduated from Marymount Manhattan College in New York with a bachelor's degree in dance. In college, she began fully identifying as a female and started to transition medically.

Cox also began acting in Off-Broadway shows and independent student films during college. In 2008, she appeared in small parts on several TV series. Her breakthrough role came in 2012 when she was cast as Sophia Burset, a transgender woman in prison on the critically acclaimed Netflix series *Orange Is the New Black.* Her portrayal of Sophia garnered widespread recognition and praise, earning her a nomination for a Primetime Emmy Award. This nomination made her the first openly transgender person to be nominated for an acting award in the history of the Emmys. Her performance not only showcased her talent but also brought much-needed visibility to transgender issues and narratives in mainstream media, and she has emerged as the face of the transgender movement in America. After *Orange Is the New Black* ended in 2019, she appeared in the films *Charlie's Angels*

(2019), *Promising Young Woman* (2020), and *Jolt* (2021). In 2020, she starred in the film *Disclosure*, a documentary examining Hollywood's portrayal of transgender people and its impact on American culture. "I was told many times that I wouldn't be able to have a mainstream career as an actor because I'm trans, because I'm Black," she said, "and here I am. And it feels really good."

Cox has been a vocal advocate for mental health awareness, sharing her own experiences with depression and suicide attempts in order to inspire and support others. Her courage in speaking openly about her struggles has helped to reduce stigma and encourage conversations about mental health within the LGBTQ+ community and beyond.

Cheryl Crawford (1902–1986)

Theater Producer, Director

Cheryl Crawford was a pioneering American theater producer and director whose innovative contributions significantly shaped the landscape of American theater in the 20th century. She cofounded influential theater organizations such as the Group Theatre, the Actors Studio, and the American Repertory Theater, all of which played critical roles in advancing theatrical arts in the United States. Her dedication to producing socially relevant and artistically groundbreaking plays brought forward new narratives that challenged societal norms and explored complex human experiences, making her a pivotal figure in the theater community, while her success as a lesbian woman in the male-dominated Broadway theater scene makes her an early LGBTQ+ trailblazer.

Born in Akron, Ohio, Crawford originally wanted to become a missionary but became interested in the theater at the age of 15 when she played Lady Macbeth in an amateur production. After graduating from Smith College in 1925, she went to New York and found work at the Theatre Guild as an actress, secretary, and assistant stage manager. By the age of 27, she had become the casting director of the Theatre Guild, working with Harold Clurman, who was serving as the play reader. Together, they left their guild positions to become directors, with Lee Strasberg, of the Group Theatre. There, she helped to introduce method acting to American audiences.

The Group Theatre became a hub for developing new plays and training actors in this emotionally truthful acting technique. Crawford acted as coproducer or codirector on many Group Theatre productions, including *Awake and Sing*, *Waiting for Lefty*, *Johnny Johnson*, and *Men in White*, which won a Pulitzer Prize. Later, at the Actors Studio, she continued to influence the craft of acting, contributing to the development of iconic actors like Marlon Brando, James Dean, and Marilyn Monroe. Her Broadway production credits include significant works such as Tennessee Williams's *The Rose Tattoo* and Rodgers and Hammerstein's *Oklahoma!*

She regarded her 1947 production of *Brigadoon* as her personal favorite, saying, "Looking back, the best time I ever had as a producer was on the morning after *Brigadoon* opened. It was the only time in my life I ever had a show that all the critics loved." Playwright Sidney Kingsley recalled, "Cheryl's contribution, though she always wanted it to be artistic, really was as den mother and producer. All her life she was best at that. She was good at raising money, settling disputes, getting in a co-producer, the thousand and one things a producer has to do."

Crawford's sexuality, while less publicly discussed during her lifetime, was an integral aspect of her identity. She was a lesbian and had several relationships with women throughout her life, including a relationship with Group Theatre actress Dorothy Patten, with whom she lived for several years in the 1930s, and with chef Ruth Norman, with whom she formed a long-term romantic partnership. In an era when LGBTQ+ identities were often stigmatized, she navigated her personal and professional life with a degree of privacy. Her sexuality, however, clearly expressed her empathetic approach to storytelling and support for diverse voices in the theater. As her biographer, Milly S. Barranger, observed, she wore her lesbian identity "undisguised in her tailored clothes, her hair style, her masculine tone of voice, and her circle of women friends."

Crawford's life and work reflected a broader commitment to authenticity and artistic integrity. Barranger summarizes her achievements: "For forty years she beat the odds that a woman could prove successful in the male-dominated establishment of American commercial theater. That success brought her mixed blessings: anxieties, disappointments, loneliness, but chiefly dreams of the next production, the next winning playwright, the next critical success." She remained active in the theater almost up until her death, which was caused by an accidental fall at the age of 84.

Mart Crowley (1935–2020)

Playwright

Edward Martino "Mart" Crowley is best known for his play *The Boys in the Band,* which opened Off-Broadway in 1968 and became one of the first American dramas to put gay characters and their experience onstage in ways not seen in a mainstream New York theater. His play neither hinted at nor demonized his characters' gayness but allowed the nine men gathering at a birthday party to discuss their lives with an honesty that was both unique and pioneering. Appearing a year before the Stonewall Uprising and running for more than two years, drawing both gay and straight audiences, including Jacqueline Kennedy and Mayor John V. Lindsay, *The Boys in the Band* was, for many in the audience, their first glimpse at unabashedly gay characters. The play has been widely credited as a catalyst for and a milestone of the gay rights movement.

Crowley was born in Vicksburg, Mississippi, to an alcoholic father and a drug-addict mother. He attended an all-boys Catholic high school and graduated from the Catholic University in Washington, D.C., in 1957 with a degree in theater. He was hired to be an assistant to director Elia Kazan, who was filming *Splendor in the Grass.* He befriended one of its stars, Natalie Wood, who hired him to be her personal assistant when she was cast in *West Side Story.*

Crowley was inspired to write *The Boys in the Band* as a response to the 1966 essay "Homosexual Drama and Its Disguises" by theater critic Stanley Kauffmann, who urged gay playwrights to address their gay experience. "Kauffman's article was 'Isn't it about time that one of these homosexual writers writes a play that's openly about his own experience?'" Crowley, who was openly gay at the time, recalled, "And I thought that was a very, very good point."

Focused on a group of gay and bi friends gathering for a birthday party in New York City, *The Boys in the Band* was not only pioneering, it was risky. "It was very different back then," Crowley said in a 2019 interview. "You could get arrested for doing the things they do in this play.... Agents said it was a career killer." As Tony Kushner, author of *Angels in America,* asserted, Crowley "courageously answered the call of a historical moment." The play reached a wider national audience in the 1970 film version, which was directed by William Friedkin.

Not all members of the gay community were happy with the play's realistic portraits of dysfunctional homosexuals. Gay playwright Edward Albee complained that straight theatergoers "were so happy to be able to see people they didn't have to respect." In its defense, Crowley maintained that he never intended to represent all gay and bisexual men or to present gay role models but rather distinctive characters treated truthfully.

Crowley wrote five additional plays, including *The Men from the Boys* (2002), a sequel to *The Boys in the Band*, as well as screenplays for television. In celebration of its 50th anniversary, *The Boys in the Band* was restaged on Broadway, earning a 2019 Tony Award for Best Revival of a Play. He said that seeing his play finally come to Broadway and win a Tony "was the highlight" of his life.

George Cukor (1899–1983)

Film Director

Called "one of the most elegant directors Hollywood ever produced," George Dewey Cukor was a prolific and influential American filmmaker whose career spanned over five decades. Renowned for his sophisticated comedies and literary adaptations, he was a master of character-driven narratives known for his ability to elicit powerful performances, particularly from female leads, earning him the title "women's director" in Hollywood. Despite his professional success, his personal life was characterized by discretion regarding his sexuality. As a gay man in Hollywood's Golden Age, he had to navigate a career in an industry that was often hostile to same-sex relationships.

Cukor was born in Manhattan. His grandfather had emigrated from Hungary in 1870 and chose his grandson's name from patriotic fervor over Admiral George Dewey's victory at Manila Bay in the Spanish–American War. He grew up on Manhattan's Upper East Side and attended public schools. "I was a stage-struck kid," he recalled, saying that he "played hooky" to see as many Broadway plays as possible in the cheapest seats. He would spend more than a decade in the professional theater, working as an assistant stage manager in a touring company; directing a stock company in Rochester, New York; and going to Broadway as a stage manager and director. He directed a hit adaptation of F. Scott Fitzgerald's *The Great Gatsby* and worked with such actors as Ethel Barrymore, Laurette Taylor, Melvyn Douglas, and Louis Calhern.

With the advent of talkies, Hollywood needed directors from the stage who were adept in dialogue, and in 1929, Cukor directed the dialogue for *All Quiet on the Western Front*. His breakthrough came with the 1933 film *Little Women*, which established him as a talented director of literary adaptations. Over the years, he directed several classic films, including *The Philadelphia Story* (1940), *Gaslight* (1944), and *Adam's Rib* (1949). One of his most acclaimed works was the musical *My Fair Lady* (1964), for which he won the Academy Award for Best Director. His ability to bring out nuanced performances from actors and meticulous attention to detail made his films enduringly popular.

Cukor bristled at the designation "women's director," saying "remember, for every Jill there was a Jack" and pointing out that he helped James Stewart, Ronal Colman, and Rex Harrison all win Oscars. As for the so-called "Cukor style," the director said, "I guess it arises out of two principal factors: my own personalized perception of the world and my ability to deal professionally with actors.... I always try to imagine setting through the best possible eyes."

Despite his professional success and acclaim, Cukor's personal life was characterized by discretion regarding his sexuality. As a gay man in Hollywood's Golden Age, he had to navigate a career in an industry that was not accepting of same-sex relationships, at least not publicly. His sexuality was an open secret in Hollywood, and he maintained a close circle of friends within the entertainment industry who shared his discretion. His home became a gathering place for other closeted celebrities and a refuge for gay and lesbian actors. He was arrested on vice charges, which were dismissed due to industry pressure.

Cukor's legacy is not only defined by his impressive body of work but also by his subtle defiance of the era's restrictive norms. His films often featured strong, complex female characters, and his direction highlighted themes of individuality and resilience. His work continues to be celebrated for its elegance, wit, and the memorable performances he drew from his actors.

Countee Cullen (1903–1946)

Poet, Novelist, Playwright

One of the leading figures of the Harlem Renaissance, Countee Cullen made fluent use of traditional English verse forms to articulate the experiences of Black Americans, a radical literary device at the time.

Born Countee LeRoy Porter, likely in Louisville, Kentucky, Cullen grew up in Harlem, New York, and was raised by Reverend Frederick A. Cullen, the pastor of Salem Methodist Episcopal Church, Harlem's largest congregation. He began publishing prize-winning poetry in high school. He graduated from New York University in 1925, the same year he published his debut volume of poetry, *Color*, and won the Witter Bynner Poetry Prize. He earned a master's degree from Harvard in 1926 and subsequently joined the editorial staff of *Opportunity* magazine. Two additional poetry volumes, *Copper Sun* and *The Ballad of the Brown Girl* (both 1927), established him as a leading light of the Harlem Renaissance. He would edit *Caroling Dusk* (1927), an anthology of poems by writers associated with the movement. He went on to publish several more poetry collections, including *The Black Christ and Other Poems* (1929) and *On These I Stand* (1947).

In 1928, Cullen married Nina Yolande Du Bois, the daughter of W. E. B. Du Bois, the famed intellectual. The marriage ended in divorce in 1930. During the 1930s, he took a position teaching French at a Harlem junior high school while attempting various literary forms, including a satirical novel, *One Way to Heaven*, and a translation of Euripides's *Medea.* He also produced theatrical works and books for children.

Even though Cullen was closeted and married a second time, it is generally believed that he was gay rather than bisexual, having had sexual relationships with men throughout his adult life and dedicating poems to the lovers and friends with whom he was infatuated. He was helped to come to terms with his sexuality by writer and philosopher Alain Locke, who introduced him to gay-affirming work by Englishman Edward Carpenter, an early gay rights activist. He wrote to Locke that Carpenter's work "opened up for me soul windows which had been closed; it threw a noble and evident light on what I had begun to believe, because of what the world believes, ignoble and unnatural. I loved myself in it." Several of his poems have coded gay imagery and meanings, including "Tableau," "Fruit of the Flower," "For a Poet," "To a Brown Boy," "The Black Christ," and "Song of Myself."

Torn between being a poet and being considered a Black poet, Cullen, perhaps more than any other writer of the Harlem Renaissance, embodied the intentions of Black intellectual leaders such as W. E. B. Du Bois and James Weldon Johnson. "In a time," Du Bois wrote in 1928, "when it is vogue to make much of the Negro's aptitude for clownishness or to depict him objectively as a serio-comic figure, it is a fine and praiseworthy act for Mr. Cullen to show through the interpretation of his own subjectivity the inner workings of the Negro soul and mind."

Merce Cunningham (1919–2009)

Dancer, Choreographer

Mercier Philip "Merce" Cunningham's innovative techniques and collaborations reshaped modern dance. Known for his avant-garde approach, he rejected traditional narrative and musical structures, instead focusing on movement itself as an expressive force. Over a career spanning more than six decades, he choreographed nearly 200 works and was pivotal in advancing the concept of dance as an independent art form. The Merce Cunningham Dance Company, founded in 1953, became a major influence in the world of contemporary dance, consistently pushing the boundaries of performance and composition.

Cunningham was born in Centralia, Washington. He took his first dance classes in Centralia and, in 1936, went to study at George Washington University in Washington, D.C. He quit after a few months, but it was there that he first saw choreography that inspired him. In 1937, he began studying at the Cornish School in Seattle, initially concentrating on theater but also starting his first formal study of modern dance, and eventually began to choreograph.

In 1938, Cunningham met the young composer John Cage, hired by the dance department as a chief accompanist and music director, and they formed a relationship that lasted until Cage's death in 1992. In 1939, Cunningham joined the Martha Graham Dance Company, performing lead roles in such productions as *El Penitente* in 1939 and *Appalachian Spring* in 1944. Also in 1944, he debuted some of his solo works that he choreographed, including *Root of an Unfocus,* featuring music by Cage. Cage's experimental music complemented Cunningham's innovative choreography, leading to performances that often used randomness as a technique to create the independent phrasing of music and dance. Cunningham also collaborated with visual artists such as Robert Rauschenberg and Andy Warhol, incorporating their designs into his productions. These interdisciplinary collaborations were revolutionary, creating a rich multimedia experience that profoundly influenced the performing arts.

In 1953, encouraged by Cage, Cunningham established the Merce Cunningham Dance Company, which toured the world to great acclaim. In 1974, he abandoned the company's repertory, which had developed over more than 20 years, for what he called "Events," excerpts from old and new dances, sometimes two or more simultaneously. In the 1990s, he began to use special animated computer programs to explore new choreography possibilities. "The computer allows you to make phrases and movements," he explained, "and then you can look at them and repeat them, over and over, in a way that you can't ask dancers to do because they get tired."

Cunningham stopped performing soon after Cage died in 1992 but continued to lead his dance company until shortly before his own death at the age of 90. During his nearly 70-year career, he won two Guggenheim fellowships—in 1954 and 1959—and in 1985, he received the Kennedy Center Honors award and the MacArthur Fellowship. His innovative spirit and his ability to integrate multiple artistic disciplines have left a lasting impact on modern dance and the performing arts. His openness about his sexuality and his pioneering work with Cage continue to inspire new generations of dancers and choreographers, cementing his legacy as a true visionary in the world of dance.

Darcelle XV

See Walter W. Cole

Ellen DeGeneres (1958–)

Actor, Comedian

Ellen DeGeneres is a renowned American comedian, television host, actress, writer, and producer who, in 1997, portrayed the first openly gay lead character on a prime-time television program when the character she played on the sitcom *Ellen* came out, mirroring her own coming out on *The Oprah Winfrey Show*. She would be featured on the cover of *Time* magazine with the headline "Yep, I'm Gay," an unprecedented platform for a gay person at the time. She faced considerable professional and personal blowback as a result but rebounded as the host of the talk show *The Ellen DeGeneres Show,* which aired from 2003 to 2022, one of the most popular daytime programs of all time, which won multiple Emmy awards and attracted a devoted audience.

Born and raised in Metairie, Louisiana, DeGeneres was raised a Christian Scientist. Her parents divorced when she was a young teenager. When her mother subsequently remarried, she moved with her mother to New Orleans. She attended the University of New Orleans but left school to work various jobs, including as a waitress, a housepainter, and a bartender.

DeGeneres began performing stand-up comedy in small clubs and coffeehouses in the early 1980s and began touring nationally, named in 1984 Showtime's funniest person in America. Her first regular TV appearance was a short-lived sitcom called *Open House.* She went on to a sitcom called *Laurie Hill* that was cancelled after only four episodes; however, it eventually led to her landing the lead role in *Ellen,* which aired from 1994 to 1998, often called the "female Seinfeld." After she came out in 1997 on *The Oprah Winfrey Show,* her character on the sitcom came out as well in what was titled "The Puppy Episode"; disguising the plotline may have been an inside joke since ABC had agreed to the plot premise and approved the episode after reviewing it. The network heavily promoted the episode, sparking rumors about what was in store, although many viewers expected her to come out. The episode attracted some 45 million viewers, and watch parties gathered around the country to see the gay reveal. Applauded by many for breaking a barrier for a gay character (and actress) on national television, she also faced hate mail, death threats, canceled sponsors, and, eventually, the show's cancellation in 1998. The experience led her to be "mired in depression," retreating from the public eye until her triumphant return in *The Ellen DeGeneres Show,* which ran to great acclaim for almost 20 years from 2003 to 2022.

Beyond her television career, DeGeneres has performed as a voice actor, notably as Dory in the animated films *Finding Nemo* (2003) and *Finding Dory* (2016). She is also a successful author, having written several best-selling books, including *My Point… and I Do Have One* (1995), *Seriously…I'm Kidding* (2011), and *Home* (2015). Her work extends to philanthropy, where she has been a vocal advocate for animal rights, environmental issues, and LGBTQ+ rights. Her generosity and commitment to social causes have solidified her reputation as a beloved public figure who uses her platform for positive change.

DeGeneres's personal life has also been a topic of great public interest, particularly her relationship with actress Portia de Rossi. The couple married in 2008 after the legalization of same-sex marriage in California, becoming one of the most high-profile LGBTQ+ couples in Hollywood. DeGeneres's openness about her sexuality has inspired many and has been instrumental in advancing LGBTQ+ visibility and acceptance.

Beauford Delaney (1901–1979)

Artist

Beauford Delaney was an influential painter whose vibrant works and unique approach to color and form left a lasting impact on modern art. Known for his expressive use of color and innovative techniques, his art transcended traditional boundaries, making him a significant figure in both the Harlem Renaissance and the broader modernist movement. His paintings, deeply infused with his experiences and emotions, continue to resonate and inspire.

Delaney was born in Knoxville, Tennessee. He was one of 10 children in a family deeply rooted in religion and music, which influenced his creative path. He displayed a talent for art at an early age, and his family supported his aspirations. He moved to Boston in 1923 to study at the Massachusetts Normal School (now the Massachusetts College of Art and Design) and the Copley Society. In 1929, he moved to New York City, where he immersed himself in the vibrant artistic community of Harlem. There, he studied at the Art Students League of New York and befriended many prominent figures of the Harlem Renaissance, including James Baldwin, who became a lifelong friend.

Delaney's career was marked by a series of notable achievements and influential works. His early paintings, such as *Can Fire in the Park* (1946), depicting a group of men gathered around a fire in a New York City park, are celebrated for their bold use of color and light to capture urban scenes and the social realism and humanistic portrayal of African American life. Another important work, *Untitled (Jazz Club)* (c. 1950), reflects the dynamic energy of a jazz club with swirling colors and abstract forms, suggesting movement and sound.

In the 1950s, Delaney moved to Paris, where his work evolved to embrace abstraction. This period saw the creation of some of his most acclaimed works, characterized by their luminous color palettes and spiritual intensity. Paintings like *Abstraction* (1958), *Untitled* (1967), and *Jazz Quartet* (1967) exemplify his mastery of abstract expressionism and innovative use of color to convey emotion and movement. His *Portrait of James Baldwin* (1965) captures the writer's intense gaze and thoughtful expression.

Living as a Black, openly gay man in both America and France, Delaney faced many challenges, but he found solace and expression through his art. His friendship with Baldwin, who was also gay, provided mutual support and inspiration. His personal struggles with mental health and identity are often reflected in his work, imbuing his paintings with a profound depth and complexity. Despite the adversities he faced, his resilience and authenticity left an enduring legacy in the art world.

Delaney's work is significant for its cultural and social impact, innovative use of color, contributions to abstract expressionism, and the emotional depth of his portraits. His paintings often depicted the African American experience, capturing the vibrancy and struggles of his community and making his work culturally relevant and socially impactful. His abstract compositions are celebrated for their spiritual and emotional resonance, influencing many artists who followed.

Paris Dupree (1950–2011)

Drag Performer, Dancer

Paris Dupree, who, according to *Out* magazine, used both he and she pronouns, was a pivotal figure in the New York City Ballroom scene, which was best known for contributing to the popularity of the dance style called "voguing." He rose to prominence during the 1980s as a legendary drag performer and the founder of the House of Dupree, where he was instrumental in shaping the Ballroom culture and community, which provided a safe space for LGBTQ+ people of color. His contributions were celebrated in the documentary *Paris Is Burning*, which brought broader attention to the struggles and talents of the Ballroom community, highlighting his importance in both LGBTQ+ history and the evolution of contemporary dance.

Dupree was raised in Philadelphia, Pennsylvania, and, during the 1980s, became a prominent figure in creating and popularizing New York City's "ball" culture, also known as the Ballroom scene, where drag queens, trans women, and gay men of color could compete in various categories, showcasing their fashion, dancing, and performance skills. These balls provided a safe and supportive space for marginalized communities to express themselves and find a sense of belonging. One of his significant contributions to the Ballroom scene was his influence on the dance style known as "voguing." Similar to hip-hop and breakdancing, voguing emerged from Black, poor, and working-class communities as a form of expression, with an emphasis on male bonding and street crews. He created the style at the dance club Footsteps in New York. He was trying to "outdance" another queen when he grabbed the *Vogue* magazine that was in his purse and began to imitate the poses that the models held in the photographs, creating a dance form that is still popular today. Voguing is a contorted, jerky, slicing style of dance, combining model-like poses and pantomimic choreography.

Dupree would be featured in Jennie Livingston's 1990 documentary *Paris Is Burning*, inspiring its title, which was best remembered for the line: "That's right! I said it! Butch queen! Boy in the day, girl at night." Filmed during the 1980s, the film chronicles the ball culture of New York City and the African American, Latino, gay, and transgender communities involved in it. The title takes its name from the Paris Is Burning Ball, held annually by Dupree. It features interviews with prominent members of the scene, including Dupree, Pepper LaBeija, Dorian Corey, Angie Xtravaganza, Willi Ninja, and others.

Dupree was openly transgender, and his sexuality and gender identity were central to his role as a trailblazer in the LGBTQ+ community. His courage to live authentically and dedication to creating spaces for others to do the same made him an iconic figure in both the drag and transgender communities.

Fred Ebb

See John Kander and Fred Ebb

Melissa Etheridge (1961–)

Singer–Songwriter

Melissa Lou Etheridge is a celebrated rock singer–songwriter known for her raspy voice, confessional lyrics, and advocacy for LGBTQ+ rights. With a career spanning over three decades, she has captivated audiences with her powerful music and courageous public stance on issues close to her heart. Her work has not only earned her critical acclaim and commercial success but also made her a significant figure in the fight for equality and representation.

Etheridge was born in Leavenworth, Kansas. From a young age, she displayed a keen interest in music, learning to play the guitar at the age of 8 and writing her first songs in her teens. She attended Berklee College of Music in Boston but left after three semesters to pursue a career in music in Los Angeles. There, she played in various clubs and honed her craft, eventually catching the attention of Island Records, which signed her in 1986.

Etheridge's self-titled debut album, *Melissa Etheridge* (1988), marked the beginning of a successful career. The album included the hit single "Bring Me Some Water," earning her a Grammy nomination. Her fourth album, *Yes I Am* (1993), featuring the hits "Come to My Window" and "I'm the Only One," brought her widespread acclaim and commercial success. This album, released after she publicly came out as a lesbian, solidified her as a voice for the LGBTQ+ community. She has won two Grammy awards and an Academy Award for Best Original Song for "I Need to Wake Up" from the documentary *An Inconvenient Truth* (2006). Her fearless exploration of personal themes and activism through her music has left a lasting impact on the industry.

Etheridge is openly lesbian and has been a prominent advocate for LGBTQ+ rights. She publicly came out at the Triangle Ball, a gay and lesbian celebration of President Bill Clinton's first inauguration in January 1993. She has been vocal about her personal experiences, including her relationships, motherhood, and her battle with breast cancer, using her platform to inspire and support others. She has four children and has been an advocate for same-sex parenting and marriage equality. Her openness about her sexuality and personal life has made her a role model for many and helped to foster greater acceptance and understanding.

Harvey Fierstein (1954–)

Playwright, Screenwriter, Actor

Harvey Forbes Fierstein claims the distinction of being one of the first openly gay celebrities in the United States. As an actor, playwright, and screenwriter, he helped to make gay and lesbian life a subject for drama, as he said, "with no apologies and climactic suicides."

Fierstein was born in Bensonhurst, Brooklyn, into a strict Jewish family. His mother was a school librarian, and his father was a handkerchief manufacturer. "When I was a kid," he recalled, "I was attracted to men. I didn't feel like a boy was supposed to feel. Then I found out about gay. So that was enough for me for then." After graduating from the High School of Art and Design, he received a BFA from the Pratt Institute in 1973. At the age of 16, he was cast in Andy Warhol's only play, *Pork* (1971), and went on to perform in more than 60 productions, often playing roles in drag. He also performed his own drag routine in Greenwich Village.

In the late 1970s, Fierstein began work on the three plays that would become *Torch Song Trilogy*. The plays center on a Jewish, homosexual drag queen and torch singer and his relationships in New York City in the late 1970s and early 1980s. *Torch Song Trilogy* debuted on Broadway in 1982 in a production starring the author himself. The work is groundbreaking for depicting the world of gay families and their struggle for self-acceptance and love. He won two Tony awards for acting and writing, and he went on to appear in the 1988 screen version. He also won a Tony for writing the book for the 1983 musical *La Cage aux Folles*, which continued to bring gay issues into the mainstream.

Fierstein won his fourth Tony Award for his performance in the stage musical version of John Waters's film *Hairspray*. He wrote the librettos for the musicals *A Catered Affair* (2007), in which he also starred; *Newsies, the Musical* (2011); and *Kinky Boots* (2012). He wrote and produced *Casa Valentina* (2014), which was about a group of heterosexual, married men in the early 1960s who met on the weekends at a Catskills resort in order to freely indulge their shared desire to dress and act like women. He then wrote and starred in *Bella Bella* (2019), a monologue play about U.S. politician Bella Abzug.

Fierstein has used his celebrity to speak out on behalf of LGBTQ+ issues. In a 1983 interview with Barbara Walters, he declared that "I assume that everyone is gay unless I'm told otherwise," and when Walters said to him, "A few years ago, I wouldn't have been able to do an interview like this," he replied in his trademark gravelly, Brooklynese accent, "You could have done it and you should have done it." In 2022, he published his memoir, *I Was Better Last Night*, which suggested that he is still questioning his sexual identity. "I'm still confused as to whether I'm a man or a woman," he revealed in an interview in *People* magazine. "But let's put it this way. I don't think I've missed anything by not making up my mind."

Tom Ford (1961-)

Fashion Designer, Filmmaker

Thomas Carlyle "Tom" Ford is a renowned American fashion designer, filmmaker, and entrepreneur who has left an indelible mark on the fashion industry and Hollywood. Known for his transformative work at Gucci and Yves Saint Laurent and for establishing his own luxury brand, he is celebrated for his sleek, modern aesthetic that blends glamour with sophistication. His foray into filmmaking has further solidified his status as a multifaceted creative force.

Ford was born in Austin, Texas. Raised in a middle-class family, his early interest in fashion was nurtured by his mother and grandmother. He initially studied architecture at the Parsons School of Design in New York but later switched to fashion after discovering his true passion. After graduating, he began his career in fashion with a brief stint at Chloé, working under Cathy Hardwick, before moving on to Perry Ellis, where he gained valuable industry experience.

Ford's career took a pivotal turn in 1990, when he joined Gucci as the brand's women's ready-to-wear designer. Within four years, he was promoted to creative director, revolutionizing the struggling brand and bringing it back to the forefront of fashion. His designs during the 1990s were marked by a bold, sexy aesthetic that became synonymous with the Gucci brand. In 2000, he took on the role of creative director at Yves Saint Laurent, further expanding his influence in the fashion world. In 2005, he launched his eponymous luxury brand Tom Ford, which includes menswear, eyewear, accessories, and beauty products. His brand quickly became a symbol of luxury and elegance, catering to a clientele that appreciates high-end, sophisticated fashion.

Ford's talents extend beyond fashion; in 2009, he made his directorial debut with the film *A Single Man*, which was critically acclaimed and earned Colin Firth an Academy Award nomination for Best Actor. He continued his success in cinema with *Nocturnal Animals* in 2016.

Ford is openly gay and has been a prominent figure in the LGBTQ+ community. He was in a long-term relationship with journalist Richard Buckley, whom he married in 2014 after 27 years together, until Buckley died in 2021. The couple had a son, Alexander John "Jack" Buckley Ford, in 2012. Ford's experiences as a gay man have influenced his work, particularly in his films, in which themes of identity, desire, and loss are explored with sensitivity and depth.

Maria Irene Fornés (1930-2018)

Playwright, Director

One of the most influential Latinx voices of the 20th century, Maria Irene Fornés was a pioneering Cuban American playwright and director who wrote over 40 plays, including acclaimed works like

Fefu and Her Friends and *Mud*, known for their experimental style and deep exploration of human relationships. She pioneered immersive theater long before the term was widely used and was an important influence on later playwrights, including Tony Kushner, Nilo Cruz, and Paula Vogel. While often referred to as "the most important writer you have never heard of," she won numerous awards, including nine Obie Awards.

Born in Havana, Cuba, Fornés immigrated to the United States in 1945, settling in New York City. She became a U.S. citizen in 1951. Initially working in a shoe factory, she took classes to learn English and became a translator. Her early years in America were characterized by a deep engagement with the arts, and she initially pursued a career as a painter. In 1954, she met writer and artist's model Harriet Sohmers. They became lovers and moved to Paris, where Fornés planned to study painting. She was overwhelmed by the world premiere production of Samuel Beckett's *Waiting for Godot*, saying "it turned my life upside down." After her relationship with Sohmers ended, she returned to New York in 1957. She turned letters written by her great-grandfather that she had brought with her from Cuba into her first play, *La Viuda* (*The Widow*, 1961). In 1959, while working on the play, she had a romantic relationship with writer Susan Sontag and attributes her career as a writer to trying to help Sontag make progress on a novel she was writing. "I might never have thought of writing," she said, "if I hadn't pretended I was going to show Susan how easy it was."

Fornés's breakthrough came with the play *Tango Palace* in 1963, which established her as a powerful, new voice in American theater. Over the next few decades, she wrote over 40 plays, including *Fefu and Her Friends* (1977), regarded as a signature work of feminist theater; *Mud* (1983), about a woman attempting to escape her life on a remote farm; *The Conduct of Life* (1985), about a Latin American solder whose job is torturing prisoners; *Abbington Square* (1987), about a young woman's emerging sexual and spiritual self-awareness; and *Enter the Night* (1993), set during the AIDS crisis. Her work was known for its experimental style, poignant exploration of human relationships, and bold commentary on social and political issues. Her plays often defied conventional narrative structures, focusing instead on the inner lives and struggles of her characters, which helped to redefine the possibilities of modern drama.

Fornés's contributions to theater were not limited to her writing. She was also a respected director and educator, mentoring many young playwrights who would go on to become significant figures in contemporary theater. Her teaching methods and workshops, particularly at the INTAR Hispanic Playwrights in Residence Laboratory, were instrumental in nurturing a generation of Latino playwrights and expanding the reach of Latino theater in the United States.

As an open lesbian, Fornés drew upon her own sexual identity in her works. Her plays often delved into themes of gender, sexuality, and identity, challenging traditional norms and offering nuanced portrayals of LGBTQ+ experiences. Her openness about her sexuality and her focus on marginalized voices have made her an enduring icon in both the LGBTQ+ and theater communities.

Diagnosed with Alzheimer's in 2005, she lived the rest of her life in care facilities and passed away in a Manhattan nursing home. Kushner summed up her achievement by saying, "She's not spoken of as an important American playwright, and she should be. She had terrifyingly high standards and was terribly blunt about what others did with her work. Her productions were unforgettable. She was really a magical maker of theater."

Roxane Gay (1974–)

Writer, Educator, Social Commentator

A contributing opinion writer at *The New York Times,* Roxane Gay is the author of the best-selling essay collection *Bad Feminist* (2014), the novel *An Untamed State* (2014), the short story collection *Difficult Women* (2017), and the memoir *Hunger* (2017). From 2016 to 2017, she collaborated with fellow writers Ta-Nehisi Coates and Yona Harvey on *Black Panther: World of Wakanda,* a comic book series from Marvel Comics. Gay and Harvey became the first Black women to write for Marvel, and the series was praised for its depiction of LGBTQ+ characters.

Gay was born in Omaha, Nebraska. Her parents were Haitian immigrants, and she spent her summers visiting family in Haiti. At the age of 12, she was raped by a gang of boys, and after attending Phillips Exeter Academy, the trauma of her sexual abuse led to her dropping out of Yale University when she was 19 years old to live with a man she had met online who was 25 years her senior, without notifying her parents about her whereabouts. They eventually located her, and she returned to Nebraska. She received a Ph.D. in rhetoric and technical communication from Michigan Technological University in 2010 and began teaching English at Eastern Illinois University. She has since taught at Purdue and Yale University.

Recalling that she began writing short stories when she was 4 years old, Gay published her first story collection, *Ayiti,* in 2011. In 2014, she published her debut novel, *An Untamed State,* and her breakthrough essay collection, *Bad Feminist.* Its title refers to the collection's challenges to the truisms of feminism in search of a wider conception. As she explained, "In each of these essays, I'm very much trying to show how feminism influences my life for better or worse. It just shows what it's like to move through the world as a woman. It's not even about feminism per se, it's about humanity and empathy."

In *Difficult Women* (2017), she highlights women who have endured traumatic experiences or whose lives make them different from societal norms. In the memoir *Hunger,* she discusses her experience with weight, body image, and sexual violence. As a result of her trauma, she confessed to coming out as a lesbian even though she was still attracted to men and receiving support from the lesbian community. She now identifies as bisexual and married artist and writer Debbie Millman in 2020.

Asked to describe her voice in her writing, Gay responded: "Messy and confident and clear—I am a Libra so I am going to straddle that fence all the time. My voice is growing. I am learning how to live in my voice more fully."

Allen Ginsberg (1926–1997)

Poet

The poet laureate of the Beat Generation whose poem "Howl" became a manifesto for the sexual revolution, Allen Ginsberg was an outspoken social and political activist on virtually every controversial issue that emerged in the second half of the 20th century from free speech to anti-war protests to gay rights. His radical literary works and advocacy for social change defined the American counterculture, coining the phrase "Flower Power."

Born and raised in New Jersey, Ginsberg was the son of a schoolteacher father and a Russian émigrée mother who was a fervent Marxist. He began writing poetry in high school under the influence of Walt Whitman. He attended Columbia University on a scholarship, and there, he became close friends with Jack Kerouac, Henry Gold, William Burroughs, and others who would become synonymous with the Beat Generation.

After leaving Columbia in 1948, he traveled widely and worked at a number of jobs, finally settling in San Francisco, where in 1954, he met Peter Orlovsky (1933–2010), who would become his lifelong partner. *Howl and Other Poems* was published in 1956 by San Francisco's City Lights bookstore. "Howl," with its famous opening line, "I saw the best minds of my generation destroyed by madness…," was daring in its exploration of sexuality (particularly homosexuality), anguish, and social issues in a nontraditional poetic form, drawing on multiple influences. As writer and critic Paul Zweig observed, "Howl" "almost singlehandedly dislocated the traditionalist poetry of the 1950s."

In 1957, customs officials seized copies of *Howl* that were being imported from England, claiming that the book was obscene; the City Lights bookstore manager was arrested and jailed for selling a copy to an undercover police officer, and poet Lawrence Ferlinghetti was later arrested for publishing the book. The subsequent trial attracted national attention, with prominent literary figures defending the poem against charges of obscenity. The judge ruled that the work was not obscene, and the notoriety provided Ginsberg with an activist platform that he rarely relinquished.

Ginsberg's other books include *Kaddish and Other Poems* (1961); *Planet News: 1961–1967* (1968); *The Fall of America: Poems of These States, 1965–1971* (1973), which won the National Book Award; and *Death & Fame, 1993–1997* (2000). His prose works have been collected in *Deliberate Prose: Selected Essays, 1952–1995* (2000). Selections from his correspondence with his partner, Peter Orlovsky, have been published in *The Letters of Allen Ginsberg* (2008), *Straight Hearts' Delight* (1980), and *My Dear Boy: Gay Love Letters through the Centuries* (1998).

Whitman's line "I am large, I contain multitudes" captures the essence of Ginsberg, a larger-than-life figure who became something of the conscience and consciousness of a generation. Writing explicitly as a gay poet at a time when homosexuality was still criminalized, he became a force for gay rights activism along with so many of the other social justice causes that he professed.

In *The Homosexual Tradition in American Poetry*, author Robert K. Martin asserts that Ginsberg "made his sexuality an integral part of his public image and his poetry" as "part of his larger attempt to undermine American society and its pretensions to respectability."

John Glines (1933–2018)

Producer, Playwright

John Glines is renowned for his contributions to LGBTQ+ representation onstage. As a playwright, producer, and advocate, he broke new ground by bringing gay themes and characters to the forefront, challenging societal norms and promoting a greater visibility and acceptance for the LGBTQ+ community.

Glines was born in Santa Maria, California, and grew up in San Francisco. He graduated from Yale with a bachelor's degree in drama in 1955. He appeared in dozens of productions in college and wrote and directed some musical revues. After graduating, he moved to New York City, where he initially worked in advertising and television. His early career included stints as a writer and producer for children's television programs, becoming in 1965 a writer for *Captain Kangaroo* and from 1978 to 1981 a writer for *Sesame Street.*

In 1972, Glines wrote a musical comedy, *God Bless Coney*, that flopped. In 1977, he cofounded The Glines, an organization dedicated to producing and promoting gay-themed plays. "One of the main goals of The Glines," he said, "was to prove that a gay play could be commercially viable.... I think playwrights should be able to use their truths. A gay playwright can write about gay people and be just as universal as a straight person." Through this platform, he produced several groundbreaking works, including the Tony Award–winning play *Torch Song Trilogy* by Harvey Fierstein. This production was a landmark in Broadway history not only for its success but also for its open portrayal of gay life and relationships. In 1983, he made history by becoming the first person to acknowledge his same-sex partner, Lawrence Lane, in a Tony Award acceptance speech, a moment that highlighted his personal and professional commitment to LGBTQ+ advocacy.

In 1985, Glines produced *As Is* by William M. Hoffman, one of the first plays to address the AIDS crisis directly. This poignant narrative follows a gay couple dealing with an AIDS diagnosis, highlighting the epidemic's devastating impact on the LGBTQ+ community. The play emphasized the importance of love, support, and understanding during one of the most challenging periods in LGBTQ+ history. In 1987, he produced *Safe Sex* by Harvey Fierstein, a trilogy of one-act plays addressing the AIDS crisis and its impact on relationships. These plays discussed safe sex practices, fear, and the necessity of communication within the LGBTQ+ community during the epidemic. He continued his trailblazing work with the production of *The Night Larry Kramer Kissed Me* by David Drake in 1992. This one-man show is a powerful exploration of a gay man's life during the AIDS crisis, blending personal and political narratives to address the challenges faced by the LGBTQ+ community.

Glines's plays include *On Tina Tuna Walk* (1980), which follows the lives of a group of eccentric characters, each dealing with their own unique struggles and triumphs. This work is significant for its engaging narrative and subtle inclusion of LGBTQ+ themes, making it accessible to a wide audience while still addressing important social issues. *The Other Side of the Closet* (1984) delves into the complexities of coming out and living authentically. This play provides an honest portrayal of the challenges faced by LGBTQ+ individuals in a society that often marginalizes them.

Glines and Lane separated in 1987, and between 1988 and 1997, Glines wrote, produced, and sometimes directed nine plays for The Glines. He then retired to Thailand, where he lived with his husband, Chaowarat Chiewvej, a former Buddhist monk, whom he married in 2014. Through his plays and productions, he played a crucial role in bringing LGBTQ+ themes to mainstream theater, offering visibility and fostering dialogue on critical issues affecting the community. His work remains a testament to the power of theater as a medium for social change and representation.

Nan Goldin (1953–)

Photographer

Nan Goldin is a highly influential American photographer known for her deeply personal and raw documentation of the LGBTQ+ community, the AIDS crisis, and the complexities of human relationships. Her work, characterized by its intimate and often provocative subject matter, has challenged conventional notions of beauty and normalcy in art. Her photographs are celebrated for their candidness and emotional depth, making her a pivotal figure in contemporary photography and a powerful voice in social activism.

Goldin was born in Washington, D.C., but grew up in the Boston suburbs. In 1965, the family had to deal with the suicide of her older sister. "I was very close to my sister and aware of some of the forces that led her to choose suicide," she recalled. "I saw the role that her sexuality and its repression played in her destruction." She left home in her early teens and lived in various foster homes. She attended the Satya Community School, where she was introduced to photography. She later studied at the School of the Museum of Fine Arts in Boston. During her early years, she was deeply immersed in the vibrant counterculture of the 1970s, which significantly shaped her artistic sensibilities. Her early work focused on the LGBTQ+ community and the underground scene in Boston and New York City, capturing the lives of her friends and acquaintances with unflinching honesty.

Goldin's first solo show was in Boston in 1973, which was based on her photographs of the city's gay and transgender communities. Her most renowned work, *The Ballad of Sexual Dependency* (1986), is a slideshow and book that documents her life and the lives of her friends from the late 1970s through the mid-1980s. This seminal work captures raw and intimate moments of love, loss, and struggle, particularly within the LGBTQ+ community, during the AIDS crisis. Her other significant projects include *The Other Side* (1993) and *I'll Be Your Mirror* (1996), which continue her exploration of themes such as identity, gender, and addiction. Her work has been exhibited globally and is part of numerous prestigious collections, including the Museum of Modern Art in New York and the Tate Modern in London. She has received numerous awards, including the Hasselblad Award in 2007.

Goldin's personal life has been as complex and multifaceted as her art. She has been open about her bisexuality and has used her photography to explore and express her own identity and relationships. Her work often reflects her intimate connections with her subjects, blurring the lines between photographer and participant. She has been a vocal advocate for LGBTQ+ rights and has used her platform to raise awareness about issues such as the AIDS epidemic and the opioid crisis. In 2017, she revealed that she was recovering from opioid addiction after being prescribed OxyContin after wrist surgery. She founded the organization P.A.I.N. (Prescription Addiction Intervention Now) in order to call out Purdue Pharma and the Sackler family for the opioid crisis. In 2022, the documentary *All the Beauty and the Bloodshed* tells the story of her life through her achievements as a photographer and activist.

Despite facing numerous personal challenges, Goldin has remained a resilient and influential figure in the art world. Her fearless exploration of intimate and often controversial subjects has not only redefined the boundaries of art but has also provided a poignant social commentary on issues such as LGBTQ+ rights, the AIDS crisis, and addiction. Through her lens, she has offered a raw and unfiltered glimpse into the human condition, making her work resonate deeply with audiences around the world.

Edward Gorey (1925–2000)

Illustrator, Author, Designer

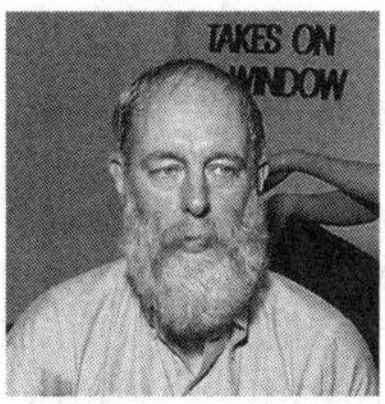

Widely celebrated for the darkly humorous, deadpan sensibility of his pen-and-ink illustrations accompanying vaguely unsettling narratives and morality tales that parodied elegant Victorian and Edwardian settings, among Edward St. John Gorey's enduringly popular picture books are *The Doubtful Guest* (1957), *The Gashlycrumb Tinies* (1963), and *The Wuggly Ump* (1963). His costume designs for the 1977 Broadway production of *Dracula* earned him a Tony Award in 1978, and during the 1980s, after decades of his books earning him a cult following, he gained fame and a national audience for his animated opening sequence of the long-running PBS series *Mystery!*

Gorey was born in Chicago to parents who divorced in 1936, when he was 11 years old. His grandmother, Helen St. John Garvey, was a greeting card illustrator, and he claimed that he inherited his artistic talent from her. In 1952, his father married cabaret singer Corinna Mura (1910–1965), who is best known for her small role in *Casablanca* (1943) as the woman guitarist playing and singing "La Marseillaise" with the band and the patrons of Rick's Café Américain. His preferred reading material as a child included Bram Stoker's *Dracula* and *Alice in Wonderland*. He attended public school in Wilmette, Illinois, where one of his classmates was John Carter, who would go on to become the actor Charlton Heston, and where some of Gorey's illustrations were featured in the school yearbook. He went on to graduate from the Francis W. Parker School in Chicago and spend a semester at the School of the Art Institute of Chicago before serving in the U.S. Army from 1944 to 1946. In 1946, after his army discharge, he entered Harvard University, where he roomed with poet Frank O'Hara and graduated in 1950.

During the early 1950s, Gorey illustrated *Case Record from a Sonnetorium* (1951) and *More Clinical Sonnets* (1953) by poet–psychiatrist Merrill Moore and, with a group of Harvard and Radcliffe graduates that included novelist Alison Lurie, poet John Ashbery, and Frank O'Hara, founded the Poets Theatre in Cambridge, Massachusetts, whose supporters were poet John Ciardi and playwright Thornton Wilder. In 1953, he moved to Manhattan, where he worked at Anchor Books, the paperback division of Doubleday, as a book cover designer, creating covers for works by Bram Stoker, Virginia Woolf, H. G. Wells, T. S. Eliot, and many other well-known authors in the literary canon. It is estimated that he illustrated over 500 covers for other authors. His first independent work, *The Unstrung Harp; or, Mr. Earbrass Writes a Novel*, was published in 1953 by Little, Brown, and Company. He would go on to produce 116 books, including volumes of his smaller titles such as *The Vinegar Works: Three Volumes of Moral Instruction* (1963), which included *The Gashlycrumb Tinies, The Insect God*, and *The West Wing* as well as four omnibus editions of his works.

Gorey led a fairly reclusive life, much of it being spent in his house in Yarmouth Port on Cape Cod, which, after his death, became a museum called the Edward Gorey House. He was a dedicated theatergoer and ballet enthusiast, never married, and was very discreet concerning his sexual identity, though his biographers have considered him asexual or celibate. In a 1980 interview with *Boston* magazine reporter Lisa Solod, he said, "Well, I'm neither one thing nor the other particularly. I suppose I'm gay. But I don't really identify with it much. I am fortunate in that I am apparently reasonably undersexed or something.... I've never said I was gay, and I've never said I wasn't.... What I'm trying to say is that I am a person before I am anything else."

Tim Gunn (1953–)

Fashion Mentor, TV Personality

Timothy MacKenzie "Tim" Gunn's significance in the fashion industry is underscored by his multifaceted contributions as a mentor, educator, and advocate for inclusivity and diversity. Through his role as a mentor on the iconic reality television series *Project Runway* and his work as an author and educator, he has solidified his reputation as a leading authority in the world of style and design. His sage advice and constructive criticism have endeared him to audiences worldwide, while his commitment to fostering inclusivity and body positivity has made him a beloved figure and role model for aspiring designers and fashion enthusiasts.

Gunn was born in Washington, D.C. His father worked for the FBI as an agent and eventually as a speechwriter for J. Edgar Hoover. Raised in a homophobic household in which homosexuals were viewed as predators and afflicted with a debilitating stutter, he endured bullying as a child. He struggled to understand his sexuality; he attempted suicide at the age of 17 and spent more than two years in a psychiatric hospital. He recalled, "A large part of what I was struggling with as a teen was my sexuality. I didn't know who I was, but I certainly knew what I *wasn't*. And I knew I wasn't a heterosexual male. The whole idea of being gay absolutely terrified me." He denied his sexual orientation until his early 20s, eventually coming out to his sister when he was 29. He earned a BFA in sculpture from the Corcoran College of Art and Design in Washington, D.C., where he served as director of admissions.

Gunn joined the faculty at New York's Parsons School of Design in 1982, serving as associate dean from 1989 to 2000 and as Fashion Design Department chair from 2000 to 2007. He left Parsons to become the chief creative officer of Liz Claiborne, Inc. He appeared on *Project Runway* during its first season as mentor to the competing young fashion designers (a role he had performed for years at Parsons), making popular his catchphrase "Make It Work." He and cohost Heidi Klum left the show after 16 seasons in 2018. They would work together on the series *Making the Cut* on Amazon. His spinoff series include *Tim Gunn's Guide to Style, Under the Gunn*, and *Project Runway: Junior*.

He participated in the It Gets Better project, founded by gay activist Dan Savage in 2010 in response to the suicides of teenagers who were bullied because they were gay. A book of more than 100 essays appeared in 2011, and a TV special aired in 2012. In it, he discussed publicly for the first time his own suicide attempt and the conflict he faced over his sexual orientation.

In 2012, Gunn made headlines by revealing that he had been celibate for 29 years. "Do I feel less of a person for it? No. Not even remotely." He attributed his sexual abstinence to a psychologically damaging past relationship as well as the AIDS epidemic, which caused him to reevaluate sex. "I think a lot of people simply retreated because they were concerned about their health. I certainly was. And I'm happy to be healthy and alive, quite frankly." He said he was more than willing to resume sexual intimacy with the right partner.

After years of struggling with his own sexuality, Gunn has become a role model both in the fashion and LGBTQ+ worlds, helping to open up both communities to a mainstream audience. "I meet so many people who are total strangers to me," he says. "They feel comfortable speaking to me, because they feel as if they know me, and, in a manner of speaking, they do."

Halston (1932–1990)

Fashion Designer

Regarded as one of the first superstar U.S. fashion designers, Halston became famous for the elegant and streamlined look that defined American fashion in the 1970s and has influenced countless subsequent designers. His innovative use of fabrics and clean, modern silhouettes, such as the Halstonette dress and the Ultrasuede shirtwaist dress, garnered a devoted following. His designs were not just about clothing; they embodied a lifestyle of effortless glamour. He became a central figure in New York's vibrant Studio 54 scene, surrounded by celebrities like Liza Minnelli, Bianca Jagger, and Andy Warhol, further cementing his status as a cultural icon.

Born Roy Halston Frowick in Des Moines, Iowa, Halston as a boy loved to alter and make clothes for his mother and sister. After studying at the School of the Art Institute of Chicago, he moved to New York City in 1957, where he initially gained fame as a milliner, designing the iconic pillbox hat worn by Jacqueline Kennedy at the presidential inauguration. This catapulted him into the spotlight and set the stage for his illustrious career in fashion design.

Halston began designing women's wear in 1966. In 1968, he established his own fashion label, Halston Ltd., and quickly became known for the minimalist, elegant designs that redefined American fashion in the 1970s. His clients included Rita Hayworth, Liza Minnelli, Marlene Dietrich, and Diana Vreeland. As the Halston plaque on the Fashion Walk of Fame reads, "The '70s belonged to Halston…. By combining clean lines and classic fabrics, Halston designed clothing that was seasonless, made for travel and looked elegant night or day."

Halston's work was further inspired by his affinity for New York City nightlife, particularly at Studio 54. His halter dress design would become a staple of the disco era. Andy Warhol considered Halston's fashion shows "the art form of the '70s." Halston was the first designer to fully license himself as a brand and, through a 1982 licensing agreement with J. C. Penney, created an affordable line of clothing. He would describe this as an opportunity "to dress America." While this democratized fashion made his designs accessible to a broader audience, it also led to tensions with high-end retailers and ultimately contributed to his losing control of his fashion house in 1984.

Halston's sexuality and lifestyle were integral parts of his identity and public persona. Openly gay, he was a prominent figure in the LGBTQ+ community and used his platform to challenge societal norms. His relationships and social circle, which included some of the most famous and influential people of the time, highlighted his ability to blend fashion with popular culture. His legacy is one of innovation, elegance, and boundary pushing, making him a pivotal figure in both the fashion industry and LGBTQ+ history.

Harmony Hammond (1944–)

Artist, Activist

Harmony Hammond is a significant figure in contemporary art, recognized for her pioneering role in the feminist and LGBTQ+ art movements. As an artist, curator, and writer, she has made substantial contributions through her paintings, sculptures, and mixed media works that explore themes of gender, identity, and marginalized experiences. Her work has been instrumental in bringing attention to women's and queer experiences in the art world, advocating for greater representation and inclusion.

Born in Hometown, Illinois, Hammond attended Milliken University in Decatur, Illinois, at the age of 17 before enrolling at the University of Minnesota, where she graduated with a B.A. in painting in 1967. She moved to New York City in 1969 just months after the Stonewall Riots. When she learned she was pregnant with her daughter, she and her husband divorced. She came out as a lesbian in 1973.

In 1972, Hammond cofounded A.I.R. Gallery in New York City, the first all-female cooperative gallery in the United States. This groundbreaking initiative provided a platform for women artists who were often marginalized in the mainstream art world. Her contributions to feminist discourse were further amplified through her role as a coeditor of *Heresies: A Feminist Publication on Art and Politics* in 1973, which became a seminal publication for feminist thought and art criticism. In 1978, she also organized the first local exhibition devoted entirely to art by gay women, calling it *A Lesbian Show*.

Hammond's artistic practice took a distinctive turn in 1978 when she began incorporating traditional women's crafts, such as weaving and quilting, into her works. This approach challenged the boundaries between fine art and craft, elevating traditionally undervalued female labor and embedding it within contemporary art practices. Her move to Galisteo, New Mexico, in 1984 marked a new phase in her career, during which she continued her artistic exploration and activism; this culminated in 1993, when she published *Lesbian Art in America: A Contemporary*

History, the first comprehensive study of lesbian art in the United States. This work solidified her role as a key historian and advocate for LGBTQ+ representation in the arts.

In the early 1990s, Hammond described herself as "an artist, a feminist, a lesbian, middle-class, white. When I'm good, I'm an artist. When I'm bad I'm a feminist. And when I'm horrid, I'm a goddam dyke. Given the current political climate around art and the threat of being artistically silenced for being queer and female, I can't afford to be quiet or to let others define who I am and what kind of art I may or may not make."

Throughout the 2000s and beyond, Hammond continued to exhibit her work internationally, contributing to the dialogue around feminism and LGBTQ+ issues in the art world. Her legacy as an artist, activist, and scholar highlights the intersection of art and social justice, making her a pivotal figure in contemporary art history.

Lorraine Hansberry (1930–1965)

Playwright

The first African American woman to have a play produced on Broadway, Lorraine Hansberry is justly revered as the foremother of Black drama and whose play, *A Raisin in the Sun*, has entered the canon of classic American family dramas of the 20th century.

Hansberry was born in Chicago, Illinois, the youngest of four children of Carl Hansberry, a successful real estate agent. In 1938, her father purchased a home in a white neighborhood, an event that provoked racial tension in legally segregated Chicago and provided the genesis for *A Raisin in the Sun*. After a brick was thrown through their window, narrowly missing the young Lorraine, the Hansberrys were evicted. With the help of the NAACP, the case went to the Supreme Court, which resulted in a decision that prohibited racially restricted real estate covenants. The Hansberrys would return to their home, but, in the words of the future playwright, endured "a hellishly hostile white neighborhood."

Hansberry attended a mostly white high school, excelled in English and history, and became president of the debate society. She went on to the University of Wisconsin for two years before moving to New York City, where she wrote for *Young Progressives of America* magazine, a radical Black monthly published in Harlem. She wrote articles on women's rights, civil rights, the arts, African history, and politics. After marrying producer Robert Nemiroff, whom she met on a picket line at New York University, she began work on three plays, including *The Crystal Stairs*, begun in 1956, changing the title to *A Raisin in the Sun* in 1957. It would take a year and a half to get the play, featuring African American central characters by an unknown African American female playwright, produced. It debuted in 1959, thanks to funding from African American cultural leaders such as Harry Belafonte, with Sidney Poitier in a lead role.

Coming at a time in which racial segregation laws were being overturned and the modern civil rights movement was taking shape, *A Raisin in the Sun* was both groundbreaking and revelatory, an unprecedented, realistic depiction of an African American family that attempts to leave the ghetto for a home in the white suburbs. The play traces the trajectory of the American Dream and the brutal discrepancy between American ideals and reality. A critical and popular success, the play ran for two years, earning Hansberry the distinction of becoming the first Black dramatist to win the New York Drama Critics' Circle Award. She would also write the screenplay for the 1961 film version of the play.

Hansberry and Nemiroff divorced in 1963. In 1965, Hansberry died after a short battle with pancreatic cancer on the day that her second play, *The Sign in Sidney Brustein's Window,* closed on Broadway. Nemiroff edited two collections of her work in *To Be Young, Gifted and Black* (1969) and *Les Blancs: The Collected Last Plays of Lorraine Hansberry* (1972). After her death, her private letters and diaries were found to contain numerous references to her attraction to women. She wrote candidly about her feelings and relationships with women, providing a clear indication of her sexual orientation. These writings were often coded or private due to the societal norms of her time, which forced lesbians and gays to remain closeted. Scholars have determined that Hansberry, who was an early member of the Daughters of Bilitis, contributed to the DOB's publication *The Ladder* under a pseudonym, discussing her thoughts on lesbian relationships, gender roles, and the challenges faced by LGBTQ+ individuals.

Keith Haring (1958–1990)

Artist

Street artist, pop artist, and muralist Keith Allen Haring became a superstar of the 1980s art scene, rising to prominence with his vibrant and dynamic graffiti-inspired artwork, which transcended traditional boundaries to become symbols of activism, joy, and social change. His images of crawling children, barking dogs, and dancing figures, displayed on T-shirts as well as in public places and museums, originated in the New York City subway system, where the young artist was inspired by the beauty and immediacy of graffiti. As a subway graffiti artist, he would become one of the most successful artists of his era, with an immediately recognizable artistic style.

Haring was born in Reading, Pennsylvania, but raised in Kutztown. His father was an engineer and amateur cartoonist, and at an early age, he spent time with his father producing creative designs. He was influenced by Walt Disney cartoons, Dr. Seuss, Charles Schulz, and the Looney Tunes characters. After graduating from a public high school in 1976, he studied commercial art at Pittsburgh's Ivy School of Professional Art until 1978, when he moved to New York City to study painting at the School of Visual Arts. He wrote in his journal in 1978: "I am becoming much more aware of movement. The importance of movement is intensified when a painting becomes a performance. The performance (the act of painting) becomes as important as the resulting painting."

Haring would find a way to join art and performance and achieve his initial public attention with graffiti art in the New York subway, where he created white chalk drawings on black, unused advertising backboards in the stations. He tagged his work with a motif known as "Radiant Baby," a crawling infant emitting rays of light, which became his most recognized symbol. As gallery owner Tony Shafrazi stated, "He was one of the most astonishing unique talents of recent times. In a short time after he arrived in New York at age 20, he practically took over Manhattan with his subway drawings, which were an instant series of signs and pictograms that everybody became familiar with."

His first solo exhibition was in 1981. As his art became better known, it was shown in galleries and museums throughout the world. He began making large, outdoor murals in Rio de Janeiro, Berlin, Melbourne, Chicago, Atlanta, and elsewhere. From 1982 to 1989, he was featured in more than 100 solo and group exhibitions and produced more than 50 public artworks, many of which were created for charities, hospitals, day care centers, and orphanages.

In 1986, he opened the Pop Shop in New York City, where he marketed products that ranged from T-shirts and buttons to original prints as a way of making his art more accessible and affordable. "My shop is an extension of what I was doing in the subway stations," he remarked, "breaking down the barriers between high and low art." He channeled his popularity and art into social activism. Openly gay, he produced images promoting safe sex and AIDS awareness. In 1988, he designed the logo for National Coming Out Day, which is still in use today for this annual awareness day.

Diagnosed with HIV in 1987 and AIDS in 1988, Haring continued to work on projects promoting AIDS awareness. Before his death at the age of 31, he established the Keith Haring Foundation to provide funding to AIDS organizations. He was one of the inaugural 50 American "pioneers, trailblazers, and heroes" to be inducted on the National LGBTQ Wall of Honor within the Stonewall National Monument in 2019.

E. Lynn Harris (1955–2009)

Novelist

Everette Lynn Harris was a publishing phenomenon as the author of a string of national best-selling novels about Black, often closeted, men with sexual identity conflicts, drawing on his own familiarity with the gay community. His publishing success crossed over to a heterosexual audience and made him both the most successful African American and gay author of his era.

Harris was born in Flint, Michigan. He grew up in Little Rock, Arkansas, and was raised by his mother and stepfather, who was abusive. He had early experiences that caused him to question his sexuality, but he kept this part of himself hidden. He attended the University of Arkansas, Fayetteville, and studied journalism. He became the first Black student to serve as editor of a publication (the yearbook) at the university and its first African American male cheerleader.

After graduation, Harris became a computer salesman with IBM, AT&T, and Hewlett-Packard. In 1991, he quit his computer sales career and started his first novel, *Invisible Life.* Unable to find a publisher for it, he self-published it in 1991, selling it mostly to Black-owned bookstores, beauty salons, and book clubs. The popularity of the book led to a contract with a mainstream publisher and 10 consecutive novels on *The New York Times* bestseller lists and more than 4 million copies of his books in print. These include *Just as I Am* (1995), *And This Too Shall Pass* (1997), *If This World Were Mine* (1988), *Not a Day Goes By* (2000), *Any Way the Wind Blows* (2002), *A Love of My Own* (2003), and *Just Too Good to Be True* (2008). They feature racy and sometimes graphic tales of affluent, ambitious, and powerful Black men—athletes, businessmen, and professionals—who struggle with their attraction to both men and women, combining the glamour of jet-setting potboilers with a topic that had received little attention: men who are publicly heterosexual but secretly have sex with men.

Harris, who was openly gay but lived for many years in denial and shame over that fact, drew on his own experiences to make credible the emotional conflicts of his characters. His books resonated particularly with women readers and, surprisingly, with a large number of heterosexual readers as well, who could identify with the emotional conflicts he depicted. Describing the success of his books, he said, "The characters and situations are so real that people learn something about themselves and about other people." This is particularly true, according to him, about members of the Black community, who believe that "certain people like upstanding or popular black people can't be gay or bisexual." Critics of his work have said that "the popularity of his novels have forced the African American community to examine this once hidden side of the black culture."

After Harris's death, he was one of the inaugural 50 American "pioneers, trailblazers, and heroes" to be inducted on the National LGBTQ Wall of Honor within the Stonewall National Monument.

Todd Haynes (1961–)

Filmmaker

Todd Haynes is an acclaimed American filmmaker and screenwriter known for his innovative and genre-defying contributions to contemporary cinema. His work often explores themes of identity, sexuality, and societal norms, earning him a reputation as a pioneering voice in the film industry. He first garnered attention with his controversial short film *Superstar: The Karen Carpenter Story* (1987), which used Barbie dolls to depict the tragic life of singer Karen Carpenter. His breakout feature film, *Poison* (1991), won the Grand Jury Prize at the Sundance Film Festival and established him as a key figure in the New Queer Cinema movement.

Born in Los Angeles, California, Haynes developed an interest in film from an early age, producing a short film, *The Suicide* (1976), while still in high school. He went on to study art and semiotics at Brown University, where he directed *Assassins: A Film Concerning Rimbaud* (1985). At Brown, he met Christine Vachon, who would go on to produce all of his feature films. He moved to New York City after graduating and became involved in the independent film scene.

Haynes made *Superstar: The Karen Carpenter Story* in 1987 while working toward his MFA at Bard College. The film showed Carpenter's struggle with anorexia and bulimia, depicting Carpenter as a Barbie doll with its face and body whittled away. Sued by Carpenter's brother Richard over the unlicensed use of Carpenter's songs, Haynes lost the lawsuit, and *Superstar* was removed from public distribution; it has not been subsequently viewed publicly except in bootlegged versions.

The notoriety gained from *Superstar*, nevertheless, helped lead to Haynes's first feature film, *Poison*, in 1991, which was based on the writings of gay writer Jean Genet in a triptych of queer-themed narratives in different cinema genres (documentary, horror, and romantic drama). The film established Haynes as an emerging talent and one of the most important voices of the emerging New Queer Cinema movement. His importance in the film industry is marked by his ability to blend rich visual storytelling with complex, often subversive narratives. Films such as *Safe* (1995), *Velvet Goldmine* (1998), and *Far from Heaven* (2002) showcase his talent for addressing social issues through a stylized lens. *Far from Heaven*, in particular, was a critical success, earning four Academy Award nominations and widespread praise for its homage to 1950s melodramas while addressing race and sexuality.

He continued to push boundaries with his films *I'm Not There* (2007), an unconventional biopic about Bob Dylan that featured multiple actors portraying the singer, and *Carol* (2015), a critically acclaimed lesbian romance that received six Academy Award nominations.

His first documentary feature, *The Velvet Underground*, about the influential rock band, was released in 2021. *May December*, loosely based on the Mary Kay Letourneau teacher–student affair scandal, opened in 2023. His 2011 HBO miniseries based on the James Cain novel *Mildred Pierce* was equally acclaimed, earning nine Emmy nominations and winning two for Outstanding Lead Actress in a Limited or Anthology Series or Movie (Kate Winslet) and Outstanding Supporting Actor in a Limited or Anthology Series or Movie (Guy Pearce).

Haynes is openly gay and has been in a relationship with archival producer Bryan O'Keefe since 2002. His films frequently explore LGBTQ+ themes and characters, contributing to a greater visibility and representation in mainstream cinema. His openness about his sexuality and commitment to telling diverse and inclusive stories have made him an important figure in both the film industry and the LGBTQ+ community, challenging audiences to reconsider their perspectives on identity, love, and societal norms.

Essex Hemphill (1957–1995)

Poet, Performance Artist

An important voice of the African American gay community, Essex Hemphill focused on the experiences of a Black gay man, addressing the issues of identity, race, sexuality, the family, and HIV/AIDS. His first full-length collection, *Ceremonies: Prose and Poetry* (1992), won the National Library Association's Gay, Lesbian, and Bisexual New Author Award. He became one of the best-known Black gay authors since James Baldwin.

Hemphill was born into a working-class family in Chicago and raised in Washington, D.C. In 1975, he enrolled at the University of Maryland to study journalism but left after his freshman year (he eventually earned his degree in English at the University of the District of Columbia) in order to focus on his involvement in the D.C. art scene, performing, working on journals, and publishing his first poetry. In 1980, he came out publicly during a poetry reading at Howard University. Describing the challenges faced by a Black gay man, he wrote, "He is inhibited by his silence or his admissions. This is what the race has depended on in being able to erase homosexuality from our recorded history.... I can't become a whole man simply on what is fed to me: watered-down versions of black life in America. I need the...truth to be told."

Hemphill set out to express "the things that I have been hungering for," especially the reflection of the Black homosexual experience. His work, following the publication of *Ceremonies*, was included in the anthologies *Gay and Lesbian Poetry in Our Time* (1986) and *Life Sentences: Writers, Artists, and AIDS* (1993). He also edited the acclaimed anthology *Brother to Brother: New Writing by Black Gay Men* (1991), which won the Lambda Literary Award. Besides his published work, in 1982, he cofounded Cinque, a spoken word group that performed in the Washington, D.C., area. Its work was later featured in the documentaries *Tongues Tied* (1989) and *Black Is...Black Ain't* (1994).

Hemphill's lover, fellow writer Joseph F. Beam, died of AIDS in 1988. He would treat Beam's death in his poem "When My Brother Fell." Hemphill died of complications from AIDS at the age of 38. In 2014, Martin Duberman documented the lives of Hemphill and activist Michael Callen in *Hold Tight Gently: Michael Callen, Essex Hemphill, and the Battlefield of AIDS.* In 2019, Hemphill was one of the inaugural 50 American "pioneers, trailblazers, and heroes" to be inducted on the National LGBTQ Wall of Honor within the Stonewall National Monument.

Jerry Herman (1931–2019)

Composer, Lyricist

Gerald Sheldon "Jerry" Herman, one of the most celebrated composers and lyricists in American musical theater, is best known for his work on classic Broadway shows such as *Hello, Dolly!*; *Mame*; and *La Cage aux Folles*, Broadway's first musical featuring gay lovers. His rich melodies and powerful lyrics stopped shows, dazzled critics, and kept audiences leaving the theater singing and returning for more. He made stage history as the first composer–lyricist to have three musicals run more than 1,500 consecutive performances on Broadway.

Herman was born in New York City and grew up in Jersey City, New Jersey. His mother, a piano teacher, introduced him to music at a young age, and he began playing the piano by the age of 6. In 1946, his parents took him to see the original Broadway production of Irving Berlin's *Annie Get Your Gun.* He remembered it as a life-altering experience. "I was truly inspired by Irving Berlin," he recalled, "by his simplicity, and by the fact that he was able to write in a vernacular that the entire country could grasp immediately."

After graduating from high school, his mother arranged an audition for him with Frank Loesser, the composer of *Guys and Dolls,* who recommended a songwriting career. He attended the University of Miami, where he studied drama and wrote his first musical, *Sketchbook,* which was produced by the university.

After graduating in 1953, Herman moved back to New York City and began working in Off-Broadway theater. He gained recognition with the revue *Parade* in 1960, which showcased his talents as both composer and lyricist. His breakthrough came in 1961 with the Broadway musical *Milk and Honey*, which earned him his first Tony Award nomination. However, it was his next show, *Hello, Dolly!*, in 1964 that catapulted him to stardom. The musical won 10 Tony awards, including Best Musical, and became one of the longest-running shows in Broadway history. He continued his success with *Mame* in 1966, which solidified his reputation for creating strong, memorable female characters and joyous, infectious songs. In 1974, he wrote *Mack & Mabel*, which, although not a commercial success, is considered by many to have one of his most beautiful scores. In 1983, he scored a triumphant success on Broadway with *La Cage aux Folles*, which tackled themes of LGBTQ+ acceptance and family. The show was a critical and commercial success, winning six Tony awards, including Best Musical, and featuring the gay anthem "I Am What I Am."

Herman was openly gay, a fact that informed much of his work. In 1983, he met Martin Finkelstein, a designer, and they were companions until Finkelstein died of AIDS in 1989. Diagnosed HIV-positive in 1985, Herman nevertheless continued to work and live a full life. His last Broadway show was *An Evening with Jerry Herman* (1998), a career retrospective in which he played the piano onstage. He received a Tony Award for Lifetime Achievement in the Theatre in 2009 and the Kennedy Center Honors in 2010. "If I had the choice of being the most brilliant and sophisticated writer that ever came down the pike," he asserted, "or of being a simple melodic songwriter that I am, I would still have chosen the latter."

bell hooks (1952–2021)

Writer

bell hooks was a Black feminist writer and social critic who pioneered the study of intersectionality: how race, gender, class, and sexuality form overlapping systems of discrimination. The author of over 30 books, she helped push feminism and gender studies beyond its white, middle-class world to include the voices of Black and working-class women.

Born Gloria Jean Watkins but better known by her pen name, bell hooks, she was one of six children of Veodis Watkins, a postal worker, and Rosa Bell Watkins, a homemaker, in Hopkinsville, Kentucky. She began her education in segregated schools and has written about the difficulties she experienced when she made the transition to an integrated, predominantly white school. After graduating from high school, she attended Stanford University, receiving her B.A. in English in 1973. She went on to earn an M.A. in English from the University of Wisconsin in 1976 and a doctorate in literature from the University of California, Santa Monica, in 1983, writing her dissertation on author Toni Morrison.

From 1976 to 1979, hooks was an English professor and lecturer in ethnic studies at the University of California, Los Angeles, where she published her first book, a poetry collection, *And There We Wept* (1978), her first use of her pen name, which she borrowed from her outspoken maternal great-grandmother. Her decision to present her pen name in lowercase letters came from her desire for readers to focus their attention on her writing rather than on herself.

hooks taught English, ethnic studies, and women's studies at a variety of colleges and universities in the 1980s and 1990s. When she was 19, she began writing what would become her first full-length book, *Ain't I a Woman?: Black Women and Feminism*, which was eventually published in 1983. The book examines the effects of racism and sexism on African American women in the context of the civil rights and feminist movements from the women's suffrage era to the 1970s. In 1992, it was named one of the most influential books of the last 20 years. Her other books include *Feminist Theory: From Margin to Center* (1984), *All About Love: New Visions* (2000), and *We Real Cool: Black Men and Masculinity* (2004). She also published numerous scholarly articles, appeared in documentary films, and lectured widely. In 2004, she returned to Kentucky and joined Berea College as a distinguished professor in residence and founded the bell hooks center as a place to provide underrepresented students, including queer students, a safe space for expression and development.

hooks argued that womanhood could not be reduced to a singular experience but had to be considered within a framework encompassing race and class while calling for a new, more inclusive feminism that recognized differences and inequalities in search of a new unity. She applied the same concepts of intersectionality to her own sexual identity, which she characterized as "queer-pas-gay," meaning "not who you're having sex with, but about being at odds with everything around it." For her, the essence of queer was oppositional, requiring the individual "to invent and create and find a place to speak and to thrive and to live"; queerness was less about sex and more about refashioning an identity in opposition to a heteronormative world. She admitted in an interview, "I don't have a partner. I've been celibate for 17 years. I would love to have a partner, but I don't think my life is less meaningful. I always tell people my life is a pie and there's a slice of the pie that's missing, but there's so much pie left over—do I really want to spend my time looking at that empty piece and judging myself by that?"

Rock Hudson (1925–1985)

Actor

Rock Hudson, who rose to fame during Hollywood's Golden Age, became a heartthrob and leading man in the 1950s and 1960s and was the star of a popular television series in the 1970s. Known for his tall, handsome appearance and charismatic screen presence, he was one of the first known Hollywood celebrities to die of AIDS-related complications, with the publicity surrounding his death drawing attention to the disease.

Hudson was born Roy Harold Scherer Jr. in Winnetka, Illinois. His parents divorced when he was 4, and his mother remarried a man whom he despised, who also divorced his mother. He attended the same high school as fellow movie stars Charlton Heston and Ann-Margret. As a teenager, he developed an interest in acting but failed to win any roles in school plays because he could not remember his lines. After graduating in 1943, he enlisted in the U.S. Navy during World War II and served as an aircraft mechanic in the Philippines. After his discharge in 1946, he went to live with his biological father in order to pursue an acting career.

Talent scout Henry Willson took an interest in him and gave him the stage name Rock (for the Rock of Gibraltar) and Hudson (for the Hudson River), a name that Hudson later confessed to hating. He signed a contract with Universal-International Pictures with a starting salary of $125 per week and was given small roles in 28 films. His breakthrough role came with the 1954 film *Magnificent Obsession*, starring opposite Jane Wyman. This success was followed by a string of hits, including *All That Heaven Allows* (1955) and *Giant* (1956), for which he received an Academy Award nomination. He also found great success in romantic comedies, particularly through his collaborations with Doris Day such as *Pillow Talk* (1959), which, ironically, had him playing a straight man pretending he was gay; *Lover Come Back* (1961); and *Send Me No Flowers* (1964). These films showcased his comedic talent and solidified his status as a versatile leading man, making him the most bankable star in Hollywood during his heyday.

Hudson's personal life was marked by the necessity of remaining closeted due to the societal norms and professional pressures of his era. Hollywood's strict moral codes and the potential for a career-damaging scandal meant that his true sexual orientation was kept private. In 1955, in order to reinforce the public's belief that one of their most profitable stars was straight, the studio arranged a "lavender marriage" between him and Phyllis Gates, who had been the secretary of his agent. The marriage ended in divorce three years later. His sexuality was an open secret within the industry. He hosted famous pool parties, described as "blond bacchanalias," and dated men like actor Lee Garlington, who recalled, "We were ordered never to have our picture taken together, because somebody would know that we were gay." His secret was kept by friends, such as his costar, Day, who insisted that she knew "nothing about his private life."

Hudson's career evolved from movies to television, including the hit 1970s series *McMillan & Wife*, which ran from 1971 to 1977. When he announced in 1985 that he had AIDS, he became one of the first major celebrities to do so and became known as the "face of AIDS." His death in the same year raised awareness of the disease and kickstarted fundraising efforts. Randy Shilts declared in his 1987 book *And the Band Played On* that "there was AIDS before Rock Hudson, and AIDS after." Hudson's bravery in facing his illness and the subsequent public acknowledgment of his sexuality helped to humanize the AIDS crisis and reduced the stigma surrounding the disease. However, as Stephen Kijak, creator of the 2023 documentary *Rock Hudson: All That Heaven Allowed*, observed, "Everyone knows he was a gay man who had AIDS, and the effect of that was incredibly positive. But did he have anything to do with it? I don't think so. Was he in control of that narrative? Most likely not. If he'd had the choice, he would have stayed in the closet."

Robert Indiana (1928–2018)

Artist

Robert Indiana, a seminal figure in the Pop Art movement, achieved iconic status through his bold, graphic style and profound exploration of American identity. Best known for his iconic *LOVE* painting and sculpture, his work transcends mere aesthetics to offer a poignant commentary on love, hope, and the human condition. Through his distinctive use of color, typography, and symbolism, he challenged conventions and inspired audiences worldwide.

Born Robert Clark in New Castle, Indiana, he was adopted as an infant, and, after his parents divorced, he eventually relocated to Indianapolis, but he recalled having moved 21 times within the state of Indiana by the age of 17. After graduating from high school in 1946, he served in the U.S. Air Force for three years before studying at the Art Institute of Chicago (1949–1953), then Edinburgh University and Edinburgh College of Art (1953–1954).

Moving to New York City to start his career as an artist, Indiana, who adopted the surname in 1958 as a celebration of his ties to the American heartland, worked at an art supply store, where he first met artist Ellsworth Kelly. The two became lovers, with Kelly helping Indiana find a loft in Lower Manhattan's South Street Seaport district, whose nautical features the artist would imitate in many of his works. One of his first important works was the 1961 oil painting *The American Dream #1*, in which four flat, colorful discs contain signs like "tilt" and "take all." He called it "a comment on the superficiality of American life." Art critic Lawrence Alloway described it as "pop poetry of the highway." Indiana's other works revolve around action words like "eat," "hug," or "die." Through his meticulous attention to typography and symbolism, he challenged viewers to reconsider the familiar, inviting them to engage with his art on both intellectual and emotional levels.

In 1964, Indiana created his most famous work—the word L-O-V-E in colorful capital letters, with the first two letters stacked on top of the other two and the "O" tilted—originally as a commentary on his breakup with Kelly. It was then turned into a Christmas card, painting, and sculpture, eventually becoming the most iconic artwork of the 1960s. It became so popular that he called it the 20th century's "most plagiarized work of art" and, ironically, led to the neglect of his other artistic achievements.

From 1978 until his death, Indiana lived on the island of Vinalhaven, Maine. While he never hid his homosexuality, it wasn't until later in his career that he began to explore themes of queer identity more explicitly in his work. His experiences as a gay man in mid-20th-century America undoubtedly influenced his artistic expression, adding depth and complexity to his exploration of love, desire, and human connection. In 2013, the Whitney Museum of American Art presented a major retrospective exhibit of his work (*Robert Indiana: Beyond LOVE*) to reveal "an artist whose work, far from being unabashedly optimistic and affirmative, addresses the most fundamental issues facing humanity—love, death, sin, and forgiveness—giving new meaning to our understanding of the ambiguities of the American Dream and the plight of the individual in a pluralistic society." He would describe himself as "an American painter of signs charting the course."

Christopher Isherwood (1904–1986)

Writer

Best known for his books about Berlin in the 1930s, British American novelist, playwright, and memoirist Christopher William Bradshaw Isherwood was a gay man who often incorporated his sexual orientation into his works, including the novel *A Single Man* (1964), which was about an openly gay professor, and his memoir, *Christopher and His Kind* (1976), which included reflections on the gay liberation movement.

Isherwood was born on his family's estate in Cheshire, England. His father was a professional soldier who died in World War I; his mother was the daughter of a successful wine merchant. He attended the boarding school Repton before enrolling at Cambridge University in 1924 to study history. He was asked to leave Cambridge in 1925 after writing joke answers on his second-year exams. Also in 1925, he was reintroduced to a prep school friend, W. H. Auden, who in turn introduced him to the young poet Stephen Spender. Eventually, they would form, along with Cecil Day-Lewis, Louis MacNeice, and others, the Auden Group or Auden Generation.

Isherwood published his first novel, *All the Conspirators*, in 1928, and in 1929, he joined Auden in Berlin, where the poet was spending a post-graduate year. His principal motivation for visiting was to experience the sexual freedom that Weimar Berlin offered, as he later wrote: "To Christopher, Berlin meant Boys." After a short visit, he returned in July and relocated there in November 1929. During the period of the chaos of the Weimar Republic collapse and the rise of the Nazis, he began to collect the material that would become *The Berlin Stories* (1945): *The Last of Mr. Norris* and *Goodbye to Berlin*, which included the novella *Sally Bowles*, in which he created his most famous character, based on a young Englishwoman, Jean Ross, with whom he briefly shared a flat. In 1951, *Goodbye to Berlin* was adapted for the New York stage by John van Druten, using the title *I Am a Camera*. The play inspired the 1966 hit Broadway musical *Cabaret* and 1972 film.

In 1932, Isherwood started a relationship with Heinz Neddermeyer, and the following year, the couple fled Nazi Germany. They traveled throughout Europe, seeking a new nationality and passport for Neddermeyer, who was arrested in 1937 by the Gestapo and sentenced to hard labor for draft evasion and homosexuality. During this period, Isherwood took movie-writing jobs and traveled with Auden to China to report the Second Sino–Japanese War. They returned via the United States and decided to immigrate there in 1939.

Settling in Hollywood, Isherwood became an American citizen in 1946 and began living with photographer William Caskey in 1947. As he wrote in 1949 to Gore Vidal, "Homosexual relationships can be and frequently are happy. Many men live together for years and share their lives and their work, just as heterosexuals do." In 1953, he met 18-year-old Don Bachardy and, despite their age difference, began a partnership that continued, with periods of separation, until the end of Isherwood's life. In 1962, he completed *Down There on a Visit*, four related stories that overlap with the period covered in his Berlin stories, which produced, in the view of many, his finest achievement, *A Single Man* (1964), about a middle-aged, gay Englishman who was a professor at a Los Angeles university. Bachardy would become a successful artist, and the story of their relationship is told in the 2008 film *Chris & Don*. In *Christopher and His Kind* (1976), Isherwood returned to the 1930s as an avowed gay man to describe the real story of his life in Berlin and relationship with Neddermeyer. The book made him a hero of gay liberation.

Marc Jacobs (1963–)

Fashion Designer

Marc Jacobs is a renowned fashion designer known for innovative and often provocative designs that have consistently pushed the boundaries of contemporary fashion. As a former creative director of Louis Vuitton and the founder of his own highly successful label, he has left an indelible mark on the fashion industry. His fearless approach to design and ability to blend high fashion with street style has made him a significant figure in the world of fashion.

Jacobs was born in New York City to parents who were agents for the William Morris talent agency. When he was 7, his father died, and his mother subsequently remarried and divorced several times, each of which required the family to relocate. When he was a teenager, he went to live with his paternal grandmother on

Manhattan's Upper West Side. His grandmother taught him how to knit and encouraged his growing interest in fashion design. By the age of 15, he was attending the High School of Art and Design and was working at the upscale clothing boutique Charivari, where he met fashion designer Perry Ellis, who became his mentor. He studied at the Parsons School of Design, where he excelled and won several prestigious awards, including the Perry Ellis Gold Thimble Award.

Jacobs's fashion career is marked by numerous achievements and influential works. In 1986, he launched his first collection under the Marc Jacobs label, which received critical acclaim. He became the youngest designer to win the Perry Ellis Award for New Fashion Talent in 1987. His groundbreaking "grunge" collection for Ellis in 1992, though controversial at the time, is now considered iconic and had a lasting impact on fashion. In 1997, he was appointed creative director of Louis Vuitton, where he transformed the brand with his innovative vision, introducing collaborations with artists like Stephen Sprouse and Takashi Murakami. Under his leadership, Louis Vuitton became one of the most influential luxury brands in the world. Jacobs's eponymous brand, known for its bold and eclectic designs, continues to thrive, solidifying his status as a fashion maverick. In 2013, he stepped down as creative director of Louis Vuitton to concentrate on his own line and to launch a makeup line, Marc Jacobs Beauty.

Jacobs is openly gay and has been a prominent figure in the LGBTQ+ community. His personal style and openness about his sexuality have made him an icon of self-expression and individuality. "For many, many years—decades now—I've lived my life very openly," he stated. "I learned somewhere along the way…that I'm only as sick as my secrets and that one thing I won't live with is shame." He has often used his platform to advocate for LGBTQ+ rights and challenge societal norms. His personal life, including his relationships and struggles, has been widely covered in the media, but he remains unapologetically authentic, inspiring many with his courage and creativity.

Jasper Johns (1930–)

Painter, Graphic Artist

One of the most influential American artists of the 20th century, Jasper Johns is renowned for his innovative use of ordinary objects as subject matter, rendered with meticulous detail and striking simplicity. His technique challenged traditional notions of representation and propelled him to the forefront of the Pop Art movement. With iconic works such as *Flag* and *Target*, he pioneered a new visual language that transcended conventional boundaries and inspired generations of artists to come.

Born in Augusta, Georgia, Johns was raised in South Carolina by his paternal grandparents after his parents divorced. He began drawing at the age of 3 and knew he wanted to be an artist very early on. After graduating from high school in 1947, he briefly attended the University of South Carolina before moving to New York City and enrolling at the Parsons School of Design. After completing his military service in the Korean War, he returned to New York City in 1953 and began to make associations with key figures in the art world, including Robert Rauschenberg, who became his lover and partner until 1961, although neither man publicly acknowledged their relationship.

In 1954, Johns began his series of American flag paintings, and in 1958, he had his first one-man show. He became famous for his paintings depicting commonplace, two-dimensional objects, such as flags, maps, numbers, and letters of the alphabet, painted in simple colors. In their willful ordinariness, his works were a radical departure from the emotional expression of the Abstract Expressionist styles that dominated the American scene and would define the emerging Pop Art movement. One of his best-known works is *Painted Bronze* (1960), a cast sculpture of two Ballantine Ale cans. From 1961, he began to affix real objects to the surface of his canvas while incorporating more fluid brushstrokes and rawer paint textures in such works as *Diver* (1962). In the 1970s, he produced paintings of parallel lines that he called "cross-hatchings" in works like *Corpse and Mirror II* (1974). In the 1980s and 1990s, he explored catenaries—curves created by a length of cord or chain hanging free from two fixed points—such as *Catenary (Jacob's Ladder)* (1999).

Following his breakup with Rauschenberg, Johns became increasingly more reclusive, almost never giving interviews. As art critic Robert Starr observed, "It is not so much that Johns wishes to be left alone, Greta Garbo–style, but simply that he is alone.... Wounded in love...in particular by his rupture with Robert Rauschenberg in the early 1960s, he has sublimated his suffering and structured his existence around what he does by himself: his art." Johns divides his time between his studios in Connecticut and on the Caribbean island of St. Martin. He was awarded the National Medal of Arts in 1990 and the Presidential Medal of Freedom in 2011. Throughout his career, he has continued to produce innovative and influential artwork, solidifying his status as one of the most significant artists of the 20th and 21st centuries.

Jill Johnston (1929–2010)

Writer, Cultural Critic

Jill Johnston, the author of *Lesbian Nation: The Feminist Solution* who spearheaded the lesbian separatist movement of the 1970s, has been called the "boldest lesbian of her time." In *Lesbian Nation*, with a no-holds-barred approach, she argued that women

should not sleep with "the enemy" (men) but should become lesbians as a revolutionary act and that "until all women are lesbians there will be no true political revolution."

Born Jill Crowe in London, Johnston was the only child of Olive Marjorie Crowe, an American nurse, and Cyril F. Johnston, an English bellfounder and clockmaker. After her father abandoned them, her mother took her to Queens, New York, where she was raised by her grandmother. She received her bachelor's degree from Tufts University in 1951 and studied dance at the University of North Carolina, Greensboro. In the mid-1950s, she moved to New York City to continue her dance studies but turned to writing dance criticism when she broke her foot. In 1959, she began writing for *The Village Voice*, remaining with the paper until 1981. Eventually, her regular dance column became a kind of weekly diary of her involvement in the New York art world. She would say of her column, "I had a forum obviously set up for covering or perpetrating all manner of outrage."

In 1958, Johnston married Richard John Lanham, with whom she had a son and a daughter before divorcing him in 1964. By 1969, she was active in the gay and feminist movements. She came out as a lesbian in a 1971 article titled "Lois Lane Is a Lesbian," the first writer of her era to do so. She also participated in the notorious 1971 panel on women's liberation held at New York City's Town Hall. Billed as a battle of the sexes, it was moderated by Norman Mailer and included panelists Germaine Greer and Diana Trilling. When she spoke, she declared, "All women are lesbians except those who don't know it yet," and she was joined onstage by two women friends hugging and kissing and rolling on the floor. An exasperated Mailer pleaded with her to "be a lady."

Johnston would become one of the first countercultural lesbian writers at *Ms.* magazine, eventually concluding that the magazine was too mainstream, trying to present feminism to "appeal to women who read *Ladies' Home Journal.*" *Lesbian Nation*, originally published as a series of essays in *The Village Voice* from 1969 to 1972, took a very different radical approach, presenting Johnston's vision of radical lesbian feminism. Kate Millet called it "the most important book to come out of the women's movement." As Johnston explained, "Once I understood the feminist doctrines, a lesbian separatist position seemed the commonsensical position."

Johnston's follow-up to *Lesbian Nation* was *Gullible's Travels* (1974). After leaving *The Village Voice* in 1982, she wrote freelance art and literary criticism. Her other books include *Secret Lives in Art* (1994) and *Jasper Johns: Privileged Information* (1996), and she published two volumes of her memoirs: *Mother Bound* (1983) and *Paper Daughter* (1985). *Admission Accomplished: The Lesbian Nation Years (1970–75)* (1998) is an anthology of her early writing. She married her longtime partner, Ingrid Nyeboe, in Denmark in 1993 and again in Connecticut in 2009, the year before her death.

June Jordan (1936–2002)

Poet, Playwright, Essayist

One of the most highly acclaimed Jamaican American writers ever, June Jordan was the author or editor of 28 books, essays, and novels for children. One of the most prominent Black woman writers of her era along with Audre Lorde, Alice Walker, and Toni Morrison, she was acclaimed for her fierce commitment to human rights and political activism in a career that spanned civil rights, women's rights, and the gay liberation movement. A Black woman who was bisexual, she dealt with and diagnosed the issues of intersectionality before it became a recognized concept.

Born in Harlem as the only child of immigrants from Jamaica and Panama, Jordan grew up in the Bedford-Stuyvesant area of Brooklyn and credits her father with passing on to her a love of literature. She began writing poetry at the age of 7. After graduating from public schools, she attended an elite preparatory school (Northfield Mount Hermon) before enrolling at Barnard College in 1953. There, she met Columbia University student Michael Meyer, whom she married in 1955, joining him at the University of Chicago, where she did graduate studies in anthropology. In 1958, she gave birth to the couple's only child, a son, whom she raised alone after the couple divorced in 1965.

Jordan's first poetry collection, *Who Look at Me*, appeared in 1969. Among her subsequent verse collections are *Things That I Do in the Dark* (1977), *Living Room* (1985), *Naming Our Destiny* (1989), *Haruko/Love Poetry* (1993), and *Kissing God Goodbye* (1997). Her poems are often deeply autobiographical and known for their immediacy and accessibility in rending complex questions of identity. She also authored children's books, plays, the memoir *Soldier: A Poet's Childhood* (2000), and the novel *His Own Where* (1971), which was nominated for the National Book Award. Her collections of political essays include *On Call* (1985), *Civil Wars* (1996), and *Affirmative Acts* (1998). Toni Morrison summarized Jordan's achievements by saying, "I am talking about a span of forty years of tireless activism coupled with and fueled by flawless art."

Jordan began her teaching career in 1967 at the City College of New York, and between 1967 and 1978, she taught at Yale, Sarah Lawrence, and Connecticut College. She directed The Poetry Center at SUNY at Stony Brook from 1978 to 1989, and from 1989 to 2002, she was a professor of English, women's studies, and African American studies at the University of California, Berkeley. She was one of the first academics to acknowledge and integrate intersectionality into her politics and writing.

Throughout her life, Jordan identified as bisexual, and in her final collection of essays, *Some of Us Did Not Die* (2003), which was published posthumously, she asserted, "Bisexuality means that I am free and I am as likely to want and to love a woman as I am likely to want and to love a man, and what about that? Isn't that what freedom implies? If you are free, you are not predictable and you are not controllable. To my mind, that is the keenly positive politicizing significance of bisexual affirmation."

Christine Jorgensen (1926–1989)

Transgender Advocate, Actor

Called the "world's first famous transsexual" and "arguably the most famous person in the world" for a few short years, Christine Jorgensen helped bring the word "transsexual" into the American vocabulary. In the early 1950s, she became one of the first people to successfully undergo gender affirmation surgery and became a media sensation. The *Daily News* headline "Ex-GI Becomes Blonde Beauty" and others like it catapulted her into the public eye. Despite the sensationalism, she used her newfound fame to advocate for transgender rights and education. She became a successful nightclub entertainer, using her platform to speak openly about her experiences.

Born George William Jorgensen Jr. in the Bronx, New York, she said she had a normal, happy childhood but was frustrated by feelings that she was a woman in a man's body. In 1945 during World War II, she was drafted into the U.S. Army, serving as a military clerk. After leaving the army in 1946, she moved to Denmark, where she learned about gender reassignment surgery. She later credited Radclyffe Hall's influential lesbian novel *The Well of Loneliness* (1929) for making her "more determined than ever to fight for this victory." Her sexual conversion began with hormone injections in 1950, which were completed in 1952. She took the first name Christine to honor Christian Hamburger, the Danish hormone expert who treated her.

Returning to the United States in 1955, Jorgensen became the first transsexual in the United States to publicly announce her change of sexual identity. Three hundred reporters met her plane in New York, and her story was sensationalized in the press with headlines such as "Bronx GI Becomes a Woman!" and "Bronx 'Boy' Is Now a Girl." In a 1970 interview, she stated, "At first I was very self-conscious and very awkward, but once the notoriety hit, it did not take me long to adjust." She turned her notoriety into a series of lucrative tours on the lecture and nightclub circuit. "I decided if they want to see me," she recalled, "they would have to pay for it." She became a successful nightclub entertainer, using her platform to speak openly about her experiences. Her autobiography, *Christine Jorgensen: A Personal Autobiography*, published in 1967, provided an intimate look at her life and struggles, helping to demystify transgender issues for the general public.

Jorgensen made headlines again in 1959 when she was denied a license to marry because her birth certificate said she was male. She subsequently made the decision to remain unmarried. She never expressed regret about her decision to change sexes and linked the public reaction to her decision to the awakening that led to the sexual revolution of the 1960s.

Jorgensen's openness about her gender identity and sexuality despite the era's conservative views helped to challenge societal norms and broaden the public's understanding of gender and sexuality. Her highly publicized transition brought attention to the field of transgender health care and paved the way for more medical research and support for transgender individuals. Her courage and advocacy work left a lasting legacy, making her a trailblazer in the LGBTQ+ community and a symbol of resilience and progress. As scholar Susan Stryker has observed, "Jorgensen's story became a lightning rod for many post–World War II anxieties about gender and sexuality, and called dramatic attention to issues that would drive the feminist and gay-rights movements in the decades ahead."

John Kander (1927-)

Composer

Fred Ebb (1928-2004)

Lyricist

John Kander

Called the Rodgers and Hart and the Rodgers and Hammerstein of the second half of the 20th century, the Broadway and film songwriting duo of John Kander and Fred Ebb dominated their field and produced the scores for such groundbreaking musicals as *Cabaret*, *Chicago*, and *Kiss of the Spider Woman*. Their most famous song is "New York, New York," the title song of the Martin Scorsese film of the same name.

Kander was born in Kansas City, Missouri, into a middle-class, Jewish family. He began studying the piano at the age of 6 and performed with family and friends. He received a bachelor's degree from Oberlin College (1951) and a master's degree from Columbia (1954), both degrees in music. He worked as a pianist, dance music arranger, and summer stock musical conductor before partnering with lyricists James and William Goldman to write the score for the musical *A Family Affair* (1962).

Ebb, a native New Yorker, graduated from New York University with a bachelor's degree in English in 1955 and gained his master's degree in English from Columbia University in 1957. He collaborated with several writing partners to produce songs such as "Heartbroken," recorded by Judy Garland in 1953, and "Don't Forget," recorded by Eddy Arnold in 1954. His first theatrical writing job was as the cowriter of the lyrics for the musical revue *Baker's Dozen* (1951). He contributed songs to the cabaret revue *Isn't America Fun* (1959) and the Broadway revue *From A to Z* (1960).

Fred Ebb

Kander and Ebb were brought together by a music publisher in 1962. The short-lived play *Flora, the Red Menace* (1965) was their Broadway debut as well as that of Liza Minnelli, who won a Tony Award for Best Performance by a Leading Actress in a Musical for her role. It was also the beginning of her long collaboration with the writing team, working together in the musicals *The Act* (1977) and *The Rink* (1984) as well as in the film version of *Cabaret* (1972).

Kander and Ebb won their first Tony Award for the score of *Cabaret* (1966), which also won the best musical award. They would receive Tony awards for their scores for *Woman of the Year* (1981) and *Kiss of the Spider Woman* (1993). Their other stage works included *The Happy Time* (1968), *Zorba the Greek* (1968), *Chicago* (1975), *Steel Pier* (1997), and *The Scottsboro Boys* (2010). Their scores brilliantly capture the flavor of a specific time and place in evocative music, with brilliantly penetrating lyrics. They readily tackled serious, challenging subjects, including Nazism, abortion, murder, capital punishment, prison torture, and greed. As critic David Richards observed, "Kander and Ebb combine razzmatazz with a political conscience, and make brazen spirits seem a kind of moral courage." Many of their songs, including "Cabaret," "New York, New York," "How Lucky Can You Get," "Maybe This Time," and "All That Jazz," have both defined their eras and entered the Great American Songbook.

Even though they have been called "the musical poets of the polymorphous perverse" for openly exploring daring sexual themes in their work, both Kander and Ebb have kept their own gayness private. Work partners for 45 years, they kept their relationship professional. Before his death in 2004, Ebb asserted that any statement that he and Kander wished to make about homosexuality had been made through their songs. In 2010, Kander married dancer and choreographer Albert Stephenson, his partner since 1977. Ebb is interred in a mausoleum in Brooklyn's Greenwood Cemetery with two other men, with an epitaph that reads "Together Forever." The grave was featured in the first gay-themed tour of Greenwood Cemetery in 2014.

Ellsworth Kelly (1923–2015)

Painter, Sculptor, Printmaker

Ellsworth Kelly, a towering figure in 20th-century American art, revolutionized abstract art with his bold use of color, shape, and form. His minimalist approach and emphasis on abstraction set him apart from his contemporaries, earning him acclaim as one of the pioneers of the postwar art movement. His enduring legacy as a master of color and form continues to influence generations of artists, cementing his place as one of the most important figures in modern art history.

Kelly was born in Newburgh, New York, but was raised in Oradell, New Jersey. There, he developed a lifelong passion for ornithology and birdwatching. He also developed a passion for form and color in his public-school art classes. He would go on to study technical art at Pratt Institute in Brooklyn from 1941 until he was inducted into the U.S. Army in 1943. During World War II, he served with other artists and designers in the Ghost Army, a deception unit that used inflatable tanks, trucks, and other constructions to mislead the Germans about the direction and disposition of Allied forces in advance of D-Day. He developed expertise in military camouflage techniques that he would later apply to his art.

From 1946 to 1947, Kelly studied at the School of the Museum of Fine Arts in Boston before returning to Europe to live and study in Paris, where he immersed himself in the postwar art scene. He recalled, "Paris was gray after the war. I liked being alone. I liked being a stranger. I didn't speak French well, and I like the silence." There, he began painting his first abstract pictures, which were derived from patterns found in sidewalk grates or configurations of pipes on the side of a building. "I started to look at the city around me," he said, "and that became my source." In the seven years he spent in Paris, however, he sold only one painting and, after being evicted from his studio, returned to New York City in 1954. He began working in a loft in a deserted section of Lower Manhattan near the South Street Seaport among fellow artists such as Robert Indiana, Jasper Johns, and Robert Rauschenberg. His works differed from the reigning Abstract Expressionism of the time as evidenced by his rejection of showing any sign of the painter's hand in works. Instead, his paintings were typically flat, consisting of adjacent geometric panels of smooth color. Among his most significant works are his iconic color field paintings, which feature large, flat expanses of color separated by clean, crisp lines. Examples include *Spectrum I* (1953) and *Red Blue Green* (1963), which exemplify his mastery of color and form. He also gained recognition for his *Plant Drawings* series, in which he meticulously rendered botanical forms with an emphasis on their abstract qualities.

In 1956 and 1957, Kelly had his first New York City exhibitions at a gallery. Three of his works, *Atlantic*, *Bar*, and *Painting in Three Panels*, were shown at the

Whitney Museum's exhibit *Young America 1957*. He began creating freestanding sculptures in the late 1950s, which, like his paintings, were geometric objects of solid colors made from industrial materials such as steel and aluminum. As his reputation grew, he received numerous commissions for large-scale sculptures such as the one he did for the New York State Pavilion at the New York World's Fair (1964).

Kelly's sexuality has been a subject of speculation and curiosity, as he was known to be discreet about his personal life. While he never publicly identified as gay during his lifetime, biographers and art historians have noted that he had several relationships with men, including photographer Jack Shear, whom he met in the 1980s and later became his partner. Artist Robert Indiana's famous *LOVE* painting was at least inspired by his relationship with Kelly in 1956; the work expressed what he felt for Kelly and was an homage to his influence in its use of geometrical shapes and color.

In 1970, Kelly moved to Spencertown in Upstate New York, later to be joined there in 1984 by his partner, Jack Shear. While there, Kelly began creating large-scale, outdoor sculptures and public artworks that appear in collections around the world in public places such as Chicago and Berlin. His work was the subject of numerous solo exhibitions and retrospectives at the Museum of Modern Art (1973), the Whitney Museum of American Art (1982), and the Guggenheim Museum (1982). His last major work was a freestanding stone secular chapel called *Austin*, which was commissioned by the Blanton Museum of Art in Austin, Texas, and constructed posthumously, opening to the public in 2018.

In a final interview before his death at the age of 92, Kelly declared, "Any good art is spiritual…it's about reaching something." He once explained, "I think what we all want from art is a sense of fixity, a sense of opposing the chaos of daily living."

Lincoln Kirstein (1907–1996)

Dance Impresario

Acknowledged as one of the most important influences in the development of American culture in the 20th century, Lincoln Edward Kirstein was a poet, novelist, historian, art collector, and critic, but it was as a ballet company director and impresario that he made his greatest contribution to American culture. As a cofounder of the New York City Ballet, his efforts to promote and support the arts have left a legacy in the world of dance and beyond.

Kirstein was born in Rochester, New York, to Jewish parents. He was raised in Boston, where his father headed Filene's Department Store. His cultivated and affluent parents encouraged their son's early interest in the arts but refused his repeated requests to attend a performance of Sergei Diaghilev's Ballets Russes in Boston because they felt that the 9-year-old was too young. While attending Harvard, he cofounded the prestigious literary magazine *Hound & Horn* and, at the same time, caught what he called "balletomania," spending summers traveling abroad to attend ballet productions. He was particularly impressed by the works of Diaghilev's youngest choreographic discovery, George Balanchine. It was Balanchine's *Apollo* that awakened in Kirstein the potential of classical ballet and the goal of establishing that level of ballet in America.

After graduating in 1930, Kirstein continued publishing *Hound & Horn* as a literary quarterly until 1934, when he decided to focus his energies on bringing Balanchine to America, establishing the School of American Ballet and a company, the American Ballet, which made its debut in 1935. From 1935 to 1938, it was the resident ballet company for the Metropolitan Opera, and some of the dance sequences that Balanchine choreographed for operatic productions mystified conservative music lovers. After the American Ballet toured South America in 1941, it disbanded.

In 1941, despite Kirstein's primary attraction to men, he married Fidelma Cadmus, the sister of artist Paul Cadmus, who had been Kirstein's lover. Their relationship, while not traditionally romantic, was based on mutual respect, affection, and shared artistic interests, and their marriage lasted for 50 years until Cadmus's death in 1991. His marriage additionally provided a socially acceptable cover that allowed him to navigate public life without the scrutiny that might have come from being openly gay. Within his private and trusted circles, his sexuality was more openly acknowledged and accepted.

In 1943 during World War II, Kirstein enlisted and was assigned to the military's Monuments, Fine Arts, and Archives (MFAA) program, which rescued and preserved European art. In Germany in 1945, he was involved with retrieving artworks around Munich and from the salt mines at Altaussee. In the 2014 film *The Monuments Men*, the character played by Bob Balaban is loosely based on Kirstein.

In 1946, Kirstein and Balanchine founded the Ballet Society, which was renamed the New York City Ballet (NYCB) in 1948 with the intention, as Kirstein stated, "to enable Balanchine to do exactly what he wants to do in the way he wants to do it." He would serve as the company's general director from 1946 to 1989. The NYCB holds a distinguished place in the history of dance, significantly impacting ballet both in the United States and internationally. Renowned for its innovative choreography, the company redefined ballet through Balanchine's focus on speed, precision, and musicality, and its repertoire includes influential works by Balanchine, Jerome Robbins, and other prominent choreographers. The NYCB has created a distinctly American style of ballet, incorporating American themes and sensibilities, and its training methods have influenced ballet across the country through the School of American Ballet. The company has played a crucial role in popularizing ballet, with performances like *The Nutcracker* becoming a holiday tradition, and, as a cultural landmark at the Lincoln Center, it attracts audiences worldwide. The NYCB has provided a platform for emerging choreographers, fostered collaborations with composers and artists, and elevated the global profile of American ballet through its tours. The enduring repertoire of ballets created for the NYCB continues to be performed globally, and its educational impact ensures the perpetuation of the Balanchine technique. The NYCB's transformative impact, cultural contributions, and global influence make it a cornerstone of the dance world, with a legacy that continues to inspire and shape contemporary ballet.

That legacy is largely the result of the vision and determination of Kirstein. Peter Martins, artistic director of the NYCB at the time of Kirstein's death, stated, "Like Balanchine, he informed, inspired, guided, and enriched not only the lives of every member of the New York City Ballet, but the lives of many generations. We have lost a founder, a father, a friend."

Larry Kramer (1935–2020)

Writer, AIDS Activist

Susan Sontag called writer and activist Laurence David "Larry" Kramer "one of America's most valuable troublemakers." His confrontational and controversial style was expressed in such works as the novel *Faggots* (1978) and his most acclaimed play, *The Normal Heart* (1985), as well as in the relentless activism that made him the conscience of the AIDS epidemic. As a founder of the Gay Men's Health Crisis and ACT UP, the protest organization targeting governmental agencies and corporations to publicize the lack of treatment and funding for people with AIDS, he justifies immunologist Anthony Fauci's statement that "in American medicine there are two eras. Before Larry and after Larry."

Kramer was born in Bridgeport, Connecticut. His father earned a law degree from Yale but was unable to make a living in law during the Great Depression. He supported his family by working in a shoe store. In 1941, he secured a government job and moved his family to Washington, D.C. In 1953, he enrolled at Yale, where he attempted suicide because he felt like he was the "only gay student on campus" but then had an affair with his German professor—his first requited romantic relationship with a man. He graduated in 1957 with a degree in English and worked as a teletype operator at Columbia Pictures, eventually winning a position in the story department reworking scripts. He wrote the 1969 screenplay for the adaptation of D. H. Lawrence's *Women in Love,* which was nominated for an Academy Award, and later wrote the screenplay for the 1973 musical remake of the 1937 Frank Capra film *Lost Horizon,* a notorious critical and commercial failure.

Kramer next began to integrate gay themes in his work, including the play *Sissies' Scrapbook* (later rewritten and retitled *Four Friends*), which is about four friends, one of whom is gay. In 1978, he completed the novel *Faggots,* a scathing look at the promiscuous lifestyle of gay men, which was attacked as exaggerated and a belittling of gay people. He defended his novel, asserting that the work was more a documentary than a work of fiction and that its message was clear: Gay men and lesbians are at risk as long as they defined themselves primarily in terms of their sexual orientation.

In the early 1980s, Kramer was one of the first people to foresee the upcoming AIDS crisis, and he began to shift his focus to activism. He hosted a meeting in his New York apartment that led to the formation of the Gay Men's Health Crisis in 1981. It would become the primary organization to raise funds for and provide services to people stricken with AIDS in the New York area. He would spend the next several years fundraising, lobbying, and confronting not only the heterosexual community but the homosexual one as well for its apathy. His landmark essay, "1,112 and Counting," appeared in 1983 in the *New York Native,* a gay newspaper. It attacked everyone connected with health care in America, politicians, and gay men for their indifference. Tony Kushner, author of *Angels in America,* a book about the impact of AIDS, described the essay by saying, "With that one piece, Larry changed my world. He changed the world for all of us."

In 1983, Kramer's confrontational style was deemed too militant for the Gay Men's Health Crisis, and he was ousted from the organization. He would convert his experience confronting the AIDS crisis into *The Normal Heart,* a play set between 1981 and 1984 that featured characters struggling both with the unknown and with a bureaucracy that ignores their plight. The play is one of the first to deal with the AIDS crisis and is widely regarded as a literary and cultural landmark in its depiction of the gay community under threat.

In 1987, Kramer called for an escalation of more direct action in dealing with the AIDS crisis, which resulted in the formation of the AIDS Coalition to Unleash Power (ACT UP), an organization that used protests and demonstrations to raise awareness and combat the political and economic forces that were impeding the development of effective treatment. These included a blockade of Wall Street, an attempt to enter FDA headquarters in 1988, and chaining members to a railing inside the New York Stock Exchange. All were efforts to shock the public, raise awareness, and facilitate treatment, which proved effective. Even Dr. Fauci, a longtime target of Kramer's wrath whom Kramer had called a killer and "an incompetent idiot," later admitted, "Once you got past the rhetoric, you found that Larry Kramer made a lot of sense, and that he had a heart of gold." Fauci credited him with playing an "essential" role in the development of drug regimens that prolonged the lives of those infected with HIV and prompting the FDA to streamline its assessment and approval of certain new drugs. Kramer himself was diagnosed with the HIV virus in 1988.

In response to this experience, Kramer would write *Just Say No: A Play About a Farce* (1988) and a sequel to *The Normal Heart, The Destiny of Me* (1992). His writings on AIDS were collected as *Reports from the Holocaust: The Making of an AIDS Activist* (1989). *The American People, Volume 1: Search for My Heart* (1989) is a revisionist history that identifies the homosexuality of numerous American figures, including George Washington, Alexander Hamilton, and Abraham Lincoln. *The American People, Volume 2: The Brutality of Fact* appeared in 2020.

In 2013, Kramer married his longtime partner, architect David Webster, in a New York hospital, where Kramer had just undergone abdominal surgery. Looking back on his life in 2017, he explained, "I was trying to make people united and angry. I was known as the angriest man in the world, mainly because that anger got you further than being nice."

Tony Kushner (1956–)

Playwright, Screenwriter

Anthony Robert "Tony" Kushner is the author of *Angels in America,* one of the most important dramas to appear in the last decade of the 20th century. That a play with the subtitle *A Gay Fantasia on National Themes* would be honored with the Pulitzer Prize and a Tony Award for Best Play suggests both the arrival on center stage of the gay experience and his genius in universalizing that experience into a profound reflection of American history and the fundamental meaning of American democracy.

Kushner was born in New York City, but his musician parents moved their family to Lake Charles, Louisiana, when he was an infant. He attributes his love of opera and literature to his father and his passion for the theater to his mother, who acted in local productions and took her son to see them at an early age. He also recollects from childhood "fairly clear memories of being gay since I was six.... By the time I was eleven there was no doubt. But I was completely in the closet." He would not come out until his 20s, after graduating from Columbia University in 1978. He worked for six years as a hotel switchboard operator before deciding to pursue a career in the theater, enrolling in New York University and earning an MFA in directing in 1984. It was the year of Ronald Reagan's reelection as president, the growing AIDS epidemic, and a number of personal setbacks for Kushner, who recalled, "The desolate political sphere mirrored in an exact and ugly way an equally desolate personal sphere." Around this moment in history and his life, he chose to set *Angels in America.*

Kushner's early works include an opera, *La Fin de la Baleine: An Opera for the Apocalypse* (1983), some children's plays, adaptations of works by Goethe and Corneille, and one-act and full-length plays, including *The Heavenly Theatre* (1986) and *Hydriotaphia* (1987). His first professional production was *A Bright Room Called Day* (1985), which was about a group of friends in Germany during the early years of Adolf Hitler's rise to power. In 1988, Oskar Eustis, artistic director of the Eureka Theatre, commissioned Kushner to write a play about the impact of AIDS on the gay community in San Francisco. This would become *Angels in America,* which grew into a seven-hour, two-part drama. The first production of both parts debuted in Los Angeles before transferring to Broadway in 1993.

Kushner stated that in *Angels in America,* he set out to write a play on "AIDS,

Mormons, and Roy Cohn," linking three disparate subjects: the disease that was destroying and isolating gays in America; the religious group that was committed to godliness but also intolerant toward gays; and the notoriously conservative power broker who, though he persecuted gays, was himself a closeted homosexual, only outed when he contracted AIDS and died in 1986. He orchestrates these elements to chronicle a particularly crucial moment in the testing of American values. The play was widely hailed as a triumph in its moral and intellectual challenges and a liberating theater experience, pointing the way for drama to reclaim a primary role as interpreter of the moment and the human condition.

Kushner's subsequent plays include *Homebody/Kabul* (1999), exploring the relationship between Afghanistan and the West, and *The Intelligent Homosexual's Guide to Capitalism and Socialism* (2009), a family drama. In addition to his work for the state, he has contributed screenplays for a number of Steven Spielberg's films, including *Munich* (2005), *Lincoln* (2012), *West Side Story* (2021), and *The Fabelmans* (2022).

Despite the centrality of his homosexuality in his life and work, Kushner confesses to not being totally at ease in the gay community: "I feel outside just by temperament and nerdishness." Much of his ambition as a writer is to synthesize the gay movement into the wider movement of American democracy. On a personal level, in 2003, he and his partner, journalist Mark Harris, held a commitment ceremony, the first same-sex commitment ceremony to be featured in the "Vows" column of *The New York Times.* In 2008, they were legally married.

Mark Lamos (1946–)

Director, Producer, Actor

Mark Lamos is a distinguished figure in the world of American theater, recognized for artistic vision and leadership that has made him a force in the evolution of American theater. Known for his innovative interpretations of both classical and contemporary works, he has made significant contributions that have earned him accolades and respect within the theatrical community. During his tenure as the artistic director of theater company the Hartford Stage from 1980 to 1998, he transformed regional theater into a nationally acclaimed institution. On Broadway, he directed productions such as *Our Country's Good* and Edward Albee's *Seascape,* both of which garnered Tony Award nominations.

Lamos was born in Melrose Park, Illinois. He developed an early interest in the arts, studying ballet and violin and participating in high school theater productions. He attended Northwestern University on a music scholarship. Offered a role in a production of Jean Anouilh's *The Lark* caused him to change his focus from music to theater. He graduated in 1969 with a degree in English and theater.

After graduation, Lamos remained in Chicago to act, but he was encouraged by a veteran New York actor to relocate to New York City to continue his career there. Within a week of arriving, he had a part in a Broadway play, and by the end of 1972, he was cast in a new Arthur Miller play, *The Creation of the World and Other Business,* and costarred with Christopher Plummer in the musical *Cyrano.*

During this time, Lamos married a female dancer, a union that lasted seven years. "I thought maybe I was bisexual," he recalled, "but maybe not. Looking back, I saw I was so uptight I could not break out of the culture at the time. It's hard for younger gay men now to know that in that day and gate it was unsafe [to come out]. When I became an actor in the '70s, and being cast as a leading man, I thought to myself, 'I cannot be gay. I have to be straight.'"

In the late 1970s, Lamos received an offer from the Arizona Theater Company to direct *Equus,* his first large-scale production. It was there that he met actor Jerry Jones, his partner since 1979. That same year, he was offered a position at the Hartford Stage and served as its artistic director from 1981 to 1998. During his tenure there, he transformed the theater into a nationally acclaimed institution. Under his direction, the Hartford Stage received a Tony Award for Outstanding Regional Theatre in 1989. He also directed productions on Broadway and Off-Broadway and has also made significant contributions to opera, directing productions for the New York City Opera and the Metropolitan Opera, including the highly praised *Madama Butterfly* and *Carmen*. In 2009, he became the artistic director of the Westport Country Playhouse in Westport, Connecticut, a position he held for 15 seasons before his retirement in 2023.

Throughout his career, Lamos has been honored with numerous awards, including the Drama Desk Award for his direction of *Our Country's Good* and the Helen Hayes Award for his work at the Shakespeare Theatre Company. In 2001, he received the prestigious John Houseman Award, recognizing his dedication to the development of classical theater. His direction of the Broadway revival of *Seascape* in 2005, which garnered four Tony Award nominations, including Best Revival of a Play, further solidified his reputation as a masterful director capable of breathing new life into classic works.

Nathan Lane (1956–)

Actor

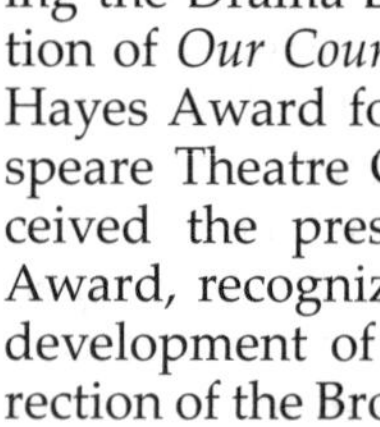

Nathan Lane is a celebrated actor known for his versatility and dynamic performances onstage and on the screen. With a career spanning several decades, he has captivated audiences with his comedic brilliance, dramatic depth, and musical talent. His work in theater, film, and television has garnered critical acclaim and numerous awards, establishing him as one of the most respected and beloved figures in entertainment.

Born Joseph Lane in Jersey City, New Jersey, Lane discovered his passion for acting at an early age and changed his first name to Nathan in honor of the character Nathan Detroit from the musical *Guys and Dolls*. He attended St. Peter's Preparatory School, where he honed his acting skills in school productions. Although he received a scholarship to attend St. Joseph's University in Philadelphia, financial constraints led him to pursue his acting career in New York City instead. His early years in New York were marked by perseverance and dedication as he worked to establish himself in the competitive world of theater.

Lane's career is highlighted by an array of notable achievements and iconic roles. He gained recognition for his 1982 Broadway debut in Nöel Coward's *Present Laughter* and received a Tony Award nomination for his breakout role as Nathan Detroit in the 1992 Broadway revival of *Guys and Dolls*. He won his first Tony Award in 1996 for his portrayal of Pseudolus in *A Funny Thing Happened on the Way to the Forum*. His performance as Max Bialystock in *The Producers* (2001) alongside Matthew Broderick became legendary, earning him another Tony Award and widespread acclaim. He won another Tony Award for his role as Roy Cohn in the Broadway revival of *Angels in America* in 2018. His extensive body of work reflects his range and ability to captivate audiences across different media. In film, he is perhaps best known for his role as Albert Goldman in *The Birdcage* (1996), which showcased his comedic talent and received critical praise. He has also voiced iconic characters such as Timon in Disney's *The Lion King* (1994) and Snowbell in *Stuart Little* (1999). His television work includes notable appearances in *Modern Family*, *The Good Wife*, and *Penny Dreadful: City of Angels*. All told, he has been the recipient of three Tony awards, seven Drama Desk awards, a Laurence Olivier Award, and a Screen Actors Guild Award for his work onstage and in film.

Lane, who came out publicly in 1999, has been a prominent advocate for LGBTQ+ rights and visibility. After a long-term relationship with his partner, Devlin Elliott, a producer and playwright, the couple married in 2015 and, together, have supported various LGBTQ+ causes and organizations.

Lane, reflecting on his goal as an actor, once said, "I want the kind of career where I can move back and forth," summarizing his desire to balance work between stage and screen and his aim to take on different types of roles and performances. His career has indeed embodied this aspiration.

Arthur Laurents (1917–2011)

Playwright, Librettist, Director, Screenwriter

Arthur Laurents made a remarkable contribution to theater and film. Known for his sharp wit, insightful storytelling, and ability to address complex social issues, his work has shaped some of the most iconic productions in American theater. He is best known for having written the book for the landmark musical *West Side Story* (1957), reimagining Shakespeare's *Romeo and Juliet* in the context of gang rivalry in New York City. He also was a distinguished screenwriter of such films as *Rope* (1948), *Anastasia* (1956), *Bonjour Tristesse* (1958), *The Way We Were* (1973), and *The Turning Point* (1977).

Born Arthur Levine in Brooklyn, New York, Laurents was the son of middle-class, Jewish parents. His father was a lawyer, and his mother was a schoolteacher. He attended Cornell University, where he studied English, and after graduation in 1937, he found work in radio writing. He was drafted into the U.S. Army during World War II and put to work writing training films and scripts. This experience honed his writing skills and set the stage for his future success in theater and film. It was also during his army service that he acted on his homosexuality with partners that he refers to in his memoir, *Original Story By: A Memoir of Broadway and Hollywood* (2000), as "those unremembered hundreds." He would eventually form a relationship with former actor Tom Hatcher that lasted for 52 years.

Laurents's first stage play, *Home of the Brave*, was produced in 1945, and its sale to a film studio led to his becoming a Hollywood screenwriter. He would be hired by Alfred Hitchcock to Americanize the British play *Rope* for the screen and, given the censorship code at the time, make the audience aware that the three main characters were gay men without blatantly saying so. The film starred Farley Granger, his lover at the time. Although he became a successful and sought-after screenwriter, his Hollywood career was suspended in the late 1940s when he was accused of Communist sympathies (largely on the basis of his first play being reviewed in the *Daily Worker*) and blacklisted for several years.

One of Laurents's most significant achievements is his work on the musical *West Side Story* (1957), for which he wrote the book. Collaborating with composer Leonard Bernstein, lyricist Stephen Sondheim, and choreographer Jerome Robbins, he helped create a groundbreaking production. The musical's critical and commercial success cemented his reputation as a masterful storyteller. Another notable work is *Gypsy* (1959), for which he again teamed up with Sondheim and Robbins, crafting a compelling narrative about the life of a vaudeville performer and her ambitious mother.

In the 1960s, Laurents was active as a Broadway director of such musicals as *I Can Get It for You Wholesale* (1962), the Broadway debut of Barbra Streisand, and

Hallelujah Baby! (1968), winning him the first of his three Tony awards. In 1983, he directed *La Cage aux Folles*, the stage production of a book by Harvey Fierstein about a gay couple who manage and perform in a Saint-Tropez nightclub. *La Cage* broke barriers for gay representation, becoming the first hit Broadway musical to be centered on a gay relationship. It was by far the greatest success of his career, running for over four years and winning him the Tony Award for Best Direction of a Musical. His final Broadway musical, *Nick & Nora* (1991), closed after only nine performances; he confessed that it was "the biggest and most public flop of my career." None of the original plays that he wrote over the next two decades—*The Radical Mystique* (1995), *Attacks on the Heart* (2003), *New Year's Eve* (2009), and *Come Back, Come Back, Wherever You Are* (2009)—made it to Broadway. In addition to *Original Story By*, he published a second book looking back on his long life and career, titled *Mainly on Directing: Gypsy, West Side Story and Other Musicals* (2009). The third memoir in the trilogy, titled *The Rest of the Story*, was published posthumously in 2012.

Eva Le Gallienne (1899–1991)

Actor, Theater Manager

Eva Le Gallienne was one of the most dominating figures of the 20th-century American stage. Dedicated to the art of the theater and a proponent of accessible and affordable quality theater for everyone, she opposed the crass, show business commercialism of Broadway and became one of the pioneering figures credited with launching the Off-Broadway and regional theater movement that would lead to the formation of some of the most renowned regional theater companies in the United States. She was openly lesbian at a time when openness was rare.

Le Gallienne was born in London, the daughter of poet and journalist Richard Le Gallienne and Julie Nørregard, a Danish journalist. Her parents divorced when she was 4 years old, and she and her mother moved to Paris. As a young girl, she saw Sarah Bernhardt act, and the experience would lead to her future acting career. In 1914, she made her stage debut in a walk-on role in the Maurice Maeterlinck play *Monna Vanna* in London and attended Tree's Academy, a drama school (later the Royal Academy of Dramatic Art) for a few months. She left school after she was cast in the role of a cockney servant in a minor comedy titled *The Laughter of Fools*, in which she received rave reviews for her role as a cockney servant. On the strength of the reviews, she and her mother left wartime London in 1915 for New York, where she struggled to establish herself onstage.

In 1920, after appearing in bit parts, performing in summer stock productions, and traveling in Europe for a time, Le Gallienne won her first starring role in Arthur Richman's play *Not so Long Ago* and, the following year, attained stardom with her role as Julie in Ferenc Molnar's *Liliom*, the play on which the musical *Carousel* was based. Her status as a star was assured after she played the lead in Molnar's *The Swan* in 1923. She became a naturalized American citizen in 1927. During the 1920s, "Miss Le G," as she was known to her colleagues in the theater, realized her dream of creating an American classical repertory theater like the Old Vic, the Comédie Française, and the Moscow Art Theatre. In 1926, she abandoned her Broadway career to found the Civic Repertory Theatre in New York City, which aimed to bring affordable, high-quality productions to a broader audience. Under her leadership, the theater produced works by such playwrights as Henrik Ibsen, Anton Chekhov, and George Bernard Shaw. Despite financial struggles, the Civic Repertory Theatre became a beacon of noncommercial theater, and her innovative approach left a lasting impact on American stagecraft. The Civic Repertory Theatre lasted for six seasons and featured her appearing in most of its plays, including the title character in *Peter Pan* and the White Queen in an adaptation of *Alice in Wonderland.* Added financial difficulties during the Great Depression forced the theater to close in 1934 after giving 1,581 performances of 34 plays, 32 of which she also directed. In 1946, Le Gallienne, with director Margaret Webster and producer Cheryl Crawford, cofounded the American Repertory Theater, which operated until 1948.

Le Gallienne's relationships with women, including Margaret Webster, silent screen star Alla Nazimova, and writer Mercedes de Acosta, were known within artistic circles. In 1934, she met actress Marion Evensen, and the two became life partners, sharing a home in Weston, Connecticut, until Evensen's death in 1971. Her openness and refusal to hide her sexual orientation made her an early icon of the LGBTQ+ arts community.

La Gallienne performed in films and on television from 1948 to 1984. In addition to her work as an actress and director, she was the author of two autobiographies, a children's book, *Flossie and Bossie* (1949), and *The Mystic in the Theatre* (1973), an analysis of the great 19th- and early 20th-century Italian tragedienne Eleanora Duse. She translated and adapted several plays, most notably Henrik Ibsen's works, and her translations are still used today. Her dedication to theater earned her numerous accolades, including a Special Tony Award in 1964 in recognition of her half century as a working actor, a Tony for her performance in a 1976 revival of the play *The Royal Family*, and an Emmy Award for the televised version of the play in 1977. In 1986, she received a National Medal of Arts, the highest honor given to artists by the U.S. government, recognizing her lifelong contributions to the arts.

Annie Leibovitz (1949–)

Photographer

Photographer Anna-Lou "Annie" Leibovitz is renowned for her capacity to infuse her portraits with emotion, depth, and meaning. Her lens has immortalized cultural luminaries and political icons, transforming mere photographs into timeless works of art that resonate across generations. From her groundbreaking contributions to *Rolling Stone* magazine in the 1970s to her iconic covers for *Vanity Fair* and *Vogue*, she has continually pushed the boundaries of photography, leaving an indelible mark on the medium and cementing her status as one of its foremost practitioners.

Leibovitz was born in Waterbury, Connecticut, and raised by her father, a lieutenant colonel in the U.S. Air Force, and her modern dance instructor mother. The family moved often and were living in the Philippines in 1967 when she enrolled in the San Francisco Art Institute to become a painter. She earned her BFA in 1971. After taking a night class in photography, she developed a passion for the medium and, while still a student in 1970, was given her first commercial assignment for *Rolling Stone* magazine: to photograph John Lennon. By 1973, she became the magazine's chief photographer, a position she would hold for the next decade. While with *Rolling Stone,* she developed her trademark technique of using bold, primary colors and surprising poses, and her famous cover photos helped to define the *Rolling Stone* look.

In 1983, Leibovitz left *Rolling Stone* to work for *Vanity Fair*, and her work included portraits of a nude, pregnant Demi Moore; Whoopi Goldberg half submerged in a bathtub of milk; a nude Sylvester Stallone in a pose inspired by Rodin's *The Thinker*; and Caitlyn Jenner in a corset after having publicly revealed her identity as a woman. In 1991, her collection of more than 200 photographs was exhibited at the National Portrait Gallery in Washington, D.C., the first woman to be so honored. In 1999, she published the book *Women*, which featured an array of female images from Supreme Court justices to Vegas showgirls to coal miners and farmers. It included an essay from her romantic partner, Susan Sontag. During Sontag's life (she died in 2004), neither one publicly disclosed that their friendship was sexual. However, when interviewed for her autobiography, *A Photographer's Life: 1990–2005* (2006), Leibovitz described her relationship with Sontag as a "love story" and, in 2009, confirmed that the descriptor "lover" was accurate: "Call us 'lovers.' I like 'lovers.' You know, 'lovers' sounds romantic. I mean, I want to be perfectly clear. I love Susan."

Leibovitz has three daughters. She gave birth to her first in 2001, when she was 52 years old. Twin girls were born to a surrogate mother in 2005. Secure in her reputation as one of the greatest contemporary portrait photographers ever, she has immortalized some of the most iconic figures of the 20th and 21st centuries from cultural icons like John Lennon and Yoko Ono to political figures such as Barack Obama and Queen Elizabeth II. When the cultural history of the last 50 years is studied, many of the most famous images of the era will be through her lens.

J. C. Leyendecker (1874–1951)

Illustrator

One of the few openly gay artists working in the early 20th century, Joseph Christian "J. C." Leyendecker was one of the most prominent American illustrators of the early 20th century and was known for his distinctive style and significant contributions to magazine and advertising art. His work, particularly his covers for *The Saturday Evening Post* and advertisements for brands like Arrow, defined the visual culture of his era. His ability to capture the essence of American life with elegance and sophistication made him a trailblazer in commercial art and illustration.

Leyendecker was born in Montabaur, Germany. His family immigrated to the United States in 1882, settling in Chicago. He displayed an artistic talent from a young age, studying at the Chicago Art Institute. In 1895, some of his posters were exhibited at a Chicago department store. He further honed his skills at the Académie Julian in Paris, where he was influenced by the European art scene, won four awards at the academy, and in 1897 had one of his paintings, *Portrait of My Brother*, exhibited at the prestigious Paris Salon. Upon returning to the United States, he and his brother, Frank, also an artist, moved to New York City to pursue their careers. He quickly made a name for himself with his illustrations for *The Century Magazine* and *Collier's Weekly*. He is best known for his work with *The Saturday Evening Post*, for which he created over 300 covers between 1899 and 1943. His most iconic creation, the Arrow Collar Man, became a cultural icon of the 1920s, epitomizing the ideal of American masculinity and style. His mastery of visual storytelling and his ability to capture contemporary fashions and trends made his work highly sought-after by advertisers and publishers. His holiday-themed covers, particularly those featuring New Year's babies, also became widely celebrated. His influence extended to other illustrators, including Norman Rockwell, who considered him a mentor and inspiration.

During the 1930s, Cluett Peabody & Company, the manufacturers of Arrow shirts, stopped using Leyendecker's illustrations in its advertisements, and his commissions for *The Saturday Evening Post*, along with new commissions, significantly declined. During World War II, he painted military recruitment and war bonds posters for the U.S. Department of War.

Although no surviving declaration exists from Leyendecker concerning his sexual orientation, historians have concluded from their research on his life and times that he was gay. He openly lived in New Rochelle, New York, with his partner, Charles Beach (1881–1954), who frequently appeared in his illustrations and served as the model for the Arrow Collar Man. The couple's nearly 50-year relationship was discreet but an open secret among their contemporaries. After his death, his estate, including his house, furnishings, and paintings, were divided between Beach and his sister, Augusta Mary. Rather than burning the paintings, as Leyendecker had directed in his will, Beach sold them at a yard sale. After his sister's death, Leyendecker's advertisements for Kellogg's cereals, as well as other family memorabilia, became the property of the Haggin Museum in Stockton, California.

Liberace (1919–1987)

Pianist, Entertainer

Liberace remains an enduring icon of American popular culture, celebrated for his extravagant performances and pioneering showmanship. With his dazzling stage presence and virtuosic piano skills, he captivated audiences around the world. With his larger-than-life persona and unapologetic embrace of opulence and excess, he set the standard for showmanship in the mid-20th century. His significance lies not only in his musical contributions but also in his role as a cultural trailblazer, challenging societal norms and paving the way for LGBTQ+ visibility in mainstream media.

Born Władziu Valentino Liberace in West Allis, Wisconsin, to Polish and Italian immigrants, Liberace, whose friends called him Lee, was the son of a grocer who played the French horn in John Philip Sousa's concert band. His mother played the piano, and he began piano lessons when he was four years old. He began his studies at Wisconsin College of Music when he was seven. As a teenager, he played the piano in silent-movie houses as "Walter Busterkeys" and at a cocktail lounge when he was 14. He appeared as a soloist in 1936 with the Chicago Symphony Orchestra at the age of 16.

In 1939 at a classical recital, the audience called out for Liberace to play the popular novelty song "Three Little Fishes," which he did to thunderous applause. This break with concert tradition—mixing the popular with classical—would provide him with the formula for his career. A virtuoso in many styles, he would mix popular music with classical works, specializing in what he called "*Reader's Digest* versions" of familiar melodies, "cutting out the dull parts." In 1952, while playing the Hollywood Bowl, he put on a set of white tails, "so they could see me in the back row." He added a gold lamé jacket in Las Vegas. When he noticed that his concert bookings and income declined when he switched back to traditional suits, he reinstated his over-the-top, sequined wardrobe and added his trademark candelabra to complete the look.

Liberace's real career breakthrough came in 1951 with the television premiere of *The Liberace Show*, which first aired locally in Los Angeles before going national a few years later. At its height during its run from 1952 to 1955, the show attracted 35 million viewers and was syndicated to more television stations than broadcast *I Love Lucy*. His largely female audience was entranced by his piano prowess, his cherubic charm, and his devotion to his mother, Frances. His brother, George, played the violin and served as his orchestral arranger. He became television's first matinee idol and the highest-earning entertainer of the 1950s and 1960s, outpacing both Elvis Presley and Frank Sinatra.

Liberace took up a decades-long residence in Las Vegas, becoming one of the city's most popular performers and one of its top-paid stars. Often derided for his showmanship, he famously quipped after one particularly caustic review, "My manager and I laughed all the way to the bank." To maintain his overwhelmingly female fanbase, he consistently denied allegations that he was gay. He famously sued the British *Daily Mirror* in 1959 and swore under oath that he was neither gay nor ever taken part in homosexual activity. The jury ruled in his favor. In 1985, it was alleged that he was diagnosed with HIV, which he denied. Eventually, after his death at the age of 67, it was revealed that, indeed, AIDS was responsible, and several of his closest friends, such as actress Betty White, publicly acknowledged his homosexuality.

The HBO biopic *Behind the Candelabra* (2013) depicted the affair between Liberace and Scott Thorson, his former chauffeur and younger lover. When Liberace ended their relationship, Thorson attempted to sue him in the first same-sex palimony case in U.S. history. The judge dismissed the claim, but Liberace settled anyway. His motto was "too much of a good thing is wonderful," which he fully embodied both in his showmanship and his lifestyle. Perhaps his most important legacy was his willingness to lean into a flamboyancy for which he was bullied as a child and make it a trademark that, in turn, made him a popular entertainer, a trailblazer for LGBTQ+ visibility in mainstream media, and a gay icon.

Little Richard (1932–2020)

Singer, Songwriter

Little Richard, often hailed as the "architect of rock and roll," revolutionized the music industry with his electrifying performances and flamboyant style. His pioneering work in the 1950s laid the foundation for rock and roll, influencing countless artists and shaping the genre's future. His unique blend of rhythm and blues, gospel, and boogie-woogie, combined with his high-energy stage presence, made him an enduring icon in the world of music.

Born Richard Wayne Penniman in Macon, Georgia, Little Richard was one of 12 children in a deeply religious family. He developed a love for music early on, singing in church choirs and listening to gospel music. His formal education was limited, but his musical education thrived through church and local performances. He left home at a young age to pursue a career in music, performing with various bands and developing his unique sound. His breakthrough came in 1955 when he recorded "Tutti Frutti," a song that catapulted him to fame and established his place in rock and roll history.

Early rock and roll was distinctly macho music, but Little Richard, who had performed in drag as a teenager, challenged the convention by appearing gaudily dressed, with his hair teased into a pompadour and wearing makeup. In later years, he was given to saying that if Elvis Presley was the king of rock and roll, then he was its queen. Offstage, he characterized himself variously as gay, bisexual, and "omnisexual."

Little Richard's career was marked by a series of groundbreaking achievements and iconic songs. His hits, including "Long Tall Sally," "Good Golly, Miss Molly," and "Lucille," became anthems of the rock and roll era. His dynamic piano playing, powerful voice, and charismatic performance style set him apart from his contemporaries. His influence extended beyond music; he broke racial barriers in a segregated America by attracting diverse audiences and paving the way for future African American artists. In addition to his musical success, he appeared in films and television shows, further solidifying his status as a cultural icon.

At the height of his fame in 1957, Little Richard walked away from rock and roll. He recalled thinking at the time, "I'm through. I am leaving show business to go back to God." He entered Oakwood College in Huntsville, Alabama, a Seventh-day Adventist school, to study for the ministry. He became a traveling evangelist, cutting his hair, getting married, and recording gospel music. He was lured back to the stage, however, in 1962, having been rediscovered by British bands. He performed in England, France, and Germany, with the Beatles and the Rolling Stones as his opening acts. He toured the United States with a band that included Jimi Hendrix on guitar. By 1977, saying he "lost my reasoning" due to alcohol and cocaine, he left the rock scene again to become a Bible salesman and disappeared from the spotlight. By the 1980s, however, he was back, performing to great acclaim, until his retirement in 2013.

Little Richard's personal life was as colorful and complex as his music. He was openly gay but often discussed his struggles with his sexuality and religious beliefs. In 1995, he declared, "I've been gay all my life and I know God is a God of love, not hate." In 2012, he said, "We are all both male and female. Sex to me is like a smorgasbord. Whatever I feel like, I go for." However, in 2017, he denounced both homosexuality and transgender identity as unnatural and ungodly. Despite these contradictions, he remained a fierce advocate for self-expression and individuality, influencing not only musicians but also serving as an inspiration to many in the LGBTQ+ community.

Audre Lorde (1934–1992)

Poet, Essayist

Self-identified as "Black, lesbian, mother, warrior, poet," Audrey Geraldine Lorde (who would later drop the "y" from her first name) was both one of the principal lesbian literary figures of the 20th century and one of the most important Black female voices in her poetry and essays. Throughout her 17 volumes of poetry, essays, and autobiography, she was a relentless opponent of racism and sexual prejudice and served as an oppositional figure as a Black feminist and a lesbian within the civil rights movement.

Lorde was born in Harlem, New York, to parents who had emigrated from Grenada. She was fascinated by poetry from a young age. "I used to speak in poetry," she recalled. "When I couldn't find the poems to express the things I was feeling, that's what started me writing poetry." She graduated from Hunter High School, where she edited its literary magazine. After an English teacher rejected one of her poems, she submitted it to *Seventeen* magazine, and it became her first professional publication. She earned her bachelor's degree from Hunter College and a master's degree in library science from Columbia. She worked as a librarian in New York City public schools from 1961 to 1968. In 1962, she married Edwin Rollins, a white, gay man, and they had two children before divorcing in 1970.

Lorde published her first volume of poetry, *The First Cities*, in 1968, the same year she became a writer in residence at Tougaloo College in Mississippi. There, she met Frances Clayton, a professor of psychology who became her partner until 1989. *Cables to Rage* (1970) explored her anger at social and personal injustice and contained her first poetic expression of her lesbianism. Subsequent collections include *From a Land Where Other People Live* (1973) and *New York Head Shop and Museum* (1974). In *The Black Unicorn* (1978), which many consider her greatest achievement, she turned from the urban themes of her early work to explore her role as a mother and daughter. *A Burst of Light* (1988) detailed her struggle with cancer and won an American Book Award. She also wrote a novel, *Zami: A New Spelling of My Name* (1982). After the collection *Undersong: Chosen Poems Old and New* (1992), her last volume of poetry,

The Marvelous Arithmetics of Distance, was published posthumously in 1993.

In 1984, Lorde published *Sister Outsider,* which included her seminal essay, "The Master's Tools Will Never Dismantle the Master's House." In it, she urges white feminists to confront racism and other forms of oppression and to celebrate difference. Her insistence that race, gender, and sexuality were critical determinants to identity would later help to define intersectional feminism and gender studies. As activist Mary Ann Adams asserted, "[Lorde] was revolutionary in speaking and writing about the complexities of identity, including race, gender, sexuality, and class, and how these intersecting identities inform one's experiences and struggles." As Lorde herself stated, "I am not one piece of myself. I cannot be simply a Black person and not be a woman too, nor can I be a woman without being a lesbian."

Charles Ludlam (1943–1987)

Playwright, Actor, Director

An influential figure in avant-garde theater, Charles Ludlam established the Ridiculous Theatrical Company and for two decades produced, directed, wrote, and starred (in both female and male roles, often with his life partner, Everett Quinton) in plays such as *The Mystery of Irma Vep* and *The Artificial Jungle.* Renowned for drag, melodrama, parodies, and satire, he and his company were at the center of the gay and avant-garde theater scene in New York for many years. *The New York Times* called him an "iconoclast among iconoclasts…[who revolutionized] downtown New York culture in the 1970s with his gender bending and outrageous theatrical sendups long before terms like 'gender bending' were common."

Ludlam was born in Queens, New York, and raised in the Long Island town of Greenlawn. He developed a passion for the theater after seeing a Punch and Judy show at a local fair and began performing in high school productions and in community and summer stock theater. In 1964, by the time he graduated from Hofstra University with a degree in dramatic literature, he was openly gay and moved to Greenwich Village, where he would live for the rest of his life.

After initially joining John Vaccaro's Playhouse of the Ridiculous, Ludlam founded his own company, the Ridiculous Theatrical Company, in 1967. Early productions included *Conquest of the Universe, or When Queens Collide*; *Eunuchs of the Forbidden City*; *The Ventriloquist's Wife*; and *The Enchanted Pig*. A master of travesty, he based many of his works on parodies of familiar genres such as the dime novel (*The Mystery of Irma Vep*), film noir (*The Artificial Jungle*), and opera (*Camille* and *Der Ring Gott Forblonjet*). His plays satirized the art world (*Le Bourgeois Avant-Garde*), psychoanalysis (*Reverse Psychology*), the cult of celebrity (*Galas*), and playwriting itself (*How to Write a Play*).

Ludlam, who wrote 29 plays and starred in most of them, saw his female impersonation as serious acting. Although most of the performers in his company were gay, he resisted calling it "gay theater" or his work as "camp." He both mocked gay stereotypes and celebrated gayness. Long before nonbinary became a concept, he explored and exploded narrow conceptions of gender and sexual identity and lifestyles. In 1991, his best-known play, *The Mystery of Irma Vep*, became the most produced play in the United States.

Ludlam died at the age of 44, a month after he was diagnosed with AIDS. The block in front of his Sheridan Square theater was renamed Charles Ludlam Lane in his honor.

Robert Mapplethorpe (1946–1989)

Photographer

One of the most influential and controversial photographers of the 20th century,

Robert Michael Mapplethorpe challenged conventions and pushed boundaries, particularly in the realms of portraiture, still life, and the exploration of the human form. His most controversial works documented the gay male BDSM subculture in New York City in the 1960s and 1970s. His depictions of male nudes, often featuring explicit scenes of bondage and fetishism, sparked outrage and debate over issues of censorship and artistic freedom. Despite the controversy surrounding his work, he remained steadfast in his commitment to exploring themes of sexuality, desire, and the human body.

Mapplethorpe was born in Floral Park, Queens, New York. His father was an electrical engineer, and he was raised Catholic. He recalled, "I come from suburban America. It was a very safe environment, and it was a good place to come from in that it was a good place to leave." After graduating from a public high school in 1963, he attended the Pratt Institute in Brooklyn from 1963 to 1970, majoring in graphic arts, but he dropped out before finishing his degree.

During the year before his death, Mapplethorpe helped found Robert Mapplethorpe, Inc., which, since his death, has raised millions of dollars to fund medical research in the fight against AIDS and HIV infection.

From 1967 to 1972, he lived with his girlfriend, artist and musician Patti Smith, in the Chelsea Hotel. After experimenting with underground filmmaking in the late 1960s, he took his first photographs using a Polaroid camera, often arranging them into collages or showing them as series. By the mid-1970s, he gained critical attention for his elegant, black-and-white photographs of his favorite subjects: still lifes, flowers, portraits of friends and celebrities, and homoerotic explorations of the male body. His muscular male models were sometimes shown engaged in sexual activity or posed with sadomasochistic props such as leather and chains.

In 1972, Mapplethorpe met art curator Sam Wagstaff, who would become his patron and lover. Jack Fritscher, Mapplethorpe's lover from 1977 to 1980, introduced him to the Mineshaft, a members-only BDSM gay leather bar and sex club in Manhattan, where he began to grow increasingly interested in documenting the New York S&M scene. As he explained in a 1988 *ARTnews* interview, "I don't like that particular word 'shocking.' I'm looking for the unexpected. I'm looking for things I've never seen before.... I was in a position to take those pictures. I felt an obligation to do them."

As Mapplethorpe's reputation grew in the 1980s, he began to focus more on still lifes and celebrity portraits rather than overtly sexual subject matter. These included a series of portraits of female bodybuilder Lisa Lyons. His work was exhibited internationally, with major shows at the Whitney Museum of American Art in New York and the National Portrait Gallery in London. In 1986, he was diagnosed with AIDS, and he would document his decline in a series of striking images. In 1989, as he was slowly dying of AIDS complications, six museums came together to organize a touring retrospective, *The Present Moment*, in which its 175 images captured the range of his subjects over his 25-year career, including nude portraits of African American men and depictions of homosexual S&M.

Touring through Chicago and Washington, D.C., controversy began to build, and when it opened in Cincinnati, 12 policemen served him with papers claiming that he had committed a misdemeanor for displaying obscenity—the first time it had ever happened to a museum. The Contemporary Arts Center refused to remove the controversial images and challenged the charges in court. After a two-week trial, it won. Podcaster Matthew Billy explained, "The lasting legacy of that is two things. First of all, it proves that art, no matter how controversial, is actually art and is not obscenity. But it also created an incentive for museums to self-censor. The trial was very, very expensive, and they lost a lot of corporate sponsorship because of all the controversy. The Contemporary Arts Center has never had a controversial exhibit like that again."

During the year before his death, Mapplethorpe helped found Robert Mapplethorpe, Inc., which, since his death, has raised millions of dollars to fund medical research in the fight against AIDS and HIV infection. Smith, in her memoir, *Just Kids* (2010), observed about her relationship with Mapplethorpe: "Robert took areas of dark human consent and made them into art. He worked without apology, investing the homosexual with grandeur, masculinity, and enviable nobility.... He was presenting something new, something not seen or explored as he saw and explored it. Robert sought to elevate aspects of male experience, to imbue homosexuality with mysticism."

Agnes Martin (1912–2004)

Artist

Abstract expressionist Agnes Bernice Martin is noted for her meticulously crafted paintings, characterized by minimalist compositions and subtle color palettes, which redefined the boundaries of the genre. During the 1950s and 1960s, she was an integral part of a small, diverse New York City community of artists, including Jasper Johns, Robert Rauschenberg, and Ellsworth Kelly, who lived in derelict shipping lofts in Lower Manhattan and created new postwar American art. Through her work, she sought to evoke universal truths and transcendental experiences, and her innovative approach has earned her widespread acclaim, solidifying her position as a leading figure in 20th-century art.

Martin was born in Macklin, Saskatchewan, Canada, a descendant of Scottish Presbyterian pioneers. Her father was a wheat farmer who died when she was two years old. Her mother supported the family by selling real estate. With an early interest in art, she opted for the financial security of teaching and, in the 1940s, moved to New York to study art education at Teachers College, Columbia University, receiving her B.A. in 1942. While living in New York, she became interested in modern art, particularly in abstract expressionism. After graduating, she attended the University of New Mexico, where she also taught art courses, before returning to Columbia to earn her MA in 1952. She became a U.S. citizen in 1950, and in 1957, she moved into a loft in Coenties Slip in Lower Manhattan, a haven for both artists and the queer community. Although she never publicly expressed her sexuality, biographers have identified several romantic relationships between Martin and other women, including art dealer Betty Parsons (1900–1982).

Martin's relationship with Parsons was instrumental in shaping her artistic career and establishing her reputation as an abstract painter. Parsons, herself a respected artist and influential art dealer, recognized Martin's talent early on and became a supportive mentor and advocate for her work. In the 1950s, Parsons gave Martin her first solo exhibition at her gallery in New York City, providing a crucial platform for her to showcase her distinctive style of abstract painting. Throughout their partnership, Parsons continued to champion Martin's art, promoting her work to collectors and curators and helping to secure important commissions and exhibitions. Beyond their professional collaboration, they shared a deep personal bond, with Martin often crediting Parsons with providing crucial guidance and encouragement during pivotal moments in her career.

From 1957 to 1967, Martin developed her signature format: 6-by-6-foot painted canvases, covered from edge to edge with meticulously penciled grids and finished with a thin layer of gesso. Her work charted new terrain from abstract expressionism and anticipated minimalism. For her, painting was "a world without objects, without interruption…or obstacle. It is to accept the necessity of…going into a field of vision as you would cross an empty beach to look at the ocean."

In 1967 at the height of her career, suffering from the growing strain of mental illness, Martin left New York for Taos, New Mexico, where she abandoned painting and devoted herself to writing and meditation. She built an adobe house with her own hands on a remote mesa.

Martin would eventually return to painting in 1974, displaying a shift in style to display bolder geometric forms, informed by the warm palette of the desert landscape, where she remained for the rest of her life. She preferred isolation but was far from a recluse. She lectured periodically around the country and became an inspiration to younger artists such as Eva Hesse and Ellen Gallagher. Her lectures were collected in the book *Writings* (1992). She continued to paint daily even after moving into a retirement community. She was awarded a National Medal of Arts in 1998 and a Lifetime Achievement Award from the Women's Caucus for Art. She would say about her work, "People who look at my painting say that it makes them happy, like the feeling when you wake up in the morning. And happiness is the goal, isn't it?"

Marshall W. Mason (1940–)

Theater Director

Marshall W. Mason is a celebrated American theater director. As the founding artistic director of the Circle Repertory Company in New York City, his innovative direction and commitment to nurturing new plays and playwrights have solidified his legacy as a transformative figure in American theater.

Mason was born in Amarillo, Texas, and discovered his passion for theater at a young age. He attended Northwestern University, where he earned a bachelor's degree in theater in 1961. While at Northwestern, at the age of 19, he received his first award for directing a production of Tennessee Williams's *Cat on a Hot Tin Roof.* After graduating, he moved to New York City, where he began working in the Off-Off-Broadway theater movement, directing numerous productions in venues such as Caffe Cino, La MaMa Experimental Theatre Club, and the Judson Poets' Theatre. He made his Off-Broadway debut in 1964 with a revival of Henrik Ibsen's *Little Eyolf* and his Broadway debut in 1976 with Jules Feiffer's *Knock Knock.*

It was while working at La MaMa that Mason first collaborated with playwright Lanford Wilson, directing his play *Balm in Gilead* (1965). He would direct over 60 acclaimed productions of Wilson's plays, including *Talley's Folly*, which won the Pulitzer Prize for Drama in 1980. His direction brought out the depth and nuance of Wilson's characters, earning him multiple accolades, including five Tony Award nominations for Best Direction of a Play.

In 1969, Mason, Wilson, director Rob Thirkield, and actress Tanya Berezin founded the Circle Repertory Company, for which Mason was the artistic director from 1969 to 1987 as well as director of over 50 of its productions. In 1974, critic Mel Gussow praised the Circle Rep as the "chief provider of new American plays." The Circle Rep would finally close in 1994.

In addition to his theater work, Mason taught theater at Arizona State University for 10 years from 1994 to 2004. He is also the author of *Creating Life on Stage: A Director's Approach to Working with Actors* (2006) and *The Transcendent Years: Circle Repertory Company & the 1960s* (2018). In 2011, immediately following New York State's enactment of its marriage equality law, he married his partner of 37 years, theater artist Daniel Irvine.

Mason's career is a testament to his passion for theater, his dedication to artistic excellence, and his commitment to fostering new talent. His impact on the theater community continues to resonate, making him a revered figure in American theater history.

Armistead Maupin (1944–)

Writer

Armistead Maupin is an acclaimed author best known for his groundbreaking *Tales of the City* series, which revolutionized LGBTQ+ literature and captivated readers around the world with its vivid characters and vibrant portrayal of San Francisco. The series and its subsequent TV adaptations would become one of the first LGBTQ+ themed works to cross over and gain a mainstream audience.

Born in Washington, D.C., Maupin grew up in a conservative Southern family and struggled with his sexuality throughout his youth and young adulthood. "I grew up believing I was mentally ill because I was gay," he recalled in a 2019 interview with the *Guardian*. "That's what I'd been taught. My father was a racist and a homophobe, and I knew that I'd be given electro-shock therapy if I told my parents. Thank God I didn't." His solace was reading, particularly *The Hardy Boys* series. "It's no accident," he remarked, "that *Tales of the City* has short chapters with snappy little titles, just like *The Hardy Boys*."

After graduating from the University of North Carolina in 1966 and, for a short time, working at a TV station in Raleigh managed by conservative future senator Jesse Helms, Maupin joined the U.S. Navy and served as a naval officer in the Mediterranean and as a civilian volunteer in the River Patrol Force in Vietnam. He subsequently worked as a newspaper reporter in Charleston, South Carolina, and in 1970, he moved to San Francisco to work as a reporter for the Associated Press. He decided to come out as gay in 1974 or, as he said, "I didn't come out. I just refused to stay in."

In 1976, Maupin began serializing *Tales of the City* as a column in the *San Francisco Chronicle*, introducing readers to the colorful residents of 28 Barbary Lane, a fictional apartment complex in the heart of the city. The series follows the lives and loves of a diverse cast of characters, anchored by three central characters—Mary Ann Singleton, a naïve young woman from Cleveland; Michael "Mouse" Tolliver, her homosexual friend; and their motherly landlady, Anna Madrigal, a transgender woman. He explains, "The premise of *Tales of the City* is that everybody has the right to love and choose the life they want. It is about all humanity, and sometimes that gets overlooked. But I am happy to stress the queer aspect because that's where the work needs to be done." The series was eventually published as a trilogy—*Tales of the City* (1978), *More Tales of the City* (1980), and *Further Tales of the City* (1982)—as well as being the origin for a number of sequels, including *Babycakes* (1984), *Significant Others* (1987), and *Sure of You* (1989). The later adventures of his characters are chronicled in *Michael Tolliver Lives* (2007), *Mary Ann in Autumn* (2010), *The Days of Anna Madrigal* (2014), and *Mona of the Manor* (2024). Despite the overriding lighthearted humor, throughout his works, he engages with serious issues, including loneliness, parenthood, the loss of a partner to AIDS, cancer, and aging.

Maupin's other novels include *Maybe the Moon* (1992) and *The Night Listener* (2000). He also wrote his memoir, *Logical Family* (2017). He had a 12-year relationship with gay rights activist Terry Anderson. Following their breakup, he married Christopher Turner, a website producer and photographer, in 2007. In 2019, Maupin, the chronicler of San Francisco, relocated to London. "San Francisco is still the most beautiful place on Earth," he stated, "but the things that gave me joy are no longer there—the bohemian friendships, and the freedom to live on any goddamn hill you wanted. People used to have their pick of the city, but not anymore. That's all because of the tech industry." His legacy, however, as a distinctive chronicler of San Francisco and all its humanity—queer and straight—remains secure.

Terrence McNally (1938–2020)

Playwright, Screenwriter

An acclaimed playwright of gay life, Terrence McNally was the four-time Tony Award-winning author of *Love! Valour! Compassion!*, *Master Class*, and *Kiss of the Spider Woman*. He also wrote several new American operas, including *Dead Man Walking*. Many of his works introduced theater audiences to gay characters and situations that most mainstream productions either ignored or played for comedy. Asked if he saw himself as brave for such depictions, he replied, "Not at all. I saw it as: These are people.... I always felt it was O.K. to be gay in the American theater."

McNally was born in St. Petersburg, Florida, to parents who ran a seaside bar and grill. When it was destroyed in a hurricane, the family relocated first to Port Chester, New York, where he first experienced theater in New York City, then to Texas. He attended a public high school before enrolling at Columbia University in 1956. After graduating in 1960, he was hired by novelist John Steinbeck to tutor his two teenage sons when the Steinbeck family took a cruise around the world.

McNally worked as the stage manager for New York's Actors Studio productions. His earliest full-length play, *This Side of the Door*, was produced by the Actors Studio in 1962. His next play, *And Things That Go Bump in the Night* (1964), which would center on a romance between two men, opened to negative reviews and the ire of conservative theater critics. His other early plays included *Bad Habits* (1971); *The Ritz* (originally produced as *The Tubs*, 1973; film, 1976), which portrays life in a Manhattan bathhouse; and *Frankie and Johnny in the Claire de Lune* (1987; film, 1991). In 1995, he won a Tony Award for Best Play for *Love! Valour! Compassion!* (film, 1997), concerning the relationships among gay men, and another the following year for *Master Class*. His librettos for *Kiss of the Spider Woman* and *Ragtime* won him Tony awards in 1993 and 1999, respectively. In 1998, his play *Corpus Christi* caused controversy for its depiction of a Christ-like character. *Mothers and Sons* (2014) examines a mother coming to terms with her late son's homosexuality, and *Fire and Air* (2018) explores the Ballets Russes and founder Sergei Diaghilev's relationship with Vaslav Nijinsky. In 2019, he received a Tony Award for Lifetime Achievement in the Theatre.

Over his long career, McNally wrote some three dozen plays as well as the books for 10 musicals, the librettos for four operas, and several screenplays for films and television. Jesse Green and Neil Genz-linger observed in McNally's obituary in *The New York Times*, "His gay stories never came across as a narrowing of theater's human focus but an expansion of it, and by inviting everyone into them he helped solidify the social change he was describing." McNally had a five-year relationship with playwright Edward Albee in the early 1960s that ended over their differing views on how to deal with their sexuality. "Edward didn't want to be reviewed as a gay playwright," he revealed, "and was never comfortable coming out."

McNally had no such reservations. He openly had a longtime relationship with playwright Gary Bonasorte, who died of AIDS in 2000. In 2003, he was joined with theater producer and lawyer Tom Kirdahy in a civil union, and the two were married in 2010. After McNally died due to complications of COVID-19, he was eulogized by actor Audra McDonald, who said, "Terrence [was] writing about what he knew, and not only unashamed but shouting to the world, 'You need to see us for everything that we are. You need to see us fully. In. The. Flesh.' In every sense of those words. There is no greater way to proclaim 'I am what I am' than in the way Terrence did."

Edna St. Vincent Millay (1892–1950)

Poet, Playwright

One of the nation's most successful and revered poets during her distinguished career, Edna St. Vincent Millay introduced into American literature the unique aspects of women's experiences and expression as well as a frank portrayal of both heterosexual and queer relationships. She was, in the words of her biographer, Nancy Milford, "the herald of the New Woman."

Millay was born in Rockland, Maine, and was raised by her divorced mother in Camden, Maine. Her middle name was derived from St. Vincent's Hospital in New York City, where her uncle's life had been saved just before her birth. Her mother encouraged her daughter's talent in writing poetry, and her first published poem appeared in 1906, when she was a young teenager. Recognition for her work first came with the publication of "Renascence" in 1912, which brought her to the attention of a benefactor who made it possible for her to attend Vassar College, where she graduated in 1917. The same year, she published her first book, *Renascence and Other Poems*, and moved to Greenwich Village in New York City.

Millay, who went by the name "Vincent," had relationships with women before and during college and included lesbian themes in *The Lamp and the Bell*, a play she wrote and starred in as an undergraduate. In Greenwich Village, she joined the Bohemian art set, worked as an actress, was associated with the Provincetown Players and the Theatre Guild, and, in her words, was "very, very poor and very, very merry." She dated both men and women and identified as bisexual, turning down several marriage proposals. Her collection *A Few Figs from Thistles* (1920) became notorious for its frank depiction of female sexuality and empowerment. The famous line "My candle burns at both ends" from the opening poem "First Fig" came to embody the hedonism of the "flaming youth" of the 1920s and helped to foster the so-called "Millay legend" of madcap youth and rebellion. In 1923, she became the first woman and the second person ever to win the Pulitzer Prize for Poetry for her poem "Ballad of the Harp-Weaver." In 1924, literary critic Harriet Monroe called her "the greatest woman poet since Sappho."

Millay's hedonistic lifestyle began to take a toll on her health. In 1923, she married Eugen Jan Boissevain, a Dutch businessman, and the couple moved to Steepletop, an isolated house in the Berkshires near Austerlitz, New York. They had an open marriage, and Millay, who continued to have female and male lovers, would celebrate her fluid and complex love life with such love sonnets as "I, Being Born a Woman" and "What Lips My Lips Have Kissed."

During the 1930s, Millay's work took on an increasing social consciousness, writing anti-totalitarian verse, radio plays, and speeches. Her political views are reflected in the dramatic narrative *Conversation at Midnight* (1937) and in the collections *Huntsman, What Quarry?* (1939), *Make Bright the Arrows* (1940), and *Murder of Lidice* (1942).

Through much of the 1940s, she struggled with health issues and a declining reputation as modernist poetic techniques found favor over her more traditional poetic forms. A final collection of her verse appeared posthumously as *Mine the Harvest* in 1954. With the rise of second-wave feminism in the 1960s, a revived interest in her life and a renewed recognition of her work occurred. Millay, the embodiment of the New Woman earlier in the 20th century, was celebrated as a feminist icon who pioneered a new set of social and sexual possibilities for women toward the end of the century.

Kate Millett (1934–2017)

Writer, Educator

A pioneering feminist author and influential figure in the women's liberation movement, Katherine Murray "Kate" Millett is best known for her landmark 1970 book *Sexual Politics* and for exploring the concept of patriarchy as a social phenomenon and a primary cause of women's oppression. In 1970, she publicly admitted that she was a lesbian even though such an admission at the time would likely discredit her as a spokesman for the women's movement, confirming skeptics' dismissal of all liberationists as lesbians.

Millett was born in St. Paul, Minnesota, into an Irish American Catholic family. Her father, an alcoholic who abused her, abandoned the family when she was 14. Her mother worked as a teacher and as an insurance sales representative. She attended parochial schools and graduated from the University of Minnesota in 1956 with a B.A. in English. She then spent two years at St. Hilda's College, Oxford, becoming the first American woman to graduate with first-class honors.

Millett began a teaching career at the University of North Carolina but left in the middle of the semester to study art in New York. From 1961 to 1963, she studied sculpture in Japan, and during her stay in Japan, she met sculptor Fumio Yoshimura, to whom she was married from 1965 to 1985.

Returning to New York, Millett earned her doctorate in English at Columbia University while teaching at Barnard College; beginning her activism, championing student rights, women's liberation, and abortion reform; and participating in anti-war and civil rights protests. Protesting Barnard's educational focus, she was dismissed from the school in 1968. She would go on to teach at Bryn Mawr College and the University of California, Berkeley.

Originating as Millett's Ph.D. dissertation, *Sexual Politics* is considered to be a classic feminist text, the first book of feminist literary criticism, and the manifesto of second-wave feminism. A bestseller, *Sexual Politics* offered a critique of patriarchy in Western society and literature, addressing the sexism and heterosexism of writers D. H. Lawrence, Henry Miller, and Norman Mailer and contrasting their perspectives from the dissenting viewpoint of the homosexual author Jean Genet.

Millett's 1971 book *The Prostitution Papers* interprets prostitution at the core of women's condition. She followed this with three autobiographical books: *Flying* (1974), a memoir about her bisexuality and her life after the success of *Sexual Politics*; *Sita* (1977), which explored her sexuality and her lesbian lover who committed suicide; and *A.D., A Memoir* (1995). Her other books include *The Basement: Meditations on a Human Sacrifice* (1979), *Going to Iran* (1982), *The Loony-Bin Trip* (1990), *The Politics of Cruelty* (1994), and *Mother Millett* (2001).

Since 1973, Millett struggled with mental illness and was involuntarily confined in mental hospitals several times. After her divorce in 1985, she formed a 39-year relationship with photojournalist Sophie Keir, whom she later married. She was a tireless advocate on behalf of women's rights, gay liberation, mental patients, and the elderly and was recognized for her work with the Yoko Ono Lennon Courage Award for the Arts and the Lambda Literary Awards' Pioneer Award. She summarized her career by saying, "My work is about people and things in cages. It's how I view women's place in society, capital, housing for the aged and the poor."

Janet Mock (1983–)

Writer, Director

Transgender rights activist Janet Mock is best known for her 2014 memoir *Redefining Realness: My Path to Womanhood, Identity, Love & So Much More* and her work on the TV series *Pose*. In 2018, she became the first transgender woman of color to write and direct an episode of television. She is a leading voice for transgender rights and has significantly influenced media representation and awareness. Named one of *Time* magazine's 100 Most Influential People, her advocacy and storytelling have made her a trailblazer in LGBTQ+ equality and visibility.

Mock was born in Honolulu, Hawaii, and named Charles after her African American father. Her mother was of Hawaiian and European descent. She recounts in her memoir that she recalls knowing at a very young age that she was a girl born in a boy's body. In high school, she began the process of hormonal transitioning. During her first year at the University of Hawaii, Manoa, she went to Thailand to have gender reassignment surgery, choosing her new first name after Janet Jackson. She graduated from college in 2004 with a degree in fashion merchandising.

Mock moved to New York to attend New York University for a journalism degree. She earned her master's degree in 2006 and began working at *People* magazine's website, becoming a web editor. In 2011, she told her story in an article published by *Marie Claire* after learning about the many transgender children who were committing suicide. She also submitted a video to the It Gets Better public service campaign. Her rise to prominence began with the publication of her memoir, *Redefining Realness: My Path to Womanhood, Identity, Love & So Much More*, in 2014. The book became a *New York Times* bestseller and was widely praised for its honest and poignant portrayal of her life as a transgender woman.

A second memoir, *Surpassing Certainty: What My Twenties Taught Me*, was published in 2017, further exploring her experiences and journey. Her memoirs not only provided visibility to transgender narratives but also challenged societal perceptions and inspired many within and outside the LGBTQ+ community.

In addition to her literary success, Mock has made significant contributions in the media and print. She produced the HBO documentary *The Trans List*, created the *Allure* magazine column "Beauty Beyond Binaries," and served as a correspondent for *Entertainment Tonight* and a host for MSNBC. She has written and directed episodes of the groundbreaking FX series *Pose*, which centers on the African American and Latino LGBTQ+ Ballroom culture in New York City during the 1980s and 1990s.

Her initial script, "Love Is the Message," made her the first trans woman of color to write and direct a television episode. Her work on *Pose* has earned her critical acclaim and multiple awards, including the prestigious Peabody Award. Signing a multi-million-dollar contract with Netflix in 2021, she became the first openly transgender woman of color to sign a deal with a major content company.

By bringing authentic transgender stories to the screen and print, Mock has played a crucial role in advancing representation and inclusivity in the entertainment industry. As an advocate, she has been a vocal proponent of transgender rights and social justice, using her platform to address issues such as discrimination, violence, and inequality faced by the transgender community.

Ryan Murphy (1965–)

Television Writer, Producer, Director

A prolific creator and director of such groundbreaking popular television series as *Nip/Tuck* (2003–2010), *Glee* (2009–2015), *American Horror Story* (2011–), and the *9-1-1* series, beginning with *9-1-1* (2018–) and, more recently, *9-1-1 Nashville*, which debuted in 2025, Ryan Patrick Murphy is also notable for the Netflix series *Ratched* (2020–2022) and for directing the films *Running with Scissors* (2006), *Eat, Pray, Love* (2010), a film adaptation of Larry Kramer's play *The Normal Heart* (2014), and the musical *The Prom* (2020). He has received six Emmy awards, a Tony Award for the Broadway revival of *The Boys in the Band* (2019), and two Grammys.

Born in Indianapolis, Indiana, Murphy was raised in a Catholic household. His mother was a writer who worked in communications, and his father was a newspaper circulation director. He attended Catholic school through 8th grade before transferring to public high school, and at the age of 15, he came out as gay. During a 2012 interview on Bravo TV's *Inside the Actors Studio*, he told host James Lipton that he had secretly dated "a lot of football players" in high school. He went on to attend Indiana University, where he sang with the Singing Hoosiers vocal group and graduated with a degree in journalism. He began his career as a journalist, writing for such publications as the *Miami Herald*, the *Los Angeles Times*, *Entertainment Weekly*, and the *Daily News*. He began screenwriting in the 1990s, selling his first script, *Why Can't I Be Audrey Hepburn?*, to Steven Spielberg. He then attracted attention as the cocreator of *Popular* (1999–2001), a cult-favorite teen comedy–drama. After his company, Ryan Murphy Productions, signed a deal with Warner Bros. Television, he created and directed the FX series *Nip/Tuck*, which earned him his first Emmy Award for Outstanding Directing for a Drama Series. In 2018, he negotiated another high-profile deal, this time with Netflix, for $300 million, one of the most lucrative deals in TV history.

During his television career, Murphy, who helped to reinvent the anthology format for the 21st century, has actively championed LGBTQ+ narratives in mainstream entertainment and worked to promote greater diversity and inclusivity in Hollywood. To that end, he founded the Half Initiative in 2018, a mentorship and education program aimed at creating equal opportunities for women and minorities behind the camera. The same year, he was a cocreator of the acclaimed series *Pose* (2018–2021), which centered on New York City Black and Latinx Ballroom culture in 1987 and featured the largest transgender cast ever assembled for a scripted series.

Murphy has been married to photographer David Miller since 2012, and the couple has three children.

Lesléa Newman (1955–)

Author

Lesléa Newman's prolific body of work has made significant contributions to the representation of LGBTQ+ themes. Her groundbreaking children's book *Heather Has Two Mommies* (1989), one of the first to depict a family with same-sex parents, sparked both widespread acclaim and controversy. With a career spanning several decades, her writing has touched on issues of identity, acceptance, and love, making her an influential voice in contemporary literature.

Born Leslie Newman in Brooklyn, New York, to Jewish parents (her pen name combines her birth name with her Hebrew name), she started writing poems when she was 8 years old to cope with her sadness when her family moved to Long Island and continued her writing interest as a teenager, competing in poetry contests sponsored by *Seventeen* magazine. She pursued her interest academically in 1973 at the University of Vermont and earned an MFA in writing from the Vermont College of Fine Arts in 1981. She also worked with Allen Ginsberg on poetry at the Naropa Institute. While she has written poetry, fiction, and nonfiction, she said that poetry has always been her first love as a writer. She came out as a lesbian in the early 1980s and was determined to write stories and poems that reflected the lives of LGBTQ+ individuals.

Newman published the groundbreaking children's book *Heather Has Two Mommies* in 1989, one of the first children's books to portray a happy, same-sex couple raising a child. It played a crucial role in promoting LGBTQ+ visibility and acceptance in children's literature. In addition to her work for children, she has authored numerous books for adults, including *The Reluctant Daughter* (2009) and *I Carry My Mother* (2015), a poignant collection of poems exploring grief and loss. Her works have earned multiple awards, including the Stonewall Book Award and the Golden Crown Literary Society Award.

Newman's poetry collections, such as *October Mourning: A Song for Matthew Shepard*, offer moving reflections on hate crimes and the need for tolerance. Additionally, *The Best Short Stories by Lesléa Newman* showcases her versatility and deep empathy for the LGBTQ+ experience. Her award-winning collection of short stories *A Letter to Harvey Milk* (2004) was adapted to stage and film. Her work is significant not only for its literary quality but also for its contributions to LGBTQ+ representation, gender diversity, and the exploration of emotional landscapes, making her a key figure in contemporary literature.

Newman lives in Holyoke, Massachusetts, with her wife, Mary Vazquez, whom she describes as "a Puerto Rican ex-nun." They solemnized their relationship in a "commitzvah" ceremony in 1989, before gay marriage was legally recognized. Newman observed, "The LGBTQ+ community is my home. It is my obligation, responsibility, and honor to do what I can to repair the world and make it a safe place for all of us." She has called her writing goal to allow "out, proud, Jewish lesbians…and others like me [to] see ourselves in a piece of literature."

Cynthia Nixon (1966–)

Actor, Activist

Cynthia Ellen Nixon is an acclaimed American actress best known for her role as Miranda Hobbes on the hit HBO series *Sex and the City*. She has also made significant contributions as an advocate for education, LGBTQ+ rights, and various social justice issues. In 2018, she ran for governor of New York, demonstrating her commitment to public service and political activism.

Nixon was born in New York City. Raised by her mother, Anne Knoll, a working actress, she was introduced to the world of theater and acting at an early age. She attended Hunter College High School and later graduated from Barnard College with a degree in English. She began her acting career as a child, appearing in commercials and theater productions. She made her Broadway debut in the 1980 revival of *The Philadelphia Story* and quickly established herself as a talented stage actress in such Broadway productions as *The Real Thing* (1983), *Hurlyburly* (1984), and *Angels in America* (1993). On film, she appeared in *Amadeus* (1984).

Nixon's breakthrough role came in 1998 when she was cast as lawyer Miranda Hobbes in *Sex and the City*. The series, which ran until 2004, became a cultural phenomenon and earned her a Primetime Emmy Award for Outstanding Supporting Actress in a Comedy Series in 2004. In 2006, she won a Tony Award for Best Performance by a Featured Actress in a Play for *Rabbit Hole.* She appeared in the 2017 revival of *The Little Foxes,* for which she won a second Tony for Best Performance by a Featured Actress in a Play. Film work has included *James White* (2015) and *A Quiet Passion* (2017), in which she portrayed poet Emily Dickinson.

In 2018, Nixon announced her candidacy for governor of New York, challenging incumbent Andrew Cuomo in the Democratic primary. Her campaign focused on issues such as educational reform, income inequality, and health care. Although she did not win the primary, her campaign brought significant attention to these issues and demonstrated her commitment to public service and advocacy.

Nixon has been open about her sexuality and is a prominent figure in the LGBTQ+ community. Regarding her sexual orientation, she stated in 2007, "I don't really feel I've changed. I'd been with men all my life, and I'd never fallen in love with a woman. But when I did, it didn't seem strange. I'm just a woman in love with another woman." She identified as bisexual in 2012 and as queer in 2018. She married education activist Christine Marinoni in 2012, and the couple has one son together. She also has two children from her previous relationship with photographer Danny Mozes.

Nixon's diverse career as an actress, activist, and politician reflects her dedication to both her craft and the causes she believes in. Her work continues to inspire and impact many both within the entertainment industry and beyond.

Richard Bruce Nugent (1906–1987)

Writer, Painter, Actor

Richard Bruce Nugent was an influential writer, painter, and actor whose contributions to the Harlem Renaissance were groundbreaking, particularly in his open exploration of LGBTQ+ themes. His work challenged societal norms and provided a bold and unique voice within the cultural movement. His artistic endeavors across various mediums have left an enduring legacy in American literature and art.

Nugent was born in Washington, D.C. Raised in a middle-class family, he showed an early interest in the arts, often drawing and writing poetry. He moved to Harlem in the 1920s, where he quickly became involved in the burgeoning cultural scene. He did not pursue formal higher education but instead immersed himself in the vibrant artistic community, where he befriended notable figures such as Langston Hughes, Zora Neale Hurston, and Wallace Thurman.

Nugent's most notable achievement is his short story "Smoke, Lilies, and Jade" (1926), published in Thurman's groundbreaking anthology *Fire!!* This work is significant for its explicit exploration of homosexuality, making it one of the first published works by an African American to openly address same-sex desire. He was also a talented painter, and his visual art, characterized by its bold use of color and form, was exhibited alongside his literary works.

He contributed to several key publications of the Harlem Renaissance, including *Opportunity* and *The Crisis,* and was involved in the theater, acting in and producing plays that showcased his multifaceted talent.

Nugent was also a talented painter, and his visual art played a crucial role in his overall artistic expression. His paintings, often characterized by vibrant colors and dynamic forms, explored themes of identity, beauty, and the human experience. His contributions to exhibitions alongside other Harlem Renaissance artists helped to push the boundaries of African American art. His visual art is significant for its integration with his literary themes and its role in expanding the artistic horizons of the Harlem Renaissance.

Nugent complemented his literary and artistic endeavors with acting and dancing. One of his most notable acting roles was in the 1929 Broadway production of *Porgy* by DuBose and Dorothy Heyward, in which he had a nonspeaking part. This production was significant, as it showcased African American performers internationally, including a cast performance in London. He also appeared as a dancer in the play *Run, Little Chillun* in 1933, a production that combined drama with African American spirituals and dance. Additionally, he was a member of Wilson William's Negro Ballet Company in the 1940s, contributing to the development of African American dance. In later years, he was featured in the 1984 documentary *Before Stonewall,* which explored the history of the LGBTQ+ community before the famous Stonewall riots, highlighting his role in the Harlem Renaissance and influence as one of the few openly gay artists of that time.

Nugent was openly gay, a rarity for his time, and this openness was reflected in both his life and work. He lived authentically despite the societal pressures and prejudices of the early 20th century. His relationships and personal experiences deeply influenced his art, allowing him to create work that was both personal and revolutionary. His candid exploration of LGBTQ+ themes provided a voice for a marginalized community within the African American cultural movement and paved the way for future generations of artists.

Rosie O'Donnell (1962–)

Entertainer, Actor

Rosie O'Donnell is a multifaceted entertainer and LGBTQ+ activist whose work

spans television, film, and theater. Known for her sharp wit, vibrant personality, and candidness, she has left an indelible mark on the entertainment industry. Her contributions extend beyond entertainment: She has been a passionate advocate for LGBTQ+ rights, children's health, and a variety of other social causes. Her career, marked by both critical acclaim and controversy, exemplifies her ability to resonate with diverse audiences and address important societal issues.

O'Donnell was born in Commack, New York, on Long Island. She experienced a challenging childhood, marked by the loss of her mother to cancer when she was just 10 years old. This tragedy deeply influenced her and later fueled her philanthropic efforts. She attended Dickinson College and later transferred to Boston University before dropping out to pursue a career in comedy. Her breakthrough came in the mid-1980s when she began performing stand-up comedy, which eventually led to appearances on the television show *Star Search,* propelling her into the national spotlight.

O'Donnell's career soared in the 1990s with her eponymous daytime talk show, *The Rosie O'Donnell Show,* which aired from 1996 to 2002. The show was a popular and critical success, earning multiple Emmy awards and cementing her status as the "queen of nice." Beyond her talk show, she has had a successful acting career, with notable roles in films such as *A League of Their Own* (1992), *Sleepless in Seattle* (1993), and *The Flintstones* (1994). She has also been involved in the theater, earning a Tony Award for producing the musical *Thoroughly Modern Millie*. Her return to television as a cohost on *The View* in the mid-2000s and her various hosting gigs further showcased her versatility and enduring appeal.

O'Donnell is an openly gay woman who has been a prominent advocate for

LGBTQ+ rights. She publicly came out in 2002, a bold move that brought significant attention to LGBTQ+ issues and rights. She has been married twice; her first marriage to Kelli Carpenter in 2004 ended in 2007, and in 2012, she married Michelle Rounds, with whom she adopted a daughter before their separation in 2015. She is a mother to five children and has been open about her struggles and triumphs in balancing her personal and professional life. Her honesty about her mental health challenges, including depression, has further endeared her to fans and advocates.

Frank O'Hara (1926–1966)

Poet, Art Critic

When Francis Russell "Frank" O'Hara died in 1966, *The New York Times*'s headline to his obituary announced, "Frank O'Hara, 40, Museum Curator; Exhibitions Aide at Modern Art Dies—Also a Poet." Posterity would reverse this afterthought to establish him as a centrally important poet of the post–World War II era who was also a museum curator. His poetry is often associated with the New York School, a movement characterized by its embrace of spontaneity, collaboration, and the blending of high and low culture. His poems are marked by their immediacy and intimacy, often capturing the rhythm and energy of urban life. He drew inspiration from his daily experiences, infusing his work with references to popular culture, jazz music, and the bustling streets of Manhattan.

Born in Baltimore, Maryland, O'Hara's family moved to Grafton, Massachusetts, at an early age. He was a serious music student who aspired to become a concert pianist. After serving aboard a destroyer in the South Pacific during World War II, he entered Harvard, changing his major from music to English and deciding to become a writer. After graduating in 1950, he earned an MA from the University of Michigan (1951) and moved to New York City, eventually sharing an apartment with fellow poet Joe LeSueur, who would become his sometime lover for the next 11 years. Immersing himself in New York's art and literary scene, he began to write reviews and art criticism for *ARTnews*. He established a long relationship with the Museum of Modern Art, first as a clerk at the information and sales desk and then becoming an assistant curator and associate curator of painting and sculpture in 1965.

Despite his involvement in art, O'Hara considered himself primarily as a poet. His first published volume was *A City Winter and Other Poems* (1952). His most celebrated collections are *Meditations in an Emergency* (1957) and *Lunch Poems* (1964). His poetry was a record of his life and a chronicle of the creative act that produces poems. Drawing on quotations, gossip, phone numbers, and commercials, he also drew inspiration from nonliterary sources, including free-form jazz and the abstract paintings of acquaintances such as Jackson Pollock and Larry River, whose work he championed in his art criticism.

O'Hara's identity as a gay man was an integral aspect of his work, although it wasn't always overtly acknowledged during his lifetime due to the social and cultural constraints of the era. While he didn't explicitly address his sexuality in all of his poetry, it often found expression through subtle references, coded language, and through his relationships with other artists and writers in the queer community. His exploration of homosexuality is most explicit in certain poems in which he directly addresses themes of desire, love, and identity. One of his most renowned works in this regard is "Homosexuality," a poem that unabashedly celebrates queer desire and intimacy. In this poem, he reflects on the joys and complexities of gay love, rejecting societal norms and embracing his sexuality with pride and defiance. Another notable poem is "A Step Away from Them," in which he paints a vivid portrait of New York City's gay subculture, capturing the energy and sensuality of urban life through the lens of the queer experience. Additionally, his collection *Lunch Poems* includes several poems that touch upon his homosexuality but often indirectly. For instance, "Poem (Lana Turner has collapsed!)" hints at queer desire amid references to Hollywood glamour and celebrity culture. Similarly, "Poem (The eager note on my door said 'Call me')" subtly alludes to same-sex attraction within the context of everyday life in New York City.

O'Hara died at the age of 40 after being struck by a jeep on a Fire Island beach after the beach taxi he had been riding in with a group of friends broke down in the dark. Despite his untimely death, his legacy endures through his poetry, which continues to inspire readers with its blend of humor, intelligence, and unabashed celebration of life. He remains a towering figure in American literature and a beloved icon of the New York art scene. Christopher Richards, in a tribute titled "Frank O'Hara's Lesson for Being Gay," observed, "What I find so essential, celebratory and let's-throw-a-parade-gay about him is [O'Hara's] ability to love whatever is aesthetically pleasurable that he comes across.... What I think I learn from his poetry...is how to like. What we prefer, what we enjoy, and what we desire are as singular as a fingerprint and in O'Hara's work having a coke with the man he loves is as sublime as a masterpiece by Leonardo or Michelangelo."

Mary Oliver (1935–2019)

Poet

Mary Oliver has been called the "poet laureate of the natural world" and contended that poetry "mustn't be fancy," specializing in presenting the often overlooked wonders of the world around us

in plain language and accessible imagery. She was a best-selling poet in America and one of its most honored, awarded the National Book Award, the Pulitzer Prize, and the Lannan Literary Award for Lifetime Achievement.

Oliver was born in Cleveland, Ohio, and grew up in a suburb of Cleveland. Her father was a teacher, and her mother was a secretary in an elementary school. In 2011, in one of her rare interviews, she spoke of being sexually abused as a child, though she did not elaborate: "I had a very dysfunctional family, and a very hard childhood. So I made a world out of words. And it was my salvation." She left home as a teenager and studied briefly at Ohio State University and Vassar College but took no degree. A fan of Edna St. Vincent Millay's poetry, she drove to Steepletop, Millay's former home in Austerlitz, New York, for a visit and wound up living there for the next six years, helping Millay's sister Norma organize Millay's papers. In the late 1950s, on a return visit to Steepletop, Oliver met Molly Malone Cook, a photographer, about whom she famously wrote, "I took one look and fell, hook and tumble." In 1964, the couple moved to Provincetown, Massachusetts, where they lived together for the next 40 years until Cook's death in 2005. She fell in love with Provincetown, "that marvelous convergence of land and water; Mediterranean light; fishermen who made their living by hard and difficult work from frightening small boats, and, both residents and sometime visitors, the many artists and writers." She would describe its surrounding woods, ponds, and harbor as "the emblem of everything," drawing her inspiration for her work from daily morning walks.

Oliver published her first collection of poems, *No Voyage and Other Poems*, in 1963, when she was 28. Her fifth collection, *American Primitive* (1983), won the Pulitzer Prize. *Dream Works* (1986) continues her search to "understand both the wonder and pain of nature." *New and Selected Poems* (1992) won the National Book Award. *Devotions: The Selected Poems of Mary Oliver* (2017) is the poet's own selection of her most representative poems.

During the 1980s, Oliver taught at Case Western Reserve University and was poet in residence at Bucknell University (1986) and Sweet Briar College (1991) before joining the faculty at Bennington College until 2001. She gave few interviews, preferring to let her poems speak for her, but often gave readings to devoted followers of her work. In a sense, her popularity cost her some critical neglect and dismissal as unchallenging. As critic Ruth Franklin observed, "Mary Oliver isn't a difficult poet. Her work is incredibly accessible, and I think that's what makes her so beloved by so many people. It doesn't feel like you have to take a seminar in order to understand Mary Oliver's poetry. She's speaking directly to you as a human being." The idea that her poetry avoids difficult questions is misleading, however. She explores, with an intense intimacy, grief following the death of her partner and was always conscious of the cost of the wonderment she found around her. She wrote in "When Death Comes": "When it's over, I want to say: all my life / I was a bride married to amazement. / I was the bridegroom, taking the world into my arms."

Cole Porter (1891–1964)

Composer, Songwriter

Cole Albert Porter effectively wrote the soundtrack of the 1930s through the 1950s, producing a vast repertoire of timeless classics that have become synonymous with the Great American Songbook. From Broadway musicals to Hollywood films, his compositions captivated audiences with their witty lyrics, sophisticated melodies, and unparalleled charm, a combination that became known as "the Cole Porter song." Iconic songs such as "Night and Day," "I've Got You Under My Skin," and "Anything Goes" solidified his reputation as one of the greatest songwriters of the 20th century.

Porter was born in Peru, Indiana, the only grandson of one of the wealthiest men in Indiana, a coal and timber speculator who dominated the family. He learned the violin at the age of 6, learned the piano at the age of 8, and wrote his first operetta at the age of 10. He defied his grandfather, who wanted him to become a lawyer, in order to pursue his interest in music at Worcester Academy in Massachusetts and Yale University (1909–1913), where he was an early member of the Whiffenpoofs, an a capella singing group, and became president of the Yale Glee Club and its principal soloist. At Yale, he wrote 300 songs, including the football fight songs "Bulldog" and "Bingo Eli Yale," which are still played at Yale. After graduating, he studied at Harvard Law School (1914) and then switched his focus to music at Yale's Graduate School of Arts and Sciences (1915–1916). He made his Broadway debut with the musical comedy *See America First*, which closed after 15 performances.

In 1917, after the United States entered World War I, Porter went to France to work for a relief organization. He would later claim to have served in the French Foreign Legion, but biographers have found no record of his serving in any branch of the military. He maintained a luxury Paris apartment and entertained lavishly with, in the words of biographer J. X. Bell, "much gay and bisexual activity, Italian nobility, cross-dressing, international musicians, and a large surplus of recreational drugs." Although he was known to be gay, he married his close friend, a wealthy, older, American divorcée, Linda Lee Thomas, in 1919. Thomas had no doubt about her husband's sexual orientation, but for her, he was the antithesis of her abusive first husband; for him, his wife established a respectable heterosexual front in an era when homosexuality was not publicly acknowledged.

In 1928, Porter wrote "Let's Do It (Let's Fall in Love)" for the Broadway musical *Paris.* It was the start of a string of hit musical comedies, including *Fifty Million Frenchmen* (1929), *Gay Divorce* (1932), *Anything Goes* (1934), *Red Hot and Blue* (1934), *Jubilee* (1935), *Dubarry Was a Lady* (1939), *Panama Hattie* (1940), *Kiss Me Kate* (1948), *Can-Can* (1953), and *Silk Stockings* (1955). Many were adapted into popular motion pictures. He would write songs and lyrics that defined a new witty sophistication in American music such as "Night and Day," "I Get a Kick Out of You," "Begin the Beguine," "I've Got You Under My Skin," "In the Still of the Night," "Just One of Those Things," "Love for Sale," "My Heart Belongs to Daddy," "Too Darn Hot," "It's De-Lovely," "I Love Paris," and "You're the Top" as well as countless others.

In 1937, a horse-riding accident left Porter a semi-invalid, necessitating 30 operations and the eventual amputation of a leg. Despite the successes that followed, he experienced another loss when his wife died in 1954. Despite his years of extramarital homosexual relationships, Thomas had been an important source of friendship and support. Although he continued to work on both Broadway shows and films, he also sought escape with alcohol and painkillers. After having his right leg amputated in 1958 and suffering several debilitating strokes, he stopped writing songs and withdrew from public life, telling friends, "I am only half a man now." His songs continue to be performed and cherished worldwide, serving as timeless reminders of his enduring talent and enduring impact on the world of music and popular culture.

Robert Rauschenberg (1925–2008)

Artist

A pivotal figure in the Neo-Dada movement of the 1950s and beyond, Milton Ernest "Robert" Rauschenberg reshaped the landscape of contemporary art by challenging conventional notions of painting, sculpture, and artistic expression. Through his innovative Combine technique and daring incorporation of found objects and everyday materials, he blurred the lines between mediums, expanding the possibilities of artistic creation and inspiring generations of artists to explore new avenues of creativity.

Rauschenberg was born in Port Arthur, Texas, to parents of German and Dutch descent. His family struggled financially, and his mother made her son shirts out of scraps of material. His first ready-made shirt was a high school graduation present. He briefly studied pharmacology at the University of Texas, Austin, before he was drafted during World War II. He saw his first paintings at the Huntington Art Gallery in California, where he was stationed as a medical technician in the Navy Hospital Corps. He first realized that he had some artistic talent when his pen portraits of comrades were admired. After his discharge, he studied at the Kansas City Art Institute (1946–1947), in Europe, at Black Mountain College in North Carolina (1948–1950), and at the Art Students League of New York (1949–1952).

Rauschenberg married fellow art student Susan Weill in 1950, with whom he had a son. They divorced in 1953, both realizing that he was attracted to men. He traveled, worked, and had an affair with painter Cy Twombly before, in 1956, he began a six-year relationship with artist Jasper Johns. Rauschenberg and Johns had studios one floor apart from each other and would comment on each other's work daily.

During this period, Rauschenberg made his most famous artwork, the Combine *Monogram*, by pushing a stuffed angora goat through a rubber tire and placing them atop a horizontal canvas. It was called by art critic Robert Hughes "one of the few great icons of male homosexual love in modern culture." *Bed* consisted of a quilt, sheet, and pillow that were covered with paint as if soaked in blood and framed on a wall. These and Rauschenberg's other artworks became icons of postwar modernism.

From the late 1950s, Rauschenberg experimented with the use of newspaper and magazine photographs in his paintings, and in about 1962, he borrowed from Andy Warhol the silkscreen stencil technique for applying photographic images to large canvases, drawing on themes from modern American history and popular culture. By the 1970s, he turned to prints on silk, cotton, and cheesecloth as well as three-dimensional constructions of cloth, paper, and bamboo. He would incorporate lithography and other printmaking techniques and rely more heavily on his own photography. The multitalented Rauschenberg defied the traditional idea that an artist must stick to one medium or style, often reconceiving all the mediums in which he worked. He was a painter, photographer, printmaker, choreographer, performance artist, set designer, and composer. Johns once declared that no American invented more than Rauschenberg. In 1970, Rauschenberg and artist Darryl Pottorf, his partner and collaborator of 25 years, moved to Captiva Island, Florida, where they lived together until Rauschenberg's death.

Adrienne Rich (1929–2012)

Poet, Essayist

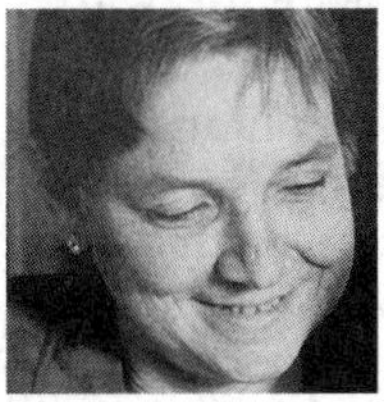

One of the most acclaimed poets of the post–World War II period, Adrienne Rich was also an important essayist and public intellectual who powerfully contributed to the debate over women's identity, sexuality, and empowerment. Critic Alison Flood credited her with bringing "the oppression of women and lesbians to the forefront of poetic discourse."

Born in Baltimore, Rich was the daughter of a pathologist who worked as a professor at Johns Hopkins Medical School. Educated at home until 4th grade, she was encouraged in her writing, and her first book, *Ariadne,* a three-act play and collection of poems, was privately printed when she was only 10 years old. She graduated from Radcliffe College in 1951, the same year that her first poetry collection, *A Change of World,* was published in the prestigious Yale Series of Younger Poets. W. H. Auden, who selected her collection for the series, declared that her poems "speak quietly but do not mumble, respects their elders, but are not cowed by them, and do not tell fibs."

In 1953, Rich married Alfred Conrad, a Harvard economist, and they had three sons between 1955 and 1959. Preoccupied with her responsibilities as a wife and mother, she saw her writing talent languish. She would break her silence in 1963 with the important collection *Snapshots of a Daughter-in-Law.* Moving to New York City, she began a teaching career at Swarthmore, Columbia, Brandeis, and City College. In 1970, her husband committed suicide, and in 1976, she came out as a lesbian with the publication of *Twenty-one Love Poems,* in which she celebrated her sexuality and love for women. At the same time, she began a lifelong relationship with writer Michelle Cliffe. During this period, she published some of her most important works, including *Leaflets* (1971), the National Book Award–winning *Diving into the Wreck* (1973), and *The Dream of Common Language* (1977).

Rich's works capture, in intense and striking images, the challenges that women face under a repressive social system that denies their human potential while expressing the urgency to achieve a liberating and autonomous self-identity. It has been argued that she accomplished in verse what Betty Friedan, author of *The Feminine Mystique*, did in prose, documenting women's disenfranchisement and erasure. She called herself "the poet of oppositional imagination" as someone who was triply marginalized—as a woman, a lesbian, and a Jew—who, early on, advocated for intersectionality and the widest possible understanding of the forces that drive gender politics.

Rich's prose works include *Of Women Born: Motherhood as Experience and Institution* (1976), *On Lies, Secrets, and Silences* (1979), *Blood, Bread, and Poetry* (1986), and *A Human Eye: Essays in Art in Society* (2009). Her most influential essay, "Compulsory Heterosexuality and the Lesbian Experience," published in 1980, condemned the erasure of lesbians from mainstream feminism. All of her essays are distinguished for their erudite, lucid, and imaginative treatment of politics, feminism, history, racism, and sexuality.

Over a long and illustrious career, she reflected at a deeply personal level the evolving women's movement, the gay liberation movement, and the major political and social changes of postwar American society. She summarized her development: "I began as an American optimist, albeit a critical one, formed by our racial legacy and by the Vietnam War.... I became an American Skeptic, not as to the long search for justice and dignity, which is part of all human history, but in the light of my nation's leading role in demoralizing and destabilizing that search, here at home and around the world. Perhaps just such a passionate skepticism, neither cynical nor nihilistic, is the ground for continuing."

Herb Ritts (1952–2002)

Photographer

Herbert "Herb" Ritts Jr. was an acclaimed American photographer who was renowned for his striking, black-and-white photography, which transformed

fashion and celebrity portraiture. His work graced the covers of major magazines such as *Vogue, Vanity Fair*, and *Rolling Stone*, and he became a key figure in popular culture through his timeless images. His photography was characterized by its clean lines, strong contrasts, and sculptural approach to the human form, which made his work instantly recognizable and highly influential in the industry.

Ritts was born in Los Angeles. His father was a furniture designer and his mother an interior designer who, together, ran a successful furniture business. He grew up in fashionable Brentwood, living next door to actor Steve McQueen, whom he regarded as a second father. His own father gave him his first camera, a Kodak Brownie, as a bar mitzvah present. In 1975, he graduated from Bard College in New York, majoring in economics with a minor in art history, and moved back to California to work in the family business. He started taking adult education classes in photography, and after photographs that he had taken of a young actor friend, Richard Gere, were published in various national magazines, his career as a portraitist was launched.

Ritts's photography was featured in numerous high-profile magazines, and he worked with some of the biggest names in Hollywood and the fashion world, capturing the 1980s era of the supermodel with images of Cindy Crawford, Christy Turlington, and Naomi Campbell. His influence extended beyond fashion photography to music videos and advertising. He directed iconic music videos for artists like Madonna ("Cherish") and Janet Jackson ("Love Will Never Do (Without You)"), which showcased his unique visual style and further cemented his reputation as a versatile and innovative artist. His ability to blend commercial appeal with artistic integrity made him a favorite among celebrities and brands alike. His work has been exhibited in prestigious galleries and museums around the world, solidifying his status as a significant figure in the art world.

Openly gay, Ritts came out publicly long before many of his colleagues in the fashion and art world did, disclosing his sexuality in 1993 on an NBC news program. He was in a relationship with entertainment lawyer Erik Hyman from 1996 until his death. He was an important figure in the LGBTQ+ community who was committed to HIV/AIDS-related causes, creating the Herb Ritts Foundation to carry on his charitable work following his death due to HIV/AIDS-related complications.

So many of Ritts's photographs have become iconic. His 1993 book *Herb Ritts: Pictures* collects many of them. Journalist Cathy Horyn observed, "You cannot imagine the 1980s and '90s in America without the photographs of Herb Ritts."

Jerome Robbins (1918–1998)

Choreographer, Director

Jerome Robbins was one of the most celebrated and innovative choreographers of the 20th century in both ballet and Broadway and Hollywood musicals. For half a century, he helped to shape the New York City Ballet with his experimental choreography in ballet's classical tradition. At the same time, he was a major creative force behind such Broadway landmark productions as *On the Town, The King and I, Gypsy, West Side Story, Fiddler on the Roof,* and many more.

Born Jerome Wilson Rabinowitz (he and his parents changed the family name legally in the 1940s) on Manhattan's Lower East Side, Robbins's father operated a delicatessen on the Upper East Side before moving his family to New Jersey, where he and his brother established the Comfort Corset Company. He showed an early aptitude for music, dancing, and theater. After graduating from high school in 1935, he matriculated at New York University but left in 1936 because his family could no longer support his education due to the Great Depression. Unwilling to work in the corset factory, he pursued a career in dance as an apprentice at Senya Gluck-Sandor's Dance Center, where his sister was a dancer. He studied various dance styles from classical ballet, modern dance, and Spanish and Asian dance forms to interpretive dancing and choreography. He would dance in the chorus of several Broadway musicals, and in 1940, he joined Ballet Theatre (now American Ballet Theatre), dancing in featured roles.

In 1944, Robbins choreographed his first successful ballet, *Fancy Free,* with a musical score by young composer Leonard Bernstein, about three American sailors on shore leave in New York City during World War II. It would be expanded into the successful Broadway musical *On the Town* (a film version appeared in 1949) and establish his uniquely divided focus as a choreographer of both ballet and musicals.

In 1949, Robbins left Ballet Theatre to join George Balanchine's newly formed New York City Ballet, where he became associate artistic director, danced in several roles for Balanchine, and choreographed such works as *The Guests* (1949), *Age of Anxiety* (1950), and *The Cage* (1951). He continued to work on Broadway, choreographing two Irving Berlin shows, *Miss Liberty* (1949) and *Call Me Madam* (1950), the latter starring Ethel Merman, and Rodgers and Hammerstein's *The King and I* (1951).

In 1953, at the height of the Red Scare, Robbins appeared before the House Un-American Activities Committee (HUAC), where he admitted to membership in the Communist Party in the 1940s and named eight fellow members. Ed Sullivan, the powerful show business columnist and popular TV show host, had threatened to reveal that Robbins was a "commie and a homosexual" if he did not come forward with his testimony, known in the argot of the HUAC hearings as "naming names." Unwilling to take the risk of being blacklisted in the entertainment industry (as those he named were), Robbins complied, an act that many of his colleagues never forgave. His decision haunted him, and he later put it at the center of an autobiographical drama, *The Poppa Piece*, which he experimented with in workshops during the 1990s.

Spared the blacklist, Robbins's career flourished. He codirected *The Pajama Game* (1954) on Broadway; conceived, directed, and choreographed *Peter Pan* (1954), starring Mary Martin; choreographed the film version of *The King and I* (1956); and created two masterpieces at the New York City Ballet: *Afternoon of a Faun* (1953) and *The Concert* (1956).

In 1957, he teamed up once again with Leonard Bernstein on *West Side Story*, which featured Robbins's street-smart choreography integrated into the action. Broadway musicals that he was involved in after *West Side Story* include *Gypsy* (1959), *A Funny Thing Happened on the Way to the Forum* (1962), *Funny Girl* (1964), and *Fiddler on the Roof* (1964). After 1964, he would focus on ballet, with an output that made him the first major American-born classical choreographer with such groundbreaking works as *Les Noces*, *Dances at a Gathering*, *Goldberg Variations*, *Glass Pieces*, and many others.

Over the course of his career, Robbins won five Tony awards, two Oscar awards, an Emmy, the Astaire Award for Lifetime Achievement in Dance, and a Kennedy Center Honors award. Despite the acclaim, he rarely felt satisfaction with his success. Mikhail Baryshnikov observed, "For Jerry, every achievement was torturous."

Robbins was equally conflicted over his sexuality and his relationships. He has been described by biographers as a gay man who loved women. His first long-term gay relationship was with actor Montgomery Clift in the late 1940s that ended when Clift left New York for film work in Hollywood. His most passionate relationship was perhaps with (female) ballet dancer Tanaquil Le Clerq. His affairs with men tended to last longer than those with women, and he expressed regret that he could not sustain a lasting relationship with either sex. Despite these disappointments, he found the outlet in dance to express himself sexually. As dance critic Maya Weiss observes, "As homosexuality was taboo in Robbins' lifetime, being involved in dance meant curbing his natural sexual desires. Yet, by using familiar dance forms, Robbins was able to present non-normative versions of sexuality on conservative stages.... Throughout his career, Robbins used dance as a way to channel and control his sexuality, creating a mix of celebration and restraint of human desire."

RuPaul (1960–)

Entertainer, Television Host

The world's most famous drag queen, RuPaul is a trailblazing figure in entertainment who is celebrated for revolutionizing drag culture and bringing it into the mainstream. His hit single "Supermodel (You Better Work)" and the success of his TV show, *RuPaul's Drag Race*, have made him a cultural icon, earning numerous awards and critical acclaim. As a versatile performer, he has excelled in singing and acting as well as hosting his popular, long-running TV series.

Born RuPaul Andre Charles in San Diego to parents who both came from Louisiana, "Ru" came from the word *roux*, the French term for the spice base for gumbo and other Creole dishes. He was the only boy of his parents' four children and began wearing his sisters' clothing and exploring cross-dressing at an early age. At the age of 15, after his parents divorced, he moved to Atlanta to study performing arts. He struggled as a musician and filmmaker during the 1980s and, in 1982, debuted on an Atlanta public access variety show and often performed as a bar dancer and backup singer.

In the mid-1980s, RuPaul moved to New York City and performed in drag. His flamboyance and ease onstage made him a hit club dancer, and by the end of the decade, he was dubbed the Queen of New York.

His first prominent national exposure came in 1989, when he danced as an extra in the video for "Love Shack" by the B-52s. He gained prominence in the 1990s with the release of his hit single "Supermodel (You Better Work)" and his debut album, *Supermodel of the World*. Other hits included "Snapshot," "WorkOut," and a 1993 duet with Elton John on a remake of "Don't Go Breaking My Heart." In 1994, he made his feature film debut in Spike Lee's *Crooklyn*. Multiple roles followed on film and television; in 1995, he published his autobiography, *Lettin' It All Hang Out*, and debuted his TV talk show, *The RuPaul Show*, which ran until 1998.

RuPaul's most significant contribution to entertainment is undoubtedly *RuPaul's Drag Race*, a reality competition show that premiered in 2009. As host and executive producer, he has transformed the show into a global phenomenon, celebrating the art of drag and providing a platform for drag queens from diverse backgrounds. The show has received critical acclaim and numerous awards and spawned international versions, solidifying his status as a cultural icon. Through *RuPaul's Drag Race*, he brought drag culture into the mainstream and promoted acceptance and understanding of LGBTQ+ identities.

In addition, RuPaul has released multiple albums, authored books, and appeared in numerous films and television shows. His distinctive style and larger-than-life persona have made him a sought-after figure in the fashion and beauty industries. His impact extends beyond entertainment; he has been an advocate for LGBTQ+ rights and visibility, using his platform to address issues such as discrimination, HIV/AIDS awareness, and the importance of self-acceptance. His motto "If you can't love yourself, how in the hell are you gonna love somebody else?" has become an empowering mantra for many.

RuPaul married his longtime partner, Australian painter Georges LeBar, in 2017. His popularity, together with his openness about his sexuality and advocacy for self-love and acceptance, have made him a pivotal figure who has left an indelible mark on popular culture in both the entertainment industry and the LGBTQ+ community. Through his work, he has not only entertained audiences and attracted many fans, he has also challenged and changed the perception of what it means to be LGBTQ+.

Sarah Schulman (1958–)

Novelist, Playwright, Activist

Sarah Schulman is an acclaimed writer and activist whose extensive work has significantly influenced LGBTQ+ literature and advocacy. As a novelist, historian, nonfiction writer, journalist, playwright, and screenwriter, she has spent the last 40 years documenting gay life in America. Known for her unflinching exploration of social issues and commitment to social justice, she has established herself as a vital voice in contemporary literature and activism. The author of more than 20 books, including the novels *The Cosmopolitans, The Mere Future, Rat Bohemia*, and *Girls, Visions and Everything*; nonfiction works such as *Conflict Is Not Abuse, Duty of Repair, AIDS and the Marketing of Gay America*, and *My American History*; and plays *Mercy* and *Carson McCullers*, she has established herself as a vital voice in contemporary literature and activism.

Schulman was born in New York City.

When asked what first got her interested in writing, she replied, "I was read to as a child, which was crucial. At an early age I was handed *The Diary of Anne Frank.* This was intended to teach me about the Holocaust, but it also let me know that girls could be writers. At the age of six I started a diary. I wrote, 'When I grow up, I will write books.'" She attended Hunter College High School and later enrolled at the University of Chicago before transferring in 1978 to Empire State College, where she earned her bachelor's degree.

Her activism began in her childhood when she protested the Vietnam War with her mother. She was active in the University of Chicago's Women's Union; a member of the Committee for Abortion Rights and Against Sterilization Abuse from 1979 to 1982; and an active member of ACT UP from 1987 to 1992, getting arrested when ACT UP occupied Grand Central Station in protest of the First Gulf War.

In 1987, she and filmmaker Jim Hubbard cofounded the New York Lesbian and Gay Experimental Film Festival, now called MIX NYC, the longest-running gay film festival in New York. She was also a cofounder of the Lesbian Avengers in 1992. A direct-action, intersectional organization dedicated to addressing the lack of lesbian visibility and LGBTQ+ rights, the Lesbian Avengers participated in such actions as protesting right-wing attempts to dismantle New York City's multicultural Children of the Rainbow Curriculum for elementary school children (1992) and opposing the Proposition 8 amendment in California (2008) that intended to ban gay marriage. One of the Avengers' most notable achievements was the establishment of the Dyke March in 1993.

Schulman published her first books in the 1980s, beginning with *The Sophie Horowitz Story* (1984), a mystery about a feminist reporter in New York City; *Girls, Visions and Everything* (1986), a lesbian coming-of-age novel set in 1980s New York City; and *After Delores* (1988), which followed a gay waitress searching for her missing ex-girlfriend in New York's East Village. Some of her most significant works include *People in Trouble* (1990), a novel set during the height of the AIDS crisis; *Rat Bohemia* (1995), which examined the lives of three friends dealing with the AIDS crisis and the gentrification of New York City; *The Gentrification of the Mind: Witness to a Lost Imagination* (2012), a nonfiction study of the impact of gentrification on the cultural life of New York City; *Conflict Is Not Abuse* (2016), which challenges the conflation of conflict with abuse, advocating a more nuanced understanding of interpersonal and community dynamics; and *Let the Record Show: A Political History of ACT UP New York, 1987–1993* (2001), a comprehensive history of ACT UP and its activism during the peak of the AIDS crisis.

Although Schulman has achieved distinction in multiple literary genres, she continues to regard herself primarily as a novelist. "My goal is to write books with an assumption of lesbianism," she said, "so that women who work all week in boring jobs where they have to be in the closet can come home, kick off their shoes, and have something to read that speaks to them. I also see myself in the tradition of populist writing, because my characters are the people who inhabit the urban scenery of New York City but who are rarely recorded in fiction or theater. My audience is composed of the same kind of people who are my characters, and that makes for a very exciting dynamic. My writing has to be emotionally authentic."

David Sedaris (1956–)

Humorist, Essayist

Known for his sharp wit and keen observations of everyday life, David Sedaris is the author of acclaimed essay collections that showcase his distinctive blend of humor and insight. His work on NPR's *This American Life* and his engaging public readings have solidified his reputation as a master storyteller, turning mundane experiences into entertaining and profound narratives.

Born in Johnson City, New York, Sedaris was the second of six children whose father was an IBM engineer and eventually moved the family to Raleigh, North Carolina. After public high school in Raleigh, where he performed in plays and wrestled with the realization that he was gay, he briefly attended Western Carolina University and Kent State University. In 1977, he dropped out of school to hitchhike around the country. He moved to Chicago in 1983 and graduated from the School of the Art Institute of Chicago in 1987.

Sedaris began keeping a diary from an early age and knew he wanted to be a writer by the age of 25. In 1987, he taught writing part-time and began reading from his diary at Chicago clubs, where he came to the attention of Ira Glass of Chicago Public Radio, who invited him to appear on his program, *The Wild Room.* Sedaris said, "I owe everything to Ira…. My life changed completely, like someone waved a magic wand." He made his National Public Radio debut in 1992, and he began to record a monthly segment on NPR based on his diary entries. Best-selling essay collections followed, including *Barrel Fever* (1994), *Naked* (1997), *Me Talk Pretty One Day* (2000), *Dress Your Family in Corduroy and Denim* (2004), *When You Are Engulfed in Flames* (2008), *Let's Explore Diabetes with Owls* (2013), and *Calypso* (2018). His work is characterized by its dark humor, self-deprecation, and insightful commentary on everyday life.

Sedaris is a frequent contributor to *The New Yorker* magazine and has been a regular performer on the public radio show *This American Life,* also hosted by Glass. His live readings and book tours draw large audiences, captivated by his engaging and humorous delivery. He is openly gay, and his sexuality is an integral part of his personal narrative and literary voice. His essays often explore themes of identity, family, and the challenges and joys of being a gay man. His candid and often humorous accounts of his experiences have resonated with a wide audience, contributing to greater visibility and acceptance of LGBTQ+ stories in mainstream media. His long-term relationship with his partner, artist and designer Hugh Hamrick, is a recurring subject in his writings, offering readers a glimpse into their life together.

In 2001, Sedaris was awarded the Thurber Prize for American Humor and named "Humorist of the Year" by *Time* magazine. His sister, Amy Sedaris, is also a well-known comedian and entertainer, and he has written several plays with her, including *One Woman Shoe* (1995) and *The Little Frieda Mysteries* (1997). He is a master of probing the inconsistencies and contradictions of modern life and distilling observations that are both funny and insightful.

Irene Sharaff (1910–1993)

Costume Designer

Irene Sharaff was a legendary costume designer whose innovative and exquisite designs graced both the Broadway stage and Hollywood films. Her work, characterized by its meticulous attention to detail and vibrant use of color, earned her numerous awards and cemented her place as one of the most influential designers in theater and film history, winning five Academy awards and one Tony. Her ability to bring characters to life through her costumes has left an enduring legacy in the world of design.

Sharaff was born in Boston, Massachusetts, to parents of Armenian descent. She showed an early interest in the arts and pursued her passion by studying at the New York School of Fine and Applied Arts (now Parsons School of Design) and the Art Students League of New York. She began her career as a muralist and painter before transitioning to costume design. Her early work in theater included designing for ballets and operas, where she quickly gained recognition for her talent and creativity.

Sharaff's career is marked by numerous notable achievements and iconic works. She made her Broadway debut as a costume designer with the production of *Alice in Wonderland* in 1932. She would be represented on Broadway with one or more productions a season for the next 40 years. Her transition to film came with the 1945 movie *Cover Girl*, which showcased her ability to blend contemporary fashion with character-specific designs. Her work on *The King and I* (1956) and *West Side Story* (1961) earned her Academy awards and widespread acclaim. Her ability to create culturally authentic and visually stunning costumes was evident in these films, making them memorable for their aesthetic as well as their storytelling. She won a total of five Academy awards and a Tony Award, highlighting her versatility and mastery across both stage and screen.

Throughout her life, Sharaff maintained a private stance on her personal relationships, but she had a lifelong relationship with illustrator and costume designer Mai-Mai Sze from the mid-1930s until Sze's death in 1992. They lived together in a New York apartment, and Sze accompanied her to filming locations in Hollywood and all over the world. Despite the fact that they were well known as a couple, neither mentions the other in their published work. Her relationship with Sze was significant, underscoring her personal life and sexuality. Although she maintained a private stance on her personal relationships, her bond with Sze remains a notable aspect of her legacy.

The Theatre Development Fund's Irene Sharaff Lifetime Achievement Award, honoring the career of a costume designer in theater, film, opera, or dance, was named for Sharaff, who was its first recipient in 1993.

Jon Reed Sims (1947–1984)

Musician, Conductor

Jon Reed Sims was an influential musician and conductor who was renowned for his pioneering efforts in the LGBTQ+ music community. As the founder of the San Francisco Gay Freedom Day Marching Band and the San Francisco Gay Men's Chorus, he created platforms that celebrated diversity, promoted LGBTQ+ visibility, and fostered a sense of community through music. His work significantly impacted the cultural landscape, providing a voice and space for LGBTQ+ musicians and artists.

Sims was born in Smith Center, Kansas, a small farming community in the geographical center of the continental United States. He developed a passion for music at a young age, mastering the piano and trumpet during his school years. He pursued his love for music academically, earning a degree in music education from Wichita State University. He later continued his studies at Indiana University, where he earned a master's degree in music. He moved to San Francisco to be a music teacher and taught high school band in Daly City before devoting himself full time to developing gay and lesbian musical groups throughout the Bay Area.

In 1978, at the height of Anita Bryant and Jerry Falwell's anti-gay movement, Sims founded the San Francisco Gay Freedom Day Marching Band and the San Francisco Gay Men's Chorus. The Marching Band was the first openly gay marching band in the world, breaking new ground for LGBTQ+ representation in the arts.

Similarly, the Gay Men's Chorus became a symbol of unity and pride, performing at significant events and gaining widespread recognition. The chorus group ultimately spawned a variety of musical offshoots, including a concert band, jazz band, swing choir, string orchestra, and ragtime ensemble. These groups not only provided a safe space for LGBTQ+ individuals to express themselves but also played a crucial role in advocating for LGBTQ+ rights and acceptance. His leadership and vision were instrumental in their success, and his legacy continues to inspire LGBTQ+ musicians and artists today.

Sims was openly gay and dedicated his life to advocating for LGBTQ+ rights and visibility through his work in the arts. He was known for his charismatic leadership and unwavering dedication to his community. His work in the music and arts sectors not only celebrated LGBTQ+ identities but also promoted a broader acceptance and understanding. In 1984, he died of the then little-known disease called AIDS. His obituary was one of the very first to attribute a death to AIDS and include a definition of the disease, expanding awareness of the disease that would go on to ravage San Francisco's gay community.

Bessie Smith (1894–1937)

Blues Singer

Bessie Smith was one of the most important figures in the history of American music. By successfully blending African and Western styles of music, she helped to transform the folk tradition of the blues into an indigenous American art form with worldwide impact. Few contemporary singers of pop, jazz, or blues have not been influenced by her. An electrifying performer, she expressively and emotionally verbalized actual life.

Smith was born into a large, poor family in Chattanooga, Tennessee. Her father was a Baptist preacher, who died soon after she was born; her mother died when she was 9 years old, and her older sister became head of the family. She soon went to work singing on street corners for tips. She won a job as a dancer in a minstrel show, and while touring with the troupe, she met blues legend Ma Rainey, who became a lifelong friend and influence on her singing style.

In 1913, Smith moved to Atlanta to become a headliner at a local club but continued to tour rural areas, performing in dance halls, cabarets, and camp meetings. In 1920, she formed her own troupe, with herself as the star. Her rich contralto and commanding stage presence projected emotional depths never heard onstage before. Her material was drawn from vernacular African American oral tradition. As one critic observed, "More than any other singer, she set the blues tradition in terms of style and quality. She not only gave a special musical aura to this tradition but her own singing and the accompaniments of the many great jazz artists who assisted her in her recordings placed it firmly in the broader jazz tradition."

Smith's recording sessions of the mid-1920s produced some of the finest work of her career. She used her impressive range and kill to turn her voice into another instrument in classics such as "Weeping Willow Blues," "The Bye Bye Blues," and "St. Louis Blues." Her material emphasized the daily plight of African Americans, including poverty, bootlegging, unemployment, eviction, and sexual betrayal. During the Great Depression, her fortunes declined, as they did for many Black performers, with venues closing and the record industry collapsing. A final recording session in 1933 produced the classic "Nobody Knows You When You're Down and Out."

Despite her professional success, Smith's personal life was marked by turbulence and complexity. She faced numerous challenges, including racial discrimination, financial difficulties, and personal tragedies. Her relationships were often tumultuous. She married security guard Jack Gee in 1923, but the marriage was marred by infidelity and ended in separation. She was known to have had relationships with women, and her bisexuality was an open secret among those who knew her. Her fearless approach to life and love despite societal norms added to her legend and mystique.

Smith's life was tragically cut short when she died of injuries sustained in a car accident in 1937 in Clarksdale, Mississippi. Her untimely death at the age of 43 marked the end of an era, but her influence can be heard in the work of later blues, jazz, and rock musicians. Writer Ralph Ellison declared, "Bessie Smith might have been a 'blues queen' to the society at large, but within the tighter Negro community where the blues were part of a total way of life, and a major expression of an attitude toward life, she was a priestess, a celebrant who affirmed the values of the group and man's ability to deal with chaos."

K. M. Soehnlein (1967–)

Novelist

Karl Michael "K. M." Soehnlein is a distinguished American novelist and LGBTQ+ rights advocate whose evocative storytelling and dedication to social justice have garnered critical acclaim. Works such as *The World of Normal Boys, You Can Say You Knew Me When, Robin and Ruby,* and *Army of Lovers* explore themes of identity, love, and community, making significant contributions to contemporary LGBTQ+ literature.

Soehnlein was born in New York City, the son of an Irish immigrant mother and a first-generation German American father. He was raised in Westwood, New Jersey, and attended Ithaca College, majoring in cinema production and graduating in 1987. After several years in New York City, he moved to San Francisco in 1992 and earned an MFA in creative writing from San Francisco State University. From 1997 to 2003, he played the clarinet in a rock band and, since 2002, has been a faculty member in the writing program at the University of San Francisco.

Soehnlein's activism preceded his literary work. In 1987, he and his then boyfriend Alan Klein attended the first meeting of ACT UP New York, the AIDS activist group, and he would become an active member, organizing demonstrations and getting arrested multiple times. In 1990, he and others founded Queer Nation, an activist group challenging homophobia in the media and the rise in anti-queer assaults in New York City. He was prompted to found Queer Nation after he was the victim of an anti-gay assault in 1989. After the mass shooting in queer nightclub Pulse in Orlando, Florida, in 2016, he launched the viral campaign #TwoMenKissing.

Soehnlein's debut novel, *The World of Normal Boys* (2000), is a coming-of-age story set in the late 1970s following 13-year-old Robin MacKenzie as he navigates the complexities of adolescence, family dynamics, and his emerging sexuality. It received critical acclaim for its authentic portrayal of a young gay boy's experiences and won the Lambda Literary Award for Gay Fiction. *You Can Say You Knew Me When* (2005) intertwines the past and present lives of Jamie, who, while dealing with the death of his estranged father, uncovers secrets about his father's hidden life and his own identity. The novel explores themes of memory, family secrets, and self-discovery. It solidified Soehnlein's reputation as a powerful voice in contemporary LGBTQ+ literature. *Robin and Ruby* (2010) is a sequel to *The World of Normal Boys,* which picks up the story of Robin and his sister Ruby a few years later in the 1980s. It follows their separate yet intertwining paths as they grapple with love, identity, and independence. It was praised for its rich character portraits and vivid portrayal of the 1980s LGBTQ+ community. *Army of Lovers* (2015) chronicles the lives of two men, Paul and Michael, who are drawn together by activism during the AIDS crisis in the 1980s. Their love story unfolds against the backdrop of political and social upheaval and is based, at least in part, on the years during which Soehnlein spent working with ACT UP.

Soehnlein's *Robin and Ruby,* which provides both a personal and historical chronicle of the LGBTQ+ recent past from the 1970s through the 1990s, registers both the cultural moments and their cost and impact on those who lived through them. He has been at work on a sequel to *Robin and Ruby* to update their stories. He lives in San Francisco with his husband, Kevin Clarke, whom he married in 2015.

Stephen Sondheim (1930–2021)

Composer, Lyricist

Stephen Joshua Sondheim is widely regarded as one of the most influential and innovative figures in American musical theater, celebrated for his sophisticated lyrics, complex musical compositions, and the emotional depth he brought to the genre. His work, which includes such landmark musicals as *West Side Story, Gypsy, A Funny Thing Happened on the Way to the Forum, Company, Follies, A Little Night Music, Sweeney Todd, Sunday in the Park with George,* and *Into the Woods,* transformed the landscape of Broadway, pushing boundaries and redefining the thematic and narrative potential of the musical form. Over his career, he won numerous accolades, including eight Tony awards, an Academy Award, and a Pulitzer Prize, solidifying his legacy in theater history.

Born in New York City, Sondheim grew up in a privileged but tumultuous family environment with parents who eventually divorced when he was 10 years old. His father owned a dressmaking company, and his mother was a designer, with whom he lived after the divorce. His introduction to theater came through a family friend, lyricist Oscar Hammerstein II, who became a mentor and greatly influenced his work. After graduating from Williams College in 1950, where he studied music composition, he further honed his craft under the guidance of composer Milton Babbitt. His early career in theater began with writing the lyrics for Leonard Bernstein's musical *West Side Story* (1957) and for Jule Styne's music in *Gypsy* (1959), both of which earned critical acclaim and established him as a gifted lyricist.

Sondheim's major works include a series of groundbreaking musicals that each showcased his unique approach to storytelling and musical composition. In *Company* (1970), he explored themes of modern relationships and marriage with a nonlinear narrative style, while *Follies* (1971) delved into aging and regret with a haunting, nostalgic tone. *Sweeney Todd* (1979), perhaps his most daring project, combined dark humor with a gothic horror story, establishing it as one of Broadway's most unique productions. In *Sunday in the Park with George* (1984), which earned him the Pulitzer Prize for Drama, he used Georges Seurat's painting style as a metaphor for artistic creation. These works, among so many others, are revered for their emotional depth, complex characters, and his revolutionary use of music and lyrics to advance narrative and character development.

Sondheim was known for his privacy, especially regarding his personal life. He came out as gay in 1970 at the age of 40 and maintained a long-term relationship with dramatist Peter Jones. He married Jeff Romley, a Broadway producer, in 2017. Though his personal relationships were rarely a focus of public discussion, his sexual orientation and experiences subtly influenced his work, particularly in his nuanced approach to themes of love, loneliness, and identity.

Sondheim died suddenly of heart failure at the age of 91. His contributions to musical theater are immeasurable, with a body of work that challenged conventions and brought a new level of sophistication and complexity to the genre. His influence extends far beyond Broadway, inspiring generations of lyricists, composers, and playwrights to pursue emotional authenticity and artistic innovation. His legacy endures not only in his celebrated musicals but also in the lasting impact he had on American theater as a visionary who elevated the musical form into high art.

Susan Sontag (1933–2004)

Novelist, Essayist, Social Critic

Described as "one of the most influential critics of her generation," Susan Sontag is perhaps best summarized as a public intellectual who, for four of the most turbulent decades in American political and cultural history, remained at the center of debate, directing in her essays and book the intellectual conversation of her time.

Born Susan Rosenblatt to a couple engaged in the fur trade in China, Sontag was raised in New York City by a nanny. She rarely saw her father, who died when she was 5 years old, and took her stepfather's surname after her mother remarried. Her family settled in California; she graduated from high school at the age of 15 and from the University of Chicago at the age of 18. There, she married her sociology instructor, Philip Rieff, a marriage that lasted for eight years. She went on to earn master's degrees in both English and philosophy from Harvard, and, after giving birth to a son in 1952, she would continue her studies at Oxford University and the University of Paris. In Paris, after divorcing her husband, she met Cuban American playwright María Irene Fornés, with whom she moved back to New York in 1959.

Sontag began her literary career at the age of 30, publishing an experimental novel, *The Benefactor* (1963), and *Death Kit* (1967). Although she would become famous for her essays and criticism, she thought of herself principally as a fiction writer. Her short story "The Way We Live Now," dealing with the AIDS epidemic, was published to great acclaim in 1986, and two historical novels followed, *The Volcano Lover* (1992) and *In America* (2000).

Sontag's chief impact and notoriety would come with her critical writing and essays. An early essay, "Notes on Camp" (1964), challenged established artistic categories while identifying irony as a prevalent response to the cultural moment. In *Against Interpretation and Other Essays* (1968), she made a case for a sensory response to art, arguing that intuitive response, not interpretation or analysis, was key to artistic understanding. She would go on to further define the 1960s zeitgeist in *Styles of Radical Will* (1969), and in *On Photography* (1967), she laid down core aesthetic principles that would help to raise photography's status as an art form. In *Illness as Metaphor* (1978) and *AIDS and Its Metaphors* (1988), she daringly treated the social and artistic perceptions of illness, reflecting her own experience battling breast cancer.

As open as Sontag was in dealing publicly with her illness, she was much more guarded about her sexuality. She became aware of her bisexuality in her early teens, writing at the age of 15 in her diary, "I feel I have lesbian tendencies (how reluctantly I write this)." After her divorce, she would have romantic relationships with both men and women, the longest being with photographer Annie Leibovitz, which lasted from 1989 until Sontag's death. They never lived together, although they each had an apartment within view of the other, and while Sontag was alive, neither woman publicly disclosed whether their relationship was a friendship or romantic. In 2006, Leibovitz confirmed that the descriptor "lover" was accurate. Sontag, who wrote so much on so many topics, expressed regret about not dealing more with her sexuality. She was quoted with characteristic candor, saying, "I grew up in a time when the modus operandi was the 'open secret.' I'm used to that, and quite OK with it. Intellectually, I know why I haven't spoken more about my sexuality, but I do wonder if I haven't repressed something there to my detriment. Maybe I could have given comfort to some people if I had dealt with the subject of my private sexuality more, but it's never been my prime mission to give comfort, unless somebody's in drastic need. I'd rather give pleasure or shake things up."

Gertrude Stein (1874–1946)

Writer

Gertrude Stein set out to liberate language for new and distinctive purposes while pursuing an equally liberating sense of gender identity, a pioneering figure both in language and sexuality. Recognized by fellow writers such as Ernest Hemingway and Sherwood Anderson and subsequent critics as one of the leading innovators in modern literature, to the wider public, who found her writing impenetrable, she was famous for being famous, dominating the Paris avant-garde arts scene between the wars from the apartment that she shared with her secretary and lover, Alice B. Toklas. Openly gay, she was perhaps the most famous lesbian in the first half of the 20th century. She has been credited with the first published use of the word "gay" in reference to same-sex relationships and those who have them.

Born in Allegheny, Pennsylvania, Stein grew up in Oakland, California, where her father made a fortune investing in real estate. Raised by governesses and tutors, she formed her principal bond with her older brother, Leo, whom she followed to Harvard, where she enrolled in what would become Radcliffe College. In 1967, she entered Johns Hopkins University Medical School, intending to become a physician, but after four years, she lost interest and dropped out. In 1903, she joined Leo in Paris at the address that would become one of the most famous in 20th-century cultural history—27 Rue de Fleurus—the most celebrated salon in Paris, a magnet for artists, writers, intellectuals, and hangers-on in the world of the avant-garde.

In 1909, Stein published her first book, *Three Lives*, in which she attempted to duplicate what modern painters were achieving in their art: tone and texture through a pattern of repetition that suggests the equal importance of each element. Her experimental approach found few readers but many admirers, including Californian Alice B. Toklas, who became her lifelong companion. Her next project, written from 1906 to 1909, was a massive, 1,000-page work, *The Making of Americans*, a history based on three generations of her family, with no dialogue or action. It remained unpublished until 1923. She published a volume of Cubist-inspired poetry, *Tender Buttons*, in 1914 that prompted one reviewer to dub her "the Mama of Dada."

Her first (and only) commercial success was *The Autobiography of Alice B. Toklas* (1933), chronicling Stein and Toklas's lives together. The book's success led to a lecture tour of America, and Stein recorded her reflections on her native country in *Everybody's Autobiography* (1937). During World War II, they remained in Paris during the Occupation, and she produced two final works based on the war years, *Wars I Have Seen* (1945) and *Brewsie and Willie* (1946). *Q.E.D.*, one of the earliest coming-out stories, was written in 1903 but published in 1950, four years after her death. Toklas outlived Stein by 21 years, dying in 1967 at the age of 89.

Stein served as a kind of mentor of literary and artistic modernism. She was also a pioneer in exploring the limits of both language itself and conventional gender roles. Often obscured in cryptic language, she developed what has been called "a grammar of lesbian domesticity" and a reimagining of fluid gender roles and sexual identities.

George Takei (1937-)

Actor, Activist

Best known as the character Hikaru Sulu, the helmsman of the *USS Enterprise* and later captain of the *USS Excelsior* in the *Star Trek* franchise, George Takei is a cultural icon who has used his fame as a platform to speak out on behalf of social justice. In the process he has become one of the most visible and respected figures in LGBTQ and Japanese American history.

Born Hosato Takei in Los Angeles, George Takei was named after George VI, who was crowned king of the United Kingdom soon after Takei's birth. Takei's parents, Norman and Fumiko, owned a thriving dry-cleaning business. In January 1942, a month after the United States declared war on Japan following that nation's attack on Pearl Harbor, Hawaii, President Franklin D. Roosevelt signed Executive Order 9066, ordering the internment of Japanese Americans. For the duration of World War II, Takei and his family lived in the Rowher War Relocation Center in Rowher, Arkansas, and were later transferred to the Tule Lake War Relocation Center in California, an experience that profoundly affected Takei and helped to shape his activism. Takei has also spoken of his family's relatives living in Japan during the war, two of whom—an aunt and infant cousin—were killed during the atomic bombing of Hiroshima in August 1945. Takei's parents lost access to their bank accounts, because the U.S. government had frozen the bank accounts of Japanese Americans, and after the war, the family was released from interment with $25 and a one-way ticket back to Los Angeles. There, they experienced poverty and homelessness for five years while Takei's parents worked to rebuild their lives.

After his graduation from Los Angeles High School, where he served as Boys Senior Board President, Takei studied architecture at the University of California, Berkeley, and then transferred to UCLA, where he received a bachelor of arts degree in theater in 1950 and a master of arts in theater in 1964. He went on to study at the Shakespeare Institute in Stratford-upon-Avon, Sophia University in Tokyo, and the Desilu Workshop in Hollywood.

Takei's early career included voiceover work dubbing Japanese films into English and roles on stage and in films and television that gradually led to his breakthrough role in *Star Trek* in the 1960s. He has enjoyed a long and varied career, reprising his role in multiple *Star Trek* films and in *Star Trek* web series, as well as appearing in the Netflix adult animated action series *Blue Eye Samurai*, which debuted in 2023. Takei's experiences as an interned Japanese American during World War II also inspired the 2012 Broadway musical *Allegiance.*

Since the 1970s Takei's sexual orientation and affiliation with LGBTQ groups had been common knowledge among his many *Star Trek* fans. In a 2005 interview with *Frontiers* magazine, he came out publicly and revealed his 18-year relationship with producer and publicist Brad Altman. The couple married in 2008 in a ceremony at the Democracy Forum of the Japanese American National Museum in Los Angeles. Their best man and "best woman" were *Star Trek* actors Walter Koenig and Nichelle Nichols.

Takei has developed a strong reputation as a public speaker, author, and social media personality over the years, using humor and clarity to connect with diverse audiences. He has served as spokesperson for the Human Rights Campaign's Coming Out Project, and in 2006 he embarked upon a nationwide speaking tour titled "Equality Trek" to share his experiences as a gay Japanese American and with *Star Trek* and the LGBTQ running and walking club Frontrunners.

His contributions have been recognized with numerous awards, including the Order of the Rising Sun from the Japanese government (2004), the LGBT Humanist Award from the American Humanist Association (2012), the GLAAD Vito Russo Award (2014), and the Distinguished Medal of Honor for Lifetime Achievement and Public Service from the Japanese American National Museum (2015).

Mickalene Thomas (1971–)

Artist

Mickalene Thomas is a renowned contemporary artist notable for her vibrant multimedia works, which explore themes of beauty, identity, and Black female empowerment. Utilizing a blend of painting, collage, photography, and video, she creates striking portraits that draw on art history, pop culture, and personal experiences. Her work not only highlights the underrepresented narratives of Black women but also contributes to broader conversations about race, gender, and sexuality in art and society.

Born in Camden, New Jersey, Thomas was raised by her mother, Sandra Bush, a former fashion model, after her parents divorced. After graduating from high school, she moved to Portland, Oregon, with her then girlfriend and enrolled at Portland State University. A visit to the Portland Art Museum and its exhibition of Carrie Mae Weems's *The Kitchen Table Series* was, she recalled, "the first time I saw contemporary art in a museum that reflected who I was. That was the moment I knew I wanted to become an artist." She returned to the East Coast to attend the Pratt Institute in Brooklyn, earning a BFA degree in 2000. She went on to earn an MFA degree at Yale in 2002.

Thomas's breakthrough came in 2008 with her first solo museum exhibition at the Santa Monica Museum of Art. Her work often draws on art history, reinterpreting classical themes and compositions through the lens of African American culture and female empowerment. One of her most acclaimed pieces, *Le déjeuner sur l'herbe: Les Trois Femmes Noires* (2011), reimagines Édouard Manet's iconic painting by placing Black women at the center, challenging traditional narratives and highlighting underrepresented voices in art history. In 2012, her solo exhibition, *Origin of the Universe* at the Brooklyn Museum, marked a significant milestone in her career, bringing her work to a wider audience and solidifying her status as a leading contemporary artist. Her inclusion in the *30 Americans* exhibition in 2013 further solidified her impact, as the exhibition highlighted prominent African American artists and toured nationally, expanding her influence. In 2018, her exhibition *Do I Look Like a Lady?* at MOCA Grand Avenue in Los Angeles delved into themes of female identity and empowerment, reflecting her ongoing commitment to challenging societal norms and advocating for diversity in the art world.

Thomas is openly gay, and her sexuality has played a significant role in both her personal life and artistic practice. Her work often explores themes of lesbian identity and representation, celebrating the beauty and complexity of Black women's lives and relationships. Her long-term relationship with artist Racquel Chevremont, who is also her collaborator, has been a vital part of her life and work. Together, they have collaborated on various projects, blending their artistic visions to create compelling and innovative works. Her openness about her sexuality and relationship has made her a role model and advocate for LGBTQ+ representation in the art world.

Lily Tomlin (1939–)

Actress

Lily Tomlin is an acclaimed American actress, comedian, writer, and produc-

er whose career has spanned over six decades. Known for her sharp wit, versatile performances, and distinctive voice, she has made significant contributions to television, film, and stage. Her groundbreaking work in comedy and ability to portray a wide array of characters have earned her a place as one of the most beloved and influential figures in American entertainment.

Tomlin was born and raised in Detroit, Michigan. Her mother was a nurse's aide, and her father was a factory worker. They moved to Detroit from Paducah, Kentucky, during the Great Depression. After graduating from public high school in 1957, she attended Wayne State University originally to study biology, but after auditioning for a play, it sparked an interest in the theater, and she changed her major. After college, she began doing stand-up comedy in Detroit clubs before moving to New York City to continue studying acting; she made her first television appearance in 1965 on *The Merv Griffin Show* and became a cast member on *The Garry Moore Show* in 1966.

Tomlin first gained national recognition in 1969 as a cast member on the sketch comedy show *Rowan & Martin's Laugh-In* as the replacement for the departing Judy Carne. She became an instant success, creating memorable characters like snarky telephone operator Ernestine and precocious child Edith Ann. Her success on *Laugh-In* led to a series of acclaimed television specials. In addition to her television work, she has had a prolific film career, with standout roles in movies such as *Nashville* (1975), *9 to 5* (1980), *All of Me* (1984), and *Grandma* (2015). She has also enjoyed a successful stage career, particularly with her one-woman show *The Search for Signs of Intelligent Life in the Universe*, which won her a Tony Award in 1986. In 2015, she starred opposite Jane Fonda in the series *Grace and Frankie*, which was about two women whose lives are disrupted after their husbands fall in love with each other.

Beyond her professional achievements, Tomlin has been a trailblazer in advocating for LGBTQ+ rights and social justice. She has been open about her sexuality for much of her career, although she only officially came out in 2001. She revealed on *The Ellen DeGeneres Show* that in 1975, after she was nominated for an Oscar for *Nashville*, *Time* magazine offered to feature her on the cover as a way of coming out (DeGeneres would appear on the cover for that reason 22 years later). "I just decided that I wasn't going to play their game," she explained. "I wanted to be recognized for my performance." She has been in a long-term relationship with writer and collaborator Jane Wagner since 1971; the couple married in 2013 after 42 years together, following the legalization of same-sex marriage. Her openness about her relationship and advocacy work has made her an important figure in the LGBTQ+ community and a role model for many.

Tomlin's legacy is distinguished by her ability to blend humor with social commentary, creating work that is both entertaining and thought provoking. Her influence on comedy and contributions to the representation of LGBTQ+ individuals in the media have left a lasting impact on American culture.

Tommy Tune (1939–)

Choreographer, Director, Dancer

Thomas James "Tommy" Tune is a celebrated American actor, dancer, choreographer, and theater director who is renowned for his significant contributions to the world of musical theater. His innovative choreography and direction have earned him numerous accolades, including 10 Tony awards, making him one of the most decorated figures in Broadway history. His work is characterized by its creativity, elegance, and a seamless blending of dance and narrative, cementing his status as a pivotal figure in American theater.

Tune (the family name was shortened from "Tunesmith") was born in Wichita Falls, Texas, and grew up in Houston, where his father worked in the oil industry. He developed a passion for dance and theater at a young age and began taking dancing lessons at the age of 5. In 1962, he earned a degree in drama from the University of Texas, Austin, and an MFA in directing from the University of Houston. He moved to New York to begin his career, fearing that his height of over 6½ feet tall would be a problem in getting roles. However, his height actually helped him to land his first part on Broadway as one of three tall men in the chorus of the musical *Baker Street* (1965). His early career saw him performing in the chorus of various Broadway productions, gradually working his way up to more prominent roles. It was his performance in *Seesaw* (1973) that earned him his first Tony Award for Best Performance by a Featured Actor in a Musical.

Tune's remarkable career has included directing and choreographing some of Broadway's most iconic productions. He received widespread acclaim for his work on *A Day in Hollywood/A Night in the Ukraine* (1980), *Nine* (1982), and *My One and Only* (1983), each earning him Tony awards for choreography and direction. His production of *Grand Hotel* (1989) and *The Will Rogers Follies* (1991) further solidified his reputation as a masterful director and choreographer. In addition to his stage work, he has appeared in movies and television.

In his memoir, *Footnotes*, published in 1997, Tune supplied an account of his life and career as a performer, choreographer, and director. He also wrote about being openly gay in the world of theater; losing his partner, choreographer David Steiger Wolfe, to AIDS in 1984; and his breakup with *A Chorus Line* actor Michel Stuart. He also described an unnamed woman as the "love of [his] life," and some in the media speculated that the description he gave appeared to fit Twiggy, with whom he worked in *My One and Only*.

Tune's illustrious career has made a lasting impact on the landscape of musical theater. His visionary direction and choreography have set new standards in Broadway productions, blending artistic innovation with captivating storytelling. His openness about his sexuality and success in a competitive industry have made him a trailblazer and inspiration to many. As he continues to contribute to the arts, his legacy remains a testament to his extraordinary talent and enduring influence on American theater.

Robin Tyler (1942-)

Comedian, Activist

Called the "mother of gay comedy," Robin Tyler made history in 1978 when she became the first out lesbian on U.S. national television on a Showtime comedy special. She is a pioneering figure in LGBTQ+ activism and a trailblazer in comedy known for her relentless advocacy for LGBTQ+ rights and groundbreaking work as an openly lesbian comedian. Her career spans decades, during which she has made significant contributions to the fight for equality and representation. Her efforts have been instrumental in advancing the visibility and rights of the LGBTQ+ community, making her a significant figure in both the activism and entertainment spheres.

Tyler was born Arlene Chernick in Winnipeg, Manitoba, Canada. As early as 1959, she demonstrated her rebellious flamboyance by standing on a busy Winnipeg street corner holding a sign proclaiming, "Gay is Good." Her family did not accept her lesbian identity, and in 1962, she moved to Toronto. There and later in New York City, she began performing in nightclubs as a Judy Garland impersonator and stand-up comic. She developed a fearlessness onstage and a confrontational attitude to sexist and homophobic heckling. In response to one drunken patron, who shouted, "Are you a lesbian?" she quipped, "Are you the alternative?" With her impression of Garland, she took drag to a different level—as a woman pretending to be a man pretending to be a woman. "I was a lesbian being a female impersonator," she recalled. "All you have to do is be female and then just add something. Just one extra gesture."

In 1969, Tyler witnessed the second night of the Stonewall Riots with her partner, Patti Harrison, and told Harrison that she would never "stand back and just watch" again. "I think that after that night…that's when Robin Tyler the activist was born." She became a U.S. citizen so that she could tour Vietnam as part of the USO. After returning, she became an anti-war activist as well. With Harrison, she formed what she called the "first and only lesbian, feminist comedy team. There was television network interest in creating a variety show around them that never materialized because they refused to conform to the limits television required, which included remaining closeted. "Closets are vertical coffins," she said. "So, by not being on television, I was able to go out and finally be open. It wasn't that I was closeted, it's that I didn't know how to make it funny."

Tyler cofounded the first lesbian feminist theater company, paving the way for future generations of LGBTQ+ performers. As an activist, she was a key organizer of the first National March on Washington for Lesbian and Gay Rights in 1979 and again in 1993, events that were pivotal in the movement for LGBTQ+ equality.

In 2004, Tyler and her partner, Diane Olsen, played a significant role in the broader movement that led to the legalization of same-sex marriage. They applied for a marriage license in Los Angeles County and, after a license was denied, became the lead plaintiffs in the landmark lawsuit that challenged the constitutionality of California's laws banning same-sex marriage. In 2008, the California Supreme Court ruled in their favor, declaring that same-sex couples have a constitutional right to marry, making California the second state to legalize same-sex marriage. Tyler and Olsen were among the first same-sex couples to legally marry on June 16, 2008, a symbolic moment in the marriage equality movement. Despite the passage of Proposition 8 in November 2008, which temporarily banned same-sex marriage, their legal battle and public visibility helped to galvanize support for marriage equality, inspiring other couples and leading to further legal victories and, finally, to the U.S. Supreme Court case *Obergefell v. Hodges* in 2015, legalizing same-sex marriage nationally.

In 2019, Tyler's comic partner, Patti Harrison, and her wife, Diane Olsen, both died. She continues to perform. "What's good about a comic," she said, "is that… you can go on as long as you can go on. That's the age limit."

Christine Vachon (1962–)

Film Producer

One of the driving forces behind the New Queer Cinema movement that emerged in the 1990s, Christine Vachon is a renowned independent film producer who is celebrated for her work on groundbreaking films that challenge social norms and explore complex themes. Cofounding Killer Films, she produced critically acclaimed films that have been pivotal in bringing LGBTQ+ stories to mainstream cinema. Her dedication to independent filmmaking has significantly influenced the industry, providing a platform for diverse voices and fostering a greater understanding of underrepresented communities. Her contributions have cemented her as a key figure in contemporary cinema.

Vachon was born in Manhattan, New York. Her father was photographer John Vachon, and she was raised in a household that fostered her passion for the arts. She graduated from Brown University in 1983, where she acquired an encyclopedic knowledge of film history and made several short films. She was befriended by fellow student and film buff Todd Haynes, and they began a longtime collaboration. After college, she returned to New York during what has been called the first golden age of independent films. She started as an unpaid intern on *Far from Poland*, an independent film by Jill Godmilow, and worked her way up to assistant director on later projects.

Vachon's career took off in the early 1990s when she cofounded the production company Killer Films with partner Pamela Koffler. Under Vachon's leadership, Killer Films became a powerhouse in independent film production and was known for taking risks on unconventional and groundbreaking projects. One of her first major successes was producing Haynes's controversial and critically acclaimed film *Poison* (1991), which won the Grand Jury Prize at the Sundance Film Festival. This success solidified her reputation as a fearless producer willing to tackle challenging subjects.

Throughout her career, Vachon has produced numerous influential films that have left an indelible mark on the film industry. Notable works include *Kids* (1995), *Velvet Goldmine* (1998), *Boys Don't Cry* (1999), *Far from Heaven* (2002), and *Carol* (2015). Her collaboration with Haynes on multiple projects has been particularly significant, with *Carol* receiving six Academy Award nominations and further establishing her status as a leading figure in independent cinema. Her films often explore themes of identity, sexuality, and social issues, reflecting her commitment to diverse and provocative storytelling. She also coproduced the well-received 2011 HBO miniseries remake of *Mildred Pierce*, starring Kate Winslet as the title character.

Vachon is openly lesbian and has been a prominent advocate for LGBTQ+ representation in film, ensuring that the stories of marginalized communities are told with authenticity and depth. Her work has been instrumental in bringing LGBTQ+ narratives to a broader audience, challenging stereotypes, and promoting greater acceptance and understanding within the mainstream. Although identified with the New Queer Cinema film movement, she said that she wants to be known as a great producer, not a gay producer. Eamonn Bowles, an executive of Miramax, said, "I think years from now Christine will be an institution. They'll talk about 'Christine Vachon films.' She is ascending, and the reason she's getting bigger is that people are coming around to her sensibility."

Gore Vidal (1925–2012)

Writer

More properly described as a man of letters, Eugene Luther Gore Vidal Jr. published some 25 novels, two memoirs, and several volumes of essays as well as plays, television dramas, and screenplays. Like Norman Mailer and Truman Capote, he was intentionally a public figure who ran for office in both the House and the Senate (losing both times), an occasional actor, and ever present on talk shows, where he engaged in the combat of wits and insults, most famously with conservative pundit William F. Buckley Jr., who called him a "queer" on national television.

Vidal was born at the U.S. Military Academy at West Point, where his father, Eugene, had been an All-American football player and track star and had returned to be a flying instructor and football coach. His father would go on to found three airlines, including one that became TWA. His mother, Nina, was an actress and socialite and the daughter of Thomas Pryor Gore, a Democratic senator from Oklahoma.

Raised in Washington, D.C., Vidal attended St. Albans School, where he formed a relationship with one of the school's best athletes, Jimmie Trimble. Vidal would later call his affair "the most important of his life." Trimble would be killed at Iwo Jima during World War II. Vidal left St. Albans in 1939 and eventually graduated from Phillips Exeter Academy in New Hampshire. Foregoing college, he enlisted in the U.S. Army and became first mate on a freight supply ship in the Aleutian Islands. His first novel, *Williwaw* (1946), was based on his experiences. His third novel, *The City and the Pillar* (1948), dedicated to Trimble, was the coming-out story of a handsome, athletic, young Virginian man who discovers that he is gay. At the time, the book caused a scandal and was denounced as corrupt and pornographic, leading him to claim that he was blacklisted because of the book and had difficulty getting his work reviewed. He turned to writing mysteries under a pseudonym and writing for television, the stage, and, later, the movies. His play *The Best Man* (1960) was a Broadway success.

During the 1960s, Vidal returned to writing novels, producing *Julian* (1964), a meticulously researched historical novel about the fourth-century Roman emperor; *Washington, D.C.* (1967), a political novel set in the 1940s; and *Myra Breckinridge* (1968), a Black comedy about a gay man who has gender reassignment surgery. He found his greatest success with historical novels, notably what became known as his *American Chronicles*: *Burr* (1973), *1876* (1976), *Lincoln* (1984), *Empire* (1987), *Hollywood* (1990), and *The Golden Age* (2000). He also produced *Myron* (1974), a sequel to *Myra Breckinridge*, and the notorious *Live from Golgotha: The Gospel According to Gore Vidal* (1992), which rewrites the Gospels with Paul as a pederast and Jesus a buffoon.

Many critics believe that Vidal's ultimate legacy is his essay collections. *The Second American Revolution* won the National Book Critics Circle Award in 1982, and *United States: Essays, 1952–1992* (1993) won the National Book Award. He also wrote the autobiographies *Palimpsest* (1995), *Point Navigation* (2006), and *Snapshots in History's Glare* (2009).

As provocative about politics and culture as he was about sexuality, Vidal admitted in his 1995 memoir, *Palimpsest*, of having had more than 1,000 sexual encounters with both men and women by the time he was 25. He declared that human beings were inherently bisexual, and although he tended toward what he called "same-sex sex," he disliked the terms "gay" and "straight" and saw them as being arbitrary and unhelpful. He never referred to himself by any orientation, believing that words like "homosexual" or "heterosexual" describe acts and not the people who perform them. For 53 years, he had a live-in companion, Howard Austen, a former advertising executive, but he said that the secret to their relationship was that they did not sleep together. In his essay "Sex Is Politics," he wrote, "Many human beings enjoy sexual relations with their own sex, many don't; many respond to both. This plurality is the fact of our nature and not worth fretting about."

Paula Vogel (1951–)

Playwright

Paula Vogel is a celebrated American playwright whose work has greatly impacted contemporary theater. Known for her fearless exploration of complex and often taboo subjects, her plays are renowned for their emotional authenticity and depth, innovative structure, and poignant social commentary. Her contributions to the world of theater have earned her numerous awards and accolades, solidifying her place as one of the most influential dramatists of her generation.

Vogel was born in Washington, D.C. She attended Bryn Mawr College but did not graduate, eventually earning her bachelor's degree in 1974 from the Catholic University of America. She later received an MA (1976) and a Ph.D. (2016) from Cornell University. She began her career as an educator, teaching playwriting at Brown University from 1984 to 2008, where she founded and ran a playwriting workshop and started a theater workshop for women in maximum security at the Adult Correctional Institutions in Cranston, Rhode Island. Her early works, such as *Desdemona, A Play About a Handkerchief* (1979), a feminist retelling of Shakespeare's *Othello*, began to establish her reputation for tackling bold themes with a unique voice.

Vogel's breakthrough came with *The Baltimore Waltz* (1992), a poignant and humorous exploration of the AIDS crisis, which won an Obie Award for Best New American Play. This play is important for its imaginative and heartfelt portrayal of the AIDS epidemic's impact on individuals and families, using humor and fantasy to address a deeply serious topic while offering a critique of the medical establishment and a poignant depiction of love and loss. Her most acclaimed work, *How I Learned to Drive* (1997), deals with the sensitive topic of sexual abuse and earned her a Pulitzer Prize for Drama. The play is celebrated for its delicate handling of a difficult subject matter and innovative narrative structure. Other significant works include *The Long Christmas Ride Home* (2003), telling the story of a dysfunctional family's road trip to a Christmas gathering. This narrative explores themes of family conflict, trauma, and the passage of time and is notable for its innovative use of puppetry to represent the characters' younger selves, creating a visually and emotionally rich theatrical experience. *Indecent* (2015) recounts the true story of the controversial 1923 Broadway production of Sholem Asch's play *God of Vengeance*, which depicted a lesbian relationship and was shut down for obscenity. By tracing the journey of Asch's play from Europe to America, *Indecent* explores themes of censorship, anti-Semitism, and LGBTQ+ representation in the arts. Vogel's play received multiple Tony Award nominations and won for Best Direction of a Play. *Mother Play* (2024) is an autobiographical reflection on her own mother and her struggles with alcohol and her gay children, one of whom, Carl, died of AIDS in 1988.

Vogel, who is openly lesbian, has been a vocal advocate for LGBTQ+ rights throughout her career. In 2004, she married Brown University professor Anne Fausto-Sterling, a noted biologist and gender studies scholar. Her personal and professional lives have intersected through her marriage as well as her dedication to social justice, her mentorship of emerging playwrights, and her contributions to LGBTQ+ representation in the arts.

Lana Wachowski (1965–) and Lilly Wachowski (1967–)

Filmmakers, Writers, Producers

Lana and Lilly Wachowski are renowned filmmakers who are best known for creating *The Matrix* trilogy, which revolutionized science fiction and action cinema with groundbreaking special effects and philosophical depth. Their other notable works include *V for Vendetta, Cloud Atlas*, and the TV series *Sense8*. They are influential figures in the industry for their innovative storytelling and have also been vocal advocates for transgender rights, both coming out as transgender women and using their platform to promote LGBTQ+ visibility and acceptance.

Known collectively as the Wachowskis, they were born as Laurence (Lana) and Andrew (Lilly) in Chicago, Illinois. After graduating from a Chicago high school known for its performing arts in 1983 and

Lilly (left) and Lana Wachowski are award-winning TV and movie writers, producers, and directors who are behind such successes as the "Matrix" series, Cloud Atlas, *and* V for Vendetta.

1985, Lana attended Bard College in New York, and Lilly went to Emerson College in Boston. Both dropped out before graduating and together ran a house-painting and construction business in Chicago.

In 1993, the Wachowskis began to submit work to comic book series and then shifted to film writing, producing a script for *Assassins* (1995). When the director, Richard Donner, had their script totally rewritten, they tried unsuccessfully to remove their names from the film, and their experience convinced them that they should become directors. They made their debut as writers and directors in the thriller *Bound* (1996), which led to *The Matrix* in 1999. The film was a revolutionary blend of philosophical concepts, cutting-edge special effects, and thrilling action sequences. The success of *The Matrix* was followed by two sequels, *The Matrix Reloaded* and *The Matrix Revolutions*, both released in 2003. The trilogy's influence extended beyond cinema, inspiring numerous works in literature, video games, and popular culture.

In addition to *The Matrix* series, the Wachowskis have been responsible for other significant projects, including *V for Vendetta* (2005), which they wrote and produced, and the ambitious and visually stunning *Cloud Atlas* (2012). Their work often explores themes of identity, transformation, and social justice, reflecting their own personal journeys and beliefs.

Lana publicly revealed her transition in 2008, and in 2012, she made her first public appearance after transitioning to discuss *Cloud Atlas*, becoming the first major Hollywood director to come out as transgender. In 2016, Lilly also came out as a transgender woman. Accepting a GLAAD Award with her sister in 2016, Lilly said, "There's a critical eye being cast back on Lana and I's work through the lens of our transness. This is a cool thing because it's an excellent reminder that art is never static. And while the ideas of identity and transformation are critical components in our work, the bedrock that all ideas rest upon is love." *The Matrix* has been judged academically as a trans allegory, and that trans identity is central to understanding the Wachowskis' body of work.

The Wachowskis' courage in publicly sharing their transitions has made them prominent figures in the LGBTQ+ community and helped to raise awareness about transgender issues. Their visibility and advocacy have been instrumental in promoting greater acceptance and understanding of transgender individuals in both the film industry and society at large.

Andy Warhol (1928–1987)

Visual Artist, Film Director, Producer

Andy Warhol, an initiator and leading exponent of the Pop Art movement of the 1960s, revolutionized the art world with his distinctive approach to creativity and cultural commentary. Best known for his earliest works—silkscreen images of Campbell's soup cans and a wood sculpture painted like a box of Brillo pads—his career embraced fine art, photography, moviemaking, writing, and magazine publishing. Soft-spoken and unapologetically strange, he came to dominate the avant-garde scene in the 1960s and 1970s, becoming both a tastemaker and a cultural icon.

Warhol was born Andrew Warhola Jr. in Pittsburgh, Pennsylvania, into a working-class family. His parents emigrated from what is now eastern Slovakia, and his father worked in a coal mine. After graduating from a public high school in 1945, he earned a BFA in pictorial design from the Carnegie Institute of Technology (now Carnegie Mellon University) in 1949 before moving to New York City to begin a career in magazine illustration and advertising.

Warhol worked as a commercial illustrator for nearly a decade before turning to fine art in the late 1950s. He gained his first notoriety in 1962 when he exhibited a series of 32 paintings, each depicting a different variety of Campbell's soup. It exemplified his fascination with mass production and consumer culture, transforming everyday objects into subjects of artistic inquiry. As art critic Robert Hughes stated, "Painting a soup can is not in itself a radical act, but what was radical in Warhol was that he adapted the means of production of soup cans to the way he produced paintings, turning them out *en masse*—consumer art mimicking the process as well as the look of consumer culture." At the heart of his artistic philosophy was his fascination with the banality of everyday life and the pervasive influence of mass media. He famously declared, "In the future, everyone will be world-famous for 15 minutes," a sentiment that encapsulates his preoccupation with fame and the commodification of identity. Through iconic works such as *Campbell's Soup Cans* and his celebrity portraits of Marilyn Monroe, Elvis Presley, and others, he challenged traditional notions of artistic expression, elevating mundane objects and cultural icons to the realm of fine art. His work placed him at the forefront of the emerging Pop Art movement in America.

In 1964, Warhol opened his own art studio, a warehouse known simply as the Factory, which quickly became one of New York's premier cultural hotspots. As the 1960s progressed, he devoted more of his energy to filmmaking, creating such works as *Chelsea Girls* (1966); *Eat* (1963), a 45-minute film showing artist Robert Indiana eating a mushroom; *Haircut* (1963), showing a Warhol groupie having his hair cut; *My Hustler* (1965); and *Blue Movie* (1969). They were characterized by their lack of plots and, at times, inordinate length (up to 25 hours). In 1968, he was shot and nearly killed by Valerie Solanas, a radical feminist and one of the various assemblages of underground film and rock stars and other hangers-on at the Factory. In 1969, after a year of recuperation, he founded *Interview* magazine, which served as a platform for his cultivation of his and others' celebrity status. He returned to the contemporary art scene as a mentor and friend to young artists, including Keith Haring, Kenny Scharf, and Jean-Michel Basquiat. His own work consisted mainly of silkscreen prints of political and Hollywood celebrities.

Although Warhol claimed that he was a lifelong virgin and asexual, he was openly gay among friends and associates in his inner circle. His exploration of queer themes can be seen in some of his art, particularly in his films and private drawings. His film *Sleep* (1963), for example, features his partner at the time, John Giorno, sleeping for several hours, capturing an intimate and tender portrayal of their relationship. Similarly, his *Torso* series of drawings, which depicts male nudes, reflects his interest in the male form and exploration of sexuality. Additionally, his social circle at the Factory included many LGBTQ+ individuals, and he often depicted them in his work. Figures such as Candy Darling, Jackie Curtis, and Holly Woodlawn, all prominent transgender women and drag queens, were central to his artistic and social milieu.

Warhol died at the age of 58 of complications following gallbladder surgery. In 2008, his portrait *Eight Elvises* eventually resold for $100 million, making it one of the most valuable paintings in world history.

John Waters (1946–)

Filmmaker

Credited with pioneering a gay film aesthetic, John Waters is known for his subversive and influential movies. He gained fame with the cult classic *Pink Flamingos* (1972) and solidified his reputation with films like *Female Trouble* (1974) and *Hairspray* (1988). His work, characterized by its dark humor and boundary-pushing content, has earned him the title "Pope of Trash." His contributions extend beyond film into literature and the visual arts. His bold storytelling and celebration of the unconventional have left a lasting impact on both independent and mainstream cinema.

Born in Baltimore, Maryland, Waters grew up in Lutherville, Maryland, a suburb of Baltimore, along with his boyhood friend, Glenn Milstead, later known as Divine. Waters, who graduated from the Boys' Latin School of Maryland, began making silent 8mm and 16mm films in the mid-1960s, screening the films at a rented church hall to audiences drawn by word of mouth and street leafleting campaigns. By the early 1970s, he was making features that he managed to get shown at midnight screenings in art cinemas.

Waters gained significant attention with his 1972 film *Pink Flamingos*, a low-budget, transgressive comedy and deliberate exercise in ultra-bad taste that became a cult classic. The film, notorious for its shocking content and campy aesthetic, starred his muse, Divine, and established his reputation as the "Pope of Trash." Following this, he directed a series of films that combined outrageous humor with social commentary, including *Female Trouble* (1974), *Desperate Living* (1977), and *Polyester* (1981). His 1988 film *Hairspray* was a critical and commercial success, which was later adapted into a hit Broadway musical and a popular 2007 film remake. Other films include *Cry-Baby* (1990), *Serial Mom* (1994), *Pecker* (1998), *Cecil B. Demented* (2000), and *A Dirty Shame* (2004). He also acted in multiple films, including *Mondo Trasho* (1969), *Sweet and Lowdown* (1999), and *Suburban Gothic* (2014).

Beyond his work in film, Waters is also

an accomplished writer and visual artist. His books, such as *Shock Value* (1981) and *Role Models* (2010), offer insight into his creative process and life philosophy, further cementing his status as a cultural icon. His art exhibitions, often featuring provocative and humorous works, have been showcased in galleries and museums worldwide. His multifaceted career reflects his ability to transcend mediums while maintaining his unique voice and vision.

Waters is openly gay and has been a vocal advocate for LGBTQ+ rights and visibility, often using his celebrity to challenge societal norms and celebrate diversity. His films frequently feature queer characters and themes, presented in a way that is both unapologetically bold and deeply humanizing. His stance as a provocateur extends to a gay culture that he worries is becoming too mainstream and polite. "I'm for gay marriage," he stated. "I don't want to do it, but I certainly think people should be allowed to, and I wouldn't vote for anybody that would be against it. But at the same time, why do we have to be good now? Why can't we be villains in movies?" His legacy is one of gentle defiance, creativity, and an unwavering belief in the power of art to provoke, entertain, and inspire.

Edmund White (1940–2025)

Writer

Edmund Valentine White is an acclaimed author, essayist, and critic who is renowned for his contributions to LGBTQ+ literature and candid exploration of gay life. His prolific career has spanned several decades, producing influential works that have provided insight into the LGBTQ+ experience and significantly enriched American literature. His fearless storytelling and literary prowess have earned him a place among the most important voices in contemporary writing.

White was born in Cincinnati, Ohio, and raised in Evanston, Illinois. His early years were marked by a passion for literature and writing. He attended the Cranbrook School, a prestigious boarding school in Michigan, before enrolling at the University of Michigan, where he earned a degree in Chinese. He declined an offer from Harvard's doctoral program in Chinese to move to New York, where he began a career as an editor and writer, working for Time-Life Books, *Newsweek*, *The Saturday Review*, and *Horizon*. From 1981 to 1984, he served as director of New York University's New York Institute for the Humanities.

White's debut novel, *Forgetting Elena* (1973), was called "a marvelous book" by Vladimir Nabokov and has been read as a coded depiction of gay culture. He cowrote, with his psychotherapist, Charles Silverstein, *The Joy of Gay Sex* (1977), a sex guide that was one of the first to provide comprehensive and positive information about gay sex and relationships, becoming an essential resource for many gay men during a time when such information was not readily available. It also made him known to a wider readership. From 1980 to 1981, he was a member of a gay writers' group, the Violet Quill.

In 1980, he produced "States of Desire," a survey of gay life in America, and in 1982, he helped found the Gay Men's Health Crisis in New York City, the same year that *A Boy's Own Story*, the first novel in an autobiographical trilogy, appeared. Chronicling the protagonist's coming-of-age and coming-out experiences, its honest portrayal of a young man's struggles and desires was groundbreaking at the time and has remained a seminal work of gay literature.

From 1983 to 1990, White lived in Paris, and in 1984, he was diagnosed as HIV positive but was one of a small percentage of cases that is "nonprogressive" and does not lead to AIDS. He continued his autobiographical trilogy with *The Beautiful Room*

Is Empty (1988), which follows the protagonist through his college years and early adulthood and explores themes of identity, love, and the gay liberation movement of the 1960s. The trilogy concludes with *The Farewell Symphony* (1997), which follows the protagonist into adulthood, detailing his experiences with love, loss, and the impact of the AIDS crisis. This novel provides a historical perspective on the gay community's struggles and triumphs from the 1970s to the 1990s, capturing the profound changes and challenges of the era.

White's other major works include *Genet: A Biography* (1993), a critically acclaimed and award-winning biography of French writer Jean Genet. His memoir, *City Boy: My Life in New York During the 1960s and '70s* (2009), offers a vivid portrayal of his experiences in New York City during a transformative period for both the city and the gay community. The memoir provides personal insights into the cultural and social dynamics of the time, capturing the vibrancy and challenges of living through such a pivotal era. The novel *Our Young Man* (2016) explores the life of a beautiful, young, French model in the fashion world of New York and Paris during the 1980s and 1990s. The novel addresses themes of beauty, aging, and the impact of AIDS, showcasing his continued engagement with complex and timely issues.

White was appointed a full professor in Princeton University's Program in Creative Writing in 1998. He directed the Program in Creative Writing from 2002 to 2006. Since 1995, he has been the partner of fellow writer Michael Carroll. They married in 2013. Despite dealing with serious health issues, including strokes and a heart attack, he continued to produce influential works for years, not only for their literary merit but also for their honest and nuanced portrayal of gay life, making significant contributions to the visibility and understanding of LGBTQ+ experiences.

He passed away on June 3, 2025, at his home in Chelsea, Manhattan.

Walt Whitman (1819–1892)

Poet, Essayist, Journalist

Complex, contradictory, and possessed with a boundless ego coupled with a limitless capacity to enter the world around him imaginatively, Walt Whitman insisted on being regarded as the American epic poet who recorded, in his own words, an "aggregated, inseparable, unprecedented, vast, composite, electric democratic nationality." He never publicly addressed his sexuality or orientation, yet he refused to censor that aspect of himself in his work. As he wrote, "Do I contradict myself?/Very well then I contradict myself,/(I am large, I contain multitudes.)"

Whitman was born on Long Island, New York, the son of a farmer and carpenter who moved his family to nearby Brooklyn, then a small city, when he was not quite 5 years old. He left school when he was 11 years old to work as an office boy before becoming an apprentice printer. By the age of 17, he was a compositor and also worked as a country schoolmaster. Printing work led to journalism, and Whitman, until the age of 31, held a number of positions as a reporter, editorial writer, and editor on various New York newspapers. Fired from his job over his paper's regressive politics, he embarked on a three-month trip to New Orleans and began to conceive of a great poetic work to celebrate the ideals of American democracy and the American experience. He also began to dress the part of the American bard, with a full beard and workingman's clothes.

The constantly evolving *Leaves of Grass* was initially self-printed in 1855, and Whitman's unconventional form, unpoetic subjection of ordinary American life, and overt sensuality ensured a hostile critical reaction and popular neglect. However, it was embraced and appreciated by such figures as Henry David Thoreau and Ralph Waldo Emerson, who wrote to him, "I greet you at the beginning of a great career."

For the rest of his life, he expanded and revised the poems of *Leaves of Grass* (there were nine subsequent editions) into a single, all-encompassing poetic sequence, incorporating his early optimism at America's democratic prospects with his increasingly tragic tone from his experience in the Civil War, nursing the wounded in a Washington military hospital. After the war, a paralyzing stroke required him to live the rest of his life at his brother's home in Camden, New Jersey, where he gave occasional readings and received admirers who regarded him as a prophet, seer, and "the good, gray poet." He died while overseeing a final edition of *Leaves of Grass* at the age of 72.

Biographers and critics continue to debate Whitman's sexuality, and he is generally described as either gay or bisexual. His poetry does celebrate the beauty of the male physical form and same-sex comradeship, but the author steadfastly denied that such friendships contained an explicit sexual component. The most obvious candidate for the love of his life was Peter Doyle, a bus conductor whom he met in 1866. The two were inseparable for several years. Oscar Wilde, who met Whitman in 1882 while on tour in the United States, later reported that "I have the kiss of Walt Whitman still on my lips." Whitman claimed sexual relationships with women and that he fathered six children, but these claims have never been corroborated.

In poems such as "Starting from Paumanok" and "Over the Carnage Rose Prophetic Voice," he idealizes a future world founded on the principles of male comradeship. Critic Arnie Kantrowitz, writing in an essay called "How Gay Was Walt Whitman?" that analyzes the evidence in Whitman's life and works, concludes, "Whitman seems the prototype of the modern gay man."

Regardless of Whitman's denials and contradictions, he has remained an important icon of the gay community based on the ways in which his great American epic, *Leaves of Grass*, is an all-inclusive work that considers all of the American experience, even experience that is repressed and condemned. His courage and vision created a new epoch for poetry and American literature. He also can be credited with being the first giant of American literature to treat the homoerotic in a compassionate and empowering way.

Tennessee Williams (1911–1983)

Playwright

Along with Eugene O'Neill and Arthur Miller, Tennessee Williams was one of the towering major American playwrights of the 20th century. One of the founders of the so-called New Drama movement, his innovative and groundbreaking dramas were heralded "as a revelation of what superb theater could be." He would also present for one of the first times on the American stage homosexual themes that led critic Hilton Als to call him "the man who queered Broadway."

Thomas Lanier Williams III, known by his pen name, Tennessee Williams, was born in Columbus, Mississippi. His grandfather was an Episcopal clergyman in a parish in Clarksdale, Mississippi, and he lived in his grandfather's rectory for much of his early childhood before the family relocated to St. Louis. From 1929 to 1931, he attended the University of Missouri studying journalism but began writing stories and plays out of boredom with his studies. After a stint at Washington University in St. Louis, he transferred to the University of Iowa, where he graduated with a B.A. in English in 1938. He moved to New York, adopted "Tennessee" as his professional name in acknowledgment of his Southern roots, and worked a string of menial jobs as he struggled to get his plays produced.

Williams's breakout success was *The Glass Menagerie* (1944), which uses expressionistic techniques and draws movingly on his own early life in St. Louis with portraits of his domineering mother and her invalid sister. In his review, Brooks Atkinson stated that "Williams's remembrance of things past gave the theater distinction as a literary medium," and theater historian Joanne Stang wrote that "the American theater, indeed theater everywhere, has never been the same" since the premiere of *The Glass Menagerie.*

After publishing a collection of one-act plays, *27 Wagons Full of Cotton* (1946), Williams produced his most celebrated play, *A Streetcar Named Desire* (1947), called by Eric Bentley the "master-drama of the generation." The play represented a seismic shift in American theater both for its sexual naturalism and for embedding into its plot the downfall of neurotic Blanche Dubois due to a homosexual revelation: Blanche was once married to a man who kills himself after she discovers him having an affair with another man. Homosexuality would be central to the family drama of *Cat on a Hot Tin Roof* (1955) as the marriage between Brick and Maggie must face the guilt that Brick feels over his romantic and sexual feelings for a college friend who has died. Williams's other plays, mostly dealing with the quest for love, sexual repression, and the tragic consequences of contradictory sexual identity, include *Summer and Smoke* (1948), *The Rose Tattoo* (1953), *Camino Real* (1953), *Sweet Bird of Youth* (1957), *Suddenly, Last Summer* (1958), and *The Night of the Iguana* (1962).

Despite suggesting gay desire on the American stage, Williams remained tormented by questions of sexual identity. The queer characters in his works almost never have a happy ending, which critics have attributed to the shame attached to homosexuality that his Southern rearing instilled in him. After some early attempts at relationships with women, by the late 1930s, he began exploring his homosexuality, but several relationships ended badly. His longest relationship was with actor Frank Merlo, which lasted for 14 years before infidelities on both sides ended it. He believed that the years spent with Merlo in an apartment in Manhattan and a small house in Key West, Florida, were his happiest and marked the most productive period of his life. Merlo died shortly after their breakup in 1963. In *Memoirs* (1965), Williams writes, "I never considered my homosexuality as anything to be disguised. Neither did I consider it a matter to be over-emphasized. I consider it an accident of nature."

Lanford Wilson (1937–2011)

Playwright

Lanford Wilson was a prolific American playwright whose works are celebrated for their lyrical language, complex characters, and profound emotional depth. As a key figure in the Off-Off-Broadway movement, his plays often explored themes of human connection, identity, and the struggles of the marginalized. His contributions to American theater have earned him numerous awards and a lasting legacy as one of the most important playwrights of the 20th century.

Wilson was born in Lebanon, Missouri, which he used as the setting for many of his plays, including *Talley's Folly.* His parents divorced when he was 5 years old and, after his mother remarried when he was 11 years old, he grew up in Ozark, Missouri, where in high school, he developed a love of film and art and acted in school plays. After beginning college at Southwest Missouri State, he moved to San Diego to live with his father, studying art and art history at San Diego State College. He explored his family life in what he called the "purely autobiographical" play *Lemon Sky* (1970), which deals with a young gay man's attempt at a reconciliation with his father. He left college in 1957 to move to Chicago, where he worked as a graphic artist in an advertising firm and began to convert the short stories he had been writing into plays.

Wilson later moved to New York City in 1962, drawn by its theater scene. He quickly became involved with the Caffe Cino, a hub for experimental theater. His early works, such as *The Madness of Lady Bright* (1964), which follows the mental disintegration of an aging drag queen, marked him as a voice for marginalized communities and garnered attention for their innovative storytelling and exploration of contemporary issues. In 1965, he began writing plays for La MaMa Experimental Theatre Club in the East Village, where he began his long association with Marshall W. Mason, who would direct most of his works' productions.

Wilson's major plays include *Balm in Gilead* (1965), which uses overlapping dialogue to depict the lives of down-and-out characters in a New York diner. The play established him as a key figure in the Off-Off-Broadway movement. *The Rimers of Eldritch* (1967) explores hypocrisy and moral decay in a small town. *The Hot L Baltimore* (1973) highlights society's outcasts in a dilapidated hotel and won the New York Drama Critics' Circle Award for its compassionate storytelling. *The Mound Builders* (1975) examines legacy and ambition through an archaeological dig in Illinois. *Fifth of July* (1978), part of the *Talley* trilogy, explores the impact of war on individuals and families and was notable for its portrayal of a gay couple. *Talley's Folly* (1979), a romantic comedy also in the *Talley* trilogy, won the Pulitzer Prize for its sensitive portrayal of love overcoming social barriers. *Talley & Son* (1981) completes the trilogy and examines generational conflicts during World War II. *Burn This* (1987) follows the tumultuous relationship between a dancer and her deceased roommate's brother, showcasing his emotional depth. *Redwood Curtain* (1993) explores identity and the lingering effects of the Vietnam War, highlighting his continued commitment to social issues.

Wilson, who was openly gay, often explored themes of homosexuality and identity in his works. His personal experiences and relationships deeply influenced his writing, allowing him to portray LGBTQ+ characters with nuance and authenticity. His contributions to gay theater were significant, providing visibility and a voice to the LGBTQ+ community at a time when such representation was rare. He was also a founding member of the Circle Repertory Company, a theater collective that became renowned for producing innovative and influential works.

Wilson's contributions to American theater have left a profound impact, with his plays continuing to be performed and studied for their emotional resonance and social relevance. His explorations of human relationships and the complexities of identity have ensured his place as a central figure in the landscape of contemporary drama.

Grant Wood (1891–1942)

Artist

Grant DeVolson Wood was an American artist known for his role in the Regionalism movement, which emphasized rural American themes and settings during the early 20th century. His most famous work, *American Gothic* (1930), is an iconic painting depicting a stern-looking farmer and his daughter (often misinterpreted as the farmer's wife), symbolizing traditional American values and the rural Midwest. His art is characterized by its meticulous detail, smooth surfaces, and a blend of realism and stylization. His works often depicted the landscapes, people, and scenes of rural America, celebrating its simplicity and resilience. His contribution to American art lies in his ability to elevate everyday rural life into subjects of artistic and cultural significance, making him a key figure in the history of American art.

Wood was born in rural Anamosa, Iowa, but his mother moved the family to Cedar Rapids, Iowa, after his father died in 1901. After graduating from a public high school, he enrolled in The Handicraft Guild, an art school run entirely by women, in Minneapolis in 1910 before enrolling at the School of the Art Institute of Chicago in 1913.

Wood's artistic journey took a significant turn during his travels to Europe in the 1920s. Exposure to Impressionist, Post-Impressionist, Gothic, and Renaissance art deeply influenced his style. Upon returning to the United States, he developed a distinctive approach that celebrated the rural American Midwest, diverging from the European avant-garde trends of the time. This regional focus culminated in 1930 with the creation of *American Gothic*, a painting that captured the spirit of American rural life and became an enduring symbol of Americana.

In 1932, Wood cofounded the Stone City Art Colony near Cedar Rapids to support artists during the Great Depression. This initiative reflected his commitment to nurturing local talent and fostering an appreciation for regional art. His dedication to art education continued with his appointment as a professor of fine arts at the University of Iowa in 1934, where he influenced a generation of artists.

Wood's sexuality, like many aspects of his personal life, was not publicly discussed during his lifetime. While it is widely believed that his friends knew he was gay, societal norms of the time kept his orientation private. He was unhappily married from 1935 to 1938 to a former opera singer, Sara Sherman. For the last six years of his life, he lived with his personal secretary, Park Rinard. Art historian and biographer R. Tripp Evans has asserted that Wood was a closeted gay man who was terrified of having his sexual orientation exposed, and his reputation was closely guarded by his sister, Nan Wood Graham (the model for the female figure in *American Gothic*). It was only after her death in 1990 that scholars began to write about his sexuality and the homoerotic symbols in his landscapes, portraits, and genre paintings.

After his death, Wood's contributions to American art were honored by naming a World War II Liberty ship after him, the establishment of the Grant Wood Art Colony in 1975, and the placement of his home in Iowa City on the National Register of Historic Places in 1978.

Media

LGBTQ+ representation in American newspapers, magazines, radio, broadcast news, podcasting, and social media owes its evolution to the first gay and lesbian organizations, which founded publications providing information that would prove crucial to the fight for queer rights and visibility. LGBTQ+-based media, starting with newspapers and magazines, would become a critical force in helping to amplify LGBTQ+ voices and issues, offering platforms for advocacy, education, and a wider public acceptance of LGBTQ+ identities. Coverage of LGBTQ+ stories and perspectives have ultimately not only served the queer community but also added much-needed diversity to mainstream media and society as a whole, offering the public a more accurate, less stereotyped understanding of the LGBTQ+ community. In 1975, Leonard Matlovich, a decorated Vietnam veteran and U.S. Air Force sergeant, became the first openly LGBTQ+ person to appear on the cover of *Time* magazine, which was, for many years, the most influential newsmagazine in the United States. The cover featured the subhead "I Am a Homosexual." *Time* would subsequently feature newly out lesbian TV star Ellen DeGeneres (1997) and trans woman actor–producer Laverne Cox (2014) on its covers. After Harvey Milk, the first openly gay elected official in California, was assassinated in 1978, his story was covered extensively in both mainstream and LGBTQ+ news media, bringing much-needed attention to LGBTQ+ rights and visibility. Extensive reporting on the marriage equality movement, together with the #LoveWins campaign, a viral social media phenomenon, demonstrated the power of news media and digital platforms in LGBTQ+ advocacy and helped to influence public and political opinion concerning the legalization of same-sex marriage in the United States.

Media platforms are crucial in informing the public and influencing public discourse on LGBTQ+ issues. Journalism helps to shape public understanding through investigative reporting, editorials, and feature stories that highlight LGBTQ+ experiences. Radio and television provide programs for both mainstream and community-driven discussions, bringing LGBTQ+ issues to audiences that might not otherwise engage with them. In more recent years, podcasts have emerged as a powerful platform for in-depth discussion and analysis of LGBTQ+ topics, offering a space for voices that are often underrepresented in other forms of media. Finally, social media, which has revolutionized the way in which news is shared and consumed, has allowed for real-time updates and a more interactive engagement with LGBTQ+ issues. The visibility of LGBTQ+ social media influencers, podcasters, journalists, and well-known TV news anchors like Anderson Cooper and Don Lemon, who are openly gay, have additionally served as powerful examples to both queer and straight parents and young people as role models who have demonstrated that LGBTQ+ identities are compatible with successful careers in the media.

Newspapers and Magazines

LGBTQ+ representation in mainstream journalism has undergone a significant transformation over the past century, evolving from near invisibility to primarily community-oriented newspapers and magazines to a more prominent role in the media landscape. In the early to mid-20th century, LGBTQ+ issues were largely ignored by mainstream journalism or, when they were covered, it was often through a lens of scandal, criminality, or moral judgment. Newspapers and magazines either completely overlooked LGBTQ+ communities or portrayed them negatively, reinforcing prejudices and stereotypes and contributing to the marginalization of LGBTQ+ individuals. Coverage of LGBTQ+ issues was scarce, and when it did occur, it often focused on salacious or sensationalized stories, such as police raids on gay bars or the arrest of LGBTQ+ individuals, framing these events as the deviant behavior of "perverts" rather than legitimately newsworthy topics.

The challenges faced by LGBTQ+ journalists during this period were considerable. Those who were openly LGBTQ+, or even suspected of being LGBTQ+,

The San Francisco Chronicle, *headquartered at 901 Mission Street, began covering LGBTQ issues in the late 1960s, the first mainstream paper to pay attention to the needs of the community.*

risked discrimination, professional ostracism, and job loss. The stigma surrounding LGBTQ+ identities meant that many LGBTQ+ journalists were forced to conceal their identities in order to maintain their careers. Even within the LGBTQ+ community, journalists who sought to cover LGBTQ+ topics in a serious and respectful manner often struggled to find outlets that were willing to publish their work. However, notable exceptions existed as well as early pioneers who pushed against these barriers. For example, Randy Shilts, one of the first openly gay journalists at a major newspaper, played a crucial role in bringing attention to the AIDS crisis with his groundbreaking work for the *San Francisco Chronicle* and his influential book *And the Band Played On* (1987). Shilts's work marked a turning point in how LGBTQ+ issues, particularly those related to health and civil rights, were covered in the media, demonstrating the power of journalism to effect change and raise awareness.

LGBTQ+ representation in journalism has seen substantial progress since the later decades of the 20th century, with a noticeable increase in both the inclusion of LGBTQ+ topics in major news outlets and the visibility of LGBTQ+ journalists themselves. When mainstream news organizations began to actively cover LGBTQ+ issues, they reflected a broader societal shift toward a greater acceptance and recognition of LGBTQ+ visibility and rights. The *San Francisco Chronicle* began covering gay rights issues with more nuance and depth during the late 1960s, even featuring an editorial titled "A New Look at Homosexual Marriage," which suggested support for gay weddings. By the 1970s, publications like *The New York Times* and *The Village Voice,* influenced by cultural imperatives such as the second women's movement and properly shamed by activists for its use of pejoratives to describe the queer community, had begun to follow suit. Mainstream newspapers would ultimately begin to regularly report on LGBTQ+-related topics, including civil rights and health care, the latter most notably concerning the AIDS epidemic, with *The New York Times* publishing its first article in 1981 on the little-understood disease that would become the virus known as HIV/AIDS but which the *Times* initially referred to as a "rare cancer" among gay men. Overall, increased mainstream coverage has not only raised awareness of the challenges faced by LGBTQ+ communities, but it has also highlighted queer journalists' contributions to society, helping to shift public perception and foster a more inclusive environment.

In addition to mainstream newspaper outlets, many LGBTQ+-focused newspapers and magazines have played a key role in representing and advocating on behalf of local and national LGBTQ+ communities. The earliest LGBTQ+ newspaper still publishing is the *Washington Blade,* founded in 1969 as *The Gay Blade,* with roots in the newsletter of the Mattachine Society's

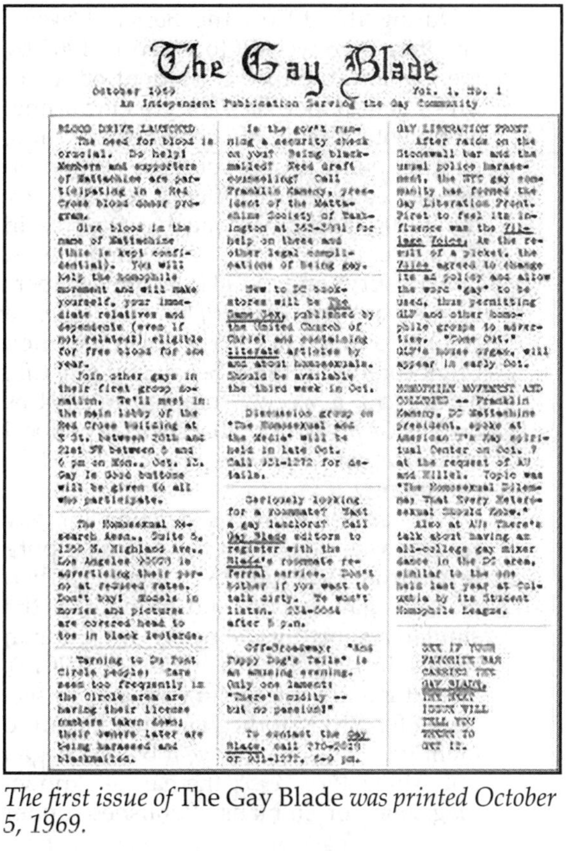

The Gay Blade

October 1969 — Vol. 1, No. 1

An Independent Publication Serving the Gay Community

BLOOD DRIVE LAUNCHED

The need for blood is crucial. Do help! Members and supporters of Mattachine are participating in a Red Cross blood donor program.

Give blood in the name of Mattachine (this is kept confidential). You will help the homophile movement and will make yourself, your immediate relatives and dependents (even if not related!) eligible for free blood for one year.

Join other gays in their first group donation. We'll meet in the main lobby of the Red Cross building at E St. between 20th and 21st NW between 2 and 6 pm on Mon., Oct. 13. Gay Is Good buttons will be given to all who participate.

The Homosexual Research Assn., Suite 5, 1350 N. Highland Ave., Los Angeles [illegible] is advertising their porno at reduced rates. Don't buy! Models in movies and pictures are covered head to toe in black leotards.

Warning to Du Pont Circle people: Cars seen too frequently in the Circle area are having their license numbers taken down; their owners later are being harassed and blackmailed.

Is the gov't running a security check on you? Being blackmailed? Need draft counseling? Call Franklin Kameny, president of the Mattachine Society of Washington at 363-3881 for help on these and other legal complications of being gay.

New to DC bookstores will be The Same Sex, published by the United Church of Christ and containing literate articles by and about homosexuals. Should be available the third week in Oct.

Discussion group on "The Homosexual and the Media" will be held in late Oct. Call 931-1272 for details.

Seriously looking for a roommate? Want a gay landlord? Call Gay Blade editors to register with the Blade's roommate referral service. Don't bother if you want to talk dirty. We won't listen. 234-6064 after 5 p.m.

Off-Broadway: "And Puppy Dog's Tails" is an amusing evening. Only one lament: "There's nudity -- but no passion!"

To contact the Gay Blade, call 270-2029 or 931-1272, 6-9 pm.

GAY LIBERATION FRONT

After raids on the Stonewall bar and the usual police harassment, the NYC gay community has formed the Gay Liberation Front. First to feel its influence was the Village Voice. As the result of a picket, the Voice agreed to change its ad policy and allow the word "gay" to be used, thus permitting GLF and other homophile groups to advertise. "Come Out," GLF's house organ, will appear in early Oct.

HOMOPHILE MOVEMENT AND COLLEGES -- Franklin Kameny, DC Mattachine president, spoke at American U's Kay Spiritual Center on Oct. 7 at the request of AU and Hillel. Topic was "The Homosexual Dilemma: That Every Heterosexual Should Know."

Also at AU: There's talk about having an all-college gay mixer dance in the DC area, similar to the one held last year at Columbia by its Student Homophile League.

SEE IF YOUR FAVORITE BAR CARRIES THE GAY BLADE. THE NEXT ISSUE WILL TELL YOU WHERE TO GET IT.

The first issue of The Gay Blade *was printed October 5, 1969.*

Washington, D.C., chapter. A social communications paper originally distributed in gay bars that featured closeted writers who used pen names, the paper was renamed in 1980 and went on to become a newspaper of record for its reporting of LGBTQ+ local, national, and international news. From 1969 to 1972, eight issues of the newspaper *Come Out!* were published in the wake of the Stonewall Uprising by the Gay Liberation Front. A voice for the GLF that was primarily sold on New York street corners, the paper focused on encouraging closeted lesbians and gays to come out, LGBTQ+ rights, and lesbian feminism and anti-sexism. In its first issue, *Come Out!* castigated *The Village Voice* for disallowing the use of the words "gay" and "homosexual" in its classified ads, words the *Voice*, despite its reputation as a progressive, alternative Greenwich Village newspaper, considered at the time to be "obscene."

During the 1970s, the *Boston Phoenix*, an alternative weekly founded in 1965 by Joe Hanlon, the former student editor of MIT's newspaper *The Tech*, was including, along with its mix of current events, arts, culture, politics, and sports, a section on the gay community (offered regularly by the 1990s) and was available for free in public venues in various cities and towns. Other surviving LGBTQ+ newspapers of note are the *Philadelphia Gay News*, a weekly founded in 1976 by Gay Liberation Front cofounder Mark Segal, and *Gay City News (gcn)*, a weekly founded in 1994 as *Lesbian Gay New York* that focuses on local and national news affecting the LGBTQ+ community.

The earliest known magazine for gay readers was *Friendship and Freedom*, published from 1924 to 1925 by Henry Gerber, an early gay activist and founder of the similarly short-lived Society for Human Rights. In 1947, Edythe Eyde (1921–2015), an editor and writer who worked as a secretary for RKO Studios and had begun to identify as a lesbian the year before, began publishing *Vice Versa*, the earliest known magazine for lesbians. Published under the pen name Lisa Ben (an anagram of "lesbian") and subtitled *America's Gayest Magazine*, Eyde founded *Vice Versa* as a forum for other lesbians to share their letters, personal stories, short fiction, and poetry. Eyde typed and printed the magazine at RKO, where she had little work and a boss who was uninterested in what she was typing as long as she "looked busy." *Vice Versa* only lasted for one year and nine issues, but journalist and historian Rodger Streitmatter, writing in the 1990s, contended that despite the magazine's lack of photographs, advertisements, or any information on its editor and writers, *Vice Versa* "set the agenda that has defined lesbian and gay journalism for 50 years."

Journalist, editor, and fiction writer Edythe Eyde (aka Lisa Ben) founded the first lesbian publication in North America, Vice Versa, *in 1947.*

The Ladder (1956–1973), published by the Daughters of Bilitis, was the first nationally distributed lesbian periodical, and the *Lesbian Tide,* which originated from the DOB Los Angeles chapter newsletter and was published from 1971 to 1980, was the first to use the word "lesbian" in its name. The *Lesbian Connection,* "for, by and about lesbians," was founded in 1974 by the lesbian feminist collective Ambitious Amazons. The Michigan-based periodical claims the distinction of being the longest-running magazine for lesbian readers in the United States.

The oldest running periodical for bisexual women is *Bi Women Quarterly,* founded in 1983 by the Boston Bisexual Women's Network, which features the life stories and creative work of women who identify as bisexual+, an inclusive term intended to encompass all the woman-aligned identities potentially contained in LGBTQ+ initialism.

Magazines founded during the homophile movement (1945–1969) by members or former members of the Mattachine Society, who had formed new organizations with different activist agendas, featured topics ranging from gay equality and rights to literary material and gay culture and included *ONE Magazine* (1953–1969), *The Mattachine Review* (1955–1967), and *Drum* (1964–1969). *The Advocate,* first published in 1967 in Los Angeles by the activist group Personal Rights in Defense and Education (PRIDE) as a newsletter for the local gay community, soon evolved into the nation's most influential LGBTQ+ newsmagazine and has remained one of the most influential LGBTQ+ publications in the United States. It has been instrumental in covering pivotal moments in LGBTQ+ history, such as the fight against HIV/AIDS, the struggle for marriage equality, and ongoing battles for transgender rights, offering a platform for stories that might not find space in mainstream media.

Out magazine, launched in 1992, has become a leading voice in LGBTQ+ culture and the experiences of LGBTQ+ individuals both in the United States and globally. In 2009, *Original Plumbing,* a lifestyle and culture magazine focusing on the stories and experiences of trans men, was founded in San Francisco to bring visibility to the trans male community and was published until 2019.

The digital age produced the informative online newsmagazine *LGBTQ Nation* in 2009. Headquartered in San Francisco, the site is affiliated with the e-zine sites *Queerly, GayCities,* and *INTO*—subtitled *A Digital Magazine for the Modern Queer World*—through its parent company, Q. Digital. The same year saw the first issue of *Frock,* an online magazine for the transgender and drag communities, which offered over 40 issues until 2017. These print and online publications have not only

One of the most successful LGBTQ magazines in America is The Advocate, *a bimonthly periodical that has been in print since 1967 and currently boasts about 175,000 subscribers.*

provided crucial information for LGBTQ+ readers but have also helped to create a sense of community and solidarity, offering over the years a space where LGBTQ+ voices can be heard and celebrated.

Although LGBTQ+ journalists in mainstream news outlets have seen success in surmounting employment barriers, such barriers do continue to exist. Discrimination, both overt and subtle, remains an issue, with many LGBTQ+ journalists encountering difficulties in advancement or feeling pressured to downplay their identities in professional settings. The media industry, like many others, has historically been dominated by cisgender, heterosexual individuals, and breaking into this space as an LGBTQ+ person often requires overcoming significant obstacles.

Additionally, LGBTQ+ journalists may face unique pressures when covering LGBTQ+ topics because they are sometimes expected to be the "voice" of the entire community, which can be both limiting and exhausting. This pressure is compounded by the fact that LGBTQ+ journalists are often the targets of harassment, particularly online, where anti-LGBTQ+ sentiments can be amplified.

Despite cultural, corporate, and political challenges, LGBTQ+ journalists continue to make invaluable contributions to the media landscape. Their work not only enriches the diversity of perspectives available to the public but also ensures that LGBTQ+ stories are told with the depth, nuance, and respect they deserve. The growing presence of LGBTQ+ journalists in newsrooms across the country is a testament to LGBTQ+ resilience and a recognition of the importance of diversity in journalism. As the industry continues to evolve, the inclusion and support of LGBTQ+ journalists will be crucial in ensuring that media coverage reflects the true diversity of the society it serves.

Radio and Television

The evolution of LGBTQ+ representation in radio and television followed a similar trajectory to print journalism, with early efforts often taking place in the margins before gradually gaining more mainstream acceptance. In the early days of radio and television, LGBTQ+ topics were rarely discussed openly, and when they were, it was often in a context that reinforced negative stereotypes. LGBTQ+ representation in radio played a significant role in the dissemination of information, advocacy, and the amplification of LGBTQ+ voices, particularly during periods when other media platforms were less inclusive. Early on, radio not only served as a lifeline for isolated LGBTQ+ individuals but also contributed to broader social change by educating all listeners about social and legal issues of concern to the LGBTQ+ community, particularly when other media platforms were less inclusive.

> ***One of the most notable LGBTQ+ radio programs is** This Way Out, **which began broadcasting in 1988 and remains one of the longest-running LGBTQ+ radio shows in the world.***

During the 1970s and 1980s, community-driven radio stations began to emerge as important platforms for LGBTQ+ voices. These stations, often run by and for the LGBTQ+ community, provided a crucial outlet for news, discussion, and advocacy that was largely absent from mainstream media. WBAI, a community radio station in New York, aired one of the first LGBTQ+ radio programs, *Gay Morning America*, in 1973. This program offered a rare space for LGBTQ+ issues to be discussed openly and respectfully, setting the stage for future positive developments in LGBTQ+ broadcasting.

One of the most notable LGBTQ+ radio programs is *This Way Out*, which began broadcasting in 1988 and remains one of the longest-running LGBTQ+ radio shows in the world. *This Way Out* was founded by Greg Gordon and Lucia Chappelle with the goal of providing news, interviews, and cultural programming for the LGBTQ+ community. The program quickly became a critical resource for listeners, offering coverage of LGBTQ+ issues that were often ignored or misrepresented in mainstream media and covering significant events such as the AIDS crisis, the fight for marriage equality, and the ongoing struggle for transgender rights, reaching an international audience through syndication. The show's impact is evident in its longevity and ability to adapt to changing media landscapes while continuing to serve as a trusted source of LGBTQ+ news and information. LGBTQ+ community radio shows have been at the forefront of providing critical content tailored specifically to LGBTQ+ communities, offering a vital platform for discussion, support, and visibility. Early on, radio not only served as a lifeline for isolated LGBTQ+ individuals but also contributed to broader social change by educating all listeners about social and legal issues of concern to the LGBTQ+ community, particularly when other media platforms were less inclusive.

National Public Radio offers news and other informational programs that often strive to integrate LGBTQ content for their audiences.

In recent years, mainstream radio has increasingly begun to address LGBTQ+ issues and include LGBTQ+ voices, though this progress has been uneven. National Public Radio (NPR), for example, has made significant strides in integrating LGBTQ+ content into its programming. Shows like *All Things Considered* and *Morning Edition* regularly feature segments on LGBTQ+ topics ranging from political and legal developments to personal stories of LGBTQ+ individuals. NPR's inclusive approach has helped to normalize LGBTQ+ issues for a broader audience, presenting them as integral components of the national conversation rather than niche topics.

However, the inclusion of LGBTQ+ voices in mainstream radio is still a work in progress. While some mainstream stations and programs have embraced LGBTQ+ content, others have been slower to do so, often relegating LGBTQ+ issues to specific segments or special broadcasts rather than integrating them fully into their regular programming. This can result in LGBTQ+ topics being treated as secondary or less important compared to other news, which can reinforce the marginalization of LGBTQ+ communities. Additionally, LGBTQ+ radio hosts and commentators are still relatively rare in mainstream radio, and those who do achieve prominence often face unique challenges, including navigating a media landscape that may not always be welcoming or supportive of their identities.

The coverage of LGBTQ+ issues as well as LGBTQ+ representation in television has evolved significantly over the years, reflecting broader societal changes and a growing acceptance of LGBTQ+ identities. In earlier decades, LGBTQ+ topics were often either ignored, marginalized, or sensationalized in television news programming. Coverage was sporadic and typi-

Rachel Maddow interviews actor Ben Affleck in an episode of The Rachel Maddow Show *on MS NOW. The popular news discussion show has won numerous awards, including three Emmys, a GLAAD Media Award, a Maggie Award from Planned Parenthood, and a Walter Cronkite Faith and Freedom Award.*

cally focused on negative aspects, such as criminal cases involving LGBTQ+ individuals or the AIDS crisis, without delving into the broader context or the humanity of those affected. However, as societal attitudes began to shift, so, too, did the approach of television news to LGBTQ+ issues. Television news programs are more likely to cover LGBTQ+ issues with the seriousness and respect they deserve. Major networks like CNN, MS NOW, and ABC News regularly feature segments on LGBTQ+ rights, health, and culture, particularly during key moments such as Pride Month or when significant legal decisions affect the LGBTQ+ community. For example, MS NOW's *The Rachel Maddow Show*, which debuted in 2008 and is hosted by openly lesbian anchor Rachel Maddow, has become a prominent platform for LGBTQ+ issues. Maddow has consistently covered LGBTQ+ topics from the fight for marriage equality to the repeal of the "Don't Ask, Don't Tell" policy, bringing these stories into the homes of millions of viewers. Similarly, CNN's *Anderson Cooper 360°*, hosted by Anderson Cooper, who publicly came out in 2012, frequently addresses LGBTQ+ issues, with Cooper using his platform to shed light on stories that might otherwise go underreported.

Despite these advances, the depth and frequency of LGBTQ+ coverage can still vary significantly between networks and programs. While some shows integrate LGBTQ+ topics into their regular programming, others may still treat these issues as special interest stories, relegating them to specific times or segments rather than fully integrating them into the news cycle. This inconsistency underscores the ongoing challenges in ensuring that LGBTQ+

issues are treated as integral parts of the broader news narrative. The presence of LGBTQ+ television broadcast journalists has helped to challenge stereotypes and demonstrate that LGBTQ+ individuals can succeed at the highest levels of journalism. This visibility has a ripple effect, influencing how LGBTQ+ people are viewed by the public and how they view themselves. When LGBTQ+ individuals see people like them on television, it sends a powerful message of acceptance and possibility, contributing to a more inclusive society.

Podcasts

Podcasts have emerged as a powerful medium for LGBTQ+ news, culture, and advocacy, providing in-depth analysis and diverse perspectives on issues that may not receive as much attention in mainstream media. The rise of LGBTQ+-focused podcasts reflects a broader trend toward personalized, on-demand content, where listeners can seek voices and stories that resonate with their experiences and interests.

One of the most popular LGBTQ+ podcasts is *LGBTQ&A*, which debuted in 2008. The podcast, produced by *The Advocate* magazine and hosted by Jeffrey Masters, features interviews with LGBTQ+ leaders, activists, and public figures. The podcast has become a vital platform for in-depth conversations about LGBTQ+ identity, politics, and culture, offering listeners a chance to hear directly from those shaping the future of LGBTQ+ rights. As of July 2022, *LGBTQ&A* had conducted over 250 interviews with such notable LGBTQ+ figures as Pete Buttigieg, Roxane Gay, Laverne Cox, and Brandi Carlile. The oral history podcast *Making Gay History*, founded by journalist Eric Marcus, who also serves as host, debuted in 2016. The podcast includes rare interviews with notable figures in LGBTQ+ history, many dating back to the 1980s. Another influential podcast is *Nancy*, which ran from 2017 to 2020

The advent of podcasting has made it possible for even rank amateurs to produce news, information, and entertainment shows that can reach thousands, even millions of people, making it a new opportunity to educate and inform audiences about the LGBTQ community.

and was produced by WNYC Studios. Hosted by Kathy Tu and Tobin Low, *Nancy* explored a wide range of LGBTQ+ topics from personal stories of coming out to broader discussions about race, religion, and family within the LGBTQ+ community. These podcasts have been praised for their ability to delve into complex issues with sensitivity and depth, providing a space for voices that are often underrepresented in other media formats.

The anonymity and reach of social media can lead to increased harassment and bullying, with LGBTQ+ individuals often targeted by hate speech and misinformation.

The impact of LGBTQ+ podcasts on the LGBTQ+ community has been significant. These shows have created new spaces for LGBTQ+ voices, offering a sense of community and connection for listeners who may feel isolated or marginalized. Podcasts allow for a more intimate and personal form of storytelling, where hosts and guests can share their experiences and perspectives in a way that feels authentic and relatable. This has not only fostered a sense of belonging among LGBTQ+ listeners but has also contributed to the broader media landscape by influencing how LGBTQ+ topics are covered in other formats. The success of LGBTQ+ podcasts has demonstrated the demand for content that speaks directly to the experiences and concerns of LGBTQ+ individuals, encouraging other media outlets to take these topics more seriously.

Social Media

Social media has revolutionized the way LGBTQ+ news is disseminated and discussed, providing a platform for real-time engagement and the amplification of LGBTQ+ voices. Platforms like Twitter, Facebook, and Instagram have become essential tools for sharing information, organizing advocacy efforts, and shaping public discourse around LGBTQ+ issues. Social media allows LGBTQ+ individuals, activists, and allies to bypass traditional media gatekeepers and connect directly with a global audience.

One of the most powerful aspects of social media is its ability to facilitate the rapid spread of information and mobilize communities around key issues. Hashtags like #LoveWins, which celebrated the U.S. Supreme Court's 2015 decision to legalize same-sex marriage nationwide, and #TransRightsAreHumanRights, which advocates for transgender equality, have played a significant role in raising awareness and rallying support for LGBTQ+ causes. Influencers like Laverne Cox, an actress and transgender rights advocate, and Jazz Jennings, a transgender teen and activist, have used social media to educate their followers, share their personal journeys, and advocate for LGBTQ+ rights. Their influence on platforms like Instagram and Twitter has helped to shape public perceptions and drive conversations around LGBTQ+ issues.

However, social media also presents challenges for LGBTQ+ content creators and journalists. The anonymity and reach of social media can lead to increased harassment and bullying, with LGBTQ+ individuals often targeted by hate speech and misinformation. This can create a hostile environment for those trying to share their stories or advocate for change. Additionally, the algorithms used by social media platforms can sometimes limit the visibility of LGBTQ+ content either by categorizing it as "sensitive" or failing to promote it in the same way as other content. These challenges underscore the need for continued vigilance and support for LGBTQ+ voices on social media.

Still, social media has revolutionized the way LGBTQ+ news is disseminated and discussed, allowing for real-time engagement and grassroots journalism and advocacy despite challenges such as harassment and algorithmic biases. LGBTQ+ individuals and organizations can use these platforms to report on issues that may be overlooked by mainstream media, share their own stories, and build networks of support and solidarity. Social media has democratized the production and dissemination of news, allowing for a more diverse and inclusive range of voices to be heard. This has been particularly important for marginalized groups within the LGBTQ+ community, such as LGBTQ+ and especially transgender people of color, who may struggle to find representation in traditional media. Through social media, these voices can reach a wider audience, contributing to a more informed and engaged public discourse on LGBTQ+ issues.

Looking forward, the future of LGBTQ+ media representation will be shaped by both challenges and opportunities. One of the key challenges will be ensuring that LGBTQ+ representation continues to expand in both depth and breadth, moving beyond tokenism to include a wider range of LGBTQ+ experiences, particularly those of marginalized groups within the community such as transgender people of color. As media landscapes continue to evolve, particularly with the rise of digital and social media platforms, opportunities will come up to reach new audiences and tell more diverse stories. However, these opportunities will need to be balanced with the ongoing need for vigilance against misinformation, harassment, and the potential for exclusionary practices, whether intentional or algorithmic.

The importance of inclusive and accurate coverage of LGBTQ+ issues in news and information platforms cannot be overstated. Media plays a critical role in shaping public perception and informing societal attitudes, and, as such, it has a responsibility to ensure that LGBTQ+ stories are told with the respect, complexity, and visibility they deserve. As the fight for LGBTQ+ rights continues, media representation will remain a crucial battleground, influencing everything from public policy to personal identity. The continued progress in LGBTQ+ media representation will depend not only on the work of LGBTQ+ journalists, content creators, and advocates but also on the broader media industry's commitment to diversity, equity, and inclusion. Fostering a media environment that truly reflects the diversity of the LGBTQ+ community can help to ensure that these voices remain at the forefront of the national conversation, driving change and advancing equality for all Americans.

BIOGRAPHIES

Charles Blow (1970–)

Journalist

Charles M. Blow is a prominent journalist, commentator, and author known for his insightful analysis and powerful commentary on social justice, politics, and race relations in the United States. As an op-ed columnist for *The New York Times*, he has become a leading voice in the national conversation on issues of equality, civil rights, and the African American experience. His work has garnered widespread acclaim for its depth, clarity, and impassioned calls for justice and reform.

Born in Gibsland, Louisiana, Blow grew up in a small rural town and was raised in a family with modest means. In high school, he founded the school newspaper and graduated as valedictorian in 1988, earning a scholarship to Grambling State University, where he studied mass communications. After graduating, he began his career as a graphics journalist, joining *The Detroit News* as a graphics artist. He moved on to *The New York Times*, where he worked as a graphics editor, eventually becoming the paper's first-ever graphics director. In 2006, he left to become the art director of *National Geographic.*

In 2008, Blow became an op-ed columnist for *The New York Times*. In his columns, he addresses a broad range of topics, including race, politics, and social justice, often drawing on his own life experiences and the broader African American experience in the United States. His writing is known for its clear, direct style and its unflinching critique of systemic racism and inequality.

Blow is also the author of the acclaimed memoir *Fire Shut Up in My Bones* (2014), which details his experiences growing up in the South, his struggles with identity, and the trauma of being sexually abused as a child. The memoir was highly praised for its honesty and courage, and it was later adapted into an opera by Terence Blanchard, becoming the first opera by a Black composer to be performed at the Metropolitan Opera in New York City. In addition to his memoir, he has written *The Devil You Know: A Black Power Manifesto* (2021), a provocative book that explores the idea of Black Americans resettling in the South to consolidate political power and create change from within.

Blow is openly bisexual, a revelation he made publicly in his memoir. Reflecting on the importance of coming out publicly, he stated, "When you are not living an honest, open, true life, you are taking advantage of a privilege granted to you by older gay, lesbian, queer people who have sacrificed tremendously so that you could come into this place. And they did so very often at great costs." His candid discussion of his sexuality as well as the challenges he faced in coming to terms with his identity have resonated with many readers and contributed to the broader conversation about LGBTQ+ issues within the Black community. His openness about his bisexuality has made him a prominent figure in advocating for the visibility and rights of bisexual individuals, particularly within communities of color.

Frank Bruni (1964–)

Journalist

Frank Anthony Bruni is a renowned journalist and author best known for his tenure as an op-ed columnist for *The New York Times*, the paper's first openly gay columnist. Over the course of his career, he has covered a wide array of topics, including politics, culture, food, and LGBTQ+ issues. His insightful and eloquent commentary, combined with his personal openness, has made him a significant voice in contemporary journalism.

Bruni was born in White Plains, New York, and grew up in a close-knit Italian American family. He attended the University of North Carolina, Chapel Hill, where he earned a B.A. in English in 1986. During his time there, he was heavily involved in student journalism, working as a writer and editor for *The Daily Tar Heel*, the university's student newspaper. After completing his undergraduate studies, he attended Columbia University's Graduate School of Journalism, where he obtained an master's degree in 1988.

Bruni began his professional journalism career at the *New York Post* and later moved to *The Detroit Free Press*. At the *Free Press*, he covered a wide range of beats, including religion and the LGBTQ+ community. In 1992, he was a runner-up for the Pulitzer Prize for Feature Writing for his profile of a convicted child molester.

In 1995, Bruni joined *The New York Times* as a metropolitan reporter. He went on to hold several prominent positions with the paper, including the Rome bureau chief and White House correspondent during the George W. Bush administration, covering Bush's 2000 presidential campaign and the subsequent administration. In 2004, he became *The New York Times*'s restaurant critic, a role in which he gained widespread acclaim for his lively, witty, and occasionally scathing reviews. His time as a restaurant critic is chronicled in his 2009 memoir, *Born Round: The Secret History of a Full-Time Eater*, in which he shares his personal struggles with food, weight, and body image.

Bruni transitioned to the role of op-ed columnist in 2011, writing on a broad spectrum of issues, including politics, education, culture, and LGBTQ+ rights. His columns often reflect his personal experiences and are marked by a distinctive blend of insight, empathy, and humor. In 2018, he published *Where You Go Is Not Who You'll Be: An Antidote to the College Admissions Mania*, a book that challenges the obsession with elite college admissions and encourages a more holistic approach to education and success. In 2021, he became a professor of journalism and public policy at Duke University.

Bruni is openly gay and has been an advocate for LGBTQ+ rights throughout his career. His openness about his sexuality and experiences as a gay man have informed much of his work, particularly his commentary on LGBTQ+ issues and the broader cultural and social dynamics surrounding them. In 2021, he faced a personal challenge when he revealed that he had been diagnosed with a rare condition called non-arteritic anterior ischemic optic neuropathy (NAION), which resulted in significant vision loss in one eye. This experience has influenced his recent work, including his 2022 memoir, *The Beauty of Dusk: On Vision Lost and Found*, which reflects on his journey of adapting to this new reality and finding resilience and perspective in the face of adversity.

Jonathan Capehart (1967–)

Television Host, Journalist

Jonathan T. Capehart is a journalist, television host, and political commentator known for his insightful analysis and commentary on politics, social issues, and LGBTQ+ rights. As a Pulitzer Prize–winning journalist and openly gay public figure, he has been a significant voice in American media, advocating for equality and inclusion. He is widely recognized for his work with *The Washington Post*, MSNBC (now MS NOW), and as the host of *The Sunday Show with Jonathan Capehart*.

Capehart was born in Newark, New Jersey. He attended Saint Benedict's Preparatory School in Newark, where he developed his skills as a writer and communicator. He went on to attend Carleton College in Northfield, Minnesota, where he earned a B.A. in political science. During his time at Carleton, he was actively involved in student journalism and developed a deep understanding of political and social issues.

After graduating, Capehart began his journalism career as a researcher for NBC's *The Today Show*. He quickly moved up the ranks, taking on roles that allowed him to develop his editorial voice and sharpen his skills as a journalist. His early career also included work as a speechwriter and policy advisor, giving him a broad perspective on political communication.

In 1993, Capehart joined the editorial board of the *Daily News*, becoming the youngest editorial board member at the age of 26. During his tenure, he was part of the team that won the Pulitzer Prize for Editorial Writing in 1999 for a series of editorials that helped save the Apollo Theater in Harlem. This achievement established him as a leading voice in American journalism.

Capehart joined *The Washington Post* as an editorial writer and member of the editorial board in 2007. His columns, which focus on politics, social justice, and LGBTQ+ issues, have garnered widespread acclaim for their clarity, depth, and commitment to advocacy. His work at *The Washington Post* has made him a prominent commentator on national and international affairs.

In addition to working in print journalism, Capehart has become a familiar face on television as a political analyst and host. He joined MSNBC as a contributor in 2009, providing political commentary and analysis on various shows, including *Morning Joe* and *Hardball with Chris Matthews*. In 2020, he was named the host of *The Sunday Show with Jonathan Capehart* on MSNBC, where he engages with newsmakers and offers in-depth discussions on current events and issues affecting the nation. He is also the host of the *Capehart* podcast on *The Washington Post* website, where he interviews prominent figures from politics, culture, and media, providing listeners with nuanced insights into today's most pressing topics.

Capehart is openly gay and has spoken candidly about his experiences as a Black gay man in America and the challenges and opportunities he has faced. He uses his platform to promote understanding and acceptance, often highlighting issues of race, sexuality, and intersectionality in his work. In 2016, he married Nick Schmit, who was the assistant chief of protocol at the U.S. Department of State under President Barack Obama. The couple's wedding was officiated by former U.S. attorney general Eric Holder, reflecting Capehart's prominent role in both the LGBTQ+ community and the political world.

As a journalist, commentator, and advocate, Capehart has used his platform to amplify marginalized voices and challenge discrimination, making him a respected and influential figure in American media and the LGBTQ+ community.

Anderson Cooper (1967–)

Television Host, Journalist

Anderson Hays Cooper is a prominent journalist, television host, and author best known as the anchor of CNN's *Anderson Cooper 360°*. With a career spanning over three decades, he has become a trusted voice in news media, recognized for his insightful reporting, empathetic interviewing style, and commitment to covering global events. His work has earned him numerous awards and accolades, making him one of the most respected journalists in the world. When he came out publicly in 2012, he became the most prominent gay journalist on American television, and in 2016, he became the first LGBTQ+ person to moderate a presidential debate.

Cooper was born in New York City to a prominent family. His mother, Gloria Vanderbilt, was a renowned fashion designer and socialite, and his father, Wyatt Emory Cooper, was a writer. His early life was marked by tragedy: his father died during heart surgery when he was 10 years old, and his older brother, Carter Vanderbilt Cooper, died by suicide in 1988. These personal experiences instilled in him a deep sense of empathy and a desire to understand the complexities of human experience.

Cooper attended the Dalton School in New York City and went on to study political science at Yale University, graduating in 1989. During college, he interned with the Central Intelligence Agency (CIA) for two summers. After graduating from Yale, he began his journalism career as a fact-checker for the small news agency Channel One. Frustrated by the lack of on-the-ground reporting opportunities, he forged his press credentials and ventured to Myanmar (Burma) on his own to cover the pro-democracy uprisings. His self-produced coverage from Myanmar, broadcast by Channel One, marked the beginning of his career as a foreign correspondent.

In 1995, Cooper joined ABC News as a correspondent and later became coanchor of the overnight news program *World News Now*. In 2001, he moved to CNN, initially as a coanchor of *American Morning*. He began anchoring *Anderson Cooper 360°* in 2003, where he quickly gained a reputation for his coverage of significant events, including the Iraq War, Hurricane Katrina, the Haiti earthquake, and the 2004 Indian Ocean tsunami. His on-the-ground reporting and emotional connection with those affected by these events showcased his commitment to human-centered journalism. In addition to his work on CNN, he is a regular correspondent for CBS's *60 Minutes*. His reporting has earned him numerous awards, including several Emmy awards, a Peabody Award, and the Edward R. Murrow Award for his journalistic excellence.

Cooper has also authored several books, including *Dispatches from the Edge: A Memoir of War, Disasters, and Survival* (2006). The memoir details his experiences covering some of the world's most challenging and dangerous stories, offering readers a glimpse into his personal and professional journey.

Cooper publicly came out as gay in 2012, allowing his friend, writer Andrew Sullivan, to publish an email from him that stated, "The fact is, I'm gay, always have been, always will be, and I couldn't be any more happy, comfortable with myself, and proud." His decision to come out was praised as a courageous and significant moment for LGBTQ+ visibility in the media. Since then, he has been an advocate for LGBTQ+ rights and has used his platform to highlight issues affecting the community. He became a father in April 2020 with the birth of his son, Wyatt Morgan Cooper, via surrogate. In 2023, he welcomed his second son, Sebastian Luke Maisani-Cooper. He coparents his children with his former partner, nightclub owner Benjamin Maisani. Cooper said that "I think being gay is one of the great blessings of my life, and it made me a better person, it made me a better reporter."

Benoit Denizet-Lewis (1975–)

Journalist, Author

Benoit Denizet-Lewis is a renowned American journalist, author, and professor whose work has largely focused on issues related to LGBTQ+ identity, addiction, and mental health. He is best known for his long-form journalism, particularly his contributions to *The New York Times Magazine*, where he has written extensively about the struggles and triumphs of marginalized communities. His thoughtful and empathetic approach to these topics has earned him a reputation as one of the leading voices in modern journalism, particularly in the context of LGBTQ+ and youth issues.

Born in France, Denizet-Lewis grew up in San Francisco, California. He attended the French American International High School, where he cofounded the school newspaper, played varsity basketball, and wrote plays. He obtained a journalism degree from Northwestern University and was a columnist and sports editor for the *Daily Northwestern*. In college, he began developing his distinctive narrative style, which blends personal storytelling with broader social analysis. Early in his career, he worked as a freelance writer, contributing to various publications and honing his skills in writing about addiction and LGBTQ+ identity. His early work in journalism laid the foundation for his later success as both a journalist and an author.

Denizet-Lewis began writing for *The New York Times Magazine* when he was 26, producing multiple cover stories and feature articles about bringing significant attention to issues like addiction, mental health, and LGBTQ+ youth. He is the author of several books, including *America Anonymous: Eight Addicts in Search of a Life* (2009), which explores the lives of people struggling with addiction across the United States. *Travels with Casey* (2014) is a memoir about his cross-country road trip with his dog, which examines the unique relationships between Americans and their dogs. His work has garnered critical acclaim and numerous accolades, solidifying his place as a journalist whose work fosters a greater empathy and understanding of often overlooked communities.

Denizet-Lewis's personal experiences as a gay man have informed much of his writing on LGBTQ+ issues. His work has often highlighted the intersection of identity, mental health, and societal acceptance, making him a significant figure in advancing a public understanding of LGBTQ+ challenges. He is also a professor at Emerson College, where he teaches journalism.

With his ability to capture deeply personal stories that resonate on a societal level, Denizet-Lewis has helped to shift the debate on addiction, mental health, and LGBTQ+ issues, encouraging greater compassion and understanding.

Cameron Esposito (1981–)

Podcaster, Comedian

Cameron Anne Young Anastasia Esposito is a comedian, actor, writer, and LGBTQ+ advocate known for her sharp wit, unique perspective, and fearless approach to comedy. With a career spanning stand-up, television, film, and podcasting, she has become a significant figure in the entertainment industry, particularly for her contributions to LGBTQ+ representation and visibility. Her work often addresses themes of sexuality, gender, and social justice, blending humor with insightful commentary. As an openly lesbian comedian, she has been a trailblazer in breaking down barriers and challenging stereotypes within the comedy world.

Esposito was born in Western Springs, Illinois, a suburb of Chicago. Raised in a Catholic family, she attended an all-girls Catholic high school, which would later serve as an inspiration for much of her comedic material. Intending a career as a social worker, she went on to study theology and English at Boston College, where she became involved in the school's improv comedy scene, sparking her interest in a career in comedy.

After college, Esposito returned to Chicago and began performing regularly at open mics, quickly gaining a reputation for her distinctive voice and engaging storytelling. She also studied and performed at The Second City and iO Theater, two of Chicago's most prestigious improvisational comedy theaters. Her career took off in the early 2010s when she began performing stand-up comedy at notable clubs and festivals around the country. Her big break came in 2013, when she made her late-night television debut on *The Late Late Show with Craig Ferguson*. During her appearance, she delivered a memorable set, including a playful interaction with fellow guest Jay Leno, which went viral and helped to catapult her career.

Esposito released her first comedy album, *Same Sex Symbol*, in 2014, which was well-received by both critics and audiences for its fresh take on LGBTQ+ issues and unapologetic humor. She followed this with several more successful albums, including *Marriage Material* (2016) and *Rape Jokes* (2018), the latter of which is a deeply personal set that addresses her own experiences with sexual assault. *Rape Jokes* was widely praised for its boldness and honesty, and all proceeds from the album were donated to RAINN (Rape, Abuse & Incest National Network).

In addition to her stand-up work, Esposito cocreated, cowrote, and starred in the semi-autobiographical TV series *Take My Wife* alongside her then wife and fellow comedian River Butcher. The series, which premiered on Seeso in 2016, was groundbreaking for its authentic portrayal of a queer relationship and focus on the experiences of LGBTQ+ comedians. Although the show was short-lived, it garnered a dedicated fanbase and critical acclaim for its representation and humor.

Esposito is also known for her podcast, *Queery*, which she launched in 2017. In *Queery*, she interviews LGBTQ+ celebrities, activists, and artists, exploring their personal experiences and discussing a wide range of topics related to identity, community, and culture. The podcast has been praised for its insightful conversations and role in highlighting diverse voices within the LGBTQ+ community. In 2021, she came out as gender fluid and revealed that she had married Katy Nishimoto, an editor for Dial Press.

Esposito continues to be a dynamic force in comedy and LGBTQ+ advocacy, using her platform to challenge norms, foster inclusivity, and encourage conversations about important social issues.

Kate Fagan (1981–)

Journalist, Author

Kate Fagan is a sports journalist, author, and former college basketball player known for her insightful coverage of sports and advocacy for mental health awareness. As a former ESPN commentator and columnist, she has become a prominent voice in sports media, particularly for her thoughtful analysis of the intersection of athletics, mental health, and LGBTQ+ issues. Her best-selling memoir, *What Made Maddy Run*, has been widely praised for shedding light on the pressures faced by student athletes and the importance of mental health support. As an openly gay woman, she has also been a strong advocate for LGBTQ+ representation and inclusion in sports.

Fagan was born in Warwick, Rhode Island, and grew up in a sports-oriented family. Her father, Chris Fagan, was a professional basketball player in Europe, and her mother was an avid runner. Growing up, she developed a passion for sports, particularly basketball, which she pursued throughout her childhood and teenage years.

Fagan attended the University of Colorado, Boulder, where she played for the Colorado Buffaloes women's basketball team from 1999 to 2004. As a standout player, she set a school record for most consecutive free throws made and was a key contributor to the team's success. During her time at Colorado, she also developed an interest in writing and journalism, which would later shape her career path.

After graduating with a degree in communications, Fagan briefly played professional basketball in Ireland before transitioning to a career in journalism. She began her career in 2006 as a sports reporter for the *Ellensburg Daily Record* and the *Glens Falls Post-Star* and later moved to the *Philadelphia Inquirer*, where she covered the Philadelphia 76ers and gained recognition for her in-depth reporting and engaging storytelling.

In 2012, Fagan joined ESPN as a columnist and on-air talent, where she quickly became known for her insightful commentary on a wide range of topics, including the NBA, the WNBA, and college sports. She was a regular panelist on ESPN's *Around the Horn* and frequently appeared on other network programs, including *Outside the Lines* and *SportsCenter*. Her work at ESPN was marked by her ability to bring a nuanced perspective to sports journalism, focusing not only on the games themselves but also on the human stories behind them.

Fagan's most significant contribution to sports journalism came in 2014 as the author of *The Reappearing Act: Coming Out as Gay on a College Basketball Team Led by Born-Again Christians*, chronicling her experiences on the Colorado women's basketball team, and in 2017 with *What Made Maddy Run: The Secret Struggles and Tragic Death of an All-American Teen*. The book explores the life and death of Madison Holleran, a University of Pennsylvania track star who died by suicide in 2014. Drawing from her own experiences as a college athlete and extensive interviews with Holleran's family and friends, Fagan examines the pressures faced by student athletes and the impact of social media on mental health. The book was widely acclaimed for its sensitive handling of a difficult subject and its call for greater awareness and support for mental health issues among young people.

In addition to her writing, Fagan has been a vocal advocate for LGBTQ+ rights and visibility in sports. She publicly came out as gay in 2017 and has since used her platform to speak out about the importance of inclusion and representation for LGBTQ+ athletes and sports professionals. She is married to fellow writer and former ESPN producer Kathryn Budig. The couple met while working at ESPN and have since collaborated on various projects, including a podcast called *Free Cookies*, in which they discuss a range of topics from sports and wellness to culture and current events.

Janet Flanner (1892–1978)

Journalist, Author

Janet Flanner was a writer and journalist best known for her role as the Paris correspondent for *The New Yorker* magazine. Writing under the pen name Genêt, her vivid, insightful, and often witty dispatches from France offered American readers a window into the cultural, political, and social life of Paris from the 1920s to the 1970s. Her work is notable not only for its literary style and keen observations but also for capturing the spirit of an era marked by significant cultural and historical events. Along with her longtime partner, Solita Solano, she was called "a defining force in the creative expat scene in Paris."

Flanner was born in Indianapolis, Indiana, into a family of affluence and cultural engagement. Her father was a mortician who also ran a crematorium, while her mother was a homemaker with a strong interest in the arts. She was introduced to literature and culture from a young age, developing a keen interest in writing and the arts. "I was looking for beauty with a capital B," she recalled, "and I couldn't find it in Indiana."

Flanner attended the University of Chicago in 1912 but left after a year, finding the academic environment stifling. She returned to Indianapolis and began her writing career with a position as the assistant drama critic for the *Indianapolis Star*. In 1921, she moved to New York City, where she became part of the city's vibrant literary and artistic scene. It was there that she met Solano, a fellow writer and journalist with whom she would have a lifelong romantic relationship. In 1922, seeking new experiences and a change of scenery, they moved to Paris, a city that would become Flanner's home for much of her life.

Flanner began her career at *The New Yorker* in 1925, shortly after the magazine was founded. Her first column, published under the pseudonym Genêt, set the tone for what would become her signature style: an elegant, engaging mix of reportage, cultural commentary, and personal insight. Her columns covered a wide range of topics from art and literature to politics and social issues, all written with a distinctive voice that combined a journalist's eye for detail with a novelist's flair for storytelling. One of her most notable pieces was "The Fall of Paris," written in June 1940, which poignantly described the city's capture by Nazi forces during World War II. Her writing captured the mood of a city under occupation and the profound impact of the war on its residents. She remained in Europe for much of the war, later returning to France as a correspondent for *The New Yorker* to report on the liberation of Paris and the postwar recovery.

Flanner's writing was not limited to war correspondence. She also wrote extensively about the cultural and artistic life of Paris, profiling figures such as Pablo Picasso, Henri Matisse, and Coco Chanel. Her pieces provided readers with intimate glimpses into the lives of some of the 20th century's most influential artists and thinkers. In 1972, she published a collection of her letters from Paris, titled *Paris Was Yesterday, 1925–1939*, which has since become a classic of literary journalism. In

1975, she won the National Book Award for the collection *Paris Journal, 1944–1965*.

Flanner was openly lesbian, a rare and courageous stance for a woman of her time. Her long-term relationship with Solano was central to her life and work, and the two were part of a vibrant expatriate community of artists, writers, and intellectuals in Paris. This circle included other notable lesbian couples, such as Gertrude Stein and Alice B. Toklas, who were also prominent figures in the Paris literary scene.

Flanner's sexuality and her experiences as an expatriate in Paris deeply influenced her writing, contributing to her unique perspective on both American and European cultures. She remained in Paris for much of her life, returning to New York only in her later years.

Ina Fried (1974–)

Journalist

Ina Fried is a journalist and technology reporter known for her insightful coverage of the tech industry and her advocacy for LGBTQ+ rights and transgender visibility. As one of the most prominent openly transgender journalists in the United States, she has become a leading voice in technology journalism, bringing a unique perspective to the industry through her reporting and commentary. Her work has helped to increase awareness about the intersection of technology, media, and social issues, and she has been a strong advocate for diversity and inclusion within the tech world.

Fried was born Ian Fried in Akron, Ohio. During the 1980s, as Ian, she was a child actor and had several notable roles, including a minor part as a young boy in *Rocky III* (1982) and the character Eliot in *Gremlins* (1984). She also appeared in an episode of the television series *Highway to Heaven* (1985) and played Young Mike Brody in *Jaws: The Revenge* (1987). Her acting career was brief; she developed an interest in journalism and technology early on and, inspired by the dynamic of the rapidly evolving tech landscape around her, she eventually transitioned to a successful career in journalism and technology reporting.

After graduating from Miami University in Ohio, Fried began her journalism career at *CNET*, a major tech news website. At *CNET*, she covered a wide range of technology topics, including mobile devices, software, and internet policy. Her work quickly gained recognition for its depth and clarity, establishing her as a rising star in tech journalism.

Fried's career took a significant turn in 2008, when she joined *AllThingsD*, a technology news website founded by veteran journalists Walt Mossberg and Kara Swisher. At *AllThingsD* (later rebranded as *Re/code*), she became one of the lead reporters covering the tech industry, focusing on major companies such as Apple, Google, and Microsoft. Her reporting provided readers with detailed insights into the strategies and innovations driving the tech world.

In 2017, Fried moved to Axios, a digital media company known for its succinct and straightforward news coverage. For the Axios website, she serves as the chief technology correspondent and writes the daily Axios AI+ (originally called Axios Login) newsletter, which covers the latest developments in technology and its impact on society. Her reporting at *Axios* has continued to be highly regarded for its clarity, accuracy, and focus on both industry trends and broader social implications.

Beyond her reporting, Fried has been a vocal advocate for transgender rights and LGBTQ+ visibility in journalism and the tech industry. She publicly came out as transgender in 2003 while working at *CNET*, making her one of the first openly transgender journalists in the tech field.

Her openness about her identity has been influential in encouraging greater diversity and inclusion in tech journalism and beyond.

Ashley Gavin (1987–)

Podcaster, Comedian, Author

Ashley Gavin is a comedian, writer, and podcast host known for her bold, unfiltered comedy and commitment to LGBTQ+ representation in the entertainment industry. As an openly gay performer, she uses her platform to challenge stereotypes, advocate for LGBTQ+ rights, and share her experiences as a queer woman. She has gained a significant following for her stand-up performances and her popular podcast, *We're Having Gay Sex*, which explores queer life and relationships with humor and honesty.

Gavin began acting in a theater club at the age of 11 and wanted to be a comedian from a young age. Despite barely passing mathematics in high school, she went on to earn a B.A. from Bryn Mawr College in 2010 with a major in computer science. After college, she pursued a career in tech, working as a software engineer and a computer science educator. However, her love for comedy eventually led her to leave her job and pursue stand-up comedy full time. She quickly made a name for herself in the New York comedy scene with her sharp wit, observational humor, and fearless approach to tackling controversial topics.

Gavin's stand-up comedy has been featured on several major platforms, including SiriusXM, and she has performed at renowned comedy clubs such as the Comedy Cellar in New York City. Her comedy often focuses on her experiences as a gay woman, navigating relationships, and the challenges of coming out. Her relatable and unapologetic style has earned her a loyal following among both LGBTQ+ and mainstream audiences.

In 2020, Gavin launched her podcast, *We're Having Gay Sex*, which quickly gained popularity for its candid conversations about sex, relationships, and queer life. The podcast features guests from various backgrounds and explores a wide range of topics with humor and sensitivity, breaking down stereotypes and promoting inclusivity. *We're Having Gay Sex* has been praised for its honest discussions and ability to tackle serious subjects with a comedic lens.

Gavin has spoken openly about her journey to self-acceptance and coming out. She often incorporates her personal experiences into her comedy, using humor to address the complexities of LGBTQ+ identity and relationships. Her openness about her sexuality has resonated with many fans, making her a relatable and influential figure within the LGBTQ+ community.

Chris Geidner (1977–)

Journalist, Blogger, Legal Analyst

Christopher "Chris" Geidner is a prominent journalist, legal analyst, and blogger known for his in-depth reporting on legal and civil rights issues, particularly those concerning the LGBTQ+ community. A former legal editor for the news website *BuzzFeed News*, he is the publisher of the *Law Dork* newsletter and blog. His work has been influential in raising awareness about the legal battles for equality in the United States, including same-sex marriage, discrimination, and the legal intricacies surrounding LGBTQ+ rights. His commitment to social justice has made him a vital voice in media and law, providing accessible analysis of complex legal proceedings that impact marginalized communities.

Born in Ohio, Geidner developed an early interest in law and politics. He earned his undergraduate degree from Youngstown State University before attending law school at Ohio State University. His early career included legal advocacy work, but his passion for writing and explaining legal concepts to a broader audience led him to pursue journalism more actively.

In 2009, Geidner began his *Law Dork* newsletter and blog, which led to a position as a senior political writer at *Metro Weekly*, where he won awards for covering the repeal of the "Don't Ask, Don't Tell" policy in the U.S. military and for his coverage of the same-sex marriage dispute. In 2012, he started covering LGBTQ+ political and legal issues for the *BuzzFeed News* website as a senior political reporter. He wrote extensively on landmark cases like *Obergefell v. Hodges*, the Supreme Court ruling that legalized same-sex marriage nationwide in 2015. His coverage of this case, along with many others related to LGBTQ+ rights, has been praised for its depth, clarity, and accessibility. He has also contributed to several other prominent publications, including *The New Republic* and *Slate*, and has spoken at numerous legal conferences and panels about LGBTQ+ rights and media. His work has been recognized with multiple journalism awards, including the National Lesbian and Gay Journalists Association's (NLGJA) Excellence in Journalism Award.

Geidner openly identifies as gay and has been a vocal advocate for LGBTQ+ equality both in his personal life and professional career. His own experiences have informed his work, allowing him to provide unique insights into the legal struggles and triumphs of the LGBTQ+ community. His contributions to both journalism and LGBTQ+ advocacy have left a lasting impact on how legal issues affecting marginalized communities are covered in the media. His clear, informative reporting has demystified complex legal proceedings for a general audience, making it easier for the public to understand and engage with significant civil rights issues.

Glenn Greenwald (1967–)

Journalist, Author, Lawyer

Glenn Edward Greenwald is a journalist, author, and constitutional lawyer

known for his investigative reporting and outspoken views on civil liberties, freedom of the press, and government surveillance. He gained international recognition for his role in publishing the Snowden revelations in 2013, which exposed the extent of global surveillance programs conducted by the U.S. National Security Agency (NSA) and other government agencies. As an openly gay journalist, he has also been a vocal advocate for LGBTQ+ rights and has used his platform to challenge mainstream narratives and advocate for independent journalism.

Greenwald was born in Queens, New York, and raised in Lauderdale Lakes, Florida. He developed an interest in law and civil liberties at a young age, which shaped his later career in journalism and activism. While still in high school, he ran unsuccessfully for a seat on the city council. After a second unsuccessful bid for public office, he decided to focus on law school. He attended George Washington University, where he graduated with a B.A. in philosophy in 1990. He then went on to earn a J.D. from New York University School of Law in 1994. After completing his law degree, he worked as a constitutional and civil rights lawyer in New York for a decade, focusing on cases involving First Amendment rights and other civil liberties issues.

In the early 2000s, Greenwald transitioned from law to journalism, motivated by his growing concern over the erosion of civil liberties in the post-9/11 era and the expanding reach of government surveillance programs. In 2005, he started his own blog, *Unclaimed Territory*, where he wrote extensively about political and legal issues, quickly gaining a following for his incisive analysis and willingness to challenge authority. His blog caught the attention of the people behind the *Salon* website, where he began writing a regular column in 2007. His columns focused on government overreach, civil liberties, and the failures of mainstream media to hold those in power accountable.

In 2012, Greenwald joined *The Guardian* newspaper as a columnist and blogger, where he continued his investigative reporting on national security issues. His most significant work at *The Guardian* came in 2013, when he collaborated with filmmaker Laura Poitras and journalist Ewen MacAskill to publish a series of articles based on documents provided by former NSA contractor Edward Snowden. The revelations detailed the NSA's extensive global surveillance operations and sparked a global debate on privacy, security, and government overreach. The reporting on the Snowden documents earned him and his colleagues numerous awards, including the 2014 Pulitzer Prize for Public Service and the George Polk Award for National Security Reporting. The coverage also led to significant legal and policy changes worldwide, reinforcing the importance of whistleblowers and investigative journalism.

In 2014, Greenwald cofounded *The Intercept*, an online news publication dedicated to adversarial journalism and reporting on issues related to civil liberties, national security, and government transparency. He worked at *The Intercept* as a founding editor and contributor until 2020, when he resigned, citing editorial disagreements and a lack of editorial freedom.

Greenwald is also the author of several books, including *How Would a Patriot Act?* (2006), *With Liberty and Justice for Some* (2011), and *No Place to Hide* (2014), which provides an in-depth account of the Snowden revelations and their implications for global privacy and surveillance.

Greenwald has been an advocate for LGBTQ+ rights throughout his career. He has spoken openly about his experiences as a gay man and the discrimination he has faced, particularly in his early years as a lawyer and journalist. He lives in Rio de Janeiro, Brazil, with his husband, David Miranda, a Brazilian politician and LGBTQ+ activist. The couple has been involved in various advocacy efforts for LGBTQ+ rights both in Brazil and internationally. He frequently uses his platform to speak out against discrimination and promote equality, leveraging his visibility as a journalist to advance LGBTQ+ issues.

Lorena Hickok (1893–1968)

Journalist, Author

Lorena Alice Hickok was a journalist and author best known for her close friendship and possible romantic relationship with First Lady Eleanor Roosevelt. As one of the first women to achieve prominence in political reporting during the early 20th century, she broke significant barriers in journalism and played a key role in documenting the political and social landscape of the United States during the Great Depression and World War II. Her extensive correspondence with Roosevelt provides invaluable insights into the life of one of America's most influential first ladies and the social and political dynamics of the era.

Hickok was born on March 7, 1893, in East Troy, Wisconsin. She grew up in a troubled home and faced numerous challenges, including an abusive father and the early death of her mother. Forced to fend for herself from a young age, she left home in her teens and moved to Milwaukee, where she found work as a domestic servant.

Despite her difficult upbringing, Hickok was determined to make a life for herself and pursued her education and career with tenacity. She eventually attended and graduated from high school, and by the age of 20, she began working as a cub reporter at the *Battle Creek Evening News* in Michigan. This was the start of a career that would lead her to become one of the most prominent female journalists of her time. She found success as a reporter for the *Minneapolis Tribune*, where she had a byline and was the paper's chief reporter, which was rare for women at the time.

In the 1920s and 1930s, Hickok became a well-known political reporter for the Associated Press (AP), covering major events such as the Lindbergh kidnapping trial. She gained a reputation for her sharp wit, tenacity, and skill in navigating the male-dominated world of political journalism. She was one of the first women to be assigned to cover a presidential campaign, following Franklin D. Roosevelt's campaign in 1932.

It was during this time that she met his wife, Eleanor, and the two women quickly developed a deep and lasting bond. Their relationship has been the subject of much speculation, with over 3,000 letters between them suggesting an intimate and possibly romantic connection. Her friendship with Eleanor provided her with unique access to the White House and an insider's perspective on one of the most significant presidencies in American history.

In 1933, Hickok left her job at the AP to work as a confidential investigator for the Federal Emergency Relief Administration (FERA), traveling extensively to report on the conditions faced by Americans during the Great Depression. Her reports were instrumental in shaping New Deal policies and provided firsthand accounts of the hardships and resilience of the American people during this challenging time. After leaving FERA, she continued to write, producing several books and articles, including *The Story of Eleanor Roosevelt* (1958), which offers a personal account of her close friend's life and work.

Hickok lived during a time when discussions of sexuality, especially regarding same-sex relationships, were highly taboo, and, as such, much of her personal life was kept private. Over the course of her life, she had several long-term relationships with women. Whether her relationship with Roosevelt was more than just a close and intimate friendship has divided biographers and historians. Regardless, she is remembered as a woman who defied social conventions and sought to live authentically in a restrictive era. Her career and personal life offer a unique window into the history of journalism, politics, and social change in 20th-century America.

Dave Karger (1974–)

Journalist

Dave Karger is an entertainment journalist, host, and film expert known for his extensive knowledge of the movie industry and engaging presence as a host on various platforms. With a career spanning over two decades, he has become a prominent figure in entertainment journalism, particularly for his coverage of the Oscars and other major film events. As an openly gay journalist, he has also been a significant voice for LGBTQ+ representation in Hollywood, using his platform to highlight diverse stories and advocate for inclusion within the industry.

Karger was born in Yorktown, Westchester County, New York. A self-described "child of the '80s," he developed a passion for movies and entertainment, which would later shape his career path. He attended Duke University as an English major. His studies included a focus on film and media, allowing him to further cultivate his love for cinema.

After graduating from Duke in 1994, Karger was hired as an intern at *Entertainment Weekly (EW)* magazine. He eventually was promoted to senior writer. During his time at *EW*, he specialized in covering the film industry, conducting in-depth interviews with actors, directors, and producers, and providing expert commentary on movies and awards shows.

Karger's expertise in film and his engaging on-camera presence led him to become a sought-after host and commentator for various media outlets. He has appeared on NBC's *Today* show, ABC's *Good Morning America,* and other programs to provide insights into the movie industry, particularly during awards season. He is well known for his coverage of the Oscars, offering predictions, analyses, and behind-the-scenes insights. In addition to his work with *Entertainment Weekly*, he has contributed to numerous other publications and platforms, including *Access Hollywood* and *E! News.*

In 2016, Karger joined Turner Classic Movies (TCM) as a host, where he introduced classic films and interviewed stars and filmmakers about their work and its impact on the film industry. His role at TCM allowed him to share his passion for cinema with a broader audience and celebrate the rich history of filmmaking.

In 1997, Karger came out as openly gay. He has hosted TCM's Pride celebration with LGBTQ+ films and documentaries. He has called hosting the Pride programming "without doubt one of my favorite things I've gotten to do as a TCM host." His dedication to celebrating cinema and advocating for diversity and inclusion in Hollywood has made him a respected voice in the media, and his work continues to inspire audiences and aspiring film enthusiasts alike.

Kay Lahusen (1930–2021)

Photojournalist, Author

Katherine "Kay" Lahusen was a photographer, author, and pioneering LGBTQ+ rights activist. As the first openly lesbian photojournalist in the United States, she used her skills to document the early LGBTQ+ rights movement, capturing key moments, people, and events that helped to shape the fight for equality. Her photographs and writings provided visibility and representation for the lesbian community at a time when such depictions were rare and often stigmatized. Her work not only preserved the history of the movement but also helped to humanize and bring dignity to LGBTQ+ individuals during a period of widespread discrimination.

Lahusen was born in Cincinnati, Ohio. She was raised by her grandparents in a conservative environment, and she struggled with understanding her sexuality in an era when LGBTQ+ identities were not widely accepted or discussed. She first realized that she was attracted to women as an early teen, developing crushes on film actresses. She attended Ohio State University, where she studied English literature. After graduating in 1952, she moved in with her girlfriend, but their relationship soon ended.

Lahusen moved to Boston in the mid-1950s, where she began working as a researcher at *The Christian Science Monitor*. It was during this time that she became more aware of her sexual orientation and started seeking out others like herself. "I thought, 'I don't want to be cured, but I do want to find out how to meet other lesbians,'" she recalled. In 1961, after seeing a copy of *The Ladder*, she met Barbara Gittings, its editor, at a Daughters of Bilitis (DOB) event in New York City, an encounter that would change her life. The two women quickly formed a deep personal and professional partnership that lasted nearly 50 years until Gittings's death in 2007, dedicating themselves to advancing LGBTQ+ rights and visibility.

In the early 1960s, Lahusen started contributing photographs and articles to *The Ladder*. Her photographs of activists, demonstrations, and everyday life for LGBTQ+ people were groundbreaking, providing rare visibility for the community. These images helped to challenge stereotypes and present LGBTQ+ individuals as real people deserving of respect and rights. One of her most iconic images is a photograph of a woman holding a sign that reads "Denial of Equality of Opportunity is Immoral," taken during one of the first LGBTQ+ pickets in front of the White House in 1965. This photograph, along with many others, became a powerful symbol of the burgeoning LGBTQ+ rights movement.

In addition to her photography, Lahusen coauthored *The Gay Crusaders* (1972) with Randy Wicker under the pen name Kay Tobin, one of the first books to profile LGBTQ+ activists. The book provided personal stories of those fighting for LGBTQ+ rights, offering readers a firsthand look at the movement's leaders and their struggles.

In 2016, a historical marker was placed at the address in Philadelphia near the apartment that Gittings and Lahusen shared in the 1960s. After her death in 2021, she was buried next to Gittings at the Congressional Cemetery in Washington, D.C. A stone bench is engraved with the motto that they helped popularize: "Gay is Good."

Aristide Laurent (1936–2011)

Publisher, Author

Aristide "A. J." Laurent was an LGBTQ+ rights activist, writer, and publisher who played a significant role in the early LGBTQ+ liberation movement in the United States. He was a cofounder of *The Los Angeles Advocate*, which later became *The Advocate*, one of the most prominent and long-standing LGBTQ+ publications in the world. His contributions to LGBTQ+ media and advocacy for gay rights helped to shape the movement during a critical time in its development, providing a platform for visibility, communication, and activism.

Laurent was born in Magnolia Springs, Alabama, the son of a farmhand of Creole ancestry. He was an altar boy and choir leader at his local church before joining the U.S. Air Force in 1960. He served for four years as a signals intelligence operator in Turkey as well as instructor for new recruits.

After leaving the Air Force, Laurent moved to Los Angeles, came out, and joined various LGBTQ+ organizations that were emerging there. He was particularly active in the Mattachine Society, one of the earliest LGBTQ+ rights groups in the United States, which focused on advocating for the rights of gay men and lesbians through education and political action. He is believed to have participated in the Compton's Cafeteria riot in 1966 and was part of the riots that followed the brutal police raid on Los Angeles's Black Cat Tavern. In the wake of the Black Cat incident, he formed the gay group Personal Rights in Defense and Education (PRIDE).

In 1967, Laurent cofounded *The Los Angeles Advocate* with Richard Mitch, Sam Allen, and Bill Rau. The publication started as a newsletter for the PRIDE organization and was intended to inform members about events, news, and issues relevant to the LGBTQ+ community. As one of the first gay publications in the United States, *The Advocate* provided a much-needed platform for LGBTQ+ voices, fostering a sense of community and solidarity among its readers.

Under his guidance, *The Advocate* grew from a small newsletter to a nationally recognized magazine, covering a wide range of topics, including politics, culture, health, and activism. The publication became known for its bold and unapologetic approach to LGBTQ+ issues, helping to challenge stereotypes and advocate for equal rights. His commitment to providing a voice for the LGBTQ+ community through the magazine played a pivotal role in the visibility and advocacy efforts of the LGBTQ+ rights movement during the late 1960s and 1970s.

In addition to his work with *The Advocate*, Laurent was also involved in other LGBTQ+ activism and organizing efforts. He was a member of the Gay Liberation Front (GLF) and the Gay Community Services Center in Los Angeles, contributing to the broader struggle for LGBTQ+ equality and justice.

Laurent's contributions to the LGBTQ+

rights movement, particularly through his work with *The Advocate,* were instrumental in providing visibility and a voice for the LGBTQ+ community during a time of significant social and political change. His legacy as a pioneer in LGBTQ+ media and advocacy continues to inspire new generations of activists and journalists who are committed to equality and justice.

W. Dorr Legg (1904–1994)

Publisher, Educator

An activist during the homophile movement, William Lambert Dorr Legg, known as W. Dorr Legg, was a cofounder of the homophile gay rights organization ONE, Inc. (1952) and publisher of *ONE Magazine,* the first homophile magazine (1953). He was also a founder of the ONE Institute, the first gay educational and archival institution.

Legg grew up in Ann Arbor, Michigan, the son of a piano manufacturer. He studied piano and architecture at the University of Michigan, graduating in 1928, then spent the next two decades working as a private landscape architect in New York, Miami, and Detroit while also teaching architecture at the University of Oregon from 1935 to 1942. His architectural career was threatened when his interracial gay relationship with accountant Merton Bird led to police harassment, and in 1948, the two moved to Los Angeles, seeking a more tolerant atmosphere. In 1950, they founded Knights of the Clock, a social club for interracial gay couples. Soon after joining the Mattachine Society, they left the initial group, along with other members, because of the Communist affiliation among its core leadership. After cofounding ONE, Inc., Legg, under the pseudonym William Lambert, spent the next 14 years managing *ONE Magazine*'s business affairs, performing editorial duties, and contributing hundreds of articles and editorials, which, along with books written by ONE, Inc., members—some of which were published by ONE Institute Press—became valuable resources on the subject of the LGBTQ+ experience in America and Europe and helped to encourage serious scholarship on gay and lesbian issues. In 1956, he taught the first class at the ONE Institute, titled "The Homophile in Society," a forerunner of later queer studies courses. Over the next several years, he taught several other courses at the Institute, recruited instructors, and developed it into a research center and archive on the gay rights struggle.

During the 1960s and 1970s, Legg's stubborn use of the word "homophile" and his disapproval of militant protests caused clashes with gay liberation activists and damaged his credibility within the gay rights movement. However, his influential work with ONE, Inc., at the start of the battle for gay rights helped to serve as a guide for the visibility sought by later activists and the work of queer studies scholars. His influence was recognized in 2011, when the National Lesbian and Gay Journalists Association announced that he would be inducted into its Hall of Fame.

Don Lemon (1966–)

Journalist, Television Host

Don Lemon is a prominent American television journalist best known for his work as a news anchor and host on CNN, where he became one of the network's most recognizable faces. Over the years, he has covered major national and international news stories, including elections, racial justice movements, and political scandals. As an openly gay African American news anchor, he has used his platform to address issues of race, identity, and LGBTQ+ rights, making him a significant figure in both journalism and advocacy for social justice.

Lemon was born in Baton Rouge, Louisiana. His father was a prominent attorney whose firm litigated a lawsuit that successfully challenged the racial segregation of Baton Rouge's public transportation. He attended Louisiana State University before transferring to Brooklyn College in New York, where he studied broadcast journalism. He began his career in journalism working for local news stations, including stints in Philadelphia and St. Louis. His early years in the field saw him rise quickly through the ranks, as his on-air charisma and reporting skills drew attention. He joined NBC News as a correspondent for *Today* and *NBC Nightly News* before moving to CNN in 2006.

At CNN, Lemon hosted *CNN Tonight with Don Lemon* from 2014 to 2023. He covered several major events, including Hurricane Katrina, the 2008 and 2012 presidential elections, and the Black Lives Matter movement. His candid discussions on race and identity, particularly his critiques of systemic racism and calls for justice, have been both praised and criticized. He has authored two books, *Transparent* (2011), in which he publicly came out as gay, and *This Is the Fire: What I Say to My Friends About Racism* (2021), in which he addresses the continuing struggle for racial equality in America. His work earned him several awards, including an Emmy for his coverage of the D.C. sniper attacks.

In 2023, Lemon was dismissed from CNN in response to the criticism he received for comments that were deemed sexist and ageist, in which he said, "A woman is considered in her prime in her 20s and 30s and maybe 40s." After leaving CNN, he launched *The Don Lemon Show* on X (and now streamed on YouTube) in 2024, but the show was cancelled after he interviewed Elon Musk.

When Lemon publicly came out as gay in 2011, he became one of the few openly gay Black men in broadcasting. In 2024, he married real estate agent Tim Malone, whom he had begun dating in 2016.

Lemon's willingness to address controversial topics like race, politics, and LGBTQ+ rights has made him a polarizing figure but also a respected voice for social justice. His work continues to influence how the media approaches sensitive issues of identity, and his legacy will be that of a journalist who used his platform to amplify marginalized voices.

Harvey Levin (1950–)

Television Producer, Journalist

Harvey Robert Levin is a prominent television producer, lawyer, and celebrity reporter best known as the founder of TMZ, one of the most influential celebrity news platforms. His impact on the entertainment industry is significant, as TMZ redefined the speed and style of celebrity reporting with its quick, often controversial coverage. Beyond his role at TMZ, he is also recognized for his television career, legal commentary, and influence in shaping modern-day tabloid journalism. His work has attracted both positive attention for breaking major stories and criticism for its aggressive approach to privacy and celebrity culture.

Levin was born in Los Angeles, California. He attended Grover Cleveland High School in Reseda and later earned his undergraduate degree in political science from the University of California, Santa Barbara, in 1972. He then pursued a law degree at the University of Chicago Law School, graduating in 1975. Initially, he worked as a lawyer, practicing in California before teaching law at the University of Miami School of Law and later at Whittier College School of Law. His foray into media began when he became a legal analyst for a local Los Angeles TV station during the O. J. Simpson trial, marking the start of his broadcast journalism career.

Levin's most significant career achievement was the creation of TMZ in 2005. The platform quickly became known for breaking exclusive stories, including the death of Michael Jackson in 2009, which cemented TMZ's reputation as a reliable—if controversial—source for entertainment news. Prior to founding TMZ, he had already built a name for himself as the producer and host of *The People's Court*, in which he provided legal analysis on various civil cases. He also served as a legal expert on shows like *Good Day L.A.* and *Celebrity Justice*.

Levin is openly gay, having come out publicly in 2010 during a National Lesbian and Gay Journalists Association event. He has been a strong advocate for LGBTQ+ rights, using his platform to raise awareness about issues facing the community. He is known to keep his personal life private, but he has been in a long-term relationship with Andy Mauer, a chiropractor in southern California. His success as a media mogul and decision to come out have made him a significant figure not only in entertainment but also in LGBTQ+ advocacy. Initially a supporter of Donald Trump in the 2016 presidential election, he broke ties with Trump over the president's attempts to establish a transgender military ban.

Over his career, Levin has played an important role in shaping digital media's rise, particularly in the realm of celebrity journalism and transforming the public's relationship with media, news consumption, and the broader entertainment industry.

Rachel Maddow (1973–)

Television Host, Political Commentator

The first openly lesbian anchor to host a major prime-time news program in the United States, Rachel Anne Maddow is a popular television host, political commentator, and author best known for her work on *The Rachel Maddow Show* on MSNBC. Her impact on political journalism is significant, as she has shaped political discourse through her unique blend of in-depth reporting; historical context; and clear, progressive viewpoints. Her ability to translate complex political and social issues into engaging stories has earned her widespread acclaim. As one of the most prominent liberal voices in American media, she continues to influence public opinion.

Maddow was born in Castro Valley, California, and grew up in a conservative Catholic family. She was an athlete, participating in high school volleyball, basketball, and swimming. She attended Stanford University, where she earned a degree in public policy in 1994. After graduating, she received a prestigious Rhodes Scholarship, enabling her to pursue a doctorate in political science at the University of Oxford. She is considered to be the first openly gay winner of the Rhodes Scholarship. She earned a Ph.D. in politics from Oxford.

Maddow's media career began in radio, working at WRNX in Holyoke, Massachusetts, and later at WRSI in Northampton, Massachusetts, before leaving in 2004 to join the Air America radio network, where she quickly gained attention for her sharp analysis and engaging style. Her most notable achievement is *The Rachel Maddow Show*, which premiered on MSNBC in 2008. As the network's flagship program, it has been praised for its thoughtful and in-depth coverage of U.S. politics, often addressing issues that are overlooked by mainstream media.

She has received several awards for her work, including Emmy awards for her coverage of breaking news stories and critical political events. In addition to her television career, she is the author of *Drift: The Unmooring of American Military Power* (2012), which became a *New York Times* bestseller. A second book, *Blowout: Corrupted Democracy, Rogue State Russia, and the Richest, Most Destructive Industry on*

Earth, was published in 2019. Her 2020 podcast *Bag Man,* which is about political corruption during the Nixon administration, was adapted into a book. A fourth book, *Prequel: An American Fight Against Fascism,* was published in 2023.

Maddow is openly lesbian and has been a prominent advocate for LGBTQ+ rights throughout her career. She came out publicly during her college years and has spoken extensively about the challenges of coming out in a conservative environment. She has been in a long-term relationship with artist Susan Mikula since 1999. The couple met when Maddow was working on odd jobs during her early radio days. They live together in western Massachusetts and New York City. Maddow's openness about her sexuality and relationship has made her a role model for LGBTQ+ individuals, and her work often highlights issues affecting the community.

Eric Marcus (1958–)

Journalist, Author

Eric Marcus is an author, journalist, and LGBTQ+ advocate best known for his contributions to documenting and preserving LGBTQ+ history through his writing and the *Making Gay History* podcast. His work provides important insights into the lives and struggles of LGBTQ+ individuals, offering a historical perspective that ensures that their stories are remembered. His books, particularly *Making Gay History: The Half-Century Fight for Lesbian and Gay Equal Rights,* have been pivotal in educating the public about LGBTQ+ civil rights movements.

Born in New York City, Marcus grew up in the suburbs of Long Island. He attended Vassar College, where he earned his bachelor's degree in 1980, majoring in urban studies, before receiving a master's degree in journalism in 1984. Early in his career, he worked as a researcher for *CBS Morning News,* honing his skills in journalism and storytelling. His early interest in LGBTQ+ issues was sparked during his time as an undergraduate at Vassar, when he began to recognize the need for documenting the untold stories of the gay rights movement.

In the late 1980s, Marcus left his job at CBS to work on an oral history of the gay and lesbian civil rights movement. He produced two seminal books on the subject, *Making History: The Struggle for Gay and Lesbian Rights, 1945 to 1990* (1992) and *Making Gay History: The Half-Century Fight for Lesbian and Gay Equal Rights* (2002), as well as the *Making Gay History* podcast, which features audio interviews with key figures in LGBTQ+ history, ensuring that their voices continue to reach new generations. His other works include *Is It a Choice?* (1993), a guide to understanding sexual orientation; *Breaking the Surface* (1995), the best-selling autobiography of Olympic diver Greg Louganis; and *What If?: Answers to Questions about What It Means to be Gay and Lesbian* (2007).

Marcus has been involved in various LGBTQ+ advocacy initiatives, including serving on the board of directors for multiple organizations dedicated to equality and justice. He has spoken candidly about his experiences as a gay man, emphasizing the importance of sharing personal stories to promote understanding and social change. Though he keeps much of his private life out of the public eye, his long-standing commitment to LGBTQ+ history and education speaks to his deep personal connection to the community.

Stephanie Miller (1961–)

Talk Show Host, Comedian

Stephanie Catherine Miller is a political commentator, comedian, and radio talk show host known for her progressive viewpoints, sharp wit, and dynamic presence in the media. As the host of *The Stephanie Miller Show,*

a nationally syndicated progressive talk radio program, she has become a leading voice in liberal political commentary, combining humor with incisive analysis to engage her audience on a wide range of political and social issues.

Miller was born in Washington, D.C., and grew up in Lockport, New York. She is the daughter of William E. Miller, a prominent conservative politician who served as a U.S. representative from New York and was Barry Goldwater's running mate in the 1964 presidential election. Despite her father's conservative background, Stephanie developed her own progressive political views, often humorously referencing her family's political differences on her show.

Miller began performing comedy in high school, doing sketches. As she recalls, "I got my first laugh, and that was it. It's like a drug. It's always been my only drug." She attended the University of Southern California, where she earned a degree in theater and pursued her interest in comedy and performance. After graduating, she began her career in entertainment, initially focusing on stand-up comedy and later transitioning to radio and television. Her early work in comedy and broadcasting laid the foundation for her unique style of political commentary, blending humor with serious discussion.

Miller's breakthrough in radio came in the 1990s when she hosted several popular morning shows, including *The Stephanie Miller Show* in Los Angeles and *Hot 97's Morning Show* in New York City. Known for her quick wit and engaging personality, she quickly became a standout in the competitive world of radio.

In 2004, Miller launched a new iteration of *The Stephanie Miller Show*, focusing on political talk and commentary from a progressive perspective. The show quickly gained traction among liberal audiences, particularly during the political climate of the George W. Bush presidency, which saw a surge in demand for alternative, progressive media voices. Her ability to address serious political topics while maintaining a humorous and entertaining approach helped her show stand out in the crowded talk radio landscape.

Miller's show is known for its lively discussions; interviews with political figures, comedians, and activists; and her comedic take on current events. She has been a vocal critic of conservative politics and policies, using her platform to advocate for progressive causes such as LGBTQ+ rights, healthcare reform, and environmental protection.

In addition to her radio work, Miller has made numerous television appearances, including guest spots on CNN, MS NOW, and other news outlets, where she provides commentary on political events and issues. She also performed in several stand-up comedy specials and has been involved in various political and comedic live shows, including the *Sexy Liberal Comedy Tour*, which she cofounded.

Miller publicly came out as a lesbian in 2010 on her radio show, a decision that was met with support from her listeners and the broader progressive community. Her coming out was a significant moment for LGBTQ+ visibility in the media, particularly within the political talk radio space, which has often been dominated by conservative voices. She has been an outspoken advocate for LGBTQ+ rights, using her platform to support equality and inclusivity. She frequently discusses LGBTQ+ issues on her show, bringing attention to the challenges faced by the community and advocating for progressive policies and social acceptance.

Michael Musto (1955–)

Journalist, Media Commentator

Michael Musto is a journalist, author, and television personality best known for his witty and irreverent writing about New York City's nightlife, entertainment, and celebrity culture. With a career spanning over four decades, he became a prominent voice in journalism through his long-running column, "La Dolce Musto," in *The Village Voice*. His unique style, characterized by a blend of humor, gossip, and incisive cultural commentary, has made him one of the most recognizable figures in the world of entertainment journalism.

Musto was born in Brooklyn, New York, to an Italian American family. Growing up, he developed a passion for the arts, particularly theater and film. His fascination with New York City's vibrant nightlife and entertainment scene began at an early age, leading him to frequent iconic venues and events that would later become the subject of his writing.

Musto attended Columbia University, where he studied English literature and began writing for various publications, honing his skills as a journalist and developing his signature voice. After graduating, he quickly immersed himself in the world of New York City's nightlife, writing for publications like *SoHo Weekly News* and *Details* magazine. His early work captured the essence of the city's underground and alternative scenes, bringing attention to the personalities and trends that defined New York's cultural landscape.

In 1984, Musto joined the staff of *The Village Voice*, an influential alternative weekly newspaper known for its coverage of arts, culture, and politics. His column, "La Dolce Musto," quickly became a must-read for anyone interested in New York's nightlife and entertainment industry. Through his column, he chronicled the happenings of the city's club scene, celebrity gossip, and broader cultural shifts of the time, often with a humorous and sardonic twist. "La Dolce Musto" ran for nearly 30 years, making him a fixture in the world of entertainment journalism. His ability to blend gossip with cultural critique, all while maintaining a playful tone, set him apart from other columnists. He became known for his candid and often unfiltered commentary, providing readers with a unique perspective on the world of fame and celebrity.

In addition to his work at *The Village Voice*, Musto has authored several books, including *Downtown* (1986), which offers an insider's look at the cultural scene of 1980s New York, and *Fork on the Left, Knife in the Back* (2011), a memoir that combines personal stories with reflections on the entertainment industry. He has also contributed to various other publications, including *Out*, *The New York Times*, *The Daily Beast*, and *Paper* magazine.

Musto's work extends beyond print journalism. He has appeared on numerous television programs, such as *E! True Hollywood Story* and *Countdown with Keith Olbermann*, where he has offered his expertise on entertainment and pop culture. His presence in both print and television has made him a well-known figure in the media landscape.

Musto is openly gay and has been a vocal advocate for LGBTQ+ rights throughout his career. He has used his platform to support LGBTQ+ artists, promote diversity in the media, and challenge stereotypes. His columns often highlighted the contributions of LGBTQ+ individuals to the arts and entertainment, helping to bring greater visibility and acceptance to the community. He has been recognized for his contributions to LGBTQ+ advocacy and media and was honored with the Vito Russo Award at the 2014 GLAAD Media Awards, celebrating his commitment to promoting equality and LGBTQ+ visibility in journalism and entertainment.

Steve Osunsami (1971–)

Journalist

Steve Osunsami is a prominent journalist and television correspondent best known for his long tenure at ABC News. As a national correspondent, he has reported on some of the most significant news stories in recent American history, including natural disasters, political events, and social justice movements. His work has earned him respect for his compassionate reporting, particularly on issues affecting marginalized communities such as race relations, LGBTQ+ rights, and poverty. His dedication to bringing untold stories to light has made him a trusted figure in American journalism.

Osunsami was born in Washington, D.C., to Nigerian immigrant parents. He was raised in Peoria, Illinois, in a family that valued education and hard work. He participated in the Head Start preschool program for children of poverty and faced the challenges of growing up as a first-generation American and navigating life as a Black man in the Midwest. He attended the University of Illinois, Urbana–Champaign, where he earned a degree in journalism. His career in broadcasting began with local news and early stints at television stations in South Carolina and Iowa. These formative years laid the groundwork for his future success in national journalism.

Osunsami's most notable work has been as a national correspondent for ABC News, where he has reported for programs like *Good Morning America, World News Tonight with David Muir*, and *20/20*. Over the years, he has covered major stories, including Hurricane Katrina, the 2008 presidential election, the Ferguson protests, and the 2020 Black Lives Matter movement. His sensitive and insightful coverage of issues affecting African Americans and the LGBTQ+ community, particularly the intersection of race and sexuality, has earned him accolades. His journalism consistently highlights underrepresented voices, and his work has contributed to a deeper understanding of civil rights issues in America.

Osunsami identifies as gay and has been a vocal advocate for LGBTQ+ visibility in the media. He has shared parts of his personal journey, discussing the challenges he faced in coming to terms with his identity, especially as a Black man from a conservative immigrant family. He is married to Joe Remillard, and the couple lives in Atlanta, Georgia. He uses his platform to speak out on issues related to LGBTQ+ rights, often drawing connections between his personal experiences and the broader social justice issues he covers in his reporting. His openness about his sexuality has made him a role model for LGBTQ+ journalists and professionals of color.

Lydia Polgreen (1975–)

Journalist, Media Executive

Lydia Polgreen is a journalist, editor, and media executive known for her global journalism and leadership in digital media. Throughout her career, she has demonstrated a commitment to storytelling that illuminates important social, political, and cultural issues. She has been recognized for her contributions to journalism, particularly in her coverage of underreported stories from around the world and efforts to bring diverse voices to the forefront of the media landscape. She was the West Africa bureau chief for *The New York Times* from 2005 to 2009 and the editor in chief of *HuffPost* from 2016 to 2020. In 2022, she returned to *The New York Times* as an opinion columnist.

Polgreen was born in Washington, D.C., and grew up in a diverse and multicultural environment, which influenced her perspective on the world. She attended St. John's College in Annapolis, Maryland, where she studied philosophy and earned her B.A. in 1997. After college, she began her career as a reporter for small newspapers, where she gained experience covering local news and issues. She later attended Columbia University's Graduate School of Journalism.

Polgreen joined *The New York Times* in

2002 as a staff reporter. She quickly made a name for herself with her coverage of international news, particularly in Africa. As the West Africa bureau chief, she covered major stories, including civil conflicts in Liberia and the Ivory Coast, the rise of Islamic extremism in Mali, and the humanitarian crises in Darfur and Sudan. Her reporting from Africa earned her several awards and accolades, including the Livingston Award for Young Journalists and the George Polk Award for Foreign Reporting.

In 2011, Polgreen was appointed as the South Asia bureau chief for *The New York Times,* based in New Delhi, India. There, she covered significant events such as the rise of Narendra Modi, the political unrest in the Maldives, and the socioeconomic changes shaping India and its neighboring countries. In 2016, she was named editorial director of *The New York Times Global,* where she focused on expanding the newspaper's reach to international audiences. Her work in this role involved developing strategies to adapt journalism to a digital-first world, ensuring the newspaper's global relevance in an evolving media landscape.

In 2017, Polgreen left *The New York Times* to become the editor in chief of *HuffPost,* a prominent digital media company known for its focus on news, politics, and lifestyle. During her tenure, she emphasized the importance of diverse voices and perspectives, and she oversaw a major redesign of the site to enhance its digital presence. She stepped down from her role at *HuffPost* in 2020 to pursue new opportunities in media and storytelling.

Polgreen is openly gay and has been a strong advocate for diversity and inclusion in journalism. She has spoken frequently about the importance of representation in the media, emphasizing that a diverse newsroom is essential for accurately and effectively telling the stories of diverse communities. Her leadership has often been characterized by her commitment to fostering inclusive environments where a wide range of voices and experiences can be heard. She rejects rigid binaries and identifies as both Black and mixed race; as both American and African; as a woman, though with a masculine gender expression; and as a lesbian, though she has also had heterosexual romantic relationships. She is married to Candace Feit, a photojournalist who shares her passion for storytelling and global issues.

Rex Reed (1938–)

Film Critic, Author

Rex Taylor Reed is a film critic, author, and actor known for his sharp wit, distinctive voice, and controversial opinions in the world of entertainment journalism. As one of the most recognizable film critics in America, he has been a prominent figure in film criticism for decades, contributing to various major publications and appearing on television as a commentator. He is also known for his outspoken personality and has been openly gay throughout much of his career, making him a notable figure in the LGBTQ+ community.

Reed was born in Fort Worth, Texas. His father was an oil company supervisor, and the family moved throughout the American South during his childhood. He grew up in a family that appreciated the arts, and he developed an early interest in theater, music, and film. He attended Louisiana State University (LSU), where he studied journalism and began writing film and play reviews for the university's newspaper and the Baton Rouge newspaper. After graduating from LSU, he moved to New York City, where he hoped to find work as an actor. Instead, he began working as a freelance journalist and publicist. His engaging style and keen insight into film and theater quickly caught the attention of editors at various publications, helping him to establish a foothold in the competitive world of entertainment journalism.

In the 1960s, Reed began writing for high-profile publications such as *The New York Times*, *Esquire*, *Vogue*, and *GQ*. He became known for his incisive film reviews and interviews with celebrities, and his witty and sometimes acerbic style set him apart from other critics of his time. In 1968, he published *Do You Sleep in the Nude?*, a collection of his celebrity interviews that showcased his talent for getting stars to open up about their personal lives and careers. The book was a commercial success and helped to cement his reputation as one of the leading film critics and celebrity interviewers in the entertainment industry.

Reed also appeared in films, including *Myra Breckinridge* (1970), playing a dual role alongside Raquel Welch and Mae West. Although his acting career was brief, his foray into film added to his reputation as a versatile entertainment figure. For many years, he was a regular presence on television as a cohost of *At the Movies*, a film review program in which he sparred with fellow critics over the merits of current films. He was also a frequent guest on talk shows.

Throughout his career, Reed has written several books, including collections of his reviews and interviews, further showcasing his talent for storytelling and criticism. His long-running column for *The New York Observer*, where he served as the publication's film critic for over two decades, solidified his status as a leading voice in film criticism.

Reed has been openly gay for much of his career, although he has often kept his personal life private. Despite the challenges of being an openly gay man in the entertainment industry during a time when LGBTQ+ representation was limited, he has maintained a successful career and built a reputation as one of the most influential film critics of his generation.

Robin Roberts (1960–)

Journalist, Television Host

Robin René Roberts is a prominent television broadcaster known for her role as an anchor on ABC's *Good Morning America*. She is recognized not only for her groundbreaking work in journalism but also for her courage in sharing her personal health battles and coming out as a lesbian. As one of the most respected and beloved figures in American media, she has used her platform to advocate for cancer awareness, LGBTQ+ rights, and diversity.

Roberts was born in Tuskegee, Alabama, and raised in Pass Christian, Mississippi. Her parents, Lucimarian Tolliver and Colonel Lawrence E. Roberts, who was a Tuskegee Airman, instilled in her the values of discipline, hard work, and perseverance. She attended Southeastern Louisiana University, where she excelled as a student athlete, playing basketball and tennis. She graduated in 1983 with a degree in communications. Her early career in broadcasting began on local radio and television stations in Mississippi and Tennessee, where she honed her skills as a sports reporter and anchor.

Roberts joined ESPN in 1990 as a sportscaster. She quickly became known for her catchphrase "Go on with your bad self!" and insightful sports analyses. Her 15-year tenure at ESPN solidified her reputation as a top sports journalist. In 2005, she joined ABC's *Good Morning America* as a coanchor. Under her leadership, the show became the most watched morning news program in America. She was praised for her warm, relatable on-screen presence and ability to connect with viewers on a personal level.

Roberts made headlines in 2007 when she publicly shared her diagnosis of breast cancer. Her openness about her treatment and recovery inspired many and brought attention to the importance of early detection and cancer awareness. In 2012, she faced another health challenge when she was diagnosed with myelodysplastic syndrome (MDS), a rare blood disorder. Her battle with MDS, which included a bone marrow transplant from her sister, Sally-Ann, was documented in a series of emotional segments on *Good Morning America*. Her courage and resilience garnered widespread admiration and led to an increase in bone marrow donations.

In 2013, Roberts publicly came out as a lesbian in a heartfelt Facebook post, revealing her long-term relationship with Amber Laign, a massage therapist. Her announcement was met with widespread support and applause from fans and colleagues alike. Her decision to come out helped to increase visibility for LGBTQ+ individuals in the media and inspired others to live authentically.

Roberts's journey from small-town girl to national television icon is marked by her resilience, authenticity, and commitment to advocating for important causes. Her willingness to share her personal struggles and triumphs has inspired millions, making her a powerful voice for both the LGBTQ+ community and those facing health challenges.

Maer Roshan (1967–)

Journalist, Media Executive

Maer Roshan is a renowned journalist, editor, and media entrepreneur best known for founding *Radar* magazine and TheFix.com as well as for his role in revitalizing *Los Angeles* magazine as its editor in chief and as the coeditor in chief of *The Hollywood Reporter*. Throughout his career, he has been a trailblazer in the world of media, particularly with his work in digital publishing and innovative approach to covering popular culture, politics, and addiction recovery. As an openly gay journalist and editor, he has brought a unique perspective to his publications, often highlighting issues that intersect with LGBTQ+ identity, addiction, and mental health.

Roshan was born in Tehran, Iran, to an Iranian Jewish father and an American mother. He moved to New York in 1979 with his mother and siblings shortly before the Islamic Revolution. He grew up in New York City and graduated from New York University, where he studied journalism, and began his career in the industry. Early in his career, he worked as a crime reporter at the *Key West Citizen* and launched his first magazine, the gay weekly *QW* in 1991. In 1994, he became the deputy editor for *New York* magazine and later the editorial director of *Talk* magazine.

Roshan is best known for founding *Radar* magazine in 2003, a publication that quickly became known for its irreverent and provocative coverage of pop culture and politics. Although *Radar* faced financial challenges and shut down after several iterations, it left a lasting impact on the media world with its bold editorial style. In 2011, he founded TheFix.com, a website focused on addiction and recovery that has been praised for its honest and insightful reporting on the subject. Additionally, as the editor in chief of *Los Angeles* magazine starting in 2019, he helped to modernize and expand the publication's digital footprint, positioning it as a leading voice in southern California journalism. His tenure at *Los Angeles* magazine has been marked by award-winning coverage of politics, culture, and lifestyle in the region.

Openly gay, Roshan has been a vocal advocate for LGBTQ+ rights throughout his career. His identity as a gay man has influenced much of his work, particularly in his focus on issues related to addiction, recovery, and mental health, areas that disproportionately affect the LGBTQ+ community. He has also spoken about his own struggles with addiction, and his experiences have informed his creation of TheFix.com, a platform dedicated to recovery and sobriety.

Through his pioneering work in both

print and digital media, Roshan has made his publications stand out in the competitive world of magazines and online journalism. His contributions to discussions around addiction, recovery, and LGBTQ+ issues have been particularly impactful, offering a platform for voices and topics that is often overlooked in mainstream media.

Dan Savage (1964–)

Journalist, Author

Daniel Keenan "Dan" Savage is a journalist, author, media pundit, and LGBTQ+ rights activist best known for his frank and often provocative advice column, "Savage Love," and for founding the It Gets Better project to help prevent suicide among LGBTQ+ youths. Through his work, he has become a significant voice in discussions surrounding sex, relationships, and LGBTQ+ issues and is known for addressing topics that are often considered taboo. His advice column, books, and podcasts have made him a widely influential figure in sex education and activism. His work has had a lasting impact on the LGBTQ+ community, particularly in advocating for LGBTQ+ youth and fostering conversations about healthy relationships.

Savage was born in Chicago, Illinois. He grew up in a conservative Catholic household, which heavily influenced his later views on religion and sexuality. He attended the University of Illinois, Urbana–Champaign, where he earned a degree in theater. After graduation, he lived in Berlin, Germany, from 1988 to 1990 before moving to Madison, Wisconsin, and then to Seattle, Washington, where he began writing his sex advice column, "Savage Love," for the Seattle alternative weekly newspaper *The Stranger* in 1991. The column quickly gained popularity due to his candid, humorous, and unapologetic approach to discussing sex and relationships, attracting a national readership.

"Savage Love" evolved into a podcast, radio show, and syndicated column that reaches millions of readers and listeners worldwide. Savage's blunt advice on sex and relationships, especially concerning LGBTQ+ issues, has earned him both praise and controversy. In 2010, he cofounded the It Gets Better project with his husband, Terry Miller, to provide support and hope to LGBTQ+ youth experiencing bullying. The project became a viral sensation and continues to be a platform for people to share stories of overcoming adversity. He is also a prolific author, with books like *The Commitment: Love, Sex, Marriage, and My Family* and *American Savage: Insights, Slights, and Fights on Faith, Sex, Love, and Politics* addressing themes of sexuality, marriage, and politics.

Savage is openly gay and has used his personal experiences to inform much of his work. He married his long-term partner, Terry Miller, in 2005, and they adopted a son, D. J. His advocacy for LGBTQ+ rights is deeply personal, and his activism often focuses on issues like marriage equality, anti-bullying, and sex education. His public presence as a gay man, combined with his outspoken support for sexual openness and LGBTQ+ equality, has made him a prominent figure in both the media and LGBTQ+ communities.

Jeffrey Schmalz (1953–1993)

Journalist

Jeffrey Schmalz was a journalist best known for his groundbreaking work at *The New York Times*, where he became a key figure in reporting on AIDS and LGBTQ+ issues during the height of the AIDS crisis in the 1980s and early 1990s. His career was notable for his transition from being a traditional newsroom figure to being an advocate for more compassionate, in-depth coverage of the HIV/AIDS epidemic after he himself was diagnosed with the disease. His journalism not only changed the way the media covered LGBTQ+ health issues but also helped to humanize those affected by the epidemic, bringing visibility and empathy to the forefront of the conversation.

Born and raised in Pennsylvania, Schmalz was brought up by his mother, who had divorced his alcoholic father when he was 2 years old; his father died when he was a teenager. He worked on his high school newspaper and received a scholarship for fatherless sons to attend Columbia University in 1971, where he studied economics.

While still attending Columbia, Schmalz began his two-decade association with *The New York Times* as a night copy boy when he was 19. After being promoted to a copy-editor position, he dropped out of college to work full time. He joined the national staff in 1988, working as bureau chief in Miami before returning to New York in 1990 as deputy national editor. In December 1990, he suffered a brain seizure at his desk that led to the discovery that he had AIDS. Having hid his homosexuality from his superiors at the *Times,* he became an eloquent spokesman for the frustrations of people with AIDS after his illness became known and with his sexual orientation no longer a secret.

Schmalz's most notable writing emerged after his AIDS diagnosis. He wrote a series of in-depth profiles of key figures in the LGBTQ+ community, including activists, politicians, and everyday people affected by the disease. His work contributed to a shift in how major media outlets reported on AIDS, focusing on the humanity and struggles of those living with the virus rather than solely on its medical aspects. His 1992 *New York Times Magazine* article "Living with AIDS" remains one of his most celebrated pieces, showcasing his personal connection to the subject matter and commitment to using his platform for advocacy. "Now I see the world through the prism of AIDS," he wrote. "I feel an obligation to those with AIDS to write about it and an obligation to the newspaper to write what just about no other reporter in America can cover in quite the same way."

Schmalz died at the age of 39, but his legacy as a journalist and advocate for compassionate coverage of AIDS lives on. His life and career were later documented in *Dying Words: The AIDS Reporting of Jeffrey Schmalz and How It Transformed* The New York Times (2015) by Samuel G. Freedman.

Ari Shapiro (1978–)

Radio Host, Journalist

Ari Michael Shapiro is a journalist, radio host, and singer best known as one of the cohosts of NPR's *All Things Considered,* one of the most listened to news programs in the United States. His work as a journalist is marked by his versatility and depth, covering a broad range of topics from politics to culture. In addition to his work in journalism, he is also a vocalist for the band Pink Martini, showcasing his talents in both media and the arts. As an openly gay journalist, he has used his platform to bring greater visibility to LGBTQ+ issues and promote inclusivity within the industry.

Shapiro was born in Fargo, North Dakota, and raised in Beaverton, Oregon. His parents were both university professors, and he grew up in a Jewish family that emphasized education and cultural engagement. He attended Yale University, where he graduated with a degree in English in 2000. His career in journalism began with an internship at NPR, working with legal affairs correspondent Nina Totenberg, which soon led to a full-time position as a reporter for NPR's *Morning Edition*. His early reporting assignments included coverage of major political stories, which helped him quickly gain recognition for his incisive, clear reporting style. By the time he joined NPR's international desk, he had become a trusted voice in both domestic and international news.

Shapiro's most notable achievements include his tenure as a cohost of *All Things Considered*, which began in 2015. His contributions have helped to shape the program's wide-ranging coverage of politics, culture, and global events. As a White House correspondent during the Obama administration, he reported on many of the most pivotal moments of the presidency, including international trips and domestic policy decisions. His journalistic range extends beyond politics; he has covered everything from terrorist attacks to arts and culture. He has won three national Edward R. Murrow awards for his journalism and was named "Journalist of the Year" in 2023 by NLGJA, the association of LGBTQ+ journalists.

Shapiro is also a vocalist for the band Pink Martini, performing with the group on international tours and contributing to several of their albums, blending his passion for storytelling with musical expression. In 2004, he married his longtime boyfriend, Michael Gottlieb, a lawyer who worked in the Office of the White House Counsel from 2013 to 2015. In 2023, he published his memoir, *The Best Strangers in the World: Stories from a Life Spent Listening*.

Randy Shilts (1951–1994)

Journalist, Author

Called "the most significant gay journalist of the twentieth century" and the journalist who changed how we see gay America, Randy Shilts was widely recognized for his groundbreaking reporting on the AIDS epidemic and role in bringing LGBTQ+ issues to mainstream media. As one of the first openly gay journalists in the United States to cover LGBTQ+ topics extensively, his work significantly impacted public perception and policy. His investigative journalism, particularly his book *And the Band Played On*, remains seminal work in both the history of journalism and the LGBTQ+ community.

Shilts was born in Davenport, Iowa, and raised in Aurora, Illinois, in a conservative, working-class family. From a young age, he showed an interest in journalism and advocacy, reflecting his passion for social justice. He attended the University of Oregon, where he became deeply involved in student journalism, serving as the editor of the school newspaper, *The Oregon Daily Emerald*. He graduated in 1975 with a degree in journalism. Despite facing discrimination because of his sexual orientation, he remained determined to pursue a career in journalism.

As an openly gay man, Shilts struggled to find full-time employment as a journalist. He moved to San Francisco and began his career at *The Advocate*, the nation's leading LGBTQ+ magazine, where he covered various topics, including politics, civil rights, and the burgeoning gay rights movement. He quickly made a name for himself with his incisive reporting and fearless approach to controversial issues. In 1981, he joined the *San Francisco Chronicle* as one of the first openly gay journalists to work for a major American newspaper. This was at a time when few news outlets were willing to hire LGBTQ+ reporters, much less allow them to cover LGBTQ+ issues. At the *Chronicle*, he began to report on the emerging AIDS crisis, dedicating himself to covering the story when few others were willing to address it. "Any good reporter could have done this story," he recalled, "but I think the reason I did it, and no one else did, is because I am gay. It was happening to people I cared about and loved."

In 1987, Shilts published *And the Band*

Played On: Politics, People, and the AIDS Epidemic, a comprehensive account of the AIDS epidemic in the United States. The book is widely regarded as a landmark in investigative journalism and is credited with significantly raising public awareness about AIDS. His reporting highlighted the indifference and negligence of government officials, the medical community, and the media, criticizing their slow response to the crisis. The book was nominated for the National Book Award and later adapted into a critically acclaimed HBO film in 1993.

Shilts continued to write influential works, including *The Mayor of Castro Street: The Life and Times of Harvey Milk* (1982), a biography of the first openly gay elected official in California, and *Conduct Unbecoming: Gays and Lesbians in the U.S. Military* (1993), which examined the discrimination faced by LGBTQ+ individuals in the U.S. Armed Forces; he called it "my definitive book on homophobia."

Shilts himself was diagnosed with HIV in 1987. He declined to be told the results of his HIV test until he had completed the writing of *And the Band Played On*, concerned that the test would interfere with his objectivity as a writer. Despite his illness, he continued to work and write, focusing on issues affecting the LGBTQ+ community and the ongoing AIDS crisis. He remained outspoken about the importance of early diagnosis, treatment, and support for those living with HIV/AIDS before his death at the age of 42.

In an interview before his death, he said, "Every gay writer who tests positive ends up being an AIDS activist. I wanted to keep on being a reporter." Historian Garry Willis has written that *And the Band Played On* "will be to gay liberation what Betty Friedan was to early feminism and Rachel Carson's *Silent Spring* was to environmentalism."

Ellen Shub (1943–2019)

Photojournalist

Ellen Shub was a photographer and photojournalist best known for her work documenting social justice movements, particularly those related to women's rights, LGBTQ+ rights, and civil rights. Her photographs captured some of the most pivotal moments in American activism from the 1970s to the early 2000s, and her work has been instrumental in preserving the history of these movements. Her photography offers a visual narrative of the struggles and triumphs of marginalized communities, making her an essential figure in documenting activism and social change through her lens.

Born in New Jersey, Shub grew up in a Jewish family with a strong sense of social justice. She attended the University of Rochester, the University of Pennsylvania, and earned an MEd from the Harvard Graduate School of Education. She worked first as a media producer in television programming in Boston before becoming a freelance photographer, quickly gaining recognition for her ability to capture intimate, impactful moments in protests, rallies, and other social justice events. Her early career was marked by her work during the women's liberation movement and the rise of LGBTQ+ activism in the 1970s, setting the tone for her lifelong commitment to documenting social change.

Shub's photographs of women's marches, LGBTQ+ protests, and civil rights demonstrations appeared in numerous publications, exhibitions, and historical archives, providing a powerful visual record of activism in America. Some of her most iconic work includes her images of the early LGBTQ+ Pride marches and feminist protests in Boston and New York. Her work has been featured in publications like *The Boston Globe*, *The Village Voice*, and *The Advocate* as well as in books and documentaries about activism.

Shub identified as lesbian, and her

personal experiences as a member of the LGBTQ+ community deeply informed her work. She was an active participant in many of the movements she documented, which allowed her to capture them with a unique level of empathy and authenticity. Her openness about her sexuality helped her connect with the communities she photographed, giving her work a personal and powerful resonance that set it apart from other photojournalists of her time. She had one son with her longtime partner, Kathy J. Seltzer.

By documenting key moments in the fight for equality and justice, Shub ensured that the visual history of these movements would not be lost or forgotten. Her photographs serve as an enduring record of the activism that shaped modern America, preserving the faces and voices of those who fought for change. Her work is a vital resource for historians, activists, and the general public, offering an intimate window into the grassroots efforts that have shaped civil rights, feminism, and LGBTQ+ liberation.

Nate Silver (1978–)

Journalist, Statistician

Nathaniel Read "Nate" Silver is a statistician, writer, and founder of the data analysis website *FiveThirtyEight* best known for his pioneering work in statistical forecasting, particularly in politics, sports, and economics. He gained national prominence for his accurate predictions during the 2008 and 2012 U.S. presidential elections, in which his innovative use of polling data revolutionized the way political forecasts are understood. His influence has since expanded beyond politics to include sports analytics and other fields in which data-driven insights are crucial. His contributions to the fields of data journalism and political analysis have made him one of the most recognized figures in the world of predictive analytics.

Silver was born in East Lansing, Michigan, the son of a community activist mother and a father who was the chair of the political science department at Michigan State University. His early passion was for baseball and, later on, for mathematics and statistics, which led him to earn a degree in economics from the University of Chicago in 2000. After college, he initially worked as a consultant but soon shifted his focus to baseball analytics. He developed a popular system called PECOTA (Player Empirical Comparison and Optimization Test Algorithm) for forecasting the performance of Major League Baseball players. This marked his first foray into applying statistical models to real-world scenarios, laying the groundwork for his future success. His interest in political forecasting grew after this, particularly during the 2008 presidential election cycle.

Silver's most notable achievement is the founding of *FiveThirtyEight* in 2008, which quickly became one of the leading platforms for data-driven political analysis. During the 2008 U.S. presidential election, he correctly predicted the outcome in 49 of the 50 states, propelling him to national fame. He achieved even greater success in 2012 when he correctly predicted the electoral outcome in all 50 states. *FiveThirtyEight* has since expanded its coverage to include sports, economics, and culture, maintaining a reputation for rigorous data analysis. He is also the author of *The Signal and the Noise: Why So Many Predictions Fail—But Some Don't* (2012), which delves into the science of forecasting, becoming a *New York Times* bestseller.

Silver has been candid about his experiences as a member of the LGBTQ+ community in the world of politics and media. While he is more widely known for his contributions to statistical analysis, he has used his platform occasionally to discuss issues related to LGBTQ+ rights, though he is more focused on his professional work than activism. He lives in New York

City and continues to maintain a strong presence in both political and sports analytics. His identity as an openly gay statistician and media figure has made him a role model for LGBTQ+ individuals in the fields of science, technology, and journalism. When asked if he has noticed people regarding him as a "gay icon," he responded, "I've started to notice it a little bit, although so far it seems like I'm more a subject of geek affection than gay affection."

By applying rigorous statistical analysis to polling data and making complex models accessible to the public, Silver has changed the way elections are covered in the media. His work at *FiveThirtyEight* has set new standards for accuracy and transparency in data-driven reporting. His legacy is not just as a forecaster but as a trailblazer in how data is used to understand and predict real-world events.

Andrew Sullivan (1963–)

Blogger, Editor, Author

Andrew Michael Sullivan is a British American author, editor, and commentator known for his influential contributions to political and social discourse, particularly regarding LGBTQ+ issues, conservatism, and cultural criticism. As one of the first openly gay public intellectuals to advocate for same-sex marriage, his writings have had a profound impact on American politics and LGBTQ+ rights. His work spans multiple media platforms, including traditional print, online blogs, and social media, making him a pioneer in both new and old forms of journalism.

Sullivan was born in South Godstone, Surrey, England. Raised in a Roman Catholic family, he attended Reigate Grammar School before earning a scholarship to Magdalen College, Oxford, where he studied modern history and graduated with first-class honors. His academic excellence led him to Harvard University, where he pursued an MPA and a Ph.D. in government, focusing on political theory. During his time at Harvard, he became deeply interested in American politics and culture. His doctoral dissertation, "Intimations Pursued: The Voice of Practice in the Conversation of Michael Oakeshott," reflected his deep engagement with conservative philosophy and laid the foundation for his future work as a public intellectual.

In 1991, Sullivan became the youngest editor in chief of *The New Republic*, a prominent political magazine, where he made a name for himself as a fearless and provocative editor. Under his leadership, *The New Republic* published groundbreaking articles on a range of topics from the Gulf War to domestic policy and LGBTQ+ rights.

Sullivan's landmark 1989 essay, "Here Comes the Groom: A (Conservative) Case for Gay Marriage," published in *The New Republic*, is credited with sparking the modern debate over same-sex marriage in the United States. In the essay, he argued that marriage would provide stability and legitimacy for same-sex couples and was consistent with conservative values. This essay had a lasting impact, helping to shape public opinion and policy debates around marriage equality. In 1995, he began writing *Virtually Normal: An Argument About Homosexuality*, a book that explored the moral, legal, and political status of homosexuality. The book was widely praised for its nuanced analysis and became a seminal text in LGBTQ+ studies and advocacy.

Sullivan launched *The Dish* in 2000, one of the earliest and most popular political blogs, where he provided commentary on current events, politics, and culture. *The Dish* became known for its candid, unfiltered voice and its willingness to tackle controversial topics, attracting a large and loyal readership. He was one of the first journalists to experiment with a subscription-based model for online content, which proved successful.

Throughout his career, Sullivan has contributed to major publications, including *The New York Times*, *The Atlantic*, *Time*, and *New York* magazine, among others. He has written extensively on topics such as conservatism, religion, HIV/AIDS, and American politics, establishing himself as a leading voice in contemporary journalism.

Sullivan has spoken openly about his experiences as a gay man, including his diagnosis with HIV in the 1990s. His personal experiences with HIV have informed much of his writing on the subject, particularly his critiques of public health policies and calls for more compassionate and effective responses to the epidemic. In 2007, he married his husband, Aaron Tone. He has often discussed his personal life and marriage in his writings, reflecting on the significance of marriage equality and the importance of personal freedom and individual rights.

Jonathan Van Ness (1987–)

Media Celebrity

Jonathan McDonald Van Ness is a television personality, author, and hairstylist best known for the role of grooming expert on the hit Netflix series *Queer Eye*. With their infectious personality and positive approach to self-care, they have become a beloved figure in pop culture known for spreading messages of self-acceptance and empowerment. As an openly nonbinary individual and advocate for LGBTQ+ rights, they have raised awareness on issues such as HIV, mental health, and gender identity, making them a significant figure in both the entertainment industry and the LGBTQ+ community.

Van Ness (who is commonly referred to by his initials, J. V. N.) was raised in Quincy, Illinois. They came "from a family of journalists," a sixth-generation member of the family-owned newspaper the *Herald-Whig* and broadcast conglomerate Quincy Media. Raised in a conservative town, they were self-described as a "little baby queen" and often faced bullying for their gender expression and flamboyant personality. They have described enduring "years of judgment, ridicule, and trauma." They attended the University of Arizona, studying political science but eventually dropping out to pursue a career in hairstyling.

They trained at the Aveda Institute in Minneapolis before working in Arizona for five years. They eventually moved to Los Angeles, where they eventually built a strong social media presence through the web series *Gay of Thrones*, a comedic recap of the hit show *Game of Thrones*. The web series became a cult favorite and earned them several Emmy nominations and offers to be a red-carpet commentator and a host of other web series.

Van Ness's breakthrough came on the Netflix reboot of *Queer Eye*, which premiered in 2018. As the grooming expert on the show, they quickly became a fan favorite for their humor, warmth, and uplifting energy. The success of *Queer Eye* has turned them into a global celebrity, allowing them to expand their career into other areas. In 2019, they released a memoir, *Over the Top: A Raw Journey to Self-Love*, which candidly revealed their struggles with addiction, mental health, and living with HIV. The book became a bestseller and was praised for its vulnerability and honesty. They are also the host of the popular podcast *Getting Curious with Jonathan Van Ness*, which explores a wide range of topics from politics to pop culture.

Van Ness came out as nonbinary and "genderqueer" in 2019 and has been an advocate for gender inclusivity and LGBTQ+ visibility. In their memoir, they also revealed that they are HIV positive, a diagnosis they received in 2012. Since then, they have been an outspoken advocate for HIV awareness and combating the stigma surrounding the disease. Their openness about their personal life and struggles has made them an inspiration to many, especially in the LGBTQ+ community.

Norah Vincent (1968–2022)

Journalist, Columnist

Norah Mary Vincent was an author and journalist known for her insightful and often controversial explorations of gender, identity, and social issues. Her most famous work, *Self-Made Man: One Woman's Year Disguised as a Man,* chronicled her experience living as a man for 18 months and exposed the complexities of gender dynamics from a firsthand perspective. Her willingness to tackle provocative subjects through immersive journalism earned her critical acclaim and established her as an important voice in discussions around gender and identity.

Vincent was born in Detroit, Michigan. She grew up both there and in London, where her father was a lawyer for the Ford Motor Company. She attended Williams College, where she earned a degree in philosophy in 1990. It was during her undergraduate career that she realized she was a lesbian. After graduation, she spent 11 years as a graduate student in philosophy at Boston College and worked as an assistant editor at the Free Press, a Boston publisher. She eventually embarked on a career in journalism, writing for publications such as the *Los Angeles Times, The Village Voice, Salon,* and *The Advocate.* Her sharp intellect and provocative style helped her quickly gain a reputation as a fearless writer willing to explore complex and controversial topics, particularly around LGBTQ+ issues, politics, and social justice.

Vincent's most notable work is her 2006 book *Self-Made Man,* in which she spent 18 months disguised as a man in order to explore male experiences and gender roles. The book was widely praised for its thought-provoking insights into masculinity, sexism, and the difficulties men face in society. The project took a physical and emotional toll on her, but it cemented her reputation as a pioneer in immersive journalism. Following *Self-Made Man,* she wrote several other books, including *Voluntary Madness: My Year Lost and Found in the Loony Bin,* which detailed her experiences in mental health institutions and explored the stigma surrounding mental illness. Her books challenged readers to rethink assumptions about gender, mental health, and identity.

Vincent identified as lesbian, and her experiences as a queer woman informed much of her writing on gender and identity. Her personal exploration of gender roles through *Self-Made Man* not only provided insights into masculinity but also offered a unique perspective on how gender expectations affect individuals across the spectrum. Throughout her life, she was a strong advocate for LGBTQ+ rights and was unafraid to question societal norms around sexuality and identity. Despite her success, she struggled with mental health issues, and her candid writing on these topics was both personal and impactful. She died by medically assisted suicide at a clinic in Switzerland, leaving behind a legacy of challenging journalism that pushed the boundaries of societal understanding. She was 53.

Through works like *Self-Made Man* and *Voluntary Madness,* Vincent invited readers into the worlds of gender performance and mental illness with compassion, curiosity, and fearlessness. Her contributions to journalism and literature remain important for those interested in the intersections of gender studies, LGBTQ+ issues, and psychology. Her work continues to inspire discussions about the fluidity of identity and the impact of societal expectations on individuals, making her an enduring figure in contemporary thought.

Jann Wenner (1946–)

Publisher, Author

Jann Simon Wenner is a magazine publisher, media entrepreneur, and cofounder of *Rolling Stone* magazine, one of the most iconic and influential publications in music, pop culture, and political journalism. Launched in 1967, *Rolling Stone* became a cultural touchstone for generations, blending music coverage with incisive political commentary and social analysis. He played a critical role in shaping the magazine's identity, giving a voice to the counterculture movements of the 1960s and beyond. His impact on music journalism and ability to connect cultural and political currents have made him one of the most significant figures in American media.

Wenner was raised in a secular Jewish family in San Francisco. He was exposed to the nascent countercultural movement during his youth. He briefly attended the University of California, Berkeley, where he immersed himself in the emerging student activism and music scene of the 1960s. He dropped out of Berkeley in 1966 and began working as a journalist. Along with music critic Ralph J. Gleason, he cofounded *Rolling Stone* in 1967, aiming to create a publication that captured the spirit of the rock and roll generation. The magazine's launch marked the beginning of his career as a powerful figure in media.

Under Wenner's leadership, *Rolling Stone* became a cultural institution, covering iconic musicians like Bob Dylan, the Beatles, and the Rolling Stones while also tackling political and social issues. He fostered the careers of legendary journalists, including Hunter S. Thompson and Tom Wolfe, who contributed groundbreaking pieces of gonzo and New Journalism. Beyond *Rolling Stone,* he expanded his media empire by founding *Outside, Us Weekly,* and *Men's Journal,* influencing both music journalism and celebrity culture. His legacy also includes the Rock & Roll Hall of Fame, where he served as a key figure in its establishment and growth.

Wenner was married to Jane Schindelheim from 1967 to 1995, and the couple had three children. In 1995, he came out as gay and began a long-term relationship with designer Matt Nye, with whom he has three more children. His eventual openness about his sexuality, along with his influential role in shaping cultural discourse, has contributed to the visibility of LGBTQ+ figures in the media industry.

Wenner published his memoir, *Like a Rolling Stone,* in 2022. In a 2023 *New York Times* interview, he said that he had not considered Black and women musical artists "articulate" enough to be interviewed for his book, which led to his removal from the board of directors of the Rock & Roll Hall of Fame. He later issued an apology, in which he stated, "I totally understand the inflammatory nature and badly chosen words and deeply apologize and accept the consequences."

Despite the controversy, Wenner's impact on American culture is well established. Through *Rolling Stone,* he not only chronicled the lives and careers of legendary musicians but also helped to shape the cultural conversation around politics, war, and social justice. His vision for a magazine that fused music and politics resonated deeply with the Baby Boomer generation, and his commitment to quality journalism, has left an indelible mark on the industry. As a media mogul and advocate for LGBTQ+ rights, he has remained a key figure in shaping American pop culture for over five decades.

Science

Pathologization: Late-19th to Mid-20th Centuries

During the 19th century, as the pursuit of scientific knowledge began to outpace the reliance on religious norms as a method of understanding the natural, physical, and behavioral worlds, attitudes toward sexuality in general and LGBTQ+ sexual identity in particular began to shift. This shift reflected broader social changes as well as evolving perspectives within the scientific community and can be divided into several key phases: pathologization, declassification, affirmation, and current trends in research and advocacy.

During the late 19th century, the U.S. scientific community began to develop a more formalized approach to understanding sexuality, heavily influenced by European medical and psychological theories. LGBTQ+ identities were mainly viewed as deviations from the norm, and the emerging fields of psychiatry and psychology often treated these identities as pathological conditions requiring intervention.

The late 19th century saw the rise of sexology, a field dedicated to the scientific study of human sexuality. Influential European sexologists like Austrian psychiatrist Richard von Krafft-Ebing and British physician and sexologist Havelock Ellis played significant roles in shaping American perspectives on sexuality. Krafft-Ebing's *Psychopathia Sexualis* (1886), one of the first major texts to catalog and categorize sexual behaviors, was widely read in the United States. In it, he classified homosexuality as a mental disorder, a view that resonated with American physicians and psychologists of the time. Ellis, whose work was also influential in the United States, offered a somewhat more sympathetic view of homosexuality. In his series *Studies in the Psychology of Sex* (1897–1928), he suggested that homosexuality was an inborn trait rather than a moral failing. However, he still considered it a deviation from the norm, reinforcing the idea that non-heteronormative sexual orientations were somehow abnormal. These early sexology theories laid the groundwork for the pathologization of homosexuality and other LGBTQ+ identities in the United States.

In the early 20th century, Sigmund Freud, whose psychoanalytic theories had started to become highly influential in America, posited that human sexuality was fluid and that everyone had the potential for both heterosexual and homosexual attractions. However, he believed that homosexuality was often the result of developmental disturbances, particularly unresolved conflicts during the Oedipal phase of childhood. He saw homosexuality as a fixation on an early stage of psychosexual development, which could theoretically be overcome with psychoanalytic therapy. His ideas were widely adopted by American psychologists and

Germnan psychiatrist Richard von Krafft-Ebing believed that homosexuality was a mental disorder.

psychiatrists, who often viewed homosexuality through the lens of psychoanalysis. For example, psychoanalysts in the United States frequently treated homosexuality as a neurotic condition resulting from dysfunctional family dynamics such as an overly close relationship with the mother or a distant relationship with the father. This approach reinforced the idea that homosexuality was a mental disorder that could potentially be "cured" through psychotherapy.

As psychiatry and psychology developed as formal disciplines in the United States, the medicalization of homosexuality became more entrenched. The inclusion of homosexuality in the first edition of the American Psychiatric Association's *Diagnostic and Statistical Manual of Mental Disorders (DSM-I)* in 1952 exemplifies this trend. In the *DSM-I*, homosexuality was classified as a "sociopathic personality disturbance," a label that reflected the widespread belief that homosexuality was a disorder requiring medical intervention. This classification had dire implications for LGBTQ+ individuals, who were often subjected to a range of harmful and invasive treatments aimed at "curing" their sexual orientation. These treatments included psychoanalysis, aversion therapy, and even more extreme measures like electroshock therapy and lobotomies. Aversion therapy, for instance, involved pairing homoerotic images with negative stimuli,

The British physician Havelock Ellis was a progressive and a social reformer. Writing on homosexuality and transexuality, he did not consider LGBTQ people to be immoral and just felt they were following sexual inclinations they were born with.

such as electric shocks or nausea-inducing drugs, in order to create an aversion to same-sex attraction. These practices not only failed to change individuals' sexual orientation but also caused significant psychological and physical harm. The pathologization of homosexuality was not limited to adults: children and adolescents exhibiting gender nonconformity or same-sex attraction were often also subjected to psychiatric treatment. The belief that early intervention could prevent the development of homosexuality led to the use of behavioral therapies designed to reinforce traditional gender roles. For example, boys perceived as "effeminate" might be encouraged or coerced into participating in stereotypically masculine activities, while girls showing tomboyish behavior might be steered toward more traditionally feminine pursuits.

Conversion therapy, also known as "reparative therapy" or "sexual orientation change efforts," based on the belief that being gay or bisexual is abnormal and that it can be "cured" or "fixed," had many key proponents. Irving Bieber, a prominent American psychiatrist, was one of the leading figures in promoting conversion therapy. His 1962 book *Homosexuality: A Psychoanalytic Study of Male Homosexuals* argued that homosexuality was the result of dysfunctional family dynamics and could be treated through psychoanalytic therapy.

Charles Socarides, another influential psychiatrist, also played a significant role in advocating for conversion therapy. His book *The Overt Homosexual* (1968) outlined his theories on the origins and treatment of homosexuality. He cofounded the National Association for Research & Therapy of Homosexuality (NARTH) in 1992, which became a central organization promoting conversion therapy as a legitimate treatment for homosexuality. The husband-and-wife research team of William Masters and Virginia Johnson were renowned sexologists whose research into the nature of human sexual response from 1957 into the 1990s further contributed to the field by claiming to have successfully "converted" individuals from homosexual to heterosexual orientations, although their findings were later discredited.

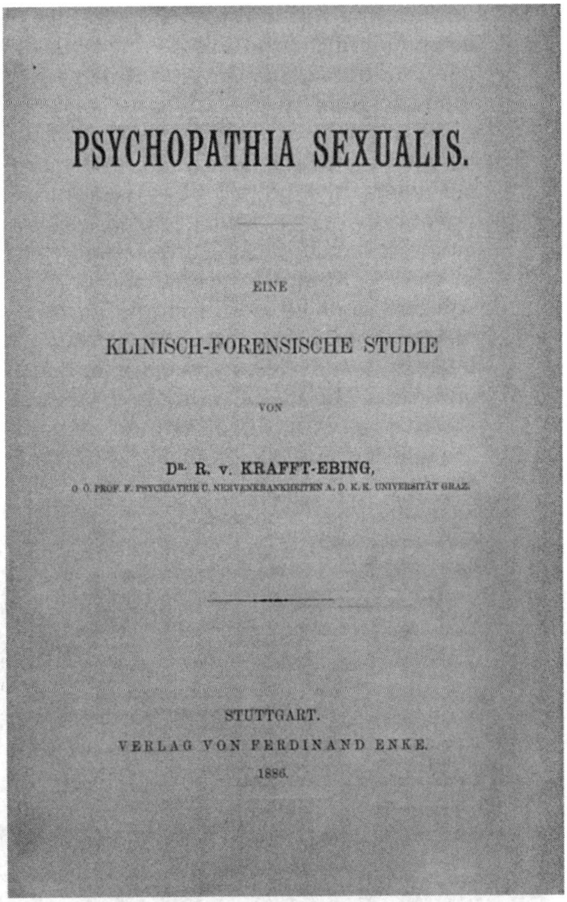

PSYCHOPATHIA SEXUALIS.

EINE

KLINISCH-FORENSISCHE STUDIE

VON

Dr. R. v. KRAFFT-EBING,

O. Ö. PROF. F. PSYCHIATRIE U. NERVENKRANKHEITEN A. D. K. K. UNIVERSITÄT GRAZ.

STUTTGART.

VERLAG VON FERDINAND ENKE.

1886.

Krafft-Ebing's Psychopathia Sexualis *was the first book of its kind to delve deeply into sexual behavior theory and was highly influential in America.*

The early 20th century also saw the influence of eugenics on the scientific understanding of homosexuality and other nonnormative sexual behaviors. Eugenics was a movement that sought to improve the human race through controlled breeding, classified homosexuality, bisexuality, and gender nonconformity as signs of degeneracy—biological flaws that needed to be eradicated in order to ensure the health of the nation. In the United States, the eugenics movement gained significant traction, leading to the forced sterilization of thousands of individuals deemed "unfit" to reproduce. LGBTQ+ individuals were often included in this category, and the idea that homosexuality was a form of degeneracy contributed to the stigmatization and medicalization of LGBTQ+ identities. Eugenicists, such as biologist Charles Davenport, psychiatrists George Henry and Edward A. Kempf, psychiatrist Henry H. Goddard, and Ellsworth Huntington, argued that homosexuality was a hereditary defect and that those who exhibited such tendencies should be mitigated through selective breeding and other interventions. The intertwining of eugenics and psychiatry further reinforced the pathologization of LGBTQ+ identities. The idea that homosexuality was not only a mental disorder but also a threat to the genetic health of the population led to increased efforts to identify, diagnose, and treat LGBTQ+ individuals in ways that often amounted to physical and emotional abuse.

Despite the dominant pathologizing views, early voices of resistance existed within the scientific community. For example, the work of Magnus Hirschfeld, a gay German physician and sexologist, influenced some American scientists and activists. Hirschfeld, who founded the Scientific-Humanitarian Committee in 1897,

The staff at Indiana University's Institute for Sex Research included (front row, left to right): Cornelia V. Christenson; Mrs. Leser; Clyde E. Martin. On steps (left to right): Mrs. Brown; Paul H. Gebhard; William Dellenback; Alfred E. Kinsey; Wardell B. Pomeroy; Dr. Davis; Eleanor Roehr; Dorothy Collins.

argued that homosexuality was a natural variation of human sexuality. Although his ideas were more widely accepted in Europe, they did find some resonance among progressive circles in the United States. In the 1940s, American sexologist Alfred Kinsey further challenged the prevailing views on homosexuality with his pioneering research on human sexual behavior. Kinsey's *Sexual Behavior in the Human Male* (1948) and *Sexual Behavior in the Human Female* (1953) revealed that same-sex behavior was far more common than previously acknowledged. Kinsey introduced the concept of a sexual orientation continuum, now known as the Kinsey Scale, which suggested that sexual orientation existed on a spectrum, with most individuals falling somewhere between exclusively heterosexual and exclusively homosexual. Although Kinsey's work was controversial and met with significant resistance from conservative elements of American society, it played a crucial role in challenging the binary understanding of sexual orientation and laid the groundwork for more progressive views on homosexuality in the latter half of the 20th century.

The Beginning of Affirmation: 1960s–1980s

The 1960s and 1970s, which marked a period of striking social and cultural change in the United States, also saw significant shifts in the scientific communi-

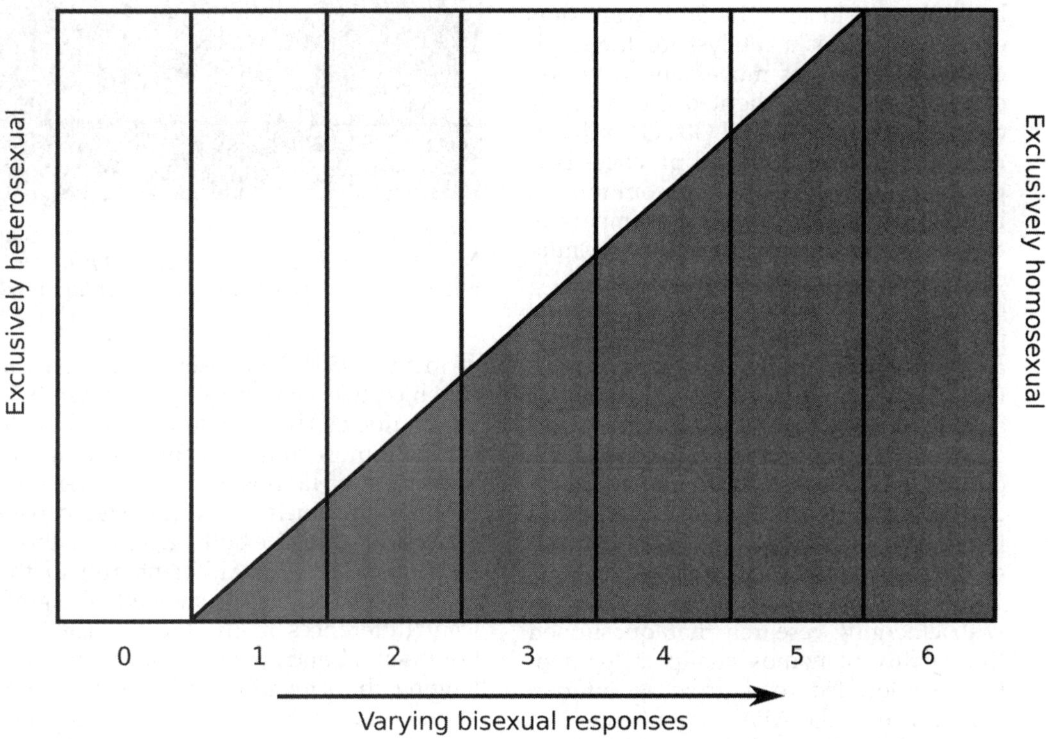

The Kinsey Scale suggests that most people fall somewhere between being exclusively heterosexual and exclusively homosexual.

The first edition of the Diagnostic and Statistical Manual *issued by the American Psychiatric Association treated homosexuality as a mental disorder.*

ty's understanding of LGBTQ+ identities. The civil rights movement, the feminist/second-wave women's rights movement, and the emerging LGBTQ+ rights movement began to challenge long-standing social norms, including the pathologization of non-heteronormative sexualities and gender identities. This period was characterized by increasing resistance to the classification of homosexuality as a mental disorder and the gradual move toward declassification and affirmation of LGBTQ+ identities.

A major turning point in the declassification of homosexuality occurred within the American Psychiatric Association (APA). The APA first classified homosexuality as a "sociopathic personality disturbance" in the *DSM-I* in 1952, reflecting the prevailing belief that homosexuality was a mental disorder requiring medical intervention. However, by the late 1960s, this view was increasingly challenged by both LGBTQ+ activists and progressive mental health professionals. The Stonewall Riots of 1969 served as a catalyst for the modern LGBTQ+ rights movement, a period of activism that highlighted the systemic discrimination faced by LGBTQ+ individuals, including the harmful practices perpetuated by the psychiatric community. LGBTQ+ activists, including members of the Gay Liberation Front and the Mattachine Society, began to target the APA directly, organizing protests at its annual meetings and demanding that the Association reconsider its stance on homosexuality. In 1970, activists disrupted the APA's annual conference, holding signs and chanting slogans like "Psychiatry is the enemy" and "Gay is Good." These actions drew significant attention to the issue and forced the APA to engage with the concerns of the LGBTQ+ community.

The pressure from activists, combined with emerging research that questioned the validity of homosexuality as a mental disorder, led to a growing internal debate within the APA. One of the most influential studies in this regard had been conducted by psychologist Evelyn Hooker in the 1950s. Her research, the results of which had been published in her 1956 paper, titled "The Adjustment of the Male Overt Homosexual," involved a comparative study of homosexual and heterosexual men in which she administered psychological tests to both groups without revealing their sexual orientation to the evaluators. The results showed no significant differences in the mental health of homosexual and heterosexual men, challenging the prevailing belief that homosexuality was inherently linked to psychopathology. Her work was groundbreaking because it provided empirical evidence that homosexuality was not associated with mental illness, undermining the rationale for its classification as a disorder.

In 1972, the APA's Nomenclature Committee, led by Dr. Robert Spitzer, began to seriously consider removing homosexuality from the *DSM-I*. Spitzer, who initially believed that homosexuality was a mental disorder, was persuaded by the evidence and arguments presented by activists and fellow psychiatrists. After extensive discussions and debates, the APA's board of trustees voted in December 1973 to remove homosexuality from the *DSM-II*, replacing it with the diagnosis of "sexual orientation disturbance," which was intended to apply only to individuals who were distressed about their sexual orientation. This decision marked a historic shift in the field of psychiatry, as it signaled the declassification of homosexuality as a mental disorder.

The declassification of homosexuality had important implications for LGBTQ+ individuals and for the field of mental health more broadly. It paved the way for the development of LGBTQ+-affirmative therapies and for the eventual condemnation of "conversion therapy."

The APA's decision was met with both support and opposition. While many in the psychiatric community welcomed the change, recognizing it as a step toward greater understanding and acceptance of sexual diversity, others resisted, arguing that homosexuality should still be considered a disorder. In response to this controversy, the APA held a referendum in 1974 in which its members voted to uphold the decision to remove homosexuality from the *DSM-II*. The final vote was 5,854 in favor of declassification and 3,810 against, confirming the APA's new position.

The declassification of homosexuality had important implications for LGBTQ+ individuals and for the field of mental health more broadly. It paved the way for the development of LGBTQ+-affirmative therapies and for the eventual condemnation of "conversion therapy." With the declassification of homosexuality, the APA and other professional organizations formally began to oppose these practices, recognizing them as both ineffective and harmful. Several scientists campaigned both for the declassification of homosexuality as a mental disorder and as vocal opponents of conversion therapy, including Dr. Judd Marmor, Dr. Charles Silverstein, Dr. Douglas Halderman, Dr. Gregory Herek, and Dr. Lawrence Hatterer.

The 1973 decision also had a ripple effect across other disciplines and institutions. In 1975, the American Psychological Association (APA) followed suit by formally endorsing the view that homosexuality was not a mental disorder. The APA also began to advocate for the rights of LGBTQ+ individuals, including the right to access nondiscriminatory mental health care. This shift in perspective contributed to a broader cultural change, as the scientific community's acceptance of homosexuality as a natural variation of human sexuality helped to reduce stigma and promote greater acceptance of LGBTQ+ individuals in society.

The declassification movement also impacted the scientific understanding of bisexuality and transgender identities, although these areas developed somewhat differently. Bisexuality had often been dismissed or misunderstood by both the general public and the scientific community, with many viewing it as a transitional or confused state rather than a legitimate sexual orientation. However, the broader shift toward recognizing sexual diversity led to a growing acceptance of bisexuality as a distinct and valid orientation. Researchers began to explore the unique experiences of bisexual individuals, including the challenges they faced in a society that often enforced a binary understanding of sexual orientation. Transgender identities, meanwhile, remained more contested within the scientific community.

The *DSM-III*, published in 1980, introduced the diagnosis of "gender identity disorder," which continued to pathologize transgender experiences by framing them as a mental health issue. However, the 1980s also saw the beginnings of a shift toward a more affirming approach to transgender identities. Some mental health professionals began to advocate for the rights of transgender individuals to access medical and psychological support in aligning their physical bodies with their gender identities. This shift was influenced by the growing recognition that gender identity is a complex and deeply ingrained aspect of human experience and that supporting individuals in their gender transitions could lead to better mental health outcomes.

The declassification of homosexuality in the 1970s marked a pivotal moment in the history of American science and LGBTQ+ rights. The removal of homosexuality from the *DSM-II* was the result of sustained activism, emerging scientific evidence, and changing cultural attitudes. This decision set the stage for the broader acceptance and affirmation of LGBTQ+ identities within the mental health community and beyond. It also laid the groundwork for future progress in the understanding and support of bisexual and transgender individuals, even as these areas continued to evolve in the decades that followed.

the Early 2000s

The 1990s and early 2000s marked a significant period of affirmation and inclusion for LGBTQ+ identities within the American scientific community. Following the declassification of homosexuality as a mental disorder in the 1970s, the scientific and medical fields began to shift their focus from pathologizing LGBTQ+ identities to understanding and affirming them as natural variations of human experience. This period was characterized by the development of LGBTQ+-affirmative therapies, the rejection of harmful practices like conversion therapy, and the increasing inclusion of bisexual and transgender identities in scientific research and health care.

One of the most significant developments during this time was the American Psychological Association's (APA) formal endorsement in 1994 of the view that homosexuality is not a mental disorder. This endorsement reinforced the declassification that had occurred two decades earlier and represented a broader commitment to supporting the mental health and well-being of LGBTQ+ individuals. The APA began actively to oppose conversion therapy, recognizing that attempts to change an individual's sexual orientation or gender identity were not only ineffective but also caused significant psychological harm. In 1998, the APA issued a statement explicitly condemning conversion therapy and urg-

Protests like this one in London have been widespread as many people believe conversion therapy is extremely harmful, causing severe psychological distress.

ing mental health professionals to avoid practices that pathologized or attempted to alter LGBTQ+ identities.

The shift toward affirmation was also reflected in the growing recognition of bisexuality as a legitimate sexual orientation rather than as a transitional phase or a form of confusion, as the scientific community became more attuned to the diversity of human sexual experiences and researchers began to explore bisexuality as a distinct orientation. Studies conducted in the 1990s and early 2000s examined the unique challenges faced by bisexual individuals such as biphobia, the tendency to experience discrimination from both heterosexual and homosexual communities, and the pressure to conform to a binary understanding of sexual orientation. These studies contributed to a more nuanced understanding of bisexuality and helped to validate the experiences of bisexual individuals.

In 1994, the publication of the DSM-IV *marked a significant step forward by replacing the diagnosis of "gender identity disorder" with "gender dysphoria." This change reflected a growing recognition that the distress experienced by transgender individuals was not inherent to their identities but rather a result of the mismatch between their gender identity and assigned sex at birth as well as the societal stigma they faced.*

The understanding and support of transgender identities also began to evolve during this period. In 1994, the publication of the *DSM-IV* marked a significant step forward by replacing the diagnosis of "gender identity disorder" with "gender dysphoria." This change reflected a growing recognition that the distress experienced by transgender individuals was not inherent to their identities but rather a result of the mismatch between their gender identity and assigned sex at birth as well as the societal stigma they faced. By focusing on the distress rather than the identity itself, the *DSM-IV* diagnosis aimed to provide transgender individuals with access to medical and psychological support without pathologizing their gender identity.

These decades also saw the emergence of standards of care for transgender individuals. The World Professional Association for Transgender Health (WPATH), formerly known as the Harry Benjamin International Gender Dysphoria Association, played a crucial role in developing these standards. WPATH's Standards of Care, first published in 1979 and updated regularly, provided guidelines for healthcare professionals on how to support transgender individuals in their gender transitions. These guidelines emphasized the importance of individualized care, informed consent, and access to gender-affirming medical interventions such as hormone therapy and surgery. The Standards of Care were widely adopted by healthcare providers and became a cornerstone of transgender health care, helping to ensure that transgender individuals received the support they needed to live in alignment with their gender identity.

In addition to changes in clinical practice, the scientific community also began to engage in research related to the development of LGBTQ+ identities. In the 1990s and early 2000s, there was a growing interest in the biological and genetic factors that might influence sexual orientation and gender identity, with research suggesting that early attempts to identify a "gay gene" or other biological determinants were often oversimplified or overstated. The result of such studies has led to the conclusion that both biological and environmental factors play a role in shaping aspects of sexual orientation and that no single cause or explanation exists for the diversity of human sexual and gender experiences.

The increased focus on LGBTQ+ health and well-being during this period also extended to public health. The HIV/AIDS epidemic, which devastated LGBTQ+

communities in the 1980s, continued to be a major public health concern in the 1990s and beyond. However, advances in medical research and treatment, particularly in the development of antiretroviral therapies, transformed HIV/AIDS from a terminal illness into a manageable chronic condition for many individuals. The scientific and medical communities worked closely with LGBTQ+ activists and organizations to improve access to HIV testing, treatment, and prevention and to combat the stigma associated with the disease.

The 1990s and 2000s also saw the emergence of a more intersectional approach to LGBTQ+ research and health care. Scholars and activists began to explore how race, gender, class, and other social factors intersected with sexual orientation and gender identity, shaping the experiences of LGBTQ+ individuals in complex ways. This intersectional perspective highlighted the need for more inclusive and culturally competent care as well as the importance of addressing the specific challenges faced by LGBTQ+ individuals from marginalized communities.

In addition to these developments in research and health care, the scientific community became increasingly involved in advocacy for LGBTQ+ rights. Professional organizations like the American Medical Association (AMA) and the American Psychological Association (APA) issued statements in support of LGBTQ+ rights, including the right to marry, the right to access health care without discrimination, and the right to live free from violence and harassment. These organizations also worked to promote diversity and inclusion within their own ranks, encouraging LGBTQ+ individuals to pursue careers in science and health care.

By the early 2000s, the affirmation and inclusion of LGBTQ+ identities had become a central focus of much scientific and medical work in the United States. The shift from pathologization to affirmation and inclusion, driven by a combination of factors, including activism, emerging scientific evidence, and broader cultural shifts toward greater acceptance of sexual and gender diversity, laid the groundwork for continued advancements in LGBTQ+ research, health care, and rights, even as challenges and areas of resistance persisted.

Contemporary Perspectives

The 2010s to the present have seen a continuation and deepening of the affirmation and inclusion of LGBTQ+ identities within the American scientific community, characterized by a growing emphasis on diversity, intersectionality, and ethical considerations in research and health care. This period has also been marked by significant advances in understanding the complexities of sexual orientation and gender identity alongside ongoing advocacy for LGBTQ+ rights and well-being.

Organizations like the AMA have increasingly worked to improve diversity in the health care field.

However, challenges and debates persist, particularly around the ethics of certain types of research and the need for more inclusive healthcare practices.

One of the most significant developments in recent years has been the publication of the *DSM-V* in 2013, which further refined the diagnosis of gender dysphoria, replacing the previous *DSM-IV* classification. The *DSM-V*'s approach to gender dysphoria reflects a more compassionate and affirming perspective on transgender identities, focusing on the distress that may arise from the incongruence between an individual's experienced or expressed gender and their assigned sex at birth rather than treating transgender identity itself as a disorder. This shift has been crucial in reducing stigma and promoting access to gender-affirming care, as it reaffirms an emphasis on the importance of supporting individuals in their gender transitions rather than pathologizing their identities.

The contemporary approach to transgender health care has been guided by the World Professional Association for Transgender Health (WPATH) and its Standards of Care, which have continued to evolve in response to new research and the needs of transgender individuals. The most recent version of the Standards of Care, published in 2011 and currently undergoing revisions for a new edition, emphasizes informed consent, individualized care, and the importance of access to a range of gender-affirming medical interventions, including hormone therapy and surgeries. These guidelines have been widely adopted by healthcare providers and have become the gold standard for transgender health care, helping to ensure that transgender individuals receive respectful, competent, and affirming care.

In addition to advances in transgender health care, the scientific community has made significant strides in continuing to understand sexual orientation and gender identity as complex, multifaceted phenomena. Research in fields such as genetics, neuroscience, and psychology, which included a large 2019 study on the human genome, has explored and attempted to explain the many biological, as well as environmental, factors that contribute to the development of sexual orientation and gender identity. For example, studies on brain structure and function have found subtle differences between cisgender and transgender individuals, while research on genetic influences has suggested that sexual orientation may well include a biologically hereditary component, though the 2019 study, like those before it, failed to identify a single "gay gene." These findings underscore the complexity and fluidity of sexual orientation and gender identity, challenging simplistic or reductionist explanations.

This research has also raised important ethical questions. Some scholars and activists have expressed concerns about the potential misuse of scientific findings, particularly in the context of genetic research. Some are afraid that efforts to identify the biological underpinnings of sexual orientation or gender identity could be used to justify discriminatory practices such as prenatal testing or genetic engineering aimed at preventing the birth of LGBTQ+ individuals. These concerns have led to calls for greater caution and ethical scrutiny in LGBTQ+-related research, with an emphasis on ensuring that such research is conducted in ways that respect the dignity and autonomy of LGBTQ+ individuals.

Another key area of focus in contemporary LGBTQ+ science is dealing with health disparities faced by LGBTQ+ individuals. Research has consistently shown that LGBTQ+ people experience higher rates of mental health issues, substance use, and chronic conditions compared to their heterosexual and cisgender peers. These disparities are often linked to the stress of living in a society that is still not fully accepting of LGBTQ+ identities as well as discrimination in healthcare settings. The concept of "minority stress," first developed by social psychologist Ilan Meyer, has become central to understanding the mental health challenges faced by LGBTQ+ individuals. Minority stress theory posits that the chronic stress of stigmatization, discrimination, and internalized homophobia or transphobia contributes to poorer mental health outcomes among LGBTQ+ people.

In response to these findings, more emphasis is now placed on developing and implementing LGBTQ+-affirmative interventions and policies. For example, the American Psychological Association and other professional organizations have issued guidelines for mental health professionals on how to provide culturally competent and affirming care to LGBTQ+ clients. These guidelines emphasize the importance of understanding the unique experiences and challenges faced by LGBTQ+ individuals as well as the need to create supportive and inclusive therapeutic environments.

In the realm of public health, a focus is now also being placed on addressing the specific needs of LGBTQ+ populations. This includes efforts to reduce the stigma associated with HIV/AIDS, which continues to disproportionately affect gay and bisexual men as well as transgender women. Advances in HIV prevention and treatment, such as Pre-Exposure Prophylaxis (PrEP) and antiretroviral therapy, have had a significant impact on reducing new infections and improving the quality of life for those living with HIV. Public health campaigns and initiatives have increasingly sought to reach LGBTQ+ communities with targeted messaging and resources, recognizing the importance of culturally tailored approaches to health promotion.

Advances in HIV prevention and treatment, such as Pre-Exposure Prophylaxis (PrEP) and antiretroviral therapy, have had a significant impact on reducing new infections and improving the quality of life for those living with HIV.

Additionally, scholars and activists have increasingly recognized that sexual orientation and gender identity do not exist in isolation but are intertwined with other aspects of identity such as race, ethnicity, socioeconomic status, and disability. This intersectional approach has highlighted the ways in which different forms of discrimination and marginalization intersect to create unique challenges for LGBTQ+ individuals who belong to multiple marginalized groups. For example, research has shown that LGBTQ+ people of color often face compounded stressors related to both racism and homophobia or transphobia, leading to even greater health disparities.

Efforts to address these intersectional challenges have included the development of more inclusive research methodologies and the creation of healthcare programs that specifically target the needs of LGBTQ+ individuals from marginalized communities. Additionally, a push has been made to increase the representation of LGBTQ+ individuals, particularly those from diverse backgrounds, in scientific research and healthcare professions. This push for diversity is seen as essential to ensuring that LGBTQ+-related research and health care are truly inclusive and reflective of the experiences of all LGBTQ+ individuals.

Advocacy for LGBTQ+ rights and inclusion within the scientific community has also continued to grow. Organizations such as the American Medical Association (AMA) and the American Psychological Association (APA) have taken strong stances in support of LGBTQ+ rights, including advocating for marriage equality, opposing discriminatory legislation, and promoting policies that protect LGBTQ+ individuals from discrimination in health care, employment, and housing. These organizations have also worked to promote diversity and inclusion within their own ranks, encouraging LGBTQ+ individuals to pursue careers in science, medicine, and psychology.

Despite these advances, challenges and debates remain. Issues such as the ethical implications of genetic research, the

The stigma against HIV/AIDS is lessening as more people understand the illness and the people it affects.

need for more inclusive and intersectional approaches to LGBTQ+ health, and the ongoing fight against discrimination in health care and society at large continue to be areas of active discussion and advocacy. The political landscape in the United States during the 2010s and 2020s has seen efforts in several states to roll back LGBTQ+ rights, particularly transgender rights, which has created new challenges for the scientific and medical communities as they work to protect the gains that have been made.

Gender-affirming treatments for transgender and nonbinary children and adolescents have been particularly contentious. Gender-affirming treatments, such as puberty blockers, hormone replacement therapy (HRT), and, in some cases, surgical procedures, are designed to help align a person's physical characteristics with their gender identity. Proponents of these treatments argue that they can significantly improve mental health outcomes, reduce gender dysphoria, and lower the risk of anxiety, depression, and suicide among transgender youths. They emphasize that these interventions, when guided by healthcare professionals and with informed consent from both the patient and their guardians, are critical in supporting the well-being of transgender individuals. However, opponents of gender-affirming treatments for youths raise concerns about the potential long-term effects and reversibility of these interventions. They argue that minors may not be fully capable of making such significant decisions about their bodies and that pressure to pursue medical interventions may occur too quickly without a thorough psychological evaluation and exploration of other options. Critics have called for stricter regulations, more comprehensive mental health assessments, and, in some cases, mandatory waiting periods before beginning any gender-affirming treatments.

Legislative actions reflect the divide over this issue, with some states enacting laws to protect access to gender-affirming treatments for minors, ensuring that transgender youths can receive appropriate medical care without unnecessary barriers. However, in recent years, several states have proposed or enacted laws that restrict or ban gender-affirming treatments for minors. These laws often cite concerns about safety, consent, and the need to protect children, while opponents argue that such laws are discriminatory and prevent necessary medical care. The controversy is also fueled by misinformation and social views, with cultural, religious, and political beliefs heavily influencing opinions on gender-affirming care. As a result, this topic remains a deeply polarized issue that highlights the need for nuanced, evidence-based discussions that prioritize the health and well-being of transgender and nonbinary young people.

In the future, the ongoing work of the scientific community will be essential in addressing the continuing challenges faced by LGBTQ+ individuals. This includes developing inclusive research methodologies, expanding access to culturally competent health care, and advocating for the protection and advancement of LGBTQ+ rights. The journey from pathologization to affirmation and inclusion has been marked by significant progress, but it also highlights the need for continued vigilance and commitment to ensure that all LGBTQ+ individuals can access the health care they need in an environment of support and respect.

LGBTQ+-Related Careers in Science

During most of the 20th century, LGBTQ+ scientists in the United States faced significant challenges, including widespread discrimination, stigma, and the threat of losing their careers if their sexual orientation or gender identity became known. Social norms and institutional policies often forced LGBTQ+ individuals to remain closeted, and those who were outed often faced severe professional and personal consequences, including dismissal from their jobs, loss of funding, and social ostracism. The scientific community's pathologization approach to LGBTQ+ identities further compounded these challenges, as LGBTQ+ scientists had to navigate a field that often viewed their very identities as disorders.

Today, while considerable progress has been made in terms of acceptance and inclusion, LGBTQ+ scientists still face challenges. These include underrepresentation in STEM fields, lack of mentorship, and the persistence of subtle forms of discrimination or bias. LGBTQ+ scientists may also encounter challenges related to securing funding or advancing their careers, particularly if their research focuses on LGBTQ+ issues, which can be marginalized or undervalued. Additionally, intersectional challenges remain significant, as LGBTQ+ scientists who are also people of color, women, or belong to other marginalized groups often face compounded barriers.

Despite these challenges, LGBTQ+ scientists have made significant contributions to their fields and continue to advocate for greater diversity, inclusion, and support within the scientific community. However, ongoing efforts are needed to address the remaining disparities and ensure that all LGBTQ+ scientists can thrive in their careers.

AIDS TIMELINE

This timeline integrates key scientific advancements, legislative actions, and the human toll of the HIV/AIDS epidemic in the United States, illustrating the ongoing battle against the disease and the progress that has been made in reducing its impact.

1981. The first cases of the disease that would come to be known as AIDS are reported. On June 5, the U.S. Centers for Disease Control and Prevention (CDC) publishes a report describing cases of a rare lung infection, *Pneumocystis carinii* pneumonia (PCP), in five previously healthy gay men in Los Angeles. This is the first official report of what will later become known as AIDS (Acquired Immunodeficiency Syndrome).

On July 2, the *Bay Area Reporter*, a weekly newspaper for the gay and lesbian community in San Francisco, publishes its first mention of "gay men's pneumonia." *The New York Times* then publishes an article about a rare cancer, Kaposi's sarcoma, appearing in 41 gay men in New York City and San Francisco, further raising alarm about a new health crisis. By the end of

1981, 337 reported cases of severe immune deficiency in the United States are reported, with 130 deaths by December 31.

1982. On January 4, Larry Kramer, Edmund White, and others found the Gay Men's Health Crisis, the first community-based AIDS service provider in the United States. The organization's founding is partly a response to the lack of federal interest and action regarding the growing crisis. Federal dismissal of the crisis is evident in the behavior of Larry Speakes, acting White House press secretary (1981–1987) during Ronald Reagan's presidency, and the White House Press Corps. When Speakes takes questions regarding AIDS, both Speakes and the press respond with homophobic jokes and laughter.

On May 31, the *Los Angeles Times* publishes the first front-page story on AIDS in the mainstream press: "Mysterious Fever Now an Epidemic." In June, the CDC uses the term "GRID" (Gay-Related Immune Deficiency) for the first time, but it is soon replaced due to its inaccuracy.

On September 24, the term "AIDS" (Acquired Immunodeficiency Syndrome) is officially used by the CDC to describe the disease and acknowledges that it is not confined to the gay community. By the end of the year, the cumulative total of reported AIDS cases in the United States reaches 771, with 618 deaths.

1983. In March, the U.S. Public Health Service issues guidelines recommending that people at risk of AIDS, particularly gay men and intravenous drug users, refrain from donating blood.

Larry Kramer, shown here in 2007 at work on a book, was a film producer and playwright but also wrote on gay men's health issues and worked to improve awareness of the AIDS crisis.

On March 14, AIDS activist Larry Kramer publishes "1,112 and Counting," a blistering assessment of the impact of AIDS on the gay community and the slow pace of scientific progress in finding the cause of AIDS.

On May 18, the U.S. Congress passes the first bill that includes funding specifically targeted for AIDS research and treatment. Two days later, Dr. Françoise Barré-Sinoussi and her team at the Pasteur Institute in France identify a virus they call LAV (Lymphadenopathy-Associated Virus) in a patient with AIDS. This virus will later be known as HIV (Human Immunodeficiency Virus).

The World Health Organization holds its first meeting between November 22–25 to assess the global AIDS situation and begins international surveillance. By the end of the year, approximately 2,304 cumulative AIDS cases have been reported in the United States, with over 1,300 deaths.

1984. In April, Dr. Robert Gallo of the U.S. National Cancer Institute confirms the discovery of a virus, which he calls HTLV-III (later known as HIV), as the cause of AIDS. This finding confirms the work done by the Pasteur Institute. U.S. Department of Health and Human Services secretary Margaret Heckler declares that a vaccine will be available within two years.

On October 10, San Francisco public health officials order bathhouses to be closed due to high-risk sexual activities occurring in these venues. By the end of the year, 7,699 cumulative AIDS cases have been reported in the United States, with 3,665 deaths.

1985. On March 2, the first blood test for HIV, known as the ELISA test, is approved by the U.S. Food and Drug Administration (FDA), allowing for blood screening and better diagnosis.

Larry Kramer's play *The Normal Heart* opens Off-Broadway on April 22. It dramatizes the impact of the growing AIDS epidemic on New York's gay community between 1981 and 1984.

William Hoffman's *As Is*, the first play about AIDS to make it to Broadway, debuts on May 1.

Dr. Robert Gallo figured out that HIV infection is what leads to AIDS, and he subsequently developed the HIV blood test.

Hollywood star Rock Hudson dies of AIDS on October 2. The first American celebrity to publicly admit to having AIDS, Hudson's death brings widespread public attention to the epidemic.

On November 11, NBC broadcasts *An Early Frost*, the first film on HIV/AIDS, in a prime-time TV slot.

In December, Ryan White, a teenager from Indiana with hemophilia, becomes a national symbol for the epidemic after being banned from school due to his HIV status. His case challenges misconceptions and stigma associated with AIDS. The end of the year sees the cumulative number of AIDS cases in the United States at 15,527, with 12,529 deaths.

1986. On January 14, Anthony Fauci, National Institute of Allergy and Infectious Diseases (NIAID) director, announces that "one million Americans have already been infected with the virus" and that "at least 2 to 3 million will be infected within 5 to 10 years." HIV is adopted as the name of the retrovirus that causes AIDS. The yearly death toll rises to over 24,000 in America.

1987. In February, Silence=Death posters begin to appear on New York City streets. The poster is the work of the Silence=Death Project, a New York activist art collective that created it in 1986. The slogan also appears written in chalk on New York City sidewalks.

On March 12, the AIDS Coalition to Unleash Power (ACT UP) is founded in New York City by Larry Kramer and others. ACT UP becomes known for its direct-action advocacy and civil disobedience, significantly impacting AIDS policy and awareness.

On March 19, AZT (zidovudine), the first antiretroviral drug, is approved by the FDA for the treatment of HIV. It becomes the first drug available to fight HIV/AIDS, offering hope to many.

In August, the FDA sanctions the first clinical trial to test an HIV vaccine.

On September 30, the CDC launches the first AIDS-related public service announcements in a campaign called America Responds to AIDS to kick off the newly designated AIDS Awareness Month in October.

In November, journalist Randy Shilts publishes *And the Band Played On*, which chronicles the 1980–1985 discovery and spread of HIV/AIDS. By the end of 1987, the global number of reported AIDS cases is 71,751, with over 47,022 deaths reported in the United States alone.

1988. On May 26, Surgeon General C. Everett Koop's report *Understanding AIDS* is sent to all households in the United States to provide explicit advice to U.S. citizens on how to protect themselves from AIDS.

On August 9, drug counselor David Purchase sets up the United States' first needle-exchange program to combat the spread of HIV in Tacoma, Washington. The first World AIDS Day is observed on December 1. It is initiated by the World Health Organization (WHO) to raise awareness and commemorate those who have died of the disease, becoming an annual event.

By the end of 1988, over 82,362 cumulative cases of AIDS have been reported in the United States, with approximately 61,816 deaths.

1990. In July, Congress enacts the Americans with Disabilities Act (ADA), which prohibits discrimination against individuals with disabilities, including people living with HIV/AIDS.

On August 12, Congress passes the Ryan White Comprehensive AIDS Resources Emergency (CARE) Act, providing federal funding for HIV/AIDS treatment and care for low-income, uninsured, and underinsured people. The act is named after Ryan White, who died of AIDS earlier that year at the age of 18.

By the end of 1990, over 160,969 cumulative AIDS cases have been reported in the United States, with approximately 100,777 deaths.

1991. In April, a clinical trial of zidovudine (AZT) in HIV-infected pregnant women begins. In May, Tony Kushner's acclaimed AIDS-related play *Angels in America* premieres in San Francisco.

On November 7, NBA star Magic Johnson publicly announces that he is HIV positive. The red ribbon is adopted as the international symbol of AIDS awareness, designed by the Visual AIDS Artists Caucus. It becomes a powerful emblem of support and solidarity.

By the end of 1991, global AIDS deaths reach over 1 million, with cumulative U.S. deaths at approximately 120,453.

1993. In January, the CDC adds HIV to the list of communicable diseases that restrict entry into the country, effectively banning travel and immigration for HIV-positive individuals. The National Association of People with AIDS convenes the first annual AIDS Watch, with hundreds of community members from across

Basketball great Magic Johnson, who announced he had HIV in 1991, has given and helped to raise millions of dollars towards HIV research.

the United States coming to Washington, D.C., to lobby Congress for increased funding.

On June 25, President Clinton appoints Kristine Gebbie to serve as the nation's first AIDS policy coordinator. She will lead the newly created White House Office of National AIDS Policy. In December, *Philadelphia,* a major Hollywood film starring Tom Hanks and Denzel Washington, is released. It is one of the first mainstream movies to address the AIDS crisis and is critically acclaimed for raising awareness.

By the end of 1993, global AIDS deaths had reached approximately 2.5 million, with cumulative U.S. deaths at about 194,476.

1994–1995. AIDS becomes the leading cause of death for all Americans ages 25–44, highlighting the epidemic's devastating impact on a generation.

On December 23, 1994, the FDA approves an oral HIV test, the first non-blood-based antibody test for HIV.

In June 1995, the FDA approves the first protease inhibitor, which ushers in a new era of Highly Active Antiretroviral Therapy (HAART).

By the end of 1995, 500,000 cases of AIDS have been reported in the United States, and global AIDS deaths have reached approximately 4.7 million, with cumulative U.S. deaths at about 343,000.

1996. Highly Active Antiretroviral Therapy (HAART), a combination of three or more antiretroviral drugs, is introduced. HAART significantly reduces AIDS-related deaths and is considered a turning point in the fight against HIV/AIDS. The number of new AIDS cases diagnosed in the United States declines for the first time since the beginning of the epidemic. AIDS is no longer the leading cause of death for all Americans ages 25–44, although it remains the leading cause of death for African Americans in this age group.

During the spring and summer, the FDA approves the first HIV home testing kit, a viral load test to measure the level of HIV in the blood; the first non-nucleoside reverse transcriptase inhibitor drug, nevirapine; and the first HIV urine test. The International AIDS Conference in Vancouver in July showcases the success of HAART, marking the beginning of the "chronic manageable disease" era of HIV/AIDS. Robert Gallo's discovery that some natural compounds known as chemokines can block HIV and halt the progression of AIDS is hailed as one of the year's most important scientific breakthroughs. HIV/AIDS researcher Dr. David Ho, who advocates for a new strategy for treating HIV in which patients are placed on new, more aggressive treatment regimes earlier in the course of their infection, is named *Time* magazine's "Man of the Year."

By the end of 1996, global AIDS deaths have reached approximately 6.4 million, with cumulative U.S. deaths at about 362,004.

1998. The CDC reports that African Americans account for 49 percent of U.S. AIDS-related deaths. AIDS-related mortality for African Americans is almost 10 times higher than that of whites and three times that of Hispanics.

2000. By the end of 2000, global AIDS deaths are estimated at over 20 million, with around 774,467 cumulative deaths in the United States.

2001. In June, the UN General Assembly holds a special session on HIV/AIDS and adopts the Declaration of Commitment on HIV/AIDS, emphasizing global cooperation and increased funding for the epidemic. U.S. secretary of state Colin Powell reaffirms President Clinton's 2000 statement that HIV/AIDS is a national security threat.

2002. On November 7, the FDA approves the first rapid diagnostic HIV test kit for use in the United States. The mobility and speed of the test allow for a wider use of HIV testing. Worldwide, 10 million young people aged 15–24 and almost 3 million children under the age of 15 are living with HIV. During the year, approximately 3.6 million new infections will occur in sub-Saharan Africa, and the epidemic will claim the lives of an estimated 2.4 million Africans.

2003. On January 28, the President's Emergency Plan for AIDS Relief (PEPFAR) is launched by President George W. Bush. PEPFAR is the largest commitment by any nation to address a single disease, providing billions in funding for HIV/AIDS treatment, prevention, and care in low-income countries. By 2003, global AIDS deaths are estimated at around 28 million.

2005. On January 21, the Centers for Disease Control and Prevention recommends emergency drug treatment for people exposed to HIV from rapes, accidents, or occasional unsafe sex or drug use.

2007. A San Francisco man with leukemia and HIV is cured of HIV through a bone marrow transplant. In August, Maraviroc, the first available CCR5 receptor antagonist, is approved by the FDA as an antiviral drug for the treatment of AIDS. The CDC reports that over 565,000 people have died of AIDS in the United States since 1981.

2010. In January, the Obama administration lifts the HIV travel and immigration ban, removing the final regulatory barriers to entry. In July, the iPrEx trial results are published, showing that Pre-Exposure Prophylaxis (PrEP) using antiretroviral drugs can reduce the risk of HIV infection in high-risk populations. PrEP becomes a key strategy in HIV prevention. By the end of 2010, global AIDS deaths are estimated at approximately 30 million.

2012. On July 3, the FDA approves the first at-home HIV test that will let users learn their HIV status right away. On July 16, the FDA approves Truvada for use as PrEP to prevent HIV infection in high-risk individuals, marking a significant advancement in HIV prevention efforts. The NAMES Project AIDS Memorial Quilt, with 50,000 panels, is displayed in

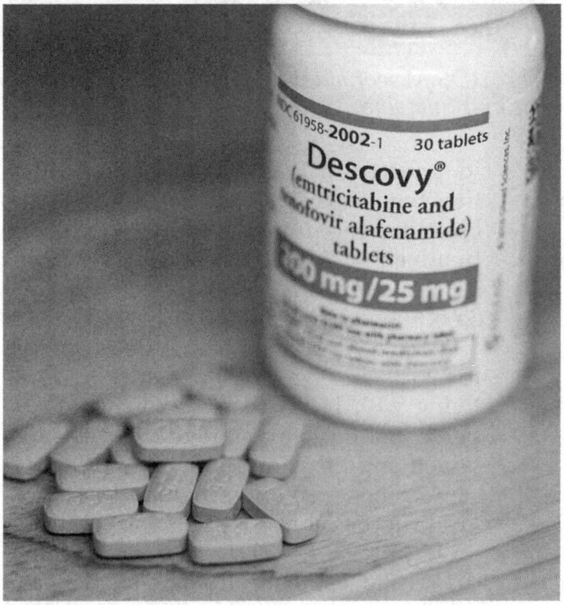

The anti-retroviral drug known as Pre-Exposure Prophylaxis (PrEP)—sold under such brands as Descovy and Truvada—has proven effective in preventing the spread of HIV.

The AIDS Memorial Quilt with its 50,000 panels is displayed in its entirety in Washington, D.C., for the first time since 1996.

its entirety in Washington, D.C., for the first time since 1996. Global AIDS deaths have decreased annually due to effective treatments for the past several years but reach a cumulative total of approximately 35 million by the end of 2012.

2015. UNAIDS sets ambitious targets for 2020, aiming for 90 percent of people living with HIV to know their status, 90 percent of those diagnosed to receive sustained antiretroviral therapy, and 90 percent of those receiving therapy to achieve viral suppression.

On July 23, the FDA approves the first diagnostic test that differentiates between different types of HIV infections (HIV-1 and HIV-2) as well as differentiating between acute and established HIV infections.

On December 23, the FDA announces that it will lift its 30-year-old ban on all blood donations by men who have sex with men and institute a policy that allows them to donate blood if they have not had sexual contact with another man in the previous 12 months. By the end of 2015, cumulative global AIDS deaths are estimated at approximately 36 million.

2016. The LATTE-2 trial demonstrates the efficacy of a long-acting injectable regimen of cabotegravir and rilpivirine, which provides an option for monthly or bimonthly HIV treatment, representing a significant advancement in simplifying HIV therapy. By the end of 2016, cumulative global AIDS deaths are estimated at approximately 36.7 million.

2017. The Undetectable=Untransmittable (U=U) campaign gains global recognition, promoting the message that people with HIV who achieve and maintain an undetectable viral load through treatment cannot sexually transmit the virus. This campaign significantly reduces stigma and promotes treatment adherence.

On June 6, *The New York Times* reports that as a group, America's Black gay and bisexual men have a higher HIV prevalence rate than any other nation in the world.

By the end of 2017, global AIDS deaths continue to decline annually, with cumulative deaths estimated at approximately 37 million.

2019. The FDA approves Descovy for PrEP, offering an alternative to Truvada for HIV prevention in certain populations. Additionally, a new long-acting injectable for HIV treatment is approved, marking the beginning of a new era in HIV care with less frequent dosing. By the end of 2019, cumulative global AIDS deaths are estimated at approximately 38 million.

2020. The COVID-19 pandemic poses new challenges to global HIV/AIDS efforts, disrupting supply chains, healthcare services, and funding. However, the global community continues to push for ending the HIV/AIDS epidemic by 2030.

By the end of 2020, the cumulative number of global AIDS deaths are estimated at approximately 38.4 million.

2021. The International AIDS Vaccine Initiative (IAVI) and Moderna announce the launch of the first efficacy trials for an HIV vaccine using mRNA technology, a significant milestone in the search for a preventative HIV vaccine.

On December 21, the FDA approves the first long-acting injectable form of HIV PrEP, Apretude. With an injection once every two months, it provides an alternative to daily oral pills.

By the end of 2021, the cumulative number of global AIDS deaths remains at approximately 38.4 million, with the annual number of deaths continuing to decline due to ongoing effective treatment and prevention efforts.

The International AIDS Vaccine Initiative (IAVI) and Moderna announce the launch of the first efficacy trials for an HIV vaccine using mRNA technology, a significant milestone in the search for a preventative HIV vaccine.

2022. Researchers continue to make progress in the search for an HIV cure with advancements in gene therapy, immune modulation, and "shock and kill" strategies. The global community remains focused on improving access to treatment, reducing stigma, and addressing inequalities in health care.

By the end of 2022, the cumulative number of global AIDS deaths remains at approximately 38.4 million.

2023. Scientists report advancements in the development of broadly neutralizing antibodies (bNAbs) for HIV prevention, showing promise in reducing the risk of HIV acquisition in clinical trials. These antibodies target multiple strains of HIV, potentially offering a new strategy for long-term prevention. A clinical trial for a preventative HIV vaccine begins. Initial results are expected to come out in late 2024.

On May 11, the FDA updates its blood donor eligibility guidance, ending long-standing discriminatory policies that excluded gay and bisexual people from donating blood.

By the end of 2023, the cumulative number of global AIDS deaths remains at approximately 38.4 million.

2024. The first HIV vaccine candidate using mRNA technology enters Phase III clinical trials, representing a significant step forward in the quest for an effective HIV vaccine. This trial marks a milestone in HIV prevention research, leveraging cutting-edge technology that was developed during the COVID-19 pandemic.

As of 2024, the cumulative number of global AIDS deaths remains at approximately 38.4 million, with continued efforts to reduce new infections and improve access to treatment globally.

BIOGRAPHIES

Bruce Alberts (1938–)

Scientist, Educator

Bruce Alberts is a renowned biochemist and educator widely recognized for his contributions to the field of molecular biology and leadership in science education. He is best known as one of the authors of the influential textbook *Molecular Biology of the Cell* and for his role as president of the National Academy of Sciences (NAS) from 1993 to 2005. He has been a vocal advocate for improving science education, promoting scientific collaboration globally, and supporting LGBTQ+ inclusion within the scientific community, making him one of the most respected figures in the scientific and educational fields.

Born in Chicago, Illinois, Alberts developed an interest in science early in life, which led him to Harvard University, where he earned a B.A. in biochemical sciences in 1960. He then pursued his graduate studies at Harvard, earning a Ph.D. in biophysics in 1965 under the mentorship of James D. Watson, codiscoverer of the structure of DNA.

After completing his doctorate, Alberts began his academic career at Princeton University, where he focused on understanding DNA replication. His work in molecular biology quickly gained recognition, leading to his appointment as a professor at the University of California, San Francisco, in 1976. He made significant contributions to the understanding of DNA replication and the protein complexes involved in this process. His research provided fundamental insights into how cells replicate their genetic material, which has implications for cancer research and biotechnology.

Alberts is perhaps best known for his book *Molecular Biology of the Cell*, a textbook first published in 1983 that has become a seminal work in the field of cell biology. The textbook is widely used in universities around the world and has been instrumental in educating generations of biologists.

As president of the National Academy of Sciences from 1993 to 2005, Alberts played a key role in promoting science education and advocating for policies that support scientific research. He was a strong proponent of inquiry-based science education, emphasizing the importance of teaching students to think critically and engage with scientific concepts actively.

Alberts, though not directly involved in LGBTQ+ advocacy, has significantly contributed to creating an inclusive and supportive environment in science, benefiting LGBTQ+ individuals. As a leader in science education and policy, he has consistently championed diversity and equity, helping to ensure that LGBTQ+ scientists can thrive without fear of discrimination. His emphasis on ethical standards and equal opportunities in scientific institutions has fostered a culture that values the contributions of LGBTQ+ individuals, advancing the cause of equality within the scientific community.

Ben Barres (1954–2017)

Scientist

Ben Barres was a pioneering neurobiologist and one of the first openly transgender scientists in academia. His groundbreaking research on glial cells, which are crucial components of the nervous system, transformed the understanding of brain function and neurodegenerative diseases. He was also an outspoken advocate for diversity and inclusion in science, particularly for women and LGBTQ+ individuals. His life and career are celebrated not only for his scientific contributions but also for his courageous and unwavering support for equality in the scientific community.

Barres was born Barbara Barres in West Orange, New Jersey. He showed an early interest in science, which led him to pursue a degree in biology at the Massachusetts Institute of Technology (MIT), where he graduated in 1976. He then earned an MD from Dartmouth Medical School in 1979, followed by a Ph.D. in neurobiology from Harvard University in 1990.

After completing his education, Barres conducted postdoctoral research at University College London and then joined the faculty at Stanford University in 1993. It was during his time at Stanford that he made significant contributions to the understanding of glial cells and their role in the nervous system. His work demonstrated that glial cells are active participants in synapse formation and function, playing a critical role in brain development and disease. This research opened new avenues for understanding neurological conditions such as Alzheimer's disease and multiple sclerosis.

In 1997, Barres transitioned from female to male, becoming one of the first openly transgender scientists in academia. His openness about his identity and the challenges he faced as a transgender man in science made him a powerful advocate for LGBTQ+ rights. He was passionate about creating an inclusive environment in academia, where individuals could pursue their scientific careers without fear of discrimination or bias. He often spoke about the importance of diversity in science, arguing that a diverse scientific community leads to more innovative and impactful research. He used his platform to advocate for the inclusion of women, LGBTQ+ individuals, and other underrepresented groups in science, working tirelessly to promote equality and support the next generation of scientists.

Sandra Bem (1944–2014)

Psychologist, Educator

Sandra Lipsitz Bem was a pioneering psychologist and feminist scholar renowned for her work on gender roles and the development of the Bem Sex-Role Inventory (BSRI). Her contributions to the understanding of gender and androgyny have had a profound impact on the fields of psychology, gender studies, and feminist theory. Her work challenged traditional notions of gender and advocated for more fluid and equitable conceptions of identity.

Bem was born in Pittsburgh, Pennsylvania. She grew up in a working-class Jewish family and demonstrated early academic promise. She attended Carnegie Mellon University, where she earned a bachelor's degree in psychology in 1965. She later pursued graduate studies at the University of Michigan, earning a Ph.D. in developmental psychology in 1968.

Bem's early career was marked by her involvement in the feminist movement and her commitment to exploring how societal expectations shape individual identity, particularly in the context of gender roles. During this time, she developed the Bem Sex-Role Inventory (BSRI), introduced in 1974. The BSRI was revolutionary in its approach to measuring masculinity and femininity as independent dimensions rather than opposing ends of a single continuum. This allowed for the identification of androgyny, a concept that she promoted as a more flexible and adaptive approach to gender identity.

Bem's book *The Lenses of Gender: Transforming the Debate on Sexual Inequality*, published in 1993, further explored the societal constructs of gender and how these "lenses" perpetuate inequality. Her work consistently advocated for a more egalitarian society, where individuals could express themselves beyond rigid gender norms.

In addition to her scholarly work, Bem was a vocal advocate for feminist issues, contributing to both academic and public discourse on gender equality. Her research and writings have influenced generations of scholars and activists in the fields of psychology, gender studies, and feminism. She was married to Daryl Bem, a fellow psychologist, and together, they raised two children in an environment that encouraged critical thinking and challenged traditional gender norms. Her personal life reflected her professional beliefs, as she and her husband sought to raise their children in a gender-neutral environment. She died by suicide in 2014 after being diagnosed with Alzheimer's disease. Upon receiving the diagnosis, she made the decision to end her life on her own terms before the disease could severely impact her cognitive abilities and sense of self. She meticulously planned her death, discussing it openly with her family, who supported her decision. Her choice to die by suicide reflected her desire to maintain control over her life and dignity, which was consistent with her lifelong commitment to autonomy and personal agency.

Harry Benjamin (1886–1986)

Scientist

Harry Benjamin was a pioneering endocrinologist and sexologist whose work laid the foundation for the modern understanding of transgender health care. He is best known for his groundbreaking contributions to the treatment and support of transgender individuals, particularly through the development of the Harry Benjamin Standards of Care, which became a cornerstone in the field of transgender medicine. His compassionate approach and scientific rigor helped to shape the medical community's response to gender dysphoria.

Benjamin was born in Berlin, Germany. He pursued his medical education in Germany, receiving his medical degree from the University of Tübingen in 1912. Initially, his career focused on endocrinology and sexology, influenced by his interest in human sexuality and the works of Magnus Hirschfeld, another pioneering figure in sexology. He immigrated to the United States in the 1920s, where he continued his medical practice and research. His interest in gender identity and transgender issues gradually became the focus of his professional life.

Benjamin's most significant contribution to the medical field was his work with transgender individuals beginning in the 1940s. He was one of the first physicians in the United States to recognize and treat gender dysphoria, offering hormone therapy and supporting patients seeking gender-affirming surgeries. His compassionate care and scientific approach helped many transgender individuals live lives that aligned with their gender identity at a time when such support was virtually nonexistent.

In 1966, Benjamin published his seminal book *The Transsexual Phenomenon*, which provided a comprehensive overview of his work with transgender patients and offered guidelines for their care. This book was instrumental in raising awareness and understanding of transgender issues within the medical community and the broader public. The Harry Benjamin Standards of Care were established in the 1970s, providing guidelines for the treatment of transgender individuals that emphasized ethical and medically appropriate care. These standards have since been adopted and evolved into what is now known as the World Professional Association for Transgender Health (WPATH) Standards of Care. Reflecting on his career treating transsexual individuals, he said in a 1975 interview, "When I began my work, there wasn't a reputable hospital in this country that would have dreamed of permitting transsexual surgery. Now there are at least 30."

Marc Breedlove (1954–)

Scientist

Stephen Marc Breedlove, a prominent neuroscientist, has made significant contributions to the understanding of sexual orientation and gender identity through his research on the biological basis of sexual differentiation. His work has provided valuable insights into how biological factors, such as hormones and brain structure, influence sexual orientation and gender identity, which has important implications for the LGBTQ+ community.

Breedlove was born in the Ozarks in southwestern Missouri. He pursued his undergraduate studies at Yale University, where he earned a BS in psychology in 1972. He then attended the University of California, Los Angeles, where he received his Ph.D. in psychology in 1982, focusing on behavioral neuroscience. After completing his doctorate, he began his academic career with faculty positions at the University of California, Berkeley, from 1982 to 2003 and at Michigan State. His research during these early years laid the groundwork for his later studies on the effects of hormones on brain development and sexual differentiation.

Breedlove's research has had a profound impact on the field of neuroscience, particularly in understanding how prenatal hormone exposure influences the development of gender identity and sexual orientation. His work has provided key insights into the biological underpinnings of sexual behavior in both animals and humans. He has published numerous influential papers and has been a key voice in discussions about the intersection of biology and sexual orientation.

One of Breedlove's most notable contributions was his research on the effects of prenatal androgens on the development of the spinal cord and the central nervous system, which has implications for understanding sexual orientation and gender identity. His findings have challenged societal norms and have provided a scientific basis for understanding the diversity of sexual orientation and gender identities.

Breedlove's research on the biological basis of sexual orientation and gender identity has sparked controversy, particularly around concerns of biological determinism and its potential to oversimplify complex human experiences. Critics worry that his findings could be misinterpreted or misused to justify rigid gender norms or pathologize nonconforming identities. Additionally, some transgender advocates caution against overemphasizing biology at the expense of social and psychological factors, fearing it could undermine the validity of diverse gender identities or lead to harmful practices. The communication of his research also raises concerns about public misinterpretation and its impact on transgender advocacy.

Breedlove has generally responded to his critics by emphasizing the importance of understanding that his research on the biological aspects of sexual orientation and gender identity is not intended to reduce complex human experiences to simple biological determinism. He argues that biology is just one piece of the puzzle in understanding sexual orientation and gender identity, and it should be considered alongside psychological, social, and cultural factors. He has also made it clear that his work is not meant to pathologize or stigmatize LGBTQ+ individuals but rather to provide a deeper scientific understanding that can contribute to greater acceptance and reduce discrimination. He acknowledges the potential for his research to be misinterpreted or misused but stresses the importance of communicating the science accurately and responsibly to avoid such issues.

Lynn Conway (1938–2024)

Computer Scientist

Lynn Ann Conway was a pioneering computer scientist who was fired from IBM in the 1960s after telling managers that she was transgender. Best known for her contributions to VLSI (Very Large Scale Integration) chip design, which revolutionized the semiconductor industry, she was among the earliest Americans to undergo transition surgery. She rebuilt her career, not revealing her former groundbreaking work for IBM, after her transition and eventually landed a position at the Xerox PARC laboratory, where she continued to make important contributions to her field. After publicly disclosing her transition in 1999, she became a prominent transgender activist.

Conway was born in Mount Vernon, New York. "Although I was born and raised as a boy," she stated, "all during my childhood years I felt like, and desperately wanted to be, a girl." From a young age, she showed a keen interest in science and technology, which led her to pursue studies in physics at the Massachusetts Institute of Technology (MIT) before transferring to Columbia University, where she earned her bachelor's and master's degrees in electrical engineering.

After graduating in the early 1960s, Conway joined IBM's research team and worked on advanced computing systems in the secretive Project Y, which was designing the world's fastest supercomputer. At IBM, she made significant contributions to computer architecture, particularly in the development of dynamic instruction scheduling, a breakthrough that would later be implemented in advanced computer processors. However, during this time, she was also grappling with gender dysphoria. In 1968, she began transitioning from male to female, but upon revealing her plans to her employer, she was fired from IBM—a common practice at the time for transgender individuals. She told her spouse about her desire to transition involving the pioneering hormonal and surgical procedures that were then being performed, but the discloser broke up the marriage, and she was barred from contact with her two daughters for several years.

Despite this setback, Conway persevered and rebuilt her career without mentioning her work for IBM. "I had to start all over pretty much from scratch technically," she recalled, "and prove myself all over again." After completing her transition in 1968, she took a position at Memorex Corporation, where she worked on digital systems. In 1973, she was recruited by Xerox PARC (Palo Alto Research Center). It was at Xerox PARC that she collaborated with Carver Mead on the development of VLSI design, a revolutionary methodology that allowed the creation of complex semiconductor chips. Their work led to the publication of the influential textbook *Introduction to VLSI Systems* in 1980, which became a cornerstone in computer science education and was instrumental in launching the personal computing revolution.

Conway's contributions to VLSI design transformed the semiconductor industry and enabled the rapid advancement of microprocessor technology. The methods she developed are still being used in chip design today, and her work laid the groundwork for modern computing.

In the 1980s, Conway joined the faculty at the University of Michigan, where she served as a professor of electrical engineering and computer science. During her tenure, she continued to influence the field through her research and mentorship of students. She retired from active teaching in the late 1990s but remained an influential figure in the tech community.

In 2002, Conway married Charles Rogers, an engineer. In 2020, IBM offered her an apology at a ceremony in which Diana Gherson, an IBM vice president, said that Conway was "probably our very first employee to come out. And for that, we deeply regret what you went through—and know I speak for all of us."

Conway's contributions to computer science and electrical engineering have left an indelible mark on the tech industry, while her courage in the face of discrimination has inspired countless individuals in the LGBTQ+ community and beyond. Her story stands as a testament to the power of perseverance and the impact that one individual can have on both their field and society at large.

Judith Glassgold (1957-)

Clinical Psychologist

Judith M. Glassgold is a clinical psychologist known for her leadership in opposing conversion therapy and advocating for the mental health and rights of LGBTQ+ individuals. She has been a prominent voice within the American Psychological Association (APA) and chaired its Task Force on Appropriate Therapeutic Responses to Sexual Orientation. Her work has significantly influenced the broader understanding and ethical considerations surrounding sexual orientation and mental health.

Glassgold spent most of her childhood in the Bronx, New York. Her father was a scientist and professor; her mother was a learning disabilities specialist. Her mother was from an Orthodox Jewish background, which she gradually rejected. In her family, educational achievement was valued, and it was expected that she would get an advanced degree in medicine or science. She received an AB from Harvard in government and a doctorate in psychology from Rutgers University in 1989.

Glassgold is best known for her role as the chair of the American Psychological Association's (APA) Task Force on Appropriate Therapeutic Responses to Sexual Orientation, which was established in response to ongoing debates and controversies surrounding conversion therapy. In 2009, the Task Force published a landmark report that condemned conversion therapy as ineffective and harmful, stating that efforts to change an individual's sexual orientation were not supported by credible evidence and were often damaging to the mental health of LGBTQ+ individuals. The report emphasized that sexual orientation is not a disorder and should not be subject to therapeutic attempts at change. Instead, it advocated for affirmative approaches that support individuals in embracing their sexual orientation and identity. Her work on this report was instrumental in shaping the APA's stance on conversion therapy and has had a lasting impact on how mental health professionals approach issues of sexual orientation.

Beyond her work with the APA, Glassgold has been involved in various advocacy efforts to protect the rights and well-being of LGBTQ+ individuals. She has contributed to numerous publications, workshops, and training programs aimed at educating mental health professionals on the importance of affirming and supportive care for LGBTQ+ clients.

Glassgold's contributions to psychology, combining advocacy, scholarship, clinical services, and teaching, have helped to shift the field toward more inclusive and affirming practices, ensuring that mental health care is supportive and empowering for all individuals regardless of sexual orientation. Her leadership has played a critical role in the ongoing efforts to ban conversion therapy and promote mental health practices that respect and affirm LGBTQ+ identities.

Richard Green (1936-2019)

Psychiatrist, Sexologist, Legal Scholar

Richard Philip Green was a psychiatrist, sexologist, and legal scholar known

for his pioneering work in gender identity and sexual orientation. As one of the earliest and most vocal critics of psychiatry's classification of homosexuality as a mental disorder, his research and activism significantly influenced the medical and legal understanding of gender identity. His work made him a key figure in the advancement of LGBTQ+ rights and the development of gender studies.

Green was born in Brooklyn, New York. He developed an early interest in psychology and medicine, leading him to pursue a bachelor's degree at Syracuse University. He then earned his medical degree from Johns Hopkins University in 1961, where he also completed his psychiatric residency.

During his time at Johns Hopkins, Green was mentored by Dr. John Money, a prominent sexologist, which sparked his interest in gender identity and sexual orientation. He also obtained a law degree from Yale Law School in 1987, reflecting his interest in the intersection of medicine, psychology, and the law.

In 1972, Green played a significant role in the declassification of homosexuality as a mental disorder. His research demonstrated that homosexuality was not inherently linked to psychopathology, and he was an outspoken critic of reparative therapy and other attempts to "cure" homosexuality. He argued that the issue of classification should be decided by "historical and cross-cultural groundings in homosexual expression, associated psychiatric features accompanying a homosexual orientation, the emotional consequences to the homosexual of societal condemnation, and behavior of other species."

Green's career was marked by his groundbreaking research on gender identity and strong advocacy for the rights of transgender individuals. In the 1960s and 1970s, he conducted some of the earliest studies on transgender identities and was one of the first psychiatrists to support gender-affirming care for transgender individuals. His work helped to lay the foundation for the medical Standards of Care that would later be adopted by organizations such as the World Professional Association for Transgender Health (WPATH).

In addition to his work in psychiatry and sexology, Green was a respected legal scholar and served as a professor of psychiatry at the University of California, Los Angeles. He authored several influential books and articles, including *Sexual Identity Conflict in Children and Adults* (1974) and *The "Sissy Boy Syndrome" and the Development of Homosexuality* (1987), which explored the development of gender identity and sexual orientation.

Green was one of the legal counsels in the ACLU's 1990 case against the Boy Scouts of America for barring a gay man from becoming an assistant scoutmaster. The Boy Scouts won, but the case became a cornerstone in eventually leading the organization to lift its ban on openly gay leaders in 2014. He also fought for a pilot to return to the cockpit after she transitioned following gender reassignment surgery and was an early supporter of gay men serving in the military and for lesbian mothers to gain custody of their children after a divorce.

In response to his research and advocacy, Green was falsely accused of being gay. He married psychiatric professor Melissa Hines in 1986. They were divorced in 2014. Their son eulogized his father by saying, "He had no interest in conforming. Beyond those he loved, I *genuinely* don't think he cared what people thought or said about him.... He had exactly no interest in social norms."

Perry N. Halkitis (1963–)

Psychologist

Perry N. Halkitis is an esteemed public health researcher, psychologist, and ad-

vocate best known for his work in the fields of HIV/AIDS, LGBTQ+ health, and substance use among sexual minorities. As a scholar and activist, he has significantly contributed to the understanding of health disparities affecting the LGBTQ+ community, particularly through his research on the intersection of identity, behavior, and health outcomes. He is the dean of the Rutgers School of Public Health and a prominent voice in public health and LGBTQ+ advocacy.

Halkitis was born in New York City to Greek immigrant parents. He pursued his undergraduate studies in biology at Columbia University, where he developed a passion for public health and psychology. He continued his education at the City University of New York, earning a master's degree in psychology in 1988 and a doctorate in educational psychology in 1993. His early career was marked by his involvement in research related to HIV/AIDS, which emerged as a critical public health crisis during his formative years as a scholar.

Halkitis is best known for his research on the psychosocial aspects of HIV/AIDS, focusing on the experiences of gay men and other sexual minorities. His work has provided valuable insights into the behavioral and mental health challenges faced by these communities. He has authored numerous books, including *The AIDS Generation: Stories of Survival and Resilience* (2013), which highlights the experiences of gay men who lived through the early years of the HIV/AIDS epidemic.

In addition to his research, Halkitis has been a strong advocate for LGBTQ+ health equity, pushing for policies and programs that address the unique needs of sexual and gender minorities. His leadership at Rutgers School of Public Health has further solidified his role as a leading figure in public health education and LGBTQ+ advocacy. In his book, *Out in Time: The Public Lives of Gay Men from Stonewall to the Queer Generation* (2019), he discusses his own experiences as a gay man, interweaving them with broader narratives of LGBTQ+ identity and struggles over several decades.

Evelyn Hooker (1907–1996)

Psychologist, Educator

Evelyn Hooker was a psychologist whose groundbreaking research fundamentally changed the understanding of homosexuality within the psychological community. Her work in the mid-20th century challenged prevailing notions that homosexuality was a mental illness, leading to the eventual declassification of homosexuality as a mental disorder by the American Psychiatric Association (APA). Her research is widely regarded as a turning point in the movement toward LGBTQ+ rights and acceptance.

Born Evelyn Gentry in North Platte, Nebraska, Hooker grew up in northeastern Colorado in a rural environment, where she developed a passion for learning and education. She earned her bachelor's degree from the University of Colorado in 1928 and went on to pursue graduate studies at Johns Hopkins University, where she completed her Ph.D. in psychology in 1932.

Hooker began her academic career teaching at the University of California, Los Angeles (UCLA) in 1939, where she developed an interest in the psychological study of sexuality. During this period, she became increasingly aware of the biases and misconceptions that dominated the field regarding homosexuality. At UCLA in the 1940s, she befriended a gay student who introduced her to his circle of friends and said, "We have let you see us as we are, and now, it is your scientific duty to make a study of people like us." Her most significant contribution to psychology was her 1957 study "The Adjustment of the Male Overt Homosexual," which challenged the assumption that homosexual men were inherently psychologically maladjusted. Her study was the first to employ standardized psychological tests (including the Rorschach test) on a group of gay men who were not institutionalized or seeking therapy, comparing their results to a matched group of heterosexual men. The study's findings revealed no significant differences between the two groups, suggesting that homosexuality was not inherently associated with psychopathology. This research was presented at the 1956 American Psychological Association (APA) convention and published in 1957. The implications of her work were profound, contributing to the eventual declassification of homosexuality as a mental disorder by the American Psychiatric Association in 1973.

In addition to her research, Hooker became a vocal advocate for the rights and acceptance of LGBTQ+ individuals. She continued to work in academia, where she influenced a new generation of psychologists and contributed to the growing movement for LGBTQ+ rights.

Hooker married fellow psychologist Donald Hooker, who supported her groundbreaking research. After retiring from UCLA in 1970, she had a private practice until the late 1970s. She also helped to establish the Placek Fund of the American Psychological Foundation, which provides money for LGBTQ+ research. She was the subject of a 1992 documentary, *Changing Our Minds: The Story of Dr. Evelyn Hooker.*

Virginia Johnson

See William Masters and Virginia Johnson

Alfred Kinsey (1894–1956)

Scientist, Sexologist, Educator

Alfred Charles Kinsey, called "the father of the sexual revolution," was a biologist and sexologist whose pioneering research in the mid-20th century fundamentally changed the understanding of human sexuality. His work, particularly through his Kinsey Reports, challenged societal norms and provided a more comprehensive view of sexual behavior, including LGBTQ+ identities. His research laid the groundwork for the modern study of human sexuality and played a crucial role in advancing LGBTQ+ acceptance by highlighting the diversity of sexual orientation and behavior.

Kinsey was born in Hoboken, New Jersey. He grew up in a conservative and religious household, which influenced his early views on sexuality. He pursued his undergraduate studies at Bowdoin College, where he earned a degree in biology in 1916. He later completed his Ph.D. in 1919 in entomology at Harvard University, where his initial research focused on gall wasps.

Kinsey began his academic career as a biology professor at Indiana University. His early work in entomology was well regarded, but his interest in human sexuality led him to shift his focus in the late 1930s. Recognizing the lack of scientific data on human sexual behavior, he sought to fill this gap through rigorous and systematic research, eventually establishing the Kinsey Institute for Research in Sex, Gender, and Reproduction.

Kinsey is best known for his two groundbreaking publications: *Sexual Behavior in the Human Male* (1948) and *Sexual Behavior in the Human Female* (1953), collectively known as the Kinsey Reports. These studies were among the first to use large-scale surveys to document the sexual behaviors of thousands of Americans, revealing a much wider range of sexual experiences and orientations than previously acknowledged. His research challenged the prevailing views of his time by showing that many behaviors considered deviant or abnormal were, in fact, common. His work highlighted that sexual orientation exists on a spectrum, leading to the creation of the Kinsey Scale, which ranges from exclusively heterosexual (0) to exclusively homosexual (6). This scale provided a more nuanced understanding of sexual orientation, moving beyond the binary categorization of people as strictly heterosexual or homosexual.

The Kinsey Reports also documented the prevalence of same-sex behavior among both men and women, bringing attention to the existence of homosexual and bisexual individuals in a way that had not been scientifically validated before. This work was groundbreaking in its inclusion of LGBTQ+ identities and contributed to the gradual destigmatization of same-sex relationships.

While Kinsey's work was controversial and faced criticism from conservative groups, it was instrumental in challenging societal norms and promoting a more open discussion about sexuality. His research provided an empirical foundation for the burgeoning LGBTQ+ rights movement and influenced later studies on sexual orientation and gender identity.

Kinsey was married to Clara McMillen, with whom he had four children. While his personal life remained largely private, his research and interviews suggest that he had a broad understanding and acceptance of diverse sexual behaviors, including those outside of traditional norms. Some biographers have speculated about his own sexual orientation, suggesting that his research may have been driven by personal as well as scientific curiosity. However, definitive details about his sexuality remain unclear.

Kinsey's work remains a cornerstone in the study of human sexuality, and his contributions to the understanding of LGBTQ+ identities were revolutionary for his time. By providing empirical evidence of the diversity of sexual behavior, he helped to lay the foundation for the modern LGBTQ+ rights movement and continues to influence the field of sexology today.

William Masters (1915-2001) and Virginia Johnson (1925-2013)

Scientists, Sexologists

William Masters and Virginia Eshelman Johnson were pioneering sexologists who transformed the understanding of human sexuality in the mid-20th century. Their collaborative research on sexual response and dysfunction challenged societal taboos and established foundational knowledge in the field of sexology. While their work was groundbreaking and significantly advanced sexual health and therapy, their involvement in controversial research on sexual orientation, particularly conversion therapy, has left a complex legacy, especially in relation to LGBTQ+ issues.

Masters was born in Cleveland, Ohio. He earned his medical degree from the University of Rochester School of Medicine and began his career as a gynecologist and obstetrician. In the 1950s, he shifted his focus to the study of human sexuality, attending Washington University in St. Louis, where he would later form a research partnership with Johnson.

Johnson was born in Springfield, Missouri. Initially pursuing a career in music, she later transitioned to studying psychology and sociology. She joined Masters's research team at Washington University in 1957 as an assistant but quickly became a full collaborator due to her intuitive understanding of human behavior and ability to connect with research participants.

Together, Masters and Johnson conducted some of the most influential research ever to be done on human sexual response. Their first major publication, *Human Sexual Response* (1966), provided a comprehensive scientific analysis of sexual function using direct observation and measurement of sexual activity. This work dispelled long-accepted myths about human sexuality, such as the notions that sexual activity stops with aging and that men are inherently more sexual than women, and laid the groundwork for modern sex therapy. In 1970, they published *Human Sexual Inadequacy*, which introduced techniques for treating sexual dysfunction that have become staples in sex therapy. Their work helped to destigmatize discussions of sexual health and brought these issues into the public eye.

However, in 1979, Masters and Johnson published *Homosexuality in Perspective*, a controversial book that endorsed conversion therapy—an attempt to change an individual's sexual orientation from homosexual to heterosexual. The claims made in this work were later discredited, and the practice of conversion therapy is now widely condemned by major medical and psychological organizations as unethical and harmful.

Despite the controversy, Masters and Johnson's broader contributions to the understanding of human sexuality were groundbreaking. Their research played a crucial role in the development of sex therapy and opened up new avenues for treating sexual dysfunction.

Masters was married twice, first to Elizabeth Ellis, with whom he had two children, and later to Johnson. The personal and professional lives of Masters and Johnson were deeply intertwined, leading to both celebrated collaborations and public scrutiny. They were married in 1971 and divorced in 1992, after which their professional partnership also dissolved.

While Masters and Johnson's contributions were groundbreaking, their involvement in controversial research on sexual orientation, particularly conversion therapy, has also left a complex legacy, especially in relation to LGBTQ+ issues.

Nergis Mavalvala (1968–)

Scientist

Nergis Mavalvala is a Pakistani American astrophysicist known for her pioneering work in gravitational wave detection. A key figure in the historic discovery of gravitational waves, she has made significant contributions to the field of astrophysics, particularly through her involvement with the Laser Interferometer Gravitational-Wave Observatory (LIGO). Beyond her scientific achievements, she is also an advocate for diversity in science and a role model for LGBTQ+ representation in STEM fields, as she is one of the few openly lesbian women of color in astrophysics.

Mavalvala was born in Lahore, Pakistan, and grew up in Karachi. She displayed an early interest in science, tinkering with mechanical objects and displaying a curiosity about the natural world. After completing her secondary education at the Convent of Jesus and Mary in Karachi, she moved to the United States to pursue higher education. She attended Wellesley College, where she earned a bachelor's degree in 1990 in physics and astronomy. Her passion for experimental physics led her to pursue a Ph.D. at the Massachusetts Institute of Technology (MIT), where she worked under the guidance of Rainer Weiss, one of the cofounders of LIGO. During her doctoral studies, she focused on developing laser interferometry techniques, which would later play a crucial role in the detection of gravitational waves.

Mavalvala is best known for her integral role in the first direct detection of gravitational waves in 2015, a discovery that confirmed a major prediction of Albert Einstein's general theory of relativity. As part of the LIGO team, she contributed to the development of the precise instrumentation needed to detect these faint ripples in spacetime caused by the collision of massive black holes. Her work on quantum measurement techniques and the development of advanced laser interferometers was critical to the success of LIGO. The detection of gravitational waves opened a new era in astronomy, allowing scientists to observe cosmic events that were previously undetectable such as the merger of black holes and neutron stars.

In recognition of her contributions, Mavalvala has received numerous awards and honors, including the 2017 MacArthur Fellowship. She has also been elected to the National Academy of Sciences.

Mavalvala describes herself as an "out, queer person of color." She and her partner have two children. She said, "I grew up in Pakistan. I'm a minority in many different ways. I'm queer, I'm an immigrant, I'm Muslim. I'm a person of color. And all of those things give me some amount of an outsider status.... But the fact is that there's a way to be who you are and still achieve success, and that's the message that I think is important." Her visibility and success have made her a role model for many aspiring scientists, particularly those from underrepresented groups.

Vivienne Ming (1971–)

Scientist, Entrepreneur

Vivienne L'Ecuyer Ming is a theoretical neuroscientist, entrepreneur, and transgender advocate who has made significant contributions to the fields of artificial intelligence (AI), machine learning, and neuroscience. She is the cofounder of Socos Labs, a think tank that applies machine learning and AI to complex global challenges, particularly in education, health, and human potential. As a transgender woman and a prominent figure in the tech community, she is also known for her advocacy for diversity and inclusion, using her platform to promote the representation and empowerment of marginalized communities in STEM fields.

Ming was born and raised as a boy, Evan Campbell Smith, in Monterey, California. Despite a strong aptitude for science and technology, which guided her academic pursuits, she suffered from gender dysphoria, which led her to drop out of college and struggle with depression, suicide, and homelessness. In 1999, she attended the University of California, San Diego, where she earned a bachelor's degree in cognitive neuroscience. She later pursued a Ph.D. in psychology and neuroscience at Carnegie Mellon University, where she conducted research on the neural mechanisms underlying perception and cognition.

In 2005, Ming told girlfriend (and later wife) Norma Chang, "My secret is that I wish I were a woman." With Chang's support, she began her transition to Vivienne Ming, the last name being a hybrid of their family names, Smith and Chang. After gender reassignment surgery, she recalled, "My body became aligned with my identity, and it was profound."

Ming cofounded several tech startups, including Socos Labs, where she served as managing partner and chief scientist. Socos Labs operates as an independent think tank that focuses on applying AI and machine learning to global challenges in areas such as education, workforce development, and health care. One of Socos Labs's most notable projects is the development of AI-driven personalized education tools designed to optimize learning outcomes for students. Her work in this area aims to harness the power of AI to create customized learning experiences that cater to the unique needs and strengths of each student. Her research has also explored the potential of AI in predicting and enhancing human potential with applications in talent development, mental health, and social impact.

In addition to her work at Socos Labs, Ming has been a frequent speaker and writer on topics related to AI, ethics, and the future of work. She has published extensively on the intersection of technology and human development, advocating for the responsible and ethical use of AI in society.

Ming's experiences of transitioning and navigating the challenges of being a transgender woman in a male-dominated research industry have informed her advocacy work. She has been outspoken about the need for greater representation of women, LGBTQ+ individuals, and other marginalized groups in STEM fields.

John Money (1921–2006)

Psychologist, Sexologist

John William Money was a New Zealand–born American psychologist and sexologist whose work on gender identity and the differentiation between biological sex and gender identity has had a profound impact on the field of sexology and the understanding of gender. He is best known for coining the terms "gender role" and "gender identity" and his controversial theories on the malleability of gender. His work laid the foundation for much of the contemporary discourse on gender, though some aspects of his legacy remain contentious.

Money was born near Auckland in Morrinsville, New Zealand. He grew up near Wellington, where he earned a bachelor's degree in psychology and education from Victoria University of Wellington before becoming a member of the psychology faculty at the University of Otago in Dunedin. In 1947, he immigrated to the United States to pursue graduate studies at Harvard University, where he earned a Ph.D. in psychology in 1952.

After completing his doctorate, Money became a professor of pediatrics and medical psychology at Johns Hopkins University from 1951 until his death. It was there that he began to develop his theories on gender identity, working with intersex and transgender patients and conducting research that would eventually make him a prominent figure in the field of sexology.

Money is most notable for his introduction of the concepts of "gender role" and "gender identity," which he used to differentiate between the social and psychological aspects of gender and the biological aspects of sex. He argued that gender identity was primarily a result of socialization and could be shaped during early childhood, a theory that influenced both medical practices and social understanding of gender. According to psychologist Dr. Kenneth J. Zucker, he "was the first scientist to provide a language to describe the psychological dimensions of human sexuality; no such language had existed before."

Money was among the first scientists to study the psychological experience of sexual confusion and grasp possible ways to relieve suffering. He was an early proponent of gender reassignment surgery for men and women who believed that their biologically given sex was at odds with their sexual identity.

One of Money's most famous and controversial cases was that of David Reimer, a boy who was raised as a girl following a botched circumcision. He used this case to support his theory that gender identity could be successfully reassigned through socialization. However, the case ended tragically, with Reimer eventually rejecting the female identity and later taking his own life. This case significantly tarnished his reputation and led to widespread criticism of his theories.

In addition to his work on gender, Money conducted research on sexual orientation, arguing that it, too, was influenced by both biological and social factors. He authored several influential books and articles, including *Transsexualism and Sex Reassignment* (1969), *Man & Woman, Boy & Girl* (1972), and *Gay, Straight, and In-Between: The Sexology of Erotic Orientation* (1988).

Money was known for his strong views on gender and sexuality, but he kept his personal life private. He was briefly married in the 1950s. His personal beliefs about gender and sexuality were reflected in his professional work, as he consistently argued for the importance of understanding and accepting a wide range of gender identities and sexual orientations. His work continues to influence debates on gender identity, sexual orientation, and the nature versus nurture discussion in sexology.

Charlotte J. Patterson

Psychologist

Charlotte J. Patterson is a renowned psychologist best known for her pioneering research on the development and well-being of children in LGBTQ+ families. Her work has been instrumental in challenging misconceptions about LGBTQ+ parenting and has provided empirical evidence supporting the notion that children raised by same-sex parents are just as well-adjusted as those raised by heterosexual parents. Her research has significantly influenced public policy and legal debates surrounding LGBTQ+ rights, particularly in the context of adoption and marriage equality.

Patterson developed a keen interest in psychology from a young age. She attended Pomona College, where she earned her B.A. in psychology in 1971. She then continued her education at Stanford University, where she obtained a Ph.D. in 1975 in psychology with a focus on developmental and social psychology.

Patterson began her academic career as a professor and researcher, focusing on child development, family dynamics, and sexual orientation. Her early work laid the foundation for her later studies on LGBTQ+ families, a topic that became increasingly relevant as social attitudes and legal frameworks regarding same-sex relationships began to evolve.

Patterson's most notable contributions are in the field of LGBTQ+ family studies, and she has been described as "the world's expert on psychological research on children and youths raised by lesbian and gay parents." Her research has been pivotal in debunking myths about the negative effects of same-sex parenting on children and consistently shows that children raised by lesbian and gay parents are just as psychologically healthy, well-adjusted, and socially competent as those raised by heterosexual parents.

One of Patterson's landmark works is a study published in 1992 that examined the psychological development of children with lesbian mothers. This study, among others, demonstrated that the sexual orientation of parents does not adversely affect the developmental outcomes of children, thereby challenging the stereotypes and biases that had historically influenced both public opinion and legal decisions.

Patterson, as a professor of psychology at the University of Virginia and chair of its interdisciplinary Department of Women, Gender & Sexuality, has authored and coauthored numerous articles and books on LGBTQ+ family issues, including *Lesbian, Gay and Bisexual Identities in Families* (1998), *Lesbian, Gay and Bisexual Identities and Youth* (2001), and *Handbook of Psychological and Sexual Orientation* (2013). Her work has been cited in key court cases, including those related to same-sex marriage and adoption rights, making her research a critical resource for advocates and policymakers.

In addition to her research, Patterson has been actively involved in professional organizations, serving in leadership roles and contributing to the advancement of LGBTQ+ issues within the field of psychology.

Virginia Prince (1912–2009)

Sexologist

Virginia Prince was a groundbreaking

sexologist and one of the earliest advocates for transgender rights in the United States. She was a pioneering figure who popularized the term "transgender" and also played a crucial role in shaping the early transgender community. Her work laid the foundation for the understanding of gender identity as distinct from sexual orientation, significantly influencing both academic discourse and the broader social movement for transgender rights.

Born Arnold Lowman in Los Angeles, California, Prince was the daughter of a surgeon father and a mother who worked in real estate. At around the age of 12, she began cross-dressing and, during high school, began passing as a girl in public. She graduated from Pomona College in 1931 and in 1939 earned a Ph.D. in pharmacology from the University of California, San Francisco. Her early career was marked by academic success, but it was her personal journey with gender identity that would define her life's work.

In the 1950s, Prince began publicly living as a woman and became an advocate for people who, like herself, identified with a gender different from their assigned sex at birth. She founded several organizations, including the Transvestia Foundation and the Society for the Second Self, which provided support and community for cross-dressers and transgender individuals. Her publication of *Transvestia* magazine starting in 1960 was particularly influential, offering a platform for transgender people to share their experiences and explore their identities. Her coining of the term "transgender" was significant, as it described those who live full time in a gender role different from their assigned sex but do not seek surgical intervention.

Prince's personal life was deeply intertwined with her advocacy. She identified as heterosexual and was twice married. Throughout her life, she remained dedicated to promoting understanding and acceptance of gender diversity. Her decision to live openly as a woman during a time of widespread misunderstanding and prejudice was both a personal and political act that inspired many others.

Robert Spitzer (1932–2015)

Psychiatrist

Robert Leopold Spitzer was an influential psychiatrist who played a critical role in the evolution of modern psychiatry, particularly through his work on the third edition of the *Diagnostic and Statistical Manual of Mental Disorders (DSM-III)*. He is perhaps best known for leading the effort to declassify homosexuality as a mental disorder, a landmark decision that had profound implications for the LGBTQ+ community and the field of psychiatry. His work laid the groundwork for more nuanced and evidence-based approaches to mental health.

Spitzer was born on May 22, 1932, in White Plains, New York. He grew up in a Jewish family and demonstrated early academic ability, particularly in the sciences. He grew up on the Upper West Side of Manhattan and earned his undergraduate degree in psychology from Cornell University in 1953, going on to obtain his medical degree from New York School of Medicine in 1957 and then completing a psychiatric residence in 1961.

After completing his medical training, Spitzer became involved in psychiatric research at Columbia University, where he quickly gained a reputation for his methodical approach to psychiatric diagnosis. His early career was marked by his involvement in revising the *DSM*, a task that would come to define much of his professional legacy. A colleague was working on a new edition of the manual, and he became fascinated with finding reliable means of measuring symptoms and behavior. "At the time," Dr. Michael

B. First, professor of clinical psychiatry at Columbia, said, "there was zero interest in assessment. [Spitzer] saw how important it was, and his whole career led to assessment being taken seriously."

Spitzer's most notable achievement was his leadership in the revision of the *DSM*, particularly the third edition, the *DSM-III*, which was published in 1980. The *DSM-III* was a transformative document that introduced a more systematic and empirical approach to psychiatric diagnosis, moving away from the psychoanalytic theories that had previously dominated the field.

One of Spitzer's most significant contributions was his role in the declassification of homosexuality as a mental disorder. In 1973, under his leadership, the American Psychiatric Association (APA) removed homosexuality from the *DSM-II*, a decision that was based on a growing body of evidence and his conviction that homosexuality was not inherently linked to psychopathology. This decision marked a turning point in the treatment of LGBTQ+ individuals and contributed to the broader movement for LGBTQ+ rights.

Later in his career, Spitzer also became known for his controversial study on "reparative therapy" for homosexuality, published in 2001. Although the study suggested that some individuals could change their sexual orientation through therapy, he later recanted these findings, acknowledging the flaws in his research and apologizing for the harm it may have caused.

Spitzer's work on the *DSM-III* and the declassification of homosexuality as a mental disorder remain his most enduring achievements, reflecting his commitment to evidence-based practice and ethical responsibility. Dr. Allen J. Francis, professor of psychiatry at Duke University, said, "Bob Spitzer was by far the most influential psychiatrist of his time. He saved the field and its millions of patients from a crisis of credibility, raising its scientific standards and rescuing it from the arbitrariness of warring and unsupported opinions." Regarding his contribution to LGBTQ+ history, Dr. Jack Drescher has asserted, "The fact that gay marriage is allowed today is in part owed to Bob Spitzer."

Bruce Voeller (1934–1994)

Scientist

Bruce Raymond Voeller was a biologist, AIDS researcher, and gay rights activist who played a pivotal role in the early fight against HIV/AIDS and advancing LGBTQ+ rights. As a cofounder of the National Gay Task Force (now the National LGBTQ Task Force) and a pioneering researcher in the study of sexually transmitted diseases, including the early identification of AIDS, his work significantly impacted public health and the LGBTQ+ community.

Voeller was born in Minneapolis, Minnesota. He was an outstanding student, graduating from Reed College with a degree in biology at the age of 18 in 1956. He won a fellowship at the Rockefeller Institute in New York City to complete his doctoral studies in biochemistry, developmental biology, and genetics. He became a research associate there in 1961, an assistant professor two years later, and an associate professor in 1966. His early research focused on cell biology and biochemistry, and he quickly established himself as a respected scientist. However, his personal experiences as a gay man led him to become increasingly involved in the gay rights movement, which would soon become the focus of his career.

Voeller's most significant contributions were in the fields of gay rights advocacy and AIDS research. He became president of the New York Gay Activists Alliance and, in 1973, cofounded the National Gay Task Force, the first national organization dedicated to advocating for the rights of LGBTQ+ individuals. As the organization's first executive director, he played a key role in lobbying for antidiscrimination laws, promoting visibility for the LGBTQ+ community, and combating homophobia.

Voeller's scientific background uniquely positioned him to address the emerging HIV/AIDS crisis in the early 1980s. He was one of the first researchers to recognize the syndrome, which was initially called GRID (Gay-Related Immune Deficiency). He was instrumental in renaming the disease to AIDS (Acquired Immune Deficiency Syndrome) in order to avoid stigmatizing the gay community and to reflect the broader population affected by the virus.

As an advocate for sexual health, Voeller also conducted important research on safer sex practices and the effectiveness of various contraceptives and barriers, such as condoms, in preventing the transmission of HIV and other sexually transmitted infections (STIs). As the coauthor of *AIDS and Sex: An Integrated Biomedical and Behavioral Approach* (1990), he helped to establish public health guidelines that are still in use today.

Voeller came out at the age of 29 and divorced his wife in 1971. He died of an AIDS- related illness at the age of 59 and in 2019 was one of the inaugural 50 people to be inducted on the National LGBTQ Wall of Honor within the Stonewall National Monument.

Law and Government

During the 19th century, American felony laws intended to punish "crimes against nature," which included cross-dressing but were primarily targeted at gay men and referred to late in the century as "homosexual sodomy," were not new laws but holdovers from the colonial era. Sodomy laws, maintained in all the states until well into the 20th century, were subject to interpretation and enforcement depending on the region and were sometimes used in the prosecution of gay men and men in drag for being "disorderly"; gathering together in a "disorderly house"; or engaging in "indecent behavior," "public indecency," or "lewd behavior." Gay and lesbian bars and other nightlife venues where LGBTQ+ people gathered would become focal points for local legislators, who added new indecen-

A gay bar such as the famous Abbey in West Hollywood would have been shut down not that long ago for allowing "public indecency."

cy laws to the old sodomy laws and applied them to LGBTQ+ gatherings, directing police to carry them out in the form of frequent raids and arrests in attempts to shut down such venues, with raids continuing even after the Stonewall Uprising of 1969 ushered in a new and more intense era of LGBTQ+ activism.

While surveillance of suspected gay men had been present earlier, the post–World War II anti-Communist Lavender Scare, which began in the late 1940s and lasted through the 1960s, considered suspected gay and lesbian federal employees to be national security risks and subjected them to surveillance, outing, persecution, and mass firings. The Model Penal Code, established in the mid-1950s, would, by 1961, lead to the eventual repeal of sodomy laws in some states. It would take the consistent and intense determination of LGBTQ+ activists, together with court cases and the efforts of elected officials, to begin the long process of legislating state and federal civil rights for LGBTQ+ Americans.

TIMELINE

1909. The New York City Police Department creates a vice squad to enforce laws against "indecency," leading to increased surveillance and arrests of LGBTQ+ individuals, particularly targeting bars, clubs, bathhouses, and other venues where LGBTQ+ individuals gathered. The concept of vice squads, specialized police units dedicated to enforcing laws against various forms of vice (including prostitution, gambling, and "indecency" such as homosexuality) spread across the United States: the Chicago Vice Commission (1911), the Los Angeles Police Vice Division (1920s), the San Francisco Moral Police Unit (1920s), the Boston Vice and Liquor Squad (1920s), the Philadelphia Vice Squad (1920s), and the Washington, D.C., Morals Squad (1930s).

1913. The American Social Hygiene Association (ASHA) is established, playing a pivotal role in promoting sexual health education, fighting sexually transmitted infections, advocating for moral hygiene, and stigmatizing LGBTQ+ individuals as part of public health campaigns.

1915–1919. The American Defense Society (ADS) includes homosexuality in its list of "social diseases" to be eradicated. The ADS is formed in 1915 as a patriotic organization founded by Charles Stewart Davison, a New York lawyer, advocating for national defense and preparedness in the context of World War I. It works to counteract any opposition to war in order to encourage enlistment and also opposes socialism, anarchism, and Communism. The movement also aims to eradicate various social issues perceived as moral threats, including prostitution, venereal disease, and homosexuality. Although its influence declines after the war, the ADS plays a significant role in shaping public opinion and policy, and its stance that homosexuality is a social disorder needing eradication was a widely held view in the early 20th century.

1916. The U.S. Articles of War are revised in the first comprehensive revision of the military code of the United States since 1806, codified by Congress to govern the conduct of the U.S. Armed Forces. Article 93 specifically criminalizes acts of sodomy, which include homosexual conduct. This means that LGBTQ+ individuals in the military are subject to courts-martial and severe penalties if they are found engaging in same-sex acts. Punishments include dishonorable discharge, imprisonment, or hard labor. This leads to a culture of stigma, discrimination, concealment, and fear among LGBTQ+ service members. The Articles of War revision in 1916 sets a precedent for military policies that continued to discriminate against LGBTQ+ service members until the repeal of the "Don't Ask, Don't Tell" policy in 2010.

1917. When the United States enters World War I in April 1917, the expansion of the military comes with a heightened

During World War I, the U.S. military classified being homosexual as a disqualifying condition preventing gay people from serving their country.

focus on maintaining discipline, morale, and the perceived moral integrity of the U.S. Armed Forces. This leads to the U.S. military explicitly addressing homosexuality as a moral and security threat. Homosexuality is classified as a disqualifying condition for military service, and individuals identified as homosexuals are either barred from enlisting or discharged if already serving. The military implements screening procedures, including psychological and medical examinations aimed at detecting homosexual tendencies. The Immigration Act of 1917 excludes homosexuals from entering the United States. This comprehensive legislation aims at restricting the immigration of certain groups deemed undesirable based on various criteria, including literacy, nationality, and physical and mental health. One of the categories under the health and morality clauses is "moral defectives," which includes individuals with perceived moral failings such as homosexuality, considered a psychiatric disorder and moral perversion at the time. Immigration officials are given broad discretion to deny entry to anyone they suspect of engaging in same-sex behavior and thus classified as a "moral defective." The Immigration Act of 1917 sets a legal precedent for the exclusion of LGBTQ+ individuals, which persists for decades until the Immigration and Nationality Act of 1965 begins to dismantle some of these discriminatory practices. Chicago enacts a new vagrancy ordinance that allows police to arrest individuals for loitering without apparent means of support or engaging in "suspicious behavior." This ordinance is subsequently used to arrest LGBTQ+ individuals.

1920. Funded by John D. Rockefeller Jr., the Bureau of Social Hygiene is established, focusing on research and policy development related to social hygiene issues, including prostitution and STIs, and publishes health education, which reinforces negative stereotypes about LGBTQ+ individuals.

1924. Also known as the Johnson-Reed Act, the Immigration Act of 1924 is passed and includes provisions by eugenics theories, restricting immigration from countries deemed to have "inferior" genetic stock. It reflects the broader application of eugenics principles to social policy, including views on LGBTQ+ individuals as morally and genetically undesirable.

1925. Established in 1924 in Chicago, the Society for Human Rights (SHR) is the first known gay rights organization in the United States advocating for the rights of homosexuals and educating the public about homosexuality. Authorities raid founder Henry Gerber's home and the organization's office, confiscating materials and records. Gerber and several other members are arrested and charged with obscenity and conspiracy to commit sodomy. Gerber fights the charges in multiple trials, which are eventually dismissed, although legal fees ultimately bankrupt him. While hosting a private party at her home in Chicago, which is attended by several other women, many of whom were also involved in the music scene, blues singer Ma Rainey is arrested in a police raid and charged with "indecent exposure" and for hosting a "lesbian party." She is bailed out by her protégé, blues singer Bessie Smith.

A street in Paris is named after Eva Kotchever, who died at Auschwitz after being deported to Poland by the Americans.

1926. Eve's Hangout, also known as Eve Adams's Tearoom, in Greenwich Village, New York, is run by Eva Kotchever (aka Eve Adams), a Polish–Jewish immigrant and lesbian. It is a popular gathering place for lesbians, artists, writers, and other members of the bohemian community. The police raid the establishment in June 1926 as part of an undercover operation in which a policewoman, posing as a customer, is sent to Eve's to gather evidence of alleged indecency and lesbian activity. Kotchever is arrested on charges of obscenity and disorderly conduct. Convicted, she is deported to Poland in 1927.

1928. Written by Maurice Bigelow, *The Social Hygiene Movement* provides a comprehensive overview of the movement's goals, methods, and achievements, emphasizing the need to combat "immoral" behaviors, including homosexuality.

1930s. Throughout the 1930s, anxieties about social stability due to the Great Depression cause law enforcement to reinforce social norms and eliminate perceived threats to public order. This took the form of enhanced enforcement of vagrancy, indecency, and sodomy laws targeting LGBTQ+ individuals. Police departments in major cities like New York, Los Angeles, San Francisco, and Chicago intensify surveillance of areas known for LGBTQ+ gatherings, including parks, bars, and nightclubs, and undercover officers frequently engage in entrapment, posing as gay men to solicit responses that could lead to arrests for indecency or vagrancy. Throughout the decade, a number of highly publicized raids also occur on suspected LGBTQ+-friendly venues.

1930. The White House Conference on Child Health and Protection addresses various issues related to child welfare, including the importance of moral and sexual education as part of broader public health efforts. LGBTQ+ individuals are often framed negatively in discussions of moral hygiene.

1932. Arrested and charged under New York's sodomy law, Martin Webster argues that the law violates his rights to privacy and personal liberty. In *Webster v. People*, the New York Court of Appeals upholds the conviction, rejecting the argument that the sodomy law violates personal liberty or privacy rights. The decision reinforces the legality of sodomy laws in New York and serves as a precedent for upholding similar laws in other jurisdictions. The ruling contributes to the continued stigmatization and marginalization of LGBTQ+ Americans, who are criminalized for their private consensual conduct.

1933. Police raid the Black Cat Bar, a popular LGBTQ+ bar in San Francisco's North Beach, as part of a broader effort to enforce public morals and crack down on LGBTQ+-friendly establishments and exemplifies the increased policing and surveillance nationwide driven by the moral hygiene movement. The repeal of Prohibition indirectly impacts the LGBTQ+ community. With the reopening of bars, some establishments begin to cater to a more diverse clientele, including LGBTQ+ patrons, providing them with more social spaces even though these spaces are often still subject to police raids and legal scrutiny. The New York State Liquor Authority begins enforcing regulations that prohibit bars from serving known homo-

Prohibition put a damper on the gay community when it closed a lot of the bars. When the ban on alcohol was lifted, many such establishments, desiring customers, became more lenient, allowing a diverse clientele.

sexuals. This effectively makes it illegal for LGBTQ+ individuals to congregate in public bars. President Franklin D. Roosevelt establishes the Civilian Conservation Corps (CCC) but bans "sexual perversion," targeting gay men for exclusion from this New Deal program.

1934. A police raid at Cherry Grove on Fire Island, New York, results in the arrests of several artists and performers known for their involvement in the LGBTQ+ community. In response to perceived moral decay, California forms a dedicated morals squad to target "immoral" activities, including homosexuality. This leads to increased raids and arrests of LGBTQ+ individuals. Hollywood adopts the Motion Picture Production Code (Hays Code), which bans the depiction of "sexual perversion" (a term used at the time to refer to homosexuality). This leads to increased censorship and a lack of positive representation of LGBTQ+ characters in the media, influencing public perception and further marginalizing the community.

1936. The American Social Hygiene Association (ASHA) conducts a national survey on sexual behavior and health. Its findings reinforce the need for continued education and intervention in sexual health and moral hygiene, often targeting LGBTQ+ individuals as part of broader societal concerns about morality. The ASHA advocates for the treatment of homosexuality as a mental illness, which leads to psychiatric treatment of LGBTQ+ individuals, including institutionalization in mental hospitals, aversion therapy, electroconvulsive therapy, and other methods aimed at "curing" homosexuality. The ASHA report further stigmatizes homosexuality by linking it to juvenile delinquency and moral corruption. In Los Angeles, police increase surveillance and raids on LGBTQ+ individuals, using vagrancy laws to arrest those found loitering in public parks and known cruising areas. Pershing Square, a popular gathering spot for gay men, is heavily policed, with undercover officers frequently arresting individuals on vagrancy charges. In *United States v. One Package of Japanese Pessaries*, the U.S. Supreme Court rules that birth control devices can be imported for medical use. This decision, while not directly related to LGBTQ+ rights, contributes to broader discussions about sexual health and personal freedoms that do affect the LGBTQ+ community by challenging existing norms around sexuality.

1937. The New York State legislature amends its penal code to include harsher penalties for acts of "public indecency" and "lewd behavior," specifically targeting LGBTQ+ individuals and increasing their risk of arrest and imprisonment. Police raid the Pirate's Den, a well-known gay bar in New York City, and patrons are arrested on charges of vagrancy and public indecency. The raid is part of a broader campaign against LGBTQ+ nightlife in the city.

1939. Police raid multiple bars and clubs in New York's Greenwich Village, a known LGBTQ+-friendly area. Dozens of individuals are arrested for "disorderly conduct" and "public indecency." It is part of the ongoing persecution of LGBTQ+ individuals driven by moral hygiene initiatives.

1940. The American Law Institute in-

Long an active hub of the LGTBQ community, New York's Greenwich Village has been a target for police crackdowns over the years.

cludes "sexual perversion" as a mental disorder in the *Diagnostic and Statistical Manual of Mental Disorders*, further stigmatizing homosexuality and reinforcing its criminalization and medical pathologization.

1941. In June, President Franklin D. Roosevelt signs Executive Order 8802, which prohibits racial discrimination in the defense industry. While the order primarily addresses race, it indirectly affects LGBTQ+ individuals working in the defense sector by setting a precedent for workplace nondiscrimination policies.

1942. The U.S. military implements policies explicitly excluding homosexuals from service: The Selective Service System classifies homosexuality as a disqualifying mental condition, leading to the discharge and exclusion of known LGBTQ+ individuals from the U.S. Armed Forces during World War II.

1943. The U.S. military revises its classifications of homosexuality, categorizing it under "unsuitability"; this designation is used to justify the discharge of LGBTQ+ service members and is a policy that remains in place for the duration of the war and beyond. Police raid New York City's Everard Baths. A popular gathering place for gay men, the Everard Baths, which opened in 1888, was the most famous and longest-operating gay bathhouse in New York City. The 1943 raid is conducted by the New York City Police Department, whose officers enter the baths, arrest patrons, and charge them with offenses such as lewd conduct, disorderly behavior, and vagrancy. Those arrested face public shaming when their names are published in local newspapers.

1946. The formation of the United Nations includes a charter promoting human rights and fundamental freedoms for all individuals and indirectly encourages discussions about LGBTQ+ rights, although

The Everard Baths operated from 1888 to 1986. This photo was taken in 2008 at 28 W. 28th Street where they were located.

the charter does not explicitly address them at the time.

1947. President Harry S. Truman issues Executive Order 9835, establishing a loyalty program for federal employees. This contributes to the Lavender Scare, in which LGBTQ+ individuals will be targeted and dismissed from government service under suspicion of being security risks due to their sexual orientation.

1948. Lafayette Park, directly north of the White House, has been a longtime popular gathering spot for various groups, including gay men. Undercover police officers, posing as gay men, engage men in conversation and attempt to elicit from them propositions or other behavior that could be construed as homosexual advances. Once a man is perceived to be making any form of advance, he is arrested on charges such as lewd conduct, vagrancy, loitering, or disorderly behavior. These entrapment operations are aimed at both reducing the presence of gay men in public spaces and identifying individuals who could be purged from government service. Many of those who are arrested lose their jobs, especially if they had been employed by the federal government. President Harry S. Truman signs Executive Order 9981, which desegregates the military, declaring that "there shall be equality of treatment of all persons in the armed services without regard to race, color, religion, or national origin." While the order does not specifically address issues related to sexual orientation or gender identity and the military continues to enforce strict policies against homosexuals, it sets a precedent for challenging discriminatory practices within federal institutions, demonstrating that change was possible in future reforms.

1950. In an infamous speech, Senator Joseph McCarthy claims to have a list of 205 individuals in the Department of State who are known members of the Communist Party, making them "security risks." The speech is the beginning of intense anti-Communist sentiment and investigations known as the Red Scare. Although McCarthy's initial focus is on Communists, the fear and suspicion he generates quickly extends to gay men, who are deemed morally weak and thus susceptible to Communist influence. It intensifies efforts to identify and remove homosexuals from government positions.

Lafayette Park is within sight of the White House and was once a popular place for gay men to gather.

McCarthy's aide during the investigations and the hearings that follow is closeted gay lawyer Roy Cohn.

1953. President Dwight D. Eisenhower signs Executive Order 10450, expanding the criteria for dismissing federal employees to include "sexual perversion," thus institutionalizing the purge of LGBTQ+ individuals from federal service. The Senate Permanent Subcommittee on Investigations, chaired by North Carolina Democratic senator Clyde R. Hoey, conducts hearings on the employment of homosexuals and other "perverts" in the government. The hearings conclude that homosexuals are security risks, further justifying discriminatory policies and practices.

1956. Two well-known gay bars in New York City, the Wagon Wheel and the Apollinaire, are raided by the police, with patrons arrested on charges of lewd conduct and disorderly behavior. Similar raids take place at the Black Cat Bar in San Francisco and the Black Cat Tavern and the Red Rouge in Los Angeles. These raids help to galvanize early LGBTQ+ activists and organizations like the Mattachine Society and the Daughters of Bilitis to begin to advocate more openly for LGBTQ+ rights.

[I]n 1958 in** One, Inc. v. Olesen, **the Supreme Court reverses the Circuit Court's ruling, declaring that** ONE Magazine **is not obscene and that its distribution is protected by the First Amendment. This is the first time that the Supreme Court rules in favor of LGBTQ+ rights....

1957. The Wolfenden Report is published in the United Kingdom, recommending decriminalization of homosexual behavior. While this report does not directly affect U.S. law, its recommendation of the decriminalization of homosexual behavior influences discussions on LGBTQ+ rights and decriminalization globally.

1958. In 1954, *ONE Magazine*, founded in 1952 by members of the Mattachine Society, including Harry Hay, Dale Jennings, and others—the first openly gay magazine in the United States—is seized by the U.S. Post Office and declared obscene and unmailable. The U.S. District Court rules in favor of the Post Office's assessment, and the 9th Circuit Court of Appeals upholds the District Court's decision. However, in 1958 in *One, Inc. v. Olesen*, the Supreme Court reverses the Circuit Court's ruling, declaring that *ONE Magazine* is not obscene and that its distribution is protected by the First Amendment. This is the first time that the Supreme Court rules in favor of LGBTQ+ rights, establishing a crucial legal precedent for the protection of LGBTQ+ publications and providing a foundation for subsequent cases challenging discriminatory laws and practices.

1959. Cooper Do-Nuts, a popular hangout spot in downtown Los Angeles that is frequented by a diverse crowd, including LGBTQ+ individuals and drag queens, is raided by Los Angeles police officers attempting to arrest several LGBTQ+ individuals there, singling out people based on their appearance. Those targeted resist arrest, and the situation escalates, with patrons and bystanders throwing debris at the police officers. The arrestees escape, and the officers are forced to leave without making any arrests. The riot draws attention to the ongoing police harassment and mistreatment of LGBTQ+ individuals in Los Angeles. It has often been cited as one of the first LGBTQ+ uprisings against police harassment in the United States, predating the Compton's Cafeteria riot in 1966 and the Stonewall Uprising in 1969.

1961. A subcommittee of the U.S. House of Representatives holds hearings to investigate the moral character of cafeteria workers in the U.S. Capitol, including allegations of homosexuality among employees. While not directly resulting in legislation, it reflects the broader societal and governmental scrutiny of LGBTQ+ individuals at the time. Illinois becomes the first U.S. state to adopt the Model Penal

Los Angeles officials held an unveiling of an historical marker for the Cooper Do-Nuts riot on June 22, 2023.

Code to decriminalize consensual same-sex sexual activity between adults.

1964. In July, Title VII of the Civil Rights Act of 1964 passes into law, prohibiting employment discrimination based on race, color, religion, sex, or national origin. Initially, "sex" was added as a protected category with the intent of derailing the bill, but it passed into law with this provision intact. At first, Title VII has a limited and indirect impact on LGBTQ+ rights since sex was not initially interpreted to include sexual orientation or gender identity, but it lays the groundwork for future legal arguments and court decisions that would eventually extend protection to LGBTQ+ individuals. However, during President Lyndon Johnson's election campaign that year, longtime White House aide and special assistant Walter Jenkins, who had been arrested for alleged "homosexual conduct," is fired. Also fired is White House secretary and Johnson family friend Robert "Bob" Waldron after a government background check discovers that he "had engaged in homosexual acts in the recent past."

1965. Members of the Mattachine Society and the Daughters of Bilitis stage the first gay rights demonstration at the White House, protesting the government's treatment of LGBTQ+ federal employees. Gay rights activist Frank Kameny files a petition with the U.S. Civil Service Commission, challenging the dismissal of employees based on their sexual orientation. Although the petition is denied, it marks one of the earliest legal challenges to federal employment discrimination against LGBTQ+ individuals.

1966. New York mayor John Lindsay issues an executive order prohibiting discrimination in city employment based on "race, color, religion, or national origin."

John Lindsay was mayor of New York City from 1966 to 1973. One of his first acts was to sign an order prohibiting discrimination by city employers.

Although sexual orientation is not included, Lindsay's executive order represents an early attempt to address employment discrimination at the municipal level. One of the first recorded LGBTQ+ riots in U.S. history occurs at Compton's Cafeteria in San Francisco. Transgender women and drag queens resist police harassment, sparking confrontation.

1967. Police raid the Black Cat Tavern in Los Angeles, leading to a significant protest in the LGBTQ+ community, which galvanizes the LGBTQ+ rights movement in Los Angeles.

1969. The Stonewall Inn in New York City is raided by police, sparking riots and protests that mark a pivotal moment in the modern LGBTQ+ rights movement. In the case of *Norton v. Macy*, the U.S. Court of Appeals rules that federal employees cannot be dismissed solely based on their sexual orientation unless it affects job performance. This decision was one of the first to challenge the dismissal of federal employees based on sexual orientation. The ruling applies specifically to federal employment and does not extend protections to LGBTQ+ individuals in private sector, state, or local government employment, and it does not result in immediate or widespread changes in how federal agencies handle LGBTQ+ employees. Enforcement of the decision is inconsistent, and many federal employees continue to face discrimination and dismissal.

1971. A decade after Illinois became the first state to decriminalize same-sex sexual activity among consenting adults, Connecticut becomes the second state to repeal its sodomy laws. Colorado and Oregon would follow in 1972. Two men who applied for a marriage license in Minnesota and were denied challenge the decision, but the Minnesota Supreme Court upholds the denial, and the U.S. Supreme Court, in *Baker v. Nelson*, dismisses the appeal "for want of a substantial federal question." This case effectively leaves the issue of same-sex marriage to the states.

1972. Congress passes the Equal Rights Amendment (ERA), which is sent to the states for ratification. The proposed amendment states: "Equality of rights un-

Richard John Baker (left) and James Michael McConnell (shown here in 1970) became the first same-sex couple to legally marry on September 3, 1971, after initially being denied by a county clerk the previous year.

der the law shall not be denied or abridged by the United States or by any State on account of sex." The ERA needs to be ratified by 38 states; Congress initially set a deadline of 1979, which is later extended to 1982. By the deadline, only 35 states had ratified the amendment. The amendment reaches the 38 states needed in 2020, but legal and political debates ensue about the validity of these late ratifications and the original deadline's legitimacy. The ERA's language of ensuring equal rights regardless of sex has been interpreted by many legal scholars to extend protections to LGBTQ+ individuals.

1973. Maryland becomes the first state to ban same-sex marriage explicitly by defining marriage as a union between a man and a woman.

1974. After the University of New Hampshire initially denies recognition to a gay student organization, the U.S. District Court, in *Gay Students Organization of the University of New Hampshire v. Bonner*, rules that the university must grant official recognition since denying it violates the students' First Amendment rights to free speech and assembly. The decision affirms the right of LGBTQ+ student groups to exist and function within educational institutions, promoting greater visibility and advocacy on college campuses. A gay man who is denied a position with the Internal Revenue Service solely based on his sexual orientation files a lawsuit, arguing that the Civil Service Commission's (CSC) policy of excluding homosexuals from federal employment is discriminatory and violates his rights under the Fifth Amendment, which guarantees equal protection and due process under the law. He is represented by lawyers from the National Gay Task Force and other LGBTQ+ organizations, marking one of the earliest instances of organized legal challenges against discrimination based on sexual orientation in federal employment. In *Singer v. United States Civil Service Commission*, the U.S. District Court rules in favor of the CSC, affirming that it had the authority to set employment standards, including those related to the moral character of applicants. Although the ruling reinforces the existing policy of discrimination against LGBTQ+ individuals in federal employment, the case galvanizes LGBTQ+ rights organizations to continue their fight against employment discrimination.

1975. The U.S. Civil Service Commission announces that it will no longer bar gay and lesbian individuals from federal employment solely based on their sexual orientation. It issues new guidelines stating that sexual orientation cannot be a factor in hiring decisions unless it directly affects job performance. The policy change opens up federal employment opportunities for LGBTQ+ individuals, allowing them to seek and maintain federal jobs without fear of automatic dismissal based on their sexual orientation. In *Doe v. Commonwealth's Attorney for the City of Richmond*, the U.S. District Court upholds Virginia's sodomy laws, which criminalize consensual same-sex activity. The Supreme Court's summary affirmation of the decision without written opinion upholds the constitutionality of state sodomy laws.

1977. Miami–Dade County, Florida, passes an ordinance prohibiting discrimination based on sexual orientation in areas such as employment, housing, and public accommodation. This prompts singer Anita Bryant to lead the Save Our Children campaign, leading to the repeal of the

Popular singer Anita Bryant campaigned vigorously against the LGBTQ community.

Ted Weiss was a U.S. congressman from New York from 1977 until his death from heart failure in 1992. He worked to prohibit sexual discrimination as an amendment to the Civil Rights Act.

ordinance, highlighting the resistance to LGBTQ+ rights at the time.

1978. The Briggs Initiative (Proposition 6) proposes a ban on gay and lesbian individuals and, potentially, anyone who supports gay rights from working in California's public schools. The initiative is defeated, thanks in part to the efforts of state LGBTQ+ activists like Harvey Milk.

1979. Discharged in 1975 for declaring that he is gay in a letter to his commanding officer, Leonard Matlovich, a decorated Air Force sergeant, files a lawsuit, arguing that his discharge was discriminatory and violated his rights. In *Matlovich v. Secretary of the Air Force*, the U.S. District Court rules that the Air Force has failed to justify Matlovich's discharge and finds procedural irregularities in how the Air Force applied its regulation to the case. The court orders his reinstatement, but the Air Force offers a financial settlement instead, which Matlovich accepts. However, his case sets a precedent and inspires other LGBTQ+ service members to challenge their discharges even though it does not immediately change military policy.

1980. In this presidential election year, the Democratic Party becomes the first major political party to include gay rights in its platform. The Equal Employment Opportunity Commission (EEOC) clarifies that Title VII of the Civil Rights Act of 1964, which prohibits sex discrimination, can cover sexual harassment, including same-sex sexual harassment. In *Fricke v. Lynch*, a federal court rules that a Rhode Island high school violated student Aaron Fricke's First Amendment rights by refusing to allow him to bring a same-sex date to the prom.

1981. Sponsored by Representative Ted Weiss (D–New York), the Equality Act is introduced to amend the Civil Rights Act of 1964 to include prohibitions on discrimination based on sexual orientation in employment, housing, and public accommodation. The bill does not pass, but it is one of the early attempts to extend federal civil rights protection to LGBTQ+ individuals.

1982. Wisconsin becomes the first state to pass a law prohibiting discrimination based on sexual orientation in employment, housing, and public accommodation. Several states follow: Massachusetts (1990), Hawaii (1991), California (1992), and Minnesota (1993).

1983. Representative Gerry Studds (D–Massachusetts) reveals his sexual orientation during a House debate on his censure for having a relationship with a male page, becoming the first openly gay member of Congress.

1984. Berkeley, California, passes the first domestic partnership ordinance in the United States, allowing same-sex couples to register their partnership and gain some legal recognition.

1985. Sponsored by Representative Barney Frank (D–Massachusetts), the Civil Rights Amendments Act aims to amend the Civil Rights Act of 1964 to include sexual orientation as a protected category, thereby prohibiting discrimination in employment, housing, and public accommodation. The bill does not pass. After media attention and a public outcry, a foster child is removed from the care of a Massachusetts gay male couple, instituting a state policy that prioritizes the placement of foster children in "traditional family settings," effectively excluding gay and lesbian couples. In *People v. Uplinger*, the Supreme Court declines to rule on a case brought by a Buffalo man pertaining to loitering with the purpose of solicitation to commit sodomy, with the result that New York's sodomy law remains intact and in place.

1986. In *Bowers v. Hardwick*, the Supreme Court upholds Georgia's sodomy law in a 5–4 decision, ruling that the Constitution does not confer fundamental rights to engage in consensual homosexual sodomy. The decision is a significant setback for LGBTQ+ rights and legitimizes anti-LGBTQ+ laws across the country.

1987. Gerry Studds (D–Massachusetts) proposes a bill extending federal employee benefits to domestic partners of federal employees similar to those provided to spouses. The bill does not pass, but it highlights the growing movement to recognize same-sex relationships and provide equitable benefits. ACT UP stages a major protest at the headquarters of the Food and Drug Administration in Rockville, Maryland, to demand the approval of new AIDS drugs. Hundreds participate, and many are arrested in one of the largest acts of civil disobedience in the history of the LGBTQ+ rights movement.

1988. ACT UP stages a protest inside St. Patrick's Cathedral in New York City during Mass to protest the Catholic Church's stance on AIDS and homosexuality. Several are arrested, drawing significant media attention and controversy. A Stop the Church Protest follows in 1989, also at St. Patrick's, that is larger and with more confrontation, leading to numerous arrests.

1989. In a groundbreaking decision in *Watkins v. U.S. Army*, a U.S. appellate court rules against the U.S. military's ban on service by gays and lesbians. The court rules that the Army cannot discharge the complainant, Perry Watkins, after allowing him to serve openly for over 14 years and repeatedly reenlisting him despite knowing his sexual orientation. The case establishes important precedents regarding the treatment of LGBTQ+ service members.

1990. Named after 13-year-old Ryan White, a hemophiliac who became infected with HIV in 1984 after a blood transfusion and died of AIDS-related pneumonia in 1990, the Ryan White Comprehensive AIDS Resources Emergency (CARE) Act is sponsored by Senator Orrin Hatch (R–Utah) and Representative Henry Waxman (D–California). The act provides federal funding for community-based care and support services for people living with HIV/AIDS. The bill passes and is signed into law, becoming a crucial source of funding for HIV/AIDS treatment and services.

Named after 13-year-old Ryan White, a hemophiliac who became infected with HIV in 1984 after a blood transfusion and died of AIDS-related pneumonia in 1990, the Ryan White Comprehensive AIDS Resources Emergency (CARE) Act is sponsored by Senator Orrin Hatch (R–Utah) and Representative Henry Waxman (D–California).

The Hate Crimes Statistics Act is signed into law by President George H. W. Bush. The act requires the Department of Justice to collect and publish data on crimes committed based on the victim's race, ethnicity, religion, or sexual orientation. As of 2025, the act remains in force.

1992. Colorado passes Amendment 2, which prohibits any city, town, or county in the state from enacting any discrimination laws protecting LGBTQ+ individuals, setting off subsequent challenges in court.

1993. Minnesota becomes the first state to include both sexual orientation and gender identity in its anti-discrimination law. President Bill Clinton signs "Don't

U.S. president Bill Clinton signed laws against discrimination in the military, against denying security clearances based solely on sexual orientation, and against banning civilians from working in the government because of their orientation. However, he also signed the Defense of Marriage Act that allowed states to ban same-sex marriages.

Ask, Don't Tell" (DADT) into law, which allows gays and lesbians to serve in the military as long as they do not disclose their sexual orientation. The policy also prohibits military officials from inquiring about a service member's sexual orientation.

1994. First introduced in Congress, the Employment Non-Discrimination Act (ENDA) seeks to prohibit discrimination in hiring and employment on the basis of sexual orientation. The bill does not pass but is reintroduced in subsequent sessions. In 2013, a version of ENDA that includes gender identity passes the Senate but does not receive a vote in the House of Representatives.

1995. In *Bottoms v. Bottoms,* Virginia's Supreme Court awards custody of Tyler Doustou to his grandmother, Kay Bottoms, because his mother, Sharon Bottoms, is a lesbian. The case exemplifies the challenges LGBTQ+ parents face in custody battles and the widespread bias in family courts. President Bill Clinton signs Executive Order 12968, which prohibits the federal government from denying security clearances based solely on the basis of sexual orientation.

1996. In *Romer v. Evans,* the Supreme Court rules that Colorado's Amendment 2, passed in 1992, is unconstitutional since it violates the Equal Protection Clause of the 14th Amendment. This landmark decision is a significant victory for LGBTQ+ rights. President Bill Clinton, who is running for reelection, signs the Defense of Marriage Act (DOMA) into law. The act defines marriage as the union between one man and one woman for federal purposes and allows states to refuse to recognize same-sex marriages performed in other states.

1997. In *Oncale v. Sundowner Offshore Services, Inc.,* the Supreme Court rules that Title VII's prohibition of sex discrimination includes protection against same-sex sexual harassment. This landmark decision extends Title VII protection to cover harassment based on sexual orientation.

1998. President Bill Clinton issues Executive Order 13087, amending previous orders to prohibit discrimination based on sexual orientation in the federal civilian workforce. The brutal murder of Matthew Shepard, a gay college student in Wyoming, brings national attention to hate crimes against LGBTQ+ individuals, and his death becomes a catalyst for a movement to pass hate crimes legislation.

1999. California enacts a law allowing same-sex couples to register as domestic partners, granting them limited legal rights. It is one of the earliest state-level recognitions of same-sex relationships. A Hate Crimes Prevention Act is proposed to expand federal hate crimes law to include crimes motivated by the victim's actual or perceived sexual orientation, gender, or disability; the bill does not pass but sets the stage for future legislation. A Military Readiness Enhancement Act is proposed to repeal "Don't Ask, Don't Tell," which would allow LGBTQ+ individuals to serve openly in the military. The act fails to be passed.

In *Baehr v. Miike,* first proposed in 1990 as *Baehr v. Lewin,* the Supreme Court of Hawaii rules that denying marriage licenses to same-sex couples violates the Constitution of Hawaii's Equal Protection Clause unless the state can show a compelling reason for the prohibition. Remanded for further proceedings, the case sparks national debate on same-sex marriage.

2000. Vermont becomes the first state to legally recognize civil unions between same-sex couples and grant them the same rights and benefits as marriage under state law.

2002. President Bill Clinton issues Executive Order 13160, which extends nondiscrimination protections to cover sexual orientation in federal civilian employment.

2003. In *Lawrence v. Texas,* the Supreme Court rules sodomy laws unconstitutional. The precedent set by cases like *Webster v. People* (1932) and affirmed in *Bowers v. Hardwick* (1986) is overturned by the Supreme Court's landmark decision ruling that sodomy laws criminalizing private consensual sexual conduct between adults are unconstitutional, effectively invalidating such laws and decriminalizing same-sex activity across the United States. Despite the ruling, sodomy laws remain on the books in 12 U.S. states as of 2023. Following the Massachusetts Supreme Judicial Court's decision in *Goodridge v. Department of Public Health,* Massachusetts becomes the first state to legalize same-sex marriage.

2008. California becomes the second state to legalize same-sex marriage after the California Supreme Court rules in favor of same-sex marriage. Later that year, voters pass Proposition 8, banning same-sex marriage, which leads to legal battles.

2009. Signed into law by President Barack Obama, the Matthew Shepard and James Byrd Jr. Hate Crimes Prevention Act expands federal hate crime laws to include crimes motivated by race (as in the murder of James Byrd Jr.) and by the victim's actual or perceived gender, sexual orientation, gender identity, or disability.

President Barack Obama repealed the "Don't Ask, Don't Tell" rule that had required military personnel to hide their identity if they wished to serve.

2010. President Barack Obama signs the repeal of "Don't Ask, Don't Tell" (DADT), allowing LGBTQ+ individuals to serve openly in the military.

2011. New York becomes the largest U.S. state to legalize same-sex marriage.

2012. In *Macy v. Holder,* the Equal Employment Opportunity Commission (EEOC) decides that discrimination based on gender identity is a form of sex discrimination under Title VII. This case involves a transgender woman who alleged that she was denied a job because of her gender identity.

2013. In *United States v. Windsor,* the Supreme Court strikes down Section 3 of the

Defense of Marriage Act (DOMA), which defined marriage as between one man and one woman for federal purposes, allowing the federal government to recognize same-sex marriages performed in states where it is legal. The EEOC implements its Strategic Enforcement Plan, which includes protections for LGBTQ+ individuals, specifically targeting sex discrimination against lesbian, gay, bisexual, and transgender individuals under Title VII.

2014. President Barack Obama signs Executive Order 13672, prohibiting discrimination based on sexual orientation and gender identity in federal civilian employment and by federal contractors.

2015. In *Baldwin v. Foxx*, the EEOC rules that discrimination based on sexual orientation is also a form of sex discrimination under Title VII. This decision marks a significant step in extending workplace protections to gay and lesbian employees.

In the landmark case of *Obergefell v. Hodges*, the Supreme Court rules that same-sex marriage is a constitutional right, legalizing it nationwide.

Kate Brown (D-OR), who is openly bisexual, becomes the first LGBTQ governor when she is sworn in to complete the former governor's term. She is elected to her first full term the following year.

2016. Elisa Rae Shupe becomes the first person in the United States to obtain legal recognition of a nonbinary identity when they successfully petitioned an Oregon court to change their gender designation to nonbinary. They are subsequently issued a birth certificate with a sex marker of "unknown." Their petition has been cited as a legal precedent for nonbinary gender markers in the passport lawsuit *Zzyym v. Pompeo*. North Carolina passes House Bill 2 (HB2), which restricts transgender individuals from using public restrooms corresponding to their preferred gender identity and nullifies local LGBTQ+ anti-discrimination protections. The bill faces widespread backlash and legal challenges.

2017. President Donald Trump announces a ban on transgender individuals serving in the military, which is met with legal challenges and partial implementation.

James Obergefell (right) with his attorney, Al Gerhardstein, after learning of their win as the U.S. Supreme Court ruled that same-sex marriages were allowed under the 14th Amendment of the U.S. Constitution.

2018. In *Masterpiece Cakeshop v. Colorado Civil Rights Commission*, the Supreme Court rules in favor of a baker who refused to make a wedding cake for a same-sex couple, citing religious beliefs. The ruling is narrow and does not establish a broad right to discriminate but opens the door for future cases. The U.S. District Court directs the Department of State to no longer rely upon its binary-only gender marker policy to withhold requested passports.

2020. In *Bostock v. Clayton County*, the Supreme Court rules that Title VII of the Civil Rights Act of 1964, which prohibits sex discrimination, includes discrimination based on sexual orientation and gender identity. This landmark decision significantly broadens federal protections for LGBTQ+ individuals in the workplace.

President Joe Biden continued to level the playing field for LGBTQ people by revoking the directive that banned trans people from military service.

2021. On January 20, President Joe Biden signs Executive Order 13988 on his first day in office. It directs federal agencies to implement the Supreme Court's ruling in *Bostock v. Clayton County* and ensure that federal laws prohibiting sex discrimination also protect against discrimination based on sexual orientation and gender identity. On January 20, 2025, the order is rescinded by Donald Trump within hours of his inauguration as president. Five days into his presidency, President Joe Biden revokes the previous administration's directive that barred transgender individuals from serving in the military, signing Executive Order 14004. The House of Representatives passes the Equality Act, which seeks to amend the Civil Rights Act of 1964 to explicitly include sexual orientation and gender identity as protected classes. The bill faces challenges in the Senate, where it does not pass. The Department of State issues the first U.S. passport recognizing nonbinary status with an "X" gender marker. The recipient is Dana Zzyym, an intersex and nonbinary U.S. Navy veteran who had sued the Department in the case of *Zzyym v. Pompeo* (et al).

2022. The U.S. Department of State begins issuing passports with an "X" gender marker option for nonbinary, intersex, and gender-nonconforming individuals.

Maura Healey of Massachusetts and Tina Kotek of Oregon become the first openly lesbian governors in U.S. history.

2023. President Joe Biden signs an executive order to advance LGBTQ+ equality, including efforts to enhance data collection on sexual orientation and gender identity (SOGI) in order to improve services and support the LGBTQ+ community.

2024–2025. Donald Trump is elected president for the second time. Trump's election and his commitment to the government overhaul outlined in the right-wing Heritage Foundation's Project 2025 raises concerns for the future of existing LGBTQ+ rights legislation and health initiatives. These concerns are justified after Trump's inauguration when his administration begins eliminating SOGI questions from surveys and the census, deletes LGBTQ+-related content from other federal websites, and shuts down the LGBTQ+ division of the 988 Suicide and Crisis Lifeline, which greatly affects LGBTQ+ youth. In January 2025, Trump signs Executive Order 14183, disingenuously titled "Prioritizing Military Excellence and Readiness," which effectively prohibits transgender people from serving in the military.

Despite significant progress in LGBTQ+ rights in the United States, major challenges remain. Many of the landmark policy changes and court decisions in this timeline remain untethered to legislation to ensure their permanence. Governance by presidential executive order is by its

Donald Trump has worked against LGBTQ+ interests in his presidency. He has banned trans people from the military, defined sex as being determined by birth biology, restricted gender-affirming health care, censored educational efforts about sexual identity, barred trans athletes from sports, and has opposed inclusive language.

nature temporary, reversible by the next president. A case in point is President Trump's order that barred transgender military personnel in 2017. In 2021, President Biden revoked the 2017 policy, affirming that no person, solely because of gender identity, should be denied enlistment or the right to continue serving in the military. The Trump administration reimposed the ban in 2025. What is clear is that without congressional legislation, executive orders are stop-gap measures.

The Equality Act, passed by the House of Representatives in 2021, sought to amend the Civil Rights Act of 1964 to include explicit protection against discrimination based on sexual orientation and gender identity. It has faced challenges in the Senate and is currently stalled. Without comprehensive federal antidiscrimination protection, LGBTQ+ individuals remain vulnerable to discrimination in states without such protections as well as to policy reversals by presidential executive orders.

Other landmark decisions that changed the LGBTQ+ landscape have been judicial. Supreme Court rulings such as the 2003 decision decriminalizing private consensual sexual conduct, the 2015 ruling that legalized same-sex marriage nationwide, or the 2020 decision that Title VII of the Civil Rights Act of 1964 prohibits discrimination based on sexual orientation and gender identity have been seismic in their impact on LGBTQ+ equal rights. But are they now settled law? As we have learned with the overturn of *Roe v. Wade* by the current court, established precedent and settled law do not mean that revisiting and overturning a decision is either unlikely or impossible. The Supreme Court in the *Masterpiece Cakeshop* decision in 2018 seems more open to arguments of religious belief to justify the erosion of equal rights won by LGBTQ+ individuals and opened the door to additional challenges.

In the absence of comprehensive federal policy on LGBTQ+ rights, some states have enacted or proposed laws that negatively impact LGBTQ+ individuals such as so-called "bathroom bills" restricting transgender individuals' access to public restrooms and laws allowing religious exemptions that permit discrimination against LGBTQ+ individuals. This can impact access to health care, adoption and foster care services, and public accommodation. In some states, laws and policies limit transgender access to gender-affirming health care, including restrictions on hormone therapy and surgeries. Several states and municipalities have banned conversion therapy for minors, but it remains legal, in the absence of a comprehensive federal ban, in many parts of the country. Despite the *Bostock v. Clayton County* ruling, workplace discrimination for LGBTQ+ individuals remains a problem. More protections are necessary for LGBTQ+ workers, particularly in states without comprehensive nondiscrimination laws.

While substantial progress has certainly been made in securing rights and protection for LGBTQ+ individuals in the United States, continued advocacy, legislative efforts, and social change are necessary to address discrimination, ensure equal rights, and improve the overall well-being of LGBTQ+ individuals. Ensuring that these protections are comprehensive and robustly enforced, both at the federal and state levels, is crucial for guaranteeing equality and justice for the LGBTQ+ community.

BIOGRAPHIES

Christine Abizaid (1979–)

Intelligence Officer

Christine Sandra Abizaid is an intelligence officer who served as the director of the National Counterterrorism Center (NCTC) from June 2021 until her resignation in July 2024. She was the first woman to lead the NCTC and its first openly gay director, overseeing efforts to integrate and analyze information to protect the United States from terrorist threats.

A Lebanese American, Abizaid is the daughter of John Abizaid, an Army general who served as a commander of the U.S. Central Command during the Iraq and Afghanistan wars and as the U.S. ambassador to Saudi Arabia under President Trump. She earned a B.A. in psychology from the University of California, San Diego, and an M.A. in international policy studies from Stanford University. As an undergraduate, she was a star player on UC San Diego's women's soccer team, which were NCAA champions. She began her career with the Defense Intelligence Agency's (DIA) Joint Intelligence Task Force Combating Terrorism, serving as a senior intelligence analyst in both the Afghanistan–Pakistan and Iraq/Middle East divisions. During this time, she deployed several times throughout the Middle East, including a tour as the senior DIA counterterrorism representative in Iraq.

In 2014, Abizaid served as deputy assistant secretary of defense for Afghanistan, Pakistan, and Central Asia during the Obama administration. She also held positions on the National Security Council staff as director for counterterrorism and senior policy advisor to the assistant to the president for homeland security and counterterrorism. In 2021, President Joe Biden nominated her as director of the NCTC, and she was confirmed by the Senate, becoming the first woman to hold this position. In 2024, she resigned from her role as NCTC director.

Abizaid disclosed on her 2021 questionnaire to the U.S. Senate Select Committee on Intelligence that she is married to a woman. Her spouse accompanied her to her Senate confirmation and was acknowledged in her remarks. Confirmed by the Senate, she became the first female and first openly gay director of the NCTC. In 2022, speaking to an audience at a Defense Intelligence Agency Pride Month event, she expressed regret at having been closeted at the agency. "I could have been more brave and placed more trust in people," she said; "frankly it's just easier" being open.

Abizaid's career exemplifies dedication to national security and intelligence, breaking barriers as the first woman and first openly gay individual to lead the NCTC. Her leadership and expertise have significantly contributed to the United States' counterterrorism efforts.

Roberta Achtenberg (1950–)

Lawyer, Political Figure

Roberta Achtenberg is a prominent civil rights attorney, activist, and former public official. She made history as the first openly LGBTQ+ person to be appointed to a Senate-confirmed federal position when President Bill Clinton nominated her to be the assistant secretary at the Office of Fair Housing and Equal Opportunity in 1993. Her career has been defined by her tireless advocacy for LGBTQ+ rights, affordable housing, and civil rights.

Born in Los Angeles, California, Achtenberg grew up in a Jewish family. Her father had emigrated from the Soviet Union, and the family owned a neighborhood grocery store in Los Angeles. She earned her undergraduate degree from the University of California, Berkeley, in 1972 and later graduated from the University of Utah College of Law in 1975. She began her career as a civil rights attorney, working on cases involving housing discrimination, and was an early advocate for LGBTQ+ inclusion in legal protections.

In 1979, Achtenberg divorced David Chavkin and soon after came out to her family as a lesbian. She met her partner and later spouse, Mary Morgan, a judge on the San Francisco Municipal Court, in 1979, and they raised a child together, becoming one of the most visible lesbian couples in San Francisco as Achtenberg began her political and activist career there.

Achtenberg served as a member of the San Francisco Board of Supervisors, where she was a vocal advocate for LGBTQ+ rights and affordable housing. As an openly lesbian elected official, she gained national attention. Her most notable achievement came when President Bill Clinton nominated her to be the assistant secretary at the Office of Fair Housing and Equal Opportunity, part of the U.S. Department of Housing and Urban Development (HUD). Despite Senator Jesse Helms's vocal refusal to vote for "that damned lesbian," she became the first out appointee to be confirmed by the Senate. In her role at HUD, she worked to eliminate housing discrimination based on race, disability, and gender. Her appointment was a groundbreaking moment for LGBTQ+ representation in the government and set a precedent for future LGBTQ+ appointments to federal positions.

In addition to her role at HUD, Achtenberg has continued to advocate for civil rights as a member of the U.S. Commission on Civil Rights, named to that position by President Obama in 2011, and through her work with nonprofit organizations. She is a cofounder of the National Center for Lesbian Rights.

Tammy Baldwin (1962–)

Political Figure

Tammy Suzanne Green Baldwin is the first openly LGBTQ+ person to be elected to the U.S. Senate, representing Wisconsin since 2013. Her election marked a major milestone in LGBTQ+ political representation, and she has been a leading advocate for healthcare reform, LGBTQ+ rights, and economic fairness throughout her career. She is known for her work on the Affordable Care Act and her role in advancing civil rights legislation.

Born in Madison, Wisconsin, Baldwin was raised by her grandparents. Her mother was 19 and going through a divorce when she was born and suffered from mental illness and opioid addiction. After public high school, graduating as the class valedictorian, she attended Smith College, where she earned a degree in mathematics and government in 1984 before going on to earn her law degree from the University of Wisconsin Law School in 1989. She was a lawyer in private practice from 1989 to 1992.

Baldwin began her political career as a member of the Dane County Board of Supervisors and the Wisconsin Assembly, serving there from 1993 to 1999. Her election to the U.S. House of Representatives in 1998 made her the first openly gay nonincumbent to be elected to Congress, the first open lesbian to be elected to Congress, and the first woman to be elected to Congress from Wisconsin. During her time in the House, she championed healthcare reform, working to ensure the passage of the Affordable Care Act (ACA), which expanded healthcare coverage to millions of Americans.

Elected to the Senate in 2012, Baldwin has continued her focus on health care, LGBTQ+ rights, and economic equality, cosponsoring and supporting several key pieces of legislation, including the Equality Act, which aims to prohibit discrimination based on sexual orientation and gender identity. She has also been a vocal advocate for expanding Medicaid and protecting access to health care for low-income and rural Americans.

Baldwin was in a relationship with Lauren Azar for 15 years, and the couple registered as domestic partners in Wisconsin in 2009 before separating in 2010. Baldwin's career has been defined by her historic election as the first openly LGBTQ+ person in the U.S. Senate and her leadership on healthcare reform and LGBTQ+ rights. Her work continues to shape policy and advocate for equality and fairness in America.

Christopher R. Barron (1973–)

Political Consultant

Christopher R. Barron is a political strategist and activist recognized for his efforts to integrate LGBTQ+ perspectives within conservative politics. He cofounded GOProud, an organization representing gay conservatives, and has been involved in various political consulting roles, including serving as president of CapSouth Consulting. He was the organizer of LGBT for Trump and the national political director for Log Cabin Republicans.

Born in Maine, Barron was raised in Goldsboro, North Carolina. He pursued higher education at the University of North Carolina, Greensboro, and East Carolina University, where he studied political science. During his senior year, a fraternity brother "outed" him, and he came out to his family before graduating in 1997. He earned a J.D. from Wake Forest University School of Law, graduating with honors.

Barron's early career included serving as the national political director for the Log Cabin Republicans, where he directed the organization's federal lobbying efforts and media relations. In 2009, he cofounded GOProud, aiming to provide a voice for gay conservatives and their allies. Under his leadership, GOProud participated in significant political events, including the Conservative Political Action Conference (CPAC), advocating for the inclusion of LGBTQ+ issues within conservative discourse.

Barron has been legally married to his husband, Shawn R. Gardner, since 2010. He is currently vice president of public relations at International Health Brands and The Wellness Company as well as CEO of Vigilant News Network. His work has been instrumental in challenging traditional conservative views on LGBTQ+ issues, promoting inclusivity, and fostering dialogue within the political landscape.

Vic Basile (1941–)

Political Consultant

The executive director of the Human Rights Campaign (HRC), which focused on AIDS research, treatment, and education,

Vic Basile was also a cofounder of the Gay & Lesbian Victory Fund, which works toward the election of gay and lesbian political candidates.

Born in Northampton, Massachusetts, the son of an insurance salesman and a homemaker, Basile attended the University of Massachusetts, Amherst, where he studied public health education. After graduating, he joined the American Lung Association, working to improve the health of low-income urban residents. In 1971, he married Mary Ann Pryor and moved to Washington, D.C., where he worked at ACTION, the umbrella agency for the Peace Corps and VISTA. In 1979, during the first march for lesbian and gay rights, he realized he was gay and shortly thereafter came out to his wife. They divorced in 1983 but remain close friends.

Basile served as executive director of Human Rights Campaign, the largest gay rights advocacy group in the United States, from 1983 to 1989 to focus on the AIDS crisis. In 1991, he cofounded with Dallas gay rights activist William Waybourn the Gay & Lesbian Victory Fund (now called the LGBTQ+ Victory Fund), a nonpartisan political action committee dedicated to increasing the number of out LGBTQ+ public officials in the United States. It has helped to elect several hundred LGBTQ+ candidates to Congress, state legislatures, school boards, and city councils.

In 2023, Basile published his memoir, *Bending Toward Justice*, a history of HRC with reflections on his decades-long involvement with the gay rights movement. He stated, "I believe that in order for us to chart a new path forward for LGBTQ+ people, we first must understand where we've been— not only celebrating the victories and the strategies that served us, but also recognizing and reconciling with our own failures as a movement to ensure that we don't repeat mistakes of the past." Former congressman Barney Frank said about the book, "Drawing on his experience as the first executive director of the Human Rights Campaign Fund, Vic Basile has written a valuable addition to the story of one of the most consequential movements in post–World War II America."

Mary Bonauto (1961–)

Lawyer

Mary L. Bonauto is a prominent civil rights attorney known for her groundbreaking work in LGBTQ+ rights, especially in the area of marriage equality. Called by Barney Frank "our Thurgood Marshall" of the LGBTQ+ movement, her advocacy played a critical role in the legal fight for same-sex marriage in the United States. Her work as lead counsel in *Goodridge v. Department of Public Health* led to the first state legalization of same-sex marriage in Massachusetts in 2003, and her contributions in *Obergefell v. Hodges* helped to achieve marriage equality nationwide in 2015.

Bonauto was born in Newburgh, New York, into a Catholic family in upstate New York. She attended Hamilton College, where she developed an interest in civil rights, and went on to earn her law degree from Northeastern University in 1985. Early in her career, she established a private practice in Maine, where she was one of three openly gay private practice lawyers in the state. She quickly became an advocate for LGBTQ+ rights, joining Gay & Lesbian Advocates & Defenders (GLAD) as their civil rights project director.

As lead counsel in the 2003 Massachusetts case *Goodridge v. Department of Public Health*, Bonauto successfully argued that denying marriage licenses to same-sex couples was unconstitutional, making Massachusetts the first state to recognize same-sex marriage. This victory paved the way for marriage equality efforts across the United States. In 2015, she served as co-counsel in *Obergefell v. Hodges* before the U.S. Supreme Court, a case that culminated in the legalization of same-sex marriage nationwide. Beyond marriage equality, she has been a tireless advocate for antidiscrimination protections, securing LGBTQ+ rights in employment, parenting, and adoption, thus broadening her impact on civil rights for diverse communities.

Bonauto is married to Jennifer Wriggins, a law professor at the University of Maine School of Law, and they have twin daughters. Her openness about her sexuality and family life has reinforced her role as a compassionate and relatable advocate whose legal work has been both personally and professionally driven.

Bonauto's work has directly improved the lives of countless Americans, ensuring that marriage equality and antidiscrimination protections are upheld. Her contributions to LGBTQ+ rights are both pioneering and lasting, marking her as one of the most influential civil rights attorneys of her generation. Through her tireless advocacy, she has created a more inclusive society and a more just legal system.

Mel Boozer (1945–1987)

Political Figure, Educator

Melvin "Mel" Boozer was a prominent gay rights and civil rights activist who broke significant ground as an advocate for LGBTQ+ rights and racial equality. In 1980, he became the first openly gay individual to be nominated for vice president of the United States by a major political party, a symbolic but powerful act that spotlighted the struggles of marginalized communities. His advocacy at the intersection of race and sexuality helped to expand the understanding of LGBTQ+ rights as integral to the broader civil rights movement.

Born in Washington, D.C., Boozer grew up in a segregated community, experiencing both racism and homophobia. These experiences shaped his commitment to social justice. After graduating as salutatorian of his class at Dunbar High School, he attended Dartmouth College, one of only three African Americans admitted in 1963. He studied for a Ph.D. at Yale University before becoming a professor of sociology at the University of Maryland.

In 1979, Boozer was elected president of the Gay Activists Alliance of Washington, D.C., the first African American to serve as GAA president. During his tenure, the GAA won unanimous passage of the Sexual Assault Reform Act by the D.C. Council, which decriminalized sodomy and repealed solicitation laws for consenting adults.

Boozer's nomination for vice president by the Democratic Party in 1980, although symbolic, was a watershed moment in American political history. Nominated by the Socialist Party USA and supported by many in the Democratic Party, he used his platform to address the overlapping prejudices faced by Black and LGBTQ+ Americans. He spoke at the Democratic National Convention in a speech televised in prime time, calling on the party to support equality for LGBTQ+ people. He received 49 votes before the balloting was suspended and then Vice President Walter Mondale was renominated by acclamation.

In 1981, Boozer served as district director and lobbyist for the National Gay Task Force. In 1982, he cofounded the Langston Hughes–Eleanor Roosevelt Democratic Club to advocate for Black LGBTQ+ people in Washington, D.C. He died of an AIDS-related illness at the age of 41.

Boozer's legacy lies in his intersectional advocacy for LGBTQ+ and racial equality. His willingness to challenge societal norms and push for greater visibility of marginalized communities set an example for future activists. His historic vice presidential nomination in 1980 brought LGBTQ+ issues to the forefront of political discourse, while his work in various advocacy organizations laid the groundwork for advancements in antidiscrimination laws. He is remembered as a trailblazer who bridged multiple civil rights movements and broadened the scope of LGBTQ+ advocacy.

Kate Brown (1960–)

Political Figure

Katherine "Kate" Brown is a transformative figure in American politics, recognized as the first openly bisexual governor in the United States. She became the first openly LGBTQ+ person to be elected secretary of state in a U.S. state and the first openly LGBTQ+ person to be elected to statewide office in any U.S. state. When she assumed the Oregon governorship in 2015, she became the first openly LGBTQ+ person to be elected governor in any U.S. state. As Oregon's 38th governor from 2015 to 2023, her administration focused on progressive reforms, particularly in criminal justice, environmental sustainability, and expanding government transparency. Her achievements reflect her commitment to social equity and environmental stewardship. Her groundbreaking judicial appointments and efforts to end the death penalty in Oregon have left a lasting impact, advancing diversity and compassion in governance.

Born in Torrejón de Ardoz, Spain, where her father was stationed with the U.S. Air Force, Brown was raised in Minnesota. After graduating from high school in 1978, she went on to study at the University of Colorado, Boulder, earning a B.A. in environmental conservation with a certificate in women's studies in 1981. She continued her studies in Portland, Oregon, where she earned a J.D. with a certificate in environmental law from Lewis & Clark Law School in 1985. Early in her career, she practiced family and juvenile law and also served as an instructor at Portland State University, developing a deep understanding of the issues facing families and communities.

Brown began her political career with an appointment to the Oregon House of Representatives in 1991, followed by election to the Oregon Senate in 1996. She served as Senate majority leader from 2004 to 2009, making substantial contributions to progressive policy initiatives. In 2008, she made history as the first openly LGBTQ+ person to be elected to statewide office in the United States when she became Oregon's secretary of state. In this role, she championed voter access, government transparency, and accountability reforms. In 2015, she assumed the governorship following the resignation of John Kitzhaber and was subsequently elected to serve out the term in 2016 before being reelected to a full term in 2018. As governor, she made over 100 judicial appointments, prioritizing diversity within the judiciary. In 2022, she commuted the sentences of all individuals on Oregon's death row, effectively ending capital punishment in the state and dismantling the execution chamber. She also signed legislation to transition Oregon to 100 percent clean energy by 2040, placing Oregon among the most environmentally forward-thinking states in the United States.

Brown is married to Dan Little, with whom she shares a family, including two stepchildren. Her openness about her bisexuality has provided inspiration to the LGBTQ+ community, making her a role model for LGBTQ+ individuals in politics. Her advocacy and representation have significantly contributed to greater inclusivity and acceptance of LGBTQ+ individuals in public roles.

Laphonza Butler (1979–)

Political Figure, Labor Leader

Laphonza Ronaique Butler is a prominent labor leader and political strategist, currently serving as the junior U.S. senator from California. Appointed by Governor Gavin Newsom in October 2023 to fill the vacancy left by the late Senator Dianne Feinstein, Butler made history as the first openly LGBTQ+ person to represent California in the Senate and the first Black lesbian to serve openly in Congress.

Born in Magnolia, Mississippi, Butler was raised in a working-class family. She earned a bachelor's degree in political science from Jackson State University in 2001. After graduation, she began her career as a union organizer, working with nurses, janitors, and hospital workers across various states. In 2009, she moved to California, where she continued her labor advocacy, notably serving as president of the Service Employees International Union (SEIU) Local 2015, the largest union in California representing long-term care workers.

During her tenure at SEIU Local 2015, Butler played a pivotal role in advocating for policies that improved the lives of workers, including efforts to raise California's minimum wage to $15 an hour and securing paid sick leave for home care workers. She also served as president of the SEIU California State Council, where she worked on initiatives to boost the state's minimum wage and raise income taxes on the wealthiest Californians.

In 2018, California governor Jerry Brown appointed Butler a regent of the University of California. She served until 2021, when she was named the third president of EMILY's List, the first Black woman to lead the organization. Also in 2018, she joined SCRB Strategies, a political consulting firm, where she advised various political campaigns, including that of Vice President Kamala Harris during her 2020 presidential bid. In October 2023, California governor Gavin Newsom chose Butler to fill the vacancy left by Senator Dianne Feinstein's death. After being sworn in, she announced that she would not seek election for a full Senate term or run in the November 2024 special election for the final two months of Feinstein's term.

Butler identifies as lesbian, and with her wife, Naneki Lee, a fellow labor organizer with the SEIU, they have a daughter. Butler's appointment to the Senate not only marked a significant milestone in representation but also underscored her lifelong commitment to advocating for workers, women, and marginalized communities.

Pete Buttigieg (1982–)

Political Figure

Peter Paul Montgomery "Pete" Buttigieg is the first openly gay person to serve as a U.S. Cabinet member, holding the position of secretary of transportation under President Joe Biden. He gained national prominence as the mayor of South Bend, Indiana, and as a Democratic candidate in the 2020 presidential election. His candidacy for president was historic as the first major openly gay candidate, and his leadership continues to break barriers for LGBTQ+ representation in the government.

Born in South Bend, Indiana, Buttigieg grew up in a Catholic family. His father, who was born in Malta, was a professor of English at the University of Notre Dame, where his mother taught linguistics. He attended Harvard University, graduating magna cum laude in 2004 with a degree in history and literature. He was later awarded a Rhodes Scholarship and attended the University of Oxford, earning a degree in philosophy, politics, and economics. After completing his studies, he worked as a consultant at McKinsey & Company before serving in the U.S. Navy Reserve, where he deployed to Afghanistan.

Buttigieg served as the mayor of South Bend, Indiana, from 2012 to 2020. During his tenure, "Mayor Pete," as he was known, focused on revitalizing the city's economy, infrastructure, and urban development. One of his signature achievements was transforming the struggling post-industrial city through initiatives such as Smart Streets, which revitalized downtown South Bend.

In 2020, Buttigieg became the first openly gay presidential candidate to win delegates in the Iowa caucuses. His candidacy represented a major milestone in LGBTQ+ representation on the national stage. In 2021, he was appointed as the U.S. secretary of transportation, where he worked to modernize infrastructure, promote sustainability, and manage transportation recovery efforts during the COVID-19 pandemic. His leadership of the Department of Transportation included overseeing the implementation of the historic Infrastructure Investment and Jobs Act.

Buttigieg came out as gay in 2015 while serving as mayor of South Bend. His openness about his sexuality was groundbreaking for a politician from a conservative state, and his marriage to Chasten Glezman in 2018 further highlighted his role as a symbol of LGBTQ+ progress in American politics. The couple welcomed twins in 2021.

Buttigieg's significance lies not only in his policy work but also in his groundbreaking role as an openly LGBTQ+ individual in high-level politics, setting a new precedent for representation. His presidential campaign inspired many young LGBTQ+ individuals and demonstrated a broader acceptance in American politics. His legacy is likely to be that of a trailblazer who helped to expand visibility and inclusion for LGBTQ+ Americans, paving the way for future leaders from diverse backgrounds.

Joanne Conte (1933–2013)

Political Figure

Joanne Conte made history in 1991 when she became one of the first transgender individuals to be elected to public office in the United States, serving on the Arvada (Colorado) City Council. Her election represented a significant breakthrough in transgender visibility in politics and helped to pave the way for future transgender politicians.

Born in Rochester, New York, Conte spent her first four decades living as Joseph J. Balone. Her family moved to Arvada, Colorado, in her adolescence, and she attended Arvada High School. Upon graduating, she enlisted to serve as a military Morse code operator in the U.S. Army and Air Force during the Korean War. After leaving the military, she attended the University of Colorado, earning a B.A. in philosophy and an MA in political science.

In 1973, Conte underwent transition surgery, changing her name and coming out as transgender to her family, who disowned her, and she publicly concealed her past and birth gender as she began her political career. Her involvement in political organizing began in the 1980s, organizing efforts to prevent a trash transfer station from being established in a local Arvada neighborhood. In 1991, she won a seat on the Arvada City Council. During her time on the Arvada City Council, she focused on local governance issues such as zoning laws, infrastructure, and community safety. Self-described as "a raging activist," her activism on behalf of the local community caused opponents to hire a private investigator to look into her background. Prior to a story outing her as transgender appeared, she came out publicly and lost her campaign to retain her seat on the Council largely because of a smear campaign run against her by opponents.

Conte went on to work as a political science professor at the University of Colorado and ran unsuccessfully for the Colorado House of Representatives. She eventually worked as an investigative radio host, covering local issues.

Conte's election to the Arvada City Council despite not having declared herself as openly transgender was still a significant moment in U.S. political history, marking one of the earliest instances of transgender representation in public office. Her work in local politics and bravery in being open about her identity in the face of bias and opposition continue to inspire transgender individuals seeking public office.

Andrew Cray (1986–2014)

Policy Analyst

Andrew S. Cray was a policy analyst and LGBTQ+ rights advocate whose work significantly advanced healthcare access and equality for the LGBTQ+ community. As a policy analyst at the Center for American Progress, he played a pivotal role in ensuring that LGBTQ+ individuals benefited from the Affordable Care Act (ACA). He cofounded Out2Enroll, an initiative aimed at connecting LGBTQ+ Americans with new health coverage options under the ACA. His efforts were instrumental in securing nondiscrimination protections for transgender individuals and removing discriminatory exclusions from health insurance plans.

Born in Chippewa Falls, Wisconsin, Cray was the valedictorian of his high school class in 2004. He pursued higher education at Northwestern University, where he was active in LGBTQ+ advocacy, serving as the activism chair for the Rainbow Alliance. He earned his bachelor's degree from Northwestern and later obtained a law degree from the University of Michigan Law School. During his time in law school, he focused on health and social policies affecting LGBTQ+ individuals, laying the groundwork for his future career in advocacy.

After coming out as a transgender man during college, Cray began his career as a legal fellow and policy analyst with the National Coalition for LGBT Health. He was lead researcher of the coalitions report on LGBTQ+ veterans' health. At the National LGBTQ Task Force in 2009, he wrote recommendations for inclusion in the health reform legislation being debated in Congress. He then became a health law and policy fellow at the National Center for Transgender Equality, where he advocated for fair access to health care for transgender people. In 2012, his work at the Center for American Progress included research on LGBTQ+ inclusion in state implementation of the ACA and efforts to obtain transgender-inclusive health insurance policies in several states and the District of Columbia. His leadership in launching Out2Enroll helped countless LGBTQ+ individuals navigate new health insurance options, ensuring broader access to necessary medical services.

Cray was married to Sarah McBride, a fellow LGBTQ+ advocate and political figure who became the first openly transgender person to be elected to Congress in November 2024. The couple married in August 2014, shortly before Cray's death. His work laid the foundation for ongoing efforts to ensure equitable healthcare access for LGBTQ+ individuals. In recognition of his contributions, the National Center for Transgender Equality established a law fellowship and award in his honor, supporting future leaders in transgender rights advocacy.

Sharice Davids (1980–)

Political Figure

Sharice Lynnette Davids is a U.S. congresswoman representing Kansas's 3rd Congressional District, one of the first two Native American women to be elected to Congress in 2018 and the first openly LGBTQ+ Native American to serve. Her election marked a historic breakthrough in representation for both Native Americans and the LGBTQ+ community in the government. She is a former mixed martial artist who brings a unique perspective to politics, championing issues like health care, infrastructure, and economic growth, particularly for her district and marginalized communities.

Born in Frankfurt, Germany, Davids grew up in Kansas and was primarily raised by her single mother, a U.S. Army veteran. She is a member of the Ho-Chunk people and attended Leavenworth High School, Haskell Indian Nations University, Johnson County Community College, and the University of Kansas before earning a B.B.A. from the University of Missouri, Kansas City, in 2007. She later received her J.D. from Cornell Law School in 2010. Before entering politics, she began competing in mixed martial arts (MMA) as an amateur in 2006 before becoming a professional in 2013. She eventually shifted her focus to work with various organizations focused on economic development, including Native American groups. Her career in law and nonprofit work, paired with her training and competition in MMA, honed her advocacy skills and commitment to social justice.

Davids's election to Congress in 2018 was a defining moment in U.S. political history. She became one of the first two Native American women (alongside Deb Haaland) to be elected to Congress and the first openly LGBTQ+ person to be elected to Congress from Kansas. Her platform focused on affordable health care, education, and fair wages, with a particular emphasis on the needs of Native American communities and LGBTQ+ individuals. She has championed policies supporting small businesses and infrastructural improvement in her district, successfully securing bipartisan support for several initiatives aimed at economic recovery and advancement. She has also been an advocate for healthcare reform, supporting measures to expand access to affordable health insurance and medication. As a member of the House Committee on Transportation and Infrastructure, she has contributed to significant policy discussions and actions related to public transportation, urban development, and climate-conscious infrastructure planning.

Davids is openly lesbian, a central aspect of her platform and advocacy in Congress. Her openness about her sexuality has been a source of inspiration for LGBTQ+ youth and has reinforced her commitment to fighting discrimination. She has not publicly disclosed specific details about her relationships, focusing instead on her public service and advocacy.

Davids's election to Congress signified a major stride toward inclusivity and representation in American politics. She represents a unique intersection of identities that enriches her legislative perspectives, making her a critical advocate for communities often overlooked by the government.

Steve Endean (1948–1993)

Lobbyist

The first professional lobbyist for gay men and lesbians in the United States, Stephen Robert "Steve" Endean was the director of the Gay Rights National Lobby in 1978 and founded the Human Rights Campaign Fund (later the Human Rights Campaign) in 1980, serving as its first executive director. It would become the nation's largest gay political organization.

Endean was born in Davenport, Iowa, and during the 1950s, he lived in Illinois. He graduated from high school in Bloomington, Minnesota, in 1966 before eventually attending the University of Minnesota, where he majored in political science. He became involved in local and state politics but feared that his sexual orientation was incompatible with public life and that, in his words, he must "stop being gay" in order to pursue a political career. Inspired by the Stonewall Uprising, he came out to his parents and decided to apply his political skills to promote gay rights through the political process.

In 1971, Endean founded Minnesota's first gay and lesbian political group, the Gay Rights Legislative Committee, and became the state's first gay and lesbian rights lobbyist. To supplement his meager salary as a lobbyist, he worked the coat check at a popular Minneapolis gay bar. His first major project was lobbying for a Minnesota bill to bar discrimination against homosexuals in the early 1970s, and he helped to pass Minneapolis's gay rights ordinances; Minnesota's statewide nondiscrimination bill finally passed just a few months before his death in 1993.

The backlash against gay rights that Endean experienced convinced him that nationwide action, especially a national gay and lesbian rights bill, was essential. He became an early cochair of the National Gay Task Force Board of Directors and in 1978 became the director of the Gay Rights National Lobby. In 1980, he created the Human Rights Campaign Fund, the first national gay rights political action committee, which eventually merged with the gay rights lobby group. In 1986, he created the Fairness Fund, an LGBTQ+ rights organization focused on grassroots political lobbying. It eventually was folded into the HRC and later renamed Speak Out.

Diagnosed HIV positive in 1985, Endean devoted his remaining years to AIDS issues through Speak Out while continuing to work on coalition building, especially with feminists and African Americans. While no national gay and lesbian rights act has yet been passed, many of its goals—in employment, health care, and domestic partnership rights—have been accomplished by other means, which was in no small measure due to his advocacy and coalition building. His memoir, *Bringing Lesbian and Gay Rights into the Mainstream*, was completed shortly before his death due to AIDS-related complications and published in 2006.

Paula Ettelbrick (1955–2011)

Lawyer

Paula Ettelbrick was a pioneering attorney and activist who played a pivotal role in advancing LGBTQ+ rights. Her leadership in organizations such as Lambda Legal, the International Gay and Lesbian Human Rights Commission (IGLHRC), and the Stonewall Community Foundation significantly influenced legal and policy frameworks supporting LGBTQ+ individuals. Her advocacy extended beyond legal battles; she was instrumental in shaping public discourse on LGBTQ+ issues, particularly concerning family law and human rights.

Born on an army base in Stuttgart, Germany, to American parents, Ettelbrick was raised in a devout Catholic family that emphasized social responsibility and equality. She earned her undergraduate degree from Northern Illinois University in DeKalb in 1978 and received a law degree in 1984 from Wayne State University. Early in her career, she worked in social services, notably at the Harbor Light Center in Boston, assisting homeless and alcoholic women. This experience deepened her commitment to social justice and led her to focus on legal advocacy for marginalized communities.

Ettelbrick's tenure as the first staff attorney and later legal director at Lambda Legal from 1988 to 1993 was marked by significant legal victories for LGBTQ+ rights. She was instrumental in developing legal strategies that challenged discriminatory laws and practices. During her tenure as legislative counsel to the Empire State Pride Agenda in New York from 1994 to 1999, she helped to push through New York City's rights for domestic partners and equal benefits to those of spouses. She said at the time, "If you're married, you can go to City Hall and file a tax appeal as a couple. Now, we can, too. It's very meaningful for those of us who live in families not joined by marriage." As executive director of the IGLHRC from 2003 to 2009, she expanded the organization's global reach, addressing human rights abuses against LGBTQ+ individuals worldwide. At the Stonewall Community Foundation, she focused on philanthropy to support LGBTQ+ causes, emphasizing community-driven initiatives.

Ettelbrick was a mother to two children,

whom she coparented with her former partner, Suzanne Goldberg. At the time of her passing, she was partnered with Marianne Haggerty. Her personal life reflected her advocacy for diverse family structures and the recognition of LGBTQ+ relationships.

Ettelbrick's legacy is characterized by an unwavering commitment to LGBTQ+ rights and social justice. Her legal expertise and strategic leadership in various organizations have left an indelible mark on the movement for equality. Her work not only advanced legal protections but also fostered a broader understanding of LGBTQ+ issues within the human rights framework.

Barney Frank (1940–)

Political Figure

Barnett "Barney" Frank is one of the most prominent openly gay politicians in U.S. history. He served in the U.S. House of Representatives from 1981 to 2013, representing Massachusetts. He is best known for his role in coauthoring the Dodd–Frank Wall Street Reform and Consumer Protection Act of 2010, which was designed to prevent another financial crisis like the one in 2008. He was also a staunch advocate for LGBTQ+ rights throughout his career, helping to advance legislation aimed at protecting LGBTQ+ individuals from discrimination.

Born in Bayonne, New Jersey, Frank grew up in a Jewish working-class family. He excelled at writing and debate in high school and attended Harvard University, earning his bachelor's degree in 1962. He would remain at Harvard for another six years, teaching undergraduate government classes while pursuing his Ph.D. in government. He left before completing his degree in 1968 to become Boston mayor Kevin White's chief assistant for three years before serving for a year as Congressman Michael J. Harrington's administrative assistant. In 1977, he graduated from Harvard Law School.

Frank began his political career in the Massachusetts legislature in 1972. By 1980, he won a seat in the U.S. House of Representatives, where he would serve for over three decades. Before he ran for Congress, he began coming out to friends as gay but remained publicly closeted until May 1987, when he was prompted to come out due to increased media attention and the death of Stewart McKinney, a closeted bisexual Republican representative from Connecticut. After McKinney's death, Frank told *The Washington Post* that "there was an unfortunate debate about 'Was he or wasn't he?'… I said to myself, I don't want that to happen to me."

In 1989, Steve Gobie, a male escort with whom Frank had a sexual relationship in 1985 and with whom he shared his apartment until 1987, when Frank evicted him after his landlord complained that Gobie was entertaining clients in the apartment, told the politically conservative newspaper the *Washington Times* about his relationship with Frank. The relatively new paper seized the opportunity to enhance its readership and promote allegations of a prominent Democrat involved with a gay prostitution ring being run out of his apartment. The article attracted the desired attention and led to calls for an investigation. Frank asked the House Committee on Ethics to investigate, with the result that in 1990, the House of Representatives voted to reprimand Frank for improper use of political influence to fix parking tickets and influence probation officers for Gobie. The House stopped short of a more serious censure, and Frank, who recovered quickly from the scandal, easily won reelection the same year.

Frank was a vocal advocate of LGBTQ+ rights. He played a leading role in efforts to repeal the "Don't Ask, Don't Tell" policy, which prevented openly gay individuals from serving in the military. He also supported the Employment Non-Discrimination Act (ENDA) and fought for marriage equality long before it was legalized nationwide.

One of Frank's most significant accomplishments was his coauthorship of the Dodd–Frank Act, which sought to overhaul the U.S. financial regulatory system in response to the 2008 financial crisis. The act introduced stricter regulations on banks and financial institutions, established the Consumer Financial Protection Bureau (CFPB), and aimed to protect consumers from predatory lending and other financial abuses. In 2012, he married his longtime partner, James Ready, becoming the first sitting U.S. congressman to marry someone of the same sex. His openness about his sexuality and leadership on LGBTQ+ issues made him a role model for many LGBTQ+ individuals in politics and public life.

In January 2013, Frank retired after more than 30 years of service in the House of Representatives. His career was chronicled in the documentary *Compared to What?: The Improbable Journey of Barney Frank* (2014) and in his autobiography, *Frank: A Life in Politics from the Great Society to Same-Sex Marriage* (2015). In 2022, author and illustrator Eric Omer released a graphic novel based on Frank's life: *Smahtguy: The Life and Times of Barney Frank.*

Phyllis Frye (1948–)

Lawyer, Judge

Phyllis Frye is a pioneering attorney and judge celebrated as the first openly transgender judge in the United States. Her extensive legal career and activism have significantly advanced transgender rights and visibility. In 2010, she was appointed as an associate judge for the City of Houston Municipal Court, marking a historic milestone in the judiciary.

Born in San Antonio, Texas, Frye was the second of three children to her engineer father and homemaker mother. She earned the rank of Eagle Scout and was a member of the Junior Reserve Officers' Training Corps during her youth. She attended Texas A&M University, where she graduated with a BS in civil engineering and an M.S. in mechanical engineering. She was also a member of the university's Corps of Cadets and the Texas A&M Singing Cadets. After graduation, she served as a first lieutenant in the U.S. Army.

While serving in West Germany, Frye disclosed her struggles with her sexual identity to her Army superiors, who sent her back to the United States in an effort to "cure" her. These efforts involved drug therapy, hypnosis, and aversion therapy. When these treatments failed, her first wife filed for divorce and took custody of their son. She was honorably discharged from the Army in 1972 after being forced to resign.

Frye began transitioning in 1976 and was repeatedly dismissed from engineering jobs after employers learned of her gender identity. She earned an M.B.A. and a J.D. from the University of Houston but could not find a firm that would hire her. She eventually took an interest in criminal defense, representing indigent defendants as a court-appointed attorney. She later represented transgender clients in name-change and discrimination cases. In 2010, Houston mayor Annise Parker appointed Frye an associate judge for the City of Houston Municipal Court. Her appointment was publicly opposed by the Houston Area Pastors Council, but Mayor Parker pushed through the appointment, citing Frye's long experience as a trial attorney. The Houston City Council unanimously approved her appointment, becoming the first openly transgender judge in the United States.

Frye was married to Patricia "Trish" Dooley Frye for 47 years until Trish's passing in 2020. She is also a parent and grandparent and identifies as a lesbian widow. She retired from the bench in January 2023.

Maura Healey (1971–)

Political Figure

In 2022, Maura Healey became one of the first openly lesbian governors of a U.S. state (alongside Oregon's Tina Kotek). She was also the first woman to be elected governor of Massachusetts. Prior to this, she had already broken barriers as the first openly gay attorney general in the United States when she was elected to that position in Massachusetts in 2015. Serving as attorney general, she made her mark as a progressive leader on issues such as civil rights, health care, and consumer protection. Her legal work has been instrumental in defending marriage equality, fighting discrimination, and challenging harmful federal policies.

Healey was born in Bethesda, Maryland, and grew up in Hampton Falls, New Hampshire. Her mother was a nurse, and her father was a captain in the U.S. Public Health Service and an engineer. After they divorced, her mother sold her wedding ring to pay for a backyard basketball court for her daughter. She attended Harvard University, where she played on the women's basketball team and graduated with a degree in government in 1992. After college, she spent two years playing professional basketball in Europe before attending Northeastern University School of Law, earning her J.D. in 1998.

Healey began her legal career as a clerk and then worked as a private attorney before joining the Massachusetts Office of the Attorney General in 2007. Her legal expertise focused on civil rights, and she played a leading role in advocating for LGBTQ+ rights during her early years as an assistant attorney general, particularly in leading the state's challenge to the federal Defense of Marriage Act.

In 2014, Healey became the first openly lesbian woman to be elected attorney general of a U.S. state and the first openly LGBTQ+ person to be elected to statewide office in Massachusetts. As attorney general, she focused on protecting civil rights, fighting the opioid crisis, and challenging the Trump administration's policies, including efforts to dismantle the Affordable Care Act and undermine environmental protections. She was a vocal advocate for gun control, women's rights, and immigrant protections, consistently positioning herself as a progressive leader.

In 2022, Healey was elected governor of Massachusetts, further cementing her as a groundbreaking figure in U.S. politics. Her leading achievements in office include passing the Affordable Homes Act to address the housing crisis, implementing the first state tax cuts in two decades, and launching free community college for residents. Her administration has prioritized public safety and justice, pardoning thousands with misdemeanor cannabis convictions and creating a commission to combat rising anti-Semitism.

Richard A. Heyman (1935–1994)

Political Figure

Richard A. Heyman was a pioneer for LGBTQ+ visibility in American politics, becoming one of the first openly gay mayors in the United States when he was elected mayor of Key West, Florida, in 1983. He was at that time among the first openly gay Americans to be elected to public office. His leadership and advocacy for LGBTQ+ rights, particularly during the early years of the AIDS epidemic, set a precedent for LGBTQ+ representation in local government.

Heyman grew up in Grand Rapids, Ohio, in a conservative era when LGBTQ+ individuals were often marginalized.

An Eagle Scout, he graduated from Ohio State University in 1957 and then served in the Army. He began his career as a schoolteacher in Grand Rapids and later founded several employment agencies in Toledo before moving to Key West in the mid-1960s. There, he cofounded the Gingerbread Square Gallery in 1972 and became a community leader and advocate for LGBTQ+ rights.

Heyman was elected to the Key West City Commission and elected mayor of Key West in 1983, marking a significant milestone in U.S. history. "When he was elected to the city commission," Key West resident Michael Dively said, "there were very few if any openly gay and lesbians who had been elected to any public office in this country." He was reelected in 1987 during a time when the AIDS crisis was devastating the LGBTQ+ community. He worked to ensure that Key West provided support and healthcare services for those affected by the epidemic. He also used his platform to raise awareness and combat the stigma surrounding HIV/AIDS. His tenure as mayor is remembered for his commitment to inclusivity, economic growth, and civil rights. Under his leadership, Key West became a more welcoming and progressive city, with a growing LGBTQ+ community that thrived under his stewardship.

Heyman died of pneumonia brought on by AIDS at the age of 59, survived by his longtime partner, artist John Kiraly. His legacy as one of the first openly gay mayors in the United States helped to pave the way for LGBTQ+ representation in the government. His leadership in Key West during the AIDS epidemic and advocacy for LGBTQ+ rights left a lasting impact on both his city and the broader LGBTQ+ movement.

Donna Hitchens (1947–)

Lawyer, Judge

Donna Hitchens is a renowned judge and civil rights attorney known for her advocacy in LGBTQ+ rights and family law. She cofounded the National Center for Lesbian Rights (NCLR) and became the first openly gay elected female judge in the United States. Her contributions to the legal landscape for LGBTQ+ families have been significant: She helped to secure legal protections for LGBTQ+ individuals, parents, and families, and her work on family law and LGBTQ+ rights has reshaped the legal possibilities for LGBTQ+ families in California and beyond.

Hitchens was born in 1947 in rural Pennsylvania and was the first in her family to complete high school. She earned a bachelor's degree in community leadership and development from Springfield College and a master's degree in counseling from there before earning a law degree in 1977 at the University of California, Berkeley, where she became actively involved in advocacy for LGBTQ+ rights. After her schooling, she worked with grassroots organizations to support marginalized groups, eventually directing her focus toward creating legal structures that would recognize and protect LGBTQ+ individuals and families.

In 1977, Hitchens cofounded the National Center for Lesbian Rights, a nonprofit organization dedicated to advocating for LGBTQ+ legal issues. Under her leadership, the NCLR tackled cases involving parenting rights, child custody, and family protections, which were pioneering legal battles at a time when LGBTQ+ families had little legal recognition. Her influence continued to grow when she was elected to the San Francisco Superior Court in 1991, becoming the first openly gay elected female judge in the United States. As a judge, she presided over family court cases with a focus on fairness and empathy, especially concerning LGBTQ+ families. She championed legal changes in adoption and parenting rights, helping to create legal precedents that ensured that LGBTQ+ families could access the same protections as other families.

Hitchens married Nancy Davis in 2008. She has often emphasized that her identity as a gay woman has been a source of strength in her career, allowing her to approach family law cases with a unique and empathetic perspective that considers the specific challenges faced by LGBTQ+ individuals. She retired after 20 years from the San Francisco Superior Court in 2010.

Hitchens's legacy is that of a trailblazer in both the legal and LGBTQ+ communities. Her pioneering work in founding the NCLR and her accomplishments on the bench have ensured that LGBTQ+ families are recognized and protected by the law. Her career represents a profound shift in the American legal system toward inclusivity and fairness for LGBTQ+ individuals, especially those seeking family rights. Her dedication to justice has made her a lasting influence in family law and LGBTQ+ advocacy.

James Hormel (1933–2021)

Diplomat, Business Executive

James Catherwood Hormel was an heir to the Hormel Foods Corporation fortune and became the first openly gay U.S. ambassador, serving in Luxembourg from 1999 to 2001. He was a successful businessman and prominent philanthropist, particularly in LGBTQ+ causes. He helped to fund the creation of the James C. Hormel LGBTQIA Center at the San Francisco Public Library.

Hormel was born in Austin, Minnesota, into the family that founded the Hormel Foods Corporation, a major American food processing company best known for products such as SPAM. He grew up in a privileged environment, but his upbringing also instilled in him a strong sense of responsibility and commitment to public service. He attended Swarthmore College, where he earned a B.A. in history in 1955. He then pursued a law degree at the University of Chicago Law School, graduating in 1958. While in law school, he served as the dean of students, and after graduating, he briefly worked in law before transitioning to a role in his family's business.

Though he was deeply connected to his family's company, Hormel's career path led him toward philanthropy, education, and public service rather than direct involvement in the day-to-day operations of the business. His most notable achievement was his appointment as the U.S. ambassador to Luxembourg by President Bill Clinton in 1999. His nomination faced considerable opposition due to his sexual orientation, making the Senate confirmation process unusually contentious. Despite the opposition, President Clinton used a recess appointment to install Hormel as ambassador, making him the first openly gay person to serve in such a role. His tenure as ambassador was widely regarded as successful, and his appointment was a groundbreaking moment for LGBTQ+ representation in the government.

Hormel was openly gay, and his visibility as a gay man in both the business and political arenas made him a trailblazer for LGBTQ+ rights. He was married to Alice McElroy Parker, with whom he had five children, before coming out as gay later in life. After his divorce, he embraced his identity and became an outspoken advocate for LGBTQ+ issues.

In addition to his diplomatic work, Hormel was a dedicated philanthropist, focusing much of his efforts on LGBTQ+ rights, education, and the arts. He established the James C. Hormel LGBTQIA Center at the San Francisco Public Library, one of the largest collections of LGBTQ+ historical documents in the United States. He was also a significant supporter of various LGBTQ+ organizations, including the Human Rights Campaign and Lambda Legal.

Hormel's personal life was marked by his commitment to his family, philanthropic endeavors, and advocacy for equality. His openness about his sexuality, particularly during a time when being openly gay was met with significant prejudice, was a powerful statement that helped to pave the way for greater acceptance and representation of LGBTQ+ individuals in public life.

Karine Jean-Pierre (1974–)

Political Figure

Karine Jean-Pierre is a prominent political strategist and activist and was the first openly gay person and first Black woman to serve as the White House press secretary. Her career spans multiple high-profile roles, including working for advocacy organizations, political campaigns, and as a senior advisor to President Joe Biden. Her historic appointment as press secretary marked a significant milestone in U.S. political history, representing both racial and LGBTQ+ diversity at one of the highest levels of government communication.

Born in Martinique to Haitian immigrant parents, Jean-Pierre's family later moved to Queens, New York, when she was 5 years old. Her father worked as a cab driver, and her mother worked as a healthcare worker. Both parents deeply influenced her views on resilience, community, and social justice. She earned her bachelor's degree from the New York Institute of Technology in 1997 and a master's degree in public affairs from Columbia University's School of International and Public Affairs in 2003. She began her career working on various political campaigns and nonprofit advocacy organizations, quickly making a name for herself as a talented strategist and communicator.

Jean-Pierre served as regional political director for the Obama presidential campaign in 2008 and was later a senior advisor for *MoveOn.org*, where she was involved in significant grassroots activism. In 2020, she joined Joe Biden's campaign as a senior advisor and later served as principal deputy press secretary before her historic appointment as White House press secretary in 2022. As press secretary, she was the face of the administration's communication efforts, responsible for articulating and defending policies on a wide range of issues from the COVID-19 pandemic to social justice and climate policy. Her role involved balancing transparency with diplomacy, which she handled with a grounded, authentic approach that resonated with diverse audiences.

Jean-Pierre identifies as lesbian and was in a relationship with Suzanne Malveaux, a CNN national correspondent, until 2023. Together, they have an adopted daughter. Her openness about her sexuality and relationship has been an inspiration to LGBTQ+ individuals and a powerful statement about visibility. Her work has amplified underrepresented voices, and her position as a barrier-breaking public official has inspired countless people, especially within the LGBTQ+ and Black communities.

Walter Jenkins (1918–1985)

Political Advisor

Walter Wilson Jenkins was a longtime political advisor and close aide to President Lyndon B. Johnson who played a key role in Johnson's political rise, particularly during the 1960 presidential campaign and Johnson's time as vice president and president. He was considered one of Johnson's most trusted aides, serving as the special assistant to the president and playing a pivotal role in policy formation and daily operations at the White House. However, his career came to an abrupt end in 1964 when he was arrested for a homosexual act, a scandal that rocked the Johnson administration during a highly sensitive election period. Jenkins's case brought attention to the discrimination faced by LGBTQ+ individuals in the government and is often cited as a key moment in LGBTQ+ history.

Jenkins was born on March 23, 1918, in Jolly, Texas. He grew up mainly in Wichita Falls, Texas, and attended Midwestern College and the University of Texas, Austin, where he studied government and journalism. He met Lyndon B. Johnson while still in college, and they formed a close professional and personal relationship. After graduating, he went to work for Johnson, helping him in his early congressional campaigns. He served in the U.S. Army Air Forces during World War II, gaining the rank of major, but returned to political life after the war, continuing his work as Johnson's trusted aide.

Jenkins was instrumental in managing the day-to-day operations of Johnson's office, particularly during Johnson's tenure as Senate majority leader and later as vice president. He was known for his organizational skills and loyalty, helping Johnson navigate complex legislative challenges and political battles.

During the 1960 presidential campaign, Jenkins played a significant role in Johnson's selection as John F. Kennedy's running mate and later in managing the vice presidential office. When Johnson became president after Kennedy's assassination in 1963, Jenkins was by his side, assisting with policy decisions during the formative years of Johnson's presidency, including the passage of landmark legislation such as the Civil Rights Act of 1964.

However, Jenkins's career was cut short when, just weeks before the 1964 presidential election, he was arrested in Washington, D.C., for engaging in a homosexual act in a YMCA bathroom. The scandal was widely publicized, and he resigned from his position. The incident, though quickly downplayed by Johnson's campaign, became a significant moment in the history of LGBTQ+ individuals in public life, highlighting the intense stigma and legal risks associated with being gay at the time.

After his resignation from the White House, Jenkins largely retreated from public life. Following the scandal surrounding his arrest, he returned to his home in Austin, Texas, where he focused on rebuilding his life away from the spotlight. He was married and fathered six children. He separated from his wife in the early 1970s but never divorced.

Despite the scandal, Johnson was elected in 1964 by a large margin over Barry Goldwater. Political commentator Theodore H. White observed in his assessment of the 1964 election campaign, "Perhaps the most amazing of all events of the campaign of 1964 is that the nation faced the fact [of Jenkins's arrest and resignation]—and shrugged its shoulders."

Barbara Jordan (1936–1996)

Political Figure, Educator

Barbara Charline Jordan was a pioneering politician, civil rights leader, and educator whose influential career broke numerous barriers for African Americans and women in the government. Serving as a member of the U.S. House of Representatives for Texas from 1973 to 1979, she was the first Black woman to be elected to the Texas Senate, the first Black person to be elected to the U.S. Congress from Texas after Reconstruction, and the first Southern Black woman to be elected to Congress. Known for her eloquence and dedication to justice, she rose to national prominence during the Watergate hearings, in which her powerful speeches underscored the importance of the Constitution and rule of law. While she never publicly came out as a lesbian, the National Archives has designated her as the first LGBTQ+ woman in Congress.

Born in Houston, Texas, Jordan grew up in Houston's impoverished Fourth Ward in a close-knit African American neighborhood. Her parents, committed to education and self-discipline, inspired her ambitions. She attended segregated public schools and graduated magna cum laude from the all-Black Texas Southern University, a historically Black college, and went on to earn her law degree from Boston University School of Law in 1959. Returning to Texas, she opened her own law practice initially from her family's dining room table and eventually in a second-story office above a print shop. She became active in local politics, and in 1966, she made history as the first Black state senator in Texas since Reconstruction, marking the beginning of her political journey.

Elected to Congress in 1972, Jordan's achievements were remarkable and influential. During her time in the U.S. House of Representatives, she was instrumental in the passage of civil rights legislation and worked on improving social services, expanding voting rights, and enhancing protections for vulnerable communities. Her electrifying speeches during the 1974 House Committee on the Judiciary hearings on the impeachment of President Richard Nixon solidified her reputation as a defender of democracy. In 1976, she became the first Black woman to deliver a keynote address at the Democratic National Convention, inspiring audiences nationwide with her calls for unity and integrity in the government. After retiring from Congress in 1979, she joined the University of Texas, Austin, as a professor and continued to advocate for civil rights, coauthoring key immigration reforms in the 1990s.

Although private about her personal life and never publicly identifying herself as a lesbian, Jordan had a two-decade relationship with Nancy Earl, an educational psychologist, with whom she shared a home. Earl was a close confidante and companion, especially during Jordan's later years when she faced serious health issues, including multiple sclerosis.

Jordan's legacy as a groundbreaking politician, civil rights advocate, and educator endures as an example of courage, eloquence, and dedication to justice. Her work in Congress championed equality, inspired reforms, and set a powerful example of integrity in public service. Her speeches and writings continue to resonate, and her life serves as an enduring model for those fighting for social justice and ethical leadership.

Roberta "Robbie" Kaplan (1966–)

Lawyer

Roberta Ann "Robbie" Kaplan is a prominent civil rights attorney celebrated for her landmark work in LGBTQ+ rights and significant role in high-profile legal battles that have advanced equality in the United States. Best known for representing Edith Windsor in *United States v. Windsor*, she played a central role in the 2013 Supreme Court decision that struck down the Defense of Marriage Act (DOMA), marking a major victory for marriage equality. Beyond her impact on LGBTQ+ rights, she has been a leader in combating hate speech and white supremacy, most notably through her representation of plaintiffs in the 2017 Charlottesville rally case. She represented E. Jean Carroll in her civil sexual assault and defamation case against Donald Trump, winning $5 million judgments against him.

Born in Cleveland, Ohio, Kaplan was raised in a Jewish family that emphasized the importance of education and justice. She attended Harvard University, where she graduated magna cum laude with a degree in Russian history and literature in 1988 and later earned her J.D. from Columbia Law School in 1991. Her dedication to civil rights law became evident early in her career, particularly as she began working with prominent law firms and established herself as an advocate for social justice. Her personal experience as a lesbian further fueled her commitment to LGBTQ+ advocacy, shaping her career in a meaningful way.

Kaplan's achievements are many and impactful, with her work on *United States v. Windsor* standing as a cornerstone of LGBTQ+ legal history. Representing Edith Windsor, who was required to pay estate taxes after the death of her spouse due to DOMA, she argued that the act was unconstitutional because it denied same-sex couples the same federal rights afforded to heterosexual couples. The Supreme Court ruled in Windsor's favor, effectively dismantling DOMA and paving the way for nationwide marriage equality in *Obergefell v. Hodges* two years later. She also co-founded the organization Time's Up Legal Defense Fund, which supports individuals facing sexual harassment, and has been a vocal critic of hate groups, representing victims of the Charlottesville Unite the Right rally in a lawsuit against its organizers. Her firm, Kaplan Hecker & Fink, is known for its dedication to public interest law and social justice, further expanding her legacy in civil rights.

Kaplan is married to Rachel Lavine, a Democratic activist and real estate executive. The couple shares a strong commitment to progressive causes and are parents to a son. She is open about her identity as a lesbian and advocates for LGBTQ+ visibility and acceptance. Her marriage and family life underscore her belief in the importance of legal protections for LGBTQ+ families and the right to equality.

Kaplan's work has left an indelible mark on American civil rights law, particularly in advancing LGBTQ+ rights and fighting hate-based movements. Her impact extends far beyond her courtroom victories, inspiring future generations of advocates to uphold justice and equality. As a fierce defender of civil rights, she continues to be a guiding force in legal battles that address discrimination and promote inclusion.

Tina Kotek (1966–)

Political Figure

Christine "Tina" Kotek has been a trailblazer in Oregon politics and a fierce advocate for progressive values. As the 39th governor of Oregon, Kotek, along with Maura Healey of Massachusetts, became the first openly lesbian governors in the United States. Her rise from Oregon House representative to the highest office in the state reflects a career built on resilience, advocacy, and a commitment to equitable public policy. Her achievements include setting ambitious goals for housing and mental health initiatives, shaping Oregon's legislative agenda as the longest-serving speaker of the House, and making history with her groundbreaking election to the governorship.

Born in York, Pennsylvania, Kotek moved to Oregon in 1987. She pursued her education at the University of Oregon, earning a BS in religious studies in 1990 before continuing to the University of Washington, earning a master's degree in international studies and comparative religion. Her early career began in public policy advocacy, working with nonprofits focused on hunger and child welfare. At the Oregon Food Bank and later as policy director for Children First for Oregon, she honed her skills in shaping policy to support vulnerable communities, sparking her eventual transition to a political career.

Kotek's political career began in 2006 when she was elected to the Oregon House of Representatives for the 44th Congressional District, covering parts of north and northeast Portland. Quickly recognized for her leadership, she held positions as Democratic whip in 2009, co-speaker pro tempore in 2011, and House Democratic leader in 2012. In 2013, she was elected speaker of the House, becoming the first openly lesbian woman in the nation to hold this position and later becoming the longest-serving speaker in Oregon's history. Her tenure was marked by critical work in passing legislation on housing, labor rights, and health care. Becoming governor in 2023, she has prioritized affordable housing, declaring a state of emergency on homelessness shortly after taking office, and introduced initiatives to build 36,000 new housing units annually. She has also placed significant emphasis on improving behavioral health services and investing in early childhood education, reflecting her commitment to addressing Oregon's most pressing challenges.

Kotek has been married to Aimee Kotek Wilson, a social worker, for over 19 years. The couple shares a commitment to public service, and Kotek's openness about her sexuality and relationship has made her an inspirational figure for LGBTQ+ representation in politics.

Kathy Kozachenko (1953–)

Political Figure

Kathy Kozachenko is a politician and activist who made history in 1974 by becoming the first openly gay person to be elected to public office in the United States. Her election to the Ann Arbor City Council marked a significant milestone in LGBTQ+ political representation.

Born in Alexandria, Virginia, Kozachenko, of Ukrainian descent, grew up mainly in Plymouth, Michigan. She attended the University of Michigan, where she became actively involved in social justice movements, including the gay liberation movement. Her political engagement deepened during her time at the university, leading her to join the Human Rights Party (HRP), a progressive third party that was focused on civil rights and social justice issues.

In the early 1970s, only 10 cities in the United States had laws specific to gay rights. Most pertained either to housing or public employment. Ann Arbor, Michigan, was an exception. The city had enacted a human rights ordinance that protected gays in housing and employment. In 1974, at the age of 21, Kozachenko ran for city council on a platform saying that the law had not been enforced. She campaigned as an openly gay candidate and won the election to represent the city's 2nd Ward by 52 votes, becoming the first openly gay person to be elected to public office in the United States. She was the first person to show that an openly gay person could run for and be elected to public office. This was a year before Elaine Noble was elected to the Massachusetts House of Representatives and three years before Harvey Milk, often mistakenly identified as the "first elected openly gay official," was elected to the San Francisco Board of Supervisors in 1977.

During her term, Kozachenko advocated for rent control, police reform, and the enforcement of the city's human rights ordinance, which protected gay and lesbian individuals in housing and employment. After serving her term, she stepped back from electoral politics but remained active in social justice advocacy. She moved to Pittsburgh, Pennsylvania, where she continued her activism and lived with her partner of over 25 years. In 2021, she was inducted into the LGBTQ Victory Hall of Fame, recognizing her pioneering role in LGBTQ+ political representation. In recognition of her contributions, the city of Ann Arbor is raising funds as of this writing (October 2025) to erect a statue in her honor.

Malcolm L. Lazin (1943–)

Lawyer

Malcolm L. Lazin is the executive director of Equality Forum, a national and international LGBTQ+ civil rights organization that coordinates LGBTQ+ History Month, produces documentary films, and leads various educational initiatives around LGBTQ+ issues. He was a federal prosecutor who led successful grand jury investigations into public corruption.

Lazin was raised in Lebanon, Pennsylvania. He attended Lebanon Valley College, majoring in biology and chemistry, before attending Boston University School of Law. After graduating in 1968, he began his career as a federal prosecutor. His early work in law focused on civil rights and justice, but his passion for LGBTQ+ equality led him to found the Equality Forum in 1993, an organization that has since become one of the leading LGBTQ+ advocacy groups in the United States. Under his leadership, it has played a pivotal role in bringing visibility to LGBTQ+ figures and historical milestones. The Equality Forum has spearheaded major initiatives such as the LGBTQ Rights Hall of Fame and LGBTQ+ History Month, which educates the public about key moments and leaders in the LGBTQ+ movement.

Lazin, who is openly gay, has also been recognized for his efforts to promote marriage equality and antidiscrimination legislation. His work has earned him numerous awards, including the Justice in Action Award and the Human Rights Campaign's Equality Award. Through his activism, he has become a key figure in the national movement for LGBTQ+ equality.

Rachel Leland Levine (1957–)

Government Official, Physician

Rachel Leland Levine is a distinguished pediatrician and public health official renowned for her significant contributions to medicine and trailblazing role as an openly transgender government leader. In 2021, she was appointed as the 17th assistant secretary for health for the U.S. Department of Health and Human Services (HHS), making history as the first openly transgender federal official to be confirmed by the Senate. In this capacity, she oversees national public health initiatives and serves as a four-star admiral in the U.S. Public Health Service Commissioned Corps, focusing on improving the health and well-being of all Americans.

Born in Wakefield, Massachusetts, Levine pursued her undergraduate studies at Harvard College, followed by a medical degree from Tulane University School of Medicine. She completed her training in pediatrics and adolescent medicine at the Mount Sinai Medical Center in New York City. Her early career was marked by her focus on the intersection of mental and physical health, particularly in treating children, adolescents, and young adults. She served as a professor of pediatrics and psychiatry at the Penn State College of Medicine and held leadership roles, including vice chair for clinical affairs for the Department of Pediatrics and chief of the Division of Adolescent Medicine and Eating Disorders at the Penn State Hershey Medical Center.

Levine's tenure as Pennsylvania's physician general beginning in 2015 and later as the state's secretary of health was marked by her leadership in addressing the opioid crisis, improving maternal health, and enhancing immunization rates among children. Notably, she issued a standing order for the anti-overdose drug Naloxone, allowing law enforcement to carry it and enabling Pennsylvanians to purchase it without a prescription, a measure credited with saving numerous lives. She led the public health response on COVID-19 in Pennsylvania.

In 2021, President Joe Biden nominated Levine to serve as assistant secretary for health. She won confirmation in the Senate when two Republicans—Susan Collins and Lisa Murkowski—joined all Democrats to confirm her nomination. The same year, she was commissioned as a four-star admiral in the U.S. Public Health Service Commissioned Corps, becoming the first female four-star admiral in the Commissioned Corps. She left office on January 20, 2025.

Levine married Martha Peaslee in 1988, and the couple raised two children together. They divorced in 2013. Her career exemplifies a steadfast commitment to public health and equality. Her leadership roles and advocacy efforts have significantly advanced healthcare policies and LGBTQ+ rights, making her a pivotal figure in contemporary American public health.

Lori Lightfoot (1962–)

Political Figure

Lori Elaine Lightfoot made history as the first Black woman and the first openly gay mayor of Chicago, elected in 2019. She was the second openly lesbian woman (after Annise Parker in Houston) to serve as mayor of one of the 10 most populous cities in the United States. Her victory represented a significant step forward for LGBTQ+ and racial representation in the third largest city in the United States.

Lightfoot was born in Massillon, Ohio. She grew up in a working-class family. Her mother was a nighttime healthcare aide; her father was a factory worker and janitor. She earned her bachelor's degree in political science from the University of Michigan in 1984 and later graduated from the University of Chicago Law School. After law school, she worked as a federal prosecutor, handling cases involving corruption, fraud, and violent crimes.

Before becoming mayor, Lightfoot served in various leadership roles in Chicago's government, including as president of the Chicago Police Board and chair of the Police Accountability Task Force. Her work focused on reforming the police department and increasing accountability. Her election as mayor of Chicago was a historic victory not only because of her identity as a Black, openly gay woman but also because she won with more than 70 percent of the vote. Her administration focused on addressing systemic inequality in Chicago, with policies aimed at increasing affordable housing, improving public safety, and reforming the city's police department.

Lightfoot took office during a challenging time, facing issues such as police misconduct, gun violence, and economic inequality. Her efforts to reform the Chicago Police Department were particularly notable, as she implemented new accountability measures and worked to rebuild trust between the police and the community. Her tenure was also marked by her response to the COVID-19 pandemic, during which she implemented measures to support public health, local businesses, and marginalized communities affected by the crisis.

Despite overwhelming support for her election to become mayor, winning every ward in the city in 2019, Lightfoot was defeated in her reelection bid in 2023, as the rising crime rate and economic fallout from the pandemic had cost her support.

Lightfoot married Amy Eshleman, a former Chicago Public Library employee, and the couple are raising an adopted daughter. Her election as the first Black woman and openly gay mayor of Chicago marked a turning point for diversity in U.S. politics. Her leadership in tackling some of the city's most pressing issues, including police reform and economic inequality, has made her a significant figure in modern urban governance.

Sean Patrick Maloney (1966–)

Political Figure, Diplomat

Sean Patrick Maloney is a lawyer and politician who served as the U.S. ambassador to the Organisation for Economic

Co-operation and Development (OECD) from April 2024 to January 2025. Prior to this role, he represented New York's 18th Congressional District in the U.S. House of Representatives from 2013 to 2023, becoming the first openly gay person to be elected to Congress from New York.

Born in Sherbrooke, Quebec, Canada, Maloney was raised in Hanover, New Hampshire. He earned a B.A. in international relations and a J.D. from the University of Virginia in 1992. He began his political career as a volunteer for Bill Clinton's 1992 presidential campaign, later serving as a senior West Wing adviser and White House staff secretary during the Clinton administration. He often called himself "the highest-ranking openly homosexual man on the White House staff."

Maloney ran unsuccessfully for the Democratic nomination for New York attorney general in 2006. In 2012, he won election to Congress in New York's 18th Congressional District, becoming the first openly gay person to be elected to Congress from New York. During his tenure in Congress, he was a member of the centrist New Democratic Coalition and chaired both the Subcommittee on Coast Guard and Maritime Transportation of the U.S. House Committee on Transportation and Infrastructure as well as the Commodity Markets, Digital Assets, and Rural Development Subcommittee of the House Committee on Agriculture. He also served on the House Permanent Select Committee on Intelligence and was elected by his colleagues to House leadership in 2020, becoming the highest ranking openly LGBTQ+ person ever to serve in the House. He authored more than 40 pieces of legislation that became law, focusing on issues such as infrastructure, agriculture, and national security. In 2024, he was confirmed by the Senate as ambassador and permanent representative to the OECD.

Maloney married his partner of 22 years, Randy Florke, in 2014. They raised three children. Maloney has been open about his sexuality, advocating for LGBTQ+ rights throughout his career.

Sarah McBride (1990–)

Political Figure

Sarah Elizabeth McBride is a pioneering politician and LGBTQ+ rights advocate who made history in November 2024 by becoming the first openly transgender person to be elected to the U.S. Congress, representing Delaware's at-large congressional district. Prior to this, she served as a Delaware state senator, where she was the nation's first openly transgender state senator. Throughout her career, she has been instrumental in advancing legislation on issues such as paid family leave, healthcare access, and LGBTQ+ equality, significantly influencing both state and national policies.

Born in Wilmington, Delaware, McBride developed an early interest in politics and advocacy. She graduated from the Cab Calloway School of the Arts in 2009, founded by her mother, and earned a bachelor's degree in government from American University in 2013. During her time at American University, she was elected student body president and, in 2012, publicly came out as transgender in a student newspaper op-ed, marking a significant moment in her personal and public advocacy journeys.

In 2012, McBride interned at the White House and was the first openly transgender woman to work there in any capacity. In 2013, she joined the board of directors of Equality Delaware and became the state's leading advocate for legal protections and hate crime legislation for transgender residents of Delaware. In 2016, she became the first openly transgender person to address a major U.S. political party convention when she spoke at the Democratic National Convention. In 2020, she was elected to the Delaware Senate, representing the 1st Congressional District, and became the nation's first openly transgender state senator. During her tenure, she successfully sponsored legislation to create a statewide paid family and medical leave insurance program and worked on bills to expand healthcare access and protect LGBTQ+ rights. In November 2024, she was elected to the U.S. House of Representatives, making her the first openly transgender person to serve in Congress.

McBride is openly transgender and has been candid about her personal experiences, including her relationship with Andrew Cray, an LGBTQ+ rights advocate. The couple married in 2014, shortly before Cray's passing due to cancer. She has spoken openly about their relationship and the impact of his death on her advocacy work, emphasizing the importance of healthcare access and LGBTQ+ rights. In 2018, she published her memoir, *Tomorrow Will Be Different: Love, Loss, and the Fight for Trans Equality*, with a foreword by Joe Biden.

McBride's election to the U.S. Congress represents a significant milestone in American politics, symbolizing progress toward greater inclusivity and representation. Her legislative achievements and advocacy work have had a profound impact on advancing equality and justice for marginalized communities. Her journey from local activism to national prominence underscores the importance of diverse voices in shaping public policy and serves as an inspiration to many.

Ken Mehlman (1966–)

Political Consultant, Business Executive

Kenneth Brian "Ken" Mehlman is a well-known political strategist, attorney, and business executive who has played significant roles in both the political and financial sectors. He is best known for his work as the campaign manager for President George W. Bush's 2004 reelection campaign and later as the chairman of the Republican National Committee (RNC). After his political career, he transitioned to the private sector, where he became a global head at Kohlberg Kravis Roberts (KKR), a leading global investment firm. He is also notable for being one of the highest-profile figures in American politics to come out as gay, and he has since become a strong advocate for LGBTQ+ rights.

Mehlman was born in Baltimore, Maryland. He grew up in a Jewish family and attended Franklin High School in Reisterstown, Maryland. His interest in politics and public service was evident from a young age, leading him to pursue studies in government. He graduated from Franklin & Marshall College in 1988 with a bachelor's degree in government. He then attended Harvard Law School, where he earned his J.D. in 1991. After law school, he worked as an attorney at the Washington, D.C., law firm Akin Gump Strauss Hauer & Feld. His legal career, however, soon gave way to his passion for politics as he began to take on roles within the Republican Party.

Mehlman's political career gained significant momentum in the late 1990s and early 2000s. He served as director of political affairs for the Bush–Cheney 2000 presidential campaign, in which he helped to organize grassroots efforts that contributed to George W. Bush's narrow victory. His success in this role led to his appointment as campaign manager for Bush's 2004 reelection campaign. As campaign manager, he was credited with orchestrating a highly disciplined and effective strategy that led to Bush's victory over Democratic challenger John Kerry. The 2004 campaign was noted for its focus on mobilizing conservative voters, suggesting such state ballot initiatives as opposing same-sex marriage and its use of data-driven techniques that would later become standard in modern political campaigns.

Following Bush's reelection, Mehlman was elected chairman of the Republican National Committee in 2005. During his tenure as RNC chairman, he focused on expanding the party's outreach to minority voters and modernizing its voter data operations. He served in this role until 2007, after which he transitioned to the private sector.

In 2008, Mehlman joined Kohlberg Kravis Roberts (KKR), a global investment firm, where he eventually became the global head of public affairs and co-head of KKR's Global Impact Fund. At KKR, he has been involved in managing the firm's environmental, social, and governance (ESG) initiatives as well as its impact investing strategies. His work at KKR has positioned the firm as a leader in responsible and sustainable investment practices.

Mehlman made headlines in 2010 when he publicly came out as gay in an interview with *The Atlantic*. His decision to come out was seen as a significant moment in American politics, given his prominent role in the Republican Party, which had often taken stances against LGBTQ+ rights. He expressed regret for not coming out sooner and for his role in supporting policies that were harmful to the LGBTQ+ community during his time in politics.

Since coming out, Mehlman has become an active advocate for LGBTQ+ rights. He supported the repeal of the "Don't Ask, Don't Tell" military policy, implemented during Bill Clinton's presidency; worked with organizations such as the American Foundation for Equal Rights (AFER); and has been involved in efforts to promote marriage equality and combat discrimination. He played a key role in attempting to organize Republican support for same-sex marriage in the hope of shifting the party's stance on the issue.

Mehlman's decision to come out as gay in 2010 marked a pivotal moment in the intersection of politics and LGBTQ+ rights, and his subsequent advocacy work has helped to advance equality and acceptance within the Republican Party and beyond.

Harvey Milk (1930–1978)

Political Figure

Harvey Bernard Milk was one of the first openly gay elected officials in the United States, serving as a member of the San Francisco Board of Supervisors. His election in 1977 marked a significant milestone in LGBTQ+ history, as he advocated for the rights of marginalized groups, particularly the LGBTQ+ community. His life and assassination in 1978 made him a martyr for LGBTQ+ rights, and his legacy continues to inspire activists worldwide. The Harvey Milk Day holiday and the Harvey Milk Foundation were established to honor his contributions to civil rights.

Milk was born in Woodmere, New York, to a middle-class, Jewish family. After graduating from the New York State College for Teachers in Albany in 1951, he served in the U.S. Navy during the Korean War and received an "other than honorable" discharge in 1955 for having engaged in sexual acts with other enlisted men. He returned to New York to become a financial analyst.

After moving to San Francisco in 1972, Milk opened a camera store while becoming more involved in activism, particularly in the Castro District, where he became a community leader and advocate for LGBTQ+ rights. His reputation grew when he challenged the city's gay leadership, which he thought was too conservative in its attempts to gain greater political rights for gays. After two unsuccessful bids for a seat on the San Francisco Board of Supervisors (its city council) in 1973 and 1976, he was elected in 1977, becoming one of the first openly gay elected officials in U.S. history. His political platform emphasized equal rights for the LGBTQ+ community, affordable housing, and civil rights for all marginalized groups. One of his key legislative successes was the gay rights ordinance, which prohibited discrimination based on sexual orientation in employment, housing, and public accommodation within San Francisco. His ability to unite diverse groups in San Francisco, including LGBTQ+ individuals, racial minorities, and labor unions, made him a powerful advocate for social justice.

In 1978, Milk and San Francisco mayor George Moscone were shot and killed by former supervisor Dan White, who had recently resigned but sought to be reinstated. After Moscone denied his request, White entered City Hall through a basement window and fatally shot both men. White's subsequent trial led to a controversial verdict of voluntary manslaughter after the so-called "Twinkie defense," in which his lawyers blamed White's impairment on his fast food dependence. The verdict sparked public outrage in San Francisco and protests known as the White Night riots.

Milk's murder cemented his legacy as a civil rights icon and galvanized the LGBTQ+ movement in the United States. His assassination highlighted the urgent need for greater protections for LGBTQ+ individuals and inspired activism and political engagement nationwide. He became a symbol of courage and resilience, with his legacy living on through annual commemorations, documentaries, and films that spread his message of hope and equality. The outcry following his death, particularly after White's lenient sentence, fueled calls for justice reform and LGBTQ+ rights, accelerating the movement for social and legislative change.

Tributes to Milk honor his unwavering advocacy for LGBTQ+ rights, his courage in facing discrimination, and his vision of a more inclusive society. Many recognize him as a pioneer who championed visibility and dignity for LGBTQ+ individuals in public life. His influence is celebrated through various tributes, including the annual Harvey Milk Day in California, the Harvey Milk Foundation, and the naming of schools, plazas, and even a U.S. Navy ship after him. Films, documentaries, and writings continue to highlight his impact, portraying him as a lasting inspiration for equality and human rights.

David Mixner (1946–2024)

Political Consultant, Author

David Mixner was a prominent American political activist and author renowned for his extensive work in anti-war movements and LGBTQ+ rights advocacy. His efforts significantly influenced public policy and societal attitudes toward the LGBTQ+ community, marking him as a pivotal figure in the fight for equality.

Born in Elmer, New Jersey, Mixner was the son of a farmworker in southern New Jersey. He became politically active during his high school years, participating in the civil rights movement and volunteering for John F. Kennedy's 1960 presidential campaign. His early activism laid the foundation for a lifelong commitment to social justice. He enrolled at Arizona State University in Tempe and soon became involved in civil rights and anti-war activism, organizing the first of many protests in 1966 on behalf of city garbage workers who were seeking to unionize. He dropped out of college to begin working on the presidential campaign of Eugene McCarthy in 1968.

In 1969, Mixner co-organized the Moratorium to End the War in Vietnam, a nationwide protest that drew millions who were against the Vietnam War. He aspired to a public service career but was convinced that his "terrible secret" of being gay would not permit it, as he explained in the memoir *Stranger Among Friends* (1996).

In the 1970s, Mixner moved to Los Angeles, worked on campaigns for Harvey Milk, and was the campaign manager for Tom Bradley's successful bid for reelection as mayor of Los Angeles in 1977. Transitioning to LGBTQ+ advocacy in the late 1970s, he played a crucial role in defeating California's Proposition 6 in 1978, which sought to ban gays and lesbians from teaching in public schools. His leadership extended to cofounding the Municipal Elections Committee of Los Angeles (MECLA), the first gay and lesbian political action committee in the United States, and the Gay & Lesbian Victory Fund, which supports LGBTQ+ political candidates.

Mixner came out as gay during the fight against Proposition 6. He was known for his close relationships with political figures, including a friendship with Bill Clinton, with whom he worked on the Vietnam Moratorium. He agreed to support Clinton's presidential bid in exchange for a promise from Clinton to end the ban on gay men and lesbians serving in the military. In office, Clinton instead compromised with the policy of "Don't Ask, Don't Tell," and Mixner, feeling betrayed, helped lead the protest over the policy. Mixner and Clinton eventually healed their rift as the military ban on gay men and women was lifted in 2011.

Mixner died of complications of long-term COVID-19 at the age of 77. His legacy is characterized by his unwavering dedication to social justice and equality. His activism not only advanced LGBTQ+ rights but also set a precedent for future generations of advocates.

Elaine Noble (1944–)

Political Figure

Elaine Noble is celebrated as a pioneering figure in LGBTQ+ political history in the United States. She became the first out lesbian to be elected to a state legislature

in the United States when she won a seat in the Massachusetts House of Representatives in 1974. It was a landmark victory that marked a significant milestone for LGBTQ+ representation in American politics. Her election not only broke barriers but also set a precedent for LGBTQ+ individuals aspiring to public office, fostering visibility and acceptance.

Born in New Kensington, Pennsylvania, Noble grew up in a conservative household, facing challenges that shaped her resilience and dedication to social justice. She moved to Boston for higher education, where she earned a degree in fine arts from Boston University in 1966, followed by a master's degree in speech and education at Emerson College in 1970 and a master's degree in education from Harvard in 1974. Noble, who came out as a lesbian after graduation, worked initially as a speech instructor and in advertising. She was also involved in LGBTQ+ rights activism in Boston as a member of the local chapter of the Daughters of Bilitis and helping to organize Boston's early Pride marches.

In 1974, Noble was elected to the state House of Representatives, winning 59 percent of the votes after a campaign in which she faced bomb threats, broken windows at her campaign headquarters, the destruction of her car, and being spit on. "I was elected in spite of being gay," she recalled. "I was elected in a largely Irish Catholic town. There was a level of animosity in all strata of society against homosexuality." Her election was a groundbreaking achievement, coming three years before Harvey Milk's election in San Francisco. Earlier in 1974, Kathy Kozachenko had become the first openly gay candidate to successfully run for public office in the United States and was elected to the city council in Ann Arbor, Michigan. Noble, running on a progressive platform, advocated for healthcare reform, affordable housing, and women's rights, often facing hostility and discrimination as an openly gay legislator. Her courage in enduring harassment and threats underscored her commitment to her constituents and the LGBTQ+ community. She would be reelected in 1976 with almost 90 percent of the vote. After a failed bid to win the Democratic nomination for the U.S. Senate in 1978, she chose not to seek reelection to the statehouse.

After her political career, Noble went to work for Boston mayor Kevin White before establishing Noble Consulting, a healthcare consulting group, in 1986. She later cofounded the Pride Institute, the first LGBTQ+-friendly treatment center for substance abuse and mental health issues, which addressed a critical need for specialized support within the community.

As an openly lesbian politician, Noble was candid about her sexuality at a time when public acceptance was limited and the risks were high. Her openness inspired others in the LGBTQ+ community to live authentically. She was in a high-profile relationship with writer and activist Rita Mae Brown, which brought added media scrutiny but also symbolized a committed partnership in advocacy and activism. By entering politics as an openly gay woman, she challenged the political status quo and opened doors for future generations of LGBTQ+ public servants.

Annise Parker (1956–)

Political Figure

Annise Danette Parker is a politician and advocate for LGBTQ+ rights best known for her tenure as the mayor of Houston, Texas, from 2010 to 2016. She made history as the first openly gay individual to lead a major U.S. city, significantly advancing LGBTQ+ representation in politics. Beyond her mayoral role, she has been instrumental in promoting equality and diversity through various leadership positions.

Born in Houston, Texas, Parker was raised in the community of Spring Branch. Her mother was a bookkeeper, and her adoptive father worked for the Red Cross. In 1971, her family moved to a U.S. Army post in Mannheim, Germany, for two years. She attended Rice University, earning a B.A. in anthropology, psychology, and sociology in 1978. After graduation, she worked in the oil and gas industry for nearly two decades as a software analyst. Her early involvement in LGBTQ+ activism included leadership roles in organizations such as the Houston Gay and Lesbian Political Caucus, serving as its president from 1995 to 1997.

After two unsuccessful runs in 1991 and 1995, Parker was elected to the Houston City Council in 1997, where she served three terms until 2003. She then became the city controller, holding the position from 2004 to 2010. In 2009, she was elected mayor of Houston. She was Houston's second female mayor (after Kathy Whitmire, who served from 1982 to 1991) and the first openly gay mayor of a major U.S. city, the most populous U.S. city to elect an openly gay mayor until Lori Lightfoot was elected mayor of Chicago in 2019.

Discussing her role as Houston's mayor, she stated, "I was a gay and lesbian activist in my college days, so that's always been part of my acknowledgment of the world. What is different as mayor is I'm not a spokesperson for the community. I am the public face and voice of the citizens of Houston. I just happen to be a lesbian when I'm doing it." She served three terms until 2016. During her tenure, she focused on economic development, infrastructure improvements, and environmental sustainability. Notably, she championed the Houston Equal Rights Ordinance (HERO) to protect against discrimination, though it was later repealed by voters.

After her mayoral service, Parker continued her advocacy as the president and

CEO of the LGBTQ+ Victory Fund and Victory Institute, organizations dedicated to increasing the number of openly LGBTQ+ officials in public office. Under her leadership, these organizations expanded their impact, supporting numerous candidates nationwide. She served in this role until March 2025.

Parker married Kathy Hubbard in 2014. The couple has been together since 1990, and they have two adopted children. Her legacy lies in her pioneering role in LGBTQ+ representation in the government and impactful policies on urban resilience and inclusivity, inspiring LGBTQ+ leaders and fostering a more inclusive political landscape.

Jared Polis (1975–)

Political Figure

Jared Schutz Polis, the 43rd governor of Colorado, became the first openly gay man to be elected governor in U.S. history. His career has been defined by his commitment to education reform, economic growth, and progressive policies. His governorship has been marked by significant reforms in health care, renewable energy, and LGBTQ+ rights, positioning him as a leader in progressive policy and social inclusivity. Prior to his governorship, he served as a U.S. representative, where he championed initiatives in education and technology. He was the first openly gay man and second LGBTQ+ person (after Tammy Baldwin) to be elected to Congress as non-incumbent.

Polis was born in Boulder, Colorado. He is the son of Stephen Schutz and Susan Polis Schutz, founders of greeting card and book publisher Blue Mountain Arts. He lived in San Diego as a high school student and graduated from Princeton University in 1996 with a degree in political science. Demonstrating an early interest in both business and public service, he founded several successful companies, including ProFlowers, which grew to become one of the largest online flower retailers in the country. His early career was shaped by his business ventures, but he quickly turned his focus to public service, founding the Jared Polis Foundation to support educational and community initiatives.

In 2000, Polis legally changed his surname to his mother's because he "liked it better." His political career began when he was elected to the Colorado State Board of Education in 2000, where he served until 2007. In 2008, he was elected to the U.S. House of Representatives, representing Colorado's 2nd Congressional District. During his time in Congress, he was a strong advocate for education reform, immigration rights, and environmental protection. His legislative efforts included support for the DREAM Act, initiatives for renewable energy, and measures to improve STEM education. In 2018, he made history as the first openly gay man to be elected governor, winning the governorship of Colorado. As governor, he has focused on issues including health care, where he implemented a public health insurance option, and clean energy, with a commitment to 100 percent renewable energy by 2040. He has also been instrumental in expanding access to early childhood education and reducing costs for families, reinforcing his dedication to social equity and sustainability. Before he left Congress in 2019, he was one of seven openly gay members of the 113th Congress.

Polis is married to Marlon Reis, a writer and animal rights advocate, and the couple has two children. He was the first openly gay parent in Congress. Their relationship has been highly publicized as a symbol of LGBTQ+ visibility in politics, and their marriage in 2021 marked a historic milestone as he became the first sitting U.S. governor to marry a same-sex partner while in office. He also became the second (after Cathy Connolly of the Wyoming House of Representatives) openly gay parent to hold a position in a state-level government office. His openness about his sexuality and family life has made him an inspiration to many, advancing LGBTQ+ acceptance in both political and social spheres.

Danica Roem (1984-)

Political Figure

Danica Roem is a journalist, politician, and transgender activist best known for being the first openly transgender person to be elected and serve in a U.S. state legislature. Elected in 2017 to the Virginia House of Delegates, her victory gained national attention as a significant milestone for transgender representation in the government and in the fight for transgender rights and equality in the United States.

Roem was born in Manassas, Virginia. Raised in a working-class family, she attended local public schools before earning her bachelor's degree in journalism from St. Bonaventure University in 2006. She pursued a career in journalism, working for over a decade at the *Gainesville Times* and the *Prince William Times*, where she reported on local politics, government, and education. She began her transition in 2013 with hormone replacement therapy. She described her friends and coworkers as being very supportive during her transition, stating that "no one cared. It was great. I could just keep doing my job." After serving as news editor at the *Montgomery County Sentinel* in Rockville, Maryland, from 2015 to 2016, she decided to run for public office.

Roem made history in 2017 when she won her election to the Virginia House of Delegates, defeating longtime incumbent Bob Marshall, a staunch opponent of LGBTQ+ rights. Her campaign focused on local issues such as fixing traffic congestion on Route 28 and improving public schools, emphasizing that her political platform was centered on the everyday concerns of her constituents rather than her gender identity. Her win was widely viewed as a rebuke of Marshall's anti-LGBTQ+ rhetoric and an affirmation of the importance of representation and inclusion. Since her election, she has successfully passed bills related to infrastructure, school meal programs, and LGBTQ+ equality. She was reelected in 2019 and 2021, and was elected state senator for the 30th District, beginning her term in 2024.

Roem has been outspoken about her experiences as a transgender woman, using her platform to promote equality and fight discrimination. She continues to be a voice for transgender rights while also emphasizing that her legislative priorities, such as improving roads and schools, are shared by all her constituents, regardless of gender identity.

Roem's success in office shows that transgender individuals can run for and win elected positions based on their qualifications and dedication to serving their communities, not just their identities. Her focus on policy over identity politics has made her a respected and effective legislator, showing that diverse voices can lead on issues that matter to all citizens.

Abby Rubenfeld (1953-)

Lawyer

Abby Rubenfeld is a prominent civil rights attorney and LGBTQ+ rights advocate known for her pivotal role in landmark cases that advanced marriage equality in the United States. Her extensive legal career and advocacy have helped to shape the legal landscape around issues of discrimination, marriage equality, and civil rights. Her work in pivotal cases, particularly her contributions to *Obergefell v. Hodges* (the case that legalized same-sex marriage in the United States), has made her a leading figure in the fight for LGBTQ+ rights.

Rubenfeld was raised in Florida, where she experienced firsthand discrimination from establishments like country clubs that excluded her family based on their Jewish heritage. She attended Princeton University for her undergraduate studies before earning her J.D. from Boston University in 1979. Early in her career, she worked with the Lambda Legal Defense and Education Fund, where she quickly gained experience handling civil rights cases focused on LGBTQ+ issues.

Rubenfeld eventually established a family law practice in Nashville, Tennessee. As an out lesbian attorney, she was sought out by the LGBTQ+ community on issues of family law, which led her to become one of the champions of the marriage equality movement. She challenged Tennessee's Homosexual Practices Act, which criminalized sodomy and was overturned in 1996. In 2013, she organized a group of attorneys and plaintiffs to challenge Tennessee's ban on same-sex marriage, which became part of the consolidated *Obergefell v. Hodges* decision in 2015. This landmark ruling by the U.S. Supreme Court legalized same-sex marriage nationwide. She has also taken on cases advocating for parental rights, adoption rights for LGBTQ+ couples, and the elimination of discriminatory practices across various states. Her work as an attorney and advocate has helped to dismantle legal barriers that restricted LGBTQ+ rights, making her a formidable presence in the fight for equality.

Rubenfeld's legacy is that of a dedicated attorney who has made an indelible impact on civil rights law, especially concerning LGBTQ+ rights. Her contributions have broadened access to equal treatment under the law for countless individuals and families, establishing her as a pivotal figure in the ongoing struggle for equality.

Richard L. Schlegel (1927–2006)

Civil Servant

Richard Lamar Schlegel was a civil servant and LGBTQ+ rights activist whose legal battle against employment discrimination in the 1960s marked a significant moment in the fight for gay rights in the United States. Fired from federal and state government jobs on account of his sexual orientation, he filed a wrongful termination suit that reached the Supreme Court in 1970. His case, *Schlegel v. United States,* is considered an early landmark in the American gay rights movement.

Born in Berrysburg, Pennsylvania, Schlegel was the only child of a construction worker and a schoolteacher and homemaker, both of Pennsylvania German descent. He attended Pennsylvania State University from 1943 to 1945 but left after being outed by a fraternity brother. Drafted into the U.S. Army Air Forces, he served for two years on bases in Texas and Florida performing office duties for the Office of the Judge Advocate General before returning to Penn State under the G.I. Bill. He graduated in 1949 with a bachelor's degree. He later earned a master's degree in political science and public administration from American University.

Schlegel's civil service career began at the Civil Aeronautics Administration in 1952 and the Federal Civil Defense Administration from 1955 to 1958. In 1960, while working for the Department of the Army in Hawaii, he was dismissed due to his sexual orientation after seeking top-secret security clearance. Military investigators found three male soldiers who confessed to having sexual relations with Schlegel. He was charged with "immoral and indecent conduct" under civil service regulations and fired in 1961.

Schlegel exhausted federal administrative appeals before filing a wrongful termination suit in 1963, declaring that the charge of "immoral and indecent conduct" was unconstitutionally vague and that his job performance was not impacted by his private life. Six years later, a seven-judge panel ruled unanimously against him, declaring that "any schoolboy knows that a homosexual act is immoral, indecent, lewd, and obscene" and that homosexual conduct undermines efficient workings of government. ACLU lawyers petitioned the Supreme Court to hear his case, but in 1970, the Court unanimously refused. Although he failed to regain his job, the case is regarded as an early landmark of gay rights, highlighting the systemic discrimination faced by LGBTQ+ individuals in government employment.

Schlegel would become an active member of the Janus Society, an early homophile organization, and founded a chapter in Harrisburg, Pennsylvania, where he worked as finance director of the Pennsylvania Department of Highways from 1963 to 1965 before resigning involuntarily when the state police opened an investigation into his sexuality. He also worked in gay magazine publishing, serving as editor and publisher of *PACE!*, a short-lived magazine published by the Philadelphia Action Committee for Equality. Later, he became a financial investor and millionaire.

Schlegel lived in Pennsylvania until his death at the age of 79. He endowed a scholarship at Bucknell University in 1999, and his will established the Richard L. Schlegel National Legion of Honor Award for an Emerging Activist at American University. In October 2021, a state historical marker was installed outside his former residence in Harrisburg, though it was later removed in 2022 following controversy.

Matthew Shepard (1976–1998)

College Student

Matthew Wayne Shepard became an international symbol of the fight against hate and for LGBTQ+ rights following his brutal murder in 1998. His death brought awareness to the violence that LGBTQ+ individuals face and inspired a global movement for equality. His legacy led to the creation of the Matthew Shepard Foundation and the eventual passage of the Matthew Shepard and James Byrd Jr. Hate Crimes Prevention Act of 2009, which expanded federal hate crime legislation to include crimes motivated by sexual orientation and gender identity.

Shepard was born in Casper, Wyoming. As a child, he was good-natured and friendly but bullied by his classmates for his size and lack of athleticsm. His father, an oil rig inspector, went to work in Saudi Arabia, and he finished high school in Switzerland, where he developed a passion for human rights and global issues. After returning to the United States, he enrolled at the University of Wyoming, where he majored in political science and international relations.

As an openly gay 21-year-old college student, Shepard was harassed, brutally attacked, and murdered in Laramie, Wyoming, in October 1998 in what became one of the most widely reported hate crimes in American history. He was approached by two men, Aaron McKinney and Russell Henderson, at a bar. The men pretended to be gay in order to gain Shepard's trust and later drove him to a remote area, where they robbed, beat, and tied him to a fence in near-freezing temperatures, leaving him severely injured. He was found 18 hours later by a passerby, still alive but in critical condition, and died of his injuries on October 12, 1998.

The crime, motivated by homophobia, sparked national outrage and led to widespread media coverage, highlighting the dangers faced by LGBTQ+ individuals. This case, described by the BBC as "the murder that changed America," became a rallying point for LGBTQ+ rights, contributing to the eventual passage of the Matthew Shepard and James Byrd Jr. Hate Crimes Prevention Act of 2009, which expanded federal hate crime legislation to include crimes motivated by sexual orientation, gender, and disability. Shepard's parents, Judy and Dennis Shepard, became prominent activists, founding the Matthew Shepard Foundation to support LGBTQ+ rights and promote awareness.

Shepard's story has been treated in books, dramas, and television and movie versions, including *The Laramie Project* (2002), an HBO film based on the play by Moises Kaufman, which explores the reaction to Shepard's death in the Laramie community; *The Matthew Shepard Story* (2002), a made-for-television film that dramatizes Shepard's life, the aftermath of his murder, and his parents becoming advocates for LGBTQ+ rights; and *Matt Shepard Is a Friend of Mine* (2013), a documentary by Michele Josue, a personal friend of Shepard, focusing on his personality and struggles beyond the events of his death. In 2009, Judy Shepard, Matthew's mother, published a memoir, *The Meaning of Matthew*, an intimate account of the impact of his death on the Shepard family and the LGBTQ+ community. Melissa Etheridge's song "Scarecrow" was inspired by Shepard's death and addresses the violence and intolerance faced by LGBTQ+ individuals, and Elton John has dedicated performances to Shepard, using his platform to advocate for LGBTQ+ rights and remembering Shepard.

On the 20th anniversary of his death in 2018, Shepard's ashes were interred at the National Cathedral in Washington, D.C., a significant honor reflecting his enduring legacy.

Amanda Simpson (1961–)

Government Official, Engineer, Business Executive

Amanda Simpson is a pioneering figure in aerospace and the U.S. government recognized as one of the highest-ranking openly transgender officials in the United States. As an aerospace engineer and businesswoman, she has held influential positions in both the corporate sector and the federal government. Her advocacy for diversity and inclusion, especially within engineering and defense, has broken new ground, demonstrating the value of diverse perspectives in STEM fields and national security. Her appointment to high-level government roles has made her a role model and trailblazer for transgender individuals in public service.

Born in Chicago, Simpson received a BS in physics from Harvey Mudd College in 1983, an M.S. in engineering from California State University, Northridge, in 1988, and an M.B.A. from the University of Arizona in 2001. Her career began in aerospace, where she worked as a test pilot and engineer, eventually joining Raytheon, where she held various leadership roles over two decades. Her expertise and dedication propelled her rise in a field historically dominated by cisgender men.

In 2010, Simpson made history as the first openly transgender woman to be appointed by a U.S. president, joining the Department of Commerce as a senior technical advisor in the Bureau of Industry and Security under President Barack Obama. Later, she served as the deputy assistant secretary of defense for operational energy, focusing on improving the military's energy efficiency, which aligned with national security priorities. At Raytheon, she led initiatives to advance missile development and testing, earning her high regard in aerospace and defense. While working at Raytheon, she came out as a transgender woman and became an activist for transgender rights, serving on the boards of the National Center for Transgender Equality and Out & Equal Workplace Advocates. She has also actively worked to improve policies for transgender inclusion within STEM fields and federal institutions.

Simpson is openly transgender and has spoken about her transition as an integral part of her personal and professional journey. She is a vocal advocate for transgender rights and has used her platform to address discrimination and underrepresentation within technical fields. Her journey has been an inspiration to many, particularly those within the LGBTQ+ community who are pursuing careers in traditionally conservative industries.

Kyrsten Sinema (1976–)

Political Figure

Kyrsten Lea Sinema is a trailblazing American politician and lawyer known for being the first openly bisexual member of the U.S. Congress and, later, the first openly bisexual U.S. senator. Her presence in the Senate has been significant in representing diverse identities in American politics, often positioning herself as a moderate voice within the Democratic Party before declaring herself an independent in 2022. Her career has been marked by her independent stance on many issues, highlighting her commitment to representing a wide spectrum of voters, including her focus on bipartisanship in key legislative debates.

Born in Tucson, Arizona, Sinema grew up in a challenging economic environment after her parents' divorce, even experiencing homelessness with her family for a period. According to her, the family lived for three years in an abandoned gas station with no toilet or electricity, a contention disputed by her mother and stepfather. She graduated as valedictorian of her public high school and earned a bachelor's degree from Brigham Young University in 1995, an MSW from Arizona State University in 1999, and eventually a law degree, also from ASU, in 2004. Before her political career, she worked as a social worker, counselor, and adjunct professor, focusing on issues of public welfare, which helped to shape her empathetic approach to public service.

Sinema's political career began in the Arizona House of Representatives in 2005, where she served until 2011 before moving to the Arizona Senate. In 2012, she was elected to the U.S. House of Representatives, and in 2018, she made history by becoming Arizona's first female U.S. senator as well as the first openly bisexual senator. She has been involved in legislation across a wide range of areas, including veteran affairs, health care, and infrastructure. Her bipartisan approach has led her to support legislation that addresses issues of importance to both parties, such as immigration reform and gun control measures. In 2021, she was instrumental in the passing of a major bipartisan infrastructure bill that distributed substantial resources for the repair and modernization of America's infrastructure. She also drew criticism by joining Republicans in opposition to portions of President Joe Biden's Build Back Better Plan, and in 2022, she announced that she had left the Democratic Party and registered as an independent, though she continued to caucus with the Democrats for committee assignments. In 2024, she announced that she would retire from Congress at the end of her term and not seek reelection, saying that her approach to foster compromise seemed to be "a model of the past."

Sinema married and later divorced her BYU classmate Blake Dain and has identified as bisexual. Her sexuality is something she has shared openly, yet she has often emphasized her desire to focus on policy rather than personal life. Her decision to come out was met with broad support from the LGBTQ+ community, although she has remained relatively private about her personal relationships, maintaining a focus on her role as a public servant.

Barbra "Babs" Siperstein (1942–2019)

Political Figure

Barbra "Babs" Casbar Siperstein was a prominent American transgender rights activist known for her groundbreaking work in LGBTQ+ advocacy, particularly for transgender rights. She made history in 2009 as the first openly transgender member of the Democratic National Committee (DNC), solidifying her role as a trailblazer for transgender political representation in the United States. Her advocacy helped to advance several significant protections for transgender individuals, and her legacy is honored through the landmark Babs Siperstein Law in New Jersey, which simplified the process for transgender individuals to amend their gender on their birth certificates. Her dedication to equality made her a revered figure within the LGBTQ+ community and a vital force in the fight for transgender rights.

Born Barry Siperstein in Jersey City, New Jersey, Barbra attended Rutgers University, where she earned a degree in business administration. She went on to earn an M.B.A. in accounting from Pace University before joining the family business, Siperstein Fords Paint Corporation. Prior to transitioning, she married Carol Siperstein and had three children, leading what was at the time considered a "traditional" life.

Siperstein was nearing 50 in the late 1980s when she told Carol that she was transgender. The two remained together, keeping her orientation a secret. "We kind of lived a double life for many years," she recalled. Her personal journey and eventual transition to female in 2001, following Carol's death, marked a significant turning point in her life, inspiring her commitment to advocating for the rights of transgender individuals across the nation.

Siperstein's major contributions to LGBTQ+ rights began with her appointment as the first openly transgender member of the Democratic National Committee in 2009. This role enabled her to push for the inclusion of transgender rights within the Democratic platform and advocate for broader acceptance and understanding within political circles. In New Jersey, she was instrumental in the passage of the Babs Siperstein Law, which was signed in 2018. This law streamlined the process for transgender people to change the gender marker on their birth certificates without the requirement of surgery, a significant advancement for transgender rights in the state. She also cochaired the DNC's Transgender Advisory Committee and served on the executive board of the National Stonewall Democrats, consistently working to ensure transgender inclusion and representation. Her legislative advocacy and political efforts set a standard for other states to follow, and her work remains a foundation for transgender rights initiatives.

Siperstein, a devoted parent and grandparent, was deeply committed to her family throughout her life. While her transition presented challenges, she maintained a close relationship with her children and continued to support her family through her activism. She was also known for her kindness and dedication to mentoring other transgender individuals, providing them with guidance and resources. Her journey was marked by her openness about her transgender identity, which she embraced with courage and pride, paving the way for others to live openly and authentically.

Siperstein's legacy as a trailblazer in transgender rights and political representation endures as a powerful example of advocacy and courage. Her work within the DNC and influence on state legislation created lasting changes that expanded rights for transgender individuals and paved the way for future progress.

Addie Viola Smith (1893–1975)

Lawyer, Diplomat

Addie Viola Smith was a pioneering American attorney and diplomat recognized as the first woman to serve as a trade commissioner in the U.S. Foreign Service. An early feminist, she met her life partner, Eleanor Hinder, in Shanghai in 1926, and they lived together until Hinder's death in 1963. Her trailblazing career significantly advanced women's roles in international diplomacy and trade.

Born in Stockton, California, Smith was the daughter of Rufus Roy Smith, a publisher. She pursued a degree in business administration at Heald's Business College in San Francisco, graduating in 1908. In 1917, she moved to Washington, D.C., and worked for the U.S. Department of Labor while attending the Washington College of Law at American University. She earned her LLB in 1920.

After graduating, Smith joined the Foreign Service and was assigned to Beijing as a clerk in the trade commissioner's office. In 1922, she was promoted to assistant trade commissioner in Shanghai (the first woman to hold such a position) and was appointed trade commissioner of Shanghai in 1928, holding that position until 1939.

Smith served as consul and secretary to the U.S. Consulate in Shanghai and worked to evacuate Americans during the 1941 Japanese invasion. From 1942 to 1946, she lived and worked in Washington, D.C., as an economic specialist for the Department of State. She returned to China in 1946 to open the China–America Council of Commerce and Industry in Shanghai. She would subsequently work for the U.S. Economic Cooperation Administration in Bangkok, and from 1952 to 1964, she was the representative of the International Federation of Women Lawyers to the United Nations.

In 1926, Smith met Eleanor Hinder, an industrial secretary for the YWCA in China. The two developed a close partnership, living and working together in Shanghai until 1941. They continued their companionship in various locations, including Sydney, Australia, until Hinder's death in 1963. Smith died in New South Wales at the age of 82.

Smith's groundbreaking achievements paved the way for women in international diplomacy and trade. Her dedication to public service and advocacy for women's rights left an enduring impact on global trade relations and gender equality in the workforce.

Urvashi Vaid (1958–2022)

Lawyer, Author

Urvashi Vaid was an influential LGBTQ+ activist, attorney, and author whose groundbreaking work in advocacy, policy, and social justice helped to shape the modern LGBTQ+ rights movement in the United States. As the executive director of the National Gay and Lesbian Task Force (NGLTF) during the 1980s and 1990s, she was a powerful voice for marginalized communities, advocating for a range of issues from HIV/AIDS awareness to broader civil rights. Known for her strong stance on intersectionality and inclusivity, she emphasized the need for alliances across racial, gender, and economic lines, cementing her role as a visionary in both the LGBTQ+ and progressive movements.

Born in New Delhi, India, Vaid moved to the United States when she was a child. Her father, writer Krishna Baldev Vaid, received a teaching appointment at the State University of New York, Potsdam. She went on to attend Vassar College, graduating with a bachelor's degree in political science in 1979, and later earned her J.D. from Northeastern University School of Law in 1983. She founded the Boston Lesbian/Gay Political Alliance, and her passion for justice and equality quickly led her into LGBTQ+ advocacy, with her law background empowering her efforts to fight for legal reforms and protections.

From 1983 to 1996, Vaid was staff attorney at the National Prison Project of the American Civil Liberties Union, where she initiated the organization's work on HIV/AIDS in prisons. As the executive director of the National Gay and Lesbian Task Force (1989–1992), she led significant initiatives that broadened the scope of LGBTQ+ activism. She spearheaded campaigns that addressed not only the discrimination faced by LGBTQ+ individuals but also economic and social inequalities. Her book *Virtual Equality: The Mainstreaming of Gay and Lesbian Liberation* (1995) is considered a key text in understanding the challenges and complexities of LGBTQ+ rights in America. Beyond the NGLTF, she founded the Vaid Group, a consulting firm focused on justice and equality, and served on various boards and foundations, including the Arcus Foundation and the Gill Foundation, advocating for resources for grassroots LGBTQ+ initiatives. Her work consistently highlighted the importance of coalition building, and she advocated for an inclusive movement that addressed the intersecting identities of LGBTQ+ individuals.

Vaid was in a long-term partnership with fellow activist and comedian Kate Clinton. The two were dedicated advocates for LGBTQ+ rights and shared a deep commitment to social justice causes. She was open about her identity and experiences, frequently highlighting the personal as political and encouraging others to advocate for their rights openly and authentically. She was named in 2009 by *Out* magazine as one of the 50 most influential LGBTQ+ people in the United States. Her 2012 book *Irresistible Revolution: Confronting Race, Class and the Assumptions of LGBT Politics* critiques the racial and gender bias of the mainstream LGBTQ+ movement and argues that engagement with social justice is what will enable all parts of the LGBTQ+ community to gain equality and justice.

Vaid's legacy as a pioneering force in the LGBTQ+ rights movement endures through the many organizations, policies, and activists she inspired. Her work challenged the LGBTQ+ movement to broaden its focus, addressing issues of race, economic justice, and inclusion within the fight for equality. Her intersectional approach has influenced generations of activists and continues to shape contemporary LGBTQ+ advocacy.

Edith Windsor (1929–2017)

Computer Programmer, Spousal Rights Activist

Edith "Edie" Windsor was a trailblazing LGBTQ+ rights activist best known for her pivotal role in the landmark Supreme Court case *United States v. Windsor* (2013), which struck down key provisions of the Defense of Marriage Act (DOMA). Her advocacy catalyzed a broader national conversation on marriage equality, ultimately leading to the Supreme Court's recognition of same-sex marriage in *Obergefell v. Hodges* (2015). Her legal battle established her as a symbol of resilience and justice for the LGBTQ+ community, inspiring countless individuals worldwide.

Born Edith Schlain in Philadelphia, Pennsylvania, Windsor grew up in a Conservative Jewish family during the Great Depression. After graduating from Temple University in 1950, she married Saul Weiner (both adopted the surname Windsor) but divorced shortly thereafter, acknowledging her attraction to women. Keeping her married name, Windsor later pursued a master's degree in mathematics at New York University and learned computer programming, a field that propelled her into a distinguished career in technology. She joined IBM in 1958, where she quickly rose through the ranks to become a senior systems programmer—one of the few women to hold such a position in the male-dominated tech industry at the time. She kept her sexuality secret from her employer and work colleagues, fearful of exposure when she patronized lesbian hangouts.

In 1963, Windsor met Thea Spyer, a clinical psychologist. In 1967, Spyer proposed marriage, and the couple began what became a 40-year engagement and partnership. In 1975, Windsor took early retirement from IBM and began what she called a second career as an LGBTQ+ rights activist, marching in gay Pride parades, joining gay and lesbian organizations, and living openly as a lesbian.

In 2007, Windsor married the terminally ill Spyer, who died in 2009. Even though Spyer left her estate to Windsor, the Defense of Marriage Act (DOMA) of 1996, which barred same-sex married couples from federal recognition as "spouses," prevented her from receiving the federal spousal estate tax exemption, leaving her with a substantial tax bill. She challenged the law, arguing it was unconstitutional, and her case reached the Supreme Court. In a historic 5–4 decision, the Court ruled in her favor, declaring DOMA's federal definition of marriage as between a man and a woman unconstitutional. The ruling not only granted her the financial equality she deserved but also invalidated DOMA's discriminatory framework, significantly advancing marriage equality in the United States. Even though the Supreme Court for the first time granted same-sex marriage partners the recognition and benefits accorded married heterosexuals, its ruling fell short of declaring the constitutional right to same-sex unions, leaving in place laws in 37 states that banned such marriages. Full recognition of the constitutional legality of same-sex marriage would not come until 2015 in *Obergefell v. Hodges*. Legal experts and LGBTQ+ historians recognize *United States v. Windsor* as a crucial decision in the national battle over same-sex marriage rights.

As a result of her suit and victory, Windsor became a national celebrity, a gay rights matriarch, and a runner-up to Pope Francis for *Time* magazine's "Person of the Year" in 2013. She continued as a public advocate for same-sex marriage. In 2016, she married Judith Kasen. President Barack Obama would say following Windsor's death that the day of the 2013 Supreme Court ruling was "a great day for America—a victory for human decency, equality, freedom and justice."

Evan Wolfson (1957–)

Lawyer

Called "the man who brought gay marriage to the U.S.," Evan Wolfson is a key figure in the fight for marriage equality in the United States. As the founder and president of Freedom to Marry, he was a leading advocate for the legalization of same-sex marriage. He is widely credited with helping to shape the legal strategy that led to the U.S. Supreme Court's landmark 2015 ruling in *Obergefell v. Hodges*, which legalized same-sex marriage nationwide. His work has had a profound impact on LGBTQ+ rights and set a new precedent for civil rights in America.

Wolfson was born in Brooklyn, New York. He attended Yale University, where he earned a BA, and later graduated from Harvard Law School in 1983. Early in his legal career, he worked for Lambda Legal, where he began focusing on marriage equality and LGBTQ+ rights. In the 1990s, he wrote his influential book *Why Marriage Matters*, which argued for the necessity of legalizing same-sex marriage as a fundamental civil right.

In the 1990s, Wolfson played a pivotal role in the Hawaii Supreme Court case *Baehr v. Miike*, which was one of the first legal cases to challenge the ban on same-sex marriage. Although the case did not immediately result in nationwide marriage equality, it laid the foundation for future legal battles. His work in the legal community, alongside his public advocacy and media presence, made him one of the most prominent faces of the marriage equality movement. His most significant achievement was founding Freedom to Marry in 2003, an organization dedicated to winning marriage equality for same-sex couples. Under his leadership, the organization developed a comprehensive strategy that combined litigation, public education, and political advocacy. This approach significantly contributed to the growing public support for marriage equality, which rose from 27 percent in the mid-1990s to 63 percent by 2015. The efforts of Freedom to Marry culminated in the Supreme Court's 2015 decision in *Obergefell v. Hodges*, which legalized same-sex marriage nationwide. Following this victory, the organization concluded its mission and officially closed in February 2016.

In addition to his work with Freedom to Marry, Wolfson has been a public speaker, educator, and author, advocating for broader LGBTQ+ civil rights and providing a model for future civil rights movements. He married his longtime partner, Cheng He, in 2011.

Wolfson's role as the architect of the marriage equality movement in the United States has cemented his legacy as one of the most important civil rights figures of the 21st century. His work in the courts and advocacy have paved the way for the LGBTQ+ community to achieve equality under the law.

Business

The history of LGBTQ+ individuals in American business reflects a trajectory of gradual progress marked by significant milestones, persistent challenges, and dogged advocacy. Throughout the 20th century and into the 21st, LGBTQ+ individuals have faced numerous barriers in the workplace, including discrimination, lack of legal protections, and social stigmatization. Despite these obstacles, the LGBTQ+ community has made significant strides toward achieving equality and acceptance in the business world.

In the early decades of the 20th century, the situation for LGBTQ+ individuals in American business had changed little from what it had been throughout the 19th century, marked by moral and religious stigma, limited opportunities, and the necessity for concealment. Homosexuality remained criminalized in many parts of the United States, with sodomy laws strictly enforced, leading to potential arrest, imprisonment, and social ostracism for those who were discovered or suspected of being gay or lesbian. The dominant cultural and religious attitudes continued to view homosexuality as immoral and perverse, forcing many individuals to conceal their sexual orientation to avoid personal or professional consequences.

The lack of legal protection against discrimination based on sexual orientation meant that gays and lesbians could be fired, harassed, or otherwise discriminated against without any recourse. This lack of protection extended to all aspects of employment, making it difficult for individuals to maintain steady jobs or advance in careers if their sexual orientation became known. As a result, many gays and lesbians were forced to lead double lives or engage in "passing": presenting themselves as straight in public settings in order to safeguard their livelihoods. The professional environment for gays and lesbians was one of concealment and limited opportunities. Career advancement was often denied to those suspected of being gay, and individuals were typically forced to work in occupations where they could generally maintain a degree of anonymity. Jobs in which unmarried men and women could work without raising as much suspicion included teaching, the religious life, domestic service, nursing and other caregiving roles, military service, and literary and academic careers. Professions in arts and entertainment and the fashion industry often were more accepting of diverse lifestyles and allowed for greater personal expression. A pervasive need for secrecy, however, in all professions shaped professional lives for LGBTQ+ individuals and restricted their participation in business networks and professional relationships that were built on personal connections, which excluded openly gay individuals.

The stock market crash of 1929 and the ensuing Great Depression further exacerbated discrimination due to sexual orientation when job scarcity intensified

The business climate in the first decades of the 21st century has been much more accepting of LGBTQ company owners and executives compared to past centuries, but there is still work to do, especially given the steps backward caused by the Trump administration.

competition, and marginalized groups, including LGBTQ+ individuals, were easily scapegoated and excluded. During the 1930s, the Moral Hygiene movement, a social reform initiative, was part of a broader effort to promote public health and moral standards and focused on a range of issues, including venereal disease, prostitution, and public decency. The movement was driven by various societal concerns, including the rise of urbanization, changing gender roles, and the impact of the Great Depression on family structures and social norms. Advocates of the movement sought to promote traditional family values, sexual purity, and sobriety. This included the need to root out "sexual perverts" from various institutions, including workplaces, and led to increasing scrutiny and discrimination against LGBTQ+ individuals in employment.

Despite these challenges, the early 20th century also saw the beginning of more LGBTQ+ subcultures, particularly in urban areas. Cities like New York, Chicago, and San Francisco became centers for more vibrant, albeit clandestine, gay and lesbian communities. These urban centers offered a degree of anonymity (and therefore protection of sexual identity) as well as social and professional opportunities that were not available in smaller towns or rural areas. The development of these subcultures provided more support networks and spaces where individuals could express their sexual orientation more freely, though still with potentially significant risks.

Businesses catering to these gay and lesbian communities began to appear, most notably bars and clubs catering to an LGBTQ+ clientele. During the Prohibition Era (1920–1933), speakeasies and underground bars that were known for being LGBTQ+ friendly became popular—for example, Eve's Hangout in Greenwich Village, operated by lesbian Eve Adams. The Slide in New York City was a well-known "fairy" bar catering to gay male clientele in the 1890s.

The arts and entertainment industries continued to be more accepting of

LGBTQ+ individuals compared to other business sectors. Many gays and lesbians found careers in theater, music, and the emerging film industry, where their contributions were often celebrated, even if their personal lives had to remain discreet.

The Harlem Renaissance of the 1920s and 1930s included many openly gay and lesbian artists and writers, contributing to a rich cultural movement that challenged mainstream norms. New York's Harlem was also the location for several LGBTQ+-friendly venues, including the Clam House, the Ubangi Club, and the Hamilton Lodge, a fraternal organization that became famous for its annual drag balls that turned into significant social events for the LGBTQ+ community. These were exceptions that proved the rule for most LGBTQ+ individuals, whose lives were little changed in the early 20th century in terms of legal protection or societal acceptance. The need to remain closeted continued to shape their professional and personal lives, limiting their opportunities to earn a living and resulting in isolation and a continual fear of exposure.

President Dwight Eisenhower signed Executive Order 10450 in 1953 that banned homosexuals from serving as federal employees because they were supposedly a security risk.

Significant changes for LGBTQ+ individuals in business began to take root in the mid to late 20th century, spurred by a combination of activist movements, legal advancements, and evolving cultural attitudes. After World War II, urbanization and the growth of large cities accelerated, providing more opportunities for LGBTQ+ individuals to find communities, establish networks, and become increasingly more visible, especially in major cities like New York, San Francisco, and Los Angeles.

However, the post–World War II years of the late 1940s and 1950s, marked by significant social conservatism and paranoia brought about by Cold War anti-Communism hysteria, was a period of intense scrutiny and persecution of LGBTQ+ individuals. The Lavender Scare paralleled the Red Scare, targeting suspected homosexuals in the government, the military, and the private sector. President Dwight Eisenhower's Executive Order 10450 in 1953 banned homosexuals from federal employment, citing them as security risks. This policy led to the dismissal of thousands of federal employees and created a climate of fear and intimidation that extended into the private sector.

Then, during one of the darkest chapters in the history of LGBTQ+ discrimination and persecution, a fledging gay and lesbian rights movement set into motion radical changes that affected American culture broadly and American business specifically. The Mattachine Society, founded in 1950 by Harry Hay and others, became the first LGBTQ+ rights organization in the United States. *ONE Magazine*, the first nationally distributed LGBTQ+ publication, began in 1952. The Daughters of Bilitis, the first lesbian civil and political rights organization in the United States, was founded in 1955, with its publication *The Ladder* becoming the first nationally distributed lesbian publication in the United States in 1956. These organizations and publications served to widen the LGBTQ+ community nationwide and laid the groundwork for the larger LGBTQ+ rights movements that would gain momentum in the following decades.

In the aftermath of the Stonewall Uprising of 1969 and the formation of more confrontational gay rights organizations such as the Gay Liberation Front, the Gay Activists Alliance, and the Lesbian Feminist Liberation, momentum accelerated for legislative and policy changes for LGBTQ+ equal rights protection and antidiscrimination employment laws. In 1973, the American Psychiatric Association, under intense pressure from gay rights activists, declassified homosexuality as a mental disorder, which helped to reduce the stigma associated with being LGBTQ+ and supported workplace equality efforts.

> ***Even though federal protections are in place, the extent and enforcement of nondiscrimination laws can vary significantly by state. States like California, New York, and Massachusetts have comprehensive nondiscrimination laws that explicitly include sexual orientation and gender identity protection in employment.***

The earliest antidiscrimination employment laws were enacted on the local and state level. East Lansing, Michigan, became the first city in the United States to pass an ordinance prohibiting discrimination in hiring based on sexual orientation. Ann Arbor, Michigan, followed in 1974. In 1975, Minneapolis, Minnesota, passed the earliest comprehensive local LGBTQ+ protection laws in employment, housing, and public accommodation. In 1982, Wisconsin became the first state to enact a statewide law prohibiting discrimination based on sexual orientation in employment, housing, and public accommodation, setting a precedent for other states to follow.

Federally, Title VII of the Civil Rights Act of 1964 prohibited employment discrimination based on race, color, religion, sex, and national origin. However, it did not explicitly include sexual orientation or gender identity. In 1969, President Richard Nixon issued Executive Order 11476, which prohibited discrimination in federal employment based on race, color, religion, sex, national origin, handicap, and age. It would be amended by President Bill Clinton in 1998 to include sexual orientation and by President Barack Obama in 2014 to include gender identity. The Employment Non-Discrimination Act (ENDA) was first introduced in Congress in 1994 to prohibit discrimination in hiring and employment on the basis of sexual orientation and gender identity. Despite multiple votes, ENDA did not pass.

In 2015, the Supreme Court ruling in *Obergefell v. Hodges* legalized same-sex marriage nationwide. This landmark victory for LGBTQ+ rights also ensured that same-sex spouses could receive the same employment benefits as heterosexual couples, further promoting equality in the workplace. Finally, in 2020, the U.S. Supreme Court in *Bostock v. Clayton County* ruled that Title VII of the Civil Rights Act of 1964 also applies to discrimination based on sexual orientation and gender identity, a historic decision providing federal protections for LGBTQ+ employees against workplace discrimination.

The Equality Act was first introduced in Congress in 2015, with subsequent reintroductions aimed to amend the Civil Rights Act of 1964 to explicitly include protection against discrimination based on sexual orientation and gender identity in employment, housing, and other areas. As of 2025, the Equality Act was passed by the House of Representatives but has not yet passed the Senate.

Even though federal protections are in place, the extent and enforcement of nondiscrimination laws can vary significantly by state. States like California, New York,

Tim Cook, who came out in 2014, is the first openly gay person to run a Fortune 500 company (namely, Apple Inc.).

and Massachusetts have comprehensive nondiscrimination laws that explicitly include sexual orientation and gender identity protection in employment. As of 2025, 27 states had limited protection or no specific protections for LGBTQ+ individuals in employment. In these states, individuals must rely primarily on the federal protections provided by the *Bostock* ruling.

Other initiatives aimed at equality and inclusion came from businesses themselves. In 1984, IBM became one of the first major corporations to include sexual orientation in its equal opportunity policy, setting a precedent for other companies to follow. In 2002, the Human Rights Campaign, the largest LGBTQ+ political lobbying organization in the United States, published the first Corporate Equality Index (CEI), rating companies on their LGBTQ+-inclusive policies and practices. The CEI would become a powerful tool for companies to review their policies and promote workplace equality. In 2011, Tim Cook became CEO of Apple Inc. He publicly came out as gay in 2014, becoming the first openly gay CEO of a Fortune 500 company. Cook's openness about his sexuality and his leadership at one of the world's most influential companies have played a significant role in championing LGBTQ+ rights in the business world, leading to an increase in openly gay, lesbian, and transgender executives in American business.

Despite significant progress in recent years, LGBTQ+ individuals continue to face several challenges in the business world ranging from legal and policy issues to social and cultural barriers. While federal protections exist under the *Bostock v. Clayton County* ruling, state-level protection for LGBTQ+ individuals vary significantly. This inconsistency can create uncertainty and vulnerability for LGBTQ+ employees depending on their location. Legal challenges to existing protections and potential backlash against new policies pose ongoing threats to the stability of LGBTQ+ rights.

A case in point is the 2018 Supreme Court ruling in *Masterpiece Cakeshop v. Colorado Civil Rights Commission* in which a baker refused to make a wedding cake for a gay couple, citing his religious beliefs against same-sex marriage. The Supreme Court ruled 7–2 in favor of the baker, ruling that the Colorado Civil Rights Commission showed hostility toward the baker's religious beliefs and violated his right to free exercise of religion under the First Amendment. The decision did not address whether businesses could generally refuse service to LGBTQ+ individuals based on religious objections but left open the possibility of future cases addressing similar conflicts between religious beliefs and LGBTQ+ rights. The case highlights the tension between religious freedom and antidiscrimination laws. It also raised the possibility that changes in the political landscape could lead to attempts to roll back protections or reintroduce discriminatory legislation.

Even with current legal protections, discrimination and harassment of LGBTQ+ individuals remain prevalent in many workplaces. Microaggressions, hostile work environments, and unequal treatment can hinder career advancement for LGBTQ+ individuals, particularly transgender people, while ongoing discrimination can lead to lower job satisfaction, reduced productivity, and higher turnover rates among LGBTQ+ employees. Not all companies have adopted inclusive policies or offer benefits that fully support LGBTQ+ employees such as comprehensive healthcare coverage for transgender individuals or family leave policies that recognize same-sex partnerships.

LGBTQ+ individuals remain underrepresented in senior leadership and executive roles across many industries. This lack of representation can limit visibility of LGBTQ+ issues and advocacy within companies. LGBTQ+ employees, particularly transgender individuals and LGBTQ+ workers of color, often face significant wage gaps and economic disparities compared to their heterosexual and cisgender counterparts. Addressing these issues will require ongoing legal and social advocacy, policy development, and cultural change within organizations to foster equality and inclusion in the workplace.

BIOGRAPHIES

Sam Altman (1985–)

Entrepreneur, Business Executive

A leading figure in the tech industry, particularly in the fields of tech ecosystems and artificial intelligence (AI) innovation, Samuel Harris "Sam" Altman is most notable for cofounding OpenAI, Inc., the company that developed ChatGPT under his leadership. As of July 2025, his various enterprises had resulted in an estimated net worth of $1.8 billion.

Altman was born in Chicago, the eldest in a Jewish family of four children, and grew up in St. Louis, Missouri. His mother worked as a dermatologist, and his father was a real estate broker. After receiving his first computer, a Macintosh, at age eight, he began to learn how to code and take apart computer hardware. At 17, while attending John Burroughs School, a private school in Ladue, Missouri, he declared he was gay while speaking out after students objected to a National Coming Out Day speaker. After graduating from high school, he went to Stanford University, where he studied computer science until dropping out after two years to pursue entrepreneurship.

In 2005, when he was 19, he founded Loopt, a mobile, location-based social network, which secured some $30 million in venture capital; he sold Loopt to banking company Green Dot in 2012. The same year, he founded the venture capital firm Hydrazine Capital with his brother Jack to focus on early-stage startup investments. In 2014, he became the president of Y Combinator, a startup accelerator he had joined as a partner in 2011. As president, he oversaw growth to support startups valued at over $65 billion. He was affiliated with Y Combinator as president of the YC Group and self-titled chairman of the board until 2019. It was later revealed that the company's partners never approved his appointment as chairman.

In 2015, Altman, with funding from entrepreneurs such as Elon Musk; venture capitalists such as Jessica Livingston and Peter Thiel; and companies such as Microsoft, Amazon Web Services, and Infosys, cofounded and launched the artificial intelligence research organization OpenAI. By 2019, he was CEO of OpenAI and, after raising $1 billion from Microsoft, launched ChatGPT. He was abruptly fired by OpenAI's board in November 2023 over concerns of transparency and communication. However, a grassroots revolt by employees and investors led to his reinstatement days later.

In January 2025, soon after Donald Trump's inauguration, Altman, who had been a vocal critic of Trump in the past, aligned himself in a private-sector joint venture with the president, together with the heads of the computing company Oracle and the Japanese holding company SoftBank, to announce Stargate LLC, an initiative that had been planned since 2022. The venture's ambitious goal—to build extensive AI infrastructure, including data centers, across the United States—has been compared to the Manhattan Project of the 1940s, drawing questions concerning federal involvement and potential influence on AI development and usage, particularly in the field of data collection, as well as fueling concerns about the influence of tech companies on government policy.

Altman dated Loopt cofounder Nick Sivo until 2012 and married Australian software engineer Oliver Mulherin in 2024. The couple became parents to a son in February 2025. Altman is a lifelong vegetarian; a self-described doomsday prepper; and a signatory, with his husband, of the Giving Pledge, a commitment to giving away most of their wealth.

Stuart Appelbaum (1953-)

Labor Leader

Stuart Appelbaum is a prominent American labor leader and advocate for workers' rights best known for his role as president of the Retail, Wholesale and Department Store Union (RWDSU). He is openly gay and has been a significant figure in the labor movement, particularly in advocating for LGBTQ+ rights within the workplace. His leadership has been instrumental in pushing for fair wages, better working conditions, and inclusive policies that protect the rights of all workers regardless of their sexual orientation or gender identity.

Appelbaum was born in Brockton, Massachusetts. He grew up in a working-class family, which influenced his lifelong commitment to labor rights and social justice. He attended Brandeis University, where he earned a bachelor's degree in political science. He then went on to Harvard Law School, where he developed a deeper understanding of the intersection between law, politics, and workers' rights.

After completing his education, Appelbaum worked in various roles, including as an attorney and in political campaigns. His early career was marked by a strong commitment to social justice, which eventually led him to the labor movement. He was elected president of the RWDSU in 1998, a position he has held since. Under his leadership, the union has been at the forefront of efforts to improve wages, working conditions, and job security for workers in retail, wholesale, and other service industries. He has been a vocal critic of unfair labor practices and has led numerous campaigns to organize workers and secure better contracts.

Appelbaum has been deeply involved in political advocacy, particularly around issues that affect workers and marginalized communities. He has been a strong supporter of progressive policies, including raising the minimum wage, expanding healthcare access, and strengthening labor rights. He has worked to ensure that union contracts include protections against discrimination based on sexual orientation and gender identity. He has also been a prominent voice in the broader LGBTQ+ rights movement, advocating for marriage equality and other civil rights issues. His political work has included serving as a delegate to the Democratic National Convention and participating in numerous campaigns to elect pro-labor and pro-LGBTQ+ candidates.

In recent statements, Appelbaum has highlighted the ongoing challenges that LGBTQ+ workers face, including harassment, discrimination, and lack of recognition for their gender identities in the workplace. He has been particularly critical of employers who claim to espouse progressive values but fail to implement basic protections for LGBTQ+ employees such as recognizing preferred gender pronouns or ensuring safe and respectful work environments.

Mark Bingham (1970–2001)

Public Relations Executive, 9/11 Hero and Victim

Mark Kendall Bingham was the founder and CEO of the Bingham Group, a public relations firm based in San Francisco, California, with a satellite office in New York City that was established in 2001. A member of the gay-inclusive rugby team the San Francisco Fog as well as a business executive, he has been honored as one of the heroes of the hijacked United Airlines Flight 93 on September 11, 2001. His actions during the hijacking, together with his athletic prowess, led to a reassessment of gay stereotypes.

Bingham was born in Phoenix, Arizona, the single child of parents Alice Hoagland and Gerald Bingham. After his parents divorced when he was 2 years old, he was raised by his mother and her family in Florida, southern California, and San Jose, California, where he attended Los Gatos High School. He began playing rugby in high school and was captain of the team for two years.

After graduating from high school in 1988, he attended the University of California, Berkeley, where he played on Berkeley's championship rugby team and served as president of the Chi Psi fraternity. Upon his graduation from Berkeley in 1993, he came out as gay to his family and friends.

After opening a branch of the Bingham Group in New York City, Bingham began spending more time on the East Coast, where he discussed with his friend Scott Glaessgen plans to organize a New York rugby team to be named the Gotham Knights.

On September 11, 2001, he boarded United Airlines Flight 93 for San Francisco from Newark Airport. Apart from Bingham, the passengers included business executives Tom Burnett, Jeremy Glick, and Todd Beamer, who had also attended Los Gatos High School. When Al-Qaeda terrorists hijacked the plane and took over cockpit operations, Bingham, Burnett, Glick, and Beamer formed and carried out a plan to retake the plane, which thwarted the hijackers' intention to crash the plane into a target in Washington, D.C., and instead caused the aircraft to crash in a field near Shanksville, Pennsylvania, with the loss of all lives on board.

Bingham was survived by his parents and other family members and his former

The September 11 Memorial South Pool in New York City includes Bingham's name along with the other Flight 93 passengers.

partner of six years, Paul Holm. He received many posthumous honors, which included a September 17, 2001, ceremony for San Francisco Bay Area victims of the 9/11 attacks, during which Senators John McCain and Barbara Boxer presented a folded American flag to Holm in Bingham's honor. The following year, the Mark Kendall Bingham Memorial Tournament (known as the Bingham Cup), a biennial international rugby tournament primarily for gay and bisexual men, was established in his memory.

In 2004, singer–songwriter Melissa Etheridge dedicated the song "Tuesday Morning" on her *Breakdown* album to his memory. Bingham has been memorialized at the National 9/11 Memorial in New York and the Flight 93 National Memorial in Pennsylvania.

A 2013 feature-length documentary, *The Rugby Player*, focuses on Bingham and the bond he had with his mother, a former United Airlines flight attendant who became a champion of LGBTQ+ rights. The film's alternate title, *With You*, is a rugby term that was one of his favorite expressions.

David Bohnett (1956–)

Technology Entrepreneur, Investor

David Bohnett is the founder of the pioneering social networking site GeoCities and an investor in technology startups through his venture capital company, Baroda Ventures. A mission-driven philanthropist as well as a tech pioneer, he has helped to shape civil landscapes in the service of social empowerment.

Born in Chicago and raised in the affluent Chicago suburb of Hinsdale, Bohnett's father was a business executive and his mother a preschool teacher. His sister, Wendy Bohnett Campbell, served as president of the board of the Dayton Philharmonic, and his brother William, a retired corporate attorney, is a former board member of the Smithsonian Institution. While growing up, he showed an entrepreneurial spirit, delivering newspapers and selling Amway products. After graduating from high school, where he became interested in computers, he attended the University of Southern California, majoring in business administration and minoring in computer science. He worked several jobs to put himself through college and graduated in 1978 with a BS in business administration. He felt isolated as a closeted gay young man in his conservative hometown and as a USC college student, especially after the suicide of his first lover, who had grown up Roman Catholic in a small Indiana town. That changed when he entered Ross School of Business at the University of Michigan, where he received an M.B.A. in finance in 1980. In graduate school, he became a vocal, openly gay student and campus LGBTQ+ activist, working as a hotline counselor at the university's Lesbian and Gay Male Program Office (later renamed the Spectrum Center) and volunteering to appear in freshman psychology classes, telling students, "I'm gay, ask me anything."

Bohnett continued his LGBTQ+ activism in Los Angeles, where he worked with GLAAD and the Los Angeles Gay & Lesbian Community Services Center, came out to his parents, and worked as a staff information consultant at the accounting firm Arthur Anderson from 1980 to 1983. In 1983, he entered a long-term relationship with Rand Schrader, an openly gay municipal court judge who succumbed to AIDS in 1993, leaving Bohnett, before the legal recognition of same-sex registered domestic partnerships in 1999, with no legal spousal benefits. His partner of over a decade during the 2000s was writer and broadcaster Tom Gregory.

In 1994, Bohnett cofounded GeoCities, one of the first social networking platforms, which grew to host over 38 million pages before going public in 1998. The same year, he founded Baroda Ventures, which has invested in such tech startups as NetZero, Stamps.com, and Gay.com. In 1999, he founded the David Bohnett Foundation, which was initially endowed with $32 million and has since donated over $120 million to date. The Foundation has included such initiatives as LGBTQ+ rights, gun violence prevention, civic leadership, voting rights, animal language research, and support for the arts in Los Angeles. The Foundation's network of David Bohnett CyberCenters are safe, tech-equipped spaces at LGBTQ+ centers and universities, with over 60 locations nationwide.

Bohnett has been the recipient of several honors, including the Los Angeles Gay and Lesbian Center's Rand Schrader Award (1999), the ACLU Citizen Advocate Award (2002), GLSEN's Lifetime Achievement Award (2009), and the Brady Bear Award from the Brady Center to Prevent Gun Violence (2016). Since 1998, he has been featured numerous times in magazine lists of influential people. In 2025, *Time* magazine listed him in its TIME100 Philanthropy List.

Claudia Brind-Woody (1955–)

Business Executive

An executive at IBM, where she has successfully occupied senior leadership roles within the corporation, Claudia Lavergne Brind-Woody is also a globally recognized LGBTQ+ advocate whose commitment to diversity programming has helped to shape both the tech industry and corporate culture both nationally and internationally.

Raised in a small factory town in southern Virginia, Brind-Woody was about 12 years old when she knew she was "different," but without resources in her town library that included the words "gay" and "lesbian," she "didn't have a word for it." Looking back, she said, "I could tell that absolutely I was a lesbian." She attended Mary Baldwin College, where she was a member of Phi Beta Kappa and graduated summa cum laude in 1977. She went on to earn an M.S. in higher education administration from the University of Tennessee, Knoxville, where she shared an apartment with legendary women's basketball coach Pat Summitt, who was then coach of the Tennessee Lady Volunteers team. While completing her degree, she worked as an assistant coach for the university's women's basketball team and then served as assistant women's athletics director. She continued her education, earning an M.B.A. and pursuing Ph.D. coursework in organizational development at the University of Texas, Austin, where she also served as assistant women's athletics director and was awarded the Kozmetsky Prize for academic excellence. She finished her education with a J.D. from Georgia State University School of Law in 1996.

In 1996, Brind-Woody joined IBM as vice president and managing director of global intellectual property and licensing. Over more than two decades, she negotiated high-value technology deals, led the divestiture practice, and built IP management teams responsible for billions in revenue. From 2019 to 2022, she served as managing director for IBM's Walgreens Boots Alliance account, and as of 2022–2023, led IBM's Global Systems Integrators and strategic partnerships in the United Kingdom and Ireland. She also cochairs IBM's LGBTQ+ Executive Taskforce and has driven company-wide LGBTQ+ inclusion strategies such as ally training for 440,000 staff members and global resource groups in 42 countries. She has served on many advisory boards, including Out & Equal Workplace Advocates, Lambda Legal, Workplace Pride, Stonewall Global Diversity Champions, and OUTstanding, and has been a speaker on LGBTQ+ rights at international forums. Called by *Business Insider* "one of the most powerful gay women in business," she has received the Out & Equal Trailblazer Award and been recognized for her global leadership by *The Guardian* and *The Financial Times*.

Tim Cook (1960–)

Business Executive

Timothy Donald "Tim" Cook is the CEO of Apple Inc., one of the most valuable and influential companies in the world. As the first openly gay CEO of a Fortune 500 company, he has not only been a trailblazer in the tech industry but also an important advocate for LGBTQ+ rights and equality. His leadership at Apple has been marked by a focus on innovation, sustainability, and social responsibility, continuing the legacy of his predecessor, Steve Jobs, while carving out his own distinct path.

Cook was born in Robertsdale, Alabama. Raised in a working-class family, he developed a strong work ethic and an appreciation for education from an early age. He earned a BS in industrial engineering from Auburn University in 1982, followed by an M.B.A. from Duke University's Fuqua School of Business in 1988, where he was a Fuqua Scholar, a distinction given to the top 10 percent of the class.

Cook began his career at IBM, where he worked in the company's personal computer division. Over the next 12 years, he worked in manufacturing and supply chain management, eventually being promoted to the position of director of North American fulfillment. After IBM, he served as COO of the reseller division at Intelligent Electronics and later as vice president of corporate materials at Compaq, where he managed the company's procurement and inventory operations.

Cook joined Apple in 1998 as senior vice president for worldwide operations during a time when the company was struggling financially. His expertise in supply chain management and operational efficiency played a crucial role in turning around Apple's fortunes. He was instrumental in restructuring Apple's supply chain, reducing inventory levels, and increasing profitability. In 2007, he was promoted to COO of Apple and often served as acting CEO during Jobs's medical leaves. After Jobs's resignation due to health issues in August 2011, Cook was named CEO of Apple. Under his leadership, Apple has continued to thrive, introducing innovative products such as the Apple Watch, AirPods, and several new iterations of the iPhone, iPad, and Mac. He has also championed corporate responsibility, focusing on issues such as environmental sustainability, renewable energy, and supply chain transparency. He has overseen Apple's transition to using 100 percent renewable energy for its facilities and advocated for stronger data privacy protections for consumers.

Cook made headlines in 2014 when he publicly came out as gay in an essay published in *Bloomberg Businessweek*. In it, he stated that he was proud to be gay and considered it among the greatest gifts God had given him. His decision to come out was driven by a desire to help others struggling with their identity and advocate for equality and inclusion. His announcement made him the first openly gay CEO of a Fortune 500 company, and he has since become a prominent advocate for LGBTQ+ rights both within the corporate world and society at large.

Cook's journey from a small town in Alabama to the helm of one of the world's most influential companies is a testament to his vision, leadership, and commitment to making a positive impact on society. As the first openly gay CEO of a Fortune 500 company, he has not only transformed Apple but also used his platform to advocate for LGBTQ+ rights and social justice, making him a pivotal figure in both the tech industry and the broader movement for equality.

Jim Fitterling (1962–)

Business Executive

James R. "Jim" Fitterling is the chairman and CEO of Dow Inc., one of the world's leading materials science companies. He is recognized not only for his strategic leadership in steering Dow through significant transformations but also for his role as a prominent advocate for diversity and inclusion within the corporate world. He made history as one of the few openly gay CEOs of a Fortune 500 company, using his platform to champion LGBTQ+ rights and workplace equality.

Fitterling grew up on a small farm in Missouri. His interest in engineering and science was evident from a young age, which led him to pursue a degree in mechanical engineering. He graduated with a bachelor's degree in mechanical engineering from the University of Missouri in 1983.

Fitterling began his career at Dow in 1984, starting as a sales representative in the company's U.S. plastics business. Over the years, he held various leadership roles in different divisions of the company, gaining extensive experience in operations, business management, and strategy. His work took him to various locations around the world, including Malaysia, where he managed Dow's operations for Southeast Asia. He was appointed Dow's CEO in 2018, following the company's separation from DowDuPont into an independent entity. As CEO, he has been instrumental in positioning Dow as a leader in materials science, focusing on innovation, sustainability, and performance-driven growth. Under his leadership, Dow has advanced its commitment to environmental sustainability, emphasizing the development of products that reduce the company's carbon footprint and contribute to a circular economy.

Fitterling has also prioritized operational efficiency and technological innovation, ensuring that Dow remains competitive in the global market. His strategic vision has guided the company through challenging economic conditions, while his commitment to fostering a culture of inclusion and safety has been central to his leadership approach. In 2020, he was named chairman of Dow's board of directors, further solidifying his influence over the company's strategic direction.

Fitterling is one of the few openly gay CEOs leading a Fortune 500 company, making him a significant figure in the LGBTQ+ community. He came out publicly in 2014, inspired by the increasing visibility of LGBTQ+ leaders and a desire to be a role model for others. Since coming out, he has been a vocal advocate for LGBTQ+ inclusion in the workplace, emphasizing the importance of authenticity and representation in corporate leadership.

Fitterling, who is married to his longtime partner, Alex Lee, has spoken of the importance of diversity and inclusion in business, saying, "Being authentic and bringing your whole self to work is important not just for personal well-being, but also for the health of an organization. When people feel accepted and valued for who they are, they can truly thrive and contribute at their highest level."

Beth Ford (1964–)

Business Executive

Beth Ford is the president and CEO of Land O'Lakes, Inc., one of the largest agricultural cooperatives in the United States. She made history as the first openly gay woman to lead a Fortune 500 company, marking a significant milestone for LGBTQ+ representation in corporate leadership. She is known for her strategic vision, commitment to sustainability, and dedication to fostering diversity and inclusion within the agricultural industry and beyond.

Ford was born in Sioux City, Iowa, in a large family with seven siblings. Raised in a close-knit, working-class environment, she learned the values of hard work and perseverance from an early age. She attended Iowa State University, where she earned a bachelor's degree in business administration. She later obtained an M.B.A. from Columbia Business School.

Ford began her career in the oil and gas industry, working for Mobil Corporation. She gained extensive experience in operations, supply chain management, and logistics, holding leadership positions at a variety of companies, including PepsiCo, Kraft Foods, and Scholastic. Her diverse background in different industries provided her with a broad perspective on business management and operational efficiency.

Ford joined Land O'Lakes in 2011 as executive vice president and chief supply chain and operations officer. In this role, she was responsible for overseeing the company's supply chain, operations, and information technology, playing a crucial role in optimizing efficiency and driving growth. Her success in this position led to her promotion to president and CEO of Land O'Lakes in July 2018. As CEO, she has focused on innovation, sustainability, and supporting the cooperative's farmer members. She has championed efforts to enhance the use of technology in agriculture, emphasizing the importance of precision farming and data analytics to improve crop yields and reduce environmental impact. Under her leadership, Land O'Lakes has also strengthened its commitment to sustainability, implementing initiatives aimed at reducing greenhouse gas emissions and promoting soil health.

Ford's tenure as CEO has also been marked by a strong emphasis on diversity and inclusion. She has been a vocal advocate for creating a workplace culture that values and supports employees from all backgrounds. Her leadership extends beyond Land O'Lakes, as she serves on several boards and councils that influence national agricultural policy and corporate governance.

Ford made headlines not only for her professional achievements but also for her openness about her sexuality. When she was appointed CEO of Land O'Lakes, she became the first openly gay woman to lead a Fortune 500 company. She stated that she hopes her visibility can inspire others and help break down barriers for LGBTQ+ individuals in the corporate world. She lives in Minneapolis with her wife, Jill Schurtz, and their three children. She has spoken about the importance of being authentic in both her personal and professional life, and she continues to advocate for LGBTQ+ rights and equality. "The most important thing is that you're not afraid to be who you are," she said. "There are moments in everyone's life where you have to choose whether you're going to be silent or whether you're going to speak. For me, being open about who I am is one way I can encourage others to do the same and create a more inclusive world."

David Geffen (1943–)

Business Executive

David Lawrence Geffen is a highly influential American business magnate, producer, and philanthropist best known for his pioneering contributions to the entertainment industry. As the founder of Geffen Records, cofounder of DreamWorks SKG, and a key figure in the creation of Asylum Records, he has played a critical role in shaping modern music, film, and media. In addition to his professional achievements, he is one of the most prominent openly gay figures in the business world, and his philanthropy has made a significant impact in the arts, education, and LGBTQ+ rights.

Geffen was born in Brooklyn, New York, to a Jewish family. His parents were immigrants from Eastern Europe, and he grew up in a modest household. He attended Brooklyn's New Utrecht High School, where he showed an early interest in show business but struggled academically due to dyslexia, a condition that was not well understood at the time.

Geffen briefly attended the University of Texas, Austin, and Brooklyn College, but he dropped out to pursue a career in the entertainment industry. His first job in the industry was in the mailroom at the William Morris Agency in New York City. His determination and keen sense of opportunity quickly propelled him forward, and he soon became a talent agent, representing clients like Laura Nyro, Joni Mitchell, and Crosby, Stills, Nash & Young.

In 1970, Geffen cofounded Asylum Records with partner Elliot Roberts. The label became synonymous with the southern California sound of the 1970s, signing iconic artists such as the Eagles, Jackson Browne, Linda Ronstadt, and Joni Mitchell. Asylum Records quickly established itself as a major force in the music industry, and in 1972, it was acquired by Warner Communications. After leaving Asylum, he founded Geffen Records in 1980, further solidifying his influence in the music industry. Geffen Records became home to a diverse range of successful artists, including John Lennon, Elton John, Cher, Guns N' Roses, and Nirvana. The label was known for giving artists creative freedom and signing some of the most groundbreaking acts of the era.

Geffen publicly came out as gay in 1992, making him one of the most prominent openly gay figures in the entertainment industry at a time when few were open about their sexuality. His decision to come out was seen as a significant moment for LGBTQ+ visibility, especially in an industry known for its conservative attitudes toward sexual orientation.

In 1994, Geffen cofounded DreamWorks SKG with Steven Spielberg and Jeffrey Katzenberg. DreamWorks quickly became a major player in the film industry, producing critically acclaimed films such as *Saving Private Ryan*, *American Beauty*, and *Shrek*. The studio's success extended into animation and television, making it one of the most innovative and influential entertainment companies of its time.

Geffen's business acumen and visionary approach to entertainment have earned him a place as one of the most powerful figures in Hollywood. He has been recognized with numerous awards, including induction into the Rock & Roll Hall of Fame and receipt of the Academy Award for Best Picture as a producer of *American Beauty*.

Geffen is also known for his extensive philanthropy, particularly in the fields of education, health care, and the arts. He has donated hundreds of millions of dollars to various institutions, including UCLA, where the David Geffen School of Medicine is named in his honor, and Lincoln Center in New York City, which houses the David Geffen Hall. His contributions to HIV/AIDS research and treatment have been particularly impactful. He has been a major supporter of the Gay Men's Health Crisis, amfAR (the Foundation for AIDS Research), and other organizations dedicated to fighting the AIDS epidemic. His philanthropy has helped fund critical research and support services for those affected by the disease.

As one of the most influential and openly gay figures in Hollywood, Geffen has paved the way for greater acceptance and visibility of LGBTQ+ individuals in the business world.

Arlan Hamilton (1980–)

Venture Capitalist, Author

The founder and managing partner of Backstage Capital, a firm dedicated to investing in underrepresented business owners, including women, people of color, and LGBTQ+ entrepreneurs, Arlan Hamilton's bold approach to equity in entrepreneurship has established her as one of the most influential figures in the business world. Openly lesbian, Hamilton has spoken publicly about how her identity has shaped her sense of mission and business philosophy.

Hamilton's success was not the result of a traditional academic path into business or technology. Born into a working-class family in Dallas, Texas, she attended college but did not complete her degree; instead, during the 2000s and into the 2010s, she pursued work in the music and entertainment industries, where she served as a tour manager and production coordinator. She worked with a variety of performers, including recording artists Janine, Toni Braxton, and CeeLo Green, and was a director's assistant for television shows such as BET's *Sunday Best* and *The Biggest Loser*. She also founded and published the indie magazine *Interlude* and gained fans for her blog *Your Daily Lesbian Moment*, aimed at women seeking romantic and platonic connections with other women.

Although Hamilton lacked formal venture capital credentials, she taught herself the language and strategy of the field, often reading investment literature and watching Stanford University lectures online while living in transitional housing or sleeping at the airport. Her unorthodox path became the foundation of her later philosophy: Underestimated people are often the ones best equipped to create value and drive innovation. She launched Backstage Capital in 2015 with the mission of investing in entrepreneurs traditionally excluded from mainstream venture capital. Her initial success came after publishing a blog post titled "Dear White Venture Capitalists," which caught the attention of her first backer, angel investor Susan Kimberlin, who would become a venture partner at Backstage Capital. By 2018, after raising additional support, she began deploying funds to startups led by women, people of color, and LGBTQ+ individuals and had invested over $4 million in 100 startups. Her company eventually expanded to fund nearly 200 companies across a range of industries. In 2018, she also announced the creation of a $36 million fund dedicated exclusively to Black women founders, a historic commitment in a field where such demographics had received less than 0.2 percent of funding, and launched Backstage Studio, an accelerator program with branches in Los Angeles, Detroit, Philadelphia, and London.

In 2019, Hamilton married German composer and actress Anna Eichenauer. The same year, *Business Insider* named her as one of the 23 most powerful LGBTQ+ people in the tech industry. In 2020, she published *It's About Damn Time*, a memoir that also serves as a practical guide aimed at empowering entrepreneurs, particularly those from marginalized backgrounds. In 2021 and 2022, she was named on the Queer50 list in *Fast Company* magazine. In 2024, she was named as a strategic advisor for INPINK, an online marketplace that connects women in the music business with professionals seeking to hire diverse talented women in the industry.

Robert Hanson (1968–)

Business Executive

Robert Hanson is a prominent American business executive known for his leadership roles in the fashion and retail industries. He has held top positions at several major companies, including American Eagle Outfitters and John Hardy. He is openly gay and has been a vocal advocate for diversity and inclusion in the workplace, particularly in the fashion industry. His ability to drive brand innovation and growth while promoting corporate responsibility has made him a respected figure in the business world.

Hanson was born and raised in the Midwest, where he developed a strong work ethic and an early interest in business and marketing. He attended the University of Wisconsin, Madison, where he earned a bachelor's degree in marketing and finance.

Hanson began his career at Levi Strauss & Co., where he quickly rose through the ranks due to his keen understanding of brand management and consumer marketing. During his 23-year tenure at Levi Strauss, he held various leadership positions, including president of the Levi's brand, where he was responsible for global brand strategy, product design, and marketing. His work at Levi's was instrumental in revitalizing the brand and expanding its reach to new markets around the world.

In 2012, Hanson was appointed CEO of American Eagle Outfitters, a leading American clothing and accessories retailer known for its youthful brand image. Under his leadership, American Eagle experienced significant growth and brand expansion. He focused on enhancing the company's digital presence, improving customer engagement, and streamlining operations to increase profitability. His strategic initiatives helped American Eagle remain competitive in a rapidly changing retail environment.

After leaving American Eagle Outfitters in 2014, Hanson took on the role of CEO at John Hardy, a luxury jewelry brand based in Bali, Indonesia. At John Hardy, he was tasked with repositioning the brand to appeal to a broader, more global audience while maintaining its commitment to sustainable and ethical practices. He led efforts to enhance the brand's artisanal craftsmanship and expand its retail presence, which included opening flagship stores in key markets such as New York City and Hong Kong. In 2019, he was appointed executive vice president and president of Constellation Brands' wine and spirits division. During his tenure, he played a pivotal role in transforming the division by repositioning its brand portfolio to focus more on higher-end products aligned with consumer trends. He led initiatives to expand global, omnichannel distribution and strengthened direct-to-consumer and international sales channels. He stepped down from his position at Constellation Brands in February 2024.

Hanson's visibility as an openly gay executive in the fashion and retail industries has made him a role model for LGBTQ+ professionals. He has used his platform to promote diversity and inclusion initiatives both within the companies he has led and in the broader business community. His commitment to these values is reflected in his leadership style, which prioritizes empathy, collaboration, and respect for individual differences.

Mary Kay Henry (1958–)

Labor Leader

Mary Kay Henry is a prominent labor leader and the international president of the Service Employees International Union (SEIU), one of the largest and most influential labor unions in the United States. Elected as the first female president of SEIU in 2010, she has been a powerful advocate for workers' rights, social justice, and LGBTQ+ equality. As an openly lesbian leader, she has played a pivotal role in advancing LGBTQ+ rights within the labor movement and has been a strong voice for inclusion and diversity in the workplace.

Henry was born in Wayne, Michigan, and grew up in a large Catholic family. She attended Michigan State University, where she earned a bachelor's degree in urban planning and labor relations. Her early exposure to social justice issues, combined with her religious upbringing, inspired her to pursue a career in labor organizing. She began her career as a researcher and organizer for SEIU, quickly rising through the ranks due to her dedication and effectiveness in advocating for workers.

Henry was elected international president of SEIU in 2010, becoming the first woman to lead the union. Under her leadership, SEIU has continued to grow in influence, particularly in sectors such as health care, property services, and public services. She has been instrumental in campaigns to raise the minimum wage, improve working conditions, and expand healthcare access. She has led efforts such as the Fight for $15, which seeks to secure a $15 minimum wage for all workers in the United States. She has expanded SEIU's reach by building coalitions with other social justice organizations, faith groups, and community activists. She has been a strong proponent of intersectionality, recognizing the interconnectedness of workers' rights, racial justice, and LGBTQ+ equality. Her leadership has helped to position SEIU as a leading force in the broader movement for social and economic justice in the United States.

As an openly lesbian union leader, Henry has been a tireless advocate for LGBTQ+ rights within the labor movement and beyond. She has worked to ensure that SEIU is an inclusive and supportive environment for LGBTQ+ workers, pushing for LGBTQ+-inclusive policies in union contracts and fighting against discrimination in the workplace. She has also been a vocal supporter of marriage equality and has used her platform to advocate for broader social justice issues affecting the LGBTQ+ community.

Chris Hughes (1983–)

Business Executive

Christopher "Chris" Hughes is an entrepreneur, philanthropist, and cofounder of Facebook whose influence extends far beyond the tech industry. As an openly gay man, he has used his platform and resources to advocate for LGBTQ+ rights and social justice. His journey from helping to build one of the most influential social media platforms in history to becoming a vocal advocate for economic equality and LGBTQ+ issues highlights his deep commitment to fostering a more inclusive and just society.

Hughes was born in Hickory, North Carolina, and raised in a conservative household. His academic excellence led him to Phillips Academy in Andover, Massachusetts, and later to Harvard University in 2002. At Harvard, he met Mark Zuckerberg, Eduardo Saverin, and Dustin Moskovitz, and together, they cofounded Facebook. He majored in history and literature, but his role in the development of Facebook, particularly in user experience and communications, became a defining element of his early career.

Hughes was instrumental in shaping Facebook's user experience, playing a key role in launching the revolutionary Facebook News Feed. His work at Facebook laid the foundation for his later efforts to use technology for social good. In 2007, he left Facebook to join Barack Obama's presidential campaign and helped create My.BarackObama.com, a digital platform that mobilized millions of supporters and set new standards for digital engagement in political campaigns. As an openly gay man, he was also a strong advocate for LGBTQ+ rights within the campaign.

After Facebook's IPO in 2012, Hughes focused on philanthropy, particularly relating to economic justice and LGBTQ+ rights. He and his husband, Sean Eldridge, whom he married in 2012, have been significant supporters of marriage equality and other LGBTQ+ causes. In 2016, he bought *The New Republic* and attempted to modernize the century-old magazine by shifting its focus toward digital media and broadening its appeal to a younger audience. His efforts to transform the publication led to significant internal conflict, including the resignation of longtime editor Franklin Foer and a mass exodus of senior staff in 2014, who opposed the changes they believed undermined the magazine's journalistic integrity. Despite his intentions to revitalize the publication, his tenure was marked by controversy. In early 2016, he decided to sell *The New Re-*

public to Win McCormack, acknowledging that he was not the right person to lead it.

Since 2016, Hughes has focused on philanthropy, advocacy, and public policy, particularly in economic justice and social equity. He cofounded the Economic Security Project, advocating for guaranteed income as a solution to economic inequality, and has supported various philanthropic initiatives aimed at reducing poverty. He has also been an active public speaker and writer on these issues, promoting policy changes to address systemic economic challenges. His work emphasizes the importance of financial security and economic opportunities for marginalized communities.

Michaela Mendelsohn

Business Executive

Michaela Mendelsohn is a pioneering transgender entrepreneur, advocate, and public speaker known for her work in the restaurant industry and tireless efforts to support and uplift the transgender community. As the CEO of Pollo West Corporation, one of the largest franchises of El Pollo Loco, she has demonstrated exceptional leadership in business while also breaking barriers as a transgender woman in a traditionally conservative industry. Her advocacy work, particularly through the founding of TransCanWork, has made her a significant figure in the movement for transgender rights and workplace inclusion.

Mendelsohn was born in New York City but moved to southern California as a young child. She attended Cal State Northridge intending to become an attorney but decided to drop out of school to start her own construction business. After 30 years of marriage and with three grown children, she transitioned to female and joined the restaurant industry.

Mendelsohn acquired a franchise of El Pollo Loco, a popular fast-food chain specializing in Mexican-style grilled chicken. Her business acumen and leadership skills quickly became evident as she expanded her franchise holdings, growing Pollo West Corporation into one of the largest and most successful El Pollo Loco franchise groups in the United States. As the CEO of Pollo West Corporation, she oversees multiple El Pollo Loco locations across southern California.

Beyond her achievements in business, Mendelsohn is widely recognized for her advocacy work on behalf of the transgender community. In 2016, she founded TransCanWork, a nonprofit organization dedicated to creating safe and inclusive workplaces for transgender individuals. The organization provides training and resources to employers, helping them to better understand the needs and challenges of transgender employees and create environments where all workers can thrive.

Mendelsohn's commitment to inclusion is also reflected in her own business practices. She has made it a priority to hire and support transgender employees within her restaurants, providing them with opportunities for employment, mentorship, and career advancement. Her efforts have been instrumental in changing perceptions and fostering greater acceptance of transgender individuals in the workplace.

In addition to her work with TransCanWork, Mendelsohn serves on the board of the Trevor Project, a leading national organization providing crisis intervention and suicide prevention services to LGBTQ+ youth. She is also a sought-after public speaker, sharing her story and insights at conferences, universities, and corporate events across the country.

Mendelsohn has shown that it is possible to succeed in business while also making a meaningful difference in the lives of others. Her dedication to creating opportunities for transgender individuals and ongoing efforts to promote acceptance and equality have made her a significant figure in both the business world and LGBTQ+ communities.

Suze Orman (1951–)

Financial Advisor, Author, Podcast Host

Susan Lynn "Suze" Orman, who began as a waitress, became a stockbroker, and founded a financial advisory firm, is best known to most people as the Emmy Award–winning financial advice-dispensing host of *The Suze Orman Show*, which ran on CNBC from 2002 to 2015. She has appeared as a guest on numerous TV and radio shows, written 10 best-selling books on finance, and built a media empire centered around financial literacy.

Orman was born on Chicago's South Side to Russian immigrant parents, both of whom worked: Her mother was a rabbi's secretary, and her father worked in a chicken factory and managed a deli. She earned a B.A. in social work from the University of Illinois, Urbana–Champaign, in 1976 and after college moved to Berkeley, California, where she worked as a waitress at the Buttercup Bakery before deciding to pursue a career as a stockbroker in a profession dominated by men. She entered Merrill Lynch's executive training program in 1980 and upon completion became the first female stockbroker in northern California. She remained with the firm as an account executive until 1983, when she moved to Prudential Bache, where she served as vice president of investments at Prudential Bache Securities before founding the Suze Orman Financial Group in 1987. Her book *You've Earned It, Don't Lose It* (1995) became a bestseller and launched her career in media. Her podcast *Women & Money* has been running on platforms that include Apple Podcasts and iHeart since 2008. She has also released financial tools such as credit-score kits, identity-theft protection, and retirement guides. In 2016, she became a personal finance educator for the U.S. Army. She has been a vocal advocate for the National Domestic Violence Hotline and has spoken out against financial abuse. Her career has not been without controversy. She faced a backlash for offering a prepaid debit card in 2012 that carried high fees and misleading credit benefits before its discontinuation in 2014. She has also been criticized for overstating her credentials and teaching roles at the University of Phoenix. However, she continued to remain widely respected for her relatable, emotionally driven financial philosophy.

Orman came out publicly as a lesbian in February 2007, stating in *The New York Times Magazine* that she had been with brand manager Kathy Travis for seven years. The couple married in 2010 and have since spoken out on financial inequalities facing LGBTQ+ couples, which include inequities in estate planning, taxation, and retirement accounts. Throughout her career, she has empowered her audiences, particularly women and marginalized people, in the handling of money, with a "people-first" financial philosophy that demystifies issues such as debt, retirement, and investing and puts an emphasis on fiscal responsibility. As an openly LGBTQ+ media figure, she has helped to influence discussions on equality in law and finance.

Leanne Pittsford (1980–)

Entrepreneur, Community Organizer

Leanne Pittsford is the founder of Lesbians Who Tech (LWT), a large global community of LGBTQ+ women, trans, and nonbinary people in technology. A longtime advocate for inclusivity in tech and political organizing, she has used her platform to amplify underrepresented voices and foster pathways to leadership. She has combined social justice with innovation, making her a key architect in diversifying Silicon Valley and beyond.

Born and raised in a conservative family in San Diego, California, Pittsford did not formally come out as a lesbian until her senior year in college, where she earned her undergraduate degree in political science from California Polytechnic State University, San Luis Obispo. She later completed a master's degree in education, equity, and social justice from San Francisco State University. She entered professional life working in progressive politics and later joined Equality California, one of the state's largest LGBTQ+ civil rights organizations. At Equality California, she served as senior director of communications and helped to lead efforts to repeal Proposition 8, which had banned same-sex marriage in California. She was also a cofounder of the Lesbian Entrepreneur Mentoring Partnership and the founder and CEO of Start Somewhere, a digital agency working with nonprofits and various social enterprises.

In 2012, Pittsford founded Lesbians Who Tech, now called Lesbians Who Tech + Allies. LWT began as a grassroots effort in a single meetup in San Francisco that grew into an international network of over 70,000 members across more than 40 cities. She expanded the initiative to include the Edie Windsor Coding Scholarship Fund, named for IBM technology manager and LGBTQ+ activist Edith Windsor, who was the lead plaintiff in the case that led to the 2013 U.S. Supreme Court ruling that struck down the Defense of Marriage Act (DOMA), paving the way for the legalization of same-sex marriage in 2015. The scholarship fund has awarded hundreds of scholarships to queer and trans women pursuing careers in technology. She has also launched the Tech Jobs Tour and organized LGBTQ+ Tech and Innovation Summits at the White House in 2015 and 2016. She has hosted summits that have drawn thousands of attendees, including major corporate and government partners focused on diversity and inclusion. In 2017, she launched include.io, an online platform for underrepresented tech workers and recruiters. The same year, she married Pia Carusone, a partner at SKDK, a public affairs and strategic communications firm. In 2022, she hosted a virtual Pride Summit that drew over 30,000 participants from around the world.

Recognized by *San Francisco* magazine in 2015 as a "soldier of social change," Pittsford was named by *Business Insider* in 2019 as one of the most powerful LGBTQ+ people in the tech industry. Through Lesbians Who Tech and other initiatives, she has empowered numerous LGBTQ+ people in the tech world to thrive professionally while at the same time challenging the norms of corporate leadership.

Jennifer Pritzker (1950–)

Business Executive

Jennifer Natalya Pritzker is a pioneering executive, philanthropist, and retired military officer who made history as the first openly transgender billionaire. A member of the prominent Pritzker family, known for their business empire and philanthropic efforts, she has been a trailblazer not only in the world of finance and real estate but also in advocating for transgender rights and visibility. Her work has had a profound impact on both the LGBTQ+ community and the broader society, marking her as one of the most influential figures in modern history.

Pritzker was born James Nicholas Pritzker on August 13, 1950, in Chicago, Illinois, into the wealthy and influential Pritzker family. The Pritzker family is known for their ownership of the Hyatt hotel chain and numerous other businesses. Pritzker, who is the cousin of Illinois governor J. B. Pritzker, was raised in Chicago and attended Loyola University Chicago, where she earned a B.A. in history. She later pursued further education at the Army War College and earned a master's degree from Norwich University. Her early career was shaped by her military service; she joined the U.S. Army, serving as an officer for over two decades. During her military career, she received numerous honors and retired with the rank of lieutenant colonel.

After retiring from the military, Pritzker became deeply involved in business and philanthropy. She founded Tawani Enterprises in 1995, a private investment company focused on real estate development, historic preservation, and other ventures. Tawani Enterprises has been instrumental in restoring historic buildings and creating residential communities, particularly in the Chicago area. In addition to her business ventures, she has been a major philanthropist. Through the Tawani Foundation and the Pritzker Military Foundation, she has donated millions to causes related to military history, veterans' affairs, and the LGBTQ+ community.

Pritzker made headlines in 2013 when she publicly came out as transgender, becoming the first openly transgender billionaire. Since then, she has been a vocal advocate for transgender rights, using her platform to support organizations and initiatives that promote equality and visibility for transgender people. Her advocacy work includes significant donations to LGBTQ+ causes, including scholarships for transgender students and funding for gender confirmation surgeries for those in need.

Pritzker's life and career are marked by her achievements in business, dedication to philanthropy, and courageous advocacy for transgender rights. Her contributions have not only shaped industries but have also helped to create a more inclusive society.

Angelica Ross (1980–)

Entrepreneur, Actress

Angelica Ross is a trailblazing transgender actress, entrepreneur, and activist known for her significant contributions to the entertainment industry and advocacy for transgender rights. As the founder and

CEO of TransTech Social Enterprises, she has created opportunities for marginalized communities, particularly transgender individuals, to gain employment and skills in the tech industry. She is also recognized for her impactful roles in critically acclaimed television series such as *Pose* and *American Horror Story*, in which she has used her platform to amplify LGBTQ+ voices and issues.

Ross was born in Kenosha, Wisconsin. Growing up in a conservative household, she faced significant challenges related to her gender identity from a young age. After coming out as gay in her teens and later realizing her true identity as a transgender woman, she left home at the age of 17 to find a more accepting environment. She joined the U.S. Navy, hoping to secure financial stability and a future, but soon left the military due to the challenges of serving as a transgender person under the "Don't Ask, Don't Tell" policy.

After leaving the Navy, Ross moved to Hollywood to pursue a career in the entertainment industry, but she struggled to find acceptance and roles that reflected her identity. She eventually returned to her Midwest roots, where she began to explore opportunities in the tech industry. She taught herself coding and web development, skills that would later become the foundation of her entrepreneurial success.

In 2014, Ross founded TransTech Social Enterprises, a company that provides education, support, and job opportunities for transgender people in the tech industry. The organization focuses on helping transgender individuals develop technical skills, secure employment, and achieve financial independence. TransTech has become a vital resource for marginalized communities, offering training programs in web development, graphic design, and digital marketing, among other fields.

Ross's entrepreneurial success with TransTech Social Enterprises coincided with her rising prominence in the entertainment industry. In 2018, she gained widespread recognition for her role as Candy Ferocity on the groundbreaking FX series *Pose*, which tells the story of New York City's underground Ballroom culture in the 1980s and 1990s. *Pose* is celebrated for its authentic representation of LGBTQ+ characters, particularly transgender women of color, and Ross's portrayal of Candy earned her critical acclaim. Building on the success of *Pose*, she joined the cast of *American Horror Story* in 2019, becoming the first transgender actress to secure two series regular roles on major television networks. Her performances on *American Horror Story* have further solidified her status as a powerful and versatile actress, and she continues to use her visibility to advocate for transgender representation in Hollywood.

In addition to her work with TransTech, Ross is a public speaker and activist, regularly appearing at conferences, panels, and events to discuss issues related to LGBTQ+ rights, racial justice, and economic empowerment. She has been recognized with numerous awards for her contributions to social justice, including being named to *Out* magazine's Out100 list.

Martine Rothblatt (1954–)

Business Executive

Martine Aliana Rothblatt is a trailblazing entrepreneur, lawyer, and author renowned for her pioneering contributions to biotechnology, satellite communications, and transgender rights. As the founder of Sirius Satellite Radio and United Therapeutics, she has revolutionized industries while advocating for the rights and representation of the transgender community.

Rothblatt was born in Chicago, Illinois, and raised in a suburb of San Diego, California. She attended the University of California, Los Angeles, where she earned a B.A. in communication studies in 1977. She later obtained her J.D. from UCLA's School of Law in 1981 and an M.B.A. from UCLA's Anderson School of Management.

Rothblatt's early career was marked by her work in satellite communications. She was instrumental in the development of several key projects, including the PanAmSat international satellite system and WorldSpace, a satellite radio network aimed at underserved regions. Her most notable achievement in this field was founding Sirius Satellite Radio in 1990, which transformed the way people access music and information.

Rothblatt's achievements span multiple disciplines. After her success with Sirius, she shifted her focus to biotechnology following her daughter's diagnosis with a life-threatening illness. In response, she founded United Therapeutics in 1996, a biotechnology company that developed life-saving treatments for pulmonary arterial hypertension. The company's success has made her one of the highest-paid female CEOs in the United States.

Beyond her entrepreneurial ventures, Rothblatt is also a prolific author. Her books, such as *The Apartheid of Sex: A Manifesto on the Freedom of Gender*, challenge traditional notions of gender and advocate for a future in which gender is seen as a spectrum rather than a binary construct. Her work in this area has made her a leading voice in the transgender rights movement.

Rothblatt's personal life is as remarkable as her professional achievements. She transitioned from male to female in 1994, a journey that has been deeply personal and public. She has been married to her wife, Bina Aspen Rothblatt, since 1982, and they have four children together. Her relationship with Bina has been a cornerstone of her life, and they remain deeply committed to each other.

Rothblatt's advocacy for transgender rights is not only rooted in her personal experience but also in her broader vision of a society where individuals are free to express their identities without fear of discrimination. Her work has inspired countless individuals and has been a driving force behind increased visibility and rights for the transgender community.

Dan Schulman (1958–)

Business Executive, LGBTQ+ Ally

Dan Schulman is the president and CEO of PayPal, a leading financial technology company. Under his leadership, PayPal has become a global leader in digital payments, expanding its reach and services to millions of users worldwide. He is recognized not only for his strategic vision in the fintech industry but also for his commitment to social responsibility, particularly his advocacy for LGBTQ+ rights and inclusion. His leadership style emphasizes the importance of values-driven business practices, making him a prominent ally in the fight for equality.

Schulman was born in Newark, New Jersey. He attended Princeton University, where he earned a B.A. in economics. He later obtained an M.B.A. from New York University. He began his career at AT&T, where he spent 18 years and held various senior leadership roles, including president of the consumer markets division. He later served as the CEO of Priceline and then as group president at American Express, where he led the company's global travel and lifestyle services division. His experience in both technology and financial services laid the groundwork for his future success at PayPal.

Schulman took over as CEO of PayPal in 2014, following its separation from eBay. Under his leadership, PayPal has undergone a significant transformation, focusing on expanding its services, including Venmo, Xoom, and Braintree. He has driven the company's mission to democratize financial services, making it easier for people and businesses to manage their money and access the global economy. His leadership has also been marked by a strong commitment to social impact. He has led initiatives to improve financial health, particularly for underserved communities, and has been a vocal advocate for corporate responsibility. His efforts have helped PayPal become a leader not only in fintech but also in corporate citizenship.

Schulman is married and has two children. As an LGBTQ+ ally, he has been a powerful advocate for equality both within PayPal and beyond. He has championed policies that promote diversity and inclusion, ensuring that PayPal is a welcoming and supportive workplace for LGBTQ+ employees. Under his leadership, PayPal has consistently received high ratings on the Human Rights Campaign's Corporate Equality Index. He has also been outspoken in his opposition to discriminatory laws, including "bathroom bills" that target transgender individuals. In 2016, PayPal made headlines when it canceled a planned expansion in North Carolina in response to the state's passage of HB2, a law that restricted LGBTQ+ rights. This move underscored Schulman's commitment to standing up for LGBTQ+ rights, even when it involves difficult business decisions.

Schulman's tenure at PayPal has been marked by a commitment to innovation and social impact. His leadership in the fintech industry is matched by his dedication to promoting equality and inclusion, making him a key ally in the fight for LGBTQ+ rights. His actions demonstrate that values-driven leadership can have a powerful impact both within a company and in the broader society.

Todd G. Sears (1976–)

Business Executive

Todd Gilliam Sears is a prominent figure in the intersection of business and LGBTQ+

advocacy known for his pioneering work in promoting diversity and inclusion within the corporate world. As the founder and CEO of Out Leadership, a global LGBTQ+ business advisory organization, he has been instrumental in driving change across industries, particularly within finance. His efforts have helped to create more inclusive workplaces and established him as a key advocate for LGBTQ+ rights in the business community.

Sears was born and raised in North Carolina. His father was an executive in the textile industry; his mother was a nurse. Due to the family's frequent moves, he attended 10 schools before he graduated from high school. He attended Duke University, where he earned a degree in English in 1996. During his time at Duke, he was actively involved in campus life and developed a keen interest in finance and business, which would later lead him to a successful career on Wall Street.

Sears began his business career as an investment banker at major financial institutions, including Merrill Lynch and Credit Suisse. During his time on Wall Street, he gained valuable experience in finance and corporate strategy. During his early years at Merrill Lynch, he decided to live openly as a gay man, and it was his personal experience as a gay man in a traditionally conservative industry that sparked his interest in promoting diversity and inclusion within the corporate world. "When I came out," he said, "I realized that there were a lot of people in the financial industry who were not comfortable being open about who they were. It made me think about how we could create a better, more inclusive environment where everyone can bring their whole selves to work."

In 2002, Sears became one of the first openly gay men to work on Wall Street, and he created the first-ever diversity and inclusion business resource group at Merrill Lynch, which focused on LGBTQ+ employees. This initiative was one of the first of its kind on Wall Street and set the stage for future diversity efforts across the industry.

Building on this success, Sears founded Out on the Street in 2010, a groundbreaking initiative designed to bring together senior leaders from the financial services industry to discuss LGBTQ+ inclusion and its impact on business performance. Out on the Street quickly gained traction and led to the creation of Out Leadership, a broader organization that works with companies across various sectors to promote LGBTQ+ inclusion.

Under Sears's leadership, Out Leadership has grown into a global organization with a network of over 80 member companies, including many of the world's largest financial institutions. The organization provides advisory services, develops leadership programs, and hosts events that focus on the business case for LGBTQ+ inclusion. Out Leadership has been instrumental in driving policy changes, fostering leadership development, and creating more inclusive workplaces for LGBTQ+ individuals.

Sears's work has had a significant impact on the business world, particularly in the areas of diversity and inclusion. His leadership has not only opened doors for LGBTQ+ individuals in the corporate sector but has also helped to shape a more inclusive and equitable business environment globally.

Joel Simkhai (1976–)

Business Executive

Joel Simkhai is an entrepreneur best known as the founder of Grindr, the world's first geosocial networking app for gay, bisexual, and queer men. Launched in 2009, Grindr revolutionized the way LGBTQ+ individuals connect, making it one of the most significant technological innovations in the LGBTQ+ community. His work has had a lasting impact on social networking and the visibility of LGBTQ+ individuals globally.

Simkhai was born in Tel Aviv, Israel, and raised in New York City, where his family moved when he was young. He grew up in a traditional Jewish household, which influenced his cultural and social perspective. He earned a bachelor's degree in international relations and economics from Tufts University in Massachusetts.

Before creating Grindr, Simkhai worked in finance and real estate in Los Angeles. However, his passion for technology and a desire to create a platform that could connect LGBTQ+ individuals in a safe and easy way led him to explore the tech industry.

Grindr was created in 2009 as a geosocial networking platform specifically for gay men, using location-based technology to connect users in real time. "As a gay man," Simkhai said, "I've always wanted to create something that helps people connect, that makes people feel less alone. Grindr was born out of that desire." Grindr quickly became popular, growing from a niche app to a global phenomenon. It was the first of its kind and paved the way for other dating apps across various communities.

Under his leadership, Grindr expanded rapidly, becoming a cultural touchstone within the LGBTQ+ community. The app has been downloaded millions of times and is available in nearly every country. He also emphasized Grindr's role in promoting health and safety within the community, partnering with organizations to provide resources on issues like HIV prevention and mental health.

In 2016, Simkhai sold a majority stake in Grindr to the Chinese gaming company Beijing Kunlun Tech Co., and in 2018, he stepped down as CEO. His departure marked the end of an era for Grindr, but his influence on the app and the industry remains profound.

Since stepping down from Grindr in 2018, Simkhai has remained active in the tech and entrepreneurial space, focusing on new ventures and continuing his work in community building. In 2020, he launched *Misterb&b*, an LGBTQ+-focused travel and accommodation platform that aims to provide safe and welcoming spaces for LGBTQ+ travelers around the world. The platform offers services similar to Airbnb but with a specific emphasis on the needs and experiences of the LGBTQ+ community.

In addition to *Misterb&b*, Simkhai has explored other tech-related projects and investments, particularly those that align with his passion for social impact and community connection. He has also been involved in philanthropy, supporting causes related to LGBTQ+ rights, health, and safety. On the challenges of being a gay business executive, he said, "Being a gay entrepreneur means facing unique challenges, but it also means having a unique perspective. I've been able to see opportunities and needs in the market that others might miss."

Megan Smith (1964-)

Business Executive, Technologist

Megan Smith is a leading technologist, engineer, and entrepreneur who has made significant contributions to the fields of technology and innovation. She is best known for serving as the chief technology officer (CTO) of the United States under President Barack Obama, playing a key role in driving innovation and technological advancement within the federal government. She is also recognized for her work at Google, where she contributed to major projects like Google Earth and Google Maps. Her career has been marked by a commitment to leveraging technology for social good, making her one of the most influential figures in the tech industry.

Smith was born in Buffalo, New York, and grew up in the surrounding area. She showed an early interest in science and technology, which led her to pursue engineering studies at the Massachusetts Institute of Technology. She earned a BS in mechanical engineering from MIT in 1986, followed by an M.S. in mechanical engineering in 1988. During her time at MIT, she was involved in several engineering projects, including work on solar cars and robotics. Her passion for technology and innovation was evident from the start, setting the stage for a career that would span both the private and public sectors.

Smith joined General Magic, a pioneering company in the 1990s that worked on creating early personal digital assistants (PDAs). Although the company did not achieve commercial success, it was a breeding ground for future tech leaders, and her experience there was formative.

Smith joined Google in 2003, where she worked for over a decade in various roles. She was involved in significant projects such as Google Earth, Google Maps, and Google.org, the company's philanthropic arm. Her work at Google had a global impact, particularly in making geographical information more accessible to the public.

In 2014, Smith was appointed by President Barack Obama as the chief technology officer of the United States, becoming the first woman to hold the position. As CTO, she focused on initiatives that promoted innovation, open data, and the inclusion of women and minorities in tech. She played a crucial role in efforts to modernize government services and bring more technological expertise into the federal workforce.

After her tenure as CTO, Smith founded shift7, a company dedicated to using technology, data, and innovation to address societal challenges. Through shift7, she continues to advocate for inclusive innovation and works on projects that aim to solve some of the world's most pressing problems.

Smith is openly lesbian and has been a strong advocate for LGBTQ+ rights throughout her career. She has spoken openly about the importance of diversity and inclusion in the tech industry and has worked to create opportunities for underrepresented groups in technology.

Smith was married to Kara Swisher, a prominent tech journalist, for several years, and they have two children together. Though they later separated, they have remained close and continue to coparent their children.

Smith's leadership, both in the private sector and in the government, has had a lasting impact on innovation and inclusivity in the tech world. She said, "I think it's really important that people who are LGBT or who are from diverse backgrounds see that there are people like them in leadership roles in technology. It sends a powerful message that they, too, can thrive and lead in this industry."

Peter Staley (1961–)

Business Executive, Activist

Peter Staley is a renowned American HIV/AIDS and LGBTQ+ rights activist who leveraged his business acumen to become a powerful force in the fight against the AIDS epidemic. His transition from a successful career on Wall Street to full-time activism exemplifies how his understanding of the corporate world enabled him to craft effective strategies in advocacy, negotiation, and public relations. His work with ACT UP (AIDS Coalition to Unleash Power) and the Treatment Action Group (TAG) has had a lasting impact on public health policy and the treatment of HIV/AIDS, making him a pivotal figure in the movement for LGBTQ+ rights and healthcare reform.

Staley was born in Sacramento, California, and raised in a conservative household. He attended Oberlin College in Ohio, initially studying political science before switching to economics, reflecting his early interest in finance and business. After graduating in 1983, he entered the world of finance, securing a position as a bond trader at J. P. Morgan, one of the most prestigious investment banks in the world. His work on Wall Street provided him with a deep understanding of market dynamics, strategic thinking, and negotiation skills, all of which would later prove invaluable in his activism.

After being diagnosed with HIV in 1985, Staley became a founding member of ACT UP in 1987. He applied his business skills to orchestrate some of ACT UP's most significant actions, including the historic protest at the U.S. Food and Drug Administration (FDA) in 1988. His strategic mindset helped to ensure that these actions were not just symbolic but resulted in real, measurable changes such as the acceleration of drug approval processes for HIV treatment.

In 1992, Staley cofounded TAG, where he applied his business acumen to ensure that HIV/AIDS research and treatment were guided by rigorous scientific standards. His ability to navigate the complex relationships between the pharmaceutical industry, the government, and advocacy groups led to more effective treatments and better patient outcomes. His financial expertise was crucial in sustaining activist operations; he excelled at fundraising, managing budgets, and efficiently allocating resources, ensuring the long-term success of the initiatives he spearheaded.

Staley played a central role in the 2012 documentary *How to Survive a Plague*, which chronicles the efforts of activists, particularly from ACT UP and TAG, in the fight against the AIDS epidemic during the late 1980s and early 1990s. The film highlights his leadership and strategic activism, showcasing his work in organizing protests, negotiating with pharmaceutical companies, and pushing for faster drug approvals. His contributions were pivotal in transforming public health policy and securing life-saving treatments for people living with HIV/AIDS. The documentary portrays him as a key figure in the movement whose actions significantly impacted the course of the AIDS crisis.

Peter Thiel (1967–)

Business Executive

Peter Andreas Thiel is a German American entrepreneur, venture capitalist, and political activist known for his role in cofounding PayPal and for his early investment in Facebook, which established him as a major figure in Silicon Valley. His influence extends beyond the tech industry into politics, where he has been a vocal advocate for libertarian ideals and conservative causes. As one of the few openly gay conservatives in the tech industry, he has often found himself at the intersection of innovation, ideology, and controversy.

Thiel was born in Frankfurt, West Germany, and moved to the United States with his family when he was a child. He grew up in California, where he was a standout student, eventually attending Stanford University. He earned his bachelor's degree in philosophy in 1989 and a law degree from Stanford Law School in 1992. After law school, he briefly worked as a judicial clerk and then as a securities lawyer before moving into the finance world as a derivatives trader at Credit Suisse. However, he found his true calling in entrepreneurship and venture capital, which led him to cofound PayPal in 1998 with Max Levchin, Luke Nosek, and Elon Musk.

Under Thiel's leadership as CEO, PayPal revolutionized online transactions, eventually leading to its acquisition by eBay in 2002 for $1.5 billion. The success of PayPal cemented his reputation as a leading entrepreneur in Silicon Valley. In 2004, he made a $500,000 early investment in Facebook, becoming the company's first outside investor. This investment turned into one of the most lucrative in venture capital history, making him a billionaire and giving him significant influence in the tech industry.

After his successful early investment in Facebook, Thiel continued to shape the tech industry through a series of influential ventures. He cofounded Founders Fund, backing major startups like SpaceX and Airbnb, and cofounded Palantir Technologies, a leading data analytics company. He also founded Clarium Capital, a hedge fund, and later cofounded Mithril Capital Management and Valar Ventures, focusing on transformative and early-stage investments.

Thiel has sparked controversy with several of his positions, including his public support for Donald Trump during the 2016 presidential campaign, which was unpopular in Silicon Valley. He is a vocal critic of higher education, which he believes is overpriced, overrated, and stifles innovation, offering the Thiel Fellowship to encourage young entrepreneurs to drop out of college, and his libertarian views have led him to support initiatives like the Seasteading Institute, which explores creating autonomous, floating cities. He also secretly funded lawsuits against Gawker Media, leading to its bankruptcy, raising concerns about using wealth to silence the press. Additionally, his skepticism about the compatibility of democracy and freedom has further fueled debate over his views on governance and innovation.

Thiel is openly gay, and while he is not primarily known for LGBTQ+ advocacy, his presence as a successful, openly gay man in the tech industry is significant. He has often navigated the complex dynamics between his sexual orientation and his conservative political views. His support for LGBTQ+ rights has been nuanced; he was one of the few major donors to the fight against California's Proposition 8, which sought to ban same-sex marriage, while also aligning himself with political figures and movements that are often seen as oppositional to broader LGBTQ+ rights. His personal life remains relatively private, though he married his longtime partner, Matt Danzeisen, in 2017. His marriage further highlighted his complex positioning as a gay man within conservative circles.

Military

The history of LGBTQ+ individuals in the American military is a complex and evolving narrative marked by periods of exclusion, discrimination, and recent strides toward inclusion and equality. From the early 20th century, when gay men were explicitly barred from serving, to the implementation and subsequent repeal of the "Don't Ask, Don't Tell" policy and, finally, to the current policies allowing open service by all LGBTQ+ individuals, the journey has been fraught with challenges and milestones. This ongoing evolution reflects broader societal changes and persistent advocacy by LGBTQ+ service members and their allies to ensure equal treatment and opportunities within the U.S. Armed Forces. The narrative of LGBTQ+ inclusion in the military is not just a story of policy changes but also one of personal courage, resilience, and the ongoing struggle for acceptance and equal rights.

The first documented case of an American soldier being discharged for what was then called "sodomy" dates back to the early years of the U.S. military. Lieutenant Frederick Gotthold Enslin is believed to be the first U.S. soldier to be court-martialed and dismissed from the Continental Army for sodomy in 1778. General George Washington approved the court-martial and discharge of Enslin, and Enslin was "drummed out" of camp, a severe form of military disgrace in which he was paraded in front of the troops, accompanied by drummers and fifers, and expelled from the military camp. This public humiliation was intended to serve as a deterrent to others and reinforce military discipline and moral standards. This case is often cited as a significant early example of the military's punitive stance on same-sex relations.

During the 19th century, the U.S. military, reflecting the prevalent social norms and sodomy laws, often dealt swiftly and severely with those suspected of engaging in same-sex relationships. The charges brought against soldiers were described under such broad terms as "conduct unbecoming an officer" or "immorality." Precise estimates of the number of soldiers discharged for homosexuality during this period are difficult to determine due to the lack of detailed records and the stigma attached to such cases.

The National Defense Act of 1916 enacted a new set of Articles of War to govern the conduct and discipline of military personnel. Among the provisions was a specific focus on the prohibition of homosexual conduct within the ranks. Article 93 specified that any person subject to military law who committed any "unnatural carnal copulation" would be subject to court-martial and severe punishment. The implementation of Article 93 led to increased scrutiny of service members' private lives and behavior, and those found guilty of homosexuality faced not only legal penalties but also social stigma and the

Members of the U.S. Navy march in support of the LGBTQ community during a Pride march in San Diego. Considerable progress was being made for equal rights in the U.S. military before Donald Trump's re-election in 2024.

loss of military honors and benefits. The fear of being accused of same-sex sexual conduct created an environment of secrecy and suspicion, affecting the morale and cohesion of military units. Article 93 set a precedent for the military's treatment of homosexual conduct that persisted for much of the 20th century.

During World War I, the mobilization of large numbers of American troops led to the military conducting more thorough medical examinations and psychological screenings of recruits aimed at identifying individuals deemed unfit for service, including those suspected of homosexual tendencies, as part of a broader effort to maintain the moral and physical integrity of a larger and more diverse military force. The period between World War I and World War II saw the continuation of the military's strict policies against same-sex relationships. One documented case from this period is that of Private Eugene C. Goode, who was court-martialed and sentenced to hard labor in 1921 for engaging in homosexual acts.

The outbreak of World War II necessitated another large-scale mobilization of troops, with the military formalizing its policies aimed at excluding homosexuals from military service with more rigorous psychological screenings as part of the induction process and recruiting psychiatrists, who were instructed to identify individuals with "sexual perversions," including homosexuality. Recruits suspected of homosexual tendences were often rejected outright. The military issued explicit regulations and procedures for handling these cases, and it is believed that between 9,000 and 10,000 service members were discharged due to homosexuality. The military issued "blue discharges" or "blue tickets" to soldiers for having "undesirable habits and traits of character." This "blue discharge" system was publicly criticized, notably in an article in the *Pittsburgh Courier* in 1945, which described it as a "vicious instrument" used unfairly against American soldiers, and the practice was abolished in 1947, though not the policy to discharge homosexuals in the ranks. Reports and investigations during World War II revealed cases of lesbian relationships in the Women's Army Corps (WAC), which also led to many women who were suspected of same-sex conduct being discharged from the military.

During the Red Scare of the 1950s, the subsequent so-called Lavender Scare targeted, persecuted, and dismissed from government jobs and the military thousands of individuals because of their real or perceived homosexuality, citing security risks. In 1953, President Dwight Eisenhower issued Executive Order 10450, which expanded the criteria for determining the suitability of federal employees to include "sexual perversion," a term used at the time to describe gay and lesbian behavior. The order, which in effect equated homosexuality with disloyalty to the United States, led to intensified efforts to identify and remove gays and lesbians from government positions and prompted the military to conduct widespread investigations to identify gay and lesbian service personnel. Those found or suspected to be gay or lesbian were often dishonorably discharged, with loss of benefits, damage to reputations, and severe personal and professional consequences. This was one of the darkest chapters in American LGBTQ+ history, marked by systematic discrimination and violation of civil rights based on sexual preference. Executive Order 10450 remained in effect for decades. Its impact on the military was profound, leading to the unjust dismissal of many service members and perpetuating a military culture of intimidation and intolerance.

The 1960s saw the beginnings of organized resistance against these discriminatory policies. Frank Kameny, a World War II veteran dismissed from the Army Map Service for being gay, became a prominent advocate for LGBTQ+ rights. In 1961, Kameny cofounded the Mattachine Society of Washington, D.C., and petitioned the Supreme Court to review his discharge, although the court declined to hear the case. In 1965, Kameny and others led one of the first gay rights protests in the United States at the

Frank Kameny stands in front of a display of protest signs in this 2009 photograph. After being dismissed by the Army for being gay, he became a prominent activist for LGBTQ rights and cofounder of the Mattachine Society.

Pentagon in Arlington, Virginia, bringing attention to the government's policies of discrimination against gays, particularly in federal employment and the military. One of the signs carried in the protest read "The Pentagon: A Symbol of Government by Exclusion."

By the late 1960s, the Vietnam War's demand for military personnel led to slightly more lenient enforcement of anti-LGBTQ+ policies, although official policies remained unchanged. In 1975, Department of Defense Directive 1332.14 asserted that homosexuality is incompatible with military service and was considered grounds for immediate discharge. Service members could be dismissed with an Other Than Honorable (OTH) discharge or worse,

This 2001 training manual published by the U.S. Army explained to military personnel what procedures had to be followed in the "Don't Ask, Don't Tell" climate.

depending on circumstances. In 1981, the Department of Defense reaffirmed the 1975 directive, a policy that was enforced until 1993, when President Bill Clinton implemented a reform of the "Don't Ask, Don't Tell" policy.

"Don't Ask, Don't Tell" (DADT), formerly known as the Military Personnel Eligibility Act of 1993, was a significant and controversial chapter in the history of the U.S. military and LGBTQ+ rights. Signed into law on November 30, 1993, DADT was a compromise between those advocating for allowing LGBTQ+ individuals to serve openly and those insisting on maintaining the ban. Under DADT, military personnel would not be asked about their sexual orientation during the enlistment process or while serving. However, openly declaring one's homosexuality or engaging in same-sex sexual conduct was still grounds for discharge. The policy essentially mandated that gay service members remain closeted and not disclose their sexual orientation.

Despite its intention to allow LGBTQ+ individuals to serve in the military, DADT had significant negative consequences, forcing service members to conceal their identities, leading to stress, anxiety, and other mental health issues. The policy's enforcement varied widely, leading to uncertainty and fear among LGBTQ+ personnel about their careers and safety. According to the Servicemembers Legal Defense Network, more than 13,000 service members were discharged under DADT from 1993 to 2011.

Opposition to the DADT policy was led by a variety of groups, including legal defense groups, veterans' associations, civil rights organizations, and LGBTQ+ advocacy organizations such as the Servicemembers Legal Defense Network, the Human Rights Campaign, and OutServe. These and many other groups argued that DADT was unjust, discriminatory, and detrimental to military effectiveness and the well-being of LGBTQ+ service members. By the late 2000s, a significant shift in societal attitudes occurred in which more

Americans believed that gay, lesbian, and bisexual individuals should have the right to serve openly in the military. Greater visibility of LGBTQ+ individuals in media, politics, and everyday life helped to normalize LGBTQ+ identities and relationships, contributing to increased public support for gay rights.

A key milestone in the eventual repeal of DADT was the 2004 report by the Palm Center, a research institute focused on LGBTQ+ military issues that challenged the rationale behind DADT. In 2006, a Blue Ribbon Commission led by retired general John Shalikashvilli, a former chairman of the Joint Chiefs of Staff, called for a review of DADT, signaling growing support within military leadership.

In 2008, Barack Obama was elected president, having campaigned on a promise to repeal DADT. The pivotal year for repeal efforts came in 2010 when Admiral Mike Mullen, chairman of the Joint Chiefs of Staff, and Secretary of Defense Robert Gates testified before Congress in support of repealing DADT, marking a significant shift in military leadership's stance.

In November 2010, following the House of Representatives passing an amendment to repeal DADT, the Pentagon released a comprehensive study concluding that the repeal of DADT would have minimal impact on military effectiveness and unit cohesion, bolstering support for the repeal.

In December 2010, the Senate passed the Don't Ask, Don't Tell Repeal Act with a vote of 65–31, and on December 22, 2010, President Obama signed the Repeal Act into law. Final steps required certification that the military was ready to implement it, and on September 20, 2011, the repeal of DADT was fully implemented, allowing gay, lesbian, and bisexual individuals to serve openly in the U.S. military without fear of discharge based on sexual orientation.

The repeal of DADT was a landmark moment in the history of LGBTQ+ rights in the United States, affecting individuals, the military as an institution, and society at large. It marked the end of a discriminatory policy that forced gay, lesbian, and bisexual service members to hide their sexual orientation or face discharge. It set a significant legal precedent for LGBTQ+ rights within federal institutions and highlighted the need for equal treatment under the law. It also led to several additional changes and reforms within the U.S. military aimed to further integrate and support LGBTQ+ service members.

The repeal of "Don't Ask, Don't Tell" in 2010 marked the end of discrimination against the LGBTQ community in the military.

After the repeal, the military began recognizing same-sex marriages, allowing same-sex spouses to access the same benefits as opposite-sex spouses, including health care, housing allowances, survivor benefits, and access to military facilities. The Department of Defense updated its policies to ensure that all military personnel and their families, regardless of sexual orientation, received equal treatment and benefits. This included strengthened policies prohibiting discrimination based on sexual orientation and enhanced training to address respect, tolerance, and the rights of LGBTQ+ service members.

Building on the momentum from the repeal of DADT, the military took further steps to include transgender individuals. In 2016, under the Obama administration, the DoD lifted the ban on transgender service members, allowing them to serve openly and with access to necessary medical care. This policy faced challenges and reversals under the Trump administration, was reinstated and strengthened under the Biden administration in 2021, and became an issue again when Trump returned to office in 2025. Trump eliminated diversity, equity, and inclusion (DEI) policies in the military (including those that apply to LGBTQ, especially trans soldiers).

A major result of the repeal of DADT was the promotion of openly gay and transgender service members to high ranks in the military. In 2012, Major General Tammy Smith became the first openly gay general in the U.S. Army, with Major General Patricia Rose the highest-ranking openly lesbian officer in the Air Force in 2013 and Brigadier General Randy S. Taylor the highest-ranking openly gay soldier in the U.S. military when he came out in 2015. Lieutenant Colonel Bree Fram and Navy commander Emily Shilling are currently the highest-ranking openly transgender people in the military. Serving from 2016 to 2017, Eric Fanning made history by becoming the first openly gay secretary of the Army. Shawn Skelly was confirmed by unanimous consent as the assistant secretary of defense for readiness in 2021, making her the highest-ranking openly transgender defense official in U.S. history. Also in 2021, Gina Ortiz Jones was confirmed as undersecretary of the Air Force, becoming the first openly lesbian person to serve as undersecretary of a military branch.

While significant progress has been made in the U.S. military since the repeal of DADT, continuing challenges for LGBTQ+ service members highlight the need for ongoing efforts to promote equality, inclusion, and support within the U.S. military. Addressing these challenges requires a commitment to policy stability, robust enforcement of antidiscrimination measures, comprehensive health care, support for LGBTQ+ families, and opportunities for career advancement. Ensuring that past injustices are rectified and providing support when LGBTQ+ service members and spouses are deployed to countries with hostile attitudes toward LGBTQ+ individuals are also important aspects of this ongoing effort.

BIOGRAPHIES

Eric Alva (1970–)

Marine

Eric Fidelis Alva is a pioneering LGBTQ+ rights advocate and a decorated veteran of the U.S. Marine Corps. As the first American service member to be injured in the Iraq War, he has used his platform to advocate for LGBTQ+ rights, particularly the repeal of the "Don't Ask, Don't Tell" (DADT) policy. His courage and dedication have significantly influenced the fight for equality and acceptance within the military and beyond.

Alva was born into a military family in San Antonio, Texas. His middle name is drawn from the Marine Corps motto of *semper fidelis* ("always faithful"). After graduating from high school in 1989, he joined the Marine Corps, knowing at the time that he was gay and that the U.S. military excluded all gays and lesbians. He served for 13 years, including postings in Okinawa and Somalia.

In 2003, Alva became the first American to be wounded in the Iraq War after stepping on a landmine, resulting in the loss of his right leg. He was awarded the Purple Heart for his bravery and sacrifice. After his injury, he retired from the military and turned his attention to advocacy work. As an openly gay man, he became a prominent figure in the fight to repeal DADT, the policy that prohibited openly gay individuals from serving in the military. His testimony before Congress and public speaking engagements played a crucial role in raising awareness about the injustices of DADT and advocating for its repeal. In 2010, DADT was officially repealed, marking a significant victory for LGBTQ+ rights in the military. His efforts were instrumental in achieving this milestone, and he has continued to be an outspoken advocate for equality and acceptance in the military. He has received numerous awards and honors for his advocacy work, reflecting his dedication and impact on the LGBTQ+ community. One of the first soldiers to be discharged under DADT was Sergeant Danny Ingram, who had served in the Army for six years. Ingram and Alva met in 2010 and were married in 2017. Alva's memoir, *Radical Courage: How One Marine's Sacrifice Helped Change America*, was published in 2021.

Miriam Ben-Shalom (1948–)

Service Member

Miriam Ben-Shalom is a trailblazing advocate for lesbian rights within the U.S. military. As one of the first openly gay service members to challenge the military's ban on homosexuality and the first gay service member ever to be reinstated in the U.S. military after being discharged for their sexual orientation, her courageous fight for her right to serve set a precedent and paved the way for future advancements in military inclusion.

Ben-Shalom was born in Waukesha, Wisconsin. She grew up in a large Roman Catholic family. After her mother died in an automobile accident, she was raised by her father, a World War II veteran. After graduating from high school in 1967, she got married and had a daughter. In 1968, she converted to Judaism and left with her daughter for a five-year residence in Israel, serving in the Israel Defense Forces. In 1971, she returned to the United States, divorced, and entered the University of Wisconsin, Milwaukee, earning a B.A. and an MA in creative writing. She joined the U.S. Army Reserve in 1974.

In 1976, Ben-Shalom publicly came out as a lesbian, leading to her discharge from the Army Reserve. Determined to fight this decision, she embarked on a lengthy legal battle to challenge her discharge. In 1980, a federal judge ruled in her favor, ordering her reinstatement in the Army Reserve. Despite the ruling, the Army continued to resist her reinstatement, leading to further legal struggles.

Ben-Shalom's persistence paid off in 1987 when she was finally reinstated, making her the first openly gay service member to serve in the U.S. military after having been discharged for their sexual orientation and then reinstated. Her case drew national attention and highlighted the discriminatory policies faced by LGBTQ+ individuals in the U.S. Armed Forces. The Army appealed the decision and in 1989 won a decision that ruled against her. The Supreme Court declined to hear her appeal, and in 1990, her military career ended.

Ben-Shalom returned to Waukesha and was one of six LGBTQ+ veterans to cofound the Gay, Lesbian and Bisexual Veterans of America, today known as the American Veterans for Equal Rights. She joined the protest over DADT and was arrested in 2010 after chaining herself to the White House fence. Working as a teacher, she now lives in Milwaukee with her life partner, Karen Weiss.

Ben-Shalom's more recent advocacy has been controversial and considered transphobic. In 2017, she testified in Texas in support of a bill that would require transgender people to use bathrooms of the sex stated on a person's birth certificate.

She also cofounded the Hands Across the Aisle Coalition of "radical feminists, lesbians, Christians and conservatives who oppose gender identity legislation."

Despite views that fail to extend equality and justice to transgender individuals, Ben-Shalom should be acknowledged for her role in the military eventually ending discrimination based on sexual orientation. Her openness about her sexuality has been a powerful tool in challenging stereotypes and promoting acceptance.

Vernon E. "Copy" Berg III (1951–1999)

Naval Officer

Vernon E. "Copy" Berg III was a pioneering advocate for LGBTQ+ rights within the U.S. military. As one of the first service members to challenge the military's gay ban, his courageous legal battle set a significant precedent and paved the way for future advancements in LGBTQ+ military inclusion.

Berg was born in Port Jefferson, New York. Raised in a military family, he was called "Copy" because he was so like his father, a Navy chaplain. He developed a strong sense of duty and service from a young age and attended the U.S. Naval Academy, graduating in 1974. While at the Naval Academy, he met and fell in love with a civilian theater director working at the Academy, Lawrence Gibson. They were married in a small, private ceremony in 1975.

After graduating, Berg served as an ensign aboard the USS *Little Rock,* the flagship of the U.S. Navy 6th Fleet in the Mediterranean, based in Gaeta, Italy. When it was discovered that Gibson was sharing Berg's apartment in Gaeta, an investigation led to Berg's discharge for being gay. Refusing to accept this injustice, Berg, along with Gibson, initiated a legal battle against the Navy, challenging the discriminatory policies that led to his discharge. Gibson wrote about the incident and what followed in *Get Off My Ship: Ensign Berg v. the US Navy* (1978).

In 1976, Berg's lawsuit became one of the first cases to challenge the military's ban on being gay. Although the initial ruling upheld his discharge, the case garnered national attention and sparked a broader conversation about LGBTQ+ rights in the military. In 1978, the U.S. Court of Appeals ruled that he and former technical sergeant Leonard P. Matlovich of the Air Force had been unfairly discharged, although neither was reinstated as both sought. Berg was again discharged after an investigation revealed that he was in a gay relationship. After his suit against the Navy, the U.S. Armed Forces adopted a policy of generally granting honorable discharges to gays dismissed from the military. Kevin M. Cathcart of the Lambda Legal Defense and Education Fund stated, Berg "was one of the first to stand up to the military. People forget...what kind of courage that took. Tens of thousands of people have benefited from his fight."

After his discharge, Berg earned a master's degree in design from Pratt Institute in Brooklyn and became a successful artist in New York City. After separating from Gibson, he partnered with writer Paul Nash. When both were diagnosed with HIV, Berg focused his art on detailing the AIDS crisis and in the 1990s became active with the Estate Project for Artists with AIDS and with Visual AIDS, two organizations established to support artists living with HIV and preserve the work of those who died. Berg himself died of AIDS in 1999 at the age of 47.

Allan Bérubé (1946–2007)

Military Historian, Author

Allan Bérubé was a renowned historian and author whose work significantly ad-

vanced the understanding of LGBTQ+ history in America. Best known for his groundbreaking book *Coming Out Under Fire: The History of Gay Men and Women in World War II*, his contributions to documenting and preserving LGBTQ+ history have left a lasting impact on both the academic community and the broader movement for equality. His research and advocacy highlighted the experiences of LGBTQ+ individuals in the military and underscored the importance of preserving marginalized histories.

Bérubé was born in Springfield, Massachusetts, and grew up in a working-class French Canadian family in Bayonne, New Jersey. Living for a time in trailer parks while his father worked as a poorly paid cameraman for NBC, he graduated from the Mount Herman School for Boys in Massachusetts in 1964. He sought and received conscientious objector status after registering for the draft at the age of 18. He attended the University of Chicago from 1964 to 1968 but did not earn a degree. He moved to Boston, where he became involved in politics for the first time, opposing the Vietnam War. He came out as gay in 1969 and eventually settled in San Francisco, where he helped found the San Francisco Lesbian and Gay History Project. He was drawn to LGBTQ+ history after reading Jonathan Ned Katz's groundbreaking book *Gay American History* (1976), which sent him on the path of researching, writing, and presenting history to public audiences.

Bérubé's most notable work, *Coming Out Under Fire: The History of Gay Men and Women in World War II*, was published in 1990. The book originated from a box of letters salvaged from a dumpster—correspondence exchanged by a dozen gay G.I.s during the war who met on an Army base in Missouri but continued to correspond after being posted to different locations. The letters "really captured my heart and raised a lot of questions," he recalled, "so I started doing research." His book would be based on extensive archival research and oral histories documenting the experiences of gay and lesbian service members during the war. The book received widespread acclaim for its thorough scholarship and compelling narrative, winning the Lambda Literary Award for Gay Non-Fiction and the Allan Nevins Prize for literary distinction in the writing of history. The book was later adapted into a 1995 documentary film of the same name, further amplifying its impact.

In addition to his work in military history, Bérubé contributed to several other important projects, including participating in the development of the GLBT Historical Society in San Francisco. His essays and lectures on LGBTQ+ history and culture were influential in both academic and activist circles, helping to shape the field of queer studies.

Because he was gay, Bérubé was not allowed to testify before the Senate Committee on Armed Services when it held hearings on the exclusion of gays from the U.S. military in 1993. Instead, he provided Senator Edward Kennedy with questions to ask as well as a paper, "Historical Overview of the Origins of the Military's Ban on Homosexuals." He died before completing a draft of his next project, the story of the Marine Cooks and Stewards Union in the 1930s and 1940s, which was progressive, multiracial, and gay friendly.

Margarethe Cammermeyer (1942–)

Army Officer, Nurse

Colonel Margarethe "Grethe" Cammermeyer is a distinguished military officer and a prominent advocate for LGBTQ+ rights. Known for her courageous legal battle against the U.S. military's ban on gay service members, her story is one of resilience, integrity, and a steadfast commitment to equality. In 1992, she became the highest-ranking military officer to be discharged on the basis of sexual orientation. The landmark case that ruled that her discharge was unconstitutional not only challenged discriminatory policies but also paved the way for greater acceptance and inclusion within the U.S. Armed Forces. She returned to service as one of the few openly gay members of the U.S. military, and her case resulted in the implementation of the "Don't Ask, Don't Tell" policy.

Cammermeyer was born in Oslo, Norway. She immigrated to the United States with her family in 1951 and became a U.S. citizen in 1960. She pursued a career in nursing, earning a BS in nursing in 1963 from the University of Maryland. She subsequently earned a master's degree in 1976 and a Ph.D. in 1991 from the University of Washington School of Nursing.

Cammermeyer joined the U.S. Army Nurse Corps in 1961 and later served in the Vietnam War as head nurse of a neurosurgical intensive care unit. She was awarded the Bronze Star for her service. From 1970 to 1980, she served in the Army Reserve, and in 1988, she was appointed chief nurse of the Washington Army National Guard, achieving the rank of colonel. She was married for 15 years to a fellow soldier, Harvey Hawken, and they had four sons. She divorced in 1980. In 1988, she met the woman who later became her wife, Diane Divelbess.

In 1989, when Cammermeyer disclosed being gay during a security clearance interview, it led to her discharge from the Washington Army National Guard. She fought this decision, and her legal battle culminated in a landmark 1994 ruling by a federal judge that her dismissal was unconstitutional. This victory was a significant milestone in the fight against discrimination in the military and highlighted the challenges faced by LGBTQ+ service members. Her story was chronicled in her memoir, *Serving in Silence* (1994), which was later adapted into an Emmy Award–winning television movie starring Glenn Close in 1995.

After retiring from the military in 1997 after six years of active duty and 25 years in the Army Reserve and National Guard, Cammermeyer ran in 1998 for a congressional seat in Washington State, winning the Democratic primary but losing the general election. In 2010, she was appointed to the Defense Advisory Committee on Women in the Services.

Cammermeyer has been a vocal advocate for LGBTQ+ rights, using her platform to promote equality and challenge discriminatory practices. She married her partner, Diane Divelbess, in 2009, following the legalization of same-sex marriage in Washington State. Her advocacy extends beyond her own experiences as she continues to support and mentor LGBTQ+ individuals within the military and the broader community. Her efforts have had a lasting impact, contributing to the eventual repeal of the "Don't Ask, Don't Tell" policy in 2010.

Albert Cashier

See Jennie Irene Hodgers

Dan Choi (1981–)

Army Officer

Daniel "Dan" Choi is a prominent LGBTQ+ rights advocate and former U.S. Army officer known for his courageous efforts in challenging the "Don't Ask, Don't Tell" (DADT) policy. As one of the most visible and vocal figures in the fight for LGBTQ+ military inclusion, his activism has significantly influenced public perception and policy regarding LGBTQ+ service members.

Choi was born in Tustin, Orange County, California, to Korean American parents. He grew up in a conservative family and attended the U.S. Military Academy at West Point, where he graduated with degrees in Arabic and environmental engineering in 2003. He went on to serve as an infantry officer in Iraq in 2006 and 2007. He transferred from active duty to the New York Army National Guard in 2008.

Choi's military career was interrupted in 2009 when he publicly came out as gay on *The Rachel Maddow Show*. As a result, he received a discharge letter from the Army under the DADT policy. Refusing to accept this decision, he became a leading figure in the movement to repeal DADT, advocating for the rights of LGBTQ+ individuals to serve openly in the military.

Choi's activism included taking part in numerous protests, speaking engagements, and media appearances. He famously handcuffed himself to the White House fence on multiple occasions to draw attention to the discriminatory nature of DADT. His actions, along with those of many other activists, helped build momentum for the repeal of DADT, which was officially overturned in 2010.

In addition to his work on DADT, Choi has been involved in broader LGBTQ+ rights advocacy, supporting marriage equality and antidiscrimination legislation. Since his coming out, 38 West Point alumni followed his lead and formed Knights Out, an organization of West Point alumni who support the rights of LGBTQ+ soldiers to serve openly. He was one of the founding members and has served as its spokesperson.

Zoe Dunning (1963–)

Naval Officer

Maria Zoe Dunning is a pioneering advocate for LGBTQ+ rights within the U.S. military. As one of the few service members to successfully challenge the "Don't Ask, Don't Tell" (DADT) policy and remain in the military, her courageous efforts have had a lasting impact on military policies and the broader fight for LGBTQ+ equality.

Dunning was born in Milwaukee, Wisconsin, and raised in a family that valued military service. Both of her parents served in World War II. She attended the U.S. Naval Academy, part of the second class of admitted women, where she graduated with a degree in computer science in 1985. She went on to serve as a Supply Corps officer in the U.S. Navy, showing exceptional leadership and dedication throughout her career. At the end of her obligatory active-duty service, she transferred to the U.S. Navy Reserve and attended the Stanford Graduate School of Business.

In 1993, while at Stanford, Dunning publicly came out as a lesbian during a rally in support of LGBTQ+ rights in the military, declaring, "I am both a naval officer and a lesbian, and I refuse to live a lie anymore." Her admission led to her being one of the first service members to be investigated under the DADT policy. A Navy board recommended that she be honorably discharged. However, she fought back, challenging the discharge and ultimately winning her case, which argued that she had made a statement of status and not conduct, which did not violate DADT. (The military subsequently changed regulations that made any future use of that defense impossible.) She was allowed to remain in the Navy, making her one of the few openly gay service members at the time.

Dunning's legal victory and continued service became a symbol of hope and resilience for many LGBTQ+ individuals in the military. Her case drew national attention and played a significant role in the eventual repeal of DADT. She stood beside President Barack Obama as he signed the Don't Ask, Don't Tell Repeal Act into law in 2010. She retired as a Navy commander in 2007. Beyond her military service, she has been an active advocate for LGBTQ+ rights, participating in numerous organizations and initiatives aimed at promoting equality and acceptance.

Eric Fanning (1968–)

Secretary of the Army

Eric Kenneth Fanning is a prominent American public servant and leader known for his extensive work in national defense and historic role as the first openly gay secretary of the Army. His career in government and defense spans over two decades, during which he has held various significant positions within the Department of Defense. His leadership and advocacy for LGBTQ+ rights have made him a trailblazer in both the military and the broader public sector, contributing to a more inclusive environment within the U.S. Armed Forces.

Fanning was born in Kalamazoo, Michigan. After graduating from high school in Ohio, he attended Dartmouth College, where he earned a B.A. in history in 1990. After graduation, he worked as an associate at CBS News before beginning government service. His interest in government and politics began when he participated in the 1988 New Hampshire primary. His early career included roles on Capitol Hill, in which he served as a staff member for the House Committee on Armed Services and later as a special assistant in the Office of the Secretary of Defense and as associate director of political affairs at the White House.

Fanning's career in the Department of Defense is marked by a series of high-profile appointments. He served as the deputy undersecretary of the Navy and later as the undersecretary of the Air Force. In 2013, he was appointed acting secretary of the Air Force, becoming the second highest-ranking civilian leader of the Air Force. His most notable achievement came in 2016 when he was confirmed as the 22nd secretary of the Army, making history as the first openly gay person to hold this position or the head of any service in the U.S. military. He was nominated for the position by President Barack Obama in September 2015, but his confirmation was held up until May 2016 because of a dispute between a Republican senator and the Obama administration that was unrelated to Fanning. He was finally confirmed on a unanimous voice vote. With his confirmation, he became the only person to have held senior appointments in all three military departments: chief of staff to the secretary of defense, acting secretary of the Air Force, and deputy undersecretary of the Navy.

During his tenure as secretary of the Army until January 2017, he focused on modernization, readiness, and the well-being of soldiers and their families. He has also been an advocate for diversity and inclusion within the military, working to ensure equal opportunities for all service members. He is the current president and CEO of Aerospace Industries Association.

Fanning's personal life and openness about his sexuality have been integral to his identity and leadership. He married National Gallery of Art budget analyst Ben Mastri-Cohen in 2018. He has been a vocal advocate for LGBTQ+ rights and has worked to promote inclusivity within the military and beyond. His appointment as secretary of the Army was a significant milestone for the LGBTQ+ community, demonstrating progress toward greater acceptance and equality in the U.S. Armed Forces. He has used his platform to address issues of discrimination and support policies that protect and empower LGBTQ+ individuals.

Fanning's distinguished career and groundbreaking role as the first openly gay secretary of the Army have made a lasting impact on the U.S. military and the broader public sector. His leadership and advocacy for diversity and inclusion have helped to pave the way for a more equitable and accepting environment within the U.S. Armed Forces.

Bree Fram (1975–)

Air Force Officer

Bree Fram is a highly respected officer in the U.S. Space Force and one of the highest-ranking openly transgender individuals in the U.S. military. Her distinguished career and courageous advocacy for transgender rights have made her a significant figure in the movement for inclusivity and equality within the U.S. Armed Forces.

Fram was born in Syracuse, New York. She attended the U.S. Air Force Academy, where she graduated with a BS in astronautical engineering in 1997. Following her graduation, she was commissioned as a second lieutenant in the U.S. Air Force. She earned a BS in aerospace engineering at the University of Minnesota in 2001, a master's degree in astronautical engineering at the Air Force Institute of Technology in 2007, and a master's degree in national security and strategic studies at the Naval War College in 2021. Throughout her career, she has held numerous key positions that highlight her leadership and technical skills. She served in various capacities within the Air Force, including roles in space operations and policy development. She was deployed during Operation Iraqi Freedom in 2004.

In 2016, Fram made history by coming out as transgender while actively serving on the day the transgender ban in the military was dropped, a courageous decision that had a significant impact on the visibility and acceptance of transgender individuals in the military. She transitioned while in a command position and served through the reimposition of a transgender ban by the Trump administration from 2019 to 2021. As a lieutenant colonel, she is currently one of the highest-ranking out transgender officers in the U.S. military.

Fram transferred into the U.S. Space Force upon its establishment and has continued to excel in her career. Her notable assignments include serving as a policy advisor at the Pentagon, where she has influenced critical decisions related to space operations and national security. Her leadership extends beyond her military duties, as she is also a vocal advocate for transgender rights, working to ensure that all service members can serve authentically and with dignity. She served in leadership roles for SPARTA, a nonprofit advocacy organization for transgender military service members, from 2015 to 2023, culminating as president and board chair. Her advocacy has included public speaking, writing, and mentorship, helping to foster a culture of acceptance and respect within the U.S. Armed Forces. She is married to Peg Fram, and they have two children.

Fram's distinguished career and pioneering role as one of the highest-ranking openly transgender individuals in the U.S. military exemplify her unwavering dedication, leadership, and commitment to service. Her significant contributions to space operations, policy development, and advocacy for transgender rights have made her a respected and influential figure. "We have served since the [American] Revolution," she said. "You had amazing heroes of the Revolution who just happened to be gay. You had over 400 documented cases of transgender people serving during the Civil War for the Union. And so that history is all there, but when we're given that opportunity to do so openly, we can be even more valuable to the service."

Brenda Sue Fulton (1958–)

Army Officer

As one of the first openly gay graduates of the U.S. Military Academy at West Point, Brenda Sue Fulton has been instrumental in advocating for policy changes that support

LGBTQ+ service members.

Fulton was born in Ohio. She attended the U.S. Military Academy at West Point, graduating in 1980 as part of the first class to include women. Commissioned in the Army as a signal officer, she served as platoon leader, staff officer, and company commander in Germany until her retirement from the service as a captain.

Fulton's career is distinguished by her advocacy for LGBTQ+ rights. In 2009, she cofounded Knights Out, an organization of LGBTQ+ West Point graduates, and a year later became a founding board member of OutServe, an association of actively serving LGBTQ+ military members. In both roles, she was an active advocate for the repeal of the "Don't Ask, Don't Tell" policy. Her efforts were crucial in this historic change, as she tirelessly lobbied and worked with various organizations to support the repeal.

In 2011, President Barack Obama appointed Fulton as the first openly gay member of the West Point Board of Visitors, becoming the first female U.S. Military Academy graduate to chair the board in 2015. In 2017, she was appointed to the National Defense University Board of Visitors in Washington, D.C.

In 2012, after 17 years together, Fulton married her partner, Penelope Gnesin, in a ceremony at the U.S. Military Academy's Cadet Chapel, making history as one of the first same-sex couples to be married at West Point. This event symbolized the progress made toward equality and inclusivity in the military.

Since 2018, Fulton served in New Jersey as chief administrator of the state's Motor Vehicle Commission. President Joe Biden nominated her in 2021 to serve as assistant secretary for manpower and reserve affairs, which oversees personnel issues within the Pentagon, but her nomination was stalled for months over her past comments criticizing Republican policies and lawmakers.

After her nomination was withdrawn, she was appointed in 2022 as assistant secretary for the Office of Public and Intergovernmental Affairs in the Department of Veterans Affairs.

Kristin Goodwin (1971-)

Air Force Officer

Kristin Goodwin is a distinguished U.S. Air Force brigadier general and an influential figure in advocating for diversity and inclusion within the military. One of the highest-ranking openly gay officers in the Air Force, she made history in 2017 when she was named commandant of cadets at the Air Force Academy, the first openly gay officer to assume such a senior position at one of the service academies. Known for her exceptional leadership and dedication, she has made significant contributions to the Air Force, serving as a role model for many.

Goodwin was born in Pittsburgh, Pennsylvania. Her father was a career member of the U.S. Coast Guard, and her mother served until retirement in the Air Force Reserve. As a Coast Guard brat, she moved frequently but claimed Fairfax, Virginia, as her hometown because she attended high school there. She graduated from the U.S. Air Force Academy in 1993, earning a bachelor's degree in mechanical engineering.

Goodwin's early career in the Air Force was marked by her exemplary performance as a pilot and leader, quickly rising through the ranks. Her first assignment was assistant deputy executive officer at the Air Force Academy before flight training on multiple aircraft types from 1994 to 1995. She served in various capacities, including as a command pilot, with over 3,000 flight hours, and has flown nine different aircraft types, including the B-2 Spirit stealth bomber. She became the first woman to command the United States' largest bomb wing at Barksdale Air Force Base.

Goodwin came out as a lesbian while

serving and married Kelly Fisher, a professional cyclist and former firefighter, with whom she has two daughters. Her openness about her sexuality was both lauded and condemned when she was named in 2017 to be the next commandant of cadets at the Air Force Academy. Conservative activist Kayla Moore complained that Goodwin "does not set a proper moral example" based on Christian interpretations of marriage and human sexuality. As commandant, Goodwin was credited with instituting new discipline policies but also was reported to have a "stormy relationship with subordinates and colleagues." Before her term as commandant was up, she was dismissed for various infractions and a failure to engender an acceptable workplace environment. She challenged the decision. Her lawyer called the decision arbitrary and capricious and ignored her allegations about the "bigotry, bias and discrimination she faced as a gay married officer leading the Cadet Wing of the U.S. Air Force Academy."

Before retiring in 2024, Goodwin served as the chief of staff of the Joint Force Space Component Command at Peterson Air Force Base and the director of the North American Aerospace Defense Command and the U.S. Northern Command Transformation Office at Peterson. She was then posted to Space Operations Command.

Goodwin's legacy as a pioneering Air Force leader is marked by her exceptional service, leadership, and unwavering commitment to diversity and inclusion. Her contributions have not only advanced the Air Force but have also fostered a more accepting and supportive environment for all service members.

Jennie Irene Hodgers (Albert Cashier) (1843–1915)

Soldier

One of the most famous secretly female soldiers of the Civil War, Jennie Irene Hodgers served as a male Union soldier, participating in the Siege of Vicksburg. After the war, he continued to live as a man, prompting many to consider him the first American transgender soldier.

Hodgers was born in County Louth, Ireland, and immigrated as a young girl, settling in Illinois. Little is known about his early life, but it is said that his uncle or stepfather dressed him in boys' clothing in order to find work in an all-male shoe factory and that even before the war, he adopted the identity of Albert Cashier in order to live independently.

In 1862 at the age of 18, Cashier enlisted in the 95th Illinois Infantry Regiment. As a soldier, he participated in approximately 40 engagements. He was captured during a reconnaissance mission during the Siege of Vicksburg but managed to escape and return to his regiment. He participated in the Red River Campaign, the Battle of Brice's Crossroads, the Battle of Spring Hill and Franklin, and the defense of Nashville. His fellow soldiers recalled him as a modest young man who always kept his shirt buttoned to the chin and was teased because he was beardless. Despite his diminutive size, they recorded that he could "do as much work as anyone in the Company." His ability to maintain the guise of a male soldier throughout the war is a testament to his determination and resilience.

After the Civil War, Cashier continued to live as a man, settling in Saunemin, Illinois. Unable to read or write, with jobs for illiterate women extremely limited, as a man, he found work as a handyman, farm laborer, and janitor. He lived a quiet life, maintaining a male identity and drawing a military pension for many years.

In 1911, Cashier's health began to decline, and he was admitted to a veterans' hospital for care. It was during this time that his birth gender was discovered by hospital staff. Suffering from dementia, he was moved to the Watertown State Hospital for the Insane in Illinois. The hospital staff forced him to wear women's clothing for the first time in over 50 years. Unused to walking in long skirts, he tripped and fell, breaking a hip, which left him bedridden and hastened his decline. He died in 1915, less than a year before women gained the right to serve openly—if restrictively—in the U.S. Armed Forces.

Cashier was given an official Grand Army of the Republic funeral and buried with full military honors, with a tombstone that read, "Albert D. J. Cashier. Co. G, 95 Ill, Inf."

Helen G. James (1927–)

Air Force Service Member

Helen Grace James is a trailblazer in the fight for LGBTQ+ rights within the U.S. military. As a former member of the Air Force who was discharged due to her sexuality, she later won a significant legal battle to have her discharge upgraded. Her courageous fight for justice has inspired many and highlighted the ongoing challenges faced by LGBTQ+ service members.

James was born in Scranton, Pennsylvania. She earned a BS in health education at East Stroudsburg State College and taught for several years before enlisting in the U.S. Air Force in 1952. She served first as a radio operator and was later promoted to crew chief, eventually achieving the rank of airman second class. In 1955, during the Lavender Scare campaign to remove gay people from the government, the Office of Special Investigations (OSI) targeted her based on the rarity of women of her rank in the Air Force and placed her under arrest, threatening to disclose her sexuality to her family and friends unless she signed discharge papers from the Air Force. She received an "undesirable" discharge in 1955 and was also stripped of her commission in the Air Force Reserve.

After her discharge, James moved to California, where she got an advanced degree in physical therapy from Stanford University and worked as a physical therapist and as a member of the faculty at California State University, Fresno.

In 1960, James applied to upgrade her status from "undesirable" to "general discharge under honorable conditions," which eventually was done, but the designation did not allow her to have access to basic veteran services. In 2018, at the age of 90, she achieved a historic victory when as a result of her suit, her discharge was upgraded to "honorable" following a prolonged legal battle. This landmark decision was a significant step forward for LGBTQ+ rights and justice in the military.

James's case drew national attention and underscored the importance of rectifying past injustices. Her determination and resilience have been recognized as a catalyst for change, encouraging others who faced similar discrimination to seek justice. Beyond her legal victory, she has been an advocate for LGBTQ+ rights and has shared her story to raise awareness about the struggles and achievements of LGBTQ+ service members. "Everything that I've done has been worth it if I can help people," she said. "The more my story gets out there, the more support and understanding there will be for the LGBTQ+ community. We have to work hard to make change."

Leonard P. Matlovich (1943–1988)

Air Force Service Member

Leonard Philip Matlovich was a notable figure in the history of the U.S. military best known for being the first gay service member to openly challenge the military's ban on homosexuality. His bravery and activism have made him a symbol of courage and equality. His actions played a crucial role in the fight for LGBTQ+ rights within the military and in broader society, leaving a lasting impact on the movement for acceptance and inclusion.

Matlovich was born in Savannah, Georgia, at Hunter Air Force Base, the only son of Air Force sergeant Leonard Matlovich. He grew up living on military bases, mainly in the southern United States, which instilled in him a strong sense of duty and patriotism. After attending Catholic schools, he enlisted in the U.S. Air Force in 1963. He served with distinction during the Vietnam War, serving three tours of duty and earning numerous commendations, including the Bronze Star and the Purple Heart.

While stationed in Florida, Matlovich began frequenting gay bars, and in 1973, when he was 30, he had sex with another man for the first time. He came out to his friends but continued to conceal his sexual orientation from his commanding officer. He volunteered to teach Air Force race relations classes, convinced that the racism he had grown up around was wrong. He would gradually realize that the discrimination faced by gays was similar to that faced by African Americans.

In 1974, Matlovich read an interview in the *Air Force Times* with gay activist Frank Kameny. Matlovich contacted him, and Kameny told him that he was looking for a gay service member with a perfect record to create a test case to challenge the military's ban on gays. In 1975, Matlovich delivered a letter to his commanding officer declaring his homosexuality. This bold move led to his discharge from the Air Force, a decision he fought in a highly publicized legal battle. His case received widespread media attention, and he appeared on the cover of *Time* magazine in 1975 with the headline "I Am a Homosexual," becoming a national symbol of the struggle for gay rights. By 1980, the Air Force had failed to provide the court with an explanation of why Matlovich did not meet the criteria for an exception to its ban and was ordered to reinstate him. The Air Force offered him a financial settlement instead, which he accepted. His efforts helped to raise awareness and galvanize the LGBTQ+ rights movement. His story and activism continued to inspire many, contributing to the eventual repeal of the "Don't Ask, Don't Tell" policy in 2010.

Matlovich, a converted Mormon and church elder, was twice excommunicated by the Church of Jesus Christ of Latter-day Saints for homosexual acts: in 1985 and again in 1979. After his discharge, he moved to San Francisco, where he became an active figure in the gay rights movement. He worked with organizations like the Gay Rights National Lobby and campaigned against discriminatory policies. Despite facing significant personal and professional challenges, he remained committed to his cause. He was diagnosed with HIV/AIDS in the 1980s and became one of the earliest advocates for awareness and research related to the disease. His openness about his sexuality and health struggles further solidified his role as a trailblazer in the fight for equality. He died in 1988, less than a month before his 45th birthday. He is buried in the Congressional Cemetery in Washington, D.C., with a tombstone identifying him only as "A Gay Vietnam Veteran" with his birth and death year and the inscription, "When I was in the military, they gave me a medal for killing two men and a discharge for loving one."

Matlovich's courageous stand against discrimination and tireless advocacy for LGBTQ+ rights have left an enduring legacy. His willingness to challenge the status quo and fight for equality has inspired countless individuals and contributed to significant progress in the military and society at large. His life and work continue to serve as a powerful reminder of the importance of standing up for one's beliefs and the ongoing struggle for acceptance and inclusion.

Keith Meinhold (1963–)

Naval Officer

Volker Keith Meinhold is a retired U.S. Navy petty officer and a significant figure in the movement for LGBTQ+ rights within the military. His stand against discriminatory policies helped to pave the way for greater acceptance and inclusivity for LGBTQ+ service members. His legacy is marked by his unwavering commitment to equality and justice.

Meinhold was born in Stuart, Florida, and enlisted in the U.S. Navy in 1980 at the age of 17. He served as an air crewman and sonar operator, demonstrating exceptional skill and dedication in his duties. He flew missions throughout the Pacific and Indian oceans and the Persian Gulf while receiving "outstanding job performance" evaluations.

Meinhold realized that he was gay after enlisting and came out to his family in 1990. In 1992, he made headlines when he publicly came out as gay while still serving in the Navy. In an interview on the ABC News program *World News Tonight*, he stated, "Yes, in fact, I am gay." At the time, the military's policy banned openly gay, lesbian, and bisexual individuals from serving, and his declaration led to his discharge. He challenged his discharge in federal court, arguing that the military's policy violated the Constitution's equal protection guarantee and that the Navy board had acted unfairly by refusing to tell him whether he was being judged for acknowledging his homosexuality or for engaging in homosexual acts, which he consistently denied. In a landmark decision, a federal judge ruled in his favor, ordering his reinstatement into the Navy. This case was one of the first successful legal challenges to the military's ban on openly gay service members and set a precedent for future cases.

Meinhold would appear on the cover of *Newsweek* with the headline "Gays and the Military," and his case served as an important catalyst in the "Don't Ask, Don't Tell" (DADT) policy that allowed service to gays in the military provided that they were closeted. He returned to active duty, though he was warned that under the newly enacted DADT, if he repeated the same statement that had prompted the Navy's discharge proceedings, he would be discharged again. He continued to serve until his retirement in 1996, becoming one of the first openly gay U.S. service members to be honorably discharged.

Meinhold would speak out and advocate for the eventual repeal of the DADT policy in 2010. His actions helped to bring about significant changes in military policy, promoting a more inclusive environment for all service members. He has remained active in supporting LGBTQ+ rights and worked with various organizations to promote equality and justice. He lives in Florida with his partner, Steven Weiss.

Shane Ortega

Military Service Member

Shane Ortega is the first transgender person to serve openly in the military and the first American soldier to transition during active duty. He served three hazardous duty tours: two in Iraq with the Marine Corps as a woman and one in Afghanistan with the Army as a man. As one of the first openly transgender service members, he has played a crucial role in challenging and transforming military policies regarding transgender individuals, making significant strides toward inclusivity and equality.

Ortega was born in Patuxent River, Maryland. He is the son of two military veterans; his mother served in the Army and the Navy, and his father served in the Navy. A Native American from the Haudenosaunee-Tuscarora tribe, he enlisted as female in the U.S. Marine Corps in 2004, where he served as a helicopter crew chief. Initially barred from combat service as a woman, he still volunteered for two deployments to support infantry units in Iraq and volunteered to become a bomb technician, one of the most dangerous and psychologically demanding roles in the armed services.

Ortega later transferred to the U.S. Army, continuing his distinguished career as a helicopter crew chief and later as a staff sergeant. In 2009, he openly started taking testosterone with the knowledge of his Army physician and took other steps toward transitioning, though the Army continued to designate him as "female." He became one of the first openly transgender service members in the U.S. military before his retirement in 2017.

In 2013, Ortega cofounded SPARTA (Service Members, Partners, Allies for Respect and Tolerance for All) to provide support and advocacy for transgender service members in the military, helping to advance equal treatment and opportunities within the U.S. Armed Forces. In 2015, his case received widespread media attention, highlighting the need for policy change. His efforts contributed to the Department of Defense's decision in 2016 to lift the ban on transgender individuals serving openly, marking a historic milestone in the fight for transgender rights. He has continued his advocacy work beyond his military service. He was a vocal critic of the Trump administration's attempts to reinstate the ban on transgender service members and has worked tirelessly to support LGBTQ+ rights and inclusion in the military and society at large.

Ortega attributes his advocacy to his indigenous background. "I'm also a two-spirit person," he stated. "In my indigenous community that means I have a responsibility of walking between two worlds, two genders. There's a difference between being a trans Indian and living your western life and being two-spirited. It's an enormous role that comes with a lot of sacrifice. It's not a title I chose for myself. It's about bringing balance to the world."

Randy Phillips (1990–)

Air Force Service Member

Steven Randy Phillips, also known by his YouTube username, AreYouSurprised, is a retired U.S. Air Force senior airman who became widely known for his pub-

lic coming-out video during the repeal of the "Don't Ask, Don't Tell" (DADT) policy. His bravery and openness have made him a significant figure in the movement for LGBTQ+ rights in the military.

Phillips was born in Eclectic, Alabama. He enlisted in the U.S. Air Force in 2009, where he served as a senior airman. He was stationed at Aviano Air Base in Italy during a significant part of his military career. His early years in the Air Force coincided with the era of DADT, a policy that prohibited openly gay, lesbian, and bisexual individuals from serving in the military. A statute repealing DADT policy was enacted in 2010, but changes in the policy were delayed until the military reported its readiness for implementation in 2011.

Frustrated by the delay, Phillips, while deployed in Southwest Asia, became determined to reveal his homosexuality in a social media campaign seeking support for gay service members. Using the pseudonym AreYouSurprised, he began posting videos on YouTube documenting his experiences as a closeted gay man in the military and soliciting support to help in his coming out. His series of 13 videos, posted over five months, attracted international attention, providing a candid and personal perspective on the impact of the DADT policy.

On September 20, 2011, the day DADT was officially repealed, Phillips posted a video of himself coming out to his father over the phone. The emotional and heartfelt moment resonated with viewers around the world, garnering 4.6 million views and widespread media coverage. His courage in sharing his story publicly helped to humanize the issue and brought significant attention to the challenges faced by LGBTQ+ service members.

Following his coming out, Phillips continued to advocate for LGBTQ+ rights and inclusion within the military. He has participated in various events and initiatives aimed at supporting LGBTQ+ service members and raising awareness about the importance of equality and acceptance. He left the Air Force in 2014, settling in San Diego, where he established a boat tour business.

Elizabeth Reynard (1897–1962)

Naval Officer, Educator

Elizabeth Reynard was a prominent figure in the establishment of the U.S. Navy Reserve branch WAVES during World War II and a respected academic. She was the first woman to be appointed a lieutenant in the Navy Reserve. Her work significantly contributed to the inclusion of women in the U.S. Navy.

Born in Massachusetts, Reynard moved with her mother after her father's death. She graduated from Barnard College in 1922 and began teaching English there. By 1939, she was the head of the new American studies department.

With the U.S. entry into World War II, the Navy wanted to extend the role of women in service to positions requiring academic degrees such as doctors, lawyers, chemists, and engineers. The Navy sought advice from educators at the most prominent women's colleges on the best way to organize the new women's reserve. Victoria C. Gildersleeve (1877–1965), dean of Barnard College, was asked for the name of a faculty member to assist the Navy in developing a plan for the women's branch of the U.S. Navy Reserve, and she suggested Reynard, who began working for the Navy in 1942. One of her first assignments was to create a name for the members of this new women's branch, and she came up with WAVES (Women Accepted for Volunteer Emergency Service). Congress passed the bill establishing the women's reserve, and Reynard was sworn in as a lieutenant and the assistant director. In 1944, she would be promoted to lieutenant commander, supervising the training of nearly 86,000 WAVES members. She left active duty in 1945 and returned to her former faculty position at Barnard until her retirement due to poor health in 1947. She retired from the Navy Reserve in 1953.

Reynard and Gildersleeve would form an intimate relationship during the war years that lasted until Reynard's death. While neither identified publicly as a lesbian, referring to each other as close friends and housemates, their closest associates viewed their partnership as a "de facto marriage." They lived together in a house in Bedford, New York, and in a summer home on Cape Cod. They are buried together in Bedford.

Reynard's legacy is defined by her pioneering efforts in military service for women and her lasting impact on broadening women's roles both in the military and beyond.

Patricia Rose (1960–)

Air Force Officer

Patricia "Trish" Rose is a distinguished military figure known for her exceptional service in the U.S. Air Force and role as an advocate for LGBTQ+ rights within the U.S. Armed Forces. As the first openly gay brigadier general in the Air Force, she has been a trailblazer, paving the way for greater acceptance and inclusion in the military. Her leadership and dedication have made her a respected and influential figure both within the military and in the broader community as an advocate for equality.

Rose was born in Ellsworth, Maine. She grew up in a supportive family environment that valued service and dedication. She graduated with a B.A. in humanities from Providence College in Rhode Island in 1983. She would earn an M.S. in education from Eastern Illinois University in 1989. She joined the Air Force's Officer

Training School in 1984 and served as an aircraft maintenance officer from 1984 to 1986 and an instructor of aircraft maintenance from 1987 to 1991.

Rose's military career is marked by a series of significant achievements and leadership roles. She served in various capacities, including assignments in logistics, operational support, and command positions. Her exceptional performance and leadership led to her promotion in 2010 to brigadier general, making her the first openly gay general officer in the Air Force following the repeal of the "Don't Ask, Don't Tell" policy. In 2013, she was promoted to major general, making her the first openly LGBTQ+ officer to be promoted to this rank in the U.S. Air Force. Her promotion was a landmark event, symbolizing progress and increased acceptance within the military. Throughout her career, she has been instrumental in enhancing the efficiency and effectiveness of Air Force operations, contributing to numerous successful missions and initiatives. She retired from the military in 2017 to begin a career as a public relations and marketing director at a hospital in the Seattle area.

Rose has been open about her sexuality, becoming a prominent advocate for LGBTQ+ rights within the military. She is married to Navy officer Julie Roth. Her visibility and advocacy have played a crucial role in promoting a more inclusive environment within the U.S. Armed Forces, helping to break down barriers and foster acceptance. Beyond her military service, she continues to be active in various organizations and initiatives aimed at supporting LGBTQ+ service members and veterans.

Rose's distinguished career and pioneering role as the first openly gay general officer in the Air Force have made her a significant figure in military history. Her leadership, dedication, and advocacy for LGBTQ+ rights have helped to create a more inclusive and equitable environment within the U.S. Armed Forces. Her legacy as a trailblazer and advocate continues to inspire and influence, promoting acceptance and equality for all service members.

Josh Seefried (1986-)

Air Force Officer

Josh Seefried is a key figure in the movement for LGBTQ+ rights within the U.S. military. As a cofounder of OutServe, an organization that supports LGBTQ+ military personnel, and a captain in the Air Force, he has been instrumental in the repeal of the "Don't Ask, Don't Tell" (DADT) policy and in advancing equality and acceptance for LGBTQ+ service members. His advocacy has significantly influenced military policies and societal attitudes.

Seefried was born and raised in a military family, which instilled in him a deep respect for service from a young age. He pursued higher education at the U.S. Air Force Academy, where he graduated in 2009 with a degree in economics. His early career in the Air Force was marked by his decision to serve under the DADT policy, which prohibited openly gay individuals from serving in the military. Despite the challenges, he excelled in his duties and demonstrated exceptional leadership qualities.

Seefried's most significant achievement is cofounding OutServe in 2010, an underground network of LGBTQ+ service members that provided support and advocated for the repeal of DADT. Using the pseudonym J. D. Smith, he worked to bring visibility to the struggles of LGBTQ+ military personnel. OutServe rapidly grew into a prominent organization, with Seefried playing a crucial role in its development and operations.

In 2011, Seefried publicly revealed his identity following the repeal of DADT, becoming one of the most recognizable faces of the movement. He continued to lead OutServe, which later merged with the Servicemembers Legal Defense Network (SLDN) to form OutServe–SLDN. The organization has been a powerful advocate for LGBTQ+ rights, providing legal assistance, support, and advocacy for service members.

Seefried has also been an influential speaker and writer and is the author of *Don't Ask, Don't Tell* (2011), sharing his experiences and insights on LGBTQ+ issues in the military. His contributions have been transformative and recognized through numerous awards and honors, reflecting his dedication and impact on the movement for equality. His leadership and courage have paved the way for a more inclusive and accepting environment for all service members, ensuring that future generations can serve openly and proudly.

Emily Shilling (1980–)

Naval Officer

Emily Shilling is a highly respected officer in the U.S. Navy and one of the highest-ranking openly transgender individuals in the military. Her distinguished career is marked by her exceptional leadership, dedication, and commitment to both her country and the advancement of LGBTQ+ rights within the U.S. Armed Forces. Her courage and advocacy have made her a significant figure in the movement toward greater acceptance and inclusion in the military.

Shilling was born in Norfolk, Virginia, into a family with a strong naval tradition. From a young age, she was inspired by her family's legacy and her own passion for the sea. She attended the U.S. Naval Academy, graduating with honors in 2002 with a BS in naval engineering. Following her commissioning as an ensign, she embarked on a career that would see her excel in various challenging and rewarding assignments. She served on various naval vessels, including destroyers and aircraft carriers, where she showcased her skills in navigation, operations, and leadership. She became a naval aviator in 2007 and completed two deployments to Iraq and Afghanistan. In 2015, she graduated from the U.S. Naval Test Pilot School. Her dedication and performance have earned her multiple commendations, including the Navy and Marine Corps Commendation Medal and the Navy Achievement Medal.

Shilling came out as transgender in 2018, two days after a Trump administration policy barring trans people from serving openly in the military took effect. The policy prevented trans people from enlisting and forced "non-exempt service members" like Shilling, who came out after the ban took effect, to continue serving as their assigned sex at birth. "It was kind of like 'don't ask, don't tell,'' she stated. "I could be whoever I wanted to be at home. I just couldn't do anything at work." It would take President Joe Biden's executive order reversing the Trump transgender military ban to allow Shilling to continue her 15-year career. She is married to Lieutenant Commander John Shilling, and they have two children. She is passionate about mentoring young sailors and officers, fostering a culture of excellence and inclusion within the Navy. In 2013, she was elected president of SPARTA, a nonprofit advocacy organization representing transgender service members in the United States.

Shilling's distinguished career in the U.S. Navy exemplifies her unwavering dedication, leadership, and commitment to service. Her significant contributions to naval operations, strategic planning, and advocacy for transgender rights have made her a respected and influential figure. Her legacy as a dedicated officer, leader, and advocate continues to inspire and guide future generations of naval personnel.

Tammy Smith (1963–)

Army Officer

Tammy Smith is a trailblazing figure in the U.S. Army as the first openly gay general in the U.S. military. Her distinguished

career and dedication to service have made her a prominent advocate for diversity and inclusion within the U.S. Armed Forces. Her leadership and courage have set a precedent for future generations, highlighting the importance of equality and representation in the military.

Smith was born in Oakland, Oregon. She grew up in a small, rural community, where she developed a strong sense of duty and resilience. She has attributed her leadership skills to her participation in the Future Farmers of America. She attended the University of Oregon, where she earned a BS in history in 1986. Following her graduation, she was commissioned as a second lieutenant through the Reserve Officers' Training Corps (ROTC) program. She would eventually earn a doctorate in organizational leadership. Her early career in the Army included various leadership roles and assignments, which allowed her to prove her capabilities and commitment to service.

Throughout her military career, Smith held numerous key positions, demonstrating exceptional leadership and operational expertise. She served in various capacities, including logistics and support roles, which are critical to the Army's mission readiness. In 2012, she made history when she was promoted to brigadier general, becoming the first openly gay general officer in the U.S. military following the repeal of the "Don't Ask, Don't Tell" policy. Her promotion was a significant milestone for LGBTQ+ representation in the U.S. Armed Forces. She would be later promoted to major general in 2016. She continued to excel in her career, taking on roles that included commanding general of the 98th Training Division (Initial Entry Training) and serving as the deputy commanding general for sustainment for the 8th Army in South Korea. She retired from service in 2021.

Smith's personal life and openness about her sexuality have played a crucial role in her advocacy for LGBTQ+ rights within the military. In 2012, she married Tracey Hepner, a founder of the Military Partners and Families Coalition, an organization dedicated to supporting LGBTQ+ military families. She was forced to delay her marriage until after DADT was repealed, becoming the first openly gay U.S. flag officer to come out while serving since the repeal. Her visibility and advocacy have helped to promote a more inclusive environment in the U.S. Armed Forces, inspiring many service members to embrace their identities openly. Her efforts extend beyond her military service as she continues to work toward equality and support for all members of the LGBTQ+ community.

Smith's remarkable career and historic achievements have made her a pioneering figure in the U.S. military. Her leadership, dedication, and advocacy for LGBTQ+ rights have not only advanced the cause of equality within the U.S. Armed Forces but have also inspired countless individuals to pursue their careers with authenticity and pride. Her legacy as a trailblazer and advocate ensures that her impact will be felt for generations to come, promoting a more inclusive and equitable military environment.

Randy S. Taylor (1965-)

Army Officer

Randy S. Taylor is a distinguished military officer known for his extensive service and leadership in the U.S. Army. In addition to his professional achievements, he is one of the highest-ranking openly gay officers in the U.S. military. He has served as chief of staff of U.S. Strategic Command, which is responsible for the global command and control of U.S. strategic forces. His advocacy for LGBTQ+ rights has made him a significant figure in the movement for inclusivity and equality within the U.S. Armed Forces.

Taylor was born in Louisville, Kentucky. He enlisted in the U.S. Army at the age of 19 and later graduated from the University of Maryland with a BS in technology and management, a master's degree in telecommunications management, and a master's degree in national security and strategic studies. He graduated from the U.S. Naval War College.

After attending the Infantry Officer Basic Course in 1988, Taylor was first assigned as a rifle platoon leader. Throughout his career, he served in various capacities, including command roles, staff positions, and operational deployments. His dedication and performance have earned him multiple commendations, including the Legion of Merit, the Bronze Star, and the Meritorious Service Medal.

One of Taylor's notable assignments was serving as the chief of staff for the U.S. Army Cyber Command, in which he was responsible for overseeing operations and strategic initiatives related to cyber defense. His leadership was instrumental in enhancing the Army's cyber capabilities and ensuring the security of critical information infrastructure. In addition to his operational roles, he has contributed to policy development and strategic planning at the Pentagon, influencing key decisions that shape the Army's future.

Taylor came out as gay in 2015 and is married to Lucas Taylor. His openness about his identity has played a crucial role in promoting a more inclusive environment within the U.S. Armed Forces. His advocacy efforts have helped to pave the way for greater acceptance and support for LGBTQ+ service members, demonstrating that dedication and professionalism transcend sexual orientation.

Perry Watkins (1948–1996)

Army Military Service Member

Perry Watkins was a pioneering figure in the fight for LGBTQ+ rights within the U.S. military. As one of the first openly

gay service members to challenge discriminatory policies, his legal battles and personal courage significantly advanced the cause of equality and set important precedents for LGBTQ+ rights.

Watkins was born in Joplin, Missouri. He was open about being gay while in high school. Drafted into the military in 1967, he said that he was gay at his initial induction examination but was still categorized as "qualifies for military service." He served first as a chaplain's assistant but was reassigned as a personnel clerk. Throughout his military service, he made no secret of his sexual orientation. After being discharged in 1970, he reenlisted, again affirming his sexual orientation. Stationed in Germany, he occasionally performed in drag as a female impersonator at shows sponsored by the Army. In 1975, an investigation of his sexual orientation led to a decision that his excellent service record warranted his retention despite being gay. In 1979, he reenlisted for a third time, deciding to serve in the Army for 20 years in order to retire with a pension.

In 1981, another review of Watkins's security clearance led the Army to revoke it, preventing his promotion from staff sergeant to sergeant first class. After he appealed the denial of his security clearance, the Army moved to discharge him. In 1982, he sued the Army for attempting to discharge him on the grounds of his homosexuality. The case went through various levels of the judicial system, with Watkins ultimately achieving a significant victory in 1989 when the 9th Circuit Court of Appeals ruled in his favor. It was the first time a U.S. appellate court ruled against the U.S. military's ban on service by gays and lesbians. The court's decision was groundbreaking, as it recognized that the Army had allowed him to serve openly as a gay man for years, thus precluding the Army from discharging him based on his sexual orientation. This ruling highlighted the inconsistencies and discrimination within military policies and set an important legal precedent for future cases, contributing to the eventual repeal of the "Don't Ask, Don't Tell" policy in 2010.

Despite initially planning to reenlist, Watkins settled instead for a retroactive promotion to sergeant first class, retroactive pay, full retirement benefits, and an honorable discharge. He worked in the Tacoma, Washington, office of the Social Security Administration from 1984 to 1994. He resented the fact that advocates for allowing gays and lesbians to serve openly in the military never used his story or asked him to participate in their campaigns. In 1993, however, he was asked to serve as the grand marshal of the New York City Pride Parade, and a documentary, *SIS: The Perry Watkins Story,* was released in 1994. At the age of 47, he died of AIDS-related complications.

Sports

Of all the areas of American culture, American sports, despite making some strides toward achieving equality and acceptance of LGBTQ+ athletes, has lagged the furthest behind. As of 2026, no openly gay players are on the roster of the National Football League (NFL), Major League Baseball (MLB), the National Basketball Association (NBA), or the National Hockey League (NHL).

In 2023, Kevin Maxen, an associate strength coach for the NFL's Jacksonville Jaguars, made history by becoming the first openly gay male coach in major American professional sports. In male professional team sports, the barriers to coming out for athletes while active players have historically been insuperable. Few players came out before the 2020s.

Economist Jim Buzinski, writing in *Outsports*, the leading media platform dedicated to covering LGBTQ+ issues in sports, used the example of the MLB in 2015 to point out: "There are 30 major league baseball teams, each with 40 men on their roster … yet none of these 1,200 players have acknowledged being gay. If baseball players are as likely to be gay as other men their age—let's go with an estimate of 1 in 25—then the odds that none of these men are gay is one in two sextillion. A sextillion comes after a trillion, quadrillion and quintillion; it is a thousand billion billion." In short, Buzinski goes on to write, "Even if the proportion [of gay men in baseball] is much lower, the point remains that there are probably dozens of gay men currently playing for teams associated with Major League Baseball." If totaling up the rosters for all four major men's team sports (4,082) still adds up to zero, then the odds that none of these players is gay are infinitesimal. Clearly, the factors that limit male professional athletes from coming out remain intractable and have contrasted strikingly with the strides being made in other professional and amateur sports in America for LGBTQ+ athletes, leagues, and franchises.

Historically, gay male athletes were subjected to the same negative societal attitudes to homosexuality as any other segment of the population. Homosexuality was regarded as a moral failing and a psychological disorder, and this perspective was reflected in sports as well. Athletes had to conceal their sexual orientation in order to avoid discrimination and exclusion from teams and competition. As well-publicized role models and celebrities, athletes, whether professional or amateur, faced even closer scrutiny and pressure to conform to normative sexual and gender behavior while risking their careers, livelihoods, and private lives in coming out.

For the gay male athlete in the first half of the 20th century, no more cautionary tale about the risk of being sexually "different" existed than tennis star Bill Tilden, who dominated the world of tennis during the 1920s and 1930s, winning

Tennis star Bill Tilden (seen here in 1919) was a huge success on the courts in the 1920s and 1930s, but after his sexuality became known in the 1940s, he was convicted twice of sexual misconduct.

10 Grand Slam titles, seven U.S. championships, and three Wimbledon titles. He was, during these years, one of the most famous athletes in the world. He never married, and although he never publicly came out, his relationships with men led to speculation and scandal. In the 1940s, he faced serious legal issues regarding his sexuality. He was twice convicted on charges of sexual misconduct, resulting in prison sentences that destroyed his reputation and ability to earn an income from teaching tennis or playing professionally. Tilden's story reflects both the heights of sporting excellence and acclaim and the harsh realities of living as a gay man in a less accepting era.

Even as social attitudes began to change regarding LGBTQ+ acceptance and inclusion in other parts of American society in the 1960s and 1970s, professional male athletes faced significant barriers to coming out publicly. With the absence of precedents of openly gay role models in the professional leagues, it was more challenging for athletes to envision a successful career while being open about their sexuality.

The lack of representation perpetuates the notion that being openly gay is incompatible with a professional sports career. Other careers—in politics, arts and entertainment, media, business, and the military—could eventually point to trailblazing LGBTQ+ people in their ranks. Not so in the top four male professional sports leagues. Professional sports, especially men's leagues, often promote a hypermasculine culture that can be unwelcoming to gay athletes. Locker rooms are intimate spaces where camaraderie and team cohesion are paramount. The fear of disrupting these dynamics and facing potential ostracism from teammates can discourage athletes from coming out. In addition, numerous practical and economic considerations exist.

Negative fan and media reactions can deter athletes from coming out. Athletes may also fear that coming out could negatively impact their careers, including earnings, sponsorship deals, contract negotiations, and playing time. Some athletes may fear that being openly gay could overshadow their athletic performance and define their public image.

Despite the risks involved, a few male professional athletes have come out but significantly after their playing days were over. David Kopay, running back in the NFL for nine seasons from 1964 to 1972, became the first professional athlete to publicly come out in 1975. His 1977 autobiography, *The David Kopay Story*, details his experiences as a gay man in the NFL.

Other NFL players have come out after retiring: Roy Simmons, offensive lineman (1975), Esera Tuaola, defensive tackle (2007), Kwame Harris, offensive tackle (2013), and Ryan O'Callaghan, offensive tackle (2017).

In 2013, Robbie Rogers of Major League Soccer (MLS) came out as gay, becoming the first openly gay male athlete to compete in a professional sports team in the United States. His announcement was celebrated as a milestone for LGBTQ+ inclusion in sports, and Rogers continued to be an active player until his retirement in 2017. He was very much the exception, however, for nonparticipation by LGBTQ+ players on male professional teams.

The following year, defensive end Michael Sam came out as gay before the NFL draft and became the first openly gay player to be drafted in the NFL. He would be cut by the Los Angeles Rams at the end of the preseason and later joined the Dallas Cowboys' practice squad but did not make the active roster. In 2015, he signed with the Montreal Alouettes of the Canadian Football League (CFL) but left the team after only one game and later retired from professional football.

A former All-American college football player who went on to play professionally for teams in the United States, Canada, and Europe, Michael Sam was the first openly gay player in the NFL. He is currently a coach for the Panthers Wrocław in Poland.

In 2021, Carl Nassib, a defensive end, became the first NFL active player to come out, but he retired in 2023. In the MLB, Glenn Burke, an outfielder with the Los Angeles Dodgers and the Oakland Athletics from 1976 to 1979, was open about his sexuality with his teammates and management, and it was suspected that he was traded because of his sexual orientation. It was not until his playing career ended that he came out publicly in 1982. Other MLB players came out after retiring: Billy Bean, outfielder, in 1999 and Tyler Dunnington, pitcher, in 2015.

In 2007, four years after retiring from professional basketball after playing with several teams from 1995 to 2003, John Amaechi became the first former NBA player to come out in his memoir, *Man in the Middle*, which detailed the challenges he faced as a closeted gay athlete and the broader issues of homophobia in sports.

In 2013, Jason Collins made headlines by coming out as gay in a cover story for *Sports Illustrated*, the first openly gay active male athlete in one of the four major North American professional sports leagues. He played for the Brooklyn Nets for the remainder of the 2013–2014 season before retiring.

In 2021, defenseman Luke Prokop became the first player under contract with an NHL team to come out as gay. His announcement was met with considerable support from his teammates, the NHL, and fans. As of 2026, he continues to play in the minor leagues and is still working toward making his NHL debut.

Beyond the four major men's professional leagues, considerably more progress has been made in accommodating women athletes. The first two openly gay sports superstars emerged from tennis, both in 1981. Billie Jean King was outed when her former partner, Marilyn Barnett, filed a palimony lawsuit against her. The outing led to a media frenzy and a substantial financial loss for King, with most of her endorsements canceled overnight.

Despite these setbacks, she chose to address the issue directly and became one of the first prominent female athletes to acknowledge her sexuality publicly. Her decision to be open about her sexuality was groundbreaking and paved the way for greater acceptance of LGBTQ+ athletes in sports.

The same year, Martina Navratilova, who was ranked No. 3 in the world in women's singles at the time, came out as bisexual in an interview in the *Daily News*. She later clarified her sexuality, identifying as a lesbian. Her coming out was a significant moment in sports, as it was rare for a high-profile athlete at the top of her game to discuss her sexuality openly. Her revelation led to a mix of support and backlash. She lost some endorsements but also gained support from her peers and fans.

It's hard not to regard 1981 and the public coming out of two such respected superstar athletes as a turning point in the history of LGBTQ+ acceptance and visibility in American sports. King would go on to create the Women's Tennis Association and the Women's Sports Foundation, which have played crucial roles in promoting equality in sports. Navratilova continued to excel on the court, demonstrating that being open about one's sexuality did not hinder professional success. She would become a relentless advocate for LGBTQ+ rights, inspiring many athletes that followed to compete openly and authentically while promoting a more inclusive and equitable sports environment.

Czech-American Martina Navratilova (seen here in 1980) won nine Wimbledons and was ranked Number 1 in the world for 332 weeks (a record topped only by Chris Evert). She bravely came out as lesbian in 1981, a step that remarkably did not adversely affect her career.

Even before 1981, tennis served as a flashpoint in perhaps the earliest transgender controversy in U.S. sports history. In 1975, Richard Raskind, after excelling at tennis at Yale University, serving in the military, and becoming an ophthalmologist, completed gender reassignment surgery, adopted the name Renée Richards, and began living openly as a woman. In 1976, the U.S. Tennis Association (USTA) required genetic testing for female competitors, effectively barring her from competing in the U.S. Open. She filed a lawsuit against the USTA, arguing that the policy was discriminatory and violated her civil rights. In 1977, the New York Supreme Court ruled in Richards's favor, saying that she was legally a woman and had the right to compete in women's tennis. This landmark decision was a significant victory for transgender rights, setting a precedent for the inclusion of transgender athletes in professional sports.

If the public presence of LGBTQ+ athletes in men's professional team sports has failed to keep pace with comparable sectors of American society, some clear LGBTQ+ achievements have at least been made in women's professional team sports in the Women's National Basketball Association (WNBA) and soccer's U.S. Women's National Team (USWNT). Both have made significant strides in LGBTQ+ inclusion, with numerous active players coming out. As of 2024, of the 144 players on the active roster of the WNBA, 42 (29 percent) are openly LGBTQ+. The WNBA and the USWNT have both created supportive environments that celebrate diversity and have implemented policies and events to promote inclusivity.

Early visibility and advocacy of prominent LGBTQ+ athletes have also been crucial elements in fostering fan acceptance. WNBA star Sheryl Swoopes publicly came out as a lesbian in 2005, becoming one of the most prominent openly gay professional athletes at the time. Several more WNBA stars followed her in being open about their sexuality, such as Brittney Griner, Sue Bird, and Diana Taurasi. Layshia Clarendon is an openly nonbinary player, and former WNBA star and coach Becky Hammon, who is openly gay, became the first full-time female assistant coach in the NBA. In the USWNT, Megan Rapinoe, who came out publicly in 2012, has been the face of American women's soccer, a key player who led the USWNT to multiple World Cup victories and Olympic medals. Other openly gay players on the USWNT include Abby Wambach, Ali Krieger, Kristie Mewis, Kelley O'Hara, and Tierna Davidson.

A lower level of public attention allows LGBTQ+ athletes to come out with less fear of backlash, invasive media coverage, or losing endorsements or income.

The success of LGBTQ+ representation and inclusivity in American professional teams like the WNBA and the USWNT is evident also in amateur and Olympic athletics. Amateur sports in the United States, particularly at the high school and collegiate levels, benefit from strong educational and advocacy support. Organizations like GLSEN, the Trevor Project, and Athlete Ally work closely with schools and universities to promote LGBTQ+ inclusion and provide resources and training to create supportive environments. These organizations help to implement antidiscrimination policies, provide educational material, and offer counseling services, all of which foster a more inclusive atmosphere for young athletes.

Educational institutions have increasingly adopted comprehensive policies to protect LGBTQ+ students and athletes. The National Collegiate Athletic Association (NCAA), for example, has made significant efforts to create an inclusive environment through its policies and initiatives. The NCAA encourages athletic departments to have written nondiscrimination policies that explicitly cover sexual orientation, gender identity, and gender expression. These policies are designed to protect LGBTQ+ individuals from discrimination and create a more inclusive environment. The NCAA has guidelines for the inclusion of transgender student athletes as well, allowing them to compete in a manner consistent with their gender identity. Although not an NCAA initiative, the Athletic Equality Index (AEI) by Athlete Ally evaluates NCAA Division I athletic departments on their LGBTQ+ inclusion policies and practices. This index has helped institutions identify areas for improvement and encourages the adoption of more inclusive policies.

Other factors that have led to success at addressing LGBTQ+ issues in amateur sports include less intense media scrutiny on amateur athletes compared to professionals. A lower level of public attention allows LGBTQ+ athletes to come out with less fear of backlash, invasive media coverage, or losing endorsements or income. High schools and colleges often foster close-knit communities in which athletes can find support among their peers, creating a safe space for LGBTQ+ athletes to come out and be accepted by their teammates. Studies have shown that younger

The Gay Games were founded in 1982 in San Francisco and are held every four years like the Olympics (photo from the closing ceremonies at the 2006 games in Chicago).

generations tend to be more accepting and supporting of LGBTQ+ rights, and high school and college athletes are part of a generation that has a more progressive view on gender and sexuality compared to the often more traditional and conservative atmosphere of professional sports.

Perhaps the most important single factor in the changing LGBTQ+ landscape in amateur sports has been the increasing number of high-profile LGBTQ+ athletes in amateur sports and the Olympics, who have served as role models for young athletes. Their visibility and advocacy have helped to normalize being LGBTQ+ in sports and have encouraged others to come out. Their success and acceptance have demonstrated that being LGBTQ+ is not a barrier to achieving excellence in sports, further promoting inclusivity at the amateur level.

Several events, initiatives, and high-profile LGBTQ+ athletes can be mentioned in this regard. In 1981, Dr. Tom Waddell, a former Olympic decathlete, founded the Gay Games, an international sporting event aimed at promoting inclusion and celebrating LGBTQ+ athletes. The first Gay Games were held in San Francisco in 1982 and have since become a symbol of LGBTQ+ pride and athletic excellence. In 1994, Greg Louganis, a four-time Olympic gold medalist in diving, publicly came out as gay during the Gay Games in New York City. His announcement was particularly impactful given his status as one of the most successful and recognizable athletes of his time. He later disclosed that he was

HIV positive, further breaking barriers and reducing the stigma associated with both HIV/AIDS and being gay.

Participation in the Olympics by LGBTQ+ athletes symbolizes that you can become the best in your sport or compete with the best athletes in world regardless of your sexual orientation or gender identity. That message was clearly delivered by medalists such as Greg Louganis and others, including figure skater Adam Rippon, who won a bronze medal in 2018 after having come out in 2015. Freestyle skier Gus Kenworthy won a silver medal in 2014 and came out as gay in 2015. Brittney Griner won gold medals with the U.S. women's basketball team in 2016 and 2020 after having come out in 2013. One of the earliest high-profile figures associated with the U.S. Olympic team was Caitlyn Jenner who, as Bruce Jenner, won a gold medal in the decathlon in 1976 and came out as transgender in 2015.

At the 2014 Winter Olympics in Sochi, Russia, two openly gay athletes represented the United States as part of the official delegation: Billie Jean King and two-time ice hockey medalist Caitlin Cahow. Their participation was significant in sending a strong message opposing Russia's anti-LGBTQ+ laws at the time. The 2016 Olympics in Rio de Janeiro saw a record number of openly LGBTQ+ athletes participating, with at least 11 out athletes on the U.S. team. At the 2020 Olympics in Tokyo (held in 2021 due to COVID-19), Megan Rapinoe and Sue Bird, both openly gay athletes, were among the flag bearers for the United States during the opening ceremonies.

The inclusion of transgender athletes at the Olympics has been a topic of ongoing discussion and progress. The International Olympic Committee (IOC) has established guidelines to allow transgender athletes to compete in accordance with their gender identity, and the U.S. Olympic Committee has supported these initiatives. In 2024 at the Olympics in Paris, Nikki Hilz, a transgender and nonbinary runner, qualified for the U.S. team by winning the women's 1,500-meter race with a record-breaking time at the U.S. Olympic Trials. This marks a significant milestone for transgender visibility in the Olympics.

An important addition to LGBTQ+ sports advocacy has been the You Can Play Project, a nonprofit organization founded in 2012 by Patrick Burke, Brian Kitts, and Glenn Whitman to ensure that athletes are judged solely on their skills, work ethic, and competitive spirit regardless of sexual orientation or gender identity. The organization has worked across various levels of sports from youth leagues to professional teams to foster an environment in which LGBTQ+ athletes can compete without fear of discrimination. You Can Play has produced PSAs featuring prominent athletes from various sports leagues con-

American runner Nikki Hiltz is a nonbinary and transgender athlete who competed in the 2024 Olympics and won silver in the 2024 World Indoor Championships.

veying messages of support for LGBTQ+ athletes and encouraging a sports culture of inclusion. You Can Play has also partnered with professional sports teams to host Pride Nights celebrating LGBTQ+ inclusion and raising awareness.

Despite the progress that has been made concerning the acceptance and inclusion of LGBTQ+ athletes in American sports, numerous challenges remain. Homophobia and transphobia are still prevalent in many sports environments, manifested in the form of discriminatory language, exclusionary behavior, and hostility toward LGBTQ+ athletes. Clearly, not enough has been done, particularly in the four major men's professional teams, to mitigate the risks for LGBTQ+ athletes in coming out. Policies regarding LGBTQ+ inclusion can vary significantly among sports organizations. Some have comprehensive antidiscrimination policies, while others may lack clear guidelines for protecting LGBTQ+ athletes.

Many sports organizations also do not provide adequate resources or support systems for LGBTQ+ athletes such as counseling services, diversity training for coaches and players, and clear procedures for reporting discrimination. A notable lack of LGBTQ+ representation also exists in coaching, management, and administrative positions within sports organizations.

This absence of diverse leadership can perpetuate exclusionary practices and hinder the implementation of inclusive policies. Creating a more inclusive sports culture requires the combined efforts of athletes, coaches, administrators, and fans to challenge discriminatory behaviors, implement supportive policies, and celebrate diversity within sports.

At the amateur sports level, the current flashpoints are the challenges for transgender athletes. Numerous states have enacted laws that restrict transgender athletes' participation in sports, particularly targeting transgender women and girls. These laws vary, with some states banning transgender athletes from competing in sports consistent with their gender identity at the high school and collegiate levels. A patchwork of state laws creates inconsistent opportunities for transgender athletes across the country.

A former NCAA All-American swimmer, Riley Gaines has become an activist campaigning against trans women participating in women's sports.

The NCAA implemented new restrictive policies that regulate the use of hormones for transgender women competing in six specific sports starting in the 2024–2025 academic year. These changes come amid pressure from conservative groups and legal challenges aimed at banning transgender women from women's sports altogether. For example, a lawsuit against the NCAA, led by former All-American swimmer Riley Gaines, seeks to erase the records and awards of transgender women in NCAA sports. The National Association of Intercollegiate Athletics (NAIA), which oversees athletics for many small colleges and universities, has introduced a policy that effectively bans transgender women from competing in women's sports. Finally, the governing body for track and field, World Athletics, has instituted a ban on transgender women who have undergone male puberty from competing in female events at the elite level. This decision has set a precedent that may influence other sports federations and organizations globally.

In May 2024, Kansas City Chiefs kicker Harrison Butker sparked controversy with a commencement speech that was widely perceived as anti-LGBTQ+, sexist, and homophobic. Butker, known for his conservative traditionalist Catholic views, referred to Pride Month as celebrating "the deadly sins" while criticizing what he termed "dangerous gender ideologies." He advocated instead for traditional gender roles, stating that a woman's most important title should be "homemaker" and that their true purpose was marriage and motherhood.

The speech prompted an outcry of protest, including a petition demanding Butker's release from the Chiefs. Critics argued that his comments perpetuated harmful stereotypes about LGBTQ+ individuals and women. He received support, however, from conservatives and individuals who defended his right to free speech and the expression of his religious beliefs. The Chiefs have not taken any official action against Butker.

The controversy underscores the ongoing challenges related to LGBTQ+ inclusion and gender equality, highlighting tensions among free speech, religious expression, and the promotion of inclusive, respectful environments, particularly in high-profile settings such as professional sports. The incident serves as a reminder of the work still needed to foster a culture of acceptance for all individuals regardless of their sexual orientation or gender identity, whether in sports or in American society as a whole.

BIOGRAPHIES

John Amaechi (1970–)

Basketball Player, Psychologist

John Uzoma Ekwugha Amaechi is a former professional basketball player, psychologist, and advocate known for being the first former NBA player to publicly come out as gay. His courage and commitment to advocating for LGBTQ+ rights and mental health have made him a significant figure in both sports and social justice arenas.

Amaechi was born in Boston, Massachusetts, to an English mother and a Nigerian father. He was raised in Stockport, England. Amaechi, who first picked up a basketball while in secondary school, showed early promise in basketball, playing for youth teams in the United Kingdom before moving to the United States for high school. He attended St. John's Jesuit High School in Toledo, Ohio, and later enrolled at Vanderbilt University before transferring to Penn State University, where he became a standout player, becoming a two-time First Team Academic All-America member.

Amaechi's professional basketball career began when he went undrafted in the 1995 NBA draft but later signed with the Cleveland Cavaliers in 1995. He became the first undrafted player to start in his first NBA game as the Cavaliers' starting center. He also played for European teams, including in France and Greece, for two years before returning to the NBA with the Orlando Magic in 1999. He averaged 10.5 points per game with the Magic and later played for the Utah Jazz (2001–2003). Traded to the Houston Rockets before the 2003–2004 season, the Rockets traded him before the season to the New York Knicks, but he chose to retire. He played 301 games over five NBA seasons. He would come out of retirement in 2006 to represent England in the Commonwealth Games, helping the English team win the bronze medal.

After retiring from basketball in 2003, Amaechi pursued a career in psychology, earning a Ph.D. in the field. In 2007, he publicly came out as gay in his autobiography, *Man in the Middle*, becoming the first former NBA player to do so. His book received widespread acclaim and brought significant attention to issues of sexuality and sports. His book was both praised and condemned by former and current NBA players. Amaechi, who came out to his friends during his playing days, understands the decision of gay athletes not to come out publicly. "When you go public," he said, "you stop being the persona who scored this many goals, ran this fast—you're just the gay guy and that's disappointing."

As far as his own contributions, he stated, "I am not a hero nor am I special in any regard. I am simply doing what a good person of conscience would do, which is making people aware that gay people don't just look like Jack from *Will and Grace*, and that they don't want to jump your bones every occasion and that some are camp and some are butch and that we're different and we're useful and we are here."

Billy Bean (1964–2024)

Baseball Player

William Daro "Billy" Bean was a former MLB player who became one of the sport's most prominent advocates for LGBTQ+ inclusion. After coming out as gay, the second major league player to do so after Glenn Burke, several years after retiring from professional baseball in 1999, he dedicated his life to creating a more inclusive environment in sports, baseball's first ambassador for inclusion. His work as MLB's vice president and special assistant to the commissioner for inclusion made him a trailblazer for LGBTQ+ rights in the world of professional athletics.

Bean was born in Santa Ana, California. His parents divorced when he was six months old, and his mother, a meter maid and police dispatcher, remarried a police sergeant. Despite being the smallest player on his team, he became a Little League all-star by the time he was 12 and led his high school baseball team to a state championship. He attended Loyola Marymount University, where he played college baseball and earned a reputation as a talented outfielder with the potential for a professional career.

In 1986, Bean was drafted by the Detroit Tigers in the fourth round of the MLB draft. He made his MLB debut with the Tigers in 1987. Over the course of his career, he played for the Los Angeles Dodgers, the San Diego Padres, and briefly for the Kintetsu Buffaloes in Japan. Though he had a solid, if not spectacular, career, he often struggled with the pressure of hiding his sexual orientation in the hypermasculine environment of professional sports.

A handsome, successful athlete in high school and college, Bean dated a "classic beach girl" but did not share his "teammates' intense attraction to the opposite sex. There was always something missing." He married his girlfriend in 1989, but two years into his marriage, he had his first gay experience, and the couple divorced while he struggled to keep his sexual orientation closeted from his teammates and fans.

Weary of hiding his gay identity, he retired in 1995 at the age of 31, still convinced that he had more baseball in him, but, he wrote in his memoir, *Going the Other Way* (2003), "Baseball, I knew, wasn't ready for a guy like me." He came out to his parents in 1996 and, finally, publicly in 1999 in an interview with a gay columnist for the *Miami Herald.* He recalled his efforts to hide his sexual identity during his playing days: He "laughed at the jokes, lied about dates because I loved baseball. I still do. I'd go back in a minute. I only wish I hadn't felt so alone, that I could have told someone, and that I hadn't always felt God was going to strike me dead."

In 2014, Bean was appointed the MLB's first ambassador for inclusion, a role that was later expanded to vice president and special assistant to the commissioner for inclusion. In this position, he worked with each of the 30 major league clubs to promote diversity and inclusion within baseball, helping to educate players, coaches, and staff about LGBTQ+ issues and ensuring that the MLB was a welcoming place for everyone regardless of sexual orientation or gender identity. On Bean's passing, Rob Manfred, the baseball commissioner, said, "He made baseball a better institution, both on and off the field, by the power of his example, his empathy, his communication skills, his deep relationships inside and outside our sport, and commitment to doing the right thing."

Sue Bird (1980–)

Basketball Player

Suzanne Brigit "Sue" Bird is a basketball legend widely regarded as one of the greatest point guards in the history of the sport. With an illustrious career spanning two decades, she won numerous championships and accolades both in the WNBA and on the international stage. Beyond her achievements on the court, she is a vocal advocate for gender equality and LGBTQ+ rights, using her platform to inspire change.

Bird was born in Syosset, New York. Her family is of Russian–Jewish descent. She showed an early talent for basketball, playing in youth leagues and starring at Syosset High School before transferring to Christ the King Regional High School, where she led her team to a state championship and recognition as the top women's high school team in the United States. Her exceptional skills earned her a scholarship to the University of Connecticut (UConn), where she became a standout player, helping to lead the UConn Huskies to two NCAA championships (2000 and 2002) and was a three-time All-American player. Her leadership, vision, and playmaking abilities set her apart, and she was awarded the prestigious Naismith College Player of the Year and the Wade Trophy in her senior year.

Bird spent her entire professional career with the Seattle Storm in the WNBA, where she won four WNBA championships (2004, 2010, 2018, and 2020). She is a 13-time WNBA All-Star known for her exceptional leadership, playmaking, and clutch performances. In addition to her WNBA success, she had a stellar international career, winning five Olympic gold medals (2004, 2008, 2012, 2016, and 2021) and four FIBA World Cup titles with Team USA. She retired from professional basketball in 2022, marking the end of a legendary 21-season career, during which she became one of the most decorated and respected players in the history of women's basketball.

Bird came out publicly as a lesbian in 2017 during an interview with ESPN, in which she also revealed her relationship with soccer star Megan Rapinoe. The two have been together since 2016 and became one of the most high-profile LGBTQ+ couples in sports. They got engaged in October 2020 and were married in October 2023. Bird's openness about her sexuality and relationship with Rapinoe has made her an influential figure in the LGBTQ+ community and an exceptional role model for women's sports and LGBTQ+ representation.

Brian Boitano (1963–)

Figure Skater

Brian Anthony Boitano is a figure skater best known for winning the gold medal at the 1988 Winter Olympics in Calgary. Renowned for his powerful and technically flawless skating, he became a household name in the late 1980s and remains one of the most celebrated figures in the sport. Beyond his athletic achievements, he is also recognized for his contributions to popularizing figure skating in the United States and his work as an advocate for LGBTQ+ rights.

Boitano was born in Mountain View, California. Of Italian American descent, he began skating at the age of 8 and quickly showed promise, excelling in both the artistic and technical aspects of the sport. His early training was marked by a strong work ethic and dedication to mastering the most challenging elements of figure skating. He rose to prominence in the early 1980s, capturing the U.S. national title in 1985. He became the first American skater to land a triple Axel. He also became known for his innovative jumps, including the "Tano triple lutz," a variation of the triple lutz jump in which he extended one arm over his head, a move that became his signature. He won the U.S. Figure Skating Championships in 1985, 1986, and 1987, dominating American figure skating. Internationally, he secured the bronze medal at the 1983 World Figure Skating Championships and then claimed the gold medal at the 1986 World Championships, solidifying his status as a leading Olympic contender.

In his first Olympic appearance in 1984, Boitano finished fifth. However, he returned to claim the gold medal at the 1988 Winter Olympics in Calgary, Alberta, Canada. In one of the most famous showdowns in figure skating history, often referred to as the "battle of the Brians," he competed against Canadian skater Brian Orser. Boitano's flawless performance in the free skate, featuring eight triple jumps and his signature "Tano triple lutz," earned him the gold medal. This victory secured his place as one of the greatest figure skaters of his era.

After his 1988 Olympic gold medal win, Boitano continued to achieve significant milestones in his figure skating career. He turned professional shortly after the Olympics and dominated the professional skating circuit, winning multiple titles, including the World Professional Figure Skating Championships. He became a highly respected figure in the sport known for his artistry, technical skill, and consistency. In 1993, he returned to amateur competitions, following the reinstatement rule by the International Skating Union (ISU) that allowed professionals to compete in the Olympics again. He competed in the 1994 Winter Olympics in Lillehammer, finishing in sixth place. Following this, he continued his professional career, performing in numerous ice shows and tours, including his own productions.

Boitano's influence extended beyond competitions; he became an ambassador for the sport, contributing to its popularity through his performances, television appearances, and commentary. He also authored several books, including *Boitano's Edge: Inside the Real World of Figure Skating* (1997), in which he offers insights into the world of competitive skating.

Boitano publicly came out as gay in December 2013 in response to his selection as part of the U.S. delegation to the Winter Olympics in Sochi, Russia, a country that had recently passed anti-LGBTQ+ legislation. Having previously kept his sexual orientation private, he stated, "I don't feel that I can represent the country without revealing this incredible side of myself. This is an important moment, and to represent my country in Russia, it's a platform that is so important for me." His decision to come out was met with widespread support and seen as a powerful statement of solidarity with the LGBTQ+ community at a time when issues of discrimination were at the forefront of international attention.

Following his coming out, Boitano used his platform to raise awareness about LGBTQ+ issues, promoting inclusivity in sports and beyond. He participated in various events and discussions related to LGBTQ+ rights and has been involved with organizations that support LGBTQ+ youth and athletes. His activism has helped to further the conversation about the importance of acceptance and equality in the sports world, and he continues to be a respected voice in the movement for LGBTQ+ rights.

Glenn Burke (1952–1995)

Baseball Player

Glenn Lawrence Burke was an MLB player who is widely recognized for being one of the first openly gay athletes in professional sports. He was the first MLB player to come out as gay, announcing it in 1982 after he retired. He stated, "They can't ever say now that a gay man can't play in the majors, because I'm a gay man and I made it."

Burke was born in Oakland, California. He attended Berkeley High School, where he excelled in multiple sports, including basketball, track, and baseball. He helped the school's basketball team win the state championship and was named Northern California Player of the Year. His athletic talent earned him a scholarship to Merritt College in Oakland.

Burke began his professional baseball career when he was drafted by the Los Angeles Dodgers in 1972. He made his MLB debut with the Dodgers in 1977 as an outfielder. He is often credited with inventing the high five during a Dodgers game in 1977, a gesture that has since become ubiquitous in sports and everyday life. He made no secret of his being gay among the Dodgers players and management. The general manager, Al Campanis, allegedly attempted to bribe Burke to get married. Burke also felt pressure to overperform. "I kept saying," he recalled, "as long as I bat .300, and do what I have to do, they can't say nothing. I had to be a little better…I was always thinking about it."

In 1978, Burke was traded to the Oakland Athletics, where he played until his retirement in 1979. Despite his talent, he faced harassment and discrimination due to his sexuality. Manager Billy Martin introduced him to the team with a homophobic slur. Burke later revealed that his refusal to conceal his sexual orientation contributed to his early departure from professional baseball. "Prejudice drove me out of baseball sooner than I should have," he stated, "but I wasn't changing."

In 1982, Burke publicly acknowledged his sexuality in an interview with *Inside Sports* magazine. His openness about being gay made him a trailblazer in the LGBTQ+ community, particularly within the realm of professional sports.

Burke's post-baseball life was marked by struggles with addiction and health issues. Despite these challenges, he remained an advocate for LGBTQ+ rights and worked to support young athletes facing similar struggles. He died of AIDS-related complications at the age of 42. He was among the first class of inductees into the National Gay and Lesbian Sports Hall of Fame. In 2021, the Oakland Athletics renamed their annual Pride Night the Glenn Burke Pride Night. In 2022, they honored the late outfielder at their annual Pride Night for the first time.

Caitlin Cahow (1985–)

Hockey Player

Caitlin Kinder Cahow is a former American ice hockey player and influential advocate for LGBTQ+ rights and gender equality in sports. As a two-time Olympic medalist

and accomplished attorney, she has made significant contributions both on and off the ice, using her platform to advance the cause of inclusion and equality in athletics.

Cahow was born in New Haven, Connecticut. Her mother was a professor of surgery at Yale University. Her father, also a surgeon, died when she was 11. She developed a passion for ice hockey at a young age, switching from figure skating, and quickly became a standout player. She attended the Hotchkiss School, where she excelled academically and athletically, playing soccer, field hockey, lacrosse, and ice hockey, before enrolling at Harvard University. At Harvard, she played defense for the women's ice hockey team and earned numerous accolades, including All-American honors. She graduated with a degree in social/biological anthropology, which complemented her understanding of social dynamics in sports.

As a member of the U.S. women's national hockey team, Cahow won a bronze medal in the 2006 Winter Olympics in Turin, Italy. She played a key role in the U.S. team's victories at the IIHF Women's World Championship in 2007 and 2008. In 2010, she helped the U.S. team win a silver medal at the Winter Olympics in Vancouver. She was training to go to a third Olympics in 2014 but suffered a major concussion. She decided to retire from hockey and complete her law degree at Boston College.

In 2013, Cahow came out as a lesbian in an interview with Go! Athletes, a group that focuses on empowering LGBTQ+ athletes. When asked why she had not come out sooner, she said that no one ever asked. She insists that the focus on an athlete should be on their ability and performance, not on their sexuality and gender expression. "I do believe," she stated, "it is important for athletes to feel like they can express themselves however they want. If you want to be a spokesperson for a certain identity, then more power to you—but you should feel free to ignore inane questions that have nothing to do with your profession."

In 2014, President Barack Obama selected Cahow to join Billie Jean King and Brian Boitano as a member of the U.S. delegation to the closing ceremonies of the 2014 Winter Olympics in Sochi, Russia. It was widely speculated that this was to send a message to Russian president Vladimir Putin about the Russian Federation's new anti-gay laws. She regarded her role as "easily the greatest honor of my athletic career. Who knows what my life will hold, but it's going to be pretty hard to top this." She insisted that the presence of her and the other gay athletes does send a message that "our country is a country of diversity and we need to remember that. Our representatives really demonstrate that to the world, so I think it's a great all-around message."

After earning her law degree, Cahow went to work for Jones Day, one of the nation's largest law firms, becoming a partner and focusing on business restructuring and complex bankruptcy litigation. She also serves as a member of the USA Hockey Board of Directors.

Jason Collins (1978–)

Basketball Player

Jason Paul Collins is a former professional basketball player who made history as the first openly gay athlete to play in any of the four major North American professional sports leagues. His courage to come out while actively playing in the NBA has had a significant impact on sports and LGBTQ+ advocacy, inspiring many to embrace their identities openly.

Collins was born in Los Angeles, California. He grew up alongside his twin brother, Jarron, who also became an NBA player. Jason attended Harvard-Westlake School in Los Angeles, where he excelled in basketball, leading his high school team to two state championships. He went on to attend Stanford University, where he played college basketball from 1997 to 2001. At Stanford, he was known for his defensive skills and leadership on the court.

Collins was selected by the Houston Rockets as the 18th overall pick in the first round of the 2001 NBA draft but was traded to the New Jersey Nets, where he played from 2001 to 2008, contributing to the Nets' first-ever NBA finals against the Los Angeles Lakers in 2002. As the Nets' starting center, he helped them get back to the finals in 2003. He played for several teams during his 13-season career, including the Memphis Grizzlies, the Minnesota Timberwolves, the Atlanta Hawks, the Boston Celtics, the Washington Wizards, and the Brooklyn Nets.

In April 2013, Collins made headlines when he came out as gay in a cover story for *Sports Illustrated*. This announcement made him the first openly gay active athlete in one of the four major North American professional sports leagues. He received widespread support from the sports community and beyond, becoming a symbol of progress and acceptance. However, as a free agent, he was not invited by any team to a training camp. In February 2014, he signed a contract to rejoin the now Brooklyn Nets.

In November 2014, Collins announced his retirement from professional basketball after 13 seasons in the NBA. Reflecting on his coming out more than a decade later, many expressed surprise that only one other active player in the professional leagues, Tampa Bay Buccaneers linebacker Carl Nassib, had come out. Asked whether coming out was a relief, Collins stated, "There's a stress that you walk around with constantly when you're in the closet. When I came out, it was like I'd ripped off a Band-Aid. There was so much support from fans and teammates, so many new friends that I made, and I thought, why didn't I do this sooner?" He described his contribution as "holding a door open for somebody": "Mine was opened by Martina and Billie Jean and courageous athletes like them. It's my job to hold the door open for whoever is ready to enter the room next, at their own pace, in their own time."

Orlando Cruz (1981-)

Boxer

Orlando Cruz is a significant figure in both boxing and LGBTQ+ advocacy known for being one of the first openly gay professional boxers. Throughout his career, he achieved notable success, including winning the WBO NABO Featherweight and WBO Latino Featherweight titles and representing Puerto Rico in the 2000 Sydney Olympics. His decision to come out in 2012 was a groundbreaking moment in sports, making him a role model for LGBTQ+ athletes and contributing to greater acceptance and visibility within the traditionally conservative world of boxing.

Born in Yabucoa, Puerto Rico, Cruz grew up in a modest household and was introduced to boxing at a young age, inspired by his father and the sport's popularity on the island. He quickly showed promise as a talented boxer, honing his skills in local gyms and amateur competitions. His early career was marked by his success as an amateur boxer, gaining recognition for his speed and technical ability. His talent earned him a spot on the Puerto Rican national team, and he went on to represent Puerto Rico in the 2000 Sydney Olympics. Although he did not win a medal, his Olympic appearance set the stage for his transition to a professional career in boxing.

Cruz began his professional boxing career in 2000, shortly after representing Puerto Rico in the Sydney Olympics. He competed primarily in the featherweight and super featherweight divisions, quickly establishing himself as a skilled and determined fighter. In 2008, he won the WBO NABO Featherweight title, marking a significant milestone in his career.

Cruz made history in 2012 when he publicly came out as gay, becoming one of the first openly gay professional boxers. His announcement was groundbreaking in the world of sports, particularly in boxing, a sport traditionally dominated by machismo and often seen as unwelcoming to LGBTQ+ individuals. His decision to come out was motivated by his desire to live authentically and to be a role model for others who might be struggling with their identity. In his statement, he expressed being a "proud gay man" and emphasized that his sexual orientation did not define him as a fighter but rather as a person. The reaction to his announcement was largely supportive both from within the boxing community and the public. His courage in coming out was praised as a significant step forward for LGBTQ+ representation in sports, breaking down barriers and helping to challenge the stigma surrounding LGBTQ+ athletes.

Cruz continued to compete professionally after coming out. In 2012, he claimed the WBO Latino Featherweight title. He challenged for the WBO Featherweight World Championship in 2013 and the WBO Lightweight World Championship in 2016. While he did not win these world titles, his resilience and advocacy for LGBTQ+ rights made him a notable figure in the sport.

Shortly after coming out, Cruz married his partner, José Manuel, in 2013. He retired from professional boxing in 2018. Since his retirement, he has remained involved in the sport, focusing on mentoring young boxers and continuing his advocacy for LGBTQ+ rights within the athletic community. He uses his platform to inspire and support others, particularly from marginalized communities, by sharing his experiences and promoting inclusivity in sports.

Brittney Griner (1990–)

Basketball Player

Brittney Yvette Griner is one of the most dominant figures in women's basketball and is known for her exceptional skills on the court and her fearless advocacy off it. As a WNBA champion, Olympic gold medalist, and the first openly gay athlete to be endorsed by Nike, she has used her platform to champion LGBTQ+ rights and raise awareness about issues facing marginalized communities.

Griner was born in Houston, Texas. Her father was a deputy sheriff and two-tour Vietnam War veteran. She quickly stood out for her height (6 feet, 9 inches) and athletic abilities, playing volleyball and basketball in high school at Houston's Nimitz High School. She practiced with the boys' basketball team and worked with her school's football coach to develop her leg strength. She led her basketball team to the state championship game and gained national attention for her shot-blocking and dunking abilities. Her success continued at Baylor University, where she became one of the most dominant players in NCAA history. She led Baylor to an undefeated season and a national championship in 2012, earning the NCAA Final Four Most Outstanding Player award. She was a three-time All-American, two-time Naismith College Player of the Year, and set the NCAA record for career blocks. She also became the first NCAA player to score 2,000 points and block 500 shots, solidifying her legacy as one of the greatest college basketball players of all time.

In her professional career, Griner has been a standout player for the Phoenix Mercury and the Atlanta Dream in the WNBA, leading the Mercury to a championship in 2014. She is a multiple-time WNBA All-Star and has been named the league's Defensive Player of the Year on several occasions. Internationally, she has excelled as well, playing in Russia during the WNBA offseason and helping her teams win multiple EuroLeague and Russian Premier League titles. In the Olympics, she has represented the United States with distinction, winning gold medals in the 2016 Rio de Janeiro Olympics, the 2021 Tokyo Olympics, and the 2024 Paris Olympics, contributing significantly to the team's success with her scoring, rebounding, and shot-blocking abilities. Her achievements have solidified her status as one of the greatest female basketball players of her generation.

Griner is openly lesbian and has been a prominent advocate for LGBTQ+ rights throughout her career. She came out publicly in 2013, shortly before being selected as the No. 1 overall pick in the WNBA draft. She has spoken openly about her experiences with bullying and discrimination related to her sexuality and has used her platform to support LGBTQ+ youth and promote equality. She married Cherelle Watson in 2019. Her openness about her sexuality has made her a significant figure in both the sports and LGBTQ+ communities.

Griner was arrested in Russia in February 2022 for carrying vape cartridges containing cannabis oil in her luggage. She was convicted of drug charges and sentenced to nine years in prison. Her imprisonment became a significant international issue, with widespread calls for her release. After months of diplomatic efforts, she was freed in December 2022 in a prisoner exchange between the United States and Russia. After her release from Russian imprisonment, she rejoined the Phoenix Mercury for the 2023 season, continuing her career as one of the league's top players.

Becky Hammon (1977–)

Basketball Player, Coach

Becky Hammon is a groundbreaking figure in basketball known for her successful career as a WNBA player and for making history as the first full-time female assistant coach in the NBA, working with the San Antonio Spurs. In 2021, she became the head coach of the Las Vegas Aces in the WNBA, leading the team to significant success.

Born in Rapid City, South Dakota, Hammon excelled in basketball from an early age. In high school as a junior, she was named South Dakota Miss Basketball, and as a senior, she was voted South Dakota Player of the Year. Despite these accolades, she drew little attention from college basketball recruiters, who considered her too small and too slow.

Hammon played college basketball at Colorado State University from 1995 to 1999. As a point guard, she was a three-time All-American and was named the Western Athletic Conference (WAC) Player of the Year twice. She set numerous records at Colorado State, including becoming the school's all-time leading scorer, with 2,740 points. In her senior year, she led the Colorado State Rams to a 33–3 record and a spot in the Sweet Sixteen of the NCAA Tournament, marking the best season in the program's history. Her scoring ability, leadership, and work ethic earned her national recognition, setting the stage for her future professional career in the WNBA and coaching.

Hammon had a distinguished WNBA career, playing for 16 seasons from 1999 to 2014. She began with the New York Liberty, where she became known for her scoring ability and leadership as a point guard. After eight seasons with the Liberty, she was traded to the San Antonio Silver Stars in 2007, where she continued to excel, earning multiple All-Star selections and leading the team to the WNBA Finals in 2008. She retired as one of the league's top scorers and playmakers.

Following her retirement as a player, Hammon made history by becoming the first full-time female assistant coach in the

NBA when she joined the San Antonio Spurs' coaching staff in 2014. Under the mentorship of head coach Gregg Popovich, she quickly earned respect for her basketball acumen and coaching skills. In 2020, she broke another barrier by becoming the first woman to serve as head coach in an NBA game when she stepped in for Popovich after he was ejected. Her success as a coach has paved the way for more women to enter the coaching ranks in men's professional sports, making her a trailblazer in the industry. After her time with the Spurs, she became the head coach of the Las Vegas Aces in the WNBA in December 2021. She led the Aces to a WNBA Championship. This achievement made her the first rookie head coach in WNBA history to win a title.

Hammon is openly lesbian and has been in a relationship with Brenda Milano since 2015. This relationship highlights her personal life, which she generally keeps private, alongside her prominent and trailblazing career in basketball as both a player and coach.

Billie Jean King (1943–)

Tennis Player

One of the most admired and accomplished players in American tennis, Billie Jean King can be considered the single most influential figure in the successful fight for recognition and equal treatment of female athletes.

Billie Jean Moffit was born and raised in Long Beach, California. Both of her parents were athletes, and as a child, she played football and softball. She took up tennis at the age of 11 and, six months after taking her first lesson, played in her first tournament. Even as a youngster, she was noted for her aggressive, athletic play, which seemed to clash with the then dominant image of the ladylike tennis player.

King won her first tournament at 15 when she captured the southern California girls 15-and-under championship and advanced to the quarterfinals of the national championship. In 1960, she reached the finals of the national championship but lost to 17-year-old Karen Hantze. A year later, she teamed up with Hantze to win the women's double championship at Wimbledon. They became the youngest pair ever to win the event.

In 1965, Billie Jean married Larry King, who became her agent, business manager, and adviser. The following year, she won her first Wimbledon singles championship. Over the next 10 years, she won a record 20 Wimbledon titles: six singles, 10 doubles, and four mixed doubles. During that time, she also won four U.S. Open singles titles. In 1971, she joined the newly formed Virginia Slims tour and became the first female athlete to win $100,000 in a single year.

In 1973, King accepted a challenge to play a $100,000 winner-takes-all match against long-retired former champion Bobby Riggs, who had boasted that a female player could never beat a man, even with a great disparity in age. In front of 30,000 people at Houston's Astrodome and another 40 million TV viewers, she crushed him in three straight sets.

King was a founder and president of the Women's Tennis Association, founder of tennis and softball leagues for professional female athletes, and a publisher of *womenSports*, a magazine that reported on the progress of women athletes in a variety of sports. She was also the first woman to coach male tennis players.

In 1981, King was publicly outed when Marilyn Barnett, her former secretary and lover, filed a palimony lawsuit against her. The lawsuit alleged that King had an intimate relationship with Barnett for several years and that King had promised to support her financially. Barnett sought financial compensation. The lawsuit and the subsequent outing caused a media frenzy, and King, who had been successful in keeping her relationships private, was forced to address her sexuality publicly for the first time. As a result of the outing and the negative publicity surrounding the lawsuit, she lost several endorsements, which cost her an estimated $2 million in income. While the outing was a difficult and painful experience for her, it ultimately led her to become a more outspoken advocate for LGBTQ+ rights. Over time, she embraced her identity and used her platform to support the LGBTQ+ community, becoming one of the most prominent openly gay athletes in the world. Her courage in facing the fallout from the outing has been recognized as an important moment in the fight for LGBTQ+ visibility and rights. Her subsequent personal life has been marked by her long-term relationship with Ilana Kloss, a former tennis player and her current business partner. They married in a private ceremony in 2018.

David Kopay (1942-)

Football Player

David Kopay is a former American football player and one of the first professional athletes to publicly come out as gay. His courage and advocacy have made him a significant figure in the LGBTQ+ community, particularly within the realm of sports, where his story has inspired many others to live authentically.

Kopay was born in Chicago, Illinois, but grew up in Sherman Oaks, California. He grew up in a staunchly Catholic family and considered for a time becoming a priest, entering a seminary to "cure" his feelings for men. "But even with all my prayers and acts of contrition," he recalled, "I wasn't getting any relief or success in dealing with my deep secret." He transferred to Notre Dame High School and became an athletic standout, which led to a scholarship to the University of Washington in 1961. As a star running back for the Washington Huskies, he was named an All-American player and led the Huskies to the 1964 Rose Bowl.

Kopay was drafted by the San Francisco 49ers in 1964 and played in the NFL for nine seasons, including stints with the Detroit Lions, the Washington Redskins, the New Orleans Saints, and the Green Bay Packers. He was not a star player, often performing on special teams, but he earned his place on each roster through a combination of determination and physical courage.

After retiring from football in 1972, Kopay made headlines in 1975 by becoming one of the first professional athletes to come out as gay in an interview with *The Washington Star*. He had read a previous article that suggested that no gay players existed in professional football, and he contacted the writer to correct the record. In 1977, he published his autobiography, *The David Kopay Story*. The book detailed his experiences as a gay man in professional sports and became a bestseller, contributing significantly to discussions about sexuality and sports. "I really had no idea of just how big a thing it would become," he said, "or for how long I would have to continue to take all that hostility on. That hostility and self-loathing that had so been ingrained in me from my earliest years by the nuns and priests and my parents and society in general. When I first spoke out, you never saw any positive images of gay folks anywhere. Not that I was really identifying with gay folks at the time, but deep inside of course I really was."

Kopay believes that the notoriety of his coming out prevented him from getting coaching jobs after his retirement. Instead, he went to work for his uncle's business, a Hollywood flooring company. After retiring, he pledged $1 million to the University of Washington's Q Center, which supports LGBTQ+ students and faculty, saying, "I wanted to do something meaningful, to leave something behind that would benefit people whose experiences and feelings I shared and can understand." Asked in 1998 if he thought it would be safer and easier for players to come out in the future, he stated, "I used to think it was going to happen fairly soon, back when I wrote my book, but now I don't think it's going to happen for another generation. But I do think it will happen eventually."

Greg Louganis (1960–)

Diver

Gregory Efthimios "Greg" Louganis is widely regarded as one of the greatest divers in the history of the sport. A four-time Olympic gold medalist, his incredible athleticism and grace on the diving board captivated the world. Beyond his achievements in sports, he is also a prominent advocate for LGBTQ+ rights and HIV/AIDS awareness, having bravely shared his own experiences as a gay man living with HIV.

Louganis was born in El Cajon, California. Adopted at a young age by a Greek American family, he faced challenges early in life, including bullying and a struggle with his identity. However, he discovered a passion for diving at a young age, showing remarkable talent. He began competing in diving at the age of 9 and quickly rose through the ranks. He attended the University of Miami and later transferred to the University of California, Irvine, where he continued to excel in diving.

Louganis's early success included winning a silver medal in the 10-meter platform event at the 1976 Montreal Olympics when he was just 16 years old. Having missed the 1980 Summer Games in Russia due to the U.S. boycott, he dominated in 1984 in Los Angeles, gaining a gold medal in the 3-meter springboard and the 10-meter platform events. He would become the first Olympian to repeat those wins in successive Olympics at the Seoul Olympics in 1988. His performance in Seoul, particularly his recovery from having struck his head on the springboard during the preliminary rounds to win the gold medal, was one of the most memorable moments in Olympic history. It was even more amazing when he revealed later that he was HIV positive and enduring a grueling and at times debilitating antiretroviral treatment at the time. He said that he was "paralyzed with fear" that he would infect another competitor or the doctor who treated him for his head injury.

Despite being named by ABC's *Wild World of Sports* as Athlete of the Year in 1988, Louganis got few endorsement deals following either his 1984 or 1988 Olympic victories due, some suspect, to homophobia, since he had been rumored to be gay before he came out. In 1994, he announced publicly that he was gay at the Gay Games, announcing via video in the opening ceremony: "Welcome to the Gay Games, it's great to be out and proud." The following year, he disclosed that he had AIDS. His autobiography, *Breaking the Surface*, was published in 1995. In it, he revealed that he had been in a long-term abusive relationship with James Babbitt, who became his manager. At the time, Louganis was one of the most prominent athletes and celebrities to disclose their HIV status. Many reported having come out or gaining the strength to leave an abusive relationship because of the book. "It really empowered a lot of people," he stated. "That is the thing that I'm most proud of—that it had that kind of impact."

Following his diving career, Louganis has appeared in films and theater production and has used his celebrity in support of LGBTQ+ rights and HIV awareness.

Carl Nassib (1993–)

Football Player

Carl Paul Nassib is a professional football player who made history by becoming the first active NFL player to come out as gay. His announcement in 2021 was a landmark moment for LGBTQ+ representation in sports, particularly in the traditionally conservative and hypermasculine environment of American football. His courage in publicly embracing his identity has made him a trailblazer and an important figure in the ongoing movement for inclusivity in professional sports.

Nassib was born in West Chester, Pennsylvania. He grew up in a sports-oriented family, with both his father and brother having played college football. He attended Malvern Preparatory School, where he excelled in both academics and athletics, particularly in football. He continued his football career at Penn State University, where he played as a walk-on for the Penn State Nittany Lions. Over time, he worked his way up to a starting position and had a breakout season in 2015, leading the nation in sacks and earning multiple accolades, including the Lombardi Award and the Big Ten Defensive Player of the Year.

Nassib was drafted by the Cleveland Browns in the third round of the 2016 NFL draft. He quickly established himself as a reliable defensive end and was known for his work ethic and ability to pressure quarterbacks. He later played for the Tampa Bay Buccaneers, where he continued to perform at a high level before signing with the Las Vegas Raiders in 2020.

In June 2021, Nassib made headlines when he announced on Instagram that he was gay, making him the first active NFL player to come out publicly. His announcement was widely celebrated, and he pledged to donate $100,000 to the Trevor Project, an organization dedicated to suicide prevention efforts among LGBTQ+ youth. The NFL matched his donation, and his courage in coming out was praised by fans, teammates, and the broader sports community. His announcement sparked debate in the media about acceptance and diversity in professional sports. He became a role model for LGBTQ+ youth and athletes, showing that it is possible to live authentically while competing at the highest levels of sports.

After coming out, Nassib continued his NFL career as a defensive end with the Las Vegas Raiders, playing a key role for the Raiders during the 2021 season, including a crucial play in the team's season opener against the Baltimore Ravens. In the 2022 NFL season, he re-signed with the Tampa Bay Buccaneers and contributed to the team's defense, recording sacks and tackles, and maintained his role as an important rotational player. He retired from professional football in 2023.

Since Nassib's retirement, he has focused on advocacy and philanthropy, particularly in supporting LGBTQ+ causes. He has continued his involvement with the Trevor Project. He launched an application called Rayze, which is designed to connect people with local volunteer opportunities and nonprofit organizations. The app aims to make it easier for individuals to find ways to give back to their communities by linking them with causes that match their interests. Rayze reflects his commitment to philanthropy and community service, extending his impact beyond his football career.

Martina Navratilova (1956–)

Tennis Player

One of the greatest tennis champions ever, Martina Navratilova was born Martina Subertova in Prague, Czechoslovakia, where she was given the last name of her stepfather after her parents divorced and her mother remarried. Both her mother and grandmother were accomplished tennis players, and she began playing at an early age. She won her first professional singles title in Orlando, Florida, at the age of 17. In 1975 at the age of 18, she defected to the United States and was granted political asylum. She became a U.S. citizen in 1981.

Navratilova won her first Grand Slam singles title at Wimbledon in 1978 and captured the world No. 1 singles ranking for the first time, a ranking that she attained for a total of 332 weeks. Her playing style is characterized by her powerful serve-and-volley game, exceptional fitness, and strategic acumen on the court. She was the world No. 1 women's player in doubles for 237 weeks. She also holds records for the most singles titles (167) and the most doubles titles (177) in the U.S. Open era. In 2005, *Tennis* magazine selected her as the greatest female tennis player for the years 1975 through 2005, and she is arguably the greatest female tennis player of all time.

Navratilova's career consisted of two parts: her singles career and her doubles career. She completely dominated women's singles tennis in the late 1970s and 1980s. In 1982, she won 90 of 93 matches and the next year 86 of 87. In 1983, she won the Wimbledon title and the following six Grand Slam women's singles titles. In the 1987 U.S. Open, she won the women's singles, women's doubles, and mixed doubles matches to become the first triple-crown champion since 1970, a record that still stands. She retired from singles play in 1994.

In 1981, Navratilova found herself at the center of a significant controversy when she publicly came out as bisexual. This was a courageous move at a time when considerable stigma still existed surrounding LGBTQ+ identities, particularly in the world of professional sports. The controversy began when Navratilova, who was already one of the top tennis players in the world, revealed her sexual orientation in an interview with the *Daily News*. She admitted to having relationships with both men and women, making her one of the first prominent athletes to speak openly about her bisexuality. The reaction to her announcement was mixed. Some praised her honesty and bravery, recognizing the significance of her coming out in the early 1980s. However, she also faced considerable backlash. Sponsors were hesitant to be associated with her, leading to the loss of endorsements, and she received negative media attention. The public and media scrutiny was intense, with some questioning whether her personal life would affect her career. She would later clarify her sexual orientation as gay, becoming one of the first prominent athletes to do so.

Despite the controversy, Navratilova remained focused on her tennis career and continued to dominate the sport, winning numerous titles in doubles and mixed doubles, including a 2003 win at Wimbledon that tied Billie Jean King's record of 20 combined Wimbledon titles. She ended her career in 2006 with a mixed doubles title at the U.S. Open, making her, at the age of 49, the oldest ever major champion.

Over time, Navratilova became an icon not only for her incredible achievements on the court but also as a trailblazer for LGBTQ+ rights. In 2014, she married her long-term partner, Julia Lemigova. Her coming out in 1981 is now seen as a pivotal moment in sports history, marking the beginning of greater visibility and acceptance for LGBTQ+ athletes.

Diana Nyad (1949–)

Swimmer

Diana Nyad is a world-renowned endurance swimmer, author, and motivational speaker best known for her historic swim from Cuba to Florida in 2013 at the age of 64. Her achievements in the world of long-distance swimming, coupled with her powerful storytelling, have inspired countless people around the globe.

Born Diana Sneed in New York City, Nyad took her stepfather's name after her parents' divorce and her mother's remarriage. The family moved to Fort Lauderdale, Florida, where she began swimming seriously in 7th grade. She won three Florida state high school championships, but a serious heart infection prevented her from competing in strenuous short swim races. Instead, while in college at Lake Forest College in Illinois, she began distance and marathon swimming.

Nyad's first major win was in 1972 in the 22-mile (35-kilometer) Bay of Naples race, but she gained national prominence in 1975 with her record-setting swim around New York City's Manhattan Island: 28 miles (45 kilometers) in seven hours, 57 minutes. In 1979, she set a world record for distance swimming over open water by swimming 102 miles (164 kilometers) from North Bimini Island, Bahamas, to Juno Beach, Florida, in 27 hours, 41 minutes, a record that stood until 2006.

In 1978, Nyad made the first of five attempts to swim from Cuba to Florida. She failed twice in 2011, both times without a shark cage: During her second attempt, she was forced to quit after some 29 hours because of an asthma attack; her third attempt was cut short after 40 hours when she sustained painful jellyfish stings. A lightning storm and other obstacles foiled her fourth attempt in 2012 after she had spent 60 hours in the water. On her fifth attempt in 2013, she finally achieved her goal, swimming 110 miles (180 kilometers) between Havana and Key West in approximately 54 hours. At the age of 64, she became the first person to swim from Cuba to Florida without a shark cage or fins.

Nyad is the author of several books, including the memoirs *Other Shores* (1978) and *Find a Way* (2015), the latter of which focuses on her historic swim. In 2023, Annette Bening portrayed her in *Nyad*. Nyad is openly gay and has spoken about her experiences as a lesbian in both her personal life and professional career. She has been a vocal advocate for LGBTQ+ rights and has used her platform to raise awareness about the challenges faced by the LGBTQ+ community. She has been open about the struggles she has faced, including surviving sexual abuse by a coach during her youth, and how these experiences have fueled her determination to succeed.

Dave Pallone (1951-)

Umpire

Dave Pallone is a former MLB umpire whose career was marked by both controversy and trailblazing courage. Known for his role in a heated incident with Pete Rose and for being one of the first figures in professional sports to come out as gay, his life and career highlight the challenges and progress of LGBTQ+ individuals in the world of sports. His work as an advocate for LGBTQ+ rights following his MLB career has made him an influential figure in the fight against discrimination and for greater inclusion in sports.

Pallone was born in Waltham, Massachusetts. He developed an early interest in sports, particularly baseball, and began his career as an umpire in the minor leagues. He served as an MLB umpire from 1979 to 1988, during which he was known for his professionalism and ability to handle high-pressure situations. Over his nearly decade-long career, he officiated important games, including the 1983 National League Championship Series and the 1987 MLB All-Star Game.

Pallone's career in the MLB is most famously remembered for the 1988 incident involving Cincinnati Reds manager Pete Rose. During a game on April 30, 1988, Rose disputed a close call made by Pallone at first base. The altercation escalated when Rose shoved Pallone, leading to Rose's ejection from the game and a 30-day suspension. The incident garnered widespread media attention and remains one of the most notorious moments in MLB history.

Despite the controversy, Pallone continued to umpire until later in 1988, when he was unexpectedly dismissed by the MLB. His termination came amid rumors and speculation about his sexual orientation, though the official reasons were never fully disclosed. In 1990, two years after leaving the MLB, he publicly came out as gay with the release of his autobiography

Behind the Mask: My Double Life in Baseball. The book provided an insider's perspective on the challenges faced by LGBTQ+ individuals in the highly public and traditionally conservative world of professional sports. He also suggested that suspicion about his sexual orientation and the stigma associated with being a gay man in professional sports at that time may have influenced his dismissal.

Following his coming out, Pallone became a prominent advocate for LGBTQ+ rights, using his platform to speak out against discrimination and promote acceptance within the sports world and beyond. He began giving speeches and participating in various events where he shared his experiences as a closeted gay man in professional sports and the challenges he faced both personally and professionally.

Violet Palmer (1964–)

Referee

Violet Palmer is a trailblazing figure in sports known for being the first woman to officiate an NBA game and for her groundbreaking work as an openly lesbian official in a major U.S. sports league.

Born in Compton, California, Palmer grew up playing basketball and was a standout athlete in high school. She later attended Cal Poly Pomona, where she helped lead her team to two NCAA Division II national championships in 1985 and 1986. After graduating with a degree in recreation administration, she initially pursued a career in sports management. However, her passion for basketball led her to consider officiating as a career. She began refereeing high school and college games in the late 1980s and quickly gained a reputation for her knowledge of the game, fairness, and authority on the court.

Eventually, Palmer's success at the collegiate level, where she officiated NCAA Division I women's basketball games, caught the attention of NBA officials. In 1997, after years of honing her craft and breaking barriers in a male-dominated field, she made history when she was hired by the NBA, becoming the first female referee in any major American professional sports league. She made her NBA debut officiating a game between the Vancouver Grizzlies and the Dallas Mavericks. Her presence on the court was a groundbreaking moment for women in sports, as she proved that gender was no barrier to performing at the highest levels of officiating.

Palmer's early career was marked by her perseverance and resilience in overcoming challenges as she faced skepticism and scrutiny from players, coaches, and fans. Despite the pressure, she established herself as a respected and skilled referee, paving the way for future generations of female officials in professional sports. In 2006, she became the first woman to officiate an NBA playoff game, and she was selected to officiate the 2014 NBA All-Star Game. She would referee nearly 1,000 regular-season games in a nearly two-decade-long career.

Palmer publicly came out as a lesbian in 2014. She made the announcement ahead of her wedding to her longtime partner, Tanya Stine, whom she had been with for over 20 years. Her decision to come out was significant, as she became one of the first openly gay referees in major American professional sports. Her coming out was widely celebrated as an important step for LGBTQ+ visibility and acceptance within the sports community.

Palmer retired from on-court officiating in 2016 due to knee issues. However, her impact on the game continued as she transitioned to a supervisory role within the NBA's officiating department, where she helped to shape the future of refereeing. Her career helped change perceptions and promote diversity and inclusion in sports globally.

Megan Rapinoe (1985–)

Soccer Player

Megan Anna Rapinoe is one of the most iconic figures in American sports. She is the face of women's soccer and is known not only for her exceptional skills on the field but also for her outspoken advocacy for social justice, LGBTQ+ rights, and gender equality. As a two-time World Cup champion and Olympic gold medalist, she has used her platform to challenge norms and inspire change, making her a powerful voice in the fight for equality.

Rapinoe was born in Redding, California. Of Italian and Irish heritage, she grew up in a large, sports-loving family and developed a passion for soccer from the age of 3 after watching her older brother play. She often played with her twin sister, Rachael. She honed her skills through youth leagues before earning a scholarship to the University of Portland, where she played for the Portland Pilots and helped lead the team to an NCAA championship in 2005.

In 2009, Rapinoe was selected second overall in the inaugural draft for the Women's Professional Soccer (WPS) league, the highest division of soccer in the United States at the time. She played for the Chicago Red Stars and was named to the league's All-Star Team. She went on to play for several teams in the league, including Philadelphia Independence and magicJack before moving to the Seattle Sounders FC. Her most prominent club career has been with the OL Reign (formerly and currently the Seattle Reign FC) in the National Women's Soccer League (NWSL), where she has played since 2013. She became a key player for the Reign and was known for her leadership, playmaking abilities, and scoring prowess. Throughout her time with the Reign, she helped the team reach multiple playoff appearances and was instrumental in their 2014 and 2015 NWSL Shield victories.

Internationally, Rapinoe has been a cornerstone of the U.S. Women's National Team (USWNT) since her debut in 2006. Outside of the Olympics, her most notable achievements include winning two FIFA Women's World Cup titles in 2015 and 2019. In the 2019 World Cup, she won the Golden Boot (top scorer) and the Golden Ball (best player), cementing her status as one of the top players in the world.

Rapinoe's Olympic soccer career is highlighted by her contributions to the USWNT in three Olympic Games: 2012, 2016, and 2021. In the 2012 London Olympics, she played a crucial role in securing the gold medal, famously scoring an Olimpico goal (a goal scored directly from a corner kick) in the semifinal against Canada, helping the team reach and ultimately win the final against Japan. The 2016 Rio de Janeiro Olympics were less successful, with the USWNT being eliminated in the quarterfinals by Sweden, where Rapinoe had a limited role due to recovering from an ACL injury. In the 2021 Tokyo Olympics, she played a significant part in the team's journey to a bronze medal, scoring twice in the bronze medal match against Australia, including another Olimpico goal.

Rapinoe came out just prior to the London Olympics. "For a long time," she said, "I was the only player that was out." She has been open about her sexuality, indicating that she knew she was a lesbian by her first year in college. She met and began dating basketball star Sue Bird at the 2016 Olympics. Defining the gay sports power couple, Rapinoe and Bird were married in 2023.

Rapinoe has consistently used her celebrity as a platform for speaking out on social justice issues, including gender equality and equity for women athletes as well as LGBTQ+ and racial issues. She was one of the first white athletes to kneel during the National Anthem in solidarity with Colin Kaepernick, protesting racial injustice and police brutality. Her memoir *One Life* was published in 2020, detailing her life, career, activism, and the challenges she has faced as a professional athlete and advocate for social justice.

Renée Richards (1934–)

Tennis Player

Renée Richards, a pioneering figure in both the world of sports and transgender rights, made headlines in the 1970s for her successful legal battle to compete as a professional tennis player in women's tournaments after transitioning. Her courage and determination not only paved the way for greater acceptance of transgender athletes but also sparked important discussions about gender identity and inclusion in sports.

Born as Richard Raskind in New York City, Richards was raised, as she put it, as "a nice Jewish boy" in Forest Hills, Queens, her father an orthopedic surgeon and her mother one of the first female psychiatrists in the United States and a professor at Columbia University. She excelled both academically and in sports, attending Horace Mann School and later Yale University, where she captained the men's tennis team and was widely considered to be one of the best college tennis players in the country. After Yale, she attended the University of Rochester Medical School, graduating in 1959 and becoming an ophthalmologist. After an internship and residency in New York City, she joined the U.S. Navy to continue medical training and playing tennis, winning both the singles and doubles events in the All-Navy Championship.

Despite her academic, professional, and athletic successes, Richards struggled with her gender identity for many years. She began dressing as a woman in college, naming her female persona "Renée" (French for "reborn"). Her struggle with gender identity led to sexual confusion, depression, and suicidal tendencies. She married model Barbara Mole in 1970, and they had a son in 1972 before divorcing in 1975.

In 1975, Richards underwent gender reassignment surgery and began living as a woman. However, when she attempted to enter the 1976 U.S. Open as Renée Richards, the U.S. Tennis Association (USTA) required her to undergo chromosome testing, effectively barring her from competition. She sued the USTA, and in 1977, the New York Supreme Court ruled in her favor, a landmark decision that allowed her to compete in the women's division.

Richards's legal victory was a significant milestone in the fight for transgender rights. She went on to have a successful tennis career, reaching the doubles final of the U.S. Open in 1977 and ranking as high as 20th in the world. After retiring from tennis in 1981, she returned to her medical practice and became a respected eye surgeon. She also authored several books, including two volumes of memoirs, *Second Serve* (1983) and *No Way Renée: The Second Half of My Notorious Life* (2007), which detailed her life, transition, and experiences as a transgender athlete and ophthalmologist.

In 2019, Martina Navratilova stirred controversy, arguing that male athletes who transition to become female athletes but decline to undergo gender reassignment surgery should not be allowed to compete against women. She was criticized as transphobic, but Richards agrees with her: "It is just biology. Men have 10 times the amount of testosterone that normal women have.... And men still have a larger frame with a larger cardiac output, a larger lung capacity." Despite her status as a pioneering transgender athlete, Richards did not become the voice or the face of the transgender movement. She insists that gender is binary, does not believe in gender fluidity at the core of the trans movement, and remains skeptical of trans athletes who compete without gender reassignment surgery.

Despite such controversial stances, Richards remains a symbol of resilience and courage, her story continuing to inspire those who struggle with identity and acceptance. Her legacy as both a trailblazing athlete and a champion for transgender rights endures, making her a crucial figure in the ongoing fight for equality.

Robbie Rogers (1987–)

Soccer Player

Robbie Rogers is a former professional soccer player who made history by becoming the first openly gay man to compete in the MLS. His coming out in 2013 and subsequent return to professional soccer marked a pivotal moment in sports, challenging the stigma surrounding LGBTQ+ athletes in team sports.

Born in Rancho Palos Verdes, California, Rogers grew up in a supportive family environment that encouraged his passion for soccer. He attended Mater Dei High School, where he excelled in the sport, and played soccer for the Irvine Strikers, one of the top youth clubs in the country, and college soccer at the University of Maryland. In 2005, he helped the Maryland Terrapins win the NCAA Men's Soccer Championship, displaying his talent on a national stage.

Rogers began his professional career in 2006 with the Dutch club SC Heerenveen, though he didn't make any first-team appearances. He returned to the United States in 2007 and signed with the Columbus Crew in the MLS. During his time with the Crew, he quickly established himself as a key player, helping the team win the MLS Cup in 2008. He played for Leeds United from 2012 to 2013. He signed with the club in January 2012 and made a few appearances before mutually agreeing to part ways with the team in 2013. During his time with Leeds, he faced challenges with injuries and limited playing opportunities.

While playing for Leeds, Rogers came out as gay in 2013 through a blog post on his personal website. In the same post, he announced his retirement from professional soccer, citing the challenges of being a gay athlete in a sport where he felt he couldn't be open about his identity. He became the second male soccer player in Britain, after Justin Fashanu, to come out. His announcement was met with widespread support, and a few months later, he returned to soccer, signing with the LA Galaxy, making him the first openly gay male athlete to compete in a major North American professional sports league.

During his time with the Galaxy, Rogers transitioned from a winger to a left-back and became a key player for the team. He helped the Galaxy win the MLS Cup in 2014, adding to his earlier MLS success with the Columbus Crew. He played with the Galaxy until his retirement in 2017.

After retiring from soccer in 2017, Rogers transitioned into television and film production. He cofounded a production company and became an executive producer for projects like *Fellow Travelers*, a 2023 miniseries exploring a complex and intense romantic relationship between two men during the McCarthy era, highlighting their struggles. He has continued his advocacy for LGBTQ+ rights through his work in the entertainment industry, focusing on telling stories that address issues of identity and representation while remaining active in social activism.

Rogers's career is marked by both his on-field successes and advocacy for LGBTQ+ rights. His decision to come out as gay in February 2013 was groundbreaking. At the time, he had stepped away from soccer, but the outpouring of support he received after coming out encouraged him to return to the sport. He signed with the LA Galaxy in May 2013, making him the first openly gay male athlete to play in a top North American professional sports league.

Rogers's courage in coming out inspired many, and he became an advocate for LGBTQ+ rights, using his platform to raise awareness and promote inclusivity in sports. In 2014, he published his memoir, *Coming Out to Play*, in which he candidly discussed his struggles with his sexuality and experiences as a gay athlete. He married Greg Berlanti, a prominent television producer, in December 2017. The couple has two children together, a son born in 2016 and a daughter born in 2019.

Dale Scott (1959–)

Umpire

Dale Allan Scott is a former MLB umpire who made history as the first openly gay male umpire in a major U.S. sports league. His coming out in 2014 was a significant moment for LGBTQ+ representation in professional sports.

Born in Eugene, Oregon, Scott developed a passion for baseball at a young age and began his umpiring career at the age of 15. He attended the Joe Brinkman Umpire School and entered the minor leagues in 1981, working his way up through various levels, including the Northwest League, the Texas League, and the Pacific Coast League before making his MLB debut in 1985. Over the next three decades, he established himself as one of the most respected umpires in the league.

Scott umpired in numerous high-profile games, including three World Series (1998, 2001, and 2004); three All-Star Games (1993, 2001, and 2011); and six League Championship Series. He was known for his professionalism, consistency, and calm demeanor on the field, earning the respect of players, coaches, and fellow umpires alike.

Scott married his longtime partner, Michael Rausch, in 2013 after being together for over 28 years. In 2014, he made headlines when he publicly came out as gay, becoming the first openly gay umpire in MLB history. His decision to come out was widely praised and marked a significant moment for LGBTQ+ representation in professional sports. He continued to umpire in the MLB until his retirement in 2017, which was prompted by concerns over his health following a series of concussions.

Since retiring, Scott has remained active in the baseball community and as an advocate for LGBTQ+ rights, sharing his experiences and insights as a trailblazer in sports. His autobiography, *The Umpire Is Out: Calling the Game and Living My True Self*, was published in 2022, offering a candid look at his life and career both on and off the field.

Katie Sowers (1986–)

Football Coach

Katie Sowers is a trailblazing figure in football known for her historic role as the first openly gay coach in the NFL and the first woman to coach in a Super Bowl. Her groundbreaking achievements have made her a symbol of diversity and inclusion in a sport traditionally dominated by men, and she has become an inspiration for women and LGBTQ+ individuals in sports.

Sowers was born in Hesston, Kansas. Growing up, she developed a deep passion for sports, particularly football and basketball. She attended Goshen College in Indiana, where she played basketball and earned a degree in physical education. Despite her love for football, opportunities for women in the sport were limited, so she initially focused on basketball before playing for the Women's Football Alliance (WFA) team the West Michigan Mayhem.

After her playing career, Sowers transitioned to coaching, starting with youth football and gradually working her way up to coaching at the collegiate level. Her big break came when she joined the Atlanta Falcons as a scouting intern in 2016, thanks to the Bill Walsh Diversity Coaching Fellowship, which aims to increase opportunities for minority coaches in the NFL. In 2017, she made history when she was hired as an offensive assistant coach by the San Francisco 49ers, becoming the second woman to hold a full-time coaching position in the NFL. Her role involved working with the wide receivers, and her coaching was instrumental in the development of the team's offense.

Sowers came out as a lesbian in 2017, making her the first openly gay coach in the NFL. Her decision to come out publicly was a significant moment for LGBTQ+ representation in sports, as she challenged the stereotypes and barriers that have long existed in the world of professional football. She has been open about her experiences as a lesbian coach and has used her platform to advocate for greater inclusion and acceptance in sports.

Sowers's most notable achievement came during the 2019 season when the 49ers reached Super Bowl LIV. As the first woman and openly gay coach to participate in a Super Bowl, she broke new ground and brought significant attention to the importance of diversity in coaching. Her presence on the sidelines was a powerful statement about the evolving landscape of professional sports.

Sowers joined the Kansas City Chiefs in 2021 as an offensive assistant during their training camp. After her stint with the Chiefs, she became an assistant coach for the Ottawa University women's flag football team in Kansas, a position that allowed her to help develop and promote women's football at the collegiate level.

Sheryl Swoopes (1971–)

Basketball Player

Sheryl Denise Swoopes is one of the most iconic figures in women's basketball, often referred to as the "female Michael Jordan." A three-time WNBA MVP, she was the first player to be signed to the WNBA when the league was formed in

1996. Beyond her basketball achievements, she is also known for her role as a pioneer for LGBTQ+ visibility in sports.

Swoopes was born in Brownfield, Texas. She began playing basketball at an early age and quickly stood out for her athletic prowess. She attended Brownfield High School, where she led her team to a state championship. After a brief stint at the University of Texas, she transferred to Texas Tech University, where she made an indelible mark on the women's basketball program. In her senior year (1992–1993), she led Texas Tech to its first NCAA Women's Basketball Championship, scoring a record 47 points in the title game. Her outstanding performance earned her the Naismith College Player of the Year award.

Swoopes's professional career is filled with accolades and milestones. She was the first player to be signed to the WNBA, and her influence helped to shape the league in its early years. She played for the Houston Comets from 1997 to 2007, leading the team to four consecutive WNBA championships (1997–2000). During her illustrious career, she won the WNBA MVP award three times (2000, 2002, and 2005) and was known for her defensive prowess, earning Defensive Player of the Year honors three times as well. Her influence extended to international basketball, winning three Olympic gold medals with the U.S. women's basketball team (1996, 2000, and 2004). She was also a key player in multiple FIBA World Championship games, further solidifying her status as one of the greatest basketball players of all time.

In 2005, Swoopes made headlines when she publicly came out as gay, becoming one of the most high-profile athletes to do so at the time. Her announcement was significant not only for the LGBTQ+ community but also for the world of sports, where such revelations were (and still are) rare. Her courage in coming out while still being an active player broke barriers and helped to pave the way for greater acceptance of LGBTQ+ athletes. She retired from professional basketball in 2011. Since retiring, she has focused on coaching, serving as the head coach for Loyola University Chicago's women's basketball team from 2013 to 2016. She has also been active in mentoring young athletes and advocating for women's sports. She is also a highly demanded public speaker, sharing her experiences and advocating for women's sports, LGBTQ+ rights, and mental health awareness.

Swoopes has been married twice. She was first married to her high school sweetheart, Eric Jackson, with whom she has a son. Later, she had a relationship with a former basketball player and assistant coach, Alisa Scott. After their relationship ended, she married Chris Unclesho, a longtime male friend, in 2017, to the surprise of many but in confirmation of what she said at the time of her coming out as a lesbian: "I can't help who I fall in love with. No one can."

Diana Taurasi (1982–)

Basketball Player

Diana Lorena Taurasi is one of the most accomplished and admired players in the history of women's basketball. Known for her scoring ability, leadership, and clutch performances, she has earned the nickname "White Mamba," a nod to her fierce competitiveness. A WNBA champion, Olympic gold medalist, and international star, she has left an indelible mark on the sport while also advocating for gender equality in athletics.

Taurasi was born in Glendale, California, to parents of Argentine and Italian descent. Growing up, she developed a passion for basketball, excelling in youth leagues and at Don Antonio Lugo High School in Chino, California, where she was named the Naismith High School Player of the Year in 2000. She attended the University of Connecticut (UConn), where she became an exceptional player under coach Geno Auriemma. During her time at UConn, she led the UConn Huskies to three consecutive NCAA championships (2002, 2003, and 2004) and was twice named the Most Outstanding Player of the NCAA Tournament. Her leadership, scoring ability, and versatility made her one of the most celebrated players in college basketball history.

As a professional athlete, Taurasi spent her entire WNBA career with the Phoenix Mercury, where she won three WNBA championships (2007, 2009, and 2014) and was named WNBA Finals MVP twice. She was the WNBA's all-time leading scorer and earned multiple All-Star and All-WNBA honors. Internationally, she had a successful career playing in Russia and other countries during the WNBA offseason. In the Olympics, she was a key player for Team USA, winning six gold medals (2004, 2008, 2012, 2016, 2021, and 2024), making her one of the most decorated Olympic basketball players in history and tying her with Sue Bird and Teresa Edwards for winning the most Olympic gold medals in basketball history. After her victory at the 2024 Paris Olympics, she announced that it would be her final appearance with Team USA, marking the end of an amazing Olympic career that began in 2004.

Taurasi is openly lesbian and has been public about her sexuality for many years. She is married to Penny Taylor, a former WNBA player who was her Phoenix Mercury teammate. The couple married in May 2017. They have two children together. Taurasi's relationship with Taylor has been a significant part of her life, and they are one of the most well-known couples in women's basketball.

Lia Thomas (1999–)

Swimmer

Lia Thomas is a groundbreaking figure in collegiate sports known for becoming the first openly transgender woman to win an NCAA Division I championship in swimming. Her achievements in the pool, coupled with the controversy and debates they sparked, have made her a central figure in discussions about transgender athletes' participation in sports, gender identity, and fairness in competition.

Thomas was born William Thomas and grew up in Austin, Texas. From a young age, she showed talent in swimming, competing on her high school's swim team and eventually earning a spot on the University of Pennsylvania's men's swim team. She swam for three years on the men's team before beginning her transition.

In 2019, Thomas began hormone replacement therapy (HRT) as part of her transition to female. After one year of HRT, she sought to compete on the women's swim team at the University of Pennsylvania. Following NCAA guidelines, which required transgender women to undergo at least one year of HRT before competing in women's events, she joined the women's team in 2021. She quickly made headlines with her performances in women's swimming. In March 2022, she won the 500-yard freestyle at the NCAA Division I women's championships, making history as the first openly transgender woman to win an NCAA title. She also competed in other events at the championships, finishing fifth in the 200-yard freestyle and eighth in the 100-yard freestyle.

Thomas's success sparked significant debate regarding the inclusion of transgender athletes in women's sports, with some arguing that her participation was unfair to cisgender women. Despite the controversy, she remained focused on her goals and used her platform to advocate for transgender rights, emphasizing the importance of inclusion and equality in sports.

In January 2024, Thomas challenged the World Aquatics gender inclusion policy to allow her to compete in the Olympics. The policy, introduced in 2022, bans transgender women who have been through male puberty from competing in women's races. She argued that this policy is discriminatory, and in June 2024, the Court of Arbitration for Sport ruled that Thomas did not have standing to challenge the policy and would remain ineligible to compete. The ruling meant that she could not participate in the Olympic trials to select the women's swimming team for the 2024 Paris Olympics. She stated that the decision "is deeply disappointing. Blanket bans preventing trans women from competing are discriminatory and deprive us of valuable athletic opportunities that are central to our identities."

Bill Tilden (1893–1953)

Tennis Player

William Tatem "Bill" Tilden II, often referred to as "Big Bill," was one of the most dominant tennis players of the early 20th century. With a record of seven U.S. championships and three Wimbledon titles, his influence on the sport was profound. Many consider him to be the greatest tennis player of all time. However, his legacy is complex, marred by controversies surrounding his personal life that have sparked debate and reflection in the years since his career.

Tilden was born in Philadelphia, Pennsylvania, into a wealthy and socially prominent family. He began playing tennis at a young age but faced personal tragedies early in life, including the losses of his mother and older brother, which deeply affected him. His interest in tennis intensified during his college years at the University of Pennsylvania, where he honed his skills and began to stand out as a formidable player.

Tilden's breakthrough came in the early 1920s when he won his first U.S. National Championships (now the U.S. Open). His powerful serve, strategic mind, and towering presence on the court made him unbeatable. His success continued throughout the 1920s, and he dominated the sport like no one before him. His achievements in tennis are legendary. He won seven U.S. championships (1920–1925, 1929) and three Wimbledon titles (1920, 1921, and 1930). His ability to control matches with his strategic brilliance and flair for showmanship made him one of the first true superstars of tennis. He also won two Davis Cup titles for the United States, further cementing his place in tennis history.

In addition to his on-court achievements, Tilden was a prolific writer, contributing to the literature of the sport. He authored several books, including *Match Play and the Spin of the Ball* (1925), which became a tennis classic. His influence extended to coaching, where he mentored many young players, including future champions.

Tilden's personal life was complex and controversial. He was known to be gay at a time when homosexuality was illegal and highly stigmatized. His sexuality was an open secret in the tennis world, and it eventually led to his downfall. In the late 1940s and early 1950s, he was twice arrested and convicted on charges related to his relationships with teenage boys, which led to prison sentences. In 1946, he served seven months before being released on parole. In 1949, he received a one-year prison sentence. He was convinced in both cases that his celebrity would keep him out of jail, but it did not. The conviction tarnished his reputation, led to his exclusion from the tennis community, and significantly diminished his influence in the sport. He died in relative obscurity in 1953. His arrests and convictions, it is speculated, had a chilling effect on other gay athletes, reinforcing the stigma and fear surrounding homosexuality in sports during the mid-20th century. His fall from grace served as a cautionary tale, deterring other athletes from coming out and leading many to remain closeted in order to avoid similar repercussions. The severe consequences he faced highlighted the risks of being openly gay during a time when being gay was criminalized and widely condemned, contributing to the culture of silence and discrimination that persisted for decades.

Tom Waddell (1937–1987)

Olympic Athlete

Tom Waddell was a remarkable athlete, physician, and LGBTQ+ rights activist best known for founding the Gay Games, an international sporting event that celebrates diversity and inclusion. His contributions to both the sports and LGBTQ+ communities have left a lasting legacy, making him a pioneering figure in the fight for equality.

Born Thomas Flubacher in Paterson, New Jersey, Waddell's parents separated when he was in his teens, and at the age of 15, he went to live with Gene and Hazel Waddell, who adopted him. The Waddells were former vaudeville acrobats and encouraged him to take up gymnastics. He attended Springfield College in Massachusetts, where he excelled in gymnastics and track and field. The sudden death of his best friend and cocaptain on the gymnastics team led him to pursue a medical degree at the New Jersey College of Medicine, which he completed in 1965.

After medical school, Waddell joined the U.S. Army and served as a paratrooper and preventive medicine officer. Expecting to be deployed in Vietnam, he instead was sent by the Army to train as a decathlete for the 1968 Olympics in Mexico City.

He competed in the decathlon and finished in sixth place (out of 33 qualifiers). In a track meet in 1972, he injured his knee in a high jump, which ended his career as a competitive athlete.

Waddell set up a private practice in San Francisco. From 1974 through 1981, he was the medical director of the Whittaker Corporation, serving as a personal physician for a Saudi prince and businessman and eventually becoming the team physician for the Saudi Arabian Olympic team at the 1976 Montreal Olympics.

Waddell's most enduring legacy is his founding of the Gay Games. After joining a gay bowling league in San Francisco, he was inspired to organize a gay sporting event that was modeled on the Olympics. He envisioned an event that would bring together LGBTQ+ athletes from around the world in a spirit of inclusivity and pride. The first Gay Games, originally called the Gay Olympics, were held in San Francisco in 1982, attracting over 1,300 participants. A few weeks before the event was to begin, the International Olympic Committee sued him over the use of the word "Olympic," and the renamed "Gay Games" went forward. The event has since grown into a global movement, held every four years, and is a celebration of diversity in sports.

In addition to his work with the Gay Games, Waddell was a dedicated physician and advocate for health and wellness, particularly within the LGBTQ+ community. He worked in various medical capacities, including as a sports physician and as a practitioner focusing on HIV/AIDS care during the early years of the epidemic.

Waddell was openly gay at a time when such openness was rare, especially in the world of sports. In 1976, he and his partner, Charles Deaton, were featured in a cover article in *People* magazine, the first gay couple ever to appear on the cover of a major national magazine. In 1981, he met lesbian athlete Sara Lewinstein, and they decided to have a child together. To protect the legal rights of their daughter, Jessica, Waddell and Lewinstein were married in 1985. The same year, Waddell was diagnosed with AIDS, and he lived to see the success of Gay Games II in 1986 before his death. His battle against HIV/AIDS was featured in the award-winning 1989 documentary *Common Threads: Stories from the Quilt*. His autobiography, *Gay Olympian*, which was coauthored with Dick Schaap, was published in 1996.

Abby Wambach (1980–)

Soccer Player

Mary Abigail "Abby" Wambach is one of the greatest soccer players in history and is known for her record-breaking 184 international goals and leadership on the U.S. Women's National Team (USWNT), which included winning the 2015 FIFA Women's World Cup and two Olympic gold medals. Her significance, however, extends beyond her athletic achievements. She is a vocal advocate for gender equality in sports, a champion for LGBTQ+ rights, and a cultural icon who continues to inspire through her public speaking and writing.

Wambach was born in Rochester, New York. She was the youngest of seven siblings and began playing soccer at the age of 4. "I think I was bred to do what I do now," she said. She showed a remarkable talent for soccer, often competing with and against boys. In high school, she competed in soccer and basketball. She attended the University of Florida from 1998 to 2001, where she played soccer for the Florida Gators. During her time there, she became one of the most decorated players in NCAA history, setting numerous records and earning All-American honors.

Wambach made her debut for the USWNT in 2001 and quickly became known for her physicality, aerial ability, and knack for scoring crucial goals. Her most famous moment came during the

2011 FIFA Women's World Cup, when she scored a last-second header in the quarterfinals against Brazil, helping the United States advance to the semifinals. Over her illustrious career, she scored 184 goals in international play, making her the highest-scoring player in the history of international soccer, male or female, at the time of her retirement in 2015. She won two Olympic gold medals (2004 and 2012). She announced her retirement from soccer shortly after the USWNT won the 2015 FIFA Women's World Cup in her final tournament game.

Off the field, Wambach has become a leading voice for social justice. She has been an outspoken advocate for gender equality, LGBTQ+ rights, and pay equity in sports. In 2016, she published her memoir, *Forward*, in which she candidly discussed her struggles and triumphs both on and off the field. She has since become a sought-after speaker and cofounder of the Wolfpack Endeavor, which aims to empower women to reach their full potential.

Wambach has been open about her sexuality throughout her career, and she has used her platform to advocate for LGBTQ+ rights. She married fellow soccer player Sarah Huffman in 2013, though they later divorced. In 2017, she married author and activist Glennon Doyle. The couple's relationship has been widely celebrated, and together, they have become influential voices in the movements for social justice and equality.

Rick Welts (1953–)

Sports Executive

Rick Welts is a trailblazing sports executive known for his significant contributions to the NBA and groundbreaking decision to come out as an openly gay executive in the male-dominated sports industry, the first prominent American sports executive to do so. His leadership roles, particularly as the president and COO of the Golden State Warriors, have not only shaped the success of one of the NBA's most storied franchises but also marked a turning point for LGBTQ+ visibility in professional sports.

Welts was born in Seattle, Washington. His passion for sports was evident from a young age, and he attended the University of Washington, where he played a role in the school's sports department. He began his career in professional basketball with the Seattle SuperSonics in the late 1960s, working his way up from ball boy to a public relations position. His early career was marked by a strong work ethic and a keen understanding of sports marketing.

Welts is best known for his work with the NBA during the 1980s and 1990s, particularly as the league's executive vice president and chief marketing officer. He played a pivotal role in creating and promoting the NBA All-Star Weekend, which included the introduction of the Slam Dunk Contest, turning it into a major entertainment event. Additionally, he was instrumental in the marketing and branding of the NBA during a period of significant growth in the league's global popularity. He also had a key role in the launch of the Women's National Basketball Association (WNBA) in 1997, helping to establish it as the premier women's professional basketball league. In 1999, he became the president of the Phoenix Suns, overseeing the team's business operations and helping to solidify the franchise's success both on and off the court.

In 2011, Welts made headlines as the first senior executive in professional sports to come out as gay. His decision to come out publicly was a significant moment in the sports world, as it challenged the long-standing stigma around LGBTQ+ representation in professional sports leadership. He chose to share his story in an interview with *The New York Times*, in which he discussed his personal journey and the challenges he faced in keeping his sexuality private throughout his successful career. His coming out was widely praised as a courageous step that helped to break down barriers and foster a greater acceptance of LGBTQ+ individuals in the sports industry.

Shortly after coming out, Welts was hired as the president and COO of the Golden State Warriors. Under his leadership, the Warriors experienced success both on and off the court. During his tenure, the Warriors won three NBA championships (2015, 2017, and 2018) and became one of the most successful and valuable franchises in the league. He played a crucial role in the planning and opening of the Chase Center, the team's state-of-the-art arena in San Francisco, which opened in 2019. His efforts contributed to the Warriors' rise as a global brand, enhancing their business operations, fan engagement, and community involvement.

In 2020, Welts married Todd Gage, his partner of nine years. He stepped down as president and COO of the Warriors in April 2021. Since his retirement, he has remained active in the sports and business communities. He continues to serve as an advisor to the Warriors and is involved in various initiatives related to sports management and LGBTQ+ advocacy. He has also been engaged in public speaking, sharing his experiences and insights on leadership, diversity, and inclusion in professional sports.

Appendix: LGBTQ Rights Around the World

LGBTQ+ rights vary throughout the countries of the world, with notable differences in the treatment and acceptance of LGBTQ+ individuals. The global landscape of LGBTQ+ rights has been characterized by significant disparities, with some countries leading the way in acceptance and legal protections, while others continue to criminalize LGBTQ+ communities and enforce harsh penalties. Across the continents, key figures have emerged as champions of LGBTQ+ rights, pushing for legal reforms, societal change, and greater visibility for marginalized communities. A global milestone was reached in 2011 when the United Nations passed its first-ever resolution on LGBTQ+ rights, affirming the universal right to live free from violence and discrimination based on sexual orientation and gender identity.

While South Africa stands out as a beacon of progress, much of Africa remains deeply repressive, with activists fighting against immense odds. HIV/AIDS has devastated the continent, especially the sub-Saharan nations, over the decades due to poverty, politics, gender, social inequalities, and the lack of access to health care and education. It remains a major health issue and has been the most prevalent in South Africa, which is home to 20 percent of the world's HIV/AIDS population as of 2021.

Asia presents a mixed picture, with Taiwan's landmark achievements contrasted by severe repression in countries like Saudi Arabia, where LGBTQ+ activism is illegal.

Europe remains a leader in LGBTQ+ rights, with the Netherlands, Malta, Iceland, Belgium, Denmark, and Spain rating the highest, while Eastern Europe significantly lags behind, with queer activists pushing for change.

In North America, progress is evident in Canada and parts of the United States, but challenges persist, especially in Central America. As of 2025, however, the future of LGBTQ+ rights in the United States remains uncertain.

South America's advancements, led by activists in countries like Argentina, offer hope for further progress. Meanwhile, Australia and New Zealand continue to set high standards for LGBTQ+ rights in the Pacific.

As the fight for LGBTQ+ rights continues globally, the contributions of LGBTQ+ activists past and present serve as a reminder that progress is possible even in the face of adversity. The ongoing effort to secure equality and justice for LGBTQ+ individuals will shape the future of human rights in the United States and around the world. The hope is that the determination of activists and the good will and support of allies, families, friends, and politicians proves stronger than the ill will of potential oppressors so that we can create a world where everyone can live with dignity, respect, justice, and without fear regardless of their sexual orientation or gender identity.

LGBTQ+ Rights Status by Continent and Region

Africa

Despite pockets of progress, particularly in South Africa, the continent remains one of the most challenging regions for LGBTQ+ individuals, with many countries enforcing strict anti-LGBTQ+ laws.

Gay and Lesbian Rights

Statistics: Over 30 African countries criminalize same-sex relationships, and in at least four countries (Sudan, Somalia, Mauritania, and Nigeria), same-sex acts can result in the death penalty. Societal attitudes toward LGBTQ+ individuals are generally conservative, with widespread stigma and discrimination as the norm.

Same-Sex Marriage Status: Same-sex marriage is only legal in South Africa.

Best Country: South Africa. South Africa is a pioneer in LGBTQ+ rights on the continent, having legalized same-sex marriage in 2006. The country's constitution explicitly prohibits discrimination based on sexual orientation, making it a legal and cultural outlier in Africa.

Worst Countries: Nigeria and Uganda. Nigeria's Same-Sex Marriage Prohibition Act (2014) and Uganda's Anti-Homosexuality Act (2023) impose severe penalties, including life imprisonment and death in some cases. Societal homophobia is deeply entrenched, and violence against gay and lesbian individuals is common.

Important Milestones: In 1996, South Africa became the first country in the world to include sexual orientation protections in its constitution. In 2023, Uganda passed one of the world's harshest anti-LGBTQ+ laws, introducing the death penalty for "aggravated homosexuality."

Key Figures

Frank Mugisha (1979–): A Ugandan LGBTQ+ activist, Frank Mugisha is the executive director of Sexual Minorities Uganda (SMUG), considered the country's leading LGBTQ+ rights advocacy organization. He was a 2014 nominee for the Nobel Peace Prize.

Simon Nkoli (1957–1998): A prominent South African anti-apartheid and LGBTQ+ activist, Simon Nkoli was a founder of the Gay and Lesbian Organisation of the Witwatersrand (GLOW) and played a key role in the struggle for LGBTQ+ rights in South Africa.

Alice Nkom (1945–): A Cameroonian lawyer and human rights activist, Alice Nkom has been a leading figure in defending LGBTQ+ individuals in a country where homosexuality is criminalized.

Transgender Rights

Statistics: Transgender individuals face significant barriers, with only a few countries offering any legal recognition or protection. Societal acceptance is generally low, with transgender people often facing discrimination and violence.

Same-Sex Marriage Status: Transgender individuals in South Africa can legally marry, provided their gender is recognized under the law.

Best Country: South Africa. South Africa allows transgender individuals to change their legal gender without surgery, offering some of the most progressive gender recognition laws on the continent.

Worst Country: Egypt. Transgender people in Egypt face severe repression, including arrests, forced medical examinations, and violence. Legal recognition of gender changes is not allowed, and societal discrimination is rampant.

Important Milestones: In 2003, South Africa passed the Alteration of Sex Description and Sex Status Act, allowing individuals to change their gender on official documents without surgery.

Key Figures

Victor Mukasa (1975–): A Ugandan transgender activist, Victor Mukasa has been instrumental in advocating for the rights of transgender and gender-nonconforming people in Africa despite the region's harsh anti-LGBTQ+ laws. In 2008, thanks to the efforts of Mukasa and other LGBTQ+ activists, a Ugandan high court determined that the country's human rights laws extended to the LGBTQ+ community. However, in 2023, the Constitutional Court of Uganda implemented the Anti-Homosexuality Act, which was upheld in 2024, although restrictions on healthcare access for LGBTQ+ people were stricken from the law.

Jabulani Chen Pereira: A queer South African activist and visual artist, Jabulani Chen Pereira is the founder of Iranti, an organization dedicated to media advocacy for LGBTQ+ rights with a focus on transgender issues across Africa.

Asia

Asia presents a highly diverse landscape for LGBTQ+ rights ranging from progressive nations like Taiwan to deeply repressive environments like Saudi Arabia. Censorship of LGBTQ+ media representation in China is ongoing, and the country has cracked down on LGBTQ+ online activism. China's rationalism is that activist group initiatives are the work of foreign agents encouraging political subversion.

Gay and Lesbian Rights

Statistics: Over 20 Asian countries criminalize same-sex relationships, with penalties ranging from fines to execution. Taiwan is the only Asian country where same-sex marriage is legal. In most parts of Asia, societal attitudes toward LGBTQ+ individuals are heavily influenced by cultural and religious norms, leading to widespread discrimination.

Same-Sex Marriage Status: Same-sex marriage is legal only in Taiwan (since 2019).

Best Country: Taiwan. Taiwan leads Asia in LGBTQ+ rights, having legalized same-sex marriage in 2019 and implementing strong antidiscrimination laws.

Worst Country: Saudi Arabia. Saudi Arabia enforces the death penalty for same-sex acts under its strict interpretation of Sharia law. LGBTQ+ individuals face severe repression and have no legal protections.

Important Milestones: Taiwan's legalization of same-sex marriage in 2019 marked a historic first for Asia. In contrast, Malaysia saw a significant increase in anti-LGBTQ+ crackdowns in 2021, reflecting a broader regional trend toward repression.

Key Figures

Chi Chia-wei (1958–): A Taiwanese LGBTQ+ rights activist, Chi Chia-wei was instrumental in the fight for same-sex marriage in Taiwan, leading to its eventual legalization in 2019.

Ashok Row Kavi (1947–): A former Indian journalist and Hindu monk, Ashok Row Kavi founded *Bombay Dost* (1990), India's first gay magazine, and is the chair of Humsafar Trust (HST), an organization he cofounded in 1994 to promote LGBTQ+ rights.

Akan Santiso: An Indonesian LGBTQ+ activist, Akan Santiso has worked tirelessly to support the rights of LGBTQ+ individuals in Indonesia despite the country's increasingly hostile environment.

Transgender Rights

Statistics: Transgender individuals in Asia face varying levels of legal recognition, with only a few countries offering progressive laws. In many parts of Asia, societal acceptance is low, and transgender people often face violence and discrimination.

Same-Sex Marriage Status: In countries like Taiwan, transgender individuals can marry according to their legally recognized gender.

Best Country: India. India's Supreme Court recognized transgender people as a third gender in 2014, offering them legal protections and the right to self-identify. The Transgender Persons (Protection of Rights) Act of 2019 further codified these rights, though implementation has been inconsistent.

Worst Country: Malaysia. In Malaysia, transgender individuals face criminalization under both civil and Islamic laws.

Raids, arrests, and forced "rehabilitation" are common, and legal recognition of gender changes is not permitted.

Important Milestones: India's recognition of transgender individuals as a third gender in 2014 was a landmark ruling, significantly impacting the legal and social landscape for transgender rights in the region.

Key Figures

Nisha Ayub (1979–): A Malaysian transgender activist, Nisha Ayub has been a leading figure in the fight for transgender rights in Malaysia despite the country's harsh legal environment.

Laxmi Narayan Tripathi (1978–): An Indian transgender activist, Laxmi Narayan Tripathi has been a prominent advocate for the rights of hijras and transgender people in India, playing a key role in the 2014 Supreme Court ruling.

Europe

Europe is one of the most progressive regions globally for LGBTQ+ rights, with many countries offering comprehensive protections and legal recognition. However, challenges persist in Eastern Europe. The post–World War II years in the United Kingdom saw an aggressive campaign to discover and arrest gay men. Treatment of the accused included a choice of imprisonment for "gross indecency," probation, or chemical castration, as in the famous case of the brilliant codebreaker and computer scientist Alan Turing (born in 1912, he died of suicide in 1954). The 1957 Wolfenden Report recommended decriminalizing homosexual acts between consenting adults, which was achieved with the Sexual Offences Act of 1967. However, according to British journalist and LGBTQ+ rights activist Peter Tatchell, some 15,000 gay men were nevertheless arrested and convicted during the decades that followed. Full decriminalization was achieved in 2013, and same-sex marriage became legal in 2014.

Gay and Lesbian Rights

Statistics: Over 30 European countries have legalized same-sex marriage, and many have strong antidiscrimination laws. However, countries like Russia and Poland are increasingly hostile toward LGBTQ+ rights. Social acceptance of LGBTQ+ individuals is generally high in Western Europe but significantly lower in Eastern Europe. The increasing rise of right-wing politicians and governments in some European countries is also a cause for concern for the future of LGBTQ+ rights.

Same-Sex Marriage Status: Same-sex marriage is currently legal in most Western European countries.

Best Country: The Netherlands. The Netherlands was the first European country to legalize same-sex marriage (2001) and remains one of the most LGBTQ+-friendly nations globally, with comprehensive legal protections and high societal acceptance.

Worst Country: Russia. Russia's "gay propaganda" law has severely restricted the rights of LGBTQ+ individuals, contributing to widespread violence, discrimination, and a hostile environment for LGBTQ+ people.

Important Milestones: The Netherlands' legalization of same-sex marriage in 2001 set a global precedent. Meanwhile, in 2021, Hungary passed a law banning the depiction or promotion of LGBTQ+ content to minors, mirroring Russia's repressive policies.

Key Figures

Boris Dittrich (1955–): A Dutch politician and LGBTQ+ rights activist, Boris Dittrich was a key figure in the campaign to legalize same-sex marriage in the Netherlands, making it the first country to do so.

Igor Kochetkov (1970–): A Russian gay activist, Igor Kochetkov heads the Russian LGBT Network, an LGBTQ+ rights organization founded in 2006. The LGBT Network has 14 regional branches and sponsors 11 LGBTQ+ organizations throughout Russia. In 2014, Kochetkov was nominated for the Nobel Peace Prize.

Patrick Trevor-Roper (1916–2004): A British eye surgeon and pioneering gay rights activist, Patrick Trevor-Roper played a leading role in the decriminalization of homosexuality in the United Kingdom.

Transgender Rights

Statistics: In 1972, Sweden became the first country in the world to allow transgender individuals to legally change their gender and the first to provide free hormone therapy. Transgender individuals in many other European countries currently have access to legal recognition and gender-affirming health care, though challenges remain in Eastern Europe. Societal acceptance varies widely, with transgender people in Western Europe generally facing less discrimination than those in Eastern Europe, although the United Kingdom and other European nations have expressed some caution in allowing gender-affirming care for minors.

Same-Sex Marriage Status: In countries like Germany, transgender individuals can marry according to their legally recognized gender.

Best Country: Germany. Germany allows transgender individuals to change their legal gender without surgery and offers comprehensive healthcare services for transgender people, including access to hormone therapy and gender-affirming surgeries.

Worst Country: Poland. Poland's radical right-wing government has made it increasingly difficult for transgender individuals to legally change their gender, and societal acceptance is low, with frequent reports of discrimination and violence.

Important Milestones: Germany's 2017 law allowing individuals to change their legal gender without surgery was a significant step forward. However, Poland's 2021 law banning legal recognition of gender changes marked a severe setback for transgender rights.

Key Figures

Tessa Ganserer (1977–): A German politician, Tessa Ganserer is one of the first openly transgender members of the Bundestag and has been a strong advocate for transgender rights in Germany.

Anna Grodzka (1954–): A Polish politician and trans woman, Anna Grodzka was the first openly transgender member of Parliament as well as the third openly transgender member of a national parliament worldwide. She was the first president of the Trans-Fuzja Foundation, which she cofounded in 2008.

North America

North America has made significant advancements in LGBTQ+ rights, particularly in Canada and the United States. However, challenges persist, especially in parts of Central America and in some U.S. states, where transgender rights have been under attack; in the United States, most notably concerning gender-affirming care for minors, gender-neutral restrooms, using a restroom conforming to one's gender identity, and on the federal level, with a 2025 ban on transgender military personnel.

Gay and Lesbian Rights

Statistics: Same-sex marriage is legal across Canada, the United States, and Mexico, with varying levels of public acceptance. A 2024 survey found that over 70 percent of Canadians and Americans support same-sex marriage. However, in parts of Central America, LGBTQ+ individuals face high levels of violence and discrimination.

Same-Sex Marriage Status: Same-sex marriage is legal in Canada (since 2005), the United States (since 2015), and Mexico (since 2021).

Best Countries: Canada and the United States. Canada is a global leader in LGBTQ+ rights, with strong legal protections, societal acceptance, and government support for LGBTQ+ initiatives. Same-sex marriage has been legal since 2005, and public attitudes are overwhelmingly positive. Despite the nation's divisive politics and federal anti-LGBTQ+ initiatives such as the elimination of LGBTQ+ programs and the collection of data on health outcomes affecting the LGBTQ+ community that began with the second Trump administration in 2025, the United States is included here because of its long history of organized activism, beginning with the abolitionist and labor movements as well as the 20th-century civil rights movement and culminating in the long-fought, equally intense, and ultimately successful battle for LGBTQ+ acceptance and rights.

Worst Country: Jamaica. Jamaica has some of the most repressive laws and societal attitudes toward LGBTQ+ individuals in the Western Hemisphere. Same-sex sexual activity is criminalized, and gay and lesbian individuals face severe risks of violence and discrimination.

Important Milestones: The 2015 U.S. Supreme Court ruling in *Obergefell v. Hodges* legalized same-sex marriage nationwide, a landmark moment for LGBTQ+ rights. Meanwhile, Canada's early adoption of same-sex marriage in 2005 set a standard for LGBTQ+ rights in North America.

Key Figures

James Egan (1921–2000): An entrepreneur and early prominent Canadian LGBTQ+ rights activist, James Egan brought the issue of legal rights for same-sex couples before the Canadian Supreme Court in the case of *Egan v. Canada*. Although the court ruled against the issue of same-sex spousal benefits, it significantly ruled for the inclusion of sexual orientation as a prohibited grounds of discrimination under the Canadian Charter of Rights and Freedoms.

Sandra Morán (aka Sandra Morán Reyes) (1960–): A Guatemalan politician, artist, and feminist LGBTQ+ activist, Sandra Morán was the first out LGBTQ+ politician to be elected to the Congress of the Republic of Guatemala (2015). She organized the nation's first lesbian group in 1995 and first LGBTQ+ Pride event in 1998.

Maurice Tomlinson (1971–): A Jamaican LGBTQ+ rights activist, Maurice Tomlinson has been at the forefront of legal challenges to Jamaica's anti-LGBTQ+ laws, advocating for the rights of LGBTQ+ individuals in the Caribbean.

Edith Windsor (1929–2017): An American LGBTQ+ rights activist, Edith Windsor's case led to the 2013 U.S. Supreme Court ruling that struck down the Defense of Marriage Act (DOMA), paving the way for the legalization of same-sex marriage in 2015.

Transgender Rights

Statistics: Transgender individuals in North America face varying levels of legal recognition and access to health care, with significant disparities between different regions. Societal acceptance of transgender individuals is generally high in Canada but varies widely in the United States and Mexico.

Same-Sex Marriage Status: Transgender individuals can marry according to their legally recognized gender in Canada, the United States, and Mexico.

Best Country: Canada. Canada offers comprehensive protections for transgender individuals, including the right to change legal gender and access to gender-affirming health care. Public support for transgender rights is strong, and the government actively promotes inclusivity.

Worst Country: United States (Certain States). While the United States as a whole has made progress in transgender rights, several states have enacted laws that severely restrict transgender individuals' rights, particularly regarding access to health care and participation in sports. The status of transgender Americans promises to become an even more contentious issue in the near future.

Important Milestones: Canada's 2017 amendments to the Human Rights Act to include gender identity and expression as protected categories marked a significant advance in transgender rights. Conversely, recent U.S. state laws restricting transgender rights have highlighted ongoing challenges in the region.

Key Figures

Gwen Benaway (1987–): A Canadian transgender poet and activist, Gwen Benaway has been an important figure in advocating for transgender rights and representation in Canada.

Janet Mock (1983–): An American writer, director, and transgender rights activist, Janet Mock has been a leading voice in the transgender rights movement in the United States, advocating for greater visibility and equality.

Claudia Paz y Paz (1966–): A Guatemalan lawyer and activist, Claudia Paz y Paz has worked to advance LGBTQ+ rights in Central America, including transgender rights, often facing significant resistance.

South America

South America has made significant strides in LGBTQ+ rights, particularly in countries like Argentina and Brazil. However, disparities persist, particularly in more conservative regions.

Gay and Lesbian Rights

Statistics: As of 2024, six South American countries have legalized same-sex marriage. Public support for LGBTQ+ rights is generally high, particularly in Argentina and Brazil, although LGBTQ+ individuals still face discrimination and violence, especially in rural areas.

Same-Sex Marriage Status: Same-sex marriage is legal in Argentina (since 2010), Brazil (since 2013), Uruguay (since 2013), Colombia (since 2016), Ecuador (since 2019), and Chile (since 2022).

Best Country: Argentina. Argentina, which experienced several repressive regimes during the 20th century, became the first Latin American country to legalize same-sex marriage in 2010. The country has comprehensive antidiscrimination laws and is widely regarded as a leader in LGBTQ+ rights in the region.

Worst Country: Guyana. Guyana is the only country in South America where same-sex sexual activity remains illegal, with penalties of life imprisonment. LGBTQ+ individuals face significant discrimination, and legal protections are virtually nonexistent.

Important Milestones: Argentina's legalization of same-sex marriage in 2010 was a historic moment for LGBTQ+ rights in Latin America. In 2022, Chile became the latest South American country to legalize same-sex marriage, further solidifying the region's progress.

Key Figures

María Rachid (1974–): An Argentine politician and LGBTQ+ rights activist, María Rachid founded La Fulana, Community Space for Women Who Love Women in 1996. She coordinated health and rights campaigns for lesbian and bisexual women, participating in the creation of antidiscrimination bills. In 2006, she was a cofounder of the Federation of Argentinean Lesbian, Gay, Bisexual, and Trans (FALGBT), a coalition of organizations dedicated to the equal rights for LGBTQ+ people in Argentina.

Jean Wyllys (1974–): A Brazilian politician and LGBTQ+ rights activist, Jean Wyllys has been a vocal advocate for LGBTQ+ rights in Brazil, often facing significant opposition and threats due to his activism.

Transgender Rights

Statistics: Transgender individuals in South America face varying levels of legal recognition and access to health care, with significant progress in countries like Argentina and Brazil. Societal acceptance varies, with transgender individuals facing more discrimination in rural areas.

Same-Sex Marriage Status: In countries where same-sex marriage is legal, transgender individuals can marry according to their legally recognized gender.

Best Country: Argentina. Argentina is a global leader in transgender rights, with the 2012 Gender Identity Law allowing individuals to change their legal gender without requiring surgery. The country also provides access to gender-affirming health care and has a relatively high level of societal acceptance.

Worst Country: Bolivia. In Bolivia, transgender individuals face significant legal and societal challenges, with limited access to health care and legal recognition. Discrimination and violence against transgender people are widespread.

Important Milestones: Argentina's 2012 Gender Identity Law was a landmark piece of legislation, setting a global standard for transgender rights. In contrast, Bolivia has made limited progress in recognizing transgender rights, reflecting ongoing challenges in the region.

Key Figures

Lohana Berkins (1925–2016): An Argentine transgender (*travesti*) activist, Lohana Berkins was a key figure in the fight for transgender rights in Argentina, contributing significantly to the passage of the Gender Identity Law.

Erika Hilton (aka Erika Santos Silva) (1992–) and Duda Salabert Rosa (1981–): Erika Hilton and Duda Salabert Rosa are Brazilian politicians who became the first transgender people to be elected to the nation's Chamber of Deputies in 2022. Hilton is a Black and LGBTQ+ rights activist, while Salabert Rosa is the cofounder of Transvest, an organization dedicated to combating transphobia.

Diana Sacayán (1975–2015): An Argentine LGBTQ+ rights activist, Diana Sacayán was a leading figure in the fight for the rights of LGBTQ+ individuals, particularly transgender people. She was instrumental in the passage of Argentina's Gender Identity Law.

Oceania

Australia and New Zealand are among the most progressive countries in the Pacific region regarding LGBTQ+ rights, with comprehensive legal protections and widespread societal acceptance.

Gay and Lesbian Rights

Statistics: A 2023 survey found that 79 percent of Australians and 84 percent of New Zealanders support same-sex marriage. Both countries rank high on global LGBTQ+ equality indexes. However, challenges remain in more remote and conservative areas, where discrimination can still occur.

Same-Sex Marriage Status: Same-sex marriage has been legal in New Zealand since 2013 and in Australia since 2017.

Best Country: New Zealand. New Zealand is a global leader in LGBTQ+ rights, with strong antidiscrimination laws. Societal acceptance of LGBTQ+ individuals is high.

Worst Country: Papua New Guinea. Papua New Guinea remains one of the few Pacific countries where same-sex sexual activity is criminalized, with penalties of up to 14 years in prison. LGBTQ+ individuals face significant risks of violence and discrimination, with little to no legal protections.

Important Milestones: New Zealand's earlier adoption of same-sex marriage in 2013 set a precedent for LGBTQ+ rights in the region. Australia's legalization of same-sex marriage in 2017 followed a national postal survey showing overwhelming public support.

Key Figures

Rodney Croome (1964–): An Australian LGBTQ+ rights activist, Rodney Croome has been a leading figure in the campaign for marriage equality in Australia, playing a key role in the 2017 referendum.

Louisa Wall (1972–): A New Zealand politician, Louisa Wall was instrumental in the passage of New Zealand's same-sex marriage law in 2013, making her a key figure in the country's LGBTQ+ rights movement.

Transgender Rights

Statistics: Transgender individuals in Australia and New Zealand have access to legal gender recognition and gender-affirming health care, though challenges remain in more remote areas. Societal acceptance is generally high, particularly in urban areas.

Same-Sex Marriage Status: Transgender individuals in Australia and New Zealand can marry according to their legally recognized gender.

Best Country: New Zealand. New Zealand offers comprehensive protections for transgender individuals, including the ability to change their legal gender without requiring surgery. The country also provides access to gender-affirming health care, with strong public support for transgender rights.

Worst Country: Papua New Guinea. In Papua New Guinea, transgender individuals face severe discrimination and violence, with no legal recognition of gender changes and limited access to health care.

Important Milestones: New Zealand's ongoing reforms to improve gender recognition laws and healthcare access for transgender individuals reflect its commitment to LGBTQ+ rights. Meanwhile, the lack of progress in Papua New Guinea highlights the stark contrast in transgender rights within the region.

Key Figures

Georgina Beyer (1957–2023): A New Zealand politician, Georgina Beyer was the world's first openly transgender mayor and member of Parliament, playing a crucial role in advancing LGBTQ+ rights in New Zealand.

Norrie May-Welby (1961–): An Australian transgender activist, Norrie May-Welby is known for being the first person in the world to be officially recognized as gender-neutral, advocating for broader recognition of nonbinary identities in Australia.

Countries of the World that Criminalize LGBTQ Individuals

This list includes countries where same-sex acts are explicitly criminalized, but it's important to note that in many of these places, transgender individuals are also targeted through laws against "public morality," which include cross-dressing, or simply for expressing preferred gender identity. Discrimination, violence, and legal harassment are widespread in these regions, even in countries where LGBTQ+ rights are legally recognized on paper.

Africa

Algeria
Angola (decriminalized in 2019 but societal discrimination persists)
Botswana (decriminalized in 2019 but societal discrimination persists)
Burundi
Cameroon
Chad
Comoros
Egypt
Eritrea
Eswatini (Swaziland)
Ethiopia
Gambia
Ghana
Guinea
Kenya
Liberia
Libya
Malawi
Mauritania (death penalty for same-sex acts)
Mauritius
Morocco
Namibia (decriminalization pending due to recent court rulings but still enforced)
Nigeria (death penalty in some northern states under Sharia law)
Senegal
Sierra Leone
Somalia (death penalty in some regions)
South Sudan
Sudan (decriminalized the death penalty in 2020 but still punishes same-sex acts)
Tanzania
Togo
Tunisia
Uganda
Zambia
Zimbabwe

Asia

Afghanistan (death penalty under Taliban rule)
Bangladesh
Bhutan (decriminalized in 2021 but societal discrimination persists)
Brunei (death penalty for same-sex acts under Sharia law)
Malaysia
Maldives (Sharia law applied but not strictly enforced)
Myanmar
Pakistan (death penalty in some regions under Sharia law)
Singapore (decriminalized in 2022 but societal discrimination persists)
Sri Lanka
Turkmenistan
Uzbekistan

Middle East (Often Considered Part of Asia)

Iran (death penalty for same-sex acts)
Iraq (not explicitly illegal, but LGBTQ+ individuals face persecution and violence)
Jordan
Kuwait
Lebanon
Oman
The Palestinian Territories
Qatar
Saudi Arabia (death penalty for same-sex acts under Sharia law)
Syria
United Arab Emirates

Yemen (death penalty for same-sex acts under Sharia law)

Europe

Chechnya (Russia) (extrajudicial killings and persecution reported)
Poland (criminalization of LGBTQ+-related activities in some regions under "LGBT-free zones" though not directly criminalizing same-sex acts)
Russia (criminalization under "gay propaganda" law)

Oceania

Kiribati
Papua New Guinea
Samoa
Solomon Islands
Tonga
Tuvalu

North America

No countries in North America (including the United States, Canada, and Mexico) formally criminalize gay, lesbian, or transgender individuals at the national level, although, apart from Jamaica, discrimination still occurs at regional or local levels, particularly in parts of Central America and the Caribbean.

Caribbean and Central America

Antigua and Barbuda (decriminalized in 2022 but societal discrimination persists)
Barbados (decriminalized in 2022 but societal discrimination persists)
Dominica
Grenada
Jamaica
Saint Kitts and Nevis
Saint Lucia
Saint Vincent and the Grenadines

South America

Guyana (the only country in South America that criminalizes same-sex acts)

Glossary

Agender. An adjective used to describe someone who identifies as genderless or does not experience gender as a component of their identity.

Ally. A term describing a person who actively supports the rights and visibility of LGBTQ people. Allies can be straight, cisgender, or LGBTQ people who actively support other people within the LGBTQ community.

Asexual. Describes a person who experiences little or no sexual attraction to others and little or no desire for sexual activity.

Assigned female at birth/Assigned male at birth. Sometimes abbreviated as AFAB or AMAB, this term refers to the biological sex assigned to an infant based on its anatomical characteristics at birth. A similar term is *sex assigned at birth.*

Bigender. A gender identity in which someone variously or simultaneously experiences or identifies with two genders.

Biphobia. Describes a fear of, discomfort with, or hatred of bisexual people. *See also* Homophobia, Lesbophobia, and Transphobia.

Bisexual, Bisexuality. A sexual orientation describing someone who is physically, romantically, or emotionally attracted to both men/males and women/females. Sometimes used interchangeably with the term pansexual.

Cisgender. Describes a person whose gender identity aligns with the gender assigned to them at birth.

Coming out. A shortened form of what has sometimes been called "coming out of the closet," this term can refer both to the realization and acceptance of one's LGBTQ sexual orientation and gender identity and the process of telling other people about that orientation and/or identity.

Deadnaming. The act of accidentally or intentionally calling a transgender or non-binary person by their birth name and not their chosen name.

Drag. A term first used as British theater and music hall slang to describe women's clothing worn by male performers. In the United States, drag was first used to describe performances by female and male impersonators in 19th- and 20th-century minstrel shows, circuses, vaudeville, burlesque, legitimate theater, and nightclubs, as well as costumery at drag balls. Theatrical drag performers are known as Drag Queens and Drag Kings.

Gay. A sexual orientation that commonly describes men who are emotionally, romantically, and/or physically attracted to men but can also describe lesbians and non-binary people.

Gender. A word that refers to socially constructed personality characteristics of females and males that include gender-expressive norms, behaviors, and roles associated with being a woman, man, boy, or girl, such as femininity and masculinity. A person's gender identity may not always align with their biological sex and can be expressed as a combination of characteristics.

Gender binary. A system of gender classification that categorizes all people in only two distinct forms: female or male. The gender binary may be accompanied by assumptions and expectations regarding norms, behaviors, or roles.

Gender dysphoria. A description of the anxiety and distress experienced by some people whose gender identity does not correspond with their birth gender assignment. Gender dysphoria can negatively affect functioning in many aspects of life.

Gender fluid. Describes a person without a fixed gender identity. A gender-fluid person can change their gender identity and/or expression over time or depending on the situation. *See also* Cisgender, Gender, and Genderqueer.

Gender neutral. Describes language that does not indicate a person's gender. The use of gender-neutral pronouns and forms of address depends on an individual's preference.

Genderqueer. An umbrella term similar to Non-Binary. People who identify as genderqueer may reject notions of binary norms altogether, preferring instead to express and experience gender, and often sexual, fluidity. Genderqueer individuals are sometimes described as *gender expansive*.

Heteronormativity. The assumption that romantic and sexual relationships are, or always should be, between a man and a woman. The heteronormative view is that heterosexuality is the normal and/or preferred sexual orientation.

Heterosexuality. A sexual orientation in which woman are primarily romantically and physically attracted to men and vice versa. A heterosexual person is often referred to as *straight* and sometimes *het*. *See also:* Straight.

Homophobia. Describes discomfort with or a fear or hatred of people who are attracted to members of the same sex. *See also:* Biphobia, Lesbophobia, and Transphobia.

Homosexuality. Sexual orientation describing same-sex romantic and physical attraction. The word is generally considered outdated because of its clinical connotation dating back to a time when same-sex attraction was considered a form of mental illness. However, it is sometimes still used, particularly in a historical context. The noun/adjective *homosexual* is also considered clinical and outdated.

Intersectionality. An academic theory developed by law professor and civil rights activist Kimberlé Crenshaw. Intersectionality suggests that identities are influenced and shaped by the interconnection of race, class, ethnicity, sexuality/sexual orientation, gender/gender identity, physical disability, national origin, religion, age, and other social or physical attributes. This interconnection influences, in turn, ways in which people can be targets of discrimination or marginalization.

Intersex. Describes persons with biological sex characteristic that do not completely conform to the male or female binary. These can include chromosomes, genitals, reproductive organs, secondary sex traits, and hormonal patterns. Intersex people were once called *hermaphrodites*.

Lesbian. A sexual orientation that commonly describes women who are primarily emotionally, romantically, and/or physically attracted to women but can also describe gay men and non-binary people.

Lesbophobia. A form of Homophobia that describes discomfort with or a fear or hatred of lesbians. Lesbophobia is sometimes aligned with gynophobia, which is a fear or hatred of women. *See also:* Biphobia and Transphobia.

Misgender, misgendering. To incorrectly identify someone with pronouns and/or a gender that do not match the person's chosen pronouns or gender identity.

Non-binary. Describes a person who does not exclusively identify as a man/woman, girl/boy. Sometimes used as an umbrella term with such identities as agender, bigender, genderqueer, or gender fluid. *See also:* Transgender.

Outing. Disclosing someone's sexual orientation or gender identity to others without their permission. Outing has resulted in serious consequences for LGBTQ people in employment, personal safety, and family situations.

Pronouns. The words people use when referring to you, but not by your name: she/her/hers, he/him/his, and they/them/their/theirs. It is considered appropriate and polite to ask a person their preferred pronouns rather than assuming which pronouns to use.

QPOC. An acronym that stands for Queer Person of Color or Queer People of Color.

Queer. An umbrella term describing all aspects of LGBTQ+ sexual orientation and gender identity. Some people find the term more inclusive and fluid than traditional categories within the acronym. Historically a slur, *queer* has been reclaimed as a symbol of empowerment, although some continue to find the term offensive.

Questioning. Describes people who are unsure about or are exploring their sexual orientation and/or gender identity. In LGBTQ+ initialism, questioning sometimes appears as Q2.

Same gender loving (SGL). An Afrocentric, culturally affirmative term coined by African American activist and social architect Cleo Manago (1960–) in the early 1990s. SGL describes same-sex relationships between Black Americans and/or members of the African diaspora who prefer not to identify as gay or lesbian because of the Eurocentrism associated with those terms.

Sexual orientation. A term that refers to a person's enduring pattern of romantic and/or sexual attraction to other people, whether lesbian, gay, bisexual, or straight.

Straight. A term used to describe someone who is heterosexual. It is thought to have first appeared in the 1941 book *Sex Variants: A Study of Homosexual Patterns*, written by American psychiatrist George W. Henry, who used it as slang word to describe a person who abandoned homosexual practices to "go straight" or return to the "straight and narrow" ("correct") heterosexual relationships dictated by perceived societal norms. "Straight" is often used in the queer community to describe people who do not identify as LGBTQ+. However, some consider "heterosexual" to be a more neutral word, given the historical connotations of heteronormality associated with "straight." Individuals who mainly identify as heterosexual but who also embrace non-traditional gender and/or sexual expression sometimes use the terms "straight queer," "heteroqueer," or "queerhet."

Transgender. Describes a person whose gender identity does not align with the female or male sex assigned to them at birth. A transgender person may identify as the opposite of those traditional assignments or a combination of both. Sometimes abbreviated as *trans* and used as *trans man* or *trans woman*. A person who identifies with aspects of female or male characteristics may describe themselves as trans feminine or trans masculine.

Transitioning. The processes that some transgender people may undergo so that they can live more fully as their chosen gender. A person's transition may include name changes, pronoun preferences, legal transition, and medical transition. The latter includes hormone therapy and/or gender-affirming surgeries. People who have undergone gender affirmation treatments are sometimes described as transsexual.

Transphobia. Describes discomfort with or a fear or hatred of transgender people. *See also:* Biphobia, Homophobia, and Lesbophobia.

Two-Spirit. A culture-specific term used among some indigenous North Americans for tribal members who embody both a feminine and masculine spirit and fulfill the distinct role of a third gender in their communities. It appears in the LGBTQ+ acronym as *2S*.

Resources

A List of Organizations that Work on Behalf of LGBTQ+ Americans and Their Allies

Advocates for Trans Equality (A4TE)
An organization combining the former National Center for Transgender Equality (NCTE) and Transgender and Legal Defense Fund (NLDEF)
228 Park Avenue South, PMB 38268, New York NY 10003-1502
Call: 202-642-4542
Email: a4te@transequality.org
https://transequality.org

American Civil Liberties Union (ACL)
125 Broad Street, 18th Floor, New York, NY 10004
Call: 212-549-2500
https://www.aclu.org
For local offices: aclu.org/affiliates

Anti-Violence Project
Call/Text: 212-714-1141
https://avp.org

Bisexual Resource Center
P.O. Box 170796, Boston MA 02117
Call: 617-424-9595
Email: brc@biresource.org
https://biresource.org

CenterLink
A Community of LGBTQ centers with various programs focusing on advocacy, health, and LGBTQ youth.
https://www.lgbtqcenters.org

GLAAD (founded as the Gay & Lesbian Alliance Against Defamation)
A non-governmental media monitoring organization.
https://glaad.org

GLAD (GLBTQ Legal Advocates & Defenders)
18 Tremont Street, Suite 950, Boston, MA 02108
Call: 617-426-3594
Email: gladlaw@glad.org
https://www.glad.org

GLESN (Gay, Lesbian & Straight Education Network)
244 Madison Ave. #108, New York, NY 10016
Call: 212-727-0135, ext. 6565
https://www.glsen.org

GMHC (Gay Men's Health Crisis)
307 West 38th Street, New York, NY 10018
Call: 212-367-1000
Email: info@gmhc.org
https://www.gmhc.org

GSA (Gay Straight Alliance) Network
Information about the network of LGBTQ+ GSA school clubs across the U.S.
Call: 415-552-4229
Email: info@gsanetwork.org
https://gsanetwork.org

The Human Rights Campaign (HRC)
1640 Rhode Island Avenue NW, Washington, DC 20036-3278
Call: 202-628-4160
Toll-Free: 800-777-4723
https://www.hrc.org

Lambda Legal
Assistance with LGBTQ+ legal matters.
120 Wall Street, 19th Floor, New York, NY 10005-3919
Call: 212-809-8585
https://lambdalegal.org

LGBTQ+ Victory Fund
Supports LGBTQ+ political candidates at all levels of government
1225 I Street NW, Suite 525, Washington, DC 20005
Call: 202-VICTORY
https://victoryfund.org

Modern Military Association of America
1725 I Street NW, Suite 300, Washington, DC 20006
https://modernmilitary.org

National Center for Lesbian Rights (NCLR)
Fights for LGBTQ+ rights through legal action, policy advocacy, and public education.
870 Market Street, Suite 370, San Francisco, CA 94102
Call: 415-392-6257
Email: info@NCLRights.org
https://www.nclrights.org

National LGBTQ Task Force
1050 Connecticut Avenue NW, Suite 65500, Washington, DC 20036
Call: 202-393-5177
https://www.thetaskforce.org

National Resource Center on LGBTQ+ Aging
A division of SAGE (Services and Advocacy for Gay, Lesbian, Bisexual & Transgender Elders)
https://lgbtagingcenter.org
See also https://www.sageusa.org

Out & Equal
Works exclusively on LGBTQ+ workplace equality.
1901 Harrison Street, Suite 110, PMB 7324, Oakland, CA 94812
https://outandequal.org

PFLAG (formerly Parents, Families, and Friends of Lesbians and Gays)
Call: 202-467-8180
Email: love@pflag.org
https://pflag.org
See also the PFLAG program Straight for Equality at https://straightforequality.org

Point Foundation
Supports LGBTQ+ students
P.O. Box 60108, Los Angeles, CA 90060
Call: 833-887-6462
Email: info@pointfoundation.org
https://pointfoundation.org

Transgender Law Center
P.O. Box 70976, Oakland, CA 94612-0976
Call: 519-587-9696
Email: info@transgenderlawcenter.org
https://transgenderlawcenter.org

The Trevor Project
Advocates for LGBTQ+ youth
P.O. Box 68232, West Hollywood, CA 90069
Call: 212-695-8650
Email: advocacy@thetrevorproject.org
https://www.thetrevorproject.org

Talklines

LGBT National Help Center
Talklines for LGBTQ+ youth and adults
https://lgbthotline.org

National Suicide Prevention Lifeline
Call/text: 988
https://988lifeline.org

Trans Lifeline
877-565-8860
https://translifeline.org

Bibliography

Abraham, Amelia, ed. *We Can Do Better Than This: 35 Voices on the Future of LGBTQ+ Rights*. New York: Vintage Books, 2022.

Adam, Barry D. *The Rise of a Gay and Lesbian Movement*. New York: Twayne, 1995.

Atherton, Jeremy. *Gay Bar: Why We Went Out*. New York: Back Bay Books, 2022.

Barker, Meg-John, and Jules Scheele. *Queer: A Graphic History*. London: Icon Books, 2016.

Baume, Matt. *Hi Honey, I'm Homo!: Sitcoms, Specials, and the Queering of American Culture*. Dallas: Smart Pop Books, 2023.

Bornstein, Kate. *Gender Outlaw: On Men, Women, and the Rest of Us*. New York: Vintage Books, 2016.

Bronski, Michael. *A Queer History of the United States*. Boston: Beacon Press, 2011.

Bullock, Darryl W. *Queer Blues: The Hidden Figures of Early Blues Music*. London: Omnibus Press, 2023.

Butler, Judith. *Gender Trouble: Feminism and the Subversion of Identity*. London: Routledge Publishing, 2006.

Cervini, Eric. *The Deviant's War: The Homosexual vs. the United States of America*. New York: Picador, 2021.

Chauncey, George. *Gay New York: Gender, Urban Culture, and the Making of the Gay Male World, 1890–1940*. New York: Basic Books, 2019.

Donoghue, Emma. *Inseparable: Desire Between Women in Literature*. New York: Knopf, 2010.

Duberman, Martin. *Stonewall: The Definitive Story of the LGBTQ Uprising That Changed America*. New York: Plume Publishing, 2019.

Duralde, Alonso. *Hollywood Pride: A Celebration of LGBTQ+ Representation and Perseverance in Film*. Philadelphia: Running Press, 2024.

Embser-Herbert, Máel, and Bree Fram, eds. *with Honor and Integrity: Transgender Troops in Their Own Words*: New York: NYU Press, 2021.

Eriksen, Telaina. *Unconditional: A Guide to Loving and Supporting Your LGBTQ Child*. Miami, FL: Mango Publishing, 2022.

Faderman, Lillian. *Odd Girls and Twilight Lovers: A History of Lesbian Life in Twentieth-Century America*. New York: Columbia University Press, 2012.

____________. *Surpassing the Love of Men: Romantic Friendship and Love Between Women from the Renaissance to the Present*. New York: Harper Paperbacks, 1998.

Fielding, Jim. *All Pride, No Ego: A Queer Executive's Journey to Living and Leading Authentically*. Hoboken, NJ: Wiley, 2023.

Fleishman, Jane. *The Stonewall Generation: LGBTQ Elders on Sex, Activism, and Aging*. Boston: Skinner House Books, 2020.

Forrest, Katherine V. *Lesbian Pulp Fiction: The Sexually Intrepid World of Lesbian Paperback Novels 1950–1965*. Jersey City: Cleis Press, 2005.

France, David. *How to Survive a Plague: The Inside Story of How Citizens and Science Tamed AIDS*. New York: Vintage Books, 2016.

Gainsburg, Jeannie. *The Savvy Ally: A Guide for Becoming a Skilled LGBTQ+ Advocate*. Lanham, MD: Rowman & Littlefield, 2020.

Johnson, David K. *The Lavender Scare: The Cold War Persecution of Gays and Lesbians in the Federal Government*. Chicago: University of Chicago Press, 2023.

Johnson, Joshua Moon, and Gabriel Javier, eds. *Queer People of Color in Higher Education*. Charlotte, NC: Information Age Publishing, 2017.

Katz, Jonathan D., and David C. Ward. *Hide/Seek: Difference and Desire in Amer-*

ican Portraiture. Washington, DC: Smithsonian Books, 2010.

Madrone, Kelly Huegel. *LGBTQ: The Survival Guide for Lesbian, Gay, Bisexual, Transgender, and Questioning Teens*. Minneapolis: Free Spirit Publishing, 2018.

Mayo, Cris. *LGBTQ Youth and Education: Policies and Practices*. New York: Teachers College Press, 2013.

McBride, Sarah, and Joe Biden. *Tomorrow Will Be Different: Love, Loss, and the Fight for Trans Equality*. New York: Crown Books, 2019.

McDarrah, Fred W. *Pride: Photographs After Stonewall*. New York: OR Books, 2019.

Millett, Kate. *Sexual Politics*. New York: Columbia University Press, 2016.

Morris, Bonnie J. *Eden Built by Eves: The Culture of Women's Music Festivals*. Los Angeles: Alyson Books, 1999.

Nash, Margaret A., and Karen L. Graves. *Mad River, Marjorie Rowland, and the Quest for LGBTQ Teachers' Rights*. New Brunswick, NJ: Rutgers University Press, 2022.

Ng, Eve. *Mainstreaming Gays: Critical Convergences of Queer Media, Fan Cultures, and Commercial Television*. New Brunswick, NJ: Rutgers University Press, 2023.

Pain, Paromita, ed. *Global LGBTQ Activism: Social Media, Digital Technologies, and Protest Mechanisms*. London: Routledge Publishing, 2023.

Pilcher, Alex. *A Queer Little History of Art*. London: Tate Publishing, 2017.

Reimer, Matthew, and Leighton Brown. *We Are Everywhere: Protest, Power, and Pride in the History of Queer Liberation*. Berkeley, CA: Ten Speed Press, 2019

Rivera, David P, Roberto L. Abreu, and Kirsten A. Gonzalez, eds. *Affirming LGBTQ+ Students in Higher Education*. Washington, DC: American Psychological Association, 2022.

Rolls-Bentley, Gemma. *Queer Art: From Canvas to Club, and the Spaces Between*. London: Frances Lincoln, 2024.

Russo, Vito. *The Celluloid Closet: Homosexuality in the Movies*. New York: Harper & Row, 1987.

Sanlo, Ronni, and Kelly Watson. *LGBTQ History Alive with Ronni and Kelly: Interviews with Guests from the Podcast*. 2024.

Sharman, Zena. *The Remedy: Queer and Trans Voices on Health and Health Care*. Vancouver, BC: Arsenal Pulp Press, 2016.

Schulman, Sarah. *Stagestruck: Theater, AIDS, and the Marketing of Gay America*. Durham, NC: Duke University Press, 1998.

Schwarz, A. B. Christa. *Gay Voices of the Harlem Renaissance*. Bloomington IN: Indiana University Press, 2003.

Shilts, Randy. *And the Band Played On: Politics, People, and the AIDS Epidemic*. New York: St. Martin's Griffin, 2007.

___________. *Conduct Unbecoming: Lesbians and Gays in the U.S. Military, Vietnam to the Persian Gulf*. New York: St. Martin's Press, 1993.

Stryker, Susan. *Transgender History: The Roots of Today's Revolution*. New York: Seal Press, 2017.

Tucker, Randy. *And the Category is ... : Inside New York's Vogue, House, and Ballroom Community*. Boston: Beacon Press, 2022.

Wilcox, Melissa M. *Queer Religiosities: An Introduction to Queer and Transgender Studies in Religion*. Lanham, MD: Rowman & Littlefield, 2020.

Witt, Margaret. *Love, Defiance, and the Military Trial at the Tipping Point for Gay Rights*. Waltham, MA: ForeEdge, Brandeis University Press, 2017.

Wolf-Gould, Carolyn, Dallas Denny, Jamison Green, and Kyan Lynch, eds. *A History of Transgender Medicine in The United States: From Margins to Mainstream*. Albany, NY: State University of New York Press, 2025.

Photo Sources

27th Annual Maryland International Business Leadership Awards: p. 486.
ABC Television: p. 203.
Abraham Lincoln Presidential Library and Museum: pp. 10, 507.
The Advocate: p. 329.
AFGE: p. 141 (bottom).
Rick Aiello: p. 524.
Alansafe5 (Wikicommons): p. 232.
Keith Allison: p. 542.
Alpha Kappa Alpha: p. 136 (top).
American Foreign Service Journal: p. 461 (left column).
AmericanProgress.org: p. 433 (top).
AmericasRoof (Wikicommons): pp. 35, 150, 413 (top).
Andymiah (Wikicommons): p. 138.
Aolcdn.com: p. 261.
APnews.com: p. 111.
AuthorDragon401k (Wikicommons): p. 2.
Bangabandhu (Wikicommons): p. 309.
Barklerung (Wikicommons): p. 281.
Elvert Barnes: pp. 101, 104, 152, 451.
Bryan Berlin: p. 551.
Olga Berrios: p. 87.
BET.com: p. 74.
Beyond My Ken (Wikicommons): p. 326.
Billboard: p. 276.
Rex Block: p. 462.
Eva Blue: p. 242 (top).
Bohnettfoundation.org: p. 473.
Luca Borghi: p. 402.
Boston Globe: p. 186.
Claudia Brind-Woody: p. 474.
British National Library: p. 405.
R. W. Bullock: p. 234.
Bullybloggers.wordpress.com: p. 131.
Cahtls (Wikicommons): p. 410.
Caterpillar84 (Wikicommons): p. 37.
CBS News: p. 296.
CBS Television Network: pp. 181, 182, 202 (main photo), 229.
Chasbusch (Wikicommons): p. 221.
Cinema Center Films: p. 187.
COD Newsroom: p. 361.
Mark Coggins: p. 313.
Come Out!: p. 41.
Massimo Consoli: p. 95.
CPJ Photos: p. 356.
Peter Cunningham: p. 219.
DanDT (Wikicommons): p. 20.
DC Comics: p. 173.
Dcdjdrew (Wikicommons): p. 190.
Delorean08 (Wikicommons): p. 83.
Digitalcollections.sjlibrary.org: p. 450.
Digitaltransgenderarchive.net: p. 437.
Hans van Dijk: p. 522.
DiscoverLBJ.org: p. 441 (bottom).
Don't Hate (YouTube): p. 511.
Elsa Dorfman: p. 277.
Erik Drost: p. 538 (bottom).
Drum: p. 32.
Maxwell Storey Dubler: p. 58.
Dutch National Archives: p. 242 (bottom).
John Stephen Dwyer: p. 98.
Eisenhower Presidential Library: p. 467.
Eli Erlick: p. 62 (bottom).
Ted Eyton: pp. 148, 455.
Executive Office of the President of the United States: pp. 225 (bottom), 253 (bottom), 259, 420, 421, 423, 424, 441 (top), 454, 489.
Faerichiee (Wikicommons): p. 72.
FDNY Family Assistance Unit: p. 154.
Figge Art Museum: p. 323.
Flickr.com/photos/annaustin/8204529660/: p. 316.
Floor (Wikicommons): p. 235.
FloridaMemory.com: p. 417.
Focus Features: p. 201.
Frankfurt Book Fair: p. 300.
Fuzheado (Wikicommons): pp. 169, 350.
FX: p. 205 (top).
Fyavorsky (Wikicommons): p. 445.
Jeremiah Garcia: p, 264.
Gay Activists Alliance: p. 42.
Gay & Lesbian Center Radionetworks: p. 396.

GayGames.org: p. 550.
Gaylesf (Wikicommons): p. 36.
Pax Ahimsa Gethen: pp. 52, 65, 75, 139, 161 (top), 552.
Getty Images: pp. 317, 398.
Gilead Sciences: p. 387.
GLBT Historical Society, San Francisco: p. 43.
Gold Medal Books: p. 170.
Bill Golladay: p. 213.
Barnard Gotfryd: p. 271,
HaeB (Wikicommons): p. 147.
HazteOir.org: p. 499.
Iszac Henig: p. 549 (top).
Hennepin County Library: p. 346.
Dalton Hird: p. 311.
Honolulu Advertiser: p. 107.
Eric Huybrechts: p. 165.
Independence National Historical Park: p. 4.
Iwas4in2009 (Wikicommons): p. 293.
Jackson182043 (Wikicommons): p. 158.
Jerrye and Roy Klotz, M.D.: p. 45 (bottom).
Jimi45 (Wikicommons): p. 63.
JocularJez (Wikicommons): p. 449.
John D. and Catherine T. MacArthur Foundation: p. 400.
Frank Kameny: p. 77.
Kameny Posters: p. 495.
K. Kendall: p. 118.
Kewing1950 (Wikicommons): p. 67.
Kinsey Institute: p. 392.
Kris Klug: p. 487.
Gerard Koskovich: p. 133.
La MaMa Experimental Theatre Club: p. 183.
The Ladder: pp. 31, 103.
Jennifer Lapinel-Spincken: p. 241.
The Laura Flanders Show: pp. 268, 461 (right column).
Erik van Leeuwen: p. 525.
Library of Congress: pp. 29, 167, 176, 207, 216, 217, 222, 224, 225 (top), 237 (top), 245, 250, 272, 284, 303, 307, 320, 321, 342, 370 (bottom), 411, 416 (top), 442.
LIFE Magazine: p. 206.
Alan Light: pp. 56, 282.
Jennie Livingston: p. 237 (bottom).
Scott Long: p. 84.
LOOK Magazine: p. 416 (bottom).
John Mac: pp. 535, 548.
Cynthia MacAdams: p. 91.
Graham MacIndoe: p. 490.
Makers.com: p. 136 (bottom).
Makinggayhistory.com: pp. 90, 516.
Marcus Qwertyus (Wikicommons): p. 521.
MarriageEquality.org: p. 422.
Mary Jane May: p. 61.
Mass.gov: p. 438.
Masterworksbroadway.com: p. 263 (right column).
Sara Melekian: p. 532 (top).
Metro-Goldwyn-Mayer: p. 233.
Miss Ross, Inc.: p. 485.
Moni3 (Wikicommons): p. 348.
Moody College of Communication: p. 312.
Jim Marks: p. 253 (top).
Christopher Michel: p. 390 (top).
Tony Miller: p. 444.
Nelson Minar: p. 17.
S. Mirk: p. 228.
Montrealais (Wikicommons): p. 39.
Larry D. Moore: pp. 287 (bottom), 335.
MorganTheCamera (Wikicommons): pp. 105, 218.
Museum of Modern Art: p. 291.
Jon Morrow: p. 23.
Museum of John Paul II Collection: p. 7.
Myelin Repair Foundation: p. 390 (bottom).
MyNewsDesk.com: p. 345.
Naar fotocollectie: p. 223.
Nationaal Archief: p. 294.
National Archives and Records Administration: p. 8.
National Black Justice Coalition: p. 60.
National Cancer Institute: p. 384.
National Catholic Reporter: p. 156.
National Center for Transgender Equality: p. 79.
National Institutes of Health: p. 384.
National Media Museum (UK): p. 257.
NBC Studios: p. 204.
New Line Cinema: p. 188.
New York Historical: p. 5.
New York Times: pp. 260, 265, 360 (bottom).
Nightscream (Wikicommons): p. 472.
NOLA1982 (Wikicommons): p. 179.
Office of the Director of National Intelligence: p. 425.
Ben Olender, *Los Angeles Times*: p. 544.
Mary Oliver: p. 292.

Jenni Olson: p. 64.
ONE National Gay & Lesbian Archives: p. 328.
Open Media Ltd.: p. 285.
Steve Osunsami: p. 355.
Ovaryian (Wikicommons): p. 295.
Arturo Pardavila III: p. 528.
Paul2520 (Wikicommons): p. 129.
Nancy Pelosi: pp. 50, 440, 503.
Penguin Random House: p. 249.
Al Pereira: p. 283.
PFLAG: p. 46.
Phenomenelle: p. 68.
Photographer's Archive Los Angeles: p. 80.
Poemsstories (Wikicommons): p. 305.
Preus Museum: p. 164.
Queens Public Television: p. 57.
Queens Quarterly: p. 94.
Queer Nation: p. 51.
Trey Ratcliff: p. 365.
Queer Resistance Against the Cuts: p. 26.
The Rachel Maddow Show: p. 332.
RainbowAdvocacy.org: p. 157.
Rama (Wikicommons): p. 123.
Richardbrucenugent.com: p. 289.
RJM481: p. 397 (left column).
Josh Rodriguez: p. 360 (top).
Charles Rogers: p. 394.
Philip Romano: pp. 263 (left column), 288, 314, 318, 352.
Rosiestep (Wikicommons): p. 341.
Sylvie Rosokoff: p. 443.
Sage Ross: p. 141 (top).
Fred Sargeant: p. 97.
Maurice Seymour: p. 262.
David Shankbone: pp. 49, 110, 135, 210, 266, 319, 354, 383, 463.
Shutterstock: pp. 13, 14, 22, 27, 40, 48, 99, 112, 116, 146, 175, 177, 178, 202 (inset), 230, 236, 238, 239, 240, 244, 246, 252, 258, 270, 273, 286, 287 (top), 290, 298, 308, 310 (top), 310 (bottom), 321, 333, 338, 340, 353, 357, 358, 366, 376, 378, 381, 386, 407, 409, 412, 413 (bottom), 415, 431, 466, 469, 470, 471, 475, 483, 494, 497, 527, 529, 530, 532 (bottom), 534, 538 (top), 539, 540, 543, 545.
Sid Davis Productions: p. 114.
SigurdsSister (Wikicommons): p. 34.
SiliconANGLE theCUBE: p. 401.
Gage Skidmore: pp. 347, 480, 491, 526.
Slowking4: p. 299.
Smithsonian Institution: p. 372.
Smithsonian National Museum of African American History and Culture: p. 215.
Nikita Sokolsky: p. 364.
Scott Sommerdorf: p. 362.
Sony Pictures: p. 191.
State Library of Massachusetts: p. 452.
James Steakley: pp. 125, 501 (top).
SupportPDX (Wikicommons): p. 351.
Martha Swope: p. 214.
Sylvia Rivera Law Project: p. 92.
TechCrunch (Flickr): p. 488.
Thomson200 (Wikicommons): p. 546.
Thursday42 (Wikicommons): p. 76.
D. H. Tischler: p. 62 (top).
Kay Tobin: p. 71.
Mildred Tolbert: p. 280.
The Tomorrow Show: p. 12.
Topps Sports Cards: p. 531.
Toy Polar Bear (Wikicommons): p. 53.
TriStar Pictures: p. 199.
Two Gypsy Hearts: p. 547.
UCLA Library: pp. 208, 477.
Union Square Ventures: p. 481.
Universal Pictures: p. 255.
University of California, Berkeley: p. 121.
University of California, Davis: p. 397 (right column).
University of South Carolina: p. 520.
University of Victoria: pp. 66, 404.
U.S. Air Force: pp. 505 (top), 506, 512.
U.S. Army: pp. 484, 496, 504, 515.
U.S. Commission on Civil Rights: p. 426 (top).
U.S. Congress: p. 426 (bottom), 430 (bottom), 436, 448 (right column).
U.S. Department of Agriculture: p. 476 (bottom).
U.S. Department of Commerce: p. 458.
U.S. Department of Education: p. 128.
U.S. Department of Health and Human Services: p. 106.
U.S. Department of Homeland Security: p. 343.
U.S. Department of Housing and Urban Development: p. 447.
U.S. Department of Labor: p. 430 (top).
U.S. Department of State: pp. 337, 448 (left column).

U.S. Department of Veterans Affairs: p. 505 (bottom).
U.S. House Office of Photography: p. 433 (bottom).
U.S. Marine Corps: p. 498.
U.S. Navy: p. 500.
U.S. News & World Report: p. 96.
U.S. Office of Personnel Management: p. 427.
U.S. Senate: p. 459.
U.S. Public Health Service Commissioned Corps: p. 446.
Vajiajia (Wikicommons): p. 256.
ValleySounds: p. 368.
Varnent (Wikicommons): p. 88.
La Vie (Pennsylvania State University yearbook): p. 456.
Warner Bros.: p. 196.
Allan Warren: pp. 211, 275.
Washington Blade: p. 327.
Washington.edu: p. 374.
Gareth Watkins: p. 55.
Tony Webster: p. 18.
West Point Photography: p. 502.
Wisconsin Center for Film and Theater Research: p. 195.
Nancy Wong: p. 161 (bottom).
Woodhull Sexual Freedom Alliance: p. 102.
World Economic Forum: p. 476 (top).
Yates County History Center: p. 6.
Zblume (Wikicommons): p. 453.
Zesar2005 (Wikicommons): p. 501 (bottom).
Public domain: pp. 3, 9, 11, 16, 45 (top), 59, 130, 142, 166, 171, 184, 192, 194, 205 (bottom), 209, 212, 227, 231, 254, 274, 293, 297, 306, 370 (top), 371, 373, 418, 536, 549 (bottom).

Index

Note: (ill.) indicates photos and illustrations.

Symbols

Numbers

A

C

E

F

H

I

J

K

L

M

P

S

T

U

V

W

X–Y